Memorial Book of Kozienice

(Kozienice, Poland)

Translation of
Sefer Zikaron le-Kehilat Kosznitz

Edited by:

Baruch Kaplinski, Zelig Berman, Mordekhai Donnerstein, Ratze
Wasserman, Tzvi Madanes, Levi Mandel, Elimelekh Feigenbaum, Leibel
Fishstein, David Kestenberg

Original Yiddish and Hebrew Edition Published in Tel Aviv, Israel in 1969

Original English Edition Published in New York, 1985

Published by JewishGen

An Affiliate of the Museum of Jewish Heritage - A Living Memorial to the Holocaust
New York

Memorial Book of Kozienice (Poland)
Translation of *Sefer Zikaron le-Kehilat Kosznitz*

Copyright © 2016 by JewishGen, Inc.
All rights reserved.
First Printing: July 2016, Tamuz 5776
Second Printing: March 2019, Adar II 5779

Translation Project Coordinator: David Silver
Layout: Alan Roth
Cover Design: Rachel Kolokoff Hopper
Image Editors: Larry Gaum and Jan R. Fine
Index: Jonathan Wind

Published by JewishGen, Inc.
An Affiliate of the Museum of Jewish Heritage
A Living Memorial to the Holocaust
36 Battery Place, New York, NY 10280

"JewishGen, Inc. is not responsible for inaccuracies or omissions in the original work and makes no representations regarding the accuracy of this translation. Digital images of the original book's contents can be seen online at the New York Public Library Web site."

The mission of the JewishGen organization is to produce a translation of the original work and we cannot verify the accuracy of statements or alter facts cited.

Printed in the United States of America by Lightning Source, Inc.

Library of Congress Control Number (LCCN): 2016946127
ISBN: 978-1-939561-42-8 (hard cover: 890 pages, alk. paper)

All cover photographs are images from the original Yizkor book

JewishGen and the Yizkor-Books-in-Print Project

This book has been published by the **Yizkor-Books-in-Print Project,** as part of the **Yizkor Book Project** of **JewishGen, Inc**.

JewishGen, Inc. is a non-profit organization founded in 1987 as a resource for Jewish genealogy. Its website [www.jewishgen.org] serves as an international clearinghouse and resource center to assist individuals who are researching the history of their Jewish families and the places where they lived. JewishGen provides databases, facilitates discussion groups, and coordinates projects relating to Jewish genealogy and the history of the Jewish people. In 2003, JewishGen became an affiliate of the **Museum of Jewish Heritage - A Living Memorial to the Holocaust** in New York.

The **JewishGen Yizkor Book Project** was organized to make more widely known the existence of Yizkor (Memorial) Books written by survivors and former residents of various Jewish communities throughout the world. Later, volunteers connected to the different destroyed communities began cooperating to have these books translated from the original language—usually Hebrew or Yiddish—into English, thus enabling a wider audience to have access to the valuable information contained within them. As each chapter of these books was translated, it was posted on the JewishGen website and made available to the general public.

The **Yizkor-Books-in-Print Project** began in 2011 as an initiative to print and publish Yizkor Books that had been fully translated, so that hard copies would be available for purchase by the descendants of these communities and also by scholars, universities, synagogues, libraries, and museums.

These Yizkor books have been produced almost entirely through the volunteer effort of researchers from around the world, assisted by donations from private individuals. The books are printed and sold at near cost, so as to make them as affordable as possible. Our goal is to make this important genre of Jewish literature and history available in English in book form, so that people can have the personal histories of their ancestral towns on their bookshelves for themselves and for their children and grandchildren.

A list of all published translated Yizkor Books in the project with prices and ordering information can be found at:
http://www.jewishgen.org/Yizkor/ybip.html

Lance Ackerfeld, Yizkor Book Project Manager

Joel Alpert, Yizkor-Book-in-Print Project Coordinator

JewishGen
Yizkor Book Project

This book is presented by the
Yizkor Books in Print Project
Project Coordinator: Joel Alpert

Part of the
Yizkor Books Project of JewishGen, Inc.
Project Manager: Lance Ackerfeld

These books have been produced solely through volunteer effort
of individuals from around the world. The books are printed and
sold at near cost, so as to make them as affordable as possible.

Our goal is to make this history and important genre of Jewish
literature available in English in book form so that people can have
the near-personal histories of their ancestral towns on their bookshelves for themselves and for their children and grandchildren.

Any donations to the Yizkor Books Project are appreciated.

Please send donations to:
Yizkor Book Project
JewishGen
36 Battery Place
New York, NY 10280

JewishGen, Inc. is an affiliate of the
Museum of Jewish Heritage
A Living Memorial to the Holocaust

Title Page of Original Yizkor Book

ס פ ר · ז כ ר ו ן

לקהילת קוז'ניץ

למלאות 27 שנים לחורבנה
של עיר הולדתנו

ערך: ברוך קפלינסקי

חברי המערכת: זליק ברמן, מרדכי דונרשטיין, רצה וסרמן, צבי מדנס, לוי
מנדל, אלימלך פינגבוים, ליבל פישטין, ירחמיאל קסטנברג

בהוצאת ארגון עולי קוז'ניץ בישראל, צרפת, בלגיה, ארצות־הברית, ברזיל
ובהשתתפות יוצאי קוז'ניץ בכל תפוצות העולם.

תש״ל   *   תל־אביב   *   1969

דפוס „אורלי", רח' יסוד המעלה 27, תל־אביב.

Kozienice Yizkor Book

Translation of the Title Page of Original Yiddish Book

Memorial Book

for the Kozienice Community

Commemorating 27 years since the Destruction of our Town

Editor: Baruch Kaplinsky

Editorial Board: Zelig Berman, Mordechai Donnershtein, Ratza Wasserman, Tzvi Madnes, Levy Mandel, Elimelech Feigenboim, Leibel Fishtein, Yerachmiel Kastenberg

Published by the Kozienice Immigrants Association in Israel, France, Belgium, the United States, Brazil and with Participation of Kozienice Emigrants Worldwide

5730   *   Tel Aviv   *   1969

"Orly" Printers, 27 Yesod Hama'aleh Street, Tel Aviv

Memorial Book of Kozienice
(Kozienice, Poland)
51°35' / 21°34'

[Including Garbatke 51°29' / 21°38']

Translation of
Sefer Zikaron le-Kehilat Kosznitz

Edited by:

Baruch Kaplinski

Zelig Berman, Mordekhai Donnerstein, Ratze Wasserman, Tzvi Madanes, Levi Mandel, Elimelekh Feigenbaum, Leibel Fishstein, David Kestenberg

Original Yiddish and Hebrew Edition Published in Tel Aviv, Israel in 1969

Original English Edition Published in New York, 1985

Cover of the Original Yizkor Book

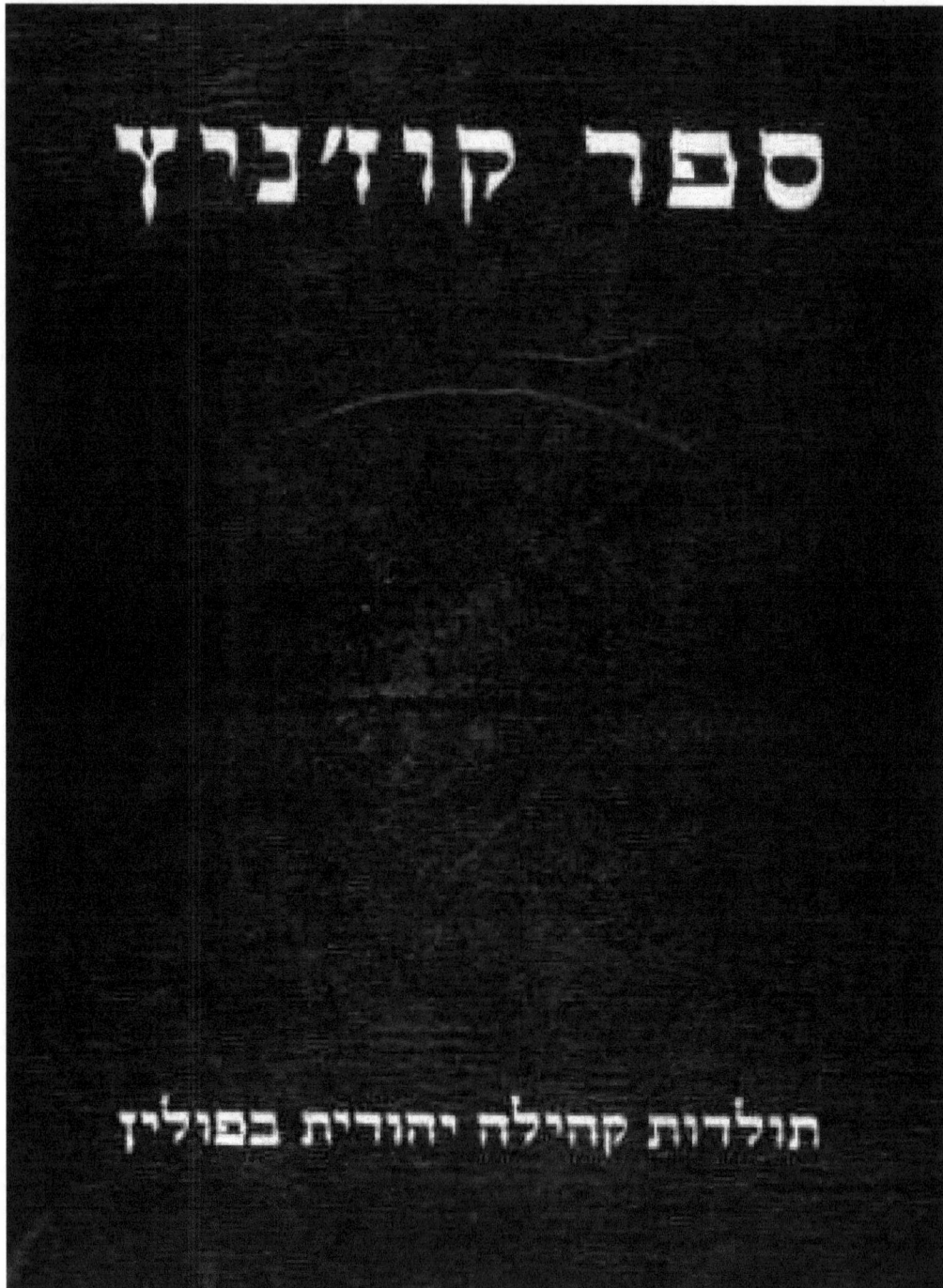

ספר קוזיניץ

תולדות קהילה יהודית בפולין

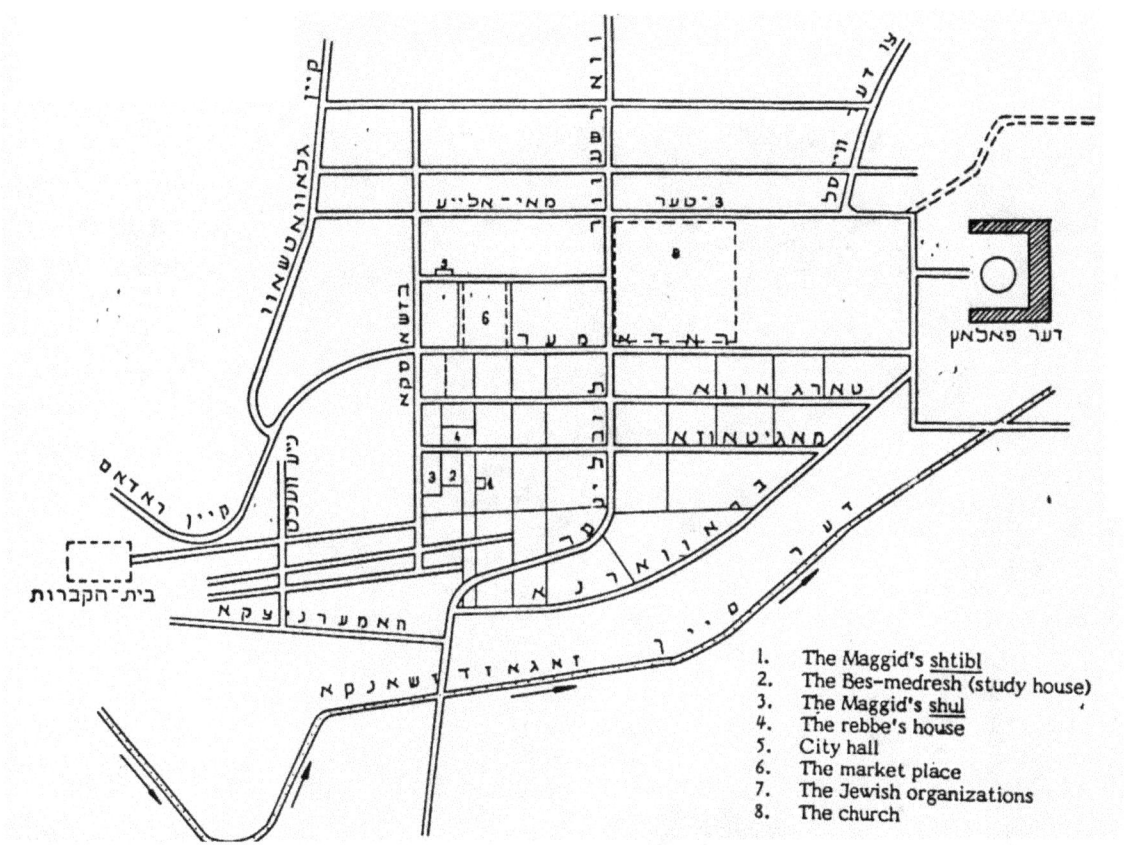

1. The Maggid's shtibl
2. The Bes-medresh (study house)
3. The Maggid's shul
4. The rebbe's house
5. City hall
6. The market place
7. The Jewish organizations
8. The church

Kozienice Town Map

דער פּלאַן פֿון קאָזשעניץ
געצייכנט פֿון זכרון דורך
מ ש ה ר אָ כ מ אַ ן.

מפת קוז׳ניץ שורטטה
מהזכרון על ידי מ ש ה
ר ו כ מ ן.

קוז׳ניץ על מפת פולין.

קאָזשעניץ אויף דער
לאנד־קארטע פֿון פּוילן.

Area Map

Acknowledgements

Our sincere appreciation to David Silver, Secretary of the Kozienitzer and Glowaczower Association, Inc. New York, for permission to put this material on the JewishGen web site and for its publication in hardcover form.

Our sincere appreciation to Seth Morgulas and Helen Rosenstein Wolf for preparing text files to facilitate the creation of this project.

This is from The book of Kozienice; <u>The Birth and the Destruction of a Jewish Community;</u> Editor: Baruch Kaplinski, Tel Aviv – New York, The Kozienice Organization, 1985 (English, 677 pages)

Special thanks to the National Yiddish Book Center in Amherst, Massachusetts and the New York Public Library for supplying the high resolution images used in this book. The original Yizkor Book may be viewed on the New York Public Library web site:

http://yizkor.nypl.org/index.php?id=1558

BALTIC SEA

LITHUANIA

Vilnius ●

RUSSIA

POLAND

BELARUS

GERMANY

● Poznan

Warsaw ●

● Lodz

Kozienice

● Prague

● Krakow

UKRAINE

CZECH REPUBLIC

SLOVAKIA

250 miles

0

0   250 Km   500 Km

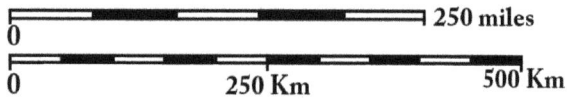

POLAND - Current Borders

Map of Poland with Kozienice indicated

Geopolitical Information:

Alternate names for the town are: Alternate names: Kozienice [Polish], Kozhenitz [Yiddish], Kozenitse [Russian], Kozhenits, Kozhnitz, Koznitz, Kozieniec

	Town	District	Province	Country
Before WWI (c. 1900):	Kozienice	Kozienice	Radom	Russian Empire
Between the wars (c. 1930):	Kozienice	Kozienice	Kielce	Poland
After WWII (c. 1950):	Kozienice			Poland
Today (c. 2000):	Kozienice			

Jewish Population in 1900: 3,764 (in 1897)

Notes:
Russian: Козенице. Yiddish: קאזשעניץ
65 miles NE of Kielce (Kieltz), 21 miles ENE of Radom.

Nearby Jewish Communities:

Garbatka 7 miles SSE
Maciejowice 8 miles N
Sieciechów 8 miles ESE
Ryczywół 9 miles NW
Stężyca 9 miles E
Sobolew 11 miles NNE
Głowaczów 11 miles WNW
Dęblin 12 miles E
Gniewoszów 13 miles SE
Irena 13 miles E
Granica 13 miles SE
Magnuszew 15 miles NNW
Łaskarzew 15 miles N
Bobrowniki 16 miles E
Ryki 16 miles ENE
Zwoleń 16 miles S
Jedlińsk 20 miles WSW
Stromiec 21 miles WNW
Puławy 21 miles ESE

Warka 21 miles NW
Kazanów 21 miles SSW
Radom 21 miles WSW
Żelechów 22 miles NE
Janowiec 22 miles SE
Mniszew 22 miles NNW
Garwolin 22 miles N
Skaryszew 23 miles SW
Ciepielów 23 miles S
Kazimierz Dolny 25 miles SE
Końskowola 25 miles ESE
Baranów 25 miles E
Sobienie Jeziory 26 miles NNW
Białobrzegi 27 miles W
Parysów 27 miles N
Osieck 27 miles NNW
Lipsko 29 miles S
Wolanów 29 miles WSW
Przytyk 30 miles WSW

A Short History of the Jewish Community of Kozienice

We have chosen to repeat an article from the interior of the translated Yizkor book that provides a good introduction to the history of this community:

This Is How the Jews of Kozienice Perished

by A. Rotkovsky

A very long time ago, Jews already lived in Kozienice and enjoyed the right to sojourn there.

A Bit of Statistics

The first Polish document in which Jews are mentioned is an illustrated Protocol of the year 1611. It is indicated there that in Kozienice there are 2 houses owned by Jews and 2 rented ones. In them are to be found 5 proprietors, 10 rent collectors, 6 butchers and 6 distillers of whiskey. At the start of the 1700's the Jews of Kozienice were occupied with the slaughter of cattle, the selling of meat and also with distilling whiskey. In 1765 there were 1365 Jews in Kozienice and the surrounding villages who paid the head tax. In 1856, there were 2885 inhabitants, of whom 1961 were Jews. In 1860 there were 1950 Jews out of a total population of 3000. According to the census of 1897 there were 3700 Jews of a total population of 6882. Right before the outbreak of World War II there were about 5000 Jews, who were mainly handworkers. The majority of Jews made a living from the shoe industry, which sold it's products to the east.

Small businessmen and merchants were but a small percent of the Jewish population. They were also mostly connected to the shoe industry. Besides this there were in the city a brewery, a mill and 2 sawmills, whose proprietors were Jews. During the fighting in 1939, Kozienice was heavily bombed by the German Luftwaffe.

Many Jewish Houses Were Destroyed

Better-situated Jews left the city, and went to relatives in other cities. The census of Jews that was carried out at the orders of the Germans, by the local Judenraat in January, 1940, indicated that there were only 4,208 Jews living in the city. The material situation of the Jewish population, right from the beginning of the occupation, was very bad. They didn't have the means to live. Because of the shortage in raw material (leather), the shoemakers had to cease working, trade died out, and occupation forces requisitioned the larger Jewish enterprises. In addition the Hitlerites levied on the Jewish community a number of "contributions" (in money and goods). Up until January, 1940, the Jews "contributed" 26,000 Zlotys of a total of 126,000 Zlotys. Besides this they had to provide, on a daily basis 300 unpaid workers to do forced labor.

[Page 523]

The Ghetto

The Ghetto was set up earlier than in other cities, in the winter of 1939–40. This was a so–called "Mopen Ghetto." Because of the bombing and the shortage of apartments, the Nazis removed a few hundred Jewish families from the central streets and squeezed them into the already densely crowded Jewish quarters. In these unsanitary conditions (a few families to a room), disease and epidemics spread. The greatest number of Jews died of hunger. Many would willingly go to the various German "points", because there they distributed a bit of hot soup and a piece of bread. During the heavy winter frosts, tattered, barefoot Jews, worked at various labor. Many collapsed from frostbitten hands and feet.

The Camp in Yedlin

Besides this, the German authorities sent out of Kozienice about 150 young Jews to forced labor in Yedlin (about 20 kilometers from Kozienice). There they worked 12 hours a day building roads and railroad lines. From the work camp in Yedlin, two Jews once escaped at night. They came back to the Kozienice Ghetto and hid in one of the attics. At the orders of the Nazis, the Judenraat and the Jewish Police turned them over to the occupying forces. They were returned to Yedlin, and there in front of all, they were shot to death. They were buried in the field near Yedlin. This was to be a warning to the remaining Jews.

Twenty Jews Shot

One of the Jewish survivors of Kozienice, Yitzhak Eliyahu Pearlstein, recalls that on Yom Kippur, 1942, 20 religious Jews refused to go to work. The commandant of the camp brought the Gestapo from Kozienice and they shot the 20 contrary Jews.

13,000 Jews in the Ghetto of Kozienice

There lived about 4,000 Jews in the Kozienice Ghetto. A short while before the great deportation, a few thousand Jews from Magnushev, Glovatshev, Ritshival, Shetshechov, Volya Klashtorna and other communities wre settled in the Ghetto. By August of 1942 there already lived in the Ghetto about 13,000 Jews. The Ghetto was hermetically sealed with barbed wire and guarded.

[Page 524]

The Selection

On the 27th of September, 1942 (it was Succos) all the Jews were driven out of their homes to an assembly point. A selection was made, and they were driven to the railroad cars that stood at the train station ramp. During the "action" the Nazis killed on the spot more than 100 Jews, in the hospital, in their homes or on the street. On that day two transports of Jews from Kozienice were carried off to the extermination camp at Treblinka (altogether about 12,000 people).

What Did The Clean–Up Commandos Tell?

The clean–up commando, which consisted of 70 young Jews, afterwards gathered the corpses from the streets and the hospital, loaded them on wagons and brought them to the Jewish cemetery, where they were buried in a common grave. For two weeks the commando gathered up and arranged the things in the abandoned Jewish homes. In one such home – Yitzhak Eliyahu Pearlstein tells – "we found a decomposing body of a woman. She was lying on a bed. She was probably shot by the Gestapo on Succos during the great selection."

Furniture, bedding, laundry, clothing, shoes and so forth were carried on trucks to a German warehouse on Koshtshelne and Radomer Streets. After checking, the better things were sent away, and the worse ones sold to the Folk–Germans and the populace of the surrounding villages. The Jews who were occupied with this work, were later sent to Dombruvke (5 kilometers from Kozienice), where they dug a canal. A short while later they were taken in a military vehicle to the camp "Hasag" in Skarzshisko.

Kozienice in Judenrein

The old Jewish city of Kozienice became Judenrein. The few still left alive, vegetated or died in the German labor–camps in Pionki, Blizshin, Starachovitz, Skarzshisko and Ostrovtze. A few of them went through the hell of Auschwitz and Buchenwald. Only a counted few lived to see liberation in 1945. All the remainder suffered a horrible death at the end of September, 1942 (Succos) in the gas chamber and crematoria of Treblinka!

Notes to the Reader:

Within the text the reader will note "{34}" standing ahead of a paragraph. This indicates that the material translated below was on page 34 of the original book. However, when a paragraph was split between two pages in the original book, the marker is placed in this book after the end of the paragraph for ease of reading.

Also please note that all references within the text of the book to page numbers, refer to the page numbers of the original Yizkor Book.

The original Yizkor Book may be viewed on the New York Public Library web site:

http://yizkor.nypl.org/index.php?id=1558

Table of Contents

Kozienice Yizkor Book

NECROLOGY

Kozienice Yizkor Book

Following is the translation of the Original Yizkor Book

[Page IV]

A Message to the
Second Generation of the Survivors
Sam Goldstein

During the years when the book of Kozienice was prepared for print, our children were still small. We didn't realize that most of our children in the United States, after they will grow up will not read Yiddish or Hebrew. We had therefore to translate this book into English, so that our children would be able to read about their heritage and understand why they don't have a family like all other people of this world.

We the survivors of the Holocaust have now reached the age of retirement and we know that someday our children will take over and continue the work we would never finish. Those who died in the Holocaust had left a message "never to forget them". We turn this message over to you, and ask you to "remember". The martyrs that died from hatred should not be forgotten for generations to come.

We had lost 6 million people and one million Jewish children among them. Our nation needs the help of each one of you. Think of your people first and stretch out a helping hand. If you are Jewish, stand up and be counted. Join any Jewish organization and become active. Preserve Jewish heritage and Jewish tradition because without it there will be no Jewish nation.

Be vigilant against our enemies. Those "Neo Nazis" or whatever names they hide under, are not just playing soldiers. They are preparing themselves for the day when they will be able to slaughter you, your children and every Jew they could get their hands on. We were as naïve as some of you may be. Even those who were sent to the gas chambers did not believe that such a thing is possible in a civilized world. But it was possible and it is still possible even here in the United States.

And now a few words about this book.

This book is translated for you the children of the survivors. You will find in this book stories, sometimes repeated, or sometimes contradicted. The people that wrote these articles are not trained authors. They wrote these stories as they remembered them.

But read this book anyway. Find out how your grandparents lived and how they died. Read about the life of their town and especially about the destruction and the Holocaust. Try to understand how a peaceful decent civilian population, unarmed, was suddenly caught by a brutal army, armed to its teeth and destroyed. Find out how they were betrayed by so many of their neighbors and how some had, at the risk of their own lives helped them. Should the death of our Jewish martyrs serve as a warning to the living to stand on guard and assure that another Holocaust will never happen again.

[Page V]

In Place of an Introduction

I have never been to Kozienice.

I have not seen Magitowa Street, nor gone walking on Lublin Street. I have not looked into the Maggid's <u>shtibl,</u> have not set foot upon the doorstep of the Cold Shul and the great <u>bes-medrash.</u>

I do not know where Yossel Citrin's barracks stood, and I never paid a visit there "on the sand". (OIFN ZAMD)

I have not drunk from the running well (Plimpl), not strolled along the avenues and green lawns of the Liarsky Palace with the lovers.

I have never gone along with the groups of Hasidim who came on the twelfth of Elul to visit the Maggid's tomb, eat with the rebbe and run from one rebbe tot eh next with written requests and donations.

I never secretly read the heretical Peretz with the study-house boys at Itche Nashelsker's, and I never talked politics in Yankel Zeigermacher's shop.

I never saw the specialty shoemakers, the boot makers and makers of uppers for shoes at work.

I never met the shoe hammerers and shoe shiners, the button-sewers and box-makers whose Kozienice shoes were worn in Nizhni Novogorod, Smolensk and Odessa.

To this day I do not know by what miracles the agents, home manufacturers, water-carriers, porters, messengers, carters and plain people of Kozienice managed to make a living.

Yet I see them alive and vibrant in my mind's eye, as if we were old friends.

I see them going about their business, running and bustling, buying and selling, and having nothing to make <u>shabbes</u> with.

I see them now rocking piously at the <u>shabbes</u> table, drawing out the melody of <u>Menukha ve-Simkha</u> (a Sabbath song) with great devotion, and dancing a <u>mitzvah</u> dance to the tune of <u>Paidyom.</u>

Now I see them in the study house between the afternoon and evening services, getting the news from old Zalmen-Barukh, who reads the <u>Ha-Tzfirah</u>, is well acquainted with every minister, and knows exactly whether he's good or bad for the Jews.

Now I see Hasidim in long capotes marching with a <u>sefer-torah</u> under a flag. They are singing under a flag. They are singing <u>Od lo avdah</u> to the tune of the closing service for Yom Kippur, and are going to Israel to redeem the swampy soil from desolation.

Now I see them at Yisroel Ziferman's house on Warsaw Street, at the local headquarters of the Zionist organization, having a friendly discussion or an evening of questions and answers.

Now, too, I see the band of strikers at the 1926 May Day demonstration. Their flags blush red, the banners cry "Down with Fascism!" The next morning the shackled demonstrators are taken to prison in Radom.

And here are the girls who monogram and embroider pillow-cases and blouses, and fight against Black Ethel for an eight-hour working day.

Where are they all? Where?

The soil of Kozienice, Pionki, Wullsa and Skarzysko has soaked up their blood. The wind has scattered their bones, dispersed them in the field of Starachowice, Szydlowiec, Blizin and Wolanow. Their ashes have fertilized the field of Treblinka, Auschwitz and Bergen-Belsen.

Only a small group of Kozienicers managed to save themselves. They live today in Israel, France, Belgium, the United States, Australia and everywhere else.

I write these few words to you, the surviving Kozienicers, spread over the entire world:

Jews of Kozienice!

All that remains of Kozienice's Hasidim and preaching, Zionism and socialism, its leaders and common people, societies and organizations is the parcel of memories, the pages and few pictures of the book which we are bringing before you.

Where you are – in Jerusalem or Paris, Brussels or New York, Rio de Janeiro or Melbourne—open this book, leaf through its pages, look at its pictures. Remember Kozienice, and do not forget its martyrs. Remember their daily struggle for Jewish survival, for Israel, for freedom and for independence of the Jewish people.

Tel-Aviv, November, 1969
Barukh Kaplinsky

Warsaw Steet. The families of Manes Bayer and Bezalel Kreizenberg lived here. The offices of the
People's Party and Yoine Mintzberg's Jewish credit bank were located in this house

The running faucet well (*plimpl*) on Lubin Street. Standing beside it is Avrum Gutmacher. Children used
to come here for a fresh, cold drink, and Jewish mothers kosher and soak their Passover dishes.

Stara-wiesh, the neighborhood of the Kozhenitz train station. On the 26th and 27th of September 1943 a train arrived here from Trablinka and too the Jews of Kozienice to the extermination camp there. In the foreground is Avrum Tenenbaum.

Lubin Street looked like this after the Jews of Kozhenitz had been deported to Treblinka. Many houses were down, leaving the street unrecognizable.

Lubin Street. The first house belonged to Moishe Medallion and contained the Bundist shoe co-operative.

Lubin Street. The three storey house was built by Yankel Shipper, and later belonged to Liezer Itche Silberberg.

Lubin Street. Families of Yankel Shipper and Moishe Donerstaein lived in the first house. Note Litman lived wher the two men are standing.

A section of Radome Street in Kozhenitz

[Page VII]

As a native of Warsaw, I adopted
Kozienice as my second home

Sabrina Goldstein born Weinstock

After five years or more facing many difficulties, financial or technical, the book of Kozienice in English translation will finally come to light.

The book was translated by Michael Wax, Doctorial candidate of literature of Toronto University and Jack Weinstein, librarian at Ivo.

Revised and set for printing by Sam Goldstein, President of the Kozienice Association. This book was translated with thoughts and completely dedicated to the second generation, that is to our children and theirs. You will learn how your close and distant relatives lived and died. People you never knew, you will laugh with them, cry with them and love with them. You will experience feelings you never had – feelings of missing someone dear – someone like grandparents, missing their love and caresses.

But let me describe Kozienice as I knew before the war and relive the happy times.

Kozienice, as provincial town, was surrounded with the most beautiful, dense forests. Pine trees so tall and stoic in their splendor. And young trees just coming up, so green and fresh.

Extremely picturesque was the small birch forest. So unique among the vast pine trees. Tall, white trunks, branches covered with silver-green leaves. And when the sun set on them and the wind caressed the shimmering leaves, it seemed like crystal bells ringing, whispering gently. Kozienice had a waterfall, lakes and small brooks. The youth many times went swimming to cool off in the hot summer days. Kozienice, if properly cultivated, could be a resort place. Many people came for vacation, to breathe the fresh fragrance of pine. In the surrounding neighboring villages, the Polish peasant lived and worked plowing the rich, golden wheat fields.

The Jews lived in town. Having small businesses, workshops – mainly artisans, seamstresses, shoemakers, tailors – pious Jews learned Talmud.

Young men and women working in these workshops, mainly located in the very houses they lived, with extremely small earnings, dreamed of a better life. Although with education not higher than elementary, and some not even this, but intelligent, eager to read and discuss and politically aware. Kozienice had even a high school where Polish families sent their children. But very few Jewish students attended. Only sons or daughters of families with better income, which were not too many.

[Page VIII]

The town came to life on Thursday every week. This was a market day. The peasants brought their goods, butter, eggs, poultry, fresh and tasty berries. And when the Jewish housewife brought them home, the house had a sweet fragrance of fresh food. In exchange, the villages bought groceries, materials, hardware, house appliances, clothing and shoes from the Jewish merchants. Businesses were profitable both ways.

Friday was another busy day, with preparations for Sabbath – cleaning the house, baking, cooking. You could see elderly Jews in traditional Hassidic attire coming back from the house of prayers. Through the open windows in summer days, you could see the Shabbot candles and hear the zmirot singing after the meal. Young people also dressed for Sabbath and could not wait the minute after the meal to rush out in the street to meet each other.

The Lubelska and Radomska Streets was the promenade. You could see boys and girls strolling back and forth endlessly, lovers dreaming to set their lives together.

On the corners of Lubelska or Radomska Streets, groups of young adults involved in hot political discussions – from the extreme left to the extreme right. Zionists, Bundtists and even Communists. A real U.N.

With little education, they were still well read and politically informed. Around midnight the street became deserted. On Saturday, young and old spent a leisure day in the woods, having a picnic, singing, dreaming and resting. The gray weekdays brought them back to the workshops. The Jewish youth of Kozienice was an interesting group – clever, talented, worthy of proper education. The town had Misnagdim Hassidim and enlightened young people. No matter how apart they were in their way of thinking, they were close to each other. Hitler destroyed the hopes, the people and the dreams.

It is quiet now in Shtetel – deadly quiet. The woods stay abandoned – and wonder – no more singing, young laughter, no more sweet whispers of lovers. It is quiet now in Shtetel – deadly quiet.

And to the Jewish people of the town Kozienice, I dedicate my poem, The Martyrs.

[Page IX]

Acknowledgement

Many, many thanks to our son, Paul, for finding a way to print this book within our finances. Without his help, the book never would be printed. We thank you, Paul.

[Page X]

The Martyrs

By Sabina Weinstock Goldstein

My head high erected

Dry eyes – they cry no more,

Feeble – a trembling voice,

Heart overflooded with grief,

I speak to you in a language

You never understood

And we did not use

You understand all the languages now

Because somewhere in all the corners

Of the world - Someone like I

speaks to you. Almost every minute

Of the day silently

And I say "You Are Not Dead!"

Your bodies just stiffen,

Your soul is alive.

Your murderers have been tickled

With vicious, brutal laughter,

When in the moments of your agony

Your scorched lips whispered the

Last Shma – called a name of your child.

And yet I say you are not dead,

Your soul is alive,

Your soul is Israel. Your soul is an inspiration

For every Jewish soldier, civilian, diplomat.

And they say: We shall never be slaughtered again,

Never again.

I bow my head now, and my body is stiffening,

Just like yours. I feel your pain, share your fortune,

And say "Be In Peace."

[Unnumbered page]

THE SURVIVIORS BID FAREWELL TO THE MARTYRS AND RETURN HOME TO ISRAEL.

OLD KOZIENICE

The Magid of Kozeniece, Rabbi Israel

THE HISTORY OF KOZIENICE

The memorial tent of the Magid in the Kozeniece cemetery. Avraham and Shifra
Kohn at the graves of their ancestors.

NECROLOGY

Martyrs of Kozienice

**Who were shot, gassed and tortured by Hitler's executioners and their henchmen
in Kozienice, Treblinka, Auschwitz and other camps in the years
1939-45.***

Surnames Starting with:
- A -

Abramovitch, Dr. Arnold, Esther and children
Abramovitch, Avrum and wife
Abramovitch, Meyer-Sholem
Adler, Gavriel
Alperman, Avrum-Meyer, Beile, Khaim and Tzippoire
Altman, Khaim, Itche and child
Arbeitman, Eliezer
Arbeitman, Pesakh, Malka and two children
Avenstern, Avrum, Rokhel-Leah and two children
Avenstern, Avrum-Leib
Avenstern, Avrum-Yitzkhok, Beile and child
Avenstern, Ben-Zion
Avenstern, Dobre and Rivke
Avenstern, Gavriel-Moishe
Avenstern, Genendel, Hersch-Ber, Mikhail and Leah
Avenstern, Hersch, Leah, Pinkhas, Eliezer, Yehoshua and Yaakov
Avenstern, Hersch-Leib, Miriam, Yekhezkel, Yitzkhok and Khanele
Avenstern, Khaim-Yoisef
Avenstern, Khaim-Yoisef, wife and child
Avenstern, Khaye-Gittel, Yaakov and four children
Avenstern, Moishe, Etta, Shmuel, Dvoire, Zainvel and Leah
Avenstern, Mordekhai and Esther
Avenstern, Nokhum, Rokhel and three children
Avenstern, Paltiel, Miriam and three children
Avenstern, Pearl, husband and four children
Avenstern, Pinkhas, wife and three children
Avenstern, Sarah
Avenstern, Sarah-Dvoire
Avenstern, Sarah-Mirel
Avenstern, Shloime and Tzirl
Avenstern, Shmuel, Khane and Zvulun
Avenstern, Shmuel, wife, Hersch, Yaakov and Pinkhas
Avenstern, Yaakov, Reizel-Mirel, Zelda, Khave, Dvoire, Yitzkhok,
Mottel and Moishe
Avenstern, Yaakov-Shabsi
Avenstern, Yoisef
Avenstern, Zainvel, wife and children

- B -

Bandman, Menakhem-Mendel, Reizel and Ben-Zion
Baran, Shmuel-Kalman
Batist, Mordekhai, Tema, Toive and two children
Baumeil, Binyomin
Baumeil, Leah and children
Baumeil, Moishe-Notte
Bayer, Elimelekh
Bayer, Mannes, Khave, Sarah, Reizel, Rokhel and Yishayahu
Bayer, Moishe, wife and two sons
Bendler, Aaron, wife, Salke and Yisroel
Bentman, Yaakov-Moishe
Berger, Toive
Berman, Clemence
Berman, Elke, Khayele and Marilke
Berman, Kalman
Berman, Khaim, Khane, Amos and Dovid
Berman, Malka
Berman, Malka and Khaye (Marilke)
Berneman, Batche and Tema
Berneman, Hinde
Berneman, Mindel
Berneman, Mordekhai
Berneman, Yekhezkel, Zelda, Gedalyahu, Reizel and Thaye
Berneman, Yerakhmiel, Herschel and Reizel
Berneman, Yisroel and Gedalyahu
Berneman, Zelig, Anshel, Pearl and Batche
Berneman, Zelig and Khaya
Berneman, Zelig,_Asher, Rokhel, Mikhail and Feigel
Bieganiec, Tzippoire and Khave
Binenthal, Moishe
Birnbaum, Ittel
Birnbaum, Khane-Golda and children
Birnbaum, Leah
Birnbaum, Moishe
Birnbaum, Moishe-Ber and Batche-Leah
Birnbaum, Monyek
Birnbaum, Pinkhas
Birnbaum, Sheindel
Birnbaum, Tema, Reizel, Khaim-Dovid, Hadassah and Mindel
Birnbaum, Yisroel
Blatman, Shmuel
Blumenzweig, Khaye-Reizel
Boorstein, Moishe
Boorstein, Yisroel
Boorstein, Yitzkhok and Reizel
Bornstein, Alter, his wife and children
Bornstein, Avniin, Esther, Shanunai and Pesakh
Bornstein, Avrum, wife and children
Bornstein, Beile

Bornstein, Binyomin and family
Bornstein, a brother of Alter's
Bornstein, Eliezer
Bornstein, Hersch
Bornstein, Hersch, Sarah-Rivke, Feige, her husband and four children
Bornstein, Kalman
Bornstein, Khaim
Bornstein, Khane-Rivke
Bornstein, Khane, Rivke and Dvoire
Bornstein, Khutshe and Meyer
Bornstein, Moishe-Yitzkhok
Bornstein, Mordekhai
Bornstein, Mordekhai, Hadassah, Yitzkhok and Shoshanna
Bornstein, Nekhe, her husband and children
Bornstein, Pola
Bornstein, Rokhel
Bornstein, Sarah-Tema, Avrum and Feige-Leah
Bornstein, Shmelke
Bornstein, Shmelke and Beile
Bornstein, Toive
Bornstein, Tzvi and Sarah-Rivke
Bornstein, Yehoshua and Khave
Brandshaft, Alte, Avrum, Rokhel, Khaim, Reizel and Pinkhas
Brandshaft, Alte-Tzippoire
Brandshaft, Azriel-Moishe
Brandspiegel, and six children
Brandspiegel, Hersch and Esther
Brandspiegel, Leib-Ber, Rivke and children
Brandspiegel, Nakhman
Brandspiegel, Oyzer, Rosa, Shmuel, Nokhum and Nekhama
Brandspiegel, Shloime
Brandspiegel, Tzvi
Brandspiegel, Yaakov, wife and children
Braun, Moishe, Tziviye, Nisser, Ber, Leib, Rokhel and Dovid
Braun, Moishe-Yoisef
Braun, Mordekhai and family
Bronstein, Moishe
Buchman, Hersch, Itte, Gittel, Rokhel and three children
Buchner, Feige, Shloime and Malka
Buchner, Leibish
Bzozovski, Zelig, Khave, Dovid, Berl, Leah and Pearl

- C -

Chanaft, Yitzkhok, Tchippe and children
Chanaft, Yitzkhok, Toive and children
Chlivner, Bezalel-Dovid, Tzime, Rokhel and Simkhe
Chmielnicki, Moishe-Tzvi, Nekhome-Leah, Toive, Sarah,
Yakhit, Rella, and Mordekhai
Chmielnicki, Yakhit and her husband
Chulish, Meyer, wife and children
Chulish, Tcharne

Cohen, Yekhezkel
Cohen, Yitzkhok and Sheindele

- D -

Danziger, Avrum-Moishe and family
Danziger, Hersch-Leib, wife and children
Danziger, Moishe-Yaak-ov, his wife and Pinkhas-Ephraim
Danziger, Yerakhmiel, Khane and children
Diament, Ephraim, Sheve and Khayele
Diament, Hersch-Mendel, Toive and Godel
Diament, Reizel and Yerakhmniel
Diament, Shmuel
Diament, Toive
Diament, Tzvi
Dickstein, Shmuel, Tzippoire and two daughters
Dotzhinsky, Isaac, wife and children
Domb, Khane
Domb, Moishe
Domerstein, Moishe, Khave, Aaron, Miriam and Tzirel
Dorfsman, Sholem, Nekhe, Moishe and Eliezer
Dorfsman, Sholem, Sarah-Nekhe,Moishe and Eliezer
Dua, Moishe-Leib

- E -

Ehrlich, Moishe
Ehrlichman, Aaron and Ettel
Ehrlichman, Schmuel, Sarah, Khane. Rokhel
and Pearl
Eichenbaum, Rokhel and Yisroel
Eidenberg, Hinda and Baby Moshe
Eisenbaum, Mordekhai-Hersch
Eisenbaum, Yisroel and Yente
Eisenberg, Khaye-Feige
Eisenmesser, Khaim, wife and children
Eisenmesser, Moishe, wife and children
Eisenmesser, Raphael
Eisenmesser, Simkhe-Peaskh and Itta-Leah
Eisenmesser, Yankel
Eisenmesser, Yitzkhok, wife and children
Epstein, Shmuel, Pearl, Rivke and Yehoshua
Epstein, Shmuel, Rivke, Yehoshua and Itte

- F -

Falberg, Shmuel-Eli, wife and daughters
Feigenbaum, Aaron-Berish and Khaye
Feigenbaum, Bernard, wife and two children
Feigenbaum, Fishel, Kasze, Khane and Mordekhai
Feigenbaum, Moishe, Tzippoire and Feige
Feigenbaum, Shloime, Rukhame and child
Feigenbaum, Yisroel, Sarah, Leah, Miriam and Moishe

Feigenbaum, Yitzkhok-Dovid and Tziviye
Finklestein, Yaakov, Tziviye, Tema, Yisroel and two children
Fishbaum, Bashe, Dovid, Borukh-Dovid and Eidel
Fishbaum, Berel and Sarah-Leah
Fishbaum, Eli
Fishbaum, Khaye
Fishbaum, Leibel, Feigel and children
Fishbaum, Yisroel, Pearl, Feige, Roize, Khaye and Ette
Fishbaum, Yissokher-Ber
Fishbaum, Yoine and Eliezer
Fishstein, Asher and Brokhe
Fishstein, Feige-Sarah
Flam, Eliezer, Feige-Mindel, Yisroel and Tirze
Flam, Gershon and Yakhit
Flam, Getzel, Golda, Khane and Yisroel
Flam, Yoisef and wife
Flamenbaum, Eliezer and Khane
Flamenbaum, Esther-Mirel
Flamenbaum, Esther-Mirel
Flamenbaum, Herschel, Genendel, Miriam and Leah
Flamenbaum, Liptsche
Flamenbaum, Menashe and Rokhel
Flamenbaum, Menashe and Rokhel
Flamenbaum, Moishe
Flamenbaum, Pearl
Flamenbaum, Yaakov, Reizel, Shloime and Leibel
Flamenbaum, Yissokher, Blume and two children
Flamenbaum, Yoisef, Malka, Mordekhai and Khaye
Fleischer, Avrum, Zelda and children
Fleischer, Eli, wife and child
Fleischer, Elimelekhm, wife and Henye
Fleischer, Khaim, Mirel and child
Fleischer, Khaim, Pearl and one child
Fleischer, Khaye, Fishel, Meyer, Khane, Roize, Pearl and Dovid
Fleischer, Melekh
Fleischer, Moishe, wife, son and daughter
Fleischer, Moishe, Sarah and two children
Fleischer, Moishe, Tema and Mindel
Fleischer, Sarah, husband, Yoisef, Khaim, Roize and Dovid
Foigel, Moishe, wife and children
Freilich, Avrum, Roize and Gittel
Freilich, Avrum, Yaakov, Roize, Tzippoire, Gittel, Yishayahu and
Naphtali-Tzvi
Freilich, Avnim-Khaim and Pinkhas
Freilich, Rabbi Ben-Zion, wife and children
Freilich, Elimelekh, Khane and Ittele
Freilich, Itte, her daughter Alte and children
Freilich, Khaye and son
Freilich, Khaye-Sarah, Pinkhas, Yerakhmiel and Moishe
Freilich, Pinkhas, Frieda and Meyer
Freilich, Sarah

Freilich, Shmuel-Eli
Freindlich, Yisroel and Gittel
Friedman, Abish
Friedman, Binyomin, wife and children
Friedman, Moishe, Feiye and children
Friedman, Motte, Tzimele and children
Friedman, Shloime, Perele, Pinkele and Abish
Frisch, Binyomin
Frisch, Menakhem-Mendel
Frisch, Menashe, Yissokher-Lieber, Elimelekh and Khane
Frisch, Mordekhai
Frisch, Yisroel-Yitzkhok, Golda and Ette-Beile
Fruman, Brokhe
Fuchs, Moishe, Roize and Yitzkhok
Funk, Mordekhai, wife and children

- G -

Garfinkle, Moishe-Leib
Garfinkle, Yehuda-Leib
Gelbard, Yaakov, Rokhel and children
Gelbard, Yoine-Gershon
Gelberg, Herschel, Pearl and children
Gelberg, Khane, Nokhum and children
Gelberg, Moishe, Sarah and four children
Gelberg, Roize, Yehoshua and children
Gelberg, Sarah, Moishe and children
Gelberg, Sime-Rokhel
Gelberg, Tzvi, Pearl and children
Gelberg, Yisroel-Menakhem and Tzime-Rokhel
Gelberg, Yisroel-Mendel
Gendzel the teacher, his wife and Marcel
Gieman, Aaron, Dobbe, Shloime and Saltche
Gieman, Moishe-Aaron
Gieman, Pearl, Malka and Velvel
Gieman, Rokhel
Gieman, Sarah
Gieman, Sheve, her husband and child
Gieman, Shloime, Bella and two children
Gieman, Shloime, Binyomin, Herschel, Rokhel and Malka
Gieman, Veve, Khane, Shloime, Esther and Sheve
Ginendel the bagel baker
Ginendel, Khaim, Rokhel, Khane and Golda
Glassman, Blume
Glassman, Reuven
Glazer, Leah
Glazer, Nekhe
Gold, Miriam, Sheindel, Bine and Menashe
Goldberg, Berel, his wife Ethel and children
Goldberg, Berel, Libe, Moishe, Rokhel and Rivke

Goldberg, Daniel
Goldberg, Khaye
Goldberg, Mordekhai-Zalman and Khane
Goldberg, Tzetl
Goldberg, Yaakov
Goldberg, Yaakov, Tziviye, Beile and Moishe
Goldberg, Yisroel-Avrum
Goldberg, Yoisef
Goldfarb, Khane
Goldfarb, Moishe
Goldfarb, Moishe, Khane, Tchippe, Pearl, her husband and two children
Goldfarb, Pearl
Goldfarb, Sara-Esther
Goldfarb, Tzippoire
Goldman, Khaim, Reizel, Avrum and Rivke
Goldman, Shabsi, Rokhel and child
Goldman, Shmuel-Leib and Molly
Goldman, Yaakov and Rivke
Goldschwartz, Yaakov
Goldstein, Dvoire
Goldstein, Freindel
Goldstein, Khaim
Goldstein, Libe
Goldstein, Minke
Goldstein, Mottel, his wife and Ettel
Goldstein, Pinkhas
Goldstein, Sarah
Goldstein, Yisroel
Goldstein, Yokheved
Goldstein, Zelig
Goldwasser, Yoisef-Khaim
Goldzweig, Leibish
Goldzweig, Moishe, Sarah-Mindel and Mekhel
Goldzweig, Pinkhas, Yaakov, Kalman and Khave
Gozhitshansky, Moishe
Gozhitshansky, Shloime
Gradovtchik, Genendel, Roize and two children
Gradovtchik, Herschel, wife and children
Gradovtchik, Itche, Libe, Hinde
Gradovtchik, Khaye, her husband Eliezer and four children
Gradovtchik, Moishe, Yoisef, Khaim, Gittel and two children
Gradovtchik, Shmuel, Adela and one child
Gradovtchik, Yoisef, Yutke and three children
Greenberg, Faivel
Greenberg, Leibish, Reizel and children
Greenberg, Nokhum
Greenberg, Naphtali-Herz
Greenberg, Reizel and nine children
Greenberg, Yisroel and Ette
Greenhaus, Yaakov, Yisroel

Greenspan, Borukh-Moishe
Greenspan, Moishe, Yakhe and three children
Greenspan, Shmerel, Tzippoire, Yitzkhok and Yekhiel
Greenspan, Shmuel, wife and children
Greenstein, Arye-Dov
Greenstein, Asher, Peske and three children
Greenstein, Dovid, Beile, Miriam and Khaim-Meyer
Greenstein, Ehpraim, Bine and five children
Greenstein, Yoisef, Sarah and three children
Greenstein, Ze'ev
Greyetz, Shifra and children
Greyetz, Yitzkhok
Grubler, Elimelekh
Grudniak, Eliezer, wife and children
Grudniak, Mendel, wife and four children
Grudniak, Meyer and Tzippoire
Grudniak, Moishe, wife and children
Grudniak, Sarah, Feige, Yekhezkel, Yisroel and Ruzhe
Grudniak, Yudel, his wife, Khave and Leizer
Gutmacher, Avrum, Sheve, Leah, Hinde and Feige
Gutmacher, Eidel-Golda and Gelle
Gutmacher, Moishe, Pesse and Leah
Gutmacher, Tevye, Shifra and children
Gutmacher, Yaakov, Golda and family

- H -

Haberman, Avrum and Frimet
Haberman, Blume
Haberman, Itche and Feige
Haberman, Khaye-Reizel, Pesse, Beile, Ilush, Yoiel and Rokhel
Haberman, Shmuel
Halputter, Mrs. and children
Hanover, Binem, Zelig and children
Hanover, Loser, wife and children
Hanover, Yoisef (the melamed), his wife and Herschel
Hershenbaum, Aaron and wife
Hershenbaum, Borukh and wife
Hershenbaum, Melekh, Beile-Rokhel, Yankel, Dovid and Avrum
Hertzberg, Ette, Milke, Pearl and Aaron
Hertzberg, Moishe-Shmuel, wife and children
Hertzberg, Yisroel and wife
Hirshenhorn, Aaron, Yudis, Kalman and Melekh
Hirshenhorn, Elimelekh, Simme, Gittel and Molekh
Hirshenhorn, Faivel, Yisroel and Meyer
Hirshenhorn, Leibel and Yisroel
Hirshenhorn, Shmuel, Feige and Mordekhai
Hirshenhorn, Yisroel and Mindel
Hoffenberg, Moishe, Rivke, Zissel, Malka, Breindel, Toive, Gittel and Shloime

Hoffenberg, Sarah, Khaye and Pearl
Hoffenberg, Toive
Hoffman, Noah, Khaye and Miriam
Honigstock, Yekhiel, Khave and six children
Honigstock, Yisroel, Hessi, Khave, Mordekhai, Miriam and Tzirl
Horowitz, Avrum, Bine and Golda
Horowitz, Dovid, wife and children
Horowitz, Leizer,Khane and children
Horowitz, Meyer, wife and children
Horowitz, Moishe, Sarah and children
Huberman, Eli, Sarah and children
Huberman, Shloime, his wife, Tzviye and two other children

- I / J -

Itzkowitz, Itche and family
Itzkowitz, Mrs. and children
Itzkowitz, Yisroel-Dovid, wife and children
Jablonka, Yaakov-Hersch, Tzippoire, Avrum, Abba, Moishe and Tziviye
Joskowitz, Yisroel-Avrum, wife, Velvel and four children, Yutt Mendel, Simkhe and two daughters

- K -

Kalb, Mottek
Kalinski, Aaron
Kalinski, Meyer
Kalinski, Miriam
Kalinski, Shmaye
Kalinski, Yoiel
Kammer, Eli and his wife
Kammer, Khane-Pearl
Kammer, Moishe and Gelle
Kammer, Shabsi, wife and children
Kammer, Yisroel, wife and children
Karent, Milly
Karp, Moishe
Karpik, Bezalel
Karpman, Moishe and Sarah
Karpman, Shmuel, Dina, Dov, Henye and Shloime
Katz, Alter, wife, Moishe, Avrum, Khaye, Gittel, Pearl and Sarah
Katz, Itche
Katz, Leib, Sarah and Yoisef
Katz, Leibel and family
Katz, Rivke, husband and child
Katz, Shabsi
Katz, Shabsi, Rokhel, Moishe and three children
Katz, Yekhiel, Zelda and Khane
Katz, Yitzkhok, Reizel, Yoisef, Yekhiel and Yitzkhok
Katz, Yoisef and parents
Kazyak, Shloime, Toive and children
Kestenberg, Avrum-Manne
Kestenberg, Dovid, Brokhe, Golda, Avrum, Shloime and Moishe

Kestenberg, Eliezer, Libe and four children
Kestenberg, Ephraim, Fishel, Leizer, Yisroel-Yaakov, Asher and Shloime
Kestenberg, Feige, husband and children
Kestenberg, Itche, Avrum, Khane and Moishe
Kestenberg, Khave-Rokhel, Aaron and Avrum
Kestenberg, Leibish and Mindel
Kestenberg, Mekhel, Esther and Golda
Kestenberg, Moishe, Rivke, Khave, Rokhel, Aaron, Avrum and Reizel
Kestenberg, Moishe, Sarah, Rosa, Yankel and three children
Kestenberg, Moishe-Yossel, wife and three children
Kestenberg, Nokhum, Rokhel and Reizel
Kestenberg, Shabsi, Khane and children
Kestenberg, Yaakov, Dovid, Khane, Yidel, Shabsi, Moishe, Zissel and Khaye
Kestenberg, Yekhiel, Eliezer and Alte
Kestenberg, Yitzkhok and sister
Kestenberg, Yudel, wife and children
Kirshenbaum, Meyer, Miriam, Yekhezkel, Feige and Sarah
Kirshenbaum, Yoisef, Khaye, Aaron, Sheve, Moishe and Falik
Kirshenblatt, Miriam and Raphael
Kirshenblatt, Yitzkhok, Leah, Faivel, Mendel, Shammai, Shloime, Simme, Dvoire
and Itte
Kleinbaum, Khaye and Ette
Kleinbaum, Khaye and Tzippoire
Kleinbaum, Zelda, Dovid, Nekhome and Nokhum
Kleinnan, Mrs. and children
Kleinman, Reizel
Kloinsky, Berish
Koffler, Nossen, wife and children
Koffman, Dina and children
Kohn, Alter, Khave, Moishe, Freida, Yissokher, Reshe, Shmuel, Yentel and Pearl
Kohn, Avrum, Batche, Reizel and two children
Kohn, Avrum, Dvoire, Sarah and his brother-in-law
Kohn, Khaim, Feige and two children
Kohn, Mendel and two children
Kohn, Moishe, wife and two children
Kohn, Moishe-Khaim and wife
Kohn, Nokhum, wife and children
Kohn, Peretz and children
Kohn,Sheve
Kohn, Shloime with his wife
Kohn, Shloime, Rivke and Sholem
Kohn, Yehoshua, Sheindel, Yoisef and Leibel
Kohn, Yehoshua-Zelig
Kohn, Yekhiel, wife, Shmuel and Pinye
Kohn, Yisroel, Roize, Tzvi, Khane, Rivke and Moishe
Kohn, Yissokher, Perele, Shmuel, Yom-Tov and Rokhel
Kohn, Yoisef and wife
Kohn, Zelig, wife, children and grandchildren
Korman, Aaron, his wife and daughter
Korman, Libe and Dvoire
Korman, Moishe and Sarah

Korman, Mordekhai
Korman, Pinkhas, Yaakov and family
Korman, Shmuel-Moishe, his wife, Tzvi, Esther, Dvoire and Khane
Korman, Yitzkhok-Eli and Alte
Kornwasser, Melekh and wife
Kramarski, Aaron, Frimet and Yerakhmiel
Kramarski, Avrum-Moishe, Brokhe and children
Kramarski, Avrum-Moishe, Brokhe, Yerakhmiel, Sarah and Tzippoire
Kreizberg, Avrum and his wife
Kreizberg, Bezalel, Bine, Ber, Khaye and Shloime
Kreizberg, Dovid
Kreizberg, Khaye, husband and children
Krishpel, Yitzkhok, Feige and Notte
Kronengoid, Dov-Berish and his wife Pearl
Kronengoid, Khaye-Leah
Kronengold, Yitzkhok, Rivke and Khaim
Kupler, Nakhman and family
Kuropatve, Dovid, Rokhel, Brokhe and Leah
Kutscher, Loser, wife and children
Kutscher, Raphael, wife and children

Index

- L -

Lederhendler, Gershon and Miriam
Lederhendler, Moishe, Gittel and two children
Lederhendler, Moishe-Aaron, Gittel, Yitzkhok-Menakhem and Pearl
Lederman, Eliezer-Mikhail
Lederman, Esther, Meyer, Sholem and Yossel-Moishe
Lederman, Gershon, Miriam and child
Lederman, Nissim, Sheindel, Miriam, Hele, Yitzkhok and Shabsi
Lenga, Mikhail, Malka and Khane
Lerman, Moishe, Miriam and daughter
Lerner, Moishe, Yankel, Beile, Sheindel and Rivke
Levi, Yekhezkel, wife and children
Levine, Velvel and Khanye
Lichtenstein, Borukh-Meyer, Khave, Yossel, Dovid and Sarah-Henye
Lichtenstein, Tema, Leah, Miriam, Yaakov and Yisroel
Lichtenstein, Yoisef and Dvoire
Lichtenstein, Yoisef and Tzippoire
Lieberman, Nossen, Rokhel, Roize, Yoisef and Khaim
Likverman, Aaron, Pinkhas and Pearl
Likverman, Kadesh, Khayele and three children
Likverman, Shimon, Yudis and children
Lippmann, Avrum, Khane-Roize, Yekhiel, Feigel, Moishe-Khonen, Rokhel, Hinde, Moishe and Yaakov-Fishel
Lippmann, Moishe-Aaron
Lippman, Tzippoire and Leah, Notte
Lippman, Yaakov, Fishel, Rekhel, Yekhiel, Feige and Moishe

Lippman, Yekhiel, Feige, Moishe and Khane
Lisband, Aaron, Sarah and child
Littman, Aaron and Rusze
Littman, Levi, Meite, Rokhel, Khave and Itche
Littman, Melekh, Toive, Dovid and Motte
Littman, Mordekhai, Sheve and children
Littman, Pinkhas, Reizel, Khave, Herschel, Mindel and Levi-Dovid
Littman, Roize and two children
Litvack, Yekhiel, wife and children
London, Aaron and family
London, Alter, wife and children
London, Khaim
Luxenberg, Leibel, Miriam, Meyer-Sholem, Daniel and Khane

- M -

Madanes, Bezalel, Sarah-Henye and children
Madanes, Yitzkhok-Meyer, Sarah-Pearl, Yaakov and Rukhama
Mandel, Aaron, wife and children
Mandel, Anshel, wife and children
Mandel, Gershon, Malka, son and daughter
Mandel, Levi, Feige and children
Mandel, Rokhel
Mandel, Shmerel, wife and children
Mandel, Tevye, Glikke, Naphtali, Khane, Mendel, Yehoshua and Tzirl
Mandel, Tzippoire, Yekhezkel and son
Mandel, Tzippoire, Yekhezkel-Gershon and children
Mandel, Yaakov-Hersch, wife, Shabsi and two sisters
Mandel, Yitzkhok, Tzirl, Yaakov, Malka, Mordekhai and family
Mandelbaum, Dvoire, Esther and Avrum
Mandelbaum, Simkhe, Miriam and Khaye
Mandeleil, Meyer and Leah
Mandelzweig, Alter, and his family
Mandelzweig, Berel, wife and son
Mandelzweig, Yissokher, wife and children
Mantelmacher, Hirsch-Leib, Dina
Margoshes, Mikhail, Golda and children
Medallion, Moishe-Yitzkhok, Breindel, Khaye-Beile, Mindel and Yekhiel
Meiden, Beile, Yaakov, and Leah
Meiden, Koppel
Meiden, Leib and his wife Miriam
Mieiden, Moishe and his wife
Meiden, Sholem and his wife Pessye
Mekler, Khaim, Khaye-Rivke, Hillel, Velvel and Libe
Meltzer, Gedalyahu, his son-in-law, wife and children
Meltzer, Moishe-Aaron, Bine, Falle, Kalman, Rokhel and Sarah
Meltzer, Yerakhmiel, wife and six children
Milberg, Moishe and Khane
Milberg, Zelig, Malka and children
Milgrom, Meyer, Freide and child
Milgrom, Yitzkhok,Miriam, Khane, Khaye-Leah, Libe and Sarah

Miller, Avrum, Miriam, Sheindel and Yoisef
Miller, Yaakov, Beile and child
Mintz, Berel and Hinde-Gittel
Mintz, Sarah and Tzime
Mintzberg, Hesse, Malka and Hillel
Muney, Yishayahu and family

- N / O -

Nachmanovith, Moishe-Mendel, wife and children
The Nagel family of eight people
Nagel, Mikhail, Khane and three children
Nashelsky, Yoisef and his family
Neudorf, Aaron
Neudorf, Avrum and Tzime
Neudorf, Elimelekh
Neudorf, Simkhe
Neudorf, Yoisef
Neunold, Moishe-Yekhezkel
Neustein, Leibish, Sarah and Shmuel
Noodleman, Itzik, wife and daughter
Noodleman, Meyer, wife and children
Noodleman, Shloime, wife and children
Noodleman, Tzvi
Noodleman, Yankel, Freide and two children
Nussbaum, Esther
Okon, Dan, Sarah, Yoisef and Sholem
Olshina, Eliezer, Leah, Pearl and Breindel
Orbach, Boruch
Orbach, Melekh, Beile-Sarah and children

- P -

Pasternak, Esther, Sarah, Genendel and Zitek
Pasternak, Yekhiel
Pearl, Herschel
Pearlstein, Gedalyahu, Khave and children
Pearlstein, Gedalyahu, Tzimmel, Khane and Shloime
Pearlstein, Moishe, wife and children
Pearlstein, Yaakov, wife and children
Peter, Elimelekh and family
Piekolek, Eliezer-Shabsi
Piekolek, Ezra, Tzippoire and four children
Piekolek, Khaim, wife, Henye, Alter, Meyer, Dovid, Yisroel, Berel,
Moishe and Pearl
Piekolek, Mendel and four children
Piekolek, Moishe-Aaron, Tzirel, Shabsi, Borukh, Godel and Pearl
Pintschever, Yitzkhok and family
Pittkowitz, Yisroel, Tevye, Rokhel, Sarah and Yaakov

Pontsch, Anshel, Reshe and children
Pontsch, Leah and Mordekhai
Popielnik, Herschel, Pearl, Yekhiel, Rokhel, Rivke and Sarah
Potasznik, Miriam, Nekhome and Rokhel
Potasznik, Yitzkhok
Potasznik, Yoisef and Esther
Purisever, Yankel and family

- R -

Rabinowitz, Shaul, Tziviye, Gittel and Yisroel
Radowitz family of ten people
Rappaport, Moishe, Khaye, Tzippoire, Mordekhai and Yitzkhok
Rechthand, Leibel
Rechthand, Menakhem-Mendel, wife and children
Rechthand, Meyer, Khaye, Aaron and Yerakhmiel
Rechthand, Yoisef, Paltiel, Dina, Yisroel and Yitzkhok-Moishe
Rechtman, Shaul, Riva, Feige, Toive, Herschel, Yisroel, Sarah and Leibel
Rechtman, Shaul, Rivke, Feige, Tzvi, Yisroel, Yudis, Arye and Sarah
Rechtman, Shloime, Rivke and three children
Reichappel, Dovid and family
Reichappel, Eliezer, Hinde, Itzik, Mendel and Dovid
Reichappel, Menashe and family
Reichappel, Mottel, wife and children
Reichappel, Yitzkhok and Shloime
Reisman, Leibish, Alte, Nekhome, Toive, Reizel, Pearl, Yekhezkel, Meyer and two children
Reisman, Nekhome, Toive, Yekhezkel and Meyer
Ring, Avrum
Rochman, Avrum, Beirekh, wife and children
Rochman, Eliezer, Rivke-Rokhel and two children
Rochman, Elimelekh, wife and children
Rochman, Khaim, Miriam and children
Rochman, Khaim, Toive and three children
Rochman, Leib, Sarah, Feige and her husband, Nekhe, Herschel, Vita, Yoisef, Yissokher and Golda
Rochman, Leibel, wife, Yankel and children
Rochman, Mendel and Khaye
Rochman, Meyer-Dov, Golda, Herschel, Shmuel, Shmelke, Esther-Ette and Eli
Rochman, Moishe, Ette, Yerakhmiel and Yitzkhok
Rochman, Yankel, wife and children
Rochman, Yisroel, wife and children
Roizman, Herschel, Yoisef, Golda and Yisroel
Roizman, Kissel
Roizman, Nekhe-Beile, Yankel and children
Roseman, Leib, Sarah, Feige and her husband
Rosen, Khane, Aaron and Rokhele
Rosen, Moishe, Feige, Eliezer and three children
Rosen, Mordekhai
Rosen, Motte and Khaye
Rosen, Peretz
Rosen, Shimen and Elimelekh
Rosen, Yoisef
Rosenbaum and his son Moishele

Rosenfeld, Ovadya, Rivke and Hinde
Rosenstock, Shmuel, Miriam, Yaakov, Yidel, Toive and Pearl
Rosenthal, Binyomin, Ettel, Yisroel, Khaye, Yom-Tov, Pearl and Moishe
Rosenthal, Herschel, Dvoire, Ezra and Khane-Sarah
Rosenthal, Herschel, Reizel, Sarah, Leah, Berel, Malka and Yekhiel
Rosenthal, Pinkhas
Rosenzweig, Avrum, Rokhel, Nekhemye, Yitzkhok, Shmelke and Libe
Rosenzweig, Leibish, Yissokher, Shmelke and Tchippe
Rosenzweig, Pesakh, wife and children
Rosenzweig, Yehoshua and Tzippoire
Rosenzweig, Yissokher
Roskoshnik, Zishe, his wife and four children
Rotman, Tzvi
Rubin, Reizel, Shimshon and Avrum
Rubin, Shimshon, Reizel and three children
Rubinstein with his family
Rubinstein, Boaz, his wife and four children
Rubinstein, Gelle
Rubinstein (Geller)
Rubinstein, Herschel and Elimelekh
Rubinstein, Leizer-Itche and Miriam
Rubinstein, Mendel, his wife and child
Rubinstein, Moishe
Rubinstein, Moishe, wife and children
Rubinstein, Moishe, Sarah and children
Rubinstein, Mordekhai
Rubinstein, Rokhel and four children

- S -

Saltzman, Eliezer, Yissokher and five children
Saltzman, Herschel, Khaye, Feige, Zelda and Khane
Saltzman, Mordekhai, Berel and Mindel
Saltzman, Naphtali, Tzirl, Shmuel-Khaim and Avrum
Saltzman, Shmuel, Gittel, Shimen, Genendel and Sarah
Saltzman, Yoisef
Salzberg, Avrum, wife and two children
Salzberg, Berel, Avrum, Khaim and three daughters
Salzberg, Berel, Khaye, Rokhel, Itel and Khaim
Salzberg, Borukh-Yoisef, Miriam and two children
Salzberg, Dobre
Salzberg, Dov, Khaye-Brokhe, Beile and Shloime
Salzberg, Feige, Esther, Simme and Pearl
Salzberg, Gershon, Tzilke, Ze'ev, Khave, Sarah, Rivke and Leah
Salzberg, Gershon, Tzippoire and Moishe-Zelig
Salzberg, Hillel, Libe and children
Salzberg, Moishe, wife and three children
Salzberg, Moishe and Simme
Salzberg, Sarah, Nekhe and Gittel
Salzberg, Shmuel, Gershon, Yissokher and Malka
Salzberg, Simkhe, Itte, Yankel and Borukh

Salzberg, Yankel-Borukh
Salzberg, Yehuda-Dov, Tzippoire and children
Salzberg, Yekhiel, Simkhe, Yankel and Khaim-Meyer
Salzberg, Yekhiel-Leizer, Simkhe, Mirel, Yoisef and Leah-Khaye
Salzberg, Yisroel, Reizel, Arye-Dov and Avruin-Moishe
Salzberg, Yissokher, Dovid, Rokhel-Leah and Dobbe
Salzberg, Yoisef, Mirel, Leah and Khaye
Saperstein, Shmuel-Zainvel, Khasye and Yitzkhok
Schuch, Yoisef and Molly (Shabbason)
Schwarzbard, Hersch, wife and children
Schwarzbard, Pinkhas, Gittel and children
Schwarzberg, Avrumn, Moishe and five children
Schwarzberg, Menashe, Sarah, Elye, Pinkhas, Binem, Yisroel and Feige
Schwarzberg, Moishe with his family
Schwarzberg, Pinkhas
Schwarzberg, Shmerel, his wife, Shmuel and Sarah-Malka
Schwarzman, Eli, Dvoire, Yaakov, Moishe, Rivke, Elke, Khele, Yoisef-Yishayahu and Kalman
Shabbason, Mottel, Rosalke, Ettel and Toive
Shabbason, Nekhe, Feige, Esther and Golda
Shabbason, Yishayahu, Leah and children
Shabbason, Yissokher and Libe
Shabbason, Zelig, Leah and Khaye
Shabbason, Zelig, Ruzhe and children
Shaff, Herschel
Shammes, Faivel, his wife and four children
Shammes, Khaye and Pearl
Shammes, Sini and his mother
Shammes, Yitzkhok, Henye and three children
Shapira, Menashe, Khaye, Yudis, Yankel, his son-in-law and children
Shapira, Moishe, wife and children
Shapira, Rivke and Leibel
Shapira, Yaakov
Shapira, the Rebbe Reb Yankele with his family, and his son-in-law Meyer Unger with his family
Shapira, Yissokher, wife and children
Shapira, Rabbi Yoisef and family
Sheinfeld, Yisroel, Yudis and child
Sherman, Aaron, Sarah, Moishe, Khane, Yoisef and Shloime
Sherman, Eli, Gedalyahu, Gittel, Shloime, Dov, Elke and Yokheved
Sherman, Yankel and Pearl
Sherman, Yankel, Tcharny, Moishe, Dvoire, Rivke, Pinkhas and Feige
Shermeister, Tzvi, Tcharny, and Khane
Shermeister, Yaakov, Tcharne, Blume, Menakhem-Moishe, Pearl, Nokhum, Mally and Rivke
Silverberg, Dovid, Rokhel and Leah
Silverberg, Eliezer-Yitzkhok, Sheindel, Malka, Avrum-Leib, Moishe, Gittel and Yoisef
Silverberg, Ette and Leah
Silverberg, Leibel
Silverberg, Leizer-Itche, Esther, Gittel and Leah
Silverberg, Meyer and wife
Silverberg, Moishe and Nekhome
Silverberg, Moishe, Pearl and Avrum

Silverberg, Yaakov, Mirel and Leibel
Silverberg, Yekhiel and Malka
Silverberg, Yidel, wife and children
Silverberg, Yisroel-Moishe, Khane-Gittel, Peretz and Yitzkhok
Silverberg, Yitzkhok-Dovid, Zissel and four children
Silverberg, Yoisef, Sarah and five children
Silverknopf, Herschel, Tzippoire-Feige, Henye, Tzviye, Brokhe, Avrum and Meyer-Akiva
Silverknopf, Yekhiel-Eliezer, Beile and Mindel
Silverman, Moishe, Sarah-Leah and Avrum
Silverstein, Aaron, Sarah and family
Silverstein, Avrum, Gittel, Zanvil, Khanine and Moishe
Silverstein, Khaim, Tzippoire, Reizel, Feige, Khaye, Pesse, Lelbel and Yissokher
Silverstein, Yitzkhok-Meyer, Perele, Zissel, Sarah, Khaim, Zelig, and Shloime
Simenhaus, Shloime
Sirota, Eliezer, his wife and children
Sirota, Leibish, his wife and two children
Sirota, Leizer and Blume
Sirota, Meyer with his family
Sirota, Meyer, his wife and four children
Sirota, Meyer, Roize, Malka and Pearl
Sirota, Meyer-Yoisef, his wife and five children
Sirota, Moishe with his family
Sirota, Mottel with his family
Sirota, Pearl-Malka
Sirota, Toive and three children
Sirota, Yitzkhok and Aaron
Smyser, Yankel, wife and children
Smyser, Yekhiel, Frimet, Rokhel, Shmuel, Leibish, Moishe and Khaim
Sobol, Eli, wife and children
Sobol, Hersch-Leib with his family
Sobol, Loser, wife and daughters
Sobol, Moishe-Leib with his family
Sochachevsky, Yerakhmiel, Leah and two children
Spiegel, Aaron and Shifre
Spiegel, Moishe, Sarah, Miriam, Velvel, Libe, Khane and Rokhel
Spiegel, Yisroel, Gittel, Aaron, Libe, Yaakov, his father-in-law, son-in-law and grandchildren
Spiegelman, Pesakh, Tzirel, Shloime, Izzy and Marcel
Spiegelman, Tevye, Khane, Rokhel, Ze'ev, Tzirel and seven grandchildren
Spiegelman, Wolf and Sarah
Statiner, Yissokher and his wife Mirel
Stecker, Pinkhas, Beile and three children
Steinbaum, Eliezer, His Wife Leah (Kopalis) and five children
Steinbaum, Menashe, Rivke-Rokhel, Ette, Brokhe and Malka
Steinbaum, Mottel, wife and children
Steinbauin, Shabsi and wife
Steinbaum, Yekhiel, His Wife Dobra (Kopalis) and five children
Steinbock, Merra, Libe and Pinkhas
Sternbaum, Eliezer, wife and children
Sternbaum, Yechiel, wife and children
Stemstein, his wife and family
Sternstein, Dora and children

Sternstein, Ette, her husband and children
Sternstein, Koppel and Itte
Sternstein, Leah, her husband and children
Sternstein, Rokhel, her husband and children
Sternstein, Yoiel, his wife and children
Streiman, Felle and four children

- T -

Tabachnik, Moishe, wife and children
Teitelbaum, Rokhel, Nokhum, Yankel and Bine
Tennenbaum, Hendel, Yerakmiel, Noah, Itche, Moishe, Toive and Leah
Tennenbaum, Moishe, Sarah, Meyer-Sholem, his wife and Khane
Tennenbaum, Reizel and Shimen
Tennenbaum, Yaakov, Rivke, Batche and Velvel
Tennenbaum, Yisroel, Menashe and Yoine
Tennenbaum, Yissokher, Genendel and children
Tennenbaum, Yoine, Tema and children
Tennenholtz, Simkhe, wife and four children
Tepper, Avrum, Reizel and Yerakhmiel
Tepper, Pinkhas, wife and children
Tepperman, Moishe, wife and children
Tepperman, Roize
Tishman, Ephraim, wife and children
Tishman, Khaim and family
Tishman, Tema, Rivke and children
Tochterman, Moishe-Yossel, Rivke, Leah and Yerakhmiel
Tuchman, Loser, Hinde, Khane-Sarah and Mindel

- W -

Walberg, Eliezer and Rivke
Walberg, Elimelekh, Shmuel, Rivke and Zelda
Walberg, Hersch, Khaim, Shmuel and Pinkhas
Waretsky, Moishe and Khaye
Waretsky, Pinkhas, Tzviye, Khaim and Khaye
Wasserman, Eliezer, Nekhe, Yitzkhok, Dovid, Mordekhai, Khave, Tcharne and family
Wasserman, Melekh
Wasserman, Moishe, his wife and Avrum
Wasserman, Mottel and Khave
Wasserman, Sholem
Wasserman, Simkhe, Rokhel-Leah and Herschel
Wasserman, Yankel, wife and children
Wasserman, Yankel and Toive
Wasserman, Yitzkhok, Shifre, Moishe, Yom-Tov and family
Waxman, Yitzkhok, wife and two children
Weinberg, Avrum, Yoiel and Leibish
Weinberg, Leib
Weinberg, Moishe
Weinberg, Mordekhai, Roize and children

Weinberg, Sarah
Weinberg, Sarah and children
Weinberg, Shmuel, Ratze and children
Weinberg, Toive the rabbi's wife
Weinberg, Velvel
Weinberg, Velvel and wife
Weinberg, Rabbi Yaakov-Hersch
Weinberg, Yoiel, wife and children
Weinberg, Yoine, Rokhel and children
Weinstock, Eliyahu and Tzirl
Weinstock, Ester
Weinstock, Frimit
Weinstock, Hershel
Weinstock, Mendel
Weinstock, Nekhemye, his daughter, son-in-law and grandchild
Weintraub, Esther, Menashe, Berish and Mendel
Weintraub, Toive
Weintraub, Yaakov-Loser, Miriam and Khaye
Weintraub, Yoiel, Gittel, Hersch and Khave
Weissbard, Moishe, Feige-Rivke, Sarah, Miriam, Yekhezkel, Khaim and Tziviye
Weissberg, Mordekhai
Weissberg, Shimen and Khane
Weissberg, Yitzkhok
Weissbrot, Koppel, Leah and her husband
Weissbrot, Miriam
Weissbrot, Moishe and Henni
Weizman, Avrum
Weizman, Avrum, Moishe and Tzirele
Weizman, Avrum, Yudis, Yekhiel and Yoiel
Weizman, Dovid
Weizman, Eliezer and Moishe-Leib
Weizman, Nossen, wife and children
Weizman, Yudis, Yekhiel and Shmuel
Werber, Leibish and son
Wildenberg, Esther and two children
Wildenberg, Faivel, Toive and Reizel
Wildenberg, Leizer, Nekhe and Mottel
Wildenberg, Moishe, Leah, Beile and children
Wildenberg, Yaakov
Wildenberg, Yaakov, Moishe and Leah
Wildman, Khane
Wildman, Moishe and Rokhele
Wiltshick, Elimelekh and Brokhe
Wolf, Mishel, Yoisef, Godel, Avigdor and Gershon
Wolf, Velvel, Dvoire and children

- Z -

Zamoysky, Loser, Rokhel and children
Zamoysky, Nekhome, Simkhe and their children
Zaterman, Leibish, Khave and children

Zaterman, Wolf and Mindel
Zaterman, Yekhiel and his wife
Zaterman, Yekhiel, Sheve, Ephraim and Urish
Zeitfinger, Alter and Rivke-Leah
Zeitfinger, Boaz
Zeitfinger, Dovid and Toive
Zeitfinger, Khaim-Yoisef and family
Zeitfinger, Moishe-Yehuda
Zeitfinger, Shifre
Zeitfinger, Shmuel, Avrum and Manek
Zemach, Yoine and Mendel
Zeman, Yisroel, Sarah and daughter
Zigelman, Beile
Zigelman, Dovid
Zigelman, Khaim, wife and children
Zigelman, Leizer, Dinah, Yankel, Simkhe, Malka, Moishe and Berish
Zimbalist, Mottel, Rokhel, Leah and children
Zimmerman, Khane
Zimmerman, Moishe
Zipperman, Tzippoire, Yente, Dobre, Yekhiel, Berel, Shloime, Leibel, Mordekhai
and Shmuel
Zipperman, Yaakov, Rokhel, Leibel, Reizel, Shmuel-Loser and Faivel
Zipperman, Yekhiel
Zucker, Avrum, Reizel, Mordekhai, Shmuel, Khaye, Rivke and Arye
Zucker, Berish, Minke and Shmuel
Zucker, Herschel with his family
Zucker, Khaim-Mordekhai
Zucker, Khaye, her sister, Sholem, Bella and their children
Zucker, Mendel, Dvoire, Pearl, Shmuel and Golda
Zucker, Moishe, wife and children
Zucker, Mottel, Shmuel, Yoisef, Khaye and Feige-Pesse
Zucker, Nekhe, Dovid and Yoisef
Zucker, Nettel, Rivke and Moishe
Zucker, Pinkhas, Altele and children
Zucker, Rukhama
Zucker, Yekhiel
Zucker, Yitzkhok-Aaron
Zucker, Yoisef, Khave, Feige and Pesse
Zuckerman, Esther-Sheindel
Zuckerman, Mendel and wife
Zuckerman, Yisroel-Isser
Zweigenberg, Avrum with his family

* Residents of Kozienice killed in Kozienice itself, as well as those deported to the
death camps where they were murdered.

Martyrs of Kozienice
Who were deported from France and killed at the Hands of the Nazi Murderers. *

- A / B / C -

Adler, Yaakov and his wife
Alterleib, Dvoire
Alterleib, Mendel
Alterleib, Miriam
Alterleib, Simone
Alterleib, Zelig
Bernman, Ida
Bernman, Itche
Bernman, Nissan
Bernman, Rosa
Bernman, Toive
Berunad, Charles
Birnbaum, Bert
Birnbaum, Meyer
Birnbaum, Sholem
Brandspiegel, Shloime
Chlivner, Solomon
Chlivner, Tzirel
Chlivner, Yaakov

- E / F / G -

Eidenbaum, Anna
Eidenbaum, Esther
Eidenbaum, Zelig
Eisenmesser, Malka, her children and husband
Eisenmesser, Sarah
Feigenbaum, Pinkhas and his wife Fishbaum, Itte-Beile
Fishbaum, Yerakhmiel
Freilich, Melekh
Friedman, Ida
Friedman, Marcel
Friedman, Melekh
Friedman, Paul
Friedman, Shmuel
Goldman, Molly
Goldman, Shmuel-Leib
Goldstein, Bernard
Goldstein, Dovid
Goldstein, Khaye
Goldstein, Shloime
Goldstein, Simon
Goldstein, Yoisef
Greenstein, Beile
Greenstein, Dovid
Greenstein, Khaim-Meyer

Greenstein, Mortka
Greenstein, Shmuel-Khaim

- H / J / K -

Hoffman, Shmuel
Hoffman, Tzippoire
Jick, Feige Jick, Gelle
Jick, Melekh
Jick, Nokhum
Jick, Yekhiel
Kalish, Paul
Kalish, Salle
Kammer, Eli
Kammer, Miriam
Kammer, Roize
Kammer, Simone
Kammer, Yoisef
Koplewitz, Yerakhmiel

- L / M / N -

Lederman, Jacques
Lederman, Mattes
Lederman, Moishe
Lederman, Paul
Lederman, Yakel's wife and five children
Lippmann, Notte

Mandel, Beile
Meltzel, Khaye
Nagel, Maurice

- P / R / S -

Pearlstein, Bernard
Pearlstein, Eli
Pearlstein, Jacqueline
Pearlstein, Salle
Pearlstein, Yerakhmiel
Potasznik, Yitzkhok
Rabin, Jacques
Rabin, Roize
Rabin, Yekhiel
Rubinstein, Rachel
Radowitz, Maurice
Radowitz, Paulette
Radowitz, Shmerel
Raphnowitz, Iris
Raphnowitz, Sheindel
Raphnowitz, Shmuel
Reichappel, Mordekhai
Reichappel, Mortka
Reichappel, Wolf
Reichappel, Yekhiel

Ring, Avrum
Rosenweiss, Moishe
Rosenzweig, Rokhel
Salzberg, Feige
Salzer, nee Kestenberg
Schneiderman, Meyer
Shammes, Dovid
Silverberg, Albert
Silverberg, Dvoire
Silverberg, Jeanette
Smyser, Denis
Smyser, Reizel
Smyser, Sarah
Sobol, Frandel
Spiegelman, Paul
Spiegelman, Sarah
Spiegelman, Wolf
Starkman, Pierre
Statwohner, Herschel
Statwohner, Myra
Statwohner, Socher
Statwohner, Yisroel
Stockfish, Cecile
Stockfish, Mary

- T / W / Z -

Tennenbaum, Annette
Tennenbaum, Meyer-Shalom
Tennenbaum, Pearl-Dina
Walberg, Yisroel
Wasserman, Mordekhai
Weinberg, Leon
Weinberg, Shmuel
Weissberg, Anna
Weissberg, Feige
Weissberg, Itche
Weizman, Dovid
Wolf, Michel
Wolfstand, Salke
Zifferman, Leib
Zifferman, Yekhiel
Zucker, Yekhiel

* Ethnic Polish Jews who were residents of Kozienice, but who had emigrated to France to work or settle there (perhaps to escape the Nazis), and who were deported from France to their deaths.

[Page 1]

SECTION 1 - Old Kozienice

Towards a History of the Jews in Kozienice
by Dr. Nakhman Blumenthal, Jerusalem

In 1966, Poland celebrated one thousand years of nationhood. These same thousand years correspond to the period of Jewish settlement there, although some few Jews had come to Poland earlier than the records indicate. Throughout the whole of our time in Poland, we were treated as strangers. "The Jews are a wandering people, here today and gone tomorrow. The Jews, "or so it was claimed," are a people with no feeling for the land. They are strangers; they feel like strangers, shut themselves off from their surroundings and separate themselves from the society in which they live. It is not surprising that the local population sees them as foreigners, distrusting them and treating them accordingly."

Was it any wonder, then, that the Jews were not recognized as fully–fledged citizens? Even when we received equal rights (on paper, at any rate) immediately after the nation's rise, we had occasion until the last minute – and this is free Poland – to h ear the constant cry, more than once accompanied by physical force, "Zydi do Palestini," "Jews to Palestine".

The people's street–cries were politely echoed by Polish diplomats. They said that there were too many Jews in Poland, that not only the Jews, but also the poorer strata of the Poles themselves had no opportunity to make a satisfactory living. If Polish peasants were seeking a livelihood in foreign countries, would it not be fairer for the Jews to leave Poland in an organized fashion – not, God forbid, in a stampede – and for their own sake? The Polish government was even prepared to give the Jews the counsel and diplomatic aid necessary to help them settle in Madagascar. Jews wouldn't care, they said. It was all the same to them, wherever they were! They were strangers of their own volition: Was there ever such a thing as a Jewish patriot?

Theoreticians who had "proven" that the Jews had lost any national attachments over the course of their lengthy exile could also be found among the Jews themselves. Today, after the holocaust, one sees that all their theories were incorrect, as hundreds and hundreds of landsmanschaft books prove. These books are devoted not only to our great misfortune in Poland, but also to memoirs and pictures of the Poland of days gone by: not only to the Jews, but to good Polish neighbours, too (and, it goes without saying, to the bad ones); to the beautiful Polish countryside and the beauty of our settlements. Even today, Jews who now live far from Poland, driven thence by the atrocities of the Second World War, boast of the beauty of Warsaw and of Cracow, of the Vistula, and the goodness of the local nobility, and the beauty

of the forest and rivers where they would bathe on Shabbes afternoon. And
with what love is this told!

Another thing which is not to be forgotten: the Polish–
Jewish landsmanschaften came into being in America, especially in New York,
at the end of the nineteenth century, half a century before the holocaust was
upon us. The landsmanschaften did not limit themselves to organizing clubs
where members could get together and talk about the old country (though this
is, of course, the psychological reason for their formation), nor did they restrict
themselves to organizing help for their impoverished homeland. How many
songs and poems in praise of the old settlement had been written even then!
No town in Poland went unhymned by a Jewish poet – how many Polish
writers did the same? The number of emigrants who have lived and are still

living outside the boundaries of Poland is considerably greater than that of the
emigrant Jews. Have they, the Poles, formed many landsmanschaften? Have
they published many landsmanschaften books? So it was before the
holocaust, and so it has remained until today.

[Page 2]

Today, the landsmanschaften books have assumed another character.
They have become tombstones for the annihilated Jewish Poland. But how
much love, love mixed with sorrow and pain, appears in the very fact of their
existence! In the best times we were treated as strangers, harassed and driven
out; in bad times we were murdered and raped.

Today, years later, when we are in our ancestral home and striking roots in
a new reality, we return from time to time, more than we would like and more
than needs be, to the old country in which our parents, our great–great-
grandparents lived and suffered. Among the many feelings which flood into
our minds, mention must be made of our love for the place, for the land which
was neither mother nor stepmother, which often betrayed us cruelly and gave
us into the hands of the Nazi executioners.

A wonderful people, indeed, the people of Israel! It cannot rid itself of its
past, bitter as it was. On the contrary, the bitterness receives the longest and
most frequent commemoration.

The History of the City of Kozienitz

The name is taken from the root koza, kozice, a goat, wild goat or stag. The
town was established in the depths of the great forests in which many
animals, mainly goats, lived. Dukes and kings used to hunt there, among
them King Zygmunt August (16th century), whose residence was in Cracow,
then the capital of Poland. The town took its name from the goats Ÿ Kozienice,
or in Yiddish, Kozienitz.

Mordekhai Donnerstein recalls a story about the town's name from school:
Once, King Zygmunt August took his wife, Barbara, hunting. The queen was

renowned for her beauty and goodness, and when the king shot at and hit a she–goat, she fainted out of pity for the animal. Wishing to comfort her, the king told her that the goat had not been hurt, in Polish <u>Kozienic.</u> The place, which was later to develop into a large settlement, thus took on the name of Kozienice. People tent to interpret place–names of whose origins they are ignorant by means of such false etymologies.

Another version of the legend is found in the first Polish encyclopedia, published by the Jew, Shmuel Orgelbrand (Warsaw, 1864), according to which the king shot and missed. His retainers cried out, "<u>Kozie–nic</u>," in other words, "You missed".

[Page 3]

The Palace of Kozienice before World War II

In fact, a village called Kozienice was already in existence at that time. It is known that King Wladislaw Jagello bought the village from on order of Wemen in 1390, and that in 1409 he ordered a wooden bridge, built on rafts, to be set up on the Vistula thee. Later, the completed bridge was floated down the Vistula to Czerwinsk, where the Polish army crossed over it to struggle against the Crusaders and win the great victory of Grunewald (Tannenberg) in 1410. The fact that the bridge was built in Kozienice proves that there were craftsmen living there, and that the settlement was occupied with something other than agriculture.

In 1466, King Kazimiez, in company with his wife, Elzbieta, stopped in Kozienice while fleeing from Cracow on account of the "bad air", or plague, which was raging there. The queen felt birth pains in Kozienice, and the court was forced to stop. She went into labour on January 1, 1467 and gave birth to a son who received the name Zygmunt. He later became king of Poland, and reigned from 1506–1549 as Zygmunt the First, also known as Zygmunt the Old, having died at the age of 83.

After the death of King Zygmunt the Old, an obelisk twenty metres high and with inscriptions in Latin was set up in front of the church which he had earlier built, and it has remained there to this day. The column was renovated at the beginning of the 18th century.

Zygmunt August (1549–1572), son of Zygmunt the First, was an enthusiastic hunter who often used to come to Kozienice, where he built himself a palace. In 1549, he gave the lord of the village, Pyotr Firlei, the governor, the right to found a city with all the rights appertaining to one, such as self-management and jurisdiction and the right to organize fairs. Over the course of fifteen years, the king also freed the town's citizens from certain taxes, thus enabling them to build brick houses. Because the king was the city's real founder, folk memory considers him the founder of the entire settlement.

Kozienice attained a certain importance due to its location between the capital, Cracow, and Lithuania. Its function as a stopover allowed the area to develop. Industry arose – a brewery, brickworks, tannery, etc. Moreover, the Vistula served as a good means of communication at the time.

Later kings were also in the habit of coming to Kozienice, where they built themselves a beautiful palace with a large garden. In fact, the town acquired a reputation for its beautiful gardens. At the time of King Zygmunt August it had 177 houses and 194 gardens, an unusual phenomenon. The last king, Stanislaw Poniatowski, also used to hunt there, and he rebuilt the wooden palace with bricks.

[Page 4]

The Town's Growth

The following figures bear witness to the town's growth:

Year	No. of Houses
1574	177
1827	243
1860	246
1880	272
1895	508

According to the 1931 census, there were 653 houses for a population of 7,793, that is, an average of 12 persons per house. At the time, the town's area was 14.2 square kilometers, while the town of Zwolen, which belonged to the same administrative district, was much larger, having 991 houses and a population of 8757.

In 1611 two houses in Kozienice were owned by Jews, and two more were rented by Jews. Altogether, there were five Jewish homeowners and ten tenants living there. Six of the Jews were butchers, and six were engaged in distilling whisky.

The town was destroyed during the 17th century war with Sweden. In 1782, a great fire left little of the old town standing, and it was rebuilt according to a new plan, this time with two markets. Arms factories, tanneries, a steam-powered mill and a factory producing tin singles were also established.

During the Napoleonic wars, the Polish army, under Prince Josef Poniatowski, took the side of Napoleon, and fought against the Austrians in Kozienice in 1809. The Polish prince remained in Kozienice for a time, and while there, he received from his troops a trophy bearing the inscription, Miles–Imperatori, the army to its commander.

Battles also took place around Kozienice during the Kosciuszko rebellion of 1794–5.

After the partition of Poland, the section of the country to which Kozienice belonged fell to the Russians. From 1807 to 1812 (i.e., under Napoleon) Kozienice belonged to the voivode province of Sandomir (the administrative center of which was in Radom) in the Principality of Warsaw. Afterwards, Kozienice went over to Russia until the outbreak of the First World War when the town was occupied by the Austrian army. It remained in Austrian hands until the fall of Austro–Hungary and the defeat of the central powers, Germany and Austria, which led to the rise of independent Poland in November, 1918.

In 1844 the provinces of Kelc and Sandomir were combined to form the province of Radom.[1] In independent Poland, the province was replaced by a state with a governor, with its capital in Kelc.

[Page 5]

The privilege of 1616

With respect to the Jews, we know for a certainty that they were already to be found in Kozienice at the beginning of the 17th century. In 1616 they received a privilege from the king entitling them to live in Kozienice. They fell back upon this privilege in 1616 when threatened with expulsion from the town. At that time there were five Jewish homeowners in Kozienice, besides ten tenant families living in the Jewish houses or in rented quarters in non–

Jewish dwellings. Figuring only five persons per family (and this is the minimum), this amounts to a Jewish population of at least 75 persons.

In 1722 the Jews of Kozienice paid 354 zlotys poll–tax, there being at least so many Jews over one year old in the town. In 1726 there were 630 Jews in Kozienice. The significant increase in population is attributable at least in part to the exercise of stricter control than was practiced by the takers of the previous census.

In 1778 the synagogue, study–house, rabbi's house and other Jewish homes burnt down.

The following facts throw some light on the position of the Jews in the country as a whole as well as in Kozienice. During the Kosciuszko rebellion, battles with the Russian army took place near Kozienice. The Russian officers demanded that the Polish authorities and the Jewish community provide them with girls, threatening to burnt he city in the event of refusal.[2] This probably came about as a punishment, as the population sympathized with and aided the Polish rebels. At the same time, the Jews of Kozienice were forced to pay the vast sum of 4,000 zlotys. After the payment had been made, the Russians left a squadron of soldiers in the town, ostensibly for its protection. The soldiers, however, occupied themselves in plundering, and especially in plundering the Jews.

At the same time a woman from Kozienice named Zelda Mordkova (i.e., the wife of Mordekhai) who was then in Warsaw appealed to the Polish government on behalf of her husband, who had been imprisoned for not having a permit to stay in Warsaw, despite the fact that he was employed in the barracks for the needs of the military (he was apparently a craftsman). Moreover, at that time every "foreign" Jew who wished to remain in Warsaw had to pay a tax of three zlotys for 14 days.

Also at that time, two representatives of the Jewish community in Kozienice, Levek Vigdorovich and Moshek Mendelovich, went to the government with the charge that Russian troops had destroyed Jewish houses and sacked Jewish property, not only in the city itself but in the entire area appertaining to the Jewish community of Kozienice.[4]

[Page 6]

After the suppression of the Kosciuszko rebellion, Poland was divided among its three great neighbours, Russia, Prussia and Austria, thus losing its independence for 125 years. Throughout this time, with the exception of the six years between 1806 and 1813 when the so–called Principality of Warsaw arose under the impetus of Napoleon, Kozienice belonged to Russia. It was during this time that Kozienice became famous (and not only among Jews) as the home of the Maggid. The Maggid and his court laid their stamp on the life of the whole town.

Demographic Information

The first reliable official source as to the number of Jews in Kozienice dates from the year 1765. In that year, a census of all the Jews in independent Poland was carried out in order to determine how much federal tax they owed. The tax was paid by the head, and was therefore called in Polish poglowna, or poll–tax.[5] Every male and female over one year old was obliged to pay the tax on a yearly basis. In the year in question, the government wished to establish whether all Jews were paying the tax, and it therefore carried out this census. Poles appointed as enumerators went from house to house to register all the Jews, their names, professions, etc. They would be joined by representatives of the community who offered additional information.

Such, at least, was the theory; the practice was often quite different. The enumerators did not visit every dwelling; they noted only those who were at home and neglected to register those who were absent. Sometimes children were completely ignored, and the aged passed off as infants of under one year old. These facts indicate that the numbers of this census, too, must be referred to with reservation; they are not exact, being, in our opinion, too small.

Professor Raphael Mahler[6], who has particularly concerned himself with this question, has established that the numbers of this census must be increased in order to arrive at the real number of Jews who were living there at the time. Firstly, the infants, for whom the law made no provision, must be taken into account. According to Professor Mahler, these amounted to 6/35% of the general Jewish population. To these must also be added the "disclaimed persons" whom the census officials had either ignored completely or the residents deliberately not reported, in order not to pay the poll–tax. Their number would amount to about 20% of the registered Jewish population. Thus, if the census states that 1365 Jews[7] were living in Kozienice and its environs, this sum must be increased by 26.35% in order to arrive at the correct figure of 175 (1365 plus 360) persons, a large enough number, especially for those times.

[Page 7]

We get the following table up to the outbreak of the war in September 1939.

No. of Jews		Total Population	
Year	In Kozienice	In Kozienice	% of Jews
1765	1365 (1725)	—	—
1827[8]	1185	2008	59
1857	1980	2902	65
1860[9]	1950	3000	65
1893	2561	4742	54
1897	3764	6392	58.9
1909	4702	8633	54.5
1910	3431	5233	65.9
1921[10]	3811	6678	55.4
1931[11]	—	7793	—
1939[12]	4780	—	—

Let us now consider the number of Jews in the Kozienice district according to the latest two censuses in Poland and one from Czarist Russia. This will give us a picture of the development of the Jewish population during this period.

Year	Population	Jews	% of Jews
1897	107,964	13,591	12.6
1921	124,527	13,021	10.5
1931[13]	143,100	14,073	9.83

The figures demonstrate that while the non–Jewish population grew–chiefly through natural increase – by 35,036 persons, or 32.7%, between 1897 and 1931, the Jewish population increased by only 492 persons, or 3.54%. The decrease in the number of Jews between 1897 and 1921 is a result of the First World War and of Jewish emigration from the region. If we add that in 1890 the percentage of Jews in the district amounted to 13.4, the decrease will become more marked.

The absolute increase of 482 persons in the region's Jewish population at this time does not even take the natural increase of the Jews of Kozienice into account. In other words, some of the Jews from the city or its surrounding villages left their dwelling places over the course of time and moved to other places, either the larger cities of the area, such as Kelc, Radom and Warsaw, or else to other countries, America in particular. Of the total number of Jews in the area, only 1584 were living in the villages in 1921; the rest lived in the two district centres Kozienice and Zwolen, the latter having 3811 Jews. While Zwolen had fewer Jews than Kozienice, it was in fact a larger town, with more non–Jewish population than in Kozienice.

[Page 8]

The rate of natural increase was lower among Jews than non–Jews; in 1921 it amounted to no more than 12 per thousand for the entire region. For every thousand Jews there were 19.8 births and 8.0 deaths. Their rate of natural increase was thus 11.8 per thousand, while that of the non–Jewish population was almost twice as great. The percentage of Jewish growth in the region amounted to only 5.7% of the general increase, even though Jews comprised 10.5% of the total population. As a result, the Jewish population had a higher proportion of elderly than the non–Jewish. The following chart will make this clear.

Children

Year	Total No. Jews	up to 10	% of Children
1897	13,790	4,357	31.6
1921	13,013	3,146	24.2

On account of a greater natural increase, the Jewish community of 1897 was younger than that of 1921. In 1897, Jewish children comprised 13.2% of the total number of children under ten years of age in the district; in 1921, only 10%.

Fortunately, the situation changed in later years. The most intelligent sectors of the Jewish population were struck by the fact that the Jews, to put it simply, had begun to have fewer children. It is well known that the urban population tends as a rule, to have fewer children than the rural, and that the Jews – as we know – are primarily city dwellers. It is to this that the greater percentage of elderly among the Jews is to be traced. In the district of Kozienice, the number of Jews of fifty years of age and over was 66.3% higher than those between thirty and forty–nine, among other nationalities. The ratio was different among other peoples: the younger age groups were many times larger than the older, an understandable phenomenon for every normal people living in normal conditions. Such conditions did not apply to Jews in the diaspora.

That Jews must refer to the official census figures only with caution was pointed out by Jewish national circles in Poland immediately after the event. There was reason enough for the census commissioners to be unable to carry their work to perfection. Since the Polish government had an interest in there being more Poles and fewer national minorities in Poland, what difficulty was there for a commissioner to register a Polish speaking Jew as a native speaker of the language? Who would go browsing through the commissioner's papers, even though he was entitled to do so? One's mother tongue had to serve as an indication of membership in the Polish race, as the census forms had no category for nationality.

On the other hand, there were also enough reasons for Jews not to line up for registration. Firstly, there were those who, for religious reasons, neither wanted to be – and could not be – counted. Secondly, there were Jews who, for a number of reasons, had no desire to come into contact with any officials. The most important of these reasons was a lack of trust that the "goy" really meant nothing but statistics. Who knew what, God Forbid, could come out of it all? It was thus more reasonable not to appear on the list.

With respect to the Jews, the statistics are not exact. They must be increased, but by how much? The problem has yet to be solved.

[Page 9]

Census was held in liberated Poland in February, 1946 in order to assess the results of the recently ended war. According to this census, the district of Kozienice had 116,900 persons, a decrease of 26,200 from the census of 1931. In fact, the population was greater, if the natural increase of the Polish people between 1931 and 1946 is taken into consideration. Of course, there was less of an increase during the war, but an increase nevertheless. The wartime losses of the Polish nation are expressed in this population decrease, but hardly to the same extent as the genocide of the Jews, who vanished from the region completely. Today, the natural increase of the Polish people has more than made up for the number of Jews who lived there before the war. The number of Jews no longer figures in Polish population statistics. Other vestiges of them – houses, study–houses, cemeteries – are likewise in the process of disappearing. Any traces of the Jews have been completely covered up.

The Dynasty of Kozienice

The founder of the dynasty was Rabbi Yisroel of Kozienice (1740 – 1815), known as the Kozienicer Maggid (i.e., Preacher). Hasidim link his birth to a miracle of the Baal Shem Tov, who blessed the poverty stricken bookbinder, Shabsi of Ostrowca, and his wife, Pearl, with a child in their old age. Tradition has it that the child was called Yisroel because the Baal Shem Tov served as godfather at his bris.

Already as a child, Yisroel was completely devoted to learning. He used to fast and afflict himself. He became thin and sickly, so much so that in his old age he was forced to stay in bed, as walking, or even standing, was painful for him. Despite his weakness, the Maggid went into raptures while praying, and the words came out of his mouth like arrows winging their way towards heaven. "Rabbi Israel was sickly all through life and often on the very of death, but his prayers were so potent that the rows of devotees gazed at that frail form of his as though at a victorious general" (Martin Buber, <u>Tales of the Hasidim</u>, vol. 1, New York, 1947, p. 31).

He studied first with Rav Shmelke Horowitz in Ricziwol. Later on, he was the youngest of the 300 pupils of the Great Maggid, Rabbi Dov Ber of Mezeritch. "At the very zenith of his life and work, he still wished to be a disciple" (Buber). After his teacher's death in 1773, he went over to Rabbi Shmelke of Nickolsburg, and after the latter's death to Rebbe Reb Elimelekh of Lizensk, despite the fact that he himself was already grown up and could by then have become a rebbe. It is told that when Rebbe Reb Elimelekh divided his heritage among his best pupils before his death (1786), he gave his eyes to the later Seer of Lublin, Yankev Yitzkhok Horowitz; his mind to the later Rebbe of Rimanov, Rabbi Menakhem–Mendel; and to Rabbi Yisroel, the future Maggid of Kozienice – his heart.

With the exception of the Baal Shem Tov himself, no other <u>Tzaddik</u> is the subject of so many miracle tales as the Kozienicer Maggid. He linked the taking of donations and performance of miracles with the teaching of the Great Maggid. Dov Ber of Mezeritch, who held that the <u>Tzaddik ha–dor</u> (the chief religious man of this generation) is the intermediary between God and men and can, with his good deeds, prayers and devotion to the Lord, destroy evil and bring redemption to the world.

[Page 10]

The Maggid's Teaching

His prayer: "Lord of the world, I beg of you to redeem Israel. And if you do not want to do that, then redeem the goyim."

Another prayer: "My Lord, I stand before you like a messenger boy, and wait for you to send me wherever you will."

Concerning his prayers, he said to his son: "Believe me, my son, there was no alien thought that did not come to me while I was praying, and with the help of God I raised them all to their upper source and root, to the place where their tent stood at the beginning."

He was once visited by a wealthy Hasid who told him how he ate no meat, only bread and water. The rebbe cut him short and commanded him – nothing other than to eat meat and drink wine. When the rich man had left, the rebbe's intimates asked him what he was doing. He answered that if the rich man were able to eat only bread, what would he give his employees and the poor who came to him for donations but stones?

There was darkness in the world. Those were the times of the Napoleonic wars, of the rise of the Principality of Warsaw (1807–13). Afterwards, the war of Gog and Magog broke out: Napoleon versus Russia. The Hasidic world split into two camps, supporters and opponents of Napoleon, even though the tzaddikim usually took pains to keep their distance from the great events of the world. Rumours were circulating among the Hasidim that the end of the world was approaching. They believed that the Messiah was coming and clung to their rebbes. These momentous events drew the Kozienicer Maggid, too, into the web of politics.

In 1808 the Polish principality, under the auspices of Napoleon, instituted compulsory military service for Jews. There was a hue and cry among the Jews: A Jew in the army? Several years' service? Certain apostasy! People ran to the two great tzaddikim in Lublin and Kozienice for help. They prayed, and the decree was rescinded. The law was changed. Instead of sending men to the army, the Jewish community was obligated to pay 70, 000 zlotys ransom money for them. The historian Dubnow observes that apart from the prayers of the tzaddikim, bribery had its effect in this case.

The same government issued a second decree in 1812, forbidding Jews to keep taverns or trade in whisky. And again it was the same story: the tzaddikim helped, and the decree was deferred for two years. In the meantime, Napoleon suffered his great defeat at the Berezina River. The Polish Principality was dissolved, the Russians returned and everything was as before. Sh9mon Dubnow attributes this miracle, too, to the power of bribery.

[Page 11]

The Maggid's name was also known among non–Jews. Eminent Polish lords used to consult him on both private and public or governmental business. It is told that Prince Adam Czartoryski went personally to the Maggid to ask for an heir. The Maggid granted his request, and he besought the Lord in the following words, "You've got plenty of goyim, one more won't hurt." The prince got his son (Tzvi Meir Horowitz, The Maggid of Kozienice, His Life and Teaching, Tel Aviv, 1944, p. 86).

On another occasion, Czartoryski came to the Maggid along with another lord who did not believe in the Kozienicer and wished to prove to the prince that his faith in the Maggid was vain. The lord made a show of requesting the recovery of his seriously ill daughter, who was not really sick at all. However, the Maggid interrupted him, and told him to go home immediately if he wished to see his daughter alive. The lord departed right away, but upon his return home his daughter was already dead.

Adam Czartoryski also turned to the Maggid on matters of state. He asked him to pray for his lord Napoleon and the Polish forces. The rebbe prayed, but Napoleon lost the war. It is reported that during the reading of the megillah on Purim, when the words nafol tipol ("he will surely fall") were read, the Maggid cried out, " Napoleon tipol" (Napoleon will fall").

The Prince Poniatowski once visited the Maggid. The Maggid wished to dissuade him from going off to war, because he did not believe that Napoleon would win. The prince was drowned in 1813.

When the great war had ended in the defeat of Napoleon, and still the Messiah had not come, the three great tzaddikim –l the Seer of Lublin, Menakhem–Mendel of Rimanov and the Kozienicer – met at the Maggid's and decided to storm heaven with their prayers and thereby force the Lord to send the Messiah down on Simkhas–Toyre. They later agreed to abolish Tisha–b'Av and remake it as a festival commemorating the coming of the Messiah (David Kandel, "The Jews in 1812," in Biblioteka Warszawska, 1912, p. 172).

The heavens were enraged at the three tzaddikim who wished to impose their will on God. The Kozienicer passed away before Sukkos, the Rimanover six months later, and the Lubiner three months after that.

It is reported concerning the latter that after the hakofes on Simkhas–Toyre he retired to his private chambers and bewailed the exile – it had already lasted so long – in a loud voice. Later, the room became quiet. The rebbetzim went in after a moment, but the rebbe was gone – he had fallen out the window and lay in the street unconscious. Thus did heaven avenge itself upon the rebbe for attempting to force the coming of the Messiah. The Hasidim called this nefilah (a falling), and were generally reluctant to discuss it.

The Lubliner lay on his deathbed for the next nine months, finally succumbing on Tisha–b'Av, 1815, the very day which was to have been transformed into a great festival...Thus ended the struggle of the three tzaddikim to bring the Messiah by the power of their prayers.

[Page 12]

The Maggid was a great adept of learning. Great scholars would approach him with questions which he answered in the twinkling of an eye. He was also a bibliophile, and left a vast library of books and manuscripts behind him. Rabbi Shmelke Horowitz of Ricziwol said to him, "This little one is among the very greatest;" and the writer reporting this saying adds that, "He found no rival in any of his predecessors for his erudition, his acuity in the sea of the gemore and his stature as a kabbalist" (Aharon Markus, Hasidism, Tel Aviv, 1954, p. 112/4). Yisroel Mafta, another reliable source, said that both the Kozienicer and his son Moishe were of the class of King David (The Sages of Israel, An Encyclopedia of the Eminent Men of Israel in Recent Generations. Ed. Rabbi David Ha–Lakhmi. Tel Aviv. 1958. P. 244).

At his passing, the Maggid left an only son, Moishe Elyakim, and a daughter, Pearl. Moishe was always in seclusion, and was not highly regarded. The Hasidim did ot wish to elect him rebbe, but instead to appoint him as cantor on account of his fine voice. But the Seer of Lublin came to his aid. While on his deathbed, he interpreted the verse, "And when the ark set out,

Moses said, "as follows: after the Maggid had passed away ("when the ark set out"), the time had come for Moses to speak. So Moishe became the rebbe in Kozienice (Markus, p. 192).

Rabbi Moishele of Kozienice was a great scholar. He left many books behind him: The Well of Moses, The Teaching of Moses, The Congregation of Moses, The Understanding of Moses. He included citations from other tzaddikim in his works. Professor Mahler writes that "he did not stir from his father's teaching," that is, he followed in his father's footsteps in learning just as in accepting donations from his Hasidim. He believed that "the Tzaddik has it in his power to bring about the redemption," and acted accordingly. He was harsher on free-thinkers than his father, who was tolerant in this matter, had been. He called them "evil men, who think to bring persecutions upon Israel." He died on the twelfth of Elul, 1828, having been rebbe for fourteen years.

Rabbi Moishe was succeeded by his son, Rabbi Eliezer, a disciple of Rebbe Reb Khaim Halberstam of Sanz. He was succeeded by Rabbi Yekhiel-Yaakev, who was followed in his turn by his son, Yerakhmiel-Moishe, who was brought up by the second Rebbe Asher of Stolin (Raphael Mahler, Hasidim and the Enlightenment, Tel Aviv, 1961, p. 293). Rabbi Yerakhmiel-Moishe died in Chzanov in 1909.

The last rebbe, the fifth from the Maggid, was Rabbi Aharon Yekhiel Hopstein, the son of Rabbi Yerakhmiel-Moishe. He was named for his grandfathers, Aharon of Karlin and Yekhiel-Yaakev of Kozienice. Rabbi Arele was born in Kozienice in 1892. "Rabbi Aharon was a remarkably talented man, astute and profound, always cheerful and of good spirits." In his eyes could be seen "a superior power of wonder, albeit incomprehensible and inexplicable." He was a riddle to all, an insoluble riddle, the riddle of a mystery which was revealed neither in his life nor in his death.[114] Like the Maggid, he was distinguished by his love for the Jewish people.

Rabbi Arele was not in Kozienice for long. He moved to Lodz, then to Warsaw and finally settled in Otwock where his Hasidim had bought him a villa. With him, the Kozienice dynasty came to a close.

[Page 13]

The Jews of Kozienice and their Livelihood

It is to be expected that in a town like Kozienice the Jews would live from craftwork and commerce. They were the only representatives of certain trades in the town, either through having their own businesses or else through acting as brokers or managers for others. There were also clergymen: a rabbi, a ritual slaughterer, a beadle, and–to draw a distinction–a bath-house attendant, who was also a barber and a medicine man who used leeches or other primitive methods to help the sick. Of course, Jews were also involved in tavern keeping and renting estates from great lords, and, due to shortages in the banks, they also lent money at interest.

The Jews had to struggle against their Christian competitors, and also to put up with various aggravations on the part of the rabble. For the right to work, a right more than once forcibly abrogated by their Christian townsmen, the Jews had to pay both the civic authorities and the guilds, as well as those who had enough "pull" to demand a payoff. They had no choice but to accede to such demands.

Moreover, there was never any lack of voices crying for the expulsion of the town's Jews, or at least for the revocation of their right to keep taverns. These, it was said, served only to spread drunkenness among the Poles and were corrupting the entire people. The truth of these allegations was never investigated, but many believed this propaganda nonetheless. Such voices were raised even during the so–called "Great Polish Sejm" (1788–92) which concerned itself, among other things, with the Jewish question in Poland.[15]

The Jews of Kozienice performed useful work. A Polish source of 1791 (Dziennik Handlowy) relates that there were active in Kozienice a Jewish stocking factory and a Jewish soap factory.[16] Soap making, like candle making, was in Jewish hands because the Jews were concerned that the products in questions be manufactured from kosher raw materials, and not from lard. However, it is clear that the products were sold to anybody.

The Polish historians have forgotten to add that Jews had established the industry in Kozienice. In the 18th century, the town was known for its royal weapons factory, in which Jews were also working.

It is also known that in those far off times there was a large number of Jews who had no means of support and lived from hand–outs. The town itself was unable to accommodate all its poor, who therefore had to wander about the country, going from door to door. One such "vagabond" was caught in Piotrkow along with his wife and sister, and sent "home" under guard.[17] The same thing happened to another Jew from Kozienice named Itzik Abramowicz, who had wandered with his wife, Leah, as far as Piotrkow.[18]

The establishment of a hasidic "court" in Kozienice brought about an economic revival. Hasidim came from near and far to seek the rebbe's advice or ask his help on ordinary Mondays or Thursdays, and to far–bring (pass some time) with him on holidays and the Days of Awe. The hasidim, who were not necessarily poor, would stay in town a few days, and receive lodging and meals from the local Jews. Jewish wagon drivers brought them to Kozienice and took them away. A few families lived entirely from this.

Even after the "discovery" of the train, Jews, and especially hasidim, persisted in going to the rebbe by wagon. Going by wagon was more "Jewish"; besides, a train goes when it wants to, a Jewish wagon–driver when he is told to. Naturally, there is no comparison between the pleasure of travelling in a wagon with a group of Jews, hearing and telling one's fill of stories, stopping for minkhe–mayrev at a Jewish inn and enjoying the inn–keeper's hospitality, than flying along in some fiendish train. Before you know where you are, you're gone. If you turn aside to rest, good luck knows where you are, but bad luck doesn't rest, especially when it sees Jews going to the rebbe for the Days of Awe.

In the second half of the 19th century the leather working industry arose in Radom, the provincial capital. This naturally led to increased employment in Kozienice: people worked in Radom, or else brought work home and delivered the finished goods to Radom.

The situation remained the same for many years. For the majority of the Jews, aside from the tiny elite, the struggle to make a living was hard at all times.

After the Rise of Poland

After the end of the First World War new nations arose from the ruins of the defeated powers. Poland inherited territories from Germany and Austria, as well as provinces which had previously belonged to Russia. Among these latter was the province of Radom, with its county–seat Kozienice, which had been occupied by Germany and Austria during the war. A new world had come into existence. The old borders ceased to exist, and new ones arose in their place.

[Page 15]

The huge export trade which had existed before between Congress Poland and Russia was no more, and Poland had to seek new markets for its manufactured goods. However, before the newly established country could switch over to another, more economically feasible production plan, it had first to discover what was in fact possible for it, and then to decide what was to be done.

The same problems faced the Jews. One had to determine what was owned by three million Jews, former members of three great nations who suddenly found themselves in a new country, what their production strength and economic base were. After examining their situation, it would be possible to devise a plan for constructive work. Such was the approach of the Joint, an American institution set up during the war, which began its rescue work immediately upon the war's end.

In 1921 the Joint carried out an inquiry among the Jews of Poland concerning their industrial undertakings. The results were elaborated and published in several volume with texts in Polish, Yiddish and English under the title, <u>Jewish Industrial Undertakings in Poland According to the Inquiry of 1921</u>, elaborated under the supervision of Eliezer Heller, engineer, Warsaw, 1923.

The inquiry did not embrace every town, but did include Kozienice, which is found in the fourth volume, devoted to the state of Kelc which replaced the earlier province of Radom. This volume is the source of the following table. The inquiry in Kozienice encompassed 224 undertakings, all of which were probably in existence before the war and were, of course, still operating at the time of the inquiry. None was shut down on account of the war. Presumably, there was no other Jewish industry in Kozienice.

A total of 497 people were employed in these undertakings, almost half of whom (224, or 45.1%) were their owners. The rest were employees. Both owners and employees were Jews.

[Page 16]

The figures indicate that the enterprises were small, averaging two workers each. They are divided thus:

Production Class	Undertakings	Employees	Owners	Family Members	Hired Workers
Metal	6	8	6	1	1
Machinery and the like	2	2	2	0	0
Wood	7	14	7	0	7
Leather, fur	6	7	6	0	1
Clothing and adornment	165	394	165	8	221 (18 women)
Paper	7	15	7	0	8
Nutrition and luxuries	24	48	24	20	4
Construction	4	5	4	0	1
Graphics	1	1	1	0	0
Sanitation	2	3	2	0	1
Total	224	497	224	29	244

The division into classes of production stands in need of some elaboration, as the classes themselves are rather too inclusive.

Appertaining to metal–work are: Blacksmithing, tinsmithing, foundries, keymaking and similar undertakings.

To machinery: Wheelwrights, dental equipment(!), watchmaking (not a terribly successful combination).

To the wood industry: Sawmills, carpentry, frame–making and box–making.

To the leather industry: Tannery, belt–making, shoemaking and purse–and–wallet–making.

[Page 17]

Adornments: Corset–making.

Paper: Bags, wallpaper, bookbinding and notebook making.

Nutrition: Flour mills, cereal mills, matzoh bakeries and slaughterhouses.

Graphics: Printing and photography.

Sanitation: Hairdressing, bathing establishments.

The statistics indicate that the proprietors alone only worked in 88 of 224 enterprises. In the other 136 there worked 136 proprietors, 29 family members and 244 hired workers. It is thus apparent that the proprietors themselves were far from wealthy–not one lived from his profits alone, without himself having to work.

The greatest number of these businesses, 165, or 73.7%, was devoted to tailoring and shoemaking. These employed 394 people, or 90.6% of all those employed. About 500 craftsman and small businessman are handling the shoe industry. Shoes are being shipped to Zaglembia and Galicia and the biggest part of the town lives from it.

Changes came about between 1921 and 1939. Many businesses closed, while few new ones (a candy factory) opened up, both on account of the general economic crisis and the increase in Jewish emigration from Kozienice. With the increase of the general population in a greater proportion, and the Jewish population in a lesser, the total number of craftsmen also increased. Nevertheless, the economic level of the Jews in Kozienice fell chiefly because of the general economic crisis, the great boycott of Jewish businesses ("Don't buy from Jews", "Support the Polish merchant, the Polish craftsman") and the anti–Semitic policies of the government (heavy taxes on Jews[19], "protocols" against them and other persecutions). As a result, the poverty and helplessness– of the Polish Jews in general–was growing.

Characteristic of the government's attitude toward the Jews in Kozienice is the fact that, in the last months before the outbreak of World War II, the government succeeded in closing a mill and a sawmill belonging to Jews. The civic authorities refused to receive a delegation of prominent Jews who wished to intervene in the matter (Haynt, May 17, 1939).

The same considerations apply to merchants as to craftsmen. Certainly, their number was not less than that of the craftsmen, but we lack precise details. Nevertheless, an inquiry made by the economic–statistical section of the Jewish Research Institute which embraced 91 towns and villages (including Kozienice), gives us a partial, but correct picture which reflects the situation in this area.

According to this inquiry, there were 126 stores in Kozienice in 1932. Of these 103–81.7%–were owned by Jews, as opposed to 1937; when only 110 of 154 stores–71.4–%–were Jewish owned. Over the course of these five years the number of non–Jewish stores went from 23 to 44 (almost double), while that of Jewish–owned stores increased by only 7. The index of Jewish participation in trade thereby decreased by 13%.

[Page 18]

More or less the same thing took place in the other towns covered by the inquiry.[20] Yankev Leshtshinsky, the reviser of the inquiry, was therefore correct to write, "The decline in the absolute number of Jews employed in all branches of retailing – village trade, market trade, the fair trade and storekeeping – can be established with complete certainty" (see Jewish economics, no. 1, May 1937, p. 7–18).

Such was the outlook until just before the war. In the last two years, 1937–39, conditions certainly did not change in favour of the Jews. An indication of the impoverishment and hopelessness of the Jews in the town is afforded by the fact that its only co–operative bank went out of business in 1937. This piece of news is found in the 1937 report of the Association of Co–operative Banks in Poland, of which the Kozienice bank had been a member.

In the final years, the last estate owner in Kozienice, Graff Larski, employed Jews at physical labour. He was no anti–Semite, and gladly employed Jews in his palace and household.

Political and Community Life

With the rise of independent Poland, Jews within and outside of the country took a positive attitude toward it, hoping to receive that which they had never obtained in Czarist Russia: civil and national rights. Jews received the right to organize a kehilla (congregation, community), although not in the fashion wished for by Jewish nationalist circles. According to Polish law, the kehilla was an institution for religious matters and social welfare, and not an all–embracing institution of Jewish autonomy. Almost all the Jewish parties, with the exception of the religious groups on the extreme right, fought against this, but without success.

Little by little, the political situation in Poland also changed. Step by step, Poland went from democracy to fascism. A clearer indication: the new constitution of 1934, as well as the official abrogation throughout Poland of the treaty concerning the rights of national minorities. It was primarily the Jews who suffered from this. The government disrupted the work of the Jewish parties, closed their meeting halls and prevented campaigning during the elections.

This was the passing of the Russian order, which recognized no kehilla but an appointed "crown" rabbi, who had no need of rabbinic ordination, no need to know anything of the religion. The new kehilla system in Kozienice led to the unfolding of a droll but true story.

[Page 19]

In 1896 the governor of Radom decreed that the birth registry was to be kept in Russian, and not as heretofore in Yiddish. The rav at that time, who was the Maggid's grandson, did not know a single word of Russian, so the community sought out a bright young man by the name of Yankev Hersch Weinberg who knew Russian and could also "learn" a little. The governor appointed him "Kozienicer Rabbiner", with a salary of 2000 rubles a year. So Weinberg kept the birth records of Kozienice, Zwolen and Gniewoszow, but the real rav, with all the attributes belonging to him as far as the Jews were concerned, remained the same as before, although the government recognized only Weinberg.

Things continued in this fashion until the outbreak of World War I. When the Austrians captured Kozienice in 1914, Yankev Hersch Weinberg ceased to be a "rabbi", and opened a printing shop and bookstore. The officials stopped paying him his stipend. Weinberg took matters into his own hands and charged those who came to him for civil documents a fee.

After the rise of independent Poland, the new kehilla administration did not insert his stipend into their budget of 1921, as he was not really a rabbi and according to Jewish law had o right to be paid for rabbinical duties. Weinberg appealed to the Governor of Kelc, who in 1925 decided that Weinberg deserved a pension because he was a rabbi. The kehilla administration appealed to the ministry. How was it that a governor should decide who is and is not a rabbi? Weinberg had no rabbinical qualifications, and had also received no pension in the past eleven years. The kehilla also took this opportunity to request that the registry books be taken from Weinberg and handed over to them.

The ministry did not corroborate the governor's edict. Weinberg appealed for an annulment of the ministry's decision to the highest administrative tribunal. The tribunal referred the matter back to the governor and everything began all over again.

The matter went to the supreme court three times, until it finally came before the Kelc district court, because Weinberg was not satisfied with the pension of 523 zlotys a year granted by order of the tribunal. He demanded 2000 zlotys a year. He also complained that he was called "crown", and not "town" rabbi.

The litigation went on for six years (and the entire matter for eleven) until finally an expert appeared before the court – Rabbi Kestenberg, the rav of Radom, who was likewise conducting a fight against the Radomerkehilla with the government's help. The court assigned "Rabbi" Weinberg a pension of 2400 zlotys a year from 1925. He received nothing for the earlier years (1914–25) because he did not submit his demands until 1921.

This was a great expense for the budget of the <u>kehilla</u>, considering that it was struggling with financial difficulties. The government had not given it a subsidy, and the Jewish population had been impoverished because of the government's economic policies (heavy taxes, the revoking of concessions from Jews, the closing of Jewish trade and industrial enterprises for "sanitary" or security reasons, and so forth).

[Page 20]

Party Life Prospers

Despite persecutions on the part of the government, an economic boycott on the part of the Polish anti–Semitic parties, and criminal attacks on Jews by the Hitlerized youth, Jewish party–life went on as normal. The vitality of the Jewish people is indicated by the fact that, regardless of the war looming between Poland and Germany, the material straits of the Polish Jews and their internal divisions, the Jewish parties carried on their party and cultural work until the eleventh hour, bringing about a spiritual revival of the Jews, who were already on the verge of destruction.

This is also to be seen clearly in Jewish Kozienice. At its January 1927 general meeting, the Zionist organization decided to re–open its library and name it after Elimelekh Neudorf, one of the founders of the organization (Haynt, January 23, 1927).

In June 1927, the Kozienice Revisionist organization celebrated the showing of its colours. A delegation of important guests came from Warsaw, and a "lecture of great significance" was given in shul on Saturday morning. There was a celebration, followed by entertainment, in the evening, and in the morning the guests were taken to the train, marching through the streets with the flag flying (Haynt, July 2, 1928).

A branch of Tarbut was also founded on this occasion, as well as a committee to celebrate the twentieth anniversary of the centre–Zionist daily newspaper, <u>The Haynt</u>.

On the other side, the Bundist organizations convened evenings, lectures, etc. In the elections for the third Sejm (1928), the Bundist organization in Kozienice received 344 votes (<u>Neue Volkszeitung</u>, March 12, 1928). At that time, however, there were no Jewish Seim representatives from the whole Kozienice district.

On the 20th and 21st of January 1934, the future hero and martyr Artur Zigelbaum visited Kozienice and lectured on the "The Labour Movement at the Crossroads" and "Kasrilevke and Menakhem–Mendel".

The Kozienice correspondent of the Warsaw <u>Haynt</u> was A. Bornstein.

From the election results of the eighteenth Zionist congress, held in Kozienice in July 1939 (<u>Haynt</u>, July 26, 1939), we get a picture of what was taking place among the Zionists immediately before the war. The division of votes was as follows:

1.	The General Zionist Organization	54
2.	Et Livnot	2
3.	Mizrahi	15
4.	The Judenstadt Party	1
5.	The Front for Labour in Eretz Yisrael	47
6.	Left Poale Zion	14
7.	Zionist Youth, members of no. 1	31
		164

[Page 21]

It goes without saying that the two larger parties in Kozienice, Agudas Yisroel and the Bund, took no part in these elections. The latter still had its representative (Councilman Opatowski) in the second last civic government. He was elected in 1934 by a coalition of the Left Poale Zion and the Communists. This common ticket pulled in a large number of votes: 500 (Neue Volkszeitung, June 2, 3, 1934).

The Jews had no representatives in the last civic elections in Kozienice in 1939 because there was but one Polish uniform ticket on the ballots, that of Ozon ("The Camp of Polish National Unity" of the ruling reactionary party), and it won every seat (Haynt, May 17, 1939). The Jews were left without any representation in the administration of the city and, as a Jewish paper expressed it at the time, the Kozienice city hall was Judenrein, anticipating that the whole town would very shortly be the same.

[Page 22]

The Bank of Kozienice

In the 1926 statistical report of the Association of Jewish Co–operative Banks in Poland, the bank of Kozienice is not yet mentioned. In the 1937 report, it is mentioned as being in liquidation. The bank, then, had a brief existence of less than ten years. It is possible that the bank existed somewhat earlier, but was not a member of the Association. Nevertheless, the fact that it went under at a time when poverty made such an institution necessary, and while the Central interest–free Credit Union (Cekabe – Centralna Kasa Bezprocentowa) was giving interest–free loans to the smaller banks and doing everything in its power to keep them going, indicates how bad economic conditions were for the Jews of Poland.

The following information about the bank of Kozienice is presented according to the <u>Statistical Reports</u> published yearly by the main office of the Co–operative Banks. The following figures refer to 1931, and are divided into two parts: one for the first half–year, one for the second. The figures for the second half–year are printed under those of the first, so that the differences may be seen at a glance.

The bank's official name was <u>Bank Spoldzielczy Creditow</u>. Its situation on July 8 and December 31, 1931 was as follows:

[Page 23]

<u>The State of the Kozhenitz Bank in 1931</u>

Receipts	Rents	Notes & Loans	Cashed Notes	Other Credits	
130	2234	22,440	14,000	49,735	
507	1065	20,890	20,000	44,862	
Movable Properties	Various Accounts	Administrative Organizational Expenses	Paid–Up Interest and Provisions	Loss from Previous Year	
1865	22,382	10,549	5,120	2,904	
1865	11,567	17,538	7,830	—	
Documents for Collection	Net Balance	Member Contributions	Reserve Fund	Deposits, Current Accounts	
148,170	256,929	9,778	117	53,506	
113,592	221,176	8,198	34	43,532	
Debts in Central Bank	Recashed Notes	Other Debts Interest	Handling on Loans	Provisions from Other Operations	Various Collections
10,000	—	4,504	4,530	6,750	167,738
10,000	4,190	5,4041	7,649	12,835	129,337

The amounts are in Polish zlotys.

Loans given out:				
Number	Sum (Global)	Average (per loan)		
134	41,450	115		
223	74,100	232		

The amounts are in Polish zlotys.

Loans given out:				
Cashing:				
Number of Documents	Sum			
1,500	42,950			
3,950	265,943			
Documents for Collection:				
Number	Sum			
6856	42,739			
826,795	1,427,258			
Members of the Bank:				
Manual Labourers	Retailers	Merchants	Various	Total
102	106	3	12	223
104	107	4	12	227

The amounts are in Polish zlotys.

A member contribution amounted to about forty zlotys.

What can be learned from the differences between the two tables?

[Page 24]

First, that the number of borrowers increased from 134 to 223, the amount of the loans growing equivalently from 41,150 zlotys to 74,100, while deposits fell from 53,560 to 43,532 zlotys. The number of cashed documents also increased significantly, from 1 500 to 3950, the sum going from 42,950 to 256,943 zlotys.

The combined facts point to an impoverishment of the Jewish population. The bank's loss for the first half–year – 2904 zlotys – likewise resulted from this: there was no money with which to return loans or buy up notes. Not only did this cause the bank to suffer, it may also have led to its ruin.

[Page 25]

Footnotes:

1. There were seven districts or counties in the province of Radom, among them that of Kozienice.

2. See Dr. E. Ringelblum, <u>Zydzi w powstaniu kosciuszkowskim</u>, Warszawa, 1938, p.89.

3. ibid., p. 109.

4. ibid., p. 146.

5. In the records of the Council of the Four Lands this tax was called <u>gilgul</u>.

6. In his work <u>Yidn in amolikn poylin likht fun tzifern</u>, Warsaw, 1958.

7. J. Kleczynski, <u>Liczba glow zydowskich w Koronie z taryf r. 1765</u>, p. 9.

8. Bohdan Wasiutynski, <u>Zydzi w Krolestwie Polskim</u>, p. 56 for the years 1827, 1857, 1893, 1909, 1910.

9. <u>Encyklopedia Judaica</u>, Kozienice, for the years 1860 1897.

10. <u>Bohdan Wasiutynski, Ludnosc zydowska w Polsce na przelomie wieku</u> XIX i XX.

11. <u>Statistiches Gemeindeverzeichnis des bisherigen polnischen Staates</u>, a German publication (Berlin) from 1939.

12. According to the materials from the Joint in Poland. Compare A. Rutkowski, "Martyrologia, walka I zaglada ludnosci zydowskiej w dystrykcie radomskim podczas okupacji hiterlwskiej," <u>Biuletyn Zydowskiego Instytutu Historycznego w Polsce</u>, 15–6 (1955) p. 167, table IX.

13. It is worth adding that there was a large number of Germans – 2498, or 1.74% of the general population, according to native tongue – in the Kozienice district.

14. <u>Eleh Ezkerah, Osef Toldot K'doshei TaSh–TaShHe</u>, edited by Yitzchok Levine, volume 3, New York (1959), p. 78/81.

15. Dr. Emanuel Ringelblum, <u>Projekty I proby przewarstwowienia Zydow w okresie stanislawowskim</u>, Warszawa, 1938, p. 11.

16. ibid., p. 43.

17. ibid., p. 53.

18. ibid., p. 26.

19. Even the club of Jewish representatives in the Polish Sejm, which was part of the Jewish National Council, intervened over this issue. (See the report of the club's activities printed under the editorship of representative Yitzkhok Greenbaum, Warsaw, 1923. After that "golden age" for the Jews in Poland, things took a great turn for the worse).

20. The material concerning Kozienice was provided by Kozienice resident and correspondent for the Economic–Statistical section, Sholem Fish.

[Page 26]

Kozienice and its Jewish Settlement
by Abraham Tennenbaum, Warsaw

The town is enclosed by the Vistula on the northeast, by the evergreen and deciduous woods of the well–known Kozienice forests on the southwest. The ancient name of the town testified that she–goats and deer lived in its forests.

In the beginning, the residents of Kozienice were the nuns of the Norbertian convent. Later, in 1390, it came into the hands of King Jagello. In 1409 he ordered a bridge built over the Vistula this enabling his forces to cross over during the attacks of the crusaders.

In 1466 King Kazimiez the Fourth sought refuge in Kozienice from the plague, and in 1467 King Zygmunt the First was born there.

Proclaimed a City in 1549

A privilege from King Zygmunt August in 1549 empowered the governor of Rias, Pyotr Pirlei, and the chief of the district of Radom to declare that section of the village lying close by the royal palace a city. At the same time, the king ordered some of the woods cut down and converted to fields and gardens.

The new city was endowed with the rights of German cities, the so–called Rights of Magdeburg, and its residents were freed from various tolls and taxes.

In the 167 houses of the entire district of Kozienice there lived: 10 distillers, 11 butchers, 20 cobblers, 4 smiths, 2 locksmiths, 2 leeches, 2 fur tailors, 6 pitch makers, 4 carpenters, 2 cabinetmakers, 2 coopers, 7 tailors and 4 bakers. There were two Jewish houses with five families living in them.

20 Houses Left after the War with Sweden

Commander Stefan Czarnecki, the castellan of Kiev, destroyed the Swedish army under General Torskild at Kozienice. All six Swedish divisions were wiped out in these battles, which took place in 1656. The town was ravaged to the extent that a census of 1660 found only twenty houses left. The Swedes destroyed the town again in 1704.

King August the Third was a frequent visitor to Kozienice, being in the habit of going there to hunt.

[Page 27]

King Stanislaw August also used to come often to Kozienice. He rebuilt the wooden palace as a brick one, and planted a large garden— still to be found there today.

Kozienice burned down in 1782. After the fire, the residents began to build brick houses, and they built a market in the centre of town.

At about the same time, crafts began to develop in Kozienice. Craftsmen came, an ammunition factory was founded with qualified workers from Germany and Belgium. An industrial region was being formed.

In 1809 General Zajonczek fought against the Austrians near Kozienice.

There is a monument near the palace, dedicated to King Zygmunt the Third. Its inscription tells of King Zygmunt the First's victory in the war with the Tatars and Wallachians. Historians deduce from this that the monument was erected toward the end of Zygmunt's reign in Poland.

Jews in Kozienice

Jews were already living in Kozienice at the time of King Zygmunt August in the second half of the sixteenth century. Restrictions against them were probably in existence at that time. We learn this from the fact that at that time there were only two Jewish houses with five owners in Kozienice. I claim therefore that there were only five Jewish families in all Kozienice.

Attitudes toward the Jews grew more liberal with time. This is to be deduced from the fact that 1365 Jews in Kozienice and its environs paid the poll–tax of 1765. If we consider that children of under one year were not paid for, we will arrive at the conviction that the Jewish population at that time numbered far more than 1365 persons.

Many factories were established in Kozienice in the nineteenth century. According to the documents, factories for sheet zinc, iron and brass, tanneries, pitcheries and a brewery were founded. This industrial development brought about a large increase in population, particularly in the Jewish population.

Jews in Kozienice

Year	1827	1857	1860	1897	1921	1931
Total	2005	2902	3000	6368	6878	7808
Jewish Population	1185	1980	1960	3764	3811	4550
% Jews	58.0	68.8	65.3	58.9	55.4	58.8

Jews in the Kozienice District

Year	1897	1921
Jewish Population	13,591	13,021
%Jews	12.6	10

According to Russian sources, 6882 persons lived in Kozienice in 1897, among them 3700 Jews, a figure which also includes eight Karaites.

[Page 28]

We see from the table that, beginning with the first half of the nineteenth century, the Jewish population of Kozienice was larger than the non–Jewish.

In 1897, number of Jews living in the neighbouring towns was as follows:

Kozienice	1961
Glowaczow	1109
Gniewaszow	1536
Zwolen	3442
Magnuszew	771
Ricziwol	492
Cieciechow	125

In the twenties of the nineteenth century, a large part of the Jewish population of Ricziwol and Cieciechow moved to the larger cities of Poland.

The Livelihood of the Jews of Kozienice in the 19th Century

In the area of employment, we have very few sources or reports. We learn From Russian sources of information that in the nineties of the nineteenth century, the pattern of Jewish employment was as follows:

In State Administration	1 Jew
In the Military	26 Jews
Rabbis	4
In Community Institutions	24
Melamdim and Teachers	11
From House Revenue and Capital	31
Bank Employees	5
Landworkers	48
Textile Workers	4
Butchers	13
Carpenters and Builders	18
Tinsmiths	12
Ceramic Workers	9
In Mills	7
Printers	7
Watchmakers	3
Workers in Religious Ritual	8
Tailors and Fur Workers	25
Shoemakers and Leather Industry	38
Construction Workers	10
Hotel and Restaurant Employees	13
In Trade	128
Various Occupations	87
TOTAL	532 Jews

[Page 29]
The Number of Jews at the Time of the Nazi Occupation

Year	1939	1940	1941
Jewish Population	4870	4208	4335

March 1942	April 1942	September 1942
4500	4756	13,000

The Growth of the Jewish Population is due to the transfer of Jews from the Surrounding Towns.

Businessmen	34 persons
Retailers	3,170
Landworkers	283
Of indefinite employment	303

The last day of the Jewish settlement in Kozienice was September 27, 1942. On that day all Jews from Kozienice and its environs were transported to the death camp of Treblinka.

[Page 30]
An Evil Wind Has Torn Up the Root
by Yissokhor Lederman, Rio de Janeiro

Our town lay in the district of Radom, almost four miles from the Vistula, and was surrounded by woods, and water, villages and towns such as Zwolen, Gniewaszow, Glowaczow, Magnuszew, Mniszow, Ricziwol, Cieciechow, Iedlnia, Garbatka and other, smaller Jewish settlements.

Before World War II, the Kozienice region with all the towns listed numbered some 15,000 Jewish souls.

Jews had been living in Kozienice for a great many years, and enjoyed many rights. The first document concerning Jews in Kozienice is an illustration record from 1611 in which it is indicated that there were two Jewish–owned houses there and two rented to Jews, in all of which there lived five landlords and ten tenants. There were six butchers and six distillers among them. They had already received the right to build a synagogue and a cemetery.

The Jews of Kozienice were slaughterers, ran small whisky and stocking factories, and traded with the neighbouring villages and landowners.

At the beginning of the eighteenth century, the settlement was growing. In 1765, the Jews of Kozienice, together with those of the neighbouring villages who belonged to the Kozienice kehilla, paid the poll–tax for 1365 people.

At the same time, the Kozienicer rebbe, Rabbi Yisroel Hopstein, revealed himself there. He was the son of Shabsi, a simple bookbinder, and was born, as the legend states, in Kozienice in the year 1737 and passed on in 1815. He was one of the pioneers of Hasidism in Poland, and his name lent itself to many tales and legends.

In 1856, there were 2885 people in Kozienice, 1961 of them Jews. In 1897, there were 3700 Jews there, out of a total population of 6882.

These, in brief, are a few details taken from historical sources. The Jewish community of Kozienice existed scarcely four hundred years. Established in 1611, it played a significant part in the economic as well as the religious, cultural and political life of Polish Jewry. An evil stormwind tore it all up by the roots.

[Page 31]

The City of Kozienice in 1895
by A. Weber

With Ricziwol behind me, I proceed to Kozienice, a city high in the estimation of our countrymen who extol the saints. The glory of the holy Maggid, his son, grandson and great–grandson resides there, and the town has remained a cradle of Hasidism to this day. Three holy shepherds, the descendants of the great men, are living there even now, and the banner of the Maggid's court, in which his household implements, his bed, his table and his chair are still preserved, will wave higher than the monument to the birth of King Zygmunt the First which likewise stands in Kozienice.

I could tarry but a few hours in the city, and did not have the opportunity to visit very many of our brethren who dwell there. I contented myself with a general view of the appearance of the city, which has been cleansed of the filth and dirt which its rulers had poured upon its streets and courtyards in days gone by, and investigated only the material condition of our brethren and the source of their livelihood. And behold! I found that trade — that is, the grain and produce markets — was slow, and that while individual merchants were making a good living due to the stationing of a division of troops in the city, the majority still complained of their situation, and the number of poor among them was great.

I turned aside to see the dwellings of the Jewish craftsmen and artisans of the town, and found, to my sorrow, that their number was small and the types of their work, aside from tailoring and cobblery, but two:

1) Pounding groats, an occupation practiced by certain individuals from days of yore. Its profits yield a meagre living, as the work is done entirely by hand, there being no machines for the workers aside from hand–turned millstones.

2) Machine sewing of shoes. I thought to myself that those employed in this profession would provide me with a great deal of material for my report, for they worked at the occupation which had so recently given birth to the Enlightenment. I considered that I would be able to learn the principles of the Enlightenment, which had found such inroads in this holy city, from them. "Let me go see how goodly and pleasant it is," in one of the low–lying streets called by the citizens Witestwa, after the bishopric which is located there.

This section of the city is like a village. In a house close to the farthest reaches of the town, a young man sits at his workbench by the machines for sewing shoes. There are three of these in the large room of his store which looks out to the street, and three youths helping him in his work. I approached the house, and the young man recognized me as a stranger and wished me good day. I returned his greeting, and began to question him about his work and occupation.

[Page 32]

"How many workshops of this type are there in the city?" "Mine is the only one," he replied.

"If so, your work must bring you a fair income, for you have as many customers as the city has residents, over 3000 people." He replied that the situation was otherwise: "I don't earn much on account of the cut–throat competition from the shoe sewers in Radom."

"How can Radom offer any competition when you live in a small town in which the finished product costs less than a workman is paid in a big city like Radom? Your prices are not forced up by as many extra costs as theirs are, and your rent is less than it would be in Radom. So how, then, can they compete with you and rob you of your livelihood?"

"It's a riddle to you and me both, but that's how it is. The competition is too heavy for me to bear."

"And if you should try to undersell the merchandise which they supply to the stores, would you make anything?"

"Nothing," he answered. "I'll lose not only the cost of my workman, but also some of the money to pay for the material which I buy for my work. My capital is too small to let me compete with them even for a month."

No sign of Enlightenment was discernible in this young man; he would never be able to solve this riddle. It would undoubtedly solve itself for me with ease after I had seen what went on among his brother craftsmen in Radom. And so I prepared myself for the trip, wished the man good–bye, and set off for Radom.

Ha–Tsfira, 1895

[Page 33]

Jews in Kozienice
by Kazimiez Mruz[1]

The earliest information about Jews in Kozienice dates from 1616. On June 13 of that year King Zygmunt the Third permitted the Jews, by means of a special Privilege, to inhabit twelve houses. In the beginning, Jews lived in two out of 167 houses, that is, 1.2% of the total.

In 1629, Jews inhabited eight houses 4.5% of the total.

In 1718, 42% of all dwellings were Jewish, 49.5% in 1729.

In 1825, Jews owned 30.7% of all dwellings.

Footnote:

1. Polish teachers in Kozienice from 1928–1945. Taken from his book <u>Schools in Kozienice</u>.

HOUSE OF THE MAGID,
RABBI ISRAEL OF KOZIENICE

בית המגיד
ר' ישראל מקוז'ניץ

המגיד מקוז'ניץ מקבל חסידים.
דער קאָושעניצער מגיד נעמט אויף חסידים.

The Magid of Kozenice receives his chassidim

THE CHASSIDIM OF KOZENIECE

קאזשעניצער
חסידות

די לויה פון ר' אהרלע האָפשטיין.
מסע ההלוויה של חרבי ר' אהרלע הופשטין.

Funeral procession of Rabbi Aharale Hofshteyn

[Page 34]

SECTION 2 – Hasidim In Kozienice

From the History of the House of Kozienice
by Rabbi Abraham Isaac Brumberg, Jerusalem

In the following article, I shall attempt to describe the entire dynasty of the House of Kozienice, as well as its two offshoots, Mogielnica and Grodzisk. Beginning with the dynasty's father and founder, Rabbi Yisrael Hopfstein, known as the Maggid of Kozienice, it concluded with his descendants, who continued the line for five generations up until the Nazi holocaust of our own times.

The Maggid of Kozienice and his contemporary, the Seer of Lublin, were the first to disseminate the teachings of the Baal Shem Tov and found hasidic centres in Poland, and they are therefore considered the fathers of Polish hasidism.

As Lublin, the headquarters of the Seer, so Kozienice, the Maggid's headquarters, attained to considerable fame over the course of the generations, because the teachings of its righteous and brilliant founder went out over the length and breadth of Poland and beyond.

The Maggid was short of stature and thin of body, nothing but skin and bones. All his life he was sickly and bedridden, wrapped in downy quilts, but his spirit stormed the heavens, and tens of thousands of Polish Jews waited upon his word. Not for nothing did he become the guide of thousands in his day, and he left a legacy behind him for the generations.

In this article, I have provided only a summary of the Maggid's activity, for it has already been documented by others. I have rather applied myself to a delineation of his descendants, who have not been written upon; I found only shapeless material before me.

Rabbi Moshe Elyakim Beriah

First of all is the Maggid's son, Rabbi Moshe Elyakim Beriah, who remained "hidden" during his father's lifetime. His character was not appreciated, and after the death of the Maggid, the townspeople wished to employ him as a bath attendant in Kozienice. Thanks only to the intervention of the Seer of Lublin, he was restored to his father's place. He led the community for thirteen years (1815–1828), and left eight books behind him. These were published in the fifty years after his death, and we can see from them that he was a master of both revealed and hidden teachings.?

[Page 35]

עמוד השער לספרו של ר' אליקים משה בּרייעה, בּנו של המגיד.

שער־בּלאט פון ספר „בּאר־משה" לר' משה אליקים בּרייעה.

The Seraph of Mogielnica

After the death of Rabbi Moshe Elyakim Beriah, the Seraph of Mogielnica, first of the Maggid's grandchildren, inherited his seat. He was the son of Perele, the Maggid's daughter, was educated at the Maggid's and was eminent in Torah and <u>khasidus</u>. He led the congregation for twenty–one years (1828–1849). Although he left no books behind him, his son, the God–fearing Rabbi Elimelekh, founder of the Grodzisk branch of the dynasty, as well as his grandson, Elimelekh's son, the saintly Rabbi Yisrael, who was killed at the hands of the Nazis, published their books in their lifetime.

Rabbi Elazar

Rabbi Elazar, the son of Rabbi Moshe Elyakim Beriah, and the Maggid's second grandson, continued the dynasty for thirteen years (1849–1862) after the death of the Seraph of Mogielnica. He was deeply versed in hasidic doctrine, but left behind him only one small book, Khidushei MaHaRa (The Novellae of our teacher Rabbi Elazar).

Rabbi Yekhiel–Yaakov

Rabbi Elazar was succeeded by his sixteen year old son, Rabbi Yekhiel–Yaakov, who began to follow his own individual path of khasidus. Of interest in this connection is his saying, "Why is it written, 'We will go in our youth and our old age' rather than the other way round? The time will come when the aged tzaddikim will go after the young ones." He was among the younger tzaddikim, but he was plucked up in the noontide of his days, at the age of twenty, having "reigned" but four years.

Rabbi Yerakhmiel Moshe

His son, Rabbi Yerakhmiel Moshe, the fifth generation of the dynasty, lost his father at the age of five and was educated in Stolin by his stepfather, Reb Asher, and his step–grandfather, the Beit Aharon. At the age of twenty–four, he returned to Kozienice, thus restoring the glory of the dynasty to its former condition. He passed away in 1909 at the age of forty–nine.

The Maggid inherited the hasidic fervour of his teacher, Rebbe Reb Elimelekh of Lizensk and this, in combination with his own keen intellect, enabled him to lay the foundations of Hasidism in Poland. He saw his task as an errand, and used to say, "I stand before the Lord like a messenger boy ready to do his bidding at any and all times." His grandson the Seraph said, "If any Jew should attain to the level of self–abnegation, and is as nothing in his own eyes, behold, he is able to receive more from heaven than from his own faculties."?

[Page 36]

Rabbi Yerakhmiel Moshe, whose spiritual development had been influenced by his great forebears of Kozienice and Stolin, was prepared to give his life for the sake of Torah and Hasidism. During the Revolution of 1905, when Jewish workers began to breach the boundaries of their faith, he stood in the breach with great self–sacrifice.

Polish Hasidism built a strong wall against any ordinary or extraordinary wind blowing upon any area of Jewish life. The teachings of the Kozienicer Maggid served the Jews of Poland as a guide and beacon in their difficult struggle for survival.

Love of the Land of Israel

An especial strain of love for the land of Israel runs like a scarlet thread through all the generations of the House of Kozienice, beginning with the Maggid himself and ending with the sixth generation of his descendants, Rabbi Yisrael Elazar, who was the originator and founder of Kfar Khasidim in Israel.

It is told that when the time of Rebbe Reb Elimelekh of Lizensk's death had drawn high, he rested his hands upon the heads of his most outstanding students, and imparted his spirit to them. To the four who were closest to him, he gave also of his faculties: his intellect to Rabbi Menakhem–Mendel of Rimanov; his power of speech to Rabbi Avraham Yehoshua Heschel of Apta; his eyesight to the Seer of Lublin; and to the Maggid of Kozienice, his heart.

The Maggid's heart was indeed on fire, and it burned with three loves: love of God, man and Torah. He joined and interwove these loves until they became one huge flame blazing like an eternal and inextinguishable fire on the altar of his heart. The fire of his own heart kindled and enflamed those of all Israel. Not for nothing was he known as the second Besht–even their names were the same, and the Maggid was born as a result of the Besht's blessing.

The Maggid's Dream

Although the Maggid was born during the Besht's lifetime and was twenty-three at the time of his passing, he differs from other disciples of the Besht in never mentioning any encounters with him. In one place only, in his book Avodot Yisrael (page 96), does he mention that he saw and spoke with the Besht in a dream.

[Page 37]

"Once," he says, "I saw the Besht in a dream and asked him why it was that at the beginning of my service, when I had first gone to learn from the tzaddikim and their deeds and had accustomed myself to serve the Lord, I felt a daily change for the better within myself as a result of study of the Torah for its own sake, concentration on my prayer, and all such remaining activities; and why I now felt no change at all, and each day seemed the same as the one before."

"He answered me with a parable: 'When a child learns the alphabet or prayers or khumesh, the change in him becomes apparent from day to day, as he learns more every day. For example, last week he learned one parsha, and now he is learning two, and so forth. Should he continue to grow, this is not the case: if he can learn three parshas with commentary by himself, he has become very acute and no change will be discernible from day to day.'"

Reb Shabtai the Bookbinder

The Maggid was born about 1737 in the town of Apta (Opatow), Poland, in the old age of his parents, Shabtai and Pearl.

His father, Reb Shabtai Hopstein, was a bookbinder who scarcely made a living from his craft. Although he was poor all his life, he did not want to have recourse to the gifts of flesh and blood, and thus never accepted anything from the poor boxes. He was a simple and upright man, and served the Lord in joy and fear.

His wife, Pearl, was also satisfied with the little her husband earned at his labour, and did not come forth with grievances or complain of their want and distress.

Reb Shabtai and his wife lived out their days in quiet and contentment. They were saddened by only one thing: they yearned greatly for a son. Even though they were already old, they did not despair of their hope's being fulfilled, and they were indeed visited with a son in their old age, the Maggid of Kozienice, who enlightened the eyes of Israel with his righteousness, teaching and piety.

His birth is enveloped in wonderful tales. It is told that once on Yom Kippur a fight broke out in the synagogue in which Reb Shabtai was praying, and the congregation hit one another with their makhzorim until they tore them. Meanwhile, Reb Shabtai was absorbed in his prayers as usual, beseeching the Lord to give him a son who would enlighten the eyes of Israel with his teaching?

[Page 38]

After the service the congregation approached and told him jokingly that he would be helped this year, that it would be a good one for him. Reb Shabtai did not understand what they were referring to, for he had neither heard the scuffle nor seen that all the makhzorim had been torn, so he took their words at face value as a blessing that he have a good year and be helped with a son, for he was childless. Thus did heaven prepare a year of prosperity for him, a year in which everyone brought him their town makhzorim for repairs, a year in which he was blessed with a son.

Golden Buttons

Poverty dwelt with Reb Shabtai. He did not have enough work to live on, and he and his wife actually starved all week. Things came to such a pass that once they did not have enough for the necessities of shabbes, and they were left without wine, Khalla and candles. They decided that if God did not want to give them enough for shabbes, they would fast, if only to avoid having to borrow.

On Friday afternoon Reb Shabtai went to the synagogue as was his wont, to read Psalms, review the week's Torah portion and prepare himself to receive the Sabbath. After the services, he stayed in the synagogue until everyone had left and then walked home alone, in order that his neighbours not besiege him with questions. What, then was his surprise on approaching his house and seeing the light of shabbes candles shining through the window? And how did his astonishment increase when he entered the house and saw the table laden with bread and wine, meat and fish, and all the delicacies of the Sabbath. He did not wish to interrogate his wife as to where all this had come from, but she nevertheless felt her husband's astonishment and dismay, and joyfully told him how the deliverance of the Lord had come upon them in the twinkling of an eye.

After Reb Shabtai had gone to the synagogue, she began to sweep the house in honour of shabbes. Suddenly there sparkled out at her from a corner some golden buttons sewn onto a pair of old gloves. She took the buttons and sold them, receiving a decent price, and then went out and bought what they needed for shabbes.

When Reb Shabtai heard his wife's story, he saw that deliverance had indeed been sent down from heaven so that their shabbes might not be just another day, and he began to dance for joy.

Why did the Besht Laugh?

Hasidic legend goes on to tell that at the same time as Reb Shabtai was dancing around his shabbes table, the Baal Shem Tov was in Medzibozh with his company of disciples, sitting at his shabbes table and celebrating the festive meal. Suddenly he started laughing. His disciples were amazed by their rebbe's strange laughter, but none dared ask what had caused it.?

[Page 39]

The next evening after havdala, the Besht's senior disciple, Reb Ze'ev Wolf Kitzes, approached him and asked for an explanation of his mysterious laughter. The Baal Shem Tov did not reply, but told him to order the wagon driver to prepare for a journey.

The Besht's disciples boarded the wagon in ignorance of both the purpose and destination of their trip. They arrived in Apta the next morning, and the Baal Shem Tov sent immediately for Reb Shabtai the bookbinder. When the latter had come, the Besht commanded him to tell what had happened to him on Friday night.

Reb Shabtai told him the story from beginning to end, and when he had finished the Besht said, "Know that the whole of the heavenly household shared in your rejoicing. And now, say what you desire, and it will be granted you." Reb Shabtai replied that he wanted neither silver nor gold. He wanted but one thing of the Lord: to be visited with a son who would live. At this, the Baal Shem Tov blessed him with a blessing which was fulfilled.

And the Child Grew

A son was born to them that year, and the Besht came and held the child at his bris. The child was named Yisrael, after the Besht, for it was by virtue of the Besht's blessing that he had come into the world.

And the child grew and became a man, and enlightened the eyes of Israel with his teaching and with his righteousness. For this was Reb Yisrael, the Maggid of Kozienice, known also by the cognomen "The Second Besht" because he was as great a wonder in his generation as the Besht had been earlier.

Although he was a feeble child, his body skinny and thin, he was distinguished by his talents. A great soul dwelt in that puny frame, a sharp mind on top of it. In his earliest childhood he was recognized as having been created for greatness. His grasp was quick, his desire to learn Torah strong. Despite his poverty and want, Reb Shabtai spared no expense in his son's education, hiring the best teachers in the city for him. The boy soaked up everything he learned and went from triumph to triumph until, still a small boy, he gained renown as a prodigy in the city of Apta.

Apta was considered a city and mother to Israel, and there were many khevrot (societies) for Torah study there. Reb Shabtai, the bookbinder, was among the directors of a khevra called Ner Tamid shel Shabbat, or The Eternal Light of the Sabbath. This was a khevra of craftsmen, and its preceptor was Rabbi Moshe Natan Shapiro. When Yisrael had attained the age of seven, his father enrolled him as a member of this society, in order that on shabbes and in the evenings he might hear the lessons of the aforementioned rav. He is listed in the khevra's register: "During the intermediate days of Passover, 1744, the young boy, Yisrael ben Shabtai, was received into the organization, his father advancing the sum of three zloty." And so the child of seven sat at the same table with already aged students to hear a lesson in Torah

[Page 40]

The boy was young in years, but could already swim the sea of the Talmud and its interpreters like one much older. He made the nights as days: by day he learnt in yeshiva, by night, after hearing the rav's lesson, he would sit learning by himself in the study house like an expert and experienced scholar. In spite of the fact that the boy wasted no time away from his studies, his father still kept an eye on him, for he burned for his son to be a great scholar.

"I did not Wish to Benefit from the Glory of the Torah"

It is told that at Chanukah time his father because anxious lest the lad be enticed to play cards with the other children in the house study, as was the custom among Jewish children during the long Chanukah nights. Since, however, the boy had promised his father that he would not play, the latter bought him a three–cent candle which would give enough light to study by but, or so he thought, go out quickly enough that there would be not time to play cards. He gave Yisrael permission to go to the study house, expecting him home again within a short while.

Nevertheless, heaven seems to have taken great joy in the sight of the prodigy absorbed in holiness and purity, in his wonderful diligence at study. A miracle was prepared for him: the candle did not go out, but burned the whole night through. As long as the candle was lit, the boy would not forbear his studies, and he kept on with them, not realizing that the night had passed.

Towards morning he returned home and went to bed. When his father saw him, he became very angry and vented his wrath upon the boy, because he suspected him of having wasted the night playing cards. What did he do? He took a leather strap and beat him until the blood flowed. The boy took it in silence. "Truly," said the Maggid, recounting this tale of his childhood, "Had I told my father that I had not played but was studying the whole time, he would have believed me and would not have beaten me. But I did not wish to benefit from the glory of the Torah."

Wandering to a Place of Torah

When Rabbi Dov Berish Ha–Cohen Katz, the grandson of the Shach (Shabtai ben Meir ha–Cohen, 1621–1662, author of a standard commentary on the Shulkhan Arukh, Yoreh Deah and Khoshen Mishpat), became rabbi of Apta, the young prodigy went to study in his yeshiva. While there, the Maggid became friendly with his son, Yitzkhok A v rah am Katz, who was later head of the rabbinical court in Pinczow and author of the responsa Keter Kehuna.?

[Page 41]

At the age of thirteen, the future Maggid left Apta to wander to a place of learning. He went first to Ostrowice, near Apta, to study in the yeshiva of Rabbi Yekhezkel, father of the author of Har Ha–Karmel. He did not remain there long, as Rabbi Yekhezkel died in 1750.

From there he wandered farther to the city of Horochow in Volhynia to study with Rabbi Mordekhai Tzvi Horowitz, son of Yitzkhok Ha–Levi Horowitz, head of the rabbinical court of Hamburg–Altona. He also studied with Rabbi Menakhem of Tarla, whom he cites in his book Tehillot Yisrael.

He became known as a sage throughout Poland, and many attempted to marry him into their families. One of the leading rabbis of the day, Rabbi Aharon bar Meir of Brisk, the author of Minkhat Aharon, came to take him home as a bridegroom after having tested him and seen his great talents. However, the match did not come about for various reasons. The Maggid married a woman in Pshiskhah. After his marriage he lived by teaching in the villages.

At His Father's Grave

In 1761, when Yisrael was twenty–four, his aged father departed this world. His tombstone is engraved as follows: "Here lies a simple and upright man, the aged Reb Shabtai son of Ze'ev Wolf, who passed away on Friday, Shevat 25, in the year 5521 since the creation of the world."

From time to time the Maggid would go to prostrate himself on the grave on his father's yortsayt. Once, he leaned against the stone and was silent. After a while, he emitted a small laugh, and said to the beadle who accompanied him, "My father was a bookbinder, and just now I, too, have bound and joined all the worlds together."

Whenever he visited his father's grave he would stay with his friend, the tzaddik Reb Avraham Yehoshua Heschel of Apta. It is told that one year there had been a great snowfall (Rev Shabtai's yortsayt falls in the winter) and Rabbi Heschel ordered his congregants to make a path in the snow from the door of his house to Reb Shabtai's grave, in order that the Maggid be able to walk there. And so it was done.

It is also told that whenever the Maggid came to prostrate himself on his father's grave in Apta, the townspeople honoured him by letting him deliver a sermon in the synagogue. Once, when they asked him to do so, he replied, "Did my previous sermon have no effect?" They were unable to answer him, and went away in great sorrow. A man from the crowd, a simple craftsman, then approached and engaged him in conversation. The rabbi has said that his sermon of last year had no effect upon us. "Well, I've come to bear witness that from the time I heard him say that every man of Israel must observe the precept of 'I have set the Lord before me always,' from that time the Lord has stood always before my eyes, like a black fire on a white fire, and I tremble and am in awe of Him."

[Page 42]

His Intimacy with Reb Shmelke Horowitz

After the death of his father, Rabbi Yisrael moved to Pshiskha, in the district of Radom. The local preacher, Rabbi Avraham, was a disciple of the Besht, and he taught Yisrael how to preach and brought him near to Hasidism.

At the same time, he made the acquaintance of the great Rebbe Reb Shmelke Horowitz, who was then rav of the nearby town of Ricziwol. Rabbi Yisrael learned both revealed Torah and khasidus from Reb Shmelke, who was among the greatest of the disciples of the Maggid of Mezritch. Reb Shmelke also showed him a new way of studying Talmud which did not depend on pilpul, and Rabbi Yisrael became very close to him.

The rav also esteemed his student greatly. It is told that at the time when Rabbi Yisrael was studying with Reb Shmelke in Ricziwol, the misnagdim sent two messengers to ask him (i.e., Shmelke) to give his consent to the placing of a ban on the hasidim. The messengers promised him that those among the hasidim who were great in Torah–himself, his brother, Pinkhas, author of Baal Ha–Hafla'ah, Rabbi Mordekhai of Neskhiz who was the grandson of the Megale Amukot, and other such–would be exempt from the ban.

"And how will you know who among the hasidim is great in Torah?" asked Reb Shmelke, and pointing out Rabbi Yisrael, who was present, he added, "Do you see this young man here? He is one of the greatest of the hasidim in Torah." The messengers went back the way they had come, and the ban was dissolved.

Another story from his time with Reb Shmelke: Once a bookseller came to Ricziwol, bringing with him a copy of Magen Avraham, which had just been republished. Rabbi Yisrael bought the book and fixed a time for its study with another young man. After the first session the hearts of both were suddenly enflamed more than usual, and they were frightened by the illumination of their faces. They decided to ask Reb Shmelke whence these lights had come. Rabbi Yisrael went in to him, and even before he had finished asking, Reb Shmelke said, "Your appearance gives you away, Yisrael. You have been studying Magen Avraham. Know that the study of this book brings great illumination to the hearts of all scholars?"

[Page 43]

Rabbi Yisrael also became known to Reb Shmelke's brother, Pinkhas, at this time, and they had dealings with one another concerning responsa.

In the "Camp" of the Maggid of Mezritch

Under the influence of the brothers Shmelke and Pinkhas, Rabbi Yisrael began to prepare himself for the journey to Mezritch and the Great Maggid Dov Baer. Before departing, he went over eight hundred books of Kabbalah, got together some money, bought a horse and wagon and hired a driver.

The journey lasted several weeks. The first time he went in to the Great Maggid, the latter asked him where he was from. "From Kozienice, near Warsaw." The Great Maggid said, "With your coming here, they will begin to say Keser Yitnu Lechah instead of Na'aritskha in the shabbes musaf in Warsaw, because the power of hasidism will be strengthened there."

And so it was. In the time of Rabbi Yisrael the Maggid, the majority of hasidim in Warsaw were Kozienicer hasidim. Among them were rich men, community leaders and important mediators with the non–Jewish world, such as Reb Mikhel Ha–Cohen, father of Rabbi Elazar, head of the rabbinical court at Poltosk, and Yaakov Moshe Muskat, father of the saintly Rabbi Yishaya Muskat of Praga.

The Maggid of Mezritch rejoiced greatly in his new student, saying to his disciple Rabbi Shneour Zalman of Ladi, author of the Tanya, "Blessed be God for sending me this young man to proofread the manuscript of the Ari's siddur!" He prevailed upon Rabbi Yisrael to proofread the siddur, and Rabbi Yisrael stayed three months in Mezritch proofreading the manuscript and preparing it for the press, besides learning Kabbala and khasidus from the Maggid of Mezritch.

While at the Maggid's, Rabbi Yisrael met and befriended many of his great and famous students, the leaders of their generation. They are mentioned in his books, especially Rabbi Avraham the Angel, son of the Mezritcher, Rabbi Avraham Kalisker, Rabbi Aharon the Great of Karlin, Rabbi Yisrael of Polotsk, Rabbi Pinkhas of Koretz, Rabbi Shneour Zalman of Ladi, Rabbi Levi Yitzkhok of Berdichev, Rabbi Elimelekh of Lizensk, and others.

And He Knew that his Ways were Pure

After the death of the Maggid of Mezritch, Rabbi Yisrael decided to attach himself to Rebbe Elimelekh of Lizensk. It was accepted among the disciples of Rebbe Reb Elimelekh that if he went out to meet them, it was proof that their conduct was governed by considerations of holiness, and if he did not, they were not yet worthy.

[Page 44]

When Rabbi Yisrael reached Rebbe Elimelekh's house, he found him asleep. He returned to his inn, greatly saddened and weeping bitterly. Suddenly he saw that Rebbe Elimelekh had come to the inn. He comforted Rabbi Yisrael and said, "An Angel awakened me, so that I could come to console you." After this, Rebbe Elimelekh asked him how many parasangs distance Kozienice was from Warsaw. "Twelve," replied Rabbi Yisrael. Rebbe Elimelekh was astounded and said, "There's a hasid like you only twelve parasangs from Warsaw?" With that, Rabbi Yisrael was comforted, and knew that his ways were pure.

His Friendship with the Seer of Lublin

Rabbi Yaakov Yitzkhok Horowitz, the Seer of Lublin, was a friend of the Maggid from the time of their youth. They met while still in Mezritch, and later became disciples of Rebbe Elimelekh of Lizensk. Both began to lead congregations in 1787, after the death of Rebbe Elimelekh. They were the first to spread the teachings of the Besht in Poland, and they founded hasidic centres in Lublin and Kozienice. Both died in the same year, first the Maggid on erev Sukkos, 1815, then the Seer on tishe–b'Av of the same year (5575 from the creation of the world). Their friendship continued for their whole lives.

And Behold, It was a Miracle

The Seer of Lublin held the Kozienicer in great esteem. When the Seer's second wife was nagging him because she had not managed to have a son by him, he advised her to go to his friend the Maggid, whose prayers and blessing would help her.

She obeyed and went to Kozienice. The Maggid commanded her to eat and drink; by doing so, his prayer would benefit her, and she would be visited with a pregnancy. He added that, at the birth of the child, he was to be godfather.

And thus it came to pass. She returned to Lublin and did as the Maggid had told her. When she had given birth to a child, the Seer sent a special emissary to Kozienice to invite the Maggid to the bris.

The Maggid's trip to Lublin excited great publicity. Thousands of people came out to greet him everywhere he passed. Prince Adam Czartoryski came in his carriage and invited the Maggid to his palace.

On his arrival at Lublin, the streets were in a tumult due to the numbers of people who had come out to greet him, among them Christians, and among these the nobility. They all wanted to see the holy man.?

[Page 45]

A certain princess came to him with her son who was suffering from polio. Both his legs were withered, and he was unable to walk. She pleaded with the Maggid to give the boy his blessing so that he would recover from his illness. The Maggid said to her, "If you promise that you will exact no increase from your Jewish tenants, and will let them remain on your manor, then I expect your son will be cured."

The princess agreed, and promised to fulfill these conditions. At once the Maggid held out his pipe to the boy and told him to bring him an ember with which to light it. As soon as the boy had taken hold of the pipe, he rose and walked upon his feet. And behold, it was a miracle.

On his return from Lublin, the Maggid, as he had promised, made a detour to the palace of Prince Czartoryski, where he was received with all the honour due a king.

Concerning the Maggid's relations with the Seer of Lublin, it is told that once, in the week during which parshas Bekhukosay (Leviticus 26:3–27:34) is read in the synagogue, the Seer said to his hasidim: "it is good to spend this Sabbath with the saint of Kozienice because he makes the curses of the Lord's rebuke into blessings." The holy Rabbi Mordekhai, author of Ma–amar Mordekhai, heard this and went to Kozienice.

That shabbes, while the Maggid was reading the Torah, Rabbi Mordekhai stood opposite him, the better to hear how he changed the curses into blessings. And when the Maggid reached the verse (Lev. 26:31), "And I will lay your cities waste, and will make your sanctuaries desolate, and I will not smell your pleasing odors," he rose and said in a loud voice, "Our father in heaven, would that we might merit to be alive at that time!"

The Maggid also esteemed his friend the Seer, and looked upon him as a holy man of God.

His Friendship with Rebbe Levi Yitzkhok of Berdichev

He held his teacher Rebbe Levi Yitzkhok of Berdichev in similar esteem, and cites him often in his books, usually referring to him as "the pious rav, our teacher Rabbi Levi Yitzkhok" rather than "my teacher and master". According to hasidic tradition, the reason underlying the Maggid's reluctance to be referred to as Rebbe Levi Yitzkhok's pupil was due to the fact that the Berdichever was said to have the soul of Rabbi Akiva, and it is well known that the disciples of Rabbi Akiva did not live long.?

[Page 46]

As is known, before his arrival in Berdichev, Reb Levi Yitzkhok suffered many persecutions at the hands of the misnagdim. Once, while he was rav in Ricziwol, he was forced to flee on Hoshanna Rabba with the four species still in his hand. He sought refuge with his friend and disciple the Maggid of Kozienice.

It is told that Reb Levi Yitzkhok once came to Kozienice for Shavues. Very early in the morning, before the sun had come up, he called to the Maggid to go with him to the mikve. The Maggid said, "I was quite apprehensive about going with him, for our ways were so different. His was ardent, a burning fire; mine was of rest and quiet." Reb Levi Yitzkhok answered him, "If so, then I will walk in your way of quiet."

They went to the mikve. The mikve was at the base of a mountain, on the "other side", and they had first to ascend, and then to go down. But when they had reached the peak, Rebbe Levi Yitzkhok said, "Lomir firn di kale in mikve arayn, let's lead the bride into the mikve," and, with no delay, he rolled down the mountain to the wall of the mikve.

Once the Maggid asked Rebbe Levi Yitzkhok when he davened shakhris. The Berdichever replied that he davened late, especially on Rosh Ha–Shana and Yom Kippur when special preparations were necessary. The Maggid said that he, on the other hand, was accustomed to daven early. Reb Levi Yitzkhok replied, Even so, I'll blow the shofar before you."

That Rosh Ha–Shana, the Maggid was preparing himself to blow the shofar when he sensed great accusations and denunciations in heaven. He plunged himself into the holy work of uniting the spheres in order to mitigate the sentence, and as a result of this effort of self–sacrifice, he grew weary and fell into a deep sleep. In his dream he saw himself in heaven, listening to dire accusations. Of a sudden, he heard a great voice splitting the firmament. "What," he asked, "is this great voice?" "The Berdichever Rebbe is on his way to immerse himself in the mikve before blowing the shofar. By doing this, he makes the evil decrees null and void." When the Maggid awoke he said, "If things stand thus, we are obliged to wait until the rebbe from Berdichev has blown the shofar and mitigated the sentence and turned the accusation away; then we will be able to blow it without any trouble."

Rebbe Levi Yitzkhok Stays with the Maggid

It is also told that the Evil One once brought a great accusation against the rebbe of Berdichev. It was said in the upper worlds that Reb Levi Yitzkhok made use of the intentions and unifications (i.e., meditations before prayer) which the High Priest used in the Temple on Yom Kippur. If such a thing were done in the Exile, then most assuredly, when the Redemption came and the Temple was restored, he would be able to raise up all the worlds. Were he to do so, the strictest justice, the letter of the law, would demand that the General Redemption of the universe follow immediately.

[Page 47]

The Evil One was furious and claimed that the Berdichever's righteousness stemmed wholly from the supernal intelligences (mokhin ila'in–in Lurianic Kabbalah, the first or upper three sefirot of keter, khokhma and bina, "the crown", wisdom and understanding) which illuminated him, and were these to be taken away, he would not be such a big shot.

Deprived of all his "levels" of sanctity, the Berdichever became a simple man, his prayer that of the man in the street. He arose and went to the Maggid, who prepared special quarters for him in which he remained for half a year. He lingered over his prayers, not on account of intentions and unifications, rather to understand the simple meanings of the words themselves.

One shabbes the Maggid was leading the prayers, and when he came to the passage "yismakh Moishe be–matnas khelkoy" ("let Moses rejoice in the gift of his portion"), he went back again and said, "yismakh Reb Levi Yitzkhok be–matnas khelkoy" ("let Reb Levi Yitzkhok rejoice ..."), and the latter was immediately restored to his pristine condition. He was filled with fervour, and began to run back and forth in the house of study, as had formerly been his wont.

After shabbes, when Reb Levi Yitzkhok felt that he was in the fullness of his spiritual strength, he went in to the Maggid in order to bid him farewell. The Maggid asked, "Where does my teacher and master wish to go?" He answered, saying that since he had been invited to a debate with the misnagdim but had not had time, he wanted to fulfil his obligation and go. The Maggid was amazed and asked, "How will you be able to debate with them?" The Berdichever replied, "What do they know that I don't? They have no knowledge which is beyond me." The Maggid said: "Well, I, too, have something to ask you. Why do you daven the shmone–esrei with your eyes open?" "Sertze, ze'en mir den?" replied Levi Yitzkhok, "You think I see anything, my dear? Said the Maggid, "You're right. We know that we see nothing while we daven the shmone–esrei because all our thoughts are given over to the upper worlds, completely removed from mundane reality, and that no sense of physical sight is at all operative. But they, the misnagdim, will not believe that my teacher is not looking about him during his prayer."

Rebbe Levi Yitzkhok admitted that the Maggid was correct, and did not go. Then the Maggid asked him to stay for Passover, and he did so.

[Page 48]

Passover Night

The first night of Passover had come. Reb Levi Yitzkhok wanted to celebrate the seder together with the Maggid, but the latter objected that, given the difference in their customs, this would be rather difficult, especially as he had no wish to make the Berdichever deviate from his normal routine. He had, therefore, arranged a table for him in a separate room, at which he could conduct the seder according to his own wishes and habits.

As soon as Reb Levi Yitzkhok had begun his <u>setter</u>, he reached the summit of his fervour; a sacred flame had taken hold of him – he overturned the table. The Maggid said that he had foreseen that such a thing would happen. Reb Levi Yitzkhok apologized, and promised that he would restrain himself henceforth and conduct his <u>seder</u> quietly.

Rabbi Yaakov Arye of Radzimin, who in his youth used to visit the Maggid and was present on this occasion, bears witness to the arrangement of this <u>seder</u>. He tells that he wished to see how each of the Great <u>tzaddikim</u> conducted his <u>seder</u>; each was in a separate room, so he stood in the doorway between these adjoining rooms, candle and <u>hagadda</u> in hand, and listened to each of them in turn. He went out that night full of enthusiasm, and told his impressions of it all his life. He used to add, "I have no more hope of hearing such a <u>seder</u> in this world. Perhaps I will be worthy to do so in the next."

The Maggid Laments his Misfortunes

Before he became known to the world, the Maggid, too, suffered great distress. Once he went to his friend and teacher, Reb Levi Yitzkhok, who was then <u>rav</u> in Zelechow, and told him of his troubles. When he departed, Reb Levi Yitzkhok went to escort him. It was winter, and very cold. The Maggid was wearing a warm overcoat, but Reb Levi Yitzkhok was clad only in a light garment. After they had gone a certain distance (it was difficult for Reb Levi Yitzkhok to part from his friend) the cold began to bother him. He asked the Maggid to lend him his coat. They went on together some distance more. Now the Maggid was beginning to feel the cold. Reb Levi Yitzkhok returned the coat and said, "Reb Yisroelkhl, warm up already." From that moment on, said the Maggid, his condition changed for the better.

Like the Berdichever Rebbe, the Maggid spoke in defense of Israel. Once a woman came to him, complaining that her husband hated her and thought her ugly. The Maggid said, "Perhaps you really are ugly." "Woe is me!" she cried. "I was pretty enough under the wedding canopy–have I all of a sudden turned ugly?"

[Page 49]

When the Maggid heard this he sighed and said, "Master of the Universe, is this not the complaint of the Congregation of Israel? When they stood before you at the foot of Mount Sinai and said, 'We will do and obey,' they were as a beautiful bride in your eyes and you chose them above all peoples. And have you now, perish the thought, grown tired of us?"

O Rock of Israel, come thou to our aid.

[Page 50]

Rabbi Yisrael Becomes Preacher of Righteousness in Kozienice

by Tzvi Meir Rabinowitz
(from his book, The Maggid of Kozienice: His Life and Teaching)

After drinking deeply of the springs of Hasidism at Mezritch and Lizensk, Rabbi Yisrael returned to the Polish interior to become "preacher of righteousness" (maggid mesharim) in Kozienice, a small town with 1300 Jews. Its Jewish settlement dated back to approximately 1661. In 1878 a great fire destroyed much of the town, including the synagogue. Even before this, the community was not numbered among the older and richer of the Polish congregations.

An Itinerant Preacher

As the Maggid's salary was too small to suffice for his livelihood, he also accepted preaching posts in the nearby communities of Magniszow and Grica, and went about the locality preaching in synagogues, admonishing the people in the ways of Torah and repentance.

Unlike the other preachers of his day who terrified their listeners with accounts of the torments of hell and the punishments of the world to come, the Maggid of Kozienice preached words of pleasantness and love. He was opposed to "the way of earlier preachers" before the age of Hasidism, and he demanded that the preacher "not reprove them (the people) with words bitter and hard as wormwood, but rather with sweet and pleasant words of appeasement." His discourses were thus liberally spiced with pleasant and homely example determined by the capabilities and concerns of his audience.

He soon gained renown as a first rate preacher. Vast multitudes flocked to hear words of awe and wisdom from his mouth, and their hearts were broken within them through reflection on repentance and good deeds.

His influence increased from day to day, and people came from far and near to hear him. His heavenly powers of abstinence and self–restraint, as well as his outward appearance, also had their influence upon the multitudes. He was thin of body, and very frail; small of stature and chronically ill; yet a youthful vigour bubbled in his soul. Day and night he studied and spread Torah among young and old; his personal prayer, uttered loudly and with fervour–the prayer, as it were, of the first Hasidim–made a particular impression.

He used to say that he experienced no pleasure like that of a good prayer well prayed. His cleaving to the divine during prayer brought him to the highest plane. He attained to a putting–off of corporeality, his entire being clove to and was fused with the upper worlds, and ascended the ladder of holy degrees in the fire of his enthusiasm, until, by means of unifications, he had reached the source of life, the light of einsof, the infinite.

Multitudes Gather at His Door

Tens of thousands soon began to flock to Kozienice to receive his blessing. There was always a great number of paupers, the oppressed and cripples hanging about his door, and as soon as he went out, they would kneel before him and ask his blessing. He was obliged to help them with charitable donations, support and intervention on their behalf. To the sick and the crippled he gave amulets. Polish gentiles also came to him to be cured, and they guarded his amulets against any contingency.

This giving of amulets aroused the wrath of the misnagdim in Kozienice, and that of the town rabbi, Rabbi Shlomo, the grandson of Rabbi Abish, head of the rabbinical court of Frankfurt, in particular. After the dispute between Rabbi Yonatan Eybeshutz and Rabbi Yaakov Emden, every giver of amulets was suspected of Sabbatianism. They therefore began to persecute him in the city and also to write letters to the rabbis of the region concerning the new baal–shem, or wonder worker, who had arisen in Poland.

The Misnagdim Restore Rabbi Yisrael

He was set upon particularly by the well–known enemy of Hasidism, David of Macow. He spent all the arrows of his wrath on the Maggid, and tried to prevent the printers in Warsaw from printing his book Zamir Aritsim (Cutting Tyrants Down to Size).

These provocations bore fruit, and the misnagdim gathered against him one shabbes and set upon him with such vehemence that he was forced to hide in a mill. After shabbes he fled from Kozienice to his friend Rebbe Levi Yitzkhok of Berdichev in Zelechow.

The Berdichever was zealous for the honour of the Maggid, and wished to excommunicate Rabbi Shlomo of Kozienice. But Hasidic legend relates that Rabbi Abish of Frankfurt came to him in a dream and warned him not to punish his grandson.

Under the influence of Rebbe Levi Yitzkhok, the misnagdim of Kozienice, with the rav at their head, repented and received Rabbi Yisrael back as preacher and restored him to his earlier honour.

[Page 52]

The Maggid continued on his new path, the path of Beshtian–Lizenskian Hasidism, with great exaltation, and his opponents gradually became his admirers.

After the death of Rebbe Dov Baer of Mezritch (1772) and Rebbe Levi Yitzkhok's reception as rav in Berdichev (1775), the Maggid of Kozienice became pre–eminent among the disseminators of Hasidism in Poland. His name spread far and wide as a leader of Hasidism, wonder worker, halakhic genius, expert in kabbalah and Jewish learning (torat yisrael), and, thanks to his manifold connections with the Polish nobility and his great influence on Polish Jewry, as a worker for the benefit of all Israel.

The Maggid of Kozienice in the Political Life of the Jews of Poland

The Maggid of Kozienice had a powerful influence in shaping the character of Jewish political life in Poland. With all his devotion to Torah and Kabbalah, to the dissemination of Hasidism and the writing of books, he yet found time to concern himself with the political and economic conditions of the Jews of Poland. In his opinion, "The way of the tzaddik is to pray for all Israel, to give freely of his soul and might and to be pained when he sees himself well off and Israel come to grief."

On this account the Maggid took part in all the activities carried on to dissolve the evil decrees of the kings, nobles and burghers of Poland, and he therefore sent special emissaries to the neighbouring towns to keep an eye on those matters which pertained to the Jews.

The Maggid sought peace, for he knew that in time of war the Jews–and the Jews of Poland were already experienced at these sorts of hardships–stood first in suffering, robbery and despoilment. It was incumbent upon them to heed the words of the king and to pray for responsible government. "We must pray," he said, "that fear of his royal majesty be placed upon the people, and that they not worship him with a love devoid of fear; if they do, they will follow their desire in all things, saying that the king loves them and will not punish them."

These words are a sign of the times, of the political realities of Polish life. In the deterioration of the king's position and the rise of the nobles, who had organized themselves into confederations engaged in internecine war, the Maggid perceived the giving over of the Jews of Poland to plunder. Although the king, Stanislaw August Poniatowski, supported the Jews, he was unable to save them from becoming lambs upon the altar of the decline of Polish kingship.

[Page 53]

His Attempt to Abolish Military Service

In their distress, the Jews appealed to the king and influential nobles to dissolve the evil decrees. The Maggid worked especially for the abolition of military service. Delegations appointed by the hasidim presented themselves to the minister of defense, Josef Poniatowski, according to hasidic legend an admirer of the Maggid, in 1812. Through his influence, military service was converted into an annual tax of seven hundred thousand pieces of gold. The Jews of Poland, and especially the hasidim, rejoiced greatly in their freedom from handing their sons over to a government which subjugated and oppressed them.

In 1811 a meeting of representatives from all the Jewish communities of Poland, similar to the Council of the Four Lands, chose twenty delegates to present themselves before the minister of finance and the king and ask that the shekhita tax (slaughter tax) imposed upon the Jews be abolished. Local government officials had been arbitrarily raising the tax and lining their own pockets with the money of the poor of Israel. Among the scholars and community leaders chosen was the Maggid of Kozienice, but the representative of the district of Radom informed the financial ministry that the Maggid was unable to take part in the delegation because of "his age and extreme sickness".

The Maggid had a great influence both in governmental circles and in the court of King Stanislaw August. Also among his hasidim were the Jewish magnates of Poland, Reb Josef a Mendelsburg of Kuzmir, Shmuel Zwitkower, Berko Bergson and his wife, Tamar, who had both access to and influence upon the king.

Reb Josefa, the Maggid's Friend

Reb Josefa was a native of Apta and a boyhood friend of the Maggid. They studied together at the Ricziwol yeshiva under Rebbe Shmelke of Nickolsburg. Nevertheless, their ways parted: the Maggid took the path of Torah and khasidus, Reb Josefa that of commerce and contracting. He settled in Josefow, in the district of Lublin, where he dealt in wood and exported trees through the port at Danzig. He also had a royally appointed monopoly on the products of salt mines. Five hundred families were employed in his industrial enterprises. He received two medals from King Stanislaw Poniatowski as a sign of friendship and esteem. Yet his wealth and nearness to the king did not distance him from the Maggid–he was among his friend's most loyal hasidim.

In his old age he settled in Kuzmir, in the district of Lublin, where he continued in the tradition of Torah study and fear of heaven based upon the teachings of Rebbe Shmelke of Nickolsburg. He chose the most brilliant young men of Poland for his daughters–one of his sons–in–law was Rabbi Meshullam Zalman Ashkenazi, head of the rabbinical court of Lublin.

[Page 54]

The Maggid received first hand reports from Reb dosefa on the government's programs concerning the Jews, and in times of need his connections gave him the opportunity to dissolve evil decrees.

Reb Shmuel Zwitkower Purchases his Portion in Paradise

Shmuel Zwitkower was considered the wealthiest Jew in Poland. He was a dealer in animals and skins, a factory owner, supplier to the army and mediator in the courts of Friedrich of Prussia and Poniatowski of Poland. He was also known for his good works on behalf of the congregation of Praga–Warsaw. He built a synagogue and <u>mikve</u>, and established a cemetery in Praga.

He attained to especial renown during the Kosciuszko rebellion of 1794. The Jews of Warsaw, under Commander Berek doselewicz, founder of a separate Jewish regiment for the defense of the capital, fought side by side with the Poles. A great battle between the Poles and Sovorov's Russians broke out near Praga.

Despite the valour of the Jews and Poles, the Russians were victorious. Fifteen thousand Poles, together with the Jewish regiment, which numbered about six hundred, fell dead on the battlements of Praga, the streets of Warsaw and the waters of the Vistula.

Legend has it that after the battle, while the Russians were still prepared to slaughter all the inhabitants of Warsaw, Reb Shmuel sat in his courtyard, a barrel on either side of him–the one filled with gold coins, the other with silver–and made a proclamation to the Cossacks that he would give three golden rubles for every living man, and one of silver for every corpse. The Russian army flocked to Reb Shmuel, bringing with them both the living and the dead. The barrels were emptied within a short time, and hundreds had been saved from death.

The Maggid of Kozienice was not satisfied with Shmuel Zwitkower's general conduct, for people grumbled against him in matters of commerce and religion. However, with his rescue of Praga, he had purchased his portion in Paradise, and the Maggid esteemed him highly for this.

The hasidim tell that one time when the Maggid came to the Sabbath prayer <u>El Adon</u>, he began to sing it to a beautiful melody they had never heard before. When they asked him to explain the tune, he said, "This is the tune with which the angels led Reb Shmuel Zwitkower to Paradise. The merits of his rescue work tipped the scales of judgment and outweighed all sins he committed, and his soul went up to Paradise in holiness and purity."

[Page 55]

The Maggid Goes to a Wedding in Warsaw

Shmuel Zwitkower's son, Berko Dov Bergson, was also a government contractor and distinguished magnate, as well as a community worker for the welfare of the Jews of Poland. He and his wife, Tamar, were admirers of the Maggid, and Tamar, especially, gave help to distinguished disciples of the Maggid and the Seer of Lublin by appointing them as officials in her business enterprises. Among those so appointed were Simkhe Bunem of Pshishkha, Yitzkhok of Worke and others.

The Maggid's influence on the Bergson family grew, and he was invited to Warsaw to officiate at the wedding of Dov Bergson's daughter to Reb Yissokher Baer Horowitz, the grandson of Rebbe Shmelke Horowitz of Ricziwol–Nickolsburg. The wedding was celebrated with great pomp, and the hasidim tell that the Maggid did not go up to the khupe until he had "repaired" the soul of Shmuel Zwitkower to make it worthy of being joined with that of the Maggid's teacher, Rebbe Shmelke.

The groom was among the most learned men of Warsaw, one of the Maggid's most distinguished pupils, and a friend of Reb Yitzkhok Meyer Alter, the Gerer Rebbe, who was likewise an outstanding student and was brought up at the Maggid's.

The Czartoryskis as Hasidim of the Maggid

Aside from his connections with the aforementioned Jewish magnates, the Maggid also had his influence among the leading figures of the Polish nobility. The well–known Czartoryski family was numbered among his followers. The head of the family, Adam Kasimir Czartoryski, was a candidate for the kingship after the death of King August in 1763, although the position finally went to his rival, Stanislaw Poniatowski. After the first partition of Poland he was appointed Marshal of the Polish army. He fought vigorously for Polish freedom, and was an opponent of Russia, which was interfering in the internal affairs of Poland.

Hasidic legend elaborated on the cordial relations obtaining between the Maggid and the Czartoryskis. The Maggid referred to Adam Czartoryski as "my Adam". Before the birth of his son, Czartoryski went to the Maggid and asked him to pray for the birth of a male child. The Maggid said, "Master of the Universe, you've got plenty of goyim, one more won't hurt."

Adam's brother, Constantine, was not a "hasid", and he expressed doubts as to the efficiency of the Maggid's wonders. He attempted once to prove to his brother that the Maggid was not gifted with the holy spirit. He devised a prank, and went to Kozienice, where he mentioned his son who, he claimed, was dangerously ill, although he was not really sick at all. But the Maggid said, "Go home quickly, while you still have a chance to see your son before his death." And thus it was – on his return home, Constantine found his son dead.

[Page 56]

When the Maggid went to see the Seer in Lublin, he was invited to Czartoryski's palace and received with great honour.

The Maggid is also mentioned in the memoirs of Anna Potocka, who tells that a Swedish astrologer and mystic came to Poland to learn Kabbalah from the renowned Rabbi of Kozienice.

The Maggid did not Reveal the Secret to Czartoryski

Leon Dembowski, one of the commanders of the Polish army, gives an interesting account in his memoirs of Prince Adam Czartoryski's visit to Kozienice.

The prince's secretary, Skowronski, was once sent to Danzig to collect eleven thousand ducats. He hid the money in a small barrel which he put between his legs during the trip back to Czartoryski's palace at Polawy. En route, Skowronski and his retinue fell into a deep slumber, during which they passed through two stations. At the third station, Skowronski awoke to find the money stolen. All his searches were in vain, and he returned to Polawy empty handed.

Several years passed, and the loss had been forgotten, when out of the blue Prince Czartoryski received a letter from the famous rabbi, the Maggid of Kozienice, who was considered a saint by the Jews, informing him that the lost money had been found and would be returned to him on three conditions: a) that the prince would pardon the thieves; b) that he would be satisfied with only ten thousand ducats, as one thousand had been lost, and c) that he would not press the Maggid to tell him how it had been recovered.

The prince agreed to these conditions and the money was returned to him. After this, the prince decided to pay a call on the Maggid. "I was present," says Dembowski, "at this visit, along with Lord Czelski. We went to Kozienice with a retinue of some number, as the prince never travelled without an escort. While we proceeded to the house of the Maggid, which was located among the town's filthy streets, a mass of Jews followed behind us, evincing their great satisfaction that the Marshal of the Austrian armies and so important a ruler had come to visit their holy man. Some let out shouts, others sang and danced. Amidst this tumult, we entered the Maggid's apartment, going straight from the corridor into his salon."

"The saint lay in bed behind a partition, swathed in bedclothes. He was an old man of about ninety (!), dressed completely in white, with a snow white beard that reached to his waist. His face was small, thin and wrinkled. The prince approached his bed and began to speak in Polish. The Maggid nodded but did not reply. Thinking that he understood no Polish, the prince tried German. He was met with the same silence. The commander then began to speak Hebrew, for he knew that language too, but with the same results."

[Page 57]

"When he realized that it was impossible to get a word out of the saint, we returned to our inn for lunch. Hordes of Jews escorted us as before, demonstrating their admiration for the Maggid. 'Our Maggid is a great sage!" they said often. I don't know whether they considered his stubborn silence to be wisdom, but in any event, the Maggid was a good and benevolent man. Wagons bringing offerings poured into Kozienice from every corner of the land. He accepted everything, but distributed it to the poor every Friday.

"We later discovered that the money had been stolen by a postal clerk who, seeing the men asleep, took the ducats and hid them under a tree. He afterwards resigned his position, got married, and spent one thousand ducats to set up housekeeping. How the Maggid came into contact with him, and how he obtained the rest of the money has remained a mystery."

It appears that Czartoryski asked the Maggid about the details of the theft. Having promised the Christian official that he would maintain secrecy, the Maggid kept his word with a wonderful dignity. He did not submit to so exalted a personable as the Marshal of the Polish army and his band of retainers, and did not answer the Prince's questions in any of the three languages. The Maggid overcame the commander with silence. A similar story is found in a slightly different version in hasidic sources.

Such connections with prominent Jews, the Polish nobility, military commanders and high governmental officials enabled the Maggid to utilize their influence to abolish compulsory military service and the prohibition of the liquor trade to Jews, two decrees which threatened to undermine both the spiritual and economic lives of the Jews of Poland.

The Hassidic Version of the Theft

The prominent Reb Shlomo of Konskiwoli used always to trade in the forests of Prince Czartoryski. Once his wagon drivers brought barrels of golden ducats from Paris to Pulawy but two barrels were missing on their arrival. The prince told Reb Shlomo to go with him to Kozienice so that the two barrels might be returned to him.

When they came to the Maggid, he said, "I am weak and bedridden, and did not steal them." The prince replied, "I know, but your prayer will restore the stolen goods." Said the Maggid, "If you promise not to ask where I got it, it will be restored to you."

By means of his prayer, a dispute broke out between the thieves and the corrupt wagon driver, and they went to the Maggid to have it settled. His teaching convinced them to sanctify the name of heaven and return what they had stolen, and they did so (Eser Orot, p. 76).?

[Page 58]

Gog and Magog

After the third partition of Poland in 1795, when there seemed to be no hope of deliverance from the predatory claims of its neighbours, Polish hope was re–awakened by the victories of Napoleon. Mighty nations bowed before his armies, great states collapsed and fell. Napoleon, who fought against the dividers of Poland–Prussia, Austria and Russia–promised the Poles a revival of their independence in return for military aid.

Twelve years after the defeat of Poland, in 1807, Napoleon took one of its territories from Austria and set up the Principality of Warsaw, with Friedrich August, King of Saxony, at its head. Two years later, after the defeat of Austria, part of that territory was also annexed to Poland.

A liberal constitution was imposed upon the new Poland which had arisen under the aegis of Napoleon. Two legislative houses, the Sejm and the Senate, as well as Napoleon's legal code, were introduced. According to this code, all citizens of the country were equal under the law, without regard to race or religion, and had equal rights and duties. The Jews of Poland began to believe that their hoped–for time had come at last, and that with the rise of Napoleonic influence on the government of Poland, their suffering was at an end.

A Song in Honour of Napoleon

When Napoleon reached Warsaw, the Jewish community presented him with a Hebrew hymn from which we can devine their attitude toward him. In it, the Jews of Warsaw express their great admiration for the victories of the conqueror who crushed nations under his foot, and their certainty that Napoleon would deal justly with the tormented and oppressed Jews of Poland:

Your hand is spread out upon lands full of injustice; the nations are bowed to the dust, they will live in your shadow; your might will prevail, nations will dwell in your hands. Behold a bright light in the heavens. And the Lord said, "Let there be light upon a land of darkness!"

We, the hunted lamb of Warsaw, have heard of your great loving kindness, Napoleon; the ends of the earth have told us. Therefore have we dared to come forth to greet you, for your goodness is greater than life itself in restoring the soul of the oppressed. "Israel shall blossom and put forth shoots, Jacob shall take root."?

[Page 59]

Orthodox Circles Afraid of Equal Rights

Only the small enlightened (maskilim) and assimilationist groups hoped to profit by the attainment of equal rights under Napoleonic law. Orthodox and hasidic circles were very much afraid of equal rights. They understood that the few economic rights, the granting of which was very doubtful, would impose numerous duties touching on the realm of religion on the Jews of Poland. The hasidim were afraid of the spirit of free thought and enlightenment which the armies of Napoleon brought to the lands they had conquered, and especially of the compulsory military service which was considered a hard blow to the Jews of Poland. Military training with goyim who despised them, eating treyf and violating shabbes in the barracks, and the removal of youth from yeshivas to battlefields were all considered by the hasidim as the hardest of the decrees of the exile.

Rebbe Schneour Zalman of Ladi gave expression to this fear in a letter to Rabbi Moshe Maisels of Vilna: "Before musaf on the first day of Rosh Ha–Shana it was shown that if Bonaparte were to win, the wealth of the Jews would be increased and their welfare exalted, but their hearts would be separated and estranged from their father in heaven. If, however, our lord Alexander (Czar of Russia) should win, poverty would increase, welfare fall for the Jews, but their hearts would be bound and tied and joined to their father in heaven. And this is a sign: we will no longer be the apple of their eye, and they will begin to take soldiers from among the children of Israel."

In the opinion of the Rav from Ladi, Napoleon "attributed everything to his own strength and might, to the power of his intellect in this manner of procedure and to organization in military matters, and to the power of his success, in that in his majesty and haughtiness he mocks faith in the Lord and dismisses providence and faith and trust in God." He was afraid that, were the French to prevail, atheism would increase in Israel, and none would remain within the faith.

The Postponement of Equal Rights

Polish hasidim shared this attitude to equal rights. Under the influence of the Seer of Lublin and the Maggid of Kozienice, the question of equal rights was deferred for ten years by virtue of Napoleon's shameful Writ of Religion of 1808, which was enacted throughout the French empire.

"Residents of the Principality of Warsaw," said the writ, "of the Mosaic persuasion, are banished for ten years from the political rights they were about to receive, in the hope that within this time they will uproot from among themselves those particular signs which so distinguish them from the rest of the population."?

[Page 60]

The government, and even such well–disposed nobles as Adam Czartoryski, considered national and cultural assimilation, the change of dress, language and customs to those of the Polish Christians, to be the sine qua non for the reception of equal rights. Naturally, the orthodox were unable to pay so high a price for the sake of a dubious equality. The effort for release from equal rights and military service continued until 1812, when the Polish dews were freed from military service. The Maggid played a leading role in this endeavor, both in the collection of funds and the persuasion of the nobility.

The Maggid Opposes Napoleon

Before the defeat of Napoleon in the Franco–Russian war, opinions were divided with respect to the war of the nations. Legend tells of the struggles between the mighty supporters and opponents of Napoleon. The tzaddikim of Poland took part in the historic battles of Moscow at Waterloo (1813), not with armed power but with prayers and unifications. The Maggid and the Seer of Lublin stood opposed to Napoleon, and tipped the balance against him.

Rebbe Menakhem Mendel of Rimanov Sides with Napoleon

The only Jewish religious figure of any importance to take the side of Napoleon was Rebbe Menakhem Mendel of Rimanov. He saw this war as the struggle of Gog and Magog, the birth pangs of the Messiah. The tzaddik, who had spent his life dissolved in tears over the hardships of the exile and the difficulties of subjugation to the nations, thought that the time of Israel's redemption had come. He used to say, "It is good that the blood of Israel be spilt, if only the end of our exile might come."

Nevertheless, his disciple, Rebbe Naphtali Tzvi of Ropschitz, opposed him with all his might and mocked his advice. Rebbe Mendel had said to his students, "Pray that the Lord might lengthen my days until after the year 1814–, and have no doubt that you will have the grace to hear the shofar of the Messiah! "

While the decisive battles between Napoleon and the Russians were raging near Moscow, Rebbe Mendel redoubled his prayers on behalf of Napoleon. He shook the worlds; almost the whole household of heaven took his side. As each matzo was taken from the oven, he said, "Another five hundred Russians have fallen!"

Napoleon was on the threshold of victory over the Russians when the Ropschitzer suddenly burst in, crying, "Rebbe, Napoleon is unclean, and the unclean is postponed until the second pesakh!" After speaking these words, he ran out of the rebbe's and travelled hurriedly to the Seer and the Maggid, so that their prayers would hasten the downfall of the unclean Napoleon. The Seer took his side, and from Lublin he went to Kozienice to enlist the Maggid in order to insure Napoleon's defeat.?

[Page 61]

The Maggid Between the Hammer and Anvil

His work was difficult indeed. Who saw the suffering and torment and depression of the exile like the Maggid? Who hoped, who waited with impatience for the redemption as he did? On the other hand, he knew that the advent of the Messiah was connected through its birth pangs with suffering and bloodshed for Israel. He thus found himself between hammer and anvil, so to speak.

Legend has it that he once announced to his household, "It is in my power to bring on the Messiah, if I wanted to."

"Nu, go ahead," replied his daughter Margalit (Perele).

"Yes, my daughter, the blood of Israel will be spilled like water. They will search for a single Jew–with candles, yet!–but will find none, not even a pearl like yourself."

"If so, then too bad for one Jew, too," she answered.

The Maggid was distressed. On the one hand, he saw the Jews suffering in the Napoleonic wars as the signs of redemption, the birth pangs of the Messiah. In his marginalia to the Maharal's G'vurat Ha–Shem, he writes: "you must understand that after the troubles that came upon us after the composition of this work, we are finished with the wars of Gog and Magog. These can be further explained only in person."

It is to be supposed that the echo of Napoleon's proclamation of the gates of Jerusalem promising the establishment of a Jewish state if the Jews were to aid him, had also reached Poland and fired the hearts of the Jews to believe that their redemption depended upon him. It appears that the Maggid bore Napoleon no love, and did not suppose that he would build Israel up. His opinion was similar to that of the Rav from Ladi.

According to hasidic tradition, twenty years before the rise of Napoleon the Maggid prophesied that "a hero and conqueror of nations who will rule the world is about to arise, but in the end he will be defeated."

The Battle Between the Maggid and the Rav from Ladi

A Chabad legend tells of the battle which broke out between the Rav from Ladi, who opposed Napoleon, and the Maggid, who supported him. Napoleon's fate hung in the balance. Neither side would budge from its opinion, so they finally agreed that on Rosh Ha–Shana each would attempt to bring the matter to a decision. Each would perform his duties in his own place and in his own way, and the one who blew the shofar first would win the palm for his side.

On the first day of Rosh Ha–Shana, the Maggid awoke early, hurried through his preparations before prayer, went to the mikve and immediately afterwards began to pray, in order to reach the shofar blowing before the Rav from Ladi would have started praying. The Maggid was to blow the shofar, and when he brought it up to his lips, his heart melted, and he realized that the Rav from Ladi had already finished his blowing.

[Page 62]

"The Litvak got there before me. He hurried and snatched the blowing from my hand, and beat me." The Rav from Ladi had decided to blow the shofar before he prayed, and by means of this device he brought Napoleon's defeat nearer.

The Maggid Prophesies: Napoleon Will Fall

Hasidim in Poland and Galicia describe the events with a legend somewhat closer to the truth. After Rebbe Naphtali–Tzvi of Ropschitz had convinced the Seer of Lublin to oppose Napoleon, he went to Kozienice. He arrived on Friday afternoon while the Maggid was at the mikve. The Ropschitzer lay down to rest in the Maggid's bed, and when the Maggid returned and found him there, the Ropschitzer refused to get up until the Maggid had prayed for Napoleon's defeat. The Maggid agreed to do so.

That night, when he reached the prayer, Mizmor Shir Le–Yom Ha–Shabbes (Psalm 92), the Maggid cried out, "They say that the French have passed from Moscow to Berzina, and I say, They are doomed to destruction forever, all evildoers shall be scattered, and Thou, O Lord, art on high forever! "

The next morning he read Exodus 18:17, navol tivol, "you will surely wither away," as Napoleon tipol, "Napoleon, you will fall".

After this historic Sabbath, Napoleon's downfall began. The Russians were victorious, the Prussians and Swedes rebelled, and Napoleon's sun began to set.

The Maggid Foresees the Subjugation of Poland

Hasidim say that the Maggid foresaw the subjugation of Poland from the first. "The Prince of Poland has no head," he used to say, "Poland has no lamp."

When Marshal Josef Poniatowski, commander of the Polish Army, passed through Kozienice, all the citizens of the town came out to meet him, with the Maggid at their head. When he asked if he would succeed in the struggle to revive Poland with the help of Napoleon, the Maggid answered in the negative. When they parted the Maggid sighed and said, "Woe to this righteous one from among the righteous of the nations! He freed the Jews from military service, but will neither return to his home nor die in his bed!"

The Maggid Weakens

These events weakened the health of the Maggid, not robust at the best of times, to the point where he could not get out of bed. In his last years he referred to himself as "a bag of bones". He stopped eating entirely, and made his condition known to the Seer of Lublin, who commanded him to endeavour to halt the progress of his illness.

[Page 63]

The "Holy Jew" once sent two of his choicest musicians to revive his spirit. The Maggid was very happy, and thanked the dew for bringing him into the world of melody. Their playing on Sabbath night restored his spirit.

The Maggid complains of his health in a letter to Rabbi Yisrael of Pikov, the son of the Berdichever Rebbe: "At present I am very weak, and, with all due thanks to the Lord who has helped me thus far, am unable to persevere in Torah and worship as I have always done. I have therefore requested that, in order to raise my memory for the better, you pray on my behalf, and also command the downhearted to go to the graves of the tzaddikim to pray for me. Is it not the glory of your blessed father to arouse the sleepers to ask mercy for me, so that the Blessed Lord will send me a complete recovery, and 1 return to my health and vigour with great strength and abundant might in order to be joined with the Lord's inheritance, which is my portion for all my labour."

The Maggid continued to weaken, and in a short time his life's objective "to be joined with the Lord's inheritance," was fulfilled. All his life he preached the basic tenets of Hasidism: clinging to the Lord, love of Torah and Israel. All who walk in this way are assured that they will die out of love of the Lord.

At the beginning of the year 5575 (late 181(f), the same year in which the Seer of Lublin and the Maggid had wished to bring on the Redemption, the angels triumphed over the mortals, and on the fourteenth of Tishre, Erev Sukkos, the Maggid passed on to a better world.

A structure was erected over his grave, and the stone bears the following inscription:

The Crown of Israel's Glory

is the man upon whom this monument has been raised. He was active in his life in performing the work of the Lord and his rulings for Israel. The Torah was on his lips, and he pulled many out of sin. He served the Lord with his strength, and enlightened the land with his glory. He was our master and teacher, the pious scholar, famous man of God, the wonder of his generation, a man of great achievements, a lover of God and of Israel, as his father Shabtai had been.

This is his memorial from generation to generation: the tzaddik and maggid mesharim of Kozienice passed away on the eve of sukkos in the year Ga'al Yisrael [5575 in gematria].

The Heads of the House of Kozienice
by M.Sh. Geshuri

The Maggid, Rabbi Yisrael of Kozienice, 1737–1815. Became preacher in Kozienice in 1765.

Rabbi Moshe Elyakim Beriah, 1757–1828. Presided in Kozienice for 33 years.

Rabbi Khaim Meir Yekhiel Shapiro, known as the Seraph of Mogielnica, 1789–1849. Presided in Kozienice for 21 years.

Rabbi Eliezer of Kozienice, died 1862. Presided in Kozienice for 13 years.

Rabbi Yekhiel–Yaakov, 1846–1863. Presided 4 years in Kozienice.

Rabbi Yerakhmiel Moshe, 1860–1909. Presided 25 years in Kozienice.

Rabbi Aharon–Yekhiel, 1889–1942. Presided in Kozienice, Otwock and Warsaw.

[Page 65]

The Music of the House of Kozienice

The Maggid of Kozienice was among the pioneers of Polish Hasidism. Having absorbed both Torah and khasides from his teachers, he became known and beloved among scholars and hasidim alike. While still in his youth, he received the "crown" of tzaddik from his followers, and rose to become one of the most important tzaddikim of his generation. His post of maggid, or preacher, preceded that of tzaddik as the Maggid.

The joy of the Sabbath played an important part in his birth, or so it is maintained by hasidic legend. As a reward for the dancing of his parents, Reb Shabsi the bookbinder and his wife, who rejoiced that the Lord had prepared a shabbes of prosperity for them after their poverty had already caused them to resign themselves to the necessity of a vokhediker shabbes, the Maggid was born. The Baal Shem Tov himself revealed to them that their dancing had caught the eye of heaven and had pleased the Lord, and that as a reward they were to be granted a son in their old age, a great son with a holy soul which he would glorify with music and joyous song.

A great difference is apparent between the melodies of Rebbe Yisroel of Kozienice and those of his friend the Seer of Lublin. Although they were members of the same school of Hasidism, both of them being students of Rebbe Shmuel–Shmelke of Nickolsburg and Rebbe Elimelekh of Lizensk, they nonetheless parted ways with respect to music.

אמר ה' ליעקב, אל תירא עבדי יעקב — לר' ישראל, המגיד מקוזיניץ.   נאַטן צו אמר ה' ליעקב — פּאָרמאָסט דורכן קאָזשעניצער מגיד.

The Influence of Polish Melodies

The Maggid's diligence in the study of Torah, of the revealed and concealed teachings, did not cause him to neglect his feeling for music. He spread Torah among the multitudes, decided questions of ritual and jurisprudence, yet was not sapped by this. Rather, he tried to blend the feelings of his heart with his keen intelligence, a mixture difficult to attain outside the realm of music.

One chord prevailed, sounding in simplicity and frankness: Polish song. Kozienice lay by the Vistula, and Polish melodies were unable to pass by the Maggid without leaving an impression on his storehouse of tunes.

From its beginnings, hasidism sought to express itself in music, and, lacking indigenous resources in this area, did so through the adaptation of non–Jewish music. This tendency passed on as a legacy to many tzaddikim who served as the originators of different styles of hasidic music. The struggle against outside musical influence is not apparent in hasidism.

[Page 66]

Kozienice was an important channel of Polish influence on hasidic life. The Maggid established ties between hasidic and Polish music, just as he revealed a fondness and inclination for Polish expressions and proverbs. Another prominent channel was thus added to the field of hasidism; because of its strangeness it remained within narrow limits and, to a definite degree, was never digested, and the hasidim were less than happy to increase its boundaries.

On Polish Music

The Poles, who were subject to Russia at the time, revealed an aptitude for music, and although they managed to make some contribution to it, nevertheless gained no renown in the musical world. Even up to the present, they have brought forth only a small number of people in this field.

Whether because of its lack of renown or on account of the prevailing political conditions, the Jews were not enthusiastic about Polish music at the time. On the other hand, Jewish musicians, who excelled as folk musicians, were accorded a respected place in Jewish life, and were often invited to the balls and parties of the Polish nobility.

The Poles boast distinguished musicians, experts in the art of counterpoint, as far back as the fifteenth century, among them Martin of Lemberg, Krist of Burek, Wilensky, and Gomulka, who was known as "the Polish Palestrina". An abundance of theory and perfection of form bear witness to their superior musical ability. The stamp of popular music is apparent in the work of many of them.

אין אדיר כאלהינו. אזוי האָט געזונגען דער קאָזשעניצער מגיד — אין אדיר כאלהינו. שר המגיד מקוזניץ בשמחת־תורה, פולונ,

The College of Choralists, an association of musicians working in a liturgical context, was founded in 1534 in association with the archiepiscopal see in Krakow, and is considered an essential factor in the development of Polish music. Upon it devolved the duty of singing matins and vespers services for the royal family.

In the following century Poland played host to important foreign composers, such as Marco Sacchi of the School of Rome, who was royal choirmaster in Poland and left three books of choral song for five voices, imitative in style, behind him. Lucca D'Arenzio also worked in Poland.

Both the intellectual classes, which had been educated in music, and the people who had shown such a liking for song and dance, were enthusiastic about the importation of opera by the Saxonian–Polish rulers at the end of the seventeenth century. In their trips between Dresden and Warsaw, they were accustomed to include theatrical troupes, singers, musicians, and dancers in their retinue. Among the members of these orchestras were such well–known Prussian musicians as Johann Joachim Quinz, the famous flautist, and Franz Benda, the principal violinist.

[Page 67]

In May, 1700, a Parisian opera troupe was invited to Warsaw. Ninety–three of its members traveled by coach from Strasburg to Ulm, then by boat to Krakow, and from Krakow to Warsaw by raft on the Vistula. August's successor put an end to the wanderings of the Polish orchestra by appointing it a permanent seat.

In the course of time, the Royal Orchestra in Warsaw gained a good reputation. With the foundation of the National Opera, Polish texts were composed for the Warsaw stage. Polish vocal art attained the fullness of its expression in Chopin. His student Mikoli (1821–1897) published Chopin's works. The Polish violinist Karl Lipinsky (1790–1861) competed against Paganini in Warsaw.

As Polish music developed, such Jews as Henry Winiawski and his brother, Josef, who founded an academy for pianists in Warsaw, began to make their voices heard. The connection between the Polish composer Moniuszkow and the Vilner Baale–bessel, the famous cantor Reb Yoel–Dovid Shtrashunsky, is still pointed to today, as are the relations of friendship and intimacy between eminent Polish and Jewish musicians.

The Wonders of the Maggid's Prayer

In the days of the Maggid there was no scarcity of hasidic music. The preceding generations had endowed it with an abundance of melodies, and the courts of eastern and western Galicia, together with those of Hungary and Congress Poland, added to this abundance. Why the Maggid then fell back on Polish melodies is not known. Even so, he knew how to preserve the purity of the traditional melodies, lest they be too greatly influenced by foreign ones.

The Maggid was eminent not only in hidden and revealed teachings, but also as the emissary of the congregation who stands before the ark leading the prayers and is able to transform prayer and music into a song of unity with the Lord. Whoever had once heard the Maggid pray before the ark was so overpowered by the strength of his singing as to be moved to visit him always in order to be warmed in the light of his prayer. Even the most vehement opponents of hasidism found themselves reconciled to the Maggid when once they had heard him float upon his sea of choral effusion. Many eminent scholars thus became enthusiastic hasidim or at least supporters of the movement within the camp of the misnagdim.

The Maggid was in the habit of leading the prayers on shabbes, and especially of prolonging the Friday evening service in order to pray with ardor and devotion, joy and jubilation, until he had extinguished any consciousness of self. The reception of the Sabbath Queen was no trifle for him, and he went out to greet her with dancing and rejoicing.

[Page 68]

He uttered the hymns until Lekha Dodi with fluency, as if the pipes of abundance and plenty had been opened and were dropping life–giving dew upon the congregation. His ardor increased from hymn to hymn, his powers of communion grew stronger, his voice more powerful–sweet, pleasant, restoring the souls of the congregation. And when the Maggid reached Lekha Dodi he opened the sluices of the source of joy and dropped pipesful of jubilation on everyone in the hall, and all were immersed in an ocean of joy.

He sang Lekha Dodi as a freilakhs, and the congregation would join in until even the walls seemed to sing along. At first, he would choose familiar tunes, so that the entire congregation could accompany him. Hasidim say that it was accepted among the tzaddikim that the Maggid's song ascended to the Throne of Glory and kindled joy in the heavenly hosts, and many contemporary tzaddikim came from near and far to listen to his shabbes prayer.

A New Melody

It happened that the Maggid changed his custom and sang Lekha Dodi to a new tune, a wedding tune used to welcome the bride and groom. No one was familiar with it, so the Maggid sang it alone. Still, the tune itself was a riddle difficult to solve. The Maggid sang the song's verses, moving his face from side to side, now towards the Sabbath Bride, now to somebody else, wonderful and invisible. When he reached the last verse, the Maggid turned toward the congregation, and signaled to the shammes to open the door for someone to whom he signaled with his finger, as if to invite him in. He then nodded his head, the shammes shut the door, and the Maggid finished the prayer in the festive tone with which he had begun.

As the tune was known to no one except the Maggid, it therefore dominated the conversation of the townspeople, who searched and burrowed and came up with no answer. Only after the Maggid' death did the shammes reveal the secret of the tune. Once, in the middle of the night, he, the shammes, heard the Maggid in conversation with the voice of one unknown who said that he had played the violin at the Maggid's wedding and lightened the hearts of the guests, and even awakened them to repent. The Maggid himself had enjoyed the tune so much that he asked the musician to play it again.

This melody was the fruit of the musician's production, and after his death he was informed that he had been one of the Levites, but that he had once defiled the song in the Temple and had therefore been sentenced to return to this world to make amends. And so he had come to the Maggid for help in rectifying the damage done by playing this tune to a group of nobles. At the Maggid's request, the deceased musician played the tune until the Maggid had absorbed it thoroughly. That night, the Maggid sang the melody. He had the power to remove any haughtiness, straighten crooked thoughts, to redeem it from the realm of the husks and raise it to the upper source. The raising of the melody to its root also rectified the musician's sin and brought rest to his lost soul.

[Page 69]

Songs of Angels from the Mouth of the Maggid

The melody was sung by many Kozienicer hasidim. Even in heaven the Maggid was considered an outstanding leader of prayer, as one "old and accustomed" who knew the job well. It is no wonder that the songs of angels, which he brought with him from time to time as gifts from heaven, were sung at his table. Some of the celestial beings saw him soaring through the upper worlds to act as a peerless master of prayer even there. Kozienicer hasidim tell many stories about these ascents.

Reb Shimon Deutsch (Ashkenazi) testified that he once fell gravely ill and was on the point of giving up the ghost. In the upper world he saw the Maggid welcoming the Sabbath. The next morning he davened shakhris, and at the shaleshides the Maggid said to him, "Descend to the lower world, for you are still a young man." Deutsch was a hasid from that time on (Sikhot Khaim).

The author of No–am Maggidim was originally an opponent of hasidism. Once, while gravely ill, he saw the Maggid in his yarmulke, praying fervently in the upper world and singing Lekha Dodi with the angels as his choir. Afterwards, he gave toyre. On his return to our world, the author of No'am Maggidim went to Kozienice and became the Maggid's disciple (Sefer Qhalei Shem).

The Maggid led the prayers during the Days of Awe every year, and did so with fervour and feeling despite his physical debility. His prayer made an impression upon the congregation and called forth an echo in the world of the tzaddikim, so that it was considered a great event. The Seer of Lublin testified that he shook all the worlds with his prayer, and perhaps this was the reason that multitudes of hasidim flocked to him for the Days of Awe, seeking assurance that their prayers be favourably received in heaven.

The Maggid reviewed all his hasidim in his memory during his prayers on the Days of Awe. Before he approached the ark, they mentioned all the members of the congregation to him. This was especially the case before Kol Nidre.

The Final Kol Nidre

The hasidim went on at particular length about the Maggid's prayer during the last year of his life. The impression left by that year's prayers on the Days of Awe was as great in heaven as it was on earth. The hasidim would expatiate greatly on this topic in order to demonstrate the auspiciousness of the Maggid's prayer.

[Page 70]

During Kol Nidre he paused before "And the Lord said, I have forgiven according to your word," and began to speak in tones supplication similar to those of Rebbe Levi–Yitzkhok of Berdichev. "Master of the Universe, who could utter or recount the greatness of your might? Your might is known to no one but you, only you know my real weakness. The proof? Every year I pray before the ark daily, but have not done so this year. It is known to you that this is due to my weakness, and yet I stood before the ark in prayer and supplication all through the month of Elul, not for myself, you know, but for the sake of your nation Israel. And therefore I ask one thing of you: Why was it so easy for me to take the yoke of your children upon myself despite my frailty, to wear myself out in prayer and holy exertion on their behalf, while for you–who has all the glory and might–for you it's hard to say two words: 'Salakhti ki–d'varekha, for I have forgiven according to your word'? If you should say that you hold back from saying it because of the lack of tzaddikim in the world, take a look! You've got Rebbe Mendele of Rimanov, who is worth all the righteous men of a generation. Maybe you refuse to say those words because there are no urim and thummim? Take a look! In Lublin you've got the Seer, Rebbe Yaakov–Yitzkhok, who shines forth like the urim and thummim fixed on Aaron's breast. And should you say there is no one willing to do penance, take a look at me. Sick as I am, I am ready to do penance for the whole congregation of Israel, and I pray you to say 'I have forgiven.☐'"

At the conclusion of this speech, he cried in a loud voice, "And the Lord said, I have forgiven according to your word," and then commanded the singers to sing sweetly, with happiness and joy.

This story is quite well–known in hasidic literature, and it received a supplement, a continuation, as it were, attributed to Rebbe Yisroel of Rizhin, who remarked upon hearing it, "I believe with perfect faith that the Maggid heard salakhti from the Lord himself, just as Moishe Rabbenu did, and that had he not heard it he would not have gone on with his prayer."

The Seer of Lublin was also moved by this stormy prayer. After mayriv at the conclusion of Yom Kippur, he said, "Would that the sun set and the good news be announced from Kozienice, for the bedridden one there has shaken all the worlds" (Tiferet Khaim).

The Maggid Overcomes his Physical Frailty

For this very reason, the Maggid found cause to complain about his success as a leader of prayer. "Perhaps because it is known in heaven that I have no pleasure or enjoyment aside from prayer," he said, "they help my prayer to ascend, so that I might receive my reward in that."

The Maggid instituted a great reform: that none among the congregation be ahead or behind in his prayers, but that they all pray together. Once when the prayer leader was going too quickly, the Maggid said, "He who speeds his prayer ahead of the congregation's is like a dog which runs before the cart" (Likutim Khadashim).

[Page 71]

Although the Maggid was chronically ill, short and weak, and had a soft voice, a mighty soul dwelt within his small frame. He served the Lord with ardor and joy, as if he were healthy. Sometimes, he was so weak as to have to be carried to the synagogue on a chair, but as soon as he arrived he was transformed, becoming powerful as a lion, his voice flashing forth flames of fire. He would leap out of his chair with ease and pray with the fervour of youth, with ardor and devotion, without feeling any traces of his infirmity.

The second Rebbe Aharon of Karl in once said to his wife, Sarah, "On account of his physical weakness, your grandfather, the Maggid, had to be carried to the synagogue; when he reached "Sing a new song to the Lord," he would gird his loins and dance like a young girl."

Music as an Aid to Worship

Music was a means of divine service for him, and he found it a suitable means of helping a man with his worship. Songs from other courts which suited the Maggid's way were sung at Kozienice, but the Maggid himself composed tunes for songs for the Sabbath and Festivals and for various prayers, just as he wrote songs whose content was a crown of praise for the Lord and for Israel.

The Admor of Radzimin, who claimed to have been present at eighteen of the Maggid's seders, testifies to the power of the music at these. During the first half of the seder it was possible to grasp and understand some of what the Maggid was saying, even though he would utter profound teachings. When he reached the second half of the seder, however, he would say things which could not be grasped, besides adding many statements in Polish. When he started Ekhad Mi Yoydea, he added in Polish, "Co wiem to powiem" (What I know I will tell).

There is a widespread belief among hasidim that a singer or player of a stringed instrument tells his listeners everything he has done in his life, and the ability to "read" music in this fashion is also attributed to the Maggid. Once, they say, one of the greatest violinists of the day, a man who had played for Czar Alexander I, was playing before the Maggid. When he finished, the Maggid reminded him of something he had forgotten to play. The hasidim were astounded to hear the Maggid criticize the famous musician, and were unable to understand the matter. After the Musician had left, the Maggid explained it to them. "Know, my children, that every singer or musician recounts all his sins and all his deeds one by one whenever he plays. So with this musician, except that he forgot one deed…"

[Page 72]

Reb Shmuel's Melody

At his Sabbath tables, the Maggid would occasionally sing new melodies which, hasidic tradition claims, came to him from the Palace of Music in heaven. To this day, the hasidim calls them "holy melodies", and they are sung with a fervour and devotion befitting their great sanctity. The originals of some of these melodies are connected with legends, the finest of which is that concerning Reb Shmuel's Melody.

Reb Shmuel Zwitkower of Praga–Warsaw, a distinguished rich man who had gained a reputation for his generosity, sanctified the Holy Name during the terrible persecution of the Jews of Praga, who were sitting ducks for the Cossacks who had just defeated the Polish army. Reb Shmuel issued a proclamation to the bloodthirsty soldiers, saying that whosoever brought him a Jew, living or dead, would receive a reward: three rubles per live Jew, and one per corpse. He was thus able to save those who had survived, and give the dead a Jewish burial. Reb Shmuel spent almost his entire fortune in this cause, and his work was extolled in expressions of thanks from the Jews of Poland.

The Khidushei Ha–Rim, Rebbe Yitzkhok–Meyer Alter of Ger, told that when he was a young boy in Kozienice the Maggid used to lead the Sabbath prayers. When he reached the hymn El Adon, his closest disciples, who stood beside him, would take up the melody, while the Maggid himself uttered only the words. One shabbes the Maggid began to sing this hymn to a beautiful and pleasant tune which his intimates had never heard. They were therefore unable to sing along. After the service, the Maggid noticed that they were still perplexed, and said, "Three years have now passed since the death of Reb Shmuel Zwitkower. Some of the angels of destruction went out to meet him, to prosecute him for his sins. Against them came an angel for the defense who had been created from his great mitzve of saving lives: 'How can it be that his great deed does not outweigh his sins? He, who has saved many Jewish lives, is worthy to go at once to the Garden of Eden.' The heavenly court ruled that he was indeed deserving of a prominent place in the Garden of Eden on account of his great labours in the rescue of Jewish lives, but that he had also to be purified of the stains of his sins before he could be admitted. This took three years, and the angels have just now escorted him to the Garden of Eden with joy and with song. And this is the song which you just heard me sing" (Me'ir Einei ha–Gola).

The Kozienice dynasty was born under the sign of music, and the spirit of the hasidim longed for melody and song. Music floated down to its founder, Rebbe Yisroel, and it occupied a respected place in prayers, songs, and festive meals. The air of Kozienice absorbed countless melodies and tunes. Some would burst forth in a still, small voice; others would flow in stormy melodies, flashing fire. No throat was sealed, no ear closed. The Maggid believed that the power of music could do great things, and in most cases he was not disappointed.

[Page 73]

The Maggid–A Fiddler

While still in his youth, the Maggid was among those who helped to establish the mood at festivities. Badkhanus, the art of the wedding jester, inclined to this function, and was therefore widespread among the tzaddikim. Rebbe Naphtali of Ropschitz, the Seer of Lublin, and Rebbe Ber of Radoschitz were all active as badkhonim, expressing marvellous ideas about the service of the Lord in their verses.

The Maggid knew how to play the violin, and there are connections between the Maggid's ability to play and the ability to play various instruments in the dynasties of Karlin and Stolin. While still a student of Rebbe Elimelekh of Lizensk, the Maggid was outstanding in his violin playing, and his teacher knew how to take advantage of this ability on various occasion.

During a cholera epidemic in Lizensk, Rebbe Elimelekh married an aging virgin to a water carrier. The Maggid played the violin at the wedding, and the Seer of Lublin acted as badkhan. At the close of the Sabbath, they went to gladden the bride and groom. Rabbi Shmuel of Korev, who was then staying with Rebbe Elimelekh, said to him, "Let us go to gladden the bride and groom."

They stood outside, and heard the Seer making rhymes. Everyone was dancing, and Rebbe Elimelekh himself danced with them for over an hour. Afterwards he said, "Lord of the Universe, as a reward for the mitzve–dance we have danced, let us merit to extinguish at least one of the coals glowing in hell (Ohel Elimelekh)."

Indeed, the Maggid understood the point of such music, without which there would be no hasidic life. Music removes inner obstacles and brings one to feelings of brotherhood. It is within its power to be raised from level to level. With its help, it is easy to banish idle thoughts, to dispel worries and sadness and to bring light to the depths of one's being.

Saved by Music

The Maggid was more than once delivered from danger to his life by the power of music. Hasidim tell that when the Holy Jew of Pshiskhe heard that the Maggid was gravely ill, he immediately sent two of his disciples, Reb Shmuel Jadlinsker and Reb Shmuel Skashiner, to Kozienice, with orders to welcome the Sabbath for him if he were still alive. They were both accomplished musicians, and had the power to return him to this world and keep him alive through their singing.

They arrived in Kozienice, told the Maggid whence they had come, and proceeded to welcome the Sabbath. The melodies, well–sung with ardour and a festive spirit, improved the Maggid's condition; his symptoms were lightened, and he realized that the melodies were a proven remedy for his illness. He said to them, "The Jew saw in a prophetic vision that I had passed through all the worlds except the world of music, and sent me these two men, so that their song might bring me back to this world" (Nifla'ot ha–Yehudi).

[Page 74]

The Maggid also used the same tunes with which he learned and prayed in his day–to–day speech. He used to sing in Polish, and Kozienicer hasidim still sing Jaki Purim, Taki Lel–Shimurim, which he would sing on Purim, and follow with a discourse on the same topic. After the meal, he said that the basis of the Purim festivities lay in the negation of the body, and he explained this with a Polish proverb, "Hulei bez kuszoli," "enjoy yourself without a shirt on your body". He also used other Polish sayings, such as "Kto rano vstaie, temu pan bog pachwali daie", "upon him who awakens early in the morning does the Lord bestow his gifts", and he intoned them all tunefully (Ohalei Shem).

He adopted acronyms even for Polish proverbs. It was said in his name that honey (dvash in Hebrew) is eaten during the month of Tishrei because dvash is an acronym for "dai boze szczenszcie," "may God send good luck." The Maggid raised the Polish sayings toward redemption by singing them, an activity resembling that of Rebbe Yitzkhok–Eisik of Kalev in Hungarian.

Paidyom le–Zion be–Rina

The Maggid employed Slavic words to erect lovely monuments to the longing for Zion. Even while reading the haggada, he did not hesitate to change a Hebrew for a Slavic word, and derive a "zionist" use from it.

Once a guest came to the Maggid on the eve of the seder, and was invited to stay over for the entire holiday. This guest spoke a bastard language, half–Russian, half–Jewish. The Maggid conducted the seder, made a tuneful and vigorous kiddush, and recited the haggada to a special tune. The guests repeated both the words and the tune, all except the one, who sat as if mute, never opening his mouth. After he had had a few cups of wine, though, he began to act with presumptuous freedom, singing various songs, some of them in Russian.

After the meal, the reading of the haggada continued. When they reached khasal siddur pesakh (the end of the prescribed portion of the seder), the guest asked the Maggid if he, the guest, might sing these lines to a tune he had learned from his father. The Maggid agreed, and the guest began to sing khasal siddur pesakh ke–hilkhasov in a pleasing voice. He continued in this fashion until he reached the verse p'duyim le-tzion be–rina (redeemed unto Zion with joy), when he began to approach the door, loudly singing "Paidyom le-tzion be–rina" ("Let's go to Zion joyously"), going back and crying, "Paidyom".

When the Maggid heard these words he hurried from the table, put on his shoes, took his staff in his hand and exclaimed with great joy, "O.K., we're ready to go to Zion, we and all of Israel, young and old–so let's go." As soon as he finished speaking, the door opened of its own accord, and the guest, who had been walking behind him, singing and dancing, went outside. The Maggid hurried after him, but when he got outside he could no longer see him, and could hear only the sound of the tune, growing faint in the distance until it had disappeared altogether (Keter ha–Yehudi).

[Page 75]

Helped by the Sanctity of Rabbi Yohai

The Maggid's way was based upon a higher clinging and occult yearnings. Ardor was a lamp unto his feet. He would arrange the hakofes on Simkhes Toyre with great ardor. Once he did so even more than usual, saying that Rabbi Shimon bar Yohai had stood by him during the hakofes, and his sanctity helped the Maggid to organize them more joyously than was usual.

Neither singing nor repentance can be taught, and the man of talent becomes a musician all by himself. The Maggid expressed this opinion in his explanation of the verse, "play skilfully with loud shouts" (Ps.33:3): "'Skilfully–by this you shall improve your ways and walk upon the good and upright path. 'Play'–you will be able to play, even though you have no musical talent. The Lord will help you on account of your righteousness, so that you will be able to honour him with your voices. It has been told me that there are righteous men among you who do not know how to 'play', despite the fact that their voices in prayer are sweeter than honeycombs. This is no simple problem, but I say to you, 'play skilfully.' What is skilful playing? 'With loud shouts,' with that which you cry out in humility, with a broken and downtrodden heart.'"

Several of the Maggid's tunes, from which some idea of the nature of his songs can be formed, have been preserved. Some are saturated with a Jewish spirit, and based on popular motifs. Another class must be connected with prayers: Tal Ten le–Ratzoys Artzekha, be–Rosh ha–Shana Yikasevun, Adam Yesoydoy me–Afar, slowly flowing melodies, expressing supplication and conciliation. As opposed to these, there are merry tunes, redolent, for the most part, of Polish motifs. Some, indeed, are Polish through and through. A pointed dissonance is apparent between these two types, with no tendency toward integration or amalgamation.

Undoubtedly, there were others besides the Maggid who enriched the court with their melodies, without calling attention to themselves. These are the anonymous composers, of whom there was a considerable number.

The Seraph of Mogielnica–the Maggid's Grandson

Rabbi Khaim Meir Yekhiel Shapira, the tzaddik of Mogielnica, was an extraordinary figure among the tzaddikim of his day. He was the song of the Maggid's only daughter, Perele, and her husband, Rabbi Ezra–Zelig, the rav of Grinic. He grew up at the Maggid's, and was his grandfather's pet. The Maggid played with him, and devoted a good deal of thought to his welfare; they learned and prayed together, and the Maggid revealed supernal mysteries to the child. The atmosphere was saturated with music, and the boy absorbed a love for it.

[Page 76]

His feel for music was deepened during sojourns with other tzaddikim. While still a child, he spent time with the Seer of Lublin and Rebbe Avraham–Yehoshua Heschel of Apta, who both prophesied that he would be a tzaddik, the Light of the Exile. He married the daughter of Rabbi Eliezer of Chmielnik, the son of Rebbe Elimelekh of Lizensk, the great Galician tzaddik who was noted for his love of Sabbath tunes.

Rebbe Khaim's biographers point out that "he was a great and famous scholar, adept in concealed and revealed teachings, holy and pious, a righteous man–the foundation of the world–the wonder and adornment of his generation– Thousands of hasidim, thirsting to lap up his holy words, flocked to learn the ways of worship from him" (Shem ha–G'dolim he–Khadash, by R. Aaron Walden, Warsaw, 1882; M'litzei eish, by R. Abraham Stern, Novozamki, 1934–). They have nonetheless omitted a salient point of his way, viz., music and dance, the melodies he composed, few though they be, and those which he revised.

He was first chosen as rav in Mogielnica, and only later received the title of tzaddik. He quickly became a force of attraction and the creator of an atmosphere suffused with tunes of joy and devotion which exalted and purified the soul. Undoubtedly, his influence must be ascribed to his personal stature, yet there were other tzaddikim at the time who did not fall below him in this respect, yet still did not attain to his level.

[Page 77]

Ardour: His Way of Worship

His way of worship was that of powerful ardour and great clinging to the Lord, and because of this he was called the Seraph by hasidim. Contemporary tzaddikim said that there had been no worship of such ardour and clinging since the time of Rebbe Levi–Yitzkhok of Berdichev.

The principle of ardour was fundamental to all his activity. He would pass before the ark on shabbas and holidays and sweeten the prayer with his strong and pleasant voice. His ardour was the medium of expression for his musical ideas and his interpretations of prayers and piyuttim.

His prayer served as a model for others and they in turn found encouragement in his example. The grandsons of Rav Moishe Stinitzer, an eminent disciple of the Seer of Lublin, told that one Rosh Ha–Shana, their grandfather was leading the musaf prayer as he usually did when his strength failed him (he was already very advanced in age) and he decided to appoint someone to take his place. But at the moment at which he wished to leave the amud, the prayer of the Seraph of Mogielnica, who was praying before the ark with great ardour, came suddenly to his ear. At once, his spirit returned, his powers revived, and he went on to complete the prayer before the amud just as he was wont to do every year.

His Boundless Love for Music

His love of music knew no bounds. He was particularly fond of melodies which were Jewish in their spirit and in their qualities in the amplification of the major–key foundation. His keen ear sought out the faults and defects of hasidic melodies, and prompted suggestions for their revision. He revitalized old melodies. Frequent use had not made them passe for him; instead, they were as well–aged wine which increases in excellence the longer it is drunk.

In the dispute concerning the older melodies, the Seraph took the side of the old, but without denigrating the value of the new. Hasidism has room for old and new alike, without any encroachment of the one upon the other.

Moreover, the Seraph himself broke free of the old melodies in order to compose his own. His melodies pulsate with the freedom of spirit characteristic of Polish hasidic music of the first epoch, in which joyousness occupies the first place.

The Seraph himself was inclined to optimism. He disliked sadness and distraction; joy and ardour were his portion. His shabbes and holiday celebrations were arranged with ardour, with the participation of the great tzaddikim of Poland, including Rebbe Yisroel–Yitzkhok of Radoshitz, Rav Shloime Rabinowitz of Radomsk, Rav Nossen–Dovid of Szidlowca, Rav Sinni of Radom, and others who were among his intimates, his disciples and his hasidim.

[Page 78]

The Tzaddik's Salutary Slap

On shabbes the Seraph would sing Tikanta Shabbas and Yismekhu be-Malkhusekho and enjoy his singing, believing that it produced pleasure in heaven. He once told the rav of Tschihow that when Leibele, his accompanist, did not confuse him during the singing of Tikanta Shabbas, the Levites in the Garden of Eden sang along with him.

While singing, he would overhear a supernal accompaniment, as it were an echo to his own singing, and feel the flutter of seraphs' wings.

It seems, however, that Leibele had a special reason to confuse the tzaddik while he was singing. During the Days of Awe and festivals, the Seraph used to pray before the ark, accompanied by a choir of hasidim under Leibele's direction. Whenever the choir hit a wrong note, Leibele would receive a resounding slap in the face from the tzaddik. Now, Leibele suffered from tuberculosis, but his illness did not interfere with his choral duties. He was positive that so long as the tzaddik lived, his illness would not be especially oppressive, and that each slap he received from the Seraph improved his health. There were those who mocked him because he would occasionally miss the right note on purpose, in order to receive a slap ... With the Seraph's passing, Leibele was left defenseless, and he too, died.

At the shaleshides, the Seraph never spoke words of Torah, as he did at the Sabbath evening and afternoon meals, but instead sang with great ardour. He used to say that with the shaleshides' zmiros, the heavenly palaces were opened to him, but he was afraid to enter them late when there was no one to let him out.

A Touch of the Turban

The joy and festivity reached its height on Purim, on which song and dance occupy the premier position. The tzaddik would be very merry at the Purim evening meal, dancing after his fashion. His custom on Purim was to make himself a turban, which he called a pidke, from one of the sleeves of his coat, its top pointed in a knot. While it was being knotted he would cry, "Jews! Pray to the Lord that the turban be built up nicely."

The hasidim used to claim that the turban was a wonderful piece of work. The Seraph would put it on his head and stand in the middle of the bes-medresh where the bima was. The hasidim would form a circle around him, dancing hand in hand until daybreak. In the middle of this dancing, the tzaddik would grab the turban and throw it into the crowd. Whoever was smited on by fortune and was struck by the turban was assured of the fulfillment of all of his wishes, of prosperity and of deliverance.

The doings with the turban circulated among Polish hasidim and many came to the Seraph to be helped by it. The term Pidke is perhaps based on the word pidyen, ransom (Sikhot Khaim by Rabbi Khaim–Meir–Yekhiel of Mogielnica, Piotrokow).

[Page 79]

The Seraph Gains Renown as a Wonder–Worker

The Seraph became renowned as a wonder–worker, a worker of salvation, an exorcist of evil spirits, and the like. Rebbe Nossen–Dovid of Szidlowca was once called to a youth in Pshiskhe. After the tzaddik had absolved the youth of an oath made to a third party who had died in the meantime, the youth proceeded to tell him of this third party, a respected and religious man, well versed in music and a fine baal–t'filla, who had approached him with an indecent proposal. The youth refused, but swore never to reveal the disgrace in public. Nevertheless, for the past week or so the spirit of the deceased baal-t'filla had been following the youth, urging him to do him a "favour".

As soon as the secret had been revealed to the tzaddik, the spirit at once entered into the youth who began singing a fine tune despite the fact that the youth had absolutely no knowledge of music. The spirit spoke rapidly in Hebrew, confessing that he had prayed before the amud. His singing was motivated by impure fantasies, and the floor where he had stood while singing had to be washed afterwards.

The tzaddik ordered the boy to go to Mogielnica, and told his father not to leave him alone. When the father went to pray in the inn the next day, the boy went outside and was possessed by the evil spirit. The spirit began to sing and speak Hebrew, and those musicians who had known the man and were familiar with his voice said that the voice of the spirit was the very voice of the man. The seraph finally drove the spirit from the boy (Toldot Nifla'ot, and see Divrei Elimelekh).

A centre of hasidism and hasidic music whose influence spread far and wide was established in Mogielnica. Song and dance were held in such esteem that they became as rituals in their worship.

The tzaddik was not graced with length of days. He died while still in his prime of the fifteenth of Iyar, 1869, in Warsaw, and was brought to rest there. He left neither manuscripts nor published books behind him, although he often gave toyre before his hasidim. Nevertheless, he is cited in many books, and his hasidim devoted several books to his personality and teachings.

Among his students were Rav Yaakov-Yitzkhok of Blandow, Rav Elimelekh, son-in-law of the tzaddik Rebbe Yerakhmiel of Pshiskha, who established a new dynasty in Grodzisk; Rav Ezra-Zelig, father of the tzaddik Reb Khaim-Meir Shapira of Drohowitz, who went to Jerusalem, where he is buried.

Rebbe Moishe–Elyakim Beriah (ob. 1828)

Kozienice hasidism brought forth a group of men who performed important work in shaping the character of this school of hasidism, but who did not fulfill their obligations in the field of music. Neglect of this area is quite marked in several cases, and an unambiguous correction of this state of affairs was to come only later.

[Page 80]

The Maggid's successors were Rav Moishe-Elyakim Beriah, Rav Elazar, Rav Yekhiel-Yaakov, and Rav Yerakhmiel-Moishe.

In their desire to express their gratitude to the great Maggid, the dews of Kozienice, concerned for the livelihood of his son, Rav Moishe-Elyakim Beriah, offered to take him on as the city's cantor.

Khazanus had always been a good opportunity for khasidus, and it often happened that khazanus was the first step in the making of a tzaddik. The first act of an enterprising hasid who aspired to lead a hasidic community was to daven before the ark; only if he passed this test would he have a chance of being promoted to tzaddik.

Rav Moishe-Elyakim Beriah was known to the townspeople as "The Master of Psalms" because he used to pour out his soul in their recitation, singing them in a sweet voice which inadvertently drew the attention of those who heard him.

The townspeople did not figure him for a learned man, for he knew how to conceal himself. Even his sister Perele doubted his fittingness to take over his father's position, but it was decided that he would be acceptable as khazan from all points of view. Decided, that is, until the congregation's board-members, with Moishe-Elyakim in tow, went to the Seer of Lublin in order to obtain his endorsement of Rav Moishe's appointment as khazan. Much to their amazement, the Seer proclaimed him worthy in every respect of taking his father's place as tzaddik, and instead of serving as khazan be entered the orchard of khasidus (Nifla'ot ha–Rabbi, by Rebbe Yaakov–Yitzkhok of Lublin).

The Rav of Apta's Respect for Him

He used to visit Rav Avraham–Yehoshua Heschel (The Rav from Apta) in Medzibozh. Rav Heschel respected him, and said to his hasidim: "Know that he is the son of the Kozienicer Maggid. The Maggid was comparable to King David, and the son is as the father." It is difficult to suppose that the Rav from Apta, who had no particular love of music, saw him as comparable to David by virtue of his musical ability; but perhaps, as a sensitive man, he did intend to refer to precisely this quality.

Once on Rosh Ha–Shana, the Rav from Apta, already late in starting his prayers, said that he would not begin until Rav Moishe started to pray. From this, we learn how far his regard for Rav Moishe reached.

Rav Moishe wrote many books, some of which have become classics. The best known are: Be'er Moshe, on the Torah; Va–Yakhel Moshe, on the Psalms; T'Filla le–Moshe, about Sukkos; Mateh Moshe on the Passover Haggada; Pirkei Moshe, on Pirkei Avot, and many other books which remained unpublished. In his writing, Rav Moishe is unconcerned with questions of brevity, and he tends to rhetorical elaboration. Although he loved music, he could not express the fact; despite the multiplicity of his writings, he never rose to the height of the tzaddikim of the first two generations of hasidism. Almost every thought and utterance of these latter touching upon music is as a dwarf bearing up a giant, and every statement about music teaches a great deal.

[Page 81]

On the other hand, there is no ignoring the little that Rav Moishe did write about music, and even this little proves him a man of ardour and inspiration.

He said: "The words of him who learns Torah for its own sake are as sweet to heaven as the voice of song with lute and harp, with timbrel, with strings and pipe." He brings proof of this from the verse "Awake, O harp and lyre!" (Ps. 57:8). By purity of heart and study of Torah, by the words of his mouth, the supernal mouth is awakened in a voice of praise and a sweet song, as the voice of song with lute and harp (Be'er Moshe, Va–Yekhi).

His ardour was clothed in musical raiment. The Book of Psalms was dear to him from his youth, and from time to time he would delve into it more deeply than into other books. He once revealed the idea expressed in the verse, "My heart is stricken (Khalal) within me" (Ps. 109:22), according to the saying of our sages, "He struck the Flute (Khalil) before them from an excess of joy." "As my own heart," added Rav Moishe, "sings ever within me just as that flute, to worship you with great joy; and there is no sluggishness or sadness in my heart" (Va–Yakhel Moshe, 109).

His townspeople discovered his pleasant voice and musical talent, but he remained unimpressed by this. He found that many must act modestly, believing that of himself he has neither the intelligence nor the ability to do anything at all–all is given by heaven, whence man derives the strength and intelligence to raise his prayer up with devotion.

Similarly for all man's advantages. Should a man have a fine voice "and know how to play on all manner of instruments", let him fulfill the verse "Honour the Lord with your substance" (mi–honkha) (Prov: 3.9), as interpreted by our sages: "Do not read mi–honkha but mi 'g 'ronkha (with your throat)." Let him believe with perfect faith that he has been favoured by heaven with a gift of grace insofar as he possesses some quality, advantage or talent beyond his fellows.

Rav Moishe bore himself up with his father's remarks on the verse, "for it is he who gives you strength to perform mighty deeds". The power to excel in a particular quality, be it in learning or be it in music, has been given you from above. It is therefore incumbent upon anybody so graced to raise the holy spark back up to its source, to the upper root from which it was taken, rather than act as "those distinguished scholars, outstanding kabbalists or musicians who sing their own praises and lift themselves above others, as if they and they alone in their time were distinguished among musicians."

Rav Moishe saw his sweet voice and musical talent as a heavenly gift bestowed upon him even though he was unworthy. The reason that he did not refuse to pray before the ark in his father's bes–medresh while still in his youth, or refuse to do so elsewhere, pleasing God and man with his voice, was to prove that by using his talent for the good of heaven, he was not ungrateful for the favour shown him, (Be'er Moshe for Yom Kippur).

[Page 82]

The Fable of the Clapper and the Bell

To what may this be likened? To the body of a bell and the clapper. The bell cannot strike without the help of the clapper inside it, and it is nothing but a vessel able to produce a sound with the clapper's help.

So it is with man: he is unable to utter songs of praise without the help of a strength rained down from heaven, for he is but a vessel for the reception of the soul. Only when heavenly light flows onto a man will the mute tongue rejoice and continually sing songs and praises to heaven (Be'er Moshe, Naso). Rav Moishe was very fond of this exemplum, and he cites it on a number of occasions in various of his books.

He cannot be considered as a creative force in the field of music, but he did continue with his father's melodies, which had become traditional in the family. They attributed especially great power to "The Angels' Melody", which was sung on special occasions and at events of the utmost gravity. A garland of legends has been wreathed about this tune, and there were those who attempted to understand the secret of its composition by the angels.

Among these was the tzaddik of Porisow, who refrained from saying that the Maggid had heard the song from angels who were singing to the Lord. In his opinion, the angels heard the song from the Maggid, and then sang it. These singing angels had been created from the Maggid's mitzvas, from his teaching and worship, all of which were performed with wonderful vitality; for the basic point of a mitzva performed with such vitality is that it leads to the creation of angels (Imrei Yehoshua by Rabbi Uri Yehoshua Asher Elkhanon, the Rabbi of Porisow, Warsaw, 1929).

Joy is a concept which has no limit. Proof of this is to be found in a wedding feast. Even though all present are joyous and happy, the arrival of the badkhan (wedding jester) with his jests and tricks makes them even happier still (Be'er Moshe, Shmini).

Rav Moishe passed away on the twelfth of Elul, 1828.

Rebbe Elazar of Kozienice

Rav Elazar of Kozienice, the son of Rebbe Moishe–Elyakim Beriah, was one of the leading lights of his time, great in Torah and fear of God, a modest and pious man in whose light many walked.

His way was to demand that the young people lead the prayers. This was a quasi–innovation among hasidim, and a signal of approach to the young. He explained this custom by saying that in their prayers the young men told him all their deeds, but the custom itself made an impression and the young endeavoured to do their duty properly, to pray pleasantly and with lovely melodies. This custom afterwards passed to Rebbe Ben–Zion Halberstam of Bobov, who gave it even greater authority, so that the young began to feel that they had equal rights in hasidism.

[Page 83]

Rebbe Elazar's own musical inclinations were but average. He took care to preserve the traditional melodies of the house of Kozienice, and did not allow undue prominence to outside melodies. He looked respectfully upon the melodies of the Seer of Lublin and the traditional melodies of other tzaddikim. In his day there was a dearth of original compositions in Kozienice.

His cantor, Abish Friedman, was known as Abish [the] Singer because of his musical talent. He composed many songs, most of the Kozienice tunes being his compositions.

Rebbe Elazar expressed his joy at the birth of his grandson, Reb Yerakhmiel–Moishe, in a conversation with Rav Raphael of Garvolin. He told him that he dreamt he saw Rav Yerakhmiel of Pshiskhe, who told him to sing Yoyn Le–Yabasha. When Rebbe Elazar told him that he could not sing it, the latter replied, "Sing, and I will help you." Rebbe Elazar then beheld his daughter–in–law, Sarah–Dvoire, giving birth, and understood what all this was hinting at. The infant was thus named Yerakhmiel.

Rebbe Elazar died on the twenty–sixth of Kislev, 1862 and left behind a small book entitled Likutei Ma–Ha–Ra, which appeared in two editions after his death.

Rebbe Yekhiel–Yaakov of Kozienice

Rebbe Elazar passed when his only son, Yekhiel–Yaakov was sixteen years of age. Yekhiel–Yaakov hesitated a long time as to whether to assume the mantle of rebbe, but finally bowed to the pressure of the hasidim and became their leader. Nevertheless, he asked that he might follow his own path of service, rather than that which lay paved before him.

He lacked the power to make any contribution in the field of music, and was forced to satisfy himself with the traditional melodies of the court of Kozienice. He established a friendship with Rav Yoisef–Barukh Epstein, the tzaddik of Neustadt, who was known as Per Guter Yid; yet his modesty forbade him from accepting written requests for help and donation–money from his followers. His teacher, Rebbe Khaim of Sanz, rebuked him often and to his face for this refusal, saying that as the scion of great and holy men he was capable of accepting such things. Rebbe Yekhiel–Yaakov answered him with the Mishnaic statement (Megilla, 2:1), "He who reads out of order has not fulfilled his obligation," and stood firm in his refusal.

Torah and prayer were the foundation of his service, and he engaged in them with great devotion and self–abnegation. He complained of the growing rapport between Jews and gentiles and of the assimilation to be expected from it. He therefore held "modern" melodies, in which there was a good deal of the spirit of the age and the music of other nations, in slight regard.

[Page 84]

Rav Yekhiel–Yaakov was not long for this world, drowning in the springtime of his years when he was dragged under the waves of the local river. He was young, not yet twenty years old. He passed away on the first day of rosh–khoydesh Tammuz, 1866. On his tombstone is inscribed "A man unique in his generation – carried off by the water; holy and merciful in serving his heavenly father." He left an only son, aged six.

Rebbe Yerakhmiel–Moishe of Kozienice (1860–1909)

Rebbe Yerakhmiel–Moishe was born in the house of his maternal grandfather, Rebbe Elimelekh of Grodzisk. At his father's premature death, he went to Kozienice to take his place. He spent many years with Rebbe Asher Perlov of Stolin and his father, Rebbe Aaron, author of Beit Aharon, whose court had become renowned in the hasidic world as a musical centre.

Rebbe Yerakhmiel–Moishe was among the most exalted of the Polish tzaddikim, a figure of glory and grandeur, a noble personality, a man pure of heart and sharp of mind. No note of music went by him without leaving an impression. For the second time in its history, the House of Kozienice experienced a turbulent and fruitful epoch.

An Architect in the Field of Music

After the Maggid, Rebbe Yerakhmiel–Moishe was the second architect of the House of Kozienice. In particular, he was not disappointing as far as music goes. He diverged from established paths and went off into the open, an act which was considered greatly daring but which ultimately won a positive appreciation.

A new and unique musical event took place with Yerakhmiel–Moishe's accession to the office of rebbe. Until his time, the history of hasidic music from the first generation on was one of development, of the emergence of styles. The Besht pioneered hasidic music, and was followed by Rebbe Duber of Mezritch, who continued with his master's tunes even while adding to them. The development of idioms and styles began with the third generation: Habad melodies attained something new in their style, while the Beshtian tendency continued its hymnal, lyrical character. Rebbe Levi–Yitzkhok of Berdichev chose an ancient style, one more suited to his spiritual aspirations. We thus see the development by generations and countries, but there is no Galician melody like the melodies of Poland, Podolia or Hungary.

The founders of the dynasties of Karlin and Kozienice were not of one mind with their successors. The music of Rebbe Aharon the Great of Karlin resembled that of Habad in style, melody and dramatic tension. Although his soul was sick with love for heaven, and resounded like a flute from the abundance of musical feeling stored up in his heart, his nature and the circumstances of his life prevented him from playing any musical instrument (at the time, hasidim regarded musical instruments as tantamount to a profanation of the sacred), whereas his grandson Rebbe Aharon the Second (author of Beit Aharon), amplified musical "worship" by admitting the playing of violin and flute.

[Page 85]

The melodies of Lithuanian Karlin were distant in their character and qualities from those of Kozienice, which had a Polish flavour. Apart from this, it must be noted that Karlin itself – Karlin the abundant in melodies – was always alive and awake in its melodies, old or new, while music's stock declined in Kozienice from one generation to the next, until it seemed that in a short while it was liable to be absorbed by the depths of oblivion.

The explanation of this lay in the fact that from the beginning the melodies of Kozienice had no solid, natural and independent foundation – in the opinion of many they gave off a scent of obsolescence. Every new style of hasidic music intensified the creative power and the substance of the music. The Maggid of Kozienice did indeed create a new musical style, but after his death, there was no discernible development of his work. His successors were not sufficiently musical to continue what had been started, and a weakness in the field of music which grew from generation to generation came about, as it were, automatically.

Changes in the music of Kozienice began with Rebbe Yerakhmiel–Moishe's accession to the dynastic throne. These were the result of his education under the tzaddikim of Stolin, with whom he spent seventeen years from the ages of seven to twenty–four. In Stolin he learned to play the violin and the reed–flute. The reed–flute was a gift from his step–grandfather, the Beit Aharon of Stolin–Karlin.

The Melody of the Revelation of Elijah

Every Saturday night after havdole he was in the habit of going into the Maggid's room with a group of hasidim and playing Eliyahu Ha–Navi on his fiddle. When he reached the words, "As it is written, Behold I send you Elijah the prophet before the advent of the great and terrible day," he would put down the fiddle and take up his flute.

These Saturday night "recitals" would be drawn out for some time and the hasidim called this melody "The Melody of the Revelation of Elijah". Rebbe Yerakhmiel–Moishe had received this melody from the Beit-Aharon, and he used to play it on special occasions, on Saturday nights during kheder vacations.

It is told that he was in the habit of playing his fiddle every Saturday night, yet in the days following Sukkos, when Jewish boys were drafted into the Czarist army, he refrained from playing out of sympathy with their suffering.

His residence in Stolin influenced him to introduce changes in the music of Kozienice, by fusing the styles of Kozienice and Stolin. Or, to put it more correctly, under his influence, the music of Kozienice became subject to that of Karlin.

[Page 86]

He constantly recalled his time in Stolin, where he grew up and studied under the supervision of the Beit Aharon, and together with his step–brother, Rav Yisroel, "The Yanuka", he suckled and absorbed the khasidus and melodies of Karlin.

He took care of the flute which Rebbe Aharon had given him as if it were a precious stone, for he – Rebbe Aharon had ushered in a now musical era in Stolin.

The musical practices of Karlin–Stolin took root in Kozienice and were a positive influence on the revival of the dynasty.

Hasidism Paved the Way for Playing on Instruments

Hasidism gradually prepared the ground for the return of hardened hearts from sorrow and trouble to music and song – one of the cultural principles of the ancient Hebrews. With the passage of time, hasidism also prepared these same hearts for playing on instruments. The most popular instrument among the Jews was the fiddle, to which the hasidim remained faithful, and the number of famous Jewish fiddlers, among them Yossel Klezmer of Lublin, Pedahzur of Berdichev and Stempenyu of Zhitomir, was sufficiently large.

In Karlin and Stolin music was also played on the flute, which had occupied an important place in pilgrimages at the time of the Second Temple. The playing of flute and fiddle was, of course, permitted only for the sake of heaven at solemn gatherings, Saturday nights, and the like. To play solely for pleasure was considered a sin.

In the days of the Maggid of Kozienice fiddle playing at weddings and similar occasions was not disparaged. One of his longest–standing and most respected hasidim, Rav Itamar of Konskovola, author of Mishmeret Itamar, was a particularly distinguished fiddler.

Playing on the fiddle was as a balm to the sick for the Maggid. Once, when one of the strings broke in the middle of a tune and Rav Itamar wanted to tie it up and go on with his playing, the Maggid was prepared to teach him "the secret of the knotting of the tefillin" as a reward. Nevertheless, it had occurred to no one that the tzaddik himself might humble himself to play the fiddle. The hearts of the hasidim had not yet been prepared for that.

Rebbe Yerakhmiel–Moishe Composed 15 Melodies

Behold now how times had changed. Four generations passed in the dynasty of Kozienice, and Rebbe Yerakhmiel–Moishe was playing the fiddle and flute. This made his court a relatively progressive one, and it exercised some influence on the surrounding courts, which now saw the necessity of transmitting the requisite musical knowledge to the children of tzaddikim. From childhood, they were taught all manner of musical instruments and how their feelings were to be expressed on them.

[Page 87]

Rebbe Yerakhmiel–Moishe endeavoured to preserve the music of Kozienice hasidism. In his opinion, the traditional was not to be changed except in cases where it would be strengthened. On the other hand, he tried to fill in the empty spaces which were to be found here and there. He injected some of the ardour of Karlin into prayer, and when he felt that the music of Kozienice had run into a dry spell, he–feeling an inspiration to compose new melodies–went and wrote them in a style similar to that of Stolin. Constraints of time allowed him to compose only fifteen melodies, among them a lengthy one for Ya Ekhsoyf, a shaleshides song, in a moderate tempo, as opposed to the slow tempo of the Karlin melodies. He put new life into the Kozienice dynasty, and granted it an increase of strength and power.

Customs of Household and Tish

A few of his customs on shabbes and festivals are described in one of the books, from which it emerges that the spiritual fusion of Stolin and Kozienice was a fact and a positive phenomenon in Kozienice.

After mayrev on Friday night, the rebbe would recite Shalom Aleikhem verse by verse, as well as Riboyn Ha–Qylamim, having prefaced these with Askinu Sudasa up until Azamer Bi–Shvakhin.

Before Kiddush he would say Eshes Khayil, and one of his table–fellows would sing the biblical refrain, so as not to diverge from established custom.

After the fish, the rebbe and his guests would recite Kol Mekadesh and Menukha Ve–Simkha responsively.

After the soup they would sing Ma Yedidus, and after the meat, Rebbe Aharon of Karlin's well–known Ya Ekhsoyf Noyam Shabbas. On occasion, they would sing this latter after finishing the turnip tzimmis which was attributed to the Besht.

At the close of the meal the Rebbe would hum Eshes Khayil and Azamer Bi–Shvakhin verse by verse and with appropriate feeling, together with his guests. After the grace after meals, they would dance in a circle to the accompaniment of singing, and the tzaddik would dance with them.

On Friday nights from Pesakh to Sahvuos, they would accompany the dancing with the song A1 Achas Kama Ve–khama from the haggada, and afterwards the tzaddik would go to his room.

Ya–Ekhsoyf – Chief Among Songs

The typical song of Karlin, Ya Ekhsoyf, was the basic one of Kozienice. It was sung not only at Sabbath and festival meals, but also outside of such gatherings. The tzaddik used to recite it after the blessings for the Torah on shabbes mornings.

[Page 88]

At the second shabbes meal the tzaddik and those at the table would recite Asader Li–Sudasa responsively, and then begin to eat. After the soup they would sing Barukh Ha–Shem Yoym Yoym responsively, and after that Barukh Kel Elyon until the verse Khemdas Ha–Yamim.

Due to its content, this last verse was considered as a song in itself in Stolin, and it served as a competition piece for hasidic composers. There are therefore a great number of tunes for it. This custom also passed to Kozienice. They would sing Yoym–La–Y abas ha during the week, and on Shabbas Zakhor and Shabbas Shekalim they would sing the liturgical poems at the meal.

Their zmiros at the shaleshides were not the same as those of the congregation. In place of these, the tzaddik and those at the table with him would say Shir Ha–Ma'aloys Esa and Ein Kelokenu in a loud voice. After Ata Hu Elokenu Ba–Shamyim U–Va–Aretz they would light the havdole candle and sing Dror Yikra to a Wallachian tune, and also Shabbas Ha–Yoym.

On Shabbas Mevarkhim they sang Yekhadshehu with the other zmiros, and of course Ya Ekhsoyf was not missing. The rebbe would draw the meal out by telling stories in order to prolong the blessing of the Sabbath. Most of his stories were taken from the lives of the giants of hasidism in the first generations. The tzaddik revealed himself to be a storyteller, and his stories always drew a great crowd until the time of the darkness at the Sabbath's end.

On Saturday nights they sang Ha–Mavdil, and after the rebbe went into the Maggid's room they would sing Eliyahu Ha–Navi. The tzaddik would play his fiddle, and sometimes even his flute. At the song's end the tzaddik would recline at the melave–malka, and in the middle of the meal would play Amar Ha–Shem Le–Ya'akov. He adorned the close of the Sabbath with music.

After the blessing of the new moon, the hasidim would dance in a circle, the tzaddik often joining them. His way home was accompanied by the songs of the hasidim, and with this the melave–malka came to an end.

His playing on Saturday nights was inspired by this time of grace, and added to the natural joy whose source is the Sabbath.

During the counting of the Omer he did not play his fiddle even on Saturday night, and he likewise did not play among those who were grieving. The absence of his playing was felt, and the days of trouble stood out all the more.

Khanuka Songs

A festive spirit would hover about the court on the first night of Khanuka during the lighting of the first candle. After the kindling, the tzaddik would say Va–Yehi Noyam seven times, and an hour later they would bring the menora into the shul, where the tzaddik would sing selected hymns.

[Page 89]

At the close of the hymn–singing they would sing a merry march. On occasion, the tzaddik would accompany the song on his fiddle. After the singing, they began to dance, singing joyously as they did so. The tzaddik was strict about attendance at the hymn–singing, as well as about their being sung in a loud voice. The first night of Khanuka passed with great festivity.

Great arrangements were made for the last day of the holiday. The morning meal lasted until night–time, and was considered a great event in the lives of the hasidim. It abounded in music and song. They would sing Aroymimkha Ha–Shem ki Dilisanu to its usual time, and then the tzaddik and the congregation would say Min Ha–Oylam Ve–Ad Ha–Oylam from Nishmas verse by verse until the end, continuing with Kol Bruei Mala to the usual tune.

There was a special order of hymns for each of the eight days of Khanuka. Each hymn was appropriate to the day in question, awakening joy at the memory of the miracle.

Joy and song adorned the Purim meal. During the meal they sang Aroymimkha Ha–Shem Ki Dilisanu to its standard melody. The rebbe rejoiced an exulted all night with songs and dances about the purity of divine service, and he also sang Kol Bruei Mala at the celebration.

His natural state was one of joy, and the spirit of his joy had its effects on his companions. His interpretation of the statement that "all Israel are responsible (arovim) for one another", is characteristic: "Sweet to one another," he said, "from the expression ve–o'rva la–ha–shem (and may it be sweet unto the Lord)."

Purim Songs

After the singing of Aroymimkha, which was sung on Khanuka and Purim alike, they would proceed to the punch, a mixture of hot water, brandy and sugar. The tzaddik would drink first, and then distribute it to the crowd.

It is a fact worthy of note that in Kozienice Shoshanas Ya'akov was always sung to a melody known as Ha–Ikar, (the Farmer). This melody marked a complete change in its character and style, in its nature and salient features from other sorts of hasidic music. This melody was not of the pretentious type which prevailed for the rest of the year. It was in a major key, gay and merry, and in a rapid three–four tempo – in every facet and detail a complete imitation of the drinking songs of the Polish peasants.

[Page 90]

How did this melody find its way into the synagogue of the tzaddikim of Kozienice? Perhaps because it bore a definite connection with the obligation to get drunk on Purim. In any event, Ha–Ikar found its "repair" in Shoshanas Ya'akov. Many legends and stories were woven about this tune according to the imagination of the tellers; on a more mundane level, the Ha–Ikar, together with the Purim rav's jesting sermon, fulfilled the program of "ad dlo yada", that a man should be so drunk on Purim as to be unable to distinguish between "blessed be Mordechai" and "cursed be Haman".

Tunes for Pesakh and the Days of Awe

The haggada was recited only in the presence of the family and their closest friends. The hasidim were not permitted to take part in the seder. The haggada was sung in a mixed Kozienice – Stolin style. Aside from the traditional ones, no melodies were sung during the first half of the seder. In the second half, Kel B'nai was sung in the Kozienice style. Oymetz G'vurasekhah was sung to its usual tune at all the Passover meals, while Ya–Ekhsoyf was sung only on the intermediate Sabbath.

The prayers for the Days of Awe were conducted in vigorously musical fashion. Apart from the traditional melodies, new ones were sung every year. The tzaddik had two distinguished leaders of prayer who had great power to draw the hearts of their hearers: Reb Mordekhai Notte, the chief shoikhet of Kozienice, led the shakhris service, and Reb Elimelekh Reb

Pinkhas's did musaf. The latter had made the singing of zmiros on Friday and Saturday nights his own. Although his voice was somewhat hoarse, he was very musical, and he organized a choir to sweeten the prayers. It was he who provided new melodies, while the tzaddik filled in the gaps in the choir. Hayoym Haras Qylam was not sung by the choir, it being the possession, so to speak, of the sons and sons–in–law of the tzaddik, who sung it as a choir themselves. After the service on Yom Kippur night, it was customary to sing

Shir Ha–Yikhud to a new tune, either as a polonaise or an exit–song; Reb Elimelekh the khazan would become anxious over having to supply such new tunes every year, and at times of need the tzaddik himself would furnish one of his own. Reb Moishe Rutman of Stozk, a respected hasid of Rebbe Elimelekh of Lizensk, always davened ne'ila.

The Maggid's tunes were not missing from the order of worship. Ha–Mamlikh Melokhim was sung to his tune. Before the Kedusha, Asei le–Ma'an Shmekha was sung to the Maggid's tune, the same tune with which the angels escorted the soul of Reb Shmuel Zwitkower to paradise, Ke–Vakaros was likewise sung to the Maggid's tune. On Yom Kippur morning, Onim Zmiros was sung to the Maggid's tune, while He'yei Im Pifiyoys was sung to the "sacred melody" of Karl in, the oldest of all Karlin melodies, which was written for Ya Ekhsoyf.

He Sang to Dull His Pain

Rebbe Yerakhmiel–Moishe did not live long. Before his death he visited the baths at Krinica in Galicia. When this produced no improvement in the state of his health, he went to Kashanow, singing Aroymimkha Ha–Shem Ki Dilisani to its Khanuka tune on the way, in order to ease his physical pain.

[Page 91]

On the evening before his death he blessed the new moon and ordered the congregation to sing and dance as they used to. He himself clapped out the rhythm of the song, sitting on a bench.

He died in Kashanow at the age of forty–nine on the thirteenth of Elul, 1909. His death left an emptiness in the dynasty, for he had been a man of energy and activity, overflowing with vigour, who had scattered light all about him with the tones of his flute and his fiddle.

His Children Continued the Tradition

His three sons kept to the path of their father. The eldest, Rav Aharon–Yekhiel (1889–1942) took over the dynastic seat in Kozienice in 1909. From there, he moved to Lodz and Warsaw, spending his last years in Otwock. From there, he was deported by the Nazis to the Warsaw ghetto, where he died.

Thousands of hasidim flocked to him, for he was wonderful in his way of life and renowned for the unique ways of working with which he influenced hasidic youth and brought it close to Torah and mitzvos. He was a wonderful fiddler, causing the hearts of his listeners to exult with the magic of his playing.

The second son, Rav Asher–Elimelekh, settled in Lublin, where he died shortly before the outbreak of the war.

Kozienice Melodies Take Hold in Israel

The youngest son, Rav Yisroel–Elazar, went to Israel and founded the moshav for Kozienicer hasidim who had decided to turn their backs on the diaspora and settle in Israel as agricultural workers living off the labour of their hands.

The three ravs continued the musical tradition, playing the flute and fiddle from time to time in both their public and private lives.

A fiddle hung on the wall of the hut in the workers' camp at Avodat Yisroel, and the sounds of Rav Yisroel–Elazar's playing sweetened the hard work of these pioneers. They called him ha–nasi (the president). The music heard in this desolate spot bore witness that a settlement which would serve as an emblem for hasidim who would later settle in the promised land was being built there. With the passage of time the moshav Avodat Yisroel became Kfar Hasidim, which is situated in the vicinity of the ancient brook, Kidron.

With the foundation of this settlement of Kozienicer hasidim, and their settlement in cities and villages, the melodies of Kozienice took hold in Israel, too. Kozienicer shtibelekh in which the Maggid's "angelic melodies" as well as marches appropriate to the rhythm of life in the new surroundings are sung, have recently been established in Tel–Aviv, Jerusalem and Haifa.

Learning from the Sages of Israel
(from Entsiklopedia li–godolei yisrael be–dorot ha–akhronism)
by Rabbi David Halakhami

Rabbi Zvi–Ber Friedman, the Maggid of Mezritch:

When he came to Mezritch, the Maggid of Kozienice said that he had learned eight hundred books of Kabbala, but that when he came to the Maggid of Mezritch, he came to the realization that he had not yet begun to understand them (p. 153).

Rebbe Elimelikh's sanctity was heralded all over, and thousands came to him in search of help and healing.

His numerous students settled in the cities of Poland and Galicia, and showed the ways of the Lord to the masses of the people. Among them were the Rebbe of Lublin, Rebbe Mendel of Rimanov, the Maggid of Kozienice, Rebbe Moishe–Leib of Sassov, Rebbe Avraham–Yehoshua Heschel of Apta, Rebbe Naphtali of Ropschitz, and others. Before his death, Rebbe Elimelekh placed his hands on the heads of his disciples and blessed them. He gave the sight of his eyes to the Rebbe of Lublin, and to the Maggid of Kozienice – the spirit of his heart (p. 165).

[Page 93]

Rebbe Yaakov–Yoysef ben ha–Rav Zvi Katz of Polnoye:

Rebbe Moishe of Kozienice told that his father, the Maggid Rebbe Yisroel of Kozienice once visited the town of Brody. While passing a certain house, he asked for an explanation of the odor of impurity emanating from it. It was explained to him that the Polnoyer's book, <u>Toldot Yaakov–Yosef</u>, had been burned beside this house, and even though a number of years had passed, traces of the deed were still discernible (p. 207).

His published works were: <u>Beit Yisrael</u>, on a number of Talmudic tractates; <u>Maggid Mesharim</u>, on the tractate Shabbat; <u>Agunat Yisrael</u>, on the granting of permission to abandoned wives to remarry; <u>Avodat Yisrael</u>; <u>Ner Yisrael</u>, on the Psalms; <u>Gvurat Yisrael</u>, and many other books on all the branches of Torah.

Rabbi Dov–Ha–levi Hurwitz in the name of Rabbi Azriel Hurwitz:

At the time of his service in Lublin, he stirred up a great dispute over the permission granted an abandoned woman to remarry by the Maggid of Kozienice, whose decision had been published with an appendix in which the leading lights of the time indicated their agreement.

Rav Azriel opposed this permission, and in a pamphlet entitled <u>Divrei Rivot</u> attempted to reject and refute the Maggid's decree, which was published in his book, <u>Agunat Yisrael</u>. The Maggid relied for this case upon the agreement of Rav Pinkhas the Wonder–Worker, but Rav Azriel expressed his doubts as to whether Rav Pinkhas was really in agreement with him.

The Maggid answered him sharply, and refuted the argument of the Rav of Lublin with decisive proofs. With respect to Rav Azriel's suspicions regarding the agreement of Rav Pinkhas, the Maggid replied, "He has permission to ask the sage himself if I have added or subtracted even a single letter from his words" (p. 223).

Rebbe Moishe–Elyakim Beriah of Kozienice

Rebbe Moishe Elyakim Beriah was the son of the Maggid and the son–in–law of Rebbe Elimelekh of Lizensk. He learned Torah from his father and spent time in the courts of other <u>tzaddikim</u>, among them Rebbe Zishe of Onipol and Rebbe Elimelekh of Lizensk.

He was renowned for his greatness in revealed and concealed learning; for his piety, reclusiveness and fear of God. At first he was the congregational preacher in Ostrowca, but after the death of his father, he was authorized by the Seer of Lublin to take his father's place in Kozienice, where thousands and tens of thousands streamed to him.

The tzaddikim of his generation told mighty things of him, and granted him great respect.

Rebbe Avraham–Yehoshua Heschel of Apta said that he (Rav Moishe) and his father were comparable to King David. Rebbe Yerakhmiel of Pshiskhe also said that Rebbe Moishe's greatness would not be revealed until the coming of the Messiah.?

[Page 94]

In this book Be'er Moshe, Rebbe Moishe describes the ways of the true tzaddikim:

"It is the way of the true tzaddikim that their hearts are always shattered within them for the sake of the poverty and sorrow of the holy shekhina. The shekhina wants with all its heart to shower an abundance of all sorts of good and treasure stores of blessing upon Israel, but Israel cannot receive it, for their deeds are not worthy of it. Is there anything more sorrowful than a mother exerting herself to suckle a sick child who is unable to suck? How great her bitterness of soul over such a torment!"

"Thus is it in thousands upon thousands of comparable cases. It is known that the cow wishes to give suck more than the calf wants to be suckled, and the wish and desire of the shekhina is to benefit us with all the benefits in the world."

"And it is over this that the tzaddik is to sicken, that his heart is to melt in his breast–continually."

He cautioned his visitors about the importance of inner intention. He was accustomed to tell a story in the name of the Baal Shem Tov entitled "And the Skies Closed off their Rains."

The rainy season had passed, and not a drop had fallen. What did the sages do? They decreed a fast, convened an assembly and prayed to the Lord with all their might. The Besht noticed one man in particular from among the simple people who was praying with great devotion, repeating the verse, "and he [God] shut up the heavens, so that there be no rain" (Deut. 11:17) several times, with tears and supplications until it became apparent that his words proceeded from his heart with purity of intention and wondrous honesty.

After he had finished, the Besht went up to him and asked him to explain the verse he had been repeating. The man answered simply, "And he shut up [atzar] the heavens, – I figured God would squeeze [ya'atzor] and wring the sky, the way you squeeze olives and grapes, until not a drop of rain would be left in it, and as far as 'there be no rain* goes, there'd be no rain in the heavens anyway because it'd all fall to the earth against its will and water the woods and vineyards."

When the Besht heard this interpretation, he said that this man's prayer had been more effective than all the others, for it had been uttered with simplicity and purity of intention.

Rebbe Moishe of Kozienice died at fifty–one. His position was filled by his son, Rebbe Elazar, the son–in–law of Rebbe Yaakov of Kolbisow, himself the son of Rebbe Naphtali of Ropschitz. His other son was Rav Yissakhar, who published the works of the Maggid. His sons–in–law: Rav Yaakov-Yoel, the grandson of Rebbe Avraham Yehoshua Heschel of Apta; Rav Yosef Unger of Dombrowa; Rav Yitzkhah–Shlomo Mazlikhov, and Rav Mordekhai–Ze'ev Hurwitz, the grandson of the Seer of Lublin.

His published books: Be'er Moshe, on the Torah; Da'at Moshe, Binat Moshe, Kahalat Moshe, Pirkei Moshe, Mateh Moshe, T'filla le–Moshe, and Va-Yakhel Moshe on the Psalms (p. 244).?

[Page 95]

A Story About Rebbe Yitzkhok–Meir Alter of Ger

The Gerer Rebbe was born in 1799 to Rav Yisrael Rotenberg, chief of the rabbinical court of Magniszow and Ger, and a hasid of Rebbe Levi–Yitzkhak of Berdichev and the Kozienicer Maggid. He achieved renown as a child prodigy and servant of the Lord, and the Maggid of Kozienice amused himself in studying Torah with the youth. One of the Maggid's hasidim once said to little Yitzkhok–Meir, "I'll give you a golden dinar if you can tell me where God dwells."

"And I'll give you two if you can tell me where he doesn't," replied Yitzkhok–Meir …

At first he frequented the Maggid, and after the latter's death, Moishe-Elyakim Beriah.

[Page 96]

The Maggid Aided the Aliya of Hasidim

Ha–Maggid Mi–Kozienice, (p. 115)

by Z.M. Rabinowitz

When the hasidic colony established in the Holy Land by Rebbe Mendele of Vitebsk found itself in financial straits, Reb Abraham Kalisker sent a special emissary to Poland in order to establish and collect a steady income for the settlement. The emissary, Reb Ephraim Fishel of Tzefat, journeyed to the courts of the Polish tzaddikim, among them that of the Maggid of Kozienice. The Maggid wrote his hasidim a letter in high style requesting support for the colony. This letter of encouragement laid the foundation for the Kolel Polin-Varsha and continued the chain of hasidic emigration and building of settlements until the time of the new aliya.

[Page 97]

The Maggid of Kozienice and His Way of Khasidus

by Aaron Zeitlin

Like his teacher, the Maggid of Mezritch, the Kozienicer Maggid was extremely frail, weak on his feet and welded to his bed.

He was born, a seven months' child, to a poor and aged bookbinder. It is inconceivable how his soul managed to sustain itself in his body, so immaterial was his very flesh. There did not seem to be even an ounce of flesh on his dried–up bones.

On a Sedan–Chair in the Bes–Medresh

He was carried into the bes–medresh on a sedan–chair. Boots were too crude for his feet, so he went about in stockings, under which a bearskin had to be laid in order for him to stand. His body was wrapped in hare–hide, and was so transparent that one rabbi said that, "the Kozienicer body has the clarity of a thousand Jewish souls."

In this weak and scarcely living body dwelt a soul of flaming fire which kept the body alive. It accepted its sufferings without protest and surrendered itself to the will of God. For its sake and because of its merits, his body did not fall apart. Yes, his body even danced ardently when such was required in the service of the Lord – but entirely through the strength of his powerful soul.

When the Maggid was carried into the bes–medresh in the morning, two beadles took him down from the sedan–chair. The assembled hasidim stood in two rows on either side of the rebbe, holding candles in their hands, and led the rebbe, garbed in talis and tefillin, to the ark.

They handed him the sefer–toyre, and he – scarcely breathing, scarcely alive – strengthened himself and danced before the ark with the To rah in his hands. Afterwards, he danced before the menorah on the amud, and put the candles into it.

After the shmone–esrei he was so exhausted that he had to lie down on the hide spread beneath him. He was barely able to finish the davening. With the last of his strength, he was then taken home to his private chamber. A lion during the davening, on the way home he was unable to move a single limb, to raise a hand or a foot.

Was His Fame Unholy?

Hasidim began to come to this Jew, this Jew who was more spirit than matter. When his renown had spread, he grew very worried: Who knows whether this renown comes from evil spirits or not?

[Page 98]

But no. Polish Jewry needed a rebbe, a spiritual leader to pray for the community and for individuals. Congress (central part of) Poland, at the beginning of the nineteenth century, was hasidic, and Jews grouped themselves around the Maggid of Kozienice and the Seer of Lublin. Reb Yisroel harnessed his frail body to the service of the Lord and of Israel.

Two Kinds of Noise

A letter of the Maggid's indicates how he was always able to strengthen himself against his illness through the power of his faith. In this letter, Reb Yisroel cites the Tikkunei Ha–Zohar to the effect that there are two types of noise (Hebrew: ra'ash, spelt resh, ayin, shin). There is one ra'ash in which God is not (lo be–ra'ash ha–shem: "and God was not in the noise/thunder", 1 Kings, 19:11), and another which is the reverse, eresh (spelt ayin, resh, shin), a bed, or more specifically, a sick–bed. Through faith, eresh is transformed into esser (ten; spelt ayin, shin, resh), corresponding to the ten sefirot, and when this takes place the shekhina is at the sick man's bedside.

The Kozienicer observed that the first sort of ra'ash, the godless sort, is the noise made by the evil man (rasha, spelt resh, shin, ayin) who is by nature unable to bear any suffering. As soon as he starts to suffer, he starts to rebel and shray gevald. The righteous man, on the other hand, the man who is pious and just, accepts his suffering in silence, with love and faith, and becomes eser oysyoys (ten letters, i.e., the ten elemental letters, corresponding to the sefirot, through which the world was created. Eres has been transformed into eser). The righteous sufferer binds his sufferings to the shekhina and the suffering of the Messiah, and thus elevates his own illness to the highest levels.

And when this world has passed away, continues the Kozienicer, then everything will be moderated (i.e., the laws will be elevated to their heavenly roots), and the sick shall stand upon their feet. This standing upon weak and sickly feet is here meant both literally and figuratively.

This teaching has a biographical value, and illuminates the Kozienicer's mystical attitude to his illness as well as his spiritual gestalt. It must be realized that the teachings of great rebbi'im generally bear a direct relation to their personal modes of being. If one wishes to know something about them, one must first go to their teachings.

Did the Kozienicer Practice Tzaddikism?

Simon Dubnow claims that the Kozienicer Maggid cultivated the tzaddikism, as he labelled it, of "children, life and a living" for which Dubnow takes umbrage with him in the same way as he does with the Seer of Lublin and the Rebbe Reb Elimelekh of Lizensk for instituting the custom of giving pidyoynes ("ransom money", the rebbe's payment for help and advice) and kvitelekh (written petitions given to the rebbe).?

[Page 99]

Nevertheless, there is a teaching in Avodat Yisrael which demonstrates that the Maggid of Kozienice was opposed to praying for "children, life, and a living". We will first examine his teaching, and afterwards see why the Kozienicer took the praying for "children, life, and a living" upon his own shoulders.

The teaching is based on the statement of the Shulkhan Arukh that all ten men of a minyan must be in one and the same place. The Kozienicer goes beyond the statement's literal sense and reads an exalted, mystic hasidic intention into it.

One place, he says, means that the minyan must concentrate itself spiritually in one place and in God's name. The principle of every prayer is the completion of God's kingdom (malkhus, also the lowest sefira) so that God might be one and his name might be one. What, then, is to be done if the ten Jews who make up the minyan begin to ramble in their thoughts, each one somewhere else, despite their being together in a single room? If instead of completing and unifying God's kingdom, which is the purpose of prayer, each one is to pray for his own needs – one for life, a second for children, a third for a living, and so on – they are no longer a real minyan, for they are not in the same place spiritually. Although they find themselves in one location they are in truth scattered and dispersed.

Consequently, Jews may not pray for the satisfaction of their own wants while they are engaged in prayers of unification. Prayer is a mystical out into which a Jew may not inject his own private concerns.

How can he be helped, then? This is where the tzaddik comes in. Only he, who has been refined from and cleansed of all earthly motives, has the right as well as the duty to pray for others. Thus does the tzaddik become one who prays for "children, life, and a living"; and in order that it not be said that the holds himself in great esteem because of his virtue, he takes a pidyen from his flock.

The tzaddik receives a pidyen so that heaven can have no complaints. If heaven should ask him, "Who are you, that you may do that which other Jews may not" the tzaddik can answer simply, "I'm a hired man."

Such humility must make an impression. Since the tzaddik does not deny that he has been hired, he must be heard out – he speaks the truth.

The Kvitel is the Ransom of Life

The pidyen given the tzaddik is the redemption or ransom of life. But, whereas deliverance must be besought for each Jew individually according to the particular root of his soul, the tzaddik who is praying for him must first examine and hear him out, identify the man's essential nature, the root of his soul. He must also know his name and that of his mother; it is from these that the kvitel derives. The fact that one is named such–and–such rather than so-and-so is no accident; there is a secret in the arrangement of the letters, a secret having once again to do with the root of the soul, with the higher, spiritual discreteness of the person who is to be helped.?

[Page 100]

Letters and their arrangement occupy an important place in kabbalah. Letters are transposed, thus mitigating laws and annuling evil decrees, increasing mercies and brightness. We have seen above how ra'ash produces eres, and eres, eser, and what the Maggid of Kozienice has to say about it.

Is this all "practical", commercialized Khasidus, as Dubnow contemptuously labels it? Nothing of the kind! Hasidism was founded on kabbalah from beginning to end, and is a direct result of the purest Baal-Shemian khasidus.

It can be asked whether kvitelekh and pidyoynos did not, with the passage of time, decline from their pristine, highly mystical level. It is, however, certain that in the time of the Maggid of Kozienice and the Seer of Lublin this matter stood on the highest rung of spirituality, despite the "observations" of misnagdim and maskilim ("the enlightened") whose vain and malevolent words have been dug up with such eagerness by Dubnow.

The Maggid was a Great Scholar

A contemporary scoffer cracked wise at the expense of the Maggid's learning, saying that the Kozienicer simply had no time for study because he was tied up helping barren women.

This is sheer nonsense. The Maggid was not only a learned man, but a genius of the first rank, as was attested by Rav Khaim Volozhiner after discussing learned matters with him for a lengthy period.

We would, of course, have been aware of this even without such proof. It is enough to look into his books to see his academic, not merely his hasidic greatness. The Kozienicer is a representative of hasidic synthesis: he reads Maimonides in the light of the Baal Shem Tov; he is as at home in kabbalah as in Talmud; binds learning to holiness and is a great master of both the mystic and the revealed traditions. He takes midrashim and builds khasidus on them; he takes Pirkei Avot and the Maharal of Prague and does likewise. Everything is threaded into the great glittering fabric of hasidism.

Looking at a kvitel is bound up with a special power of the eye, with an acuity in looking through and piercing the veil of the material. Hasidim say that Rebbe Elimelekh of Lizensk had a sharp eye, and that the Seer of Lublin's was still sharper. They say that the Seer's sight was even more acute – if such a thing is possible – than the Lizensker's.

The Duke Bows his Head to the Maggid

The Seer's friend, the Kozienicer, had a reputation for acuity of sight, although not so great as that of the Seer himself. This acuity even produced admirers among the higher aristocracy of Poland. Prince Czartoryski bowed his head meekly to the sick, poverty–stricken old Jew from Kozienice. Prince Poniatowski sought his blessing and advice.?

[Page 101]

The pale, emaciated Kozienicer, who kept himself going only through the power of faith, blessed the highly placed gentiles, but only on the condition that they do favours for the Jews. The proud, mustachioed pans trembled and gave their promise.

[Page 102]

The Maggid Argues Things out with the Lord

by Menashe Unger

Reb Yisroel Hoffstein, the Maggid of Kozienice (born approximately 1737), was raised in the town of Apt, where his father, a simple bookbinder named Shabsi, was living. In the same way as he was born when his father was already steeped in age, so Reb Yisroel was very frail even in his youth.

His father was very poor, and could not hire good teachers for him. Even so, young Yisroel displayed a great aptitude for learning, and had a great passion for Torah. Even as a boy, he knew that he did not come from a distinguished family, and that he had on that account to make even greater efforts in his studies. It is interesting that the Maggid once said that if he knew that he came from the line of Abraham, Isaac, and Jacob (i.e., a distinguished lineage, and not simply a Jewish one), he would dance in the streets with his cap cocked to the side for joy.

The Candle did not Burn Out

From childhood on, young Yisroel gained renown as a prodigy. His eagerness for learning was so great that one Khanuka, when he was seven years old, he was given a three–groschen candle so that he wouldn't linger too long in the bes–medresh, because his father was afraid that he'd end up playing cards with the other boys. As soon as Yisroel began learning, he lost track of time, but the little candle kept burning and burning until midnight.

When Yisroel finally came home, his father, assuming that he'd been playing cards, took a whip and beat him. Little Yisroel lay in bed with his pains, but said nothing. Had he but told his father that he had been sitting in the bes–medresh learning, his father would certainly have believed him; but he did not want to reveal that the candle had burned so long out of respect for his studying, so he took the blows in silence and told his father nothing.

Hasidim tells that an angel came into the bes–medresh and so enjoyed Yisroel's studying that he gave fire to the candle so that it would burn until midnight.

Yisroel Becomes a Member of Ner Tamid

When Yisroel was seven years old, his father enrolled him in the Ner Tamid society. The purpose of the society was to hear toyre from Rav Moshe Nossen–Note Shapira of Apt. Reb Shabsi the bookbinder was one of the active officials of the society. The circumstances of Yisroel's acceptance into the society are recorded in its register: "On khol ha–moed Pesakh, 1744, the young boy Yisroel ben Shabsai was received into the society, and his father gave alms of three silver zlotys." (See Le–Korol Ha–Yehudim be–Lublin, by B. Nissenbaum; Z.M. Rabinowitz, Ha–Maggid Mi–Kozienice).

[Page 103]

The young prodigy studied for a time in the yeshiva of Rav Dov Berish Katz, the Apter rav. The greatest minds of the Maggid's generation bore witness to his having been a great prodigy even in his youth. The gaon Rav Yitzkhok–Avraham, the rav of Pintschev and author of Keter Kehuna, testifies to this.

When Yisroel was somewhat older, he went from Apt to Ostrowca, to the yeshiva of Rav Yekhezkel, and from there to the Harachow yeshiva in Wohlin, headed by Rav Mordekhai–Tzvi Horowitz, the son of Rav Yitzkhakl Hamburger. After this, Yisroel wandered to many cities in Poland, Learning Torah.

Rav Aharon, the Brisker rav and author of Minkhat Aharon, wanted to arrange a marriage between Yisroel and his daughter, but nothing came of his plans.

A Melamed in Pshiskhe

Reb Shabsi passed away in 1761, and Yisroel moved to Pshiskhe in the district of Radom, which was a hasidic centre at the time. The preacher in Pshiskhe, Rav Avraham, introduced the young Yisroel to a new world full of mysteries, a world of kabbala, tzaddikim, and tales.

Reb Yisroel was popular in Pshiskhe. One of its wealthy residents, a certain Reb Yissokhor Ber, took Yisroel into his house and supported him with food and drink so that he could spend his time in study.

When Reb Yisroel –stopped eating at Reb Yissokhor Ber's, he became a melamed, and it seems that he had great pedagogical abilities, for his teachings contain many exemplar dealing with children. Thus he says in Avodat Yisrael (Parshat Ki–Tisa) that one must explain to a man how to become a good Jew by means of various examples. Just as a father who wishes to explain some concept or other to this child will package it in a familiar wrapping so that the child will understand it better—so should it likewise be done with adults.

With the money he earned from his teaching, Reb Yisroel purchased the Etz Ha–Khaim by Khaim Vital, as well as other books and manuscripts. Many books have been printed from manuscripts in the Maggid's possession, among them, Kitvei Kodesh, a florilegium; Divrei Shmuel by Rebbe Reb Shmelke of Nickolsburg; and Kedushat Levi on Pirkei Avot by Rebbe Levi–Yitzkhok of Berdichev.

Hasidim say that when the Kozienicer came to the Maggid of Mezritch for the first time, he had already learned eight hundred books of kabbala thoroughly; but as soon as he crossed the Mezritcher's threshold, he realized that he still knew nothing (see Martin Buber, Tales of the Hasidim, Vol. l, p. 287).

A Tale of a Katinka

The Kozienicer Maggid believed that a man must work on himself, by himself until he has achieved something, and he himself fulfilled this precept. He wanted to learn everything by himself, so that he would be saturated with both the revealed and concealed aspects of the Torah.?

[Page 104]

He told his Hasidim to do the same thing: If you want to achieve something, you have to do it yourself.

It is told that a woman once came to him with a kvitel, weeping that she had already been married twelve years and still had no children.

The Maggid asked her, "What do you figure to do about it?" She did not know what to say.

The Maggid told her, "When my mother was old and still childless, she heard once that the Baal Shem Tov was coming to Apt. She went to, him with a kvitel, weeping that he should pray for her to have a child."

"What do you want to do about it?" he asked her.

"What can 1 do when my husband is a poor and simple bookbinder?" she answered: "But I have one good thing which I will give the rebbe."

"She ran right home and took out her best piece of clothing, her 'Katinka', and ran back with it to the inn where the Besht was staying. On her arrival, she discovered that he had already left for Medzibozh. With nary a moment's hesitation, she set out on foot for Medzibozh, having no money to hire a horse and wagon. She travelled from town to town until she reached the Besht and gave him the 'Katinka'.

"You have done well," said the Besht, and he hung the garment on the wall

"My mother," said the Kozienicer in conclusion, "then went on foot from town to town until she returned to Apt, and within a year she was blessed with a son, and I was born."

"Well, I'll bring the rebbe a nice piece of clothing that I have at home," said the woman, "so that 1 can be blessed with a son, too."

"It won't help," said the Maggid. "You've already heard the story, but my mother had never heard any story" (Likutim Khidushim, Warsaw, 1898).

The Kozienicer Maggid was a disciple of Rebbe Reb Shmelke of Nickolsburg and Rebbe Levi–Yitzkhok of Berdichev. From the Berdichever he learned to intercede for the Jews, to chat with God in the Berdichever manner, sometimes speaking to him in Yiddish and Polish.

It is also told in Eser Orot (p.76) that the Maggid used to sing in Polish and Hebrew on Purim. For example, he used to sing a song which began, "Jaki purim, taki lel–shimurim". He also sang "Hulaj dusza bez koszuli" ("Let the Soul Dance Shirtless", the body being considered as a garment of the soul) and "Kto rano wstaje, temu pan bog pochwaly daje" ("God blesses him who gets up in the morning"). Sometimes while davening he would say in Polish, "Moj kochanku", my beloved (see Likutim Khidushim).?

[Page 105]

Why Have You Taken a Dislike to Us?

A woman once came to the Maggid and reported that her husband had thrown her out because she was ugly. "And could it be that maybe you are no beauty?" asked the Maggid ingenuously.

"Rebbe," she exclaimed, "If I was pretty enough for him under the khupe, I've now become by him ugly ?"

At once a trembling took hold of the Maggid. He gave the woman his blessing, and as soon as she had left the room began to pray to God, saying,

"Master of the Universe, remember what this woman has said, remember the people of Israel! When the Jews said, "We will obey and hear, " and you were wedded to the people .of Israel they: were "beautiful in your eyes. So why have you now taken a dislike to us?"" (Rav Naphtali Ha–Cohen Schwartz, Beit Naphtali, Munkacz, 1906).

Before Kol Nidre in the last year of his life, when he was already suffering greatly, the Maggid stood before the amud, and before he said the verse, "and the Lord said, I have forgiven according to your word," he said, "Master of the Universe! There is no limit to your greatness. You know that I have davened before the amud all month, even though I am suffering greatly; and you know well that not for my own sake have I done this, but for the sake of your people Israel. Therefore I ask you: If I could stand up to daven before you although I am suffering so many torments, is it hard for you to say but two words? Therefore I request of you say what is written, And the Lord said, I have forgiven according to your word."

The Lizensker's Disciples

Rebbe Reb Elimelekh of Lizensk raised up many disciples, but of these only three disseminated his teachings in Poland: the Maggid of Kozienice, the Seer of Lublin (Reb Yaakov–Yitzkhok Horowitz), and the Rebbe Reb Mendele of Rimanow.

These three tzaddikim walked one path of khasidus, and raised up hundreds of disciples, a large number of whom became rebbi'im in Poland and Galicia.

All three were very close to one another. Together, they issued statutes for Polish Jewry, and each held the others in great esteem. The Kozienicer wrote to the Seer of Lublin, "the rabbi, the great light of Torah and khasidus, a holy man of God."

The Seer's Wife is Helped

After the Seer of Lublin had married his second wife and she had no children, she went to receive a blessing from the Maggid of Kozienice

The Kozienicer went to Lublin for the bris.

Hasidic legend supplies all the details of how the rebbetzin came to Lublin, and thus is the story told:?

[Page 106]

The Lubliner Rebbe had a hasid named Reb Leib Mimilus who had a sister–in–law named Beile. She was descended from the Bnei Yehoshua, Rav

Yehoshua Heschel ben Falk of Lemberg, and had never been married. Reb Leib used always to submit kvitelekh in which he asked the rebbe to bless him with a worthy match for his sister–in–law, but the rebbe would always tell him to wait.

After the death of Tille, the Seer's first wife, the Seer sent a shadkhan to Reb Leib, and his sister–in–law was offered a match with the Seer of Lublin. Reb Leib and his sister–in–law both agreed to the match, and she was married to the Seer.

This second rebbetzin had no children, so she went to Kozienice and gave the Maggid a kvitel. On her arrival, the Maggid went out to meet her and said, "As long as you're here, you're no rebbetzin. As long as you're here, you'll eat and drink and then you'll listen to my prayer—and you'll be helped."

The Maggid was so frail that he referred to himself as a bag of bones, but he began davening with great ardour. After the davening, the rebbetzin went home. She became pregnant and gave birth to a son.

The Seer invited the Maggid to the bris, and the Maggid travelled to Lublin by way of Pulavy. On his arrival in Pulavy, Prince Czartoryski came out to meet him and invited him to his palace. The Maggid declined the invitation, saying that he had to go to Lublin, but that he would pay him a visit on his way back (Eser Orot, p.76).

The Halt Made to Walk

When the Maggid arrived in Lublin, the streets were full of people who had turned out to see him, among them many noblemen and noblewomen who wanted his blessing. Among these was a noblewoman with her son—he had scorched his feet and was unable to walk. The Maggid said to her, "Promise me not to raise the taxes of your Jewish tavern keepers, and your son will be helped".

The noblewoman gave her promise. The Maggid ordered her son to bring him a light for his pipe. The boy got up immediately and began to walk (Eser Orot, p.77).

Reb Hersch–Melekh Goes to Kozienice on Foot

The rebbi'im held the Kozienicer Maggid in such esteem that once the Rebbe Reb Mendele went into an ecstasy at the shaleshides, and said on his return, "I heard an oracle in heaven that whosoever lives at the time of the Maggid of Kozienice and does not see him, will not be found worthy to see the face of the Messiah."

This was heard by the Rebbe Reb Hersch–Elimelekh of Dinov, who took his pack and his staff and set out on foot for Kozienice immediately after havdole.

He wore himself out with walking; he did not want to rest, so that he would come to Kozienice as quickly as possible. He did not go to an inn on his arrival, but made straight for the Maggid.

[Page 107]

The Maggid was already very ill at this time. He lay in bed with his hasidim standing around him. As soon as the Dinover Rebbe came in, he jostle d his way to the bed and peered over a hasid's shoulder in order to behold the holy countenance of the Maggid of Kozienice. After seeing it, he said, "Praised be the blessed Lord, that I have been worthy to acquire a <u>rebbe</u> for myself with the sight of my eyes!"

A Wedding in Zelechow

The degree to which the Maggid of Kozienice was honoured in Poland is attested by the description of Reb Avraham Zussman, who lived in his time, and who, while still a young man, went to London, where he became <u>shoykhet</u> through the good offices of Rav Nossen Adler.

In one of his books (<u>Barukh Mevinim</u>, Vilna, 1869, p.97; this is cited in Z.M. Rabinowtiz, <u>Ha–Maggid Mi–Kozienice</u>, p.77, whence we have it), Zussman writes:

"When I was seven or eight years old, there was a great wedding in Zelechow between Reb Mattele, a grandson of Rebbe Yaakov–Yitzkhok of Lublin, and the daughter of the wealthy Reb Avigdor of Zelechow. The Maggid of Kozienice and the Seer of Lublin, together with their students and their students' students, were at the wedding. There were countless hasidim present; so many that the town's houses could not hold them all, and people were practically sleeping in the streets."

The ceremony was held on Friday. The Lubliner Rebbe came on Wednesday, and all the local dignitaries, in addition to a great number of hasidim, came to meet him in wagons and on foot. They accompanied him for over a mile. They came into town in the evening, and arranged all their wagons in a circle around the Lubliner's. They held a torchlight parade, going around the market a couple of times, and lights burned in every window. The celebration was enormous.

"The elderly Maggid of Kozienice arrived a day later and was accorded the same honour."

"The ceremony took place on Friday in front of the <u>shul</u>. I recall that the streets were full of rainwater that day, so they laid planks from the house where the Maggid was staying up to the shul. Rav Yaakov–Shimon Deutsch, the <u>rav</u> of Zelechow, walked in the mud beside the Maggid and held his right hand; another distinguished man walked on the other side, and held his left hand."

"The Maggid performed the blessings under the khupe, while the Rebbe from Lublin read out the marriage contract (the Maggid was smaller in stature and older than the Lubliner)."

"On shabbes before minkha, the Maggid came into the shul and delivered a sermon—the Lubliner was there listening."

This description is very characteristic, for it gives us a picture of a rebbi'ishe wedding in the time of the Maggid of Kozienice and the Seer of Lublin.?

[Page 108]

The Kozienicer Intercedes for Jews

Like all the leaders of his generation, the Maggid of Kozienice understood that peace was the best thing for the Jews. He believed that it was better for King Stanislaw August Poniatowski to rule, rather than the lesser nobility, who had united themselves in various confederations. The nobility was engaged in a series of internecine struggles, and the Jews were the perennial victims of these wars.

When a law requiring Jews to serve in the military was about to be passed in 812, the hasidim sent a delegation to Josef Poniatowski, minister of defense according to hasidic legend one, of the Maggid's non–Jewish adherents. The hasidim persuaded him to repeal the ordinance; in place of military service, it was decided that the Jews would pay a tax of 700,000 gulden a year.

In 1810, an assembly of representatives of all the Jewish communities of Poland was held, a sort of Council of the Four Lands. Twenty delegates were chosen to go before the finance minister and the king to persuade them to annul the shekhita tax which was grievously oppressing the Jewish population. Local officials exploited the tax, and were stuffing their pockets with Jewish money.

The Maggid of Kozienice was also among the representatives chosen. After the selection, however, the governor of the district of Radom announced to the finance minister that the Maggid would be unable to attend "because he is old and frail".

The Pedigree Starts With Me

Through his sayings and teachings, the Maggid of Kozienice has left us an idea of his thoughts on various subjects. So, for example, he did not think much of these Jews who fancied themselves the scions of noble lines.

Legend has it that there once came to him a Jew of distinguished family background, who was continually boasting about what great forebears he had. Said the Maggid to his hasidim, "'the difference between me and him is that one pedigree comes to an end with him, while another begins with me."

The Maggid believed that peace must prevail among the Jews. He once said, "If all Jews would make peace and take one another by the hand, their hands would all become one hand which would be able to reach the Throne of Glory."

The Maggid would on occasion make bold to speak to the Lord after the manner of Rebbe Levi–Yitzkhok of Berdichev. When he learned the Talmudic saying (Pesakhim, 87b), "God drove the Jews into exile only in order that proselytes might be added to them," the Maggid lifted his eyes to heaven and said, "Master of the Universe, of what good is interest? Better to raise the principle—take your Jews out of exile and don't wait for any interest."

[Page 109]

God is Everywhere

The Maggid once characterized hasidism in a couple of lines: "When you ask a simple Jew where God is, he will answer, 'In heaven'. When you ask an educated Jew the same question, he begins to calculate: from earth to heaven is five hundred parasangs; from one heaven to the next, another five hundred parasang s. He will calculate and calculate until he has figured out where the Throne of Glory is located. Ask a kabbalist the same question and he'll enumerate all the upper worlds until he comes to the Throne of Glory. But if you ask a hasid, he'll tell you right away: 'God is everywhere'."

What Will He Give to the Poor?

The Maggid once taught a niggardly rich man how to eat. Once, a stingy rich man came to him. The Maggid asked him, "What do you eat every day?"

"A piece of dried bread with salt and a little boiled water."

The Maggid reproved him. "That is no way to live. You must live in the world, you must eat fattened fowls and soup, and drink good wine."

The rich man said that from then on he would act as the Maggid had told him.

After the rich man had left, the hasidim asked the Maggid why he had ordered him to eat such fine meals. The Maggid replied, "Why don't you understand? If the rich man, the miser, eats fattened fowl, he'll understand that a pauper needs at least a piece of bread. But if he is satisfied with a piece of bread, then what will he give the poor?" Thus did the Maggid understand the miser's nature.

[Page 110]

The Maggid's Rebbi'im and Friends

by Rabbi Dr. Meir Schwartzman

When the Kozienicer Maggid, Reb Yisroel Hoffstein, began to study with the Rebbe Reb Shmelke of Nickolsburg, he was still living in Ricziwol, a small town not far from Kozienice. The Kozienicer went to Mezritch with Reb Shmelke, and became friendly there with the Rebbe Reb Elimelekh of Lizensk, whose student he later became.

The greatest men of his era gathered around Reb Yisroel. His students were renowned rebhi' im and tzaddikim in Poland, Galicia, Rumania, and Hungary. We will enumerate some of them here:

1. Reb Eliezer Ha–Levi, rav of Tarnograd and author of No'am Meggadim on the Torah and Imrot Tehorot on the Psalms.
2. Reb Itamar of Konskewola, author of Mishmeret Itamar.
3. Arye–Leih Lifschitz, rav of Vishnitz.
4. Reb Arye–Leihush, rav of Kishinev, author of Khomat Uriel and Gvurat Arye.
5. Reb Gavriel Malakh, the Maggid's private secretary.
6. Reb Gedalya Zelechower.
7. Reb Gershon, the rav of Ricziwol.
8. Reb Ber of Radoshitz, a great wonder–worker, a student of the Seer of Lublin and of Rebbe Meirl of Apt.
9. Reb Dovid Kharif , a son–in–law of the Maor Va–Shemesh.
10. Reb Zelig Schrentzker.
11. Reb Khaim–Meir–Yekhiel, the Seraph of Mogielnica, the Maggid's grandson.
12. Reb Yekhezkel Kozienicer, father–in–law of the Yehudi (der heiliker yid, the holy Jew) of Pshiskhe.
13. Reb Yitzkhok Meizlish, a student of Rebbe Reb Elimelekh and the Seer.
14. Reb Yitzkhok Oszerower.
15. The first Gerer Rebbe, Reb Yitzkhok–Meir Alter, author of Khidushei Ha–Rim.
16. Reb Yehuda–Leih Onipoler, author of Or Ha–Ganuz.
17. Reb Yoysef –Meir Ha–Levi, the Shpeter Rebbe.

[Page 111]

18. Reb Ydkele of Radzymin.
19. Reb Yaakov–Tzvi Yol les, the Dinever rav, an eminent scholar and kabbalist, author of Melo Ha–Ro'im.
20. Reb Yishayele Prager, author of Harei Besamim, Atzei Besam im, and Roshei Besamim.
21. Reb Mendele Morgenstern, the Kotzker Rebbe.
22. Reb Menakhem–Mendel Stern, the rav of Sighet, Hungary, author of Derekh Emuna.
23. Reb Moishe Rotenberg, rav of Wlodawe, author of She–eylot u–Teshuvot Maharam Rotenberg—Ha–Akhronim.
24. Reb Moishe Teitelbaum, rav of Ihel, Hungary, author of Yismakh Moshe, an eminent scholar and kabhalist, founder of what has become the Satmar dynasty.
25. Reb Noah–Shmuel Lipschitz, the Turbiner rav, author of Zer Zahav and Minkhat Yehuda.
26. Reb Faivel Kaminitzer.
27. Reb Pinkhas, the Gniewaszower rav.
28. Reb Hersch–Elimelekh of Dinov.
29. Reb Hershele Zidtshever.
30. Reb Sholem Belzer, founder of the Belzer dynasty.
31. Reb Bunem of Pshiskhe, likewise a student of the Seer and Yehudi.
32. Reb Shmuel, rav of Worka, author of Torat Shmuel and a student of Rabbi Akiva Eiger of Posen.
33. Teb Shmuel–Shmaryahu, rav of Ostrowca, author of Zikhron Shmuel.
34. Reb Shimon Deutsch, rav of Zelechow after Rebbe Levi–Yitzkhok left for Berdichev.

[Page 112]

Tales of the Hasidim of Kozienice

by Z.M. Rabinowitz

The Abandoned Wife

An abandoned wife, whose husband had gone to a land by the sea and disappeared, came to the Maggid and asked him to have mercy on her and to free her from the chains of being neither widow nor wife.

The Maggid asked her, "Would you recognize your husband if I showed him to you?"

"Yes," she replied.

At once a basin of water was brought before her, and the Maggid told her to look into it and tell him what she saw.

She looked and said, "I see a great city with many streets and markets, men, women and children, and a great number of craftsmen practicing their crafts."

"Look carefully at the street of the tailors," said the Maggid. "You will recognize your husband there. Snatch the iron from off the sleeve."

The woman followed his command, and grabbed both iron and sleeve. "Go to such–and–such a city," continued the Maggid, "and on such–and–such a street go into the house of the rabbi, and tell him that your husband has taken another wife and that you want him to give you a divorce. Should your husband deny this, show him the iron and the sleeve as witnesses to the truth of your words, and the rabbi will force him to divorce you."

The city in question was about three hundred parasangs from Kozienice, but the woman went by means of the power of "the shortening of the way" and arrived there in a few minutes. She went to the house of the rabbi, and made her request in the name of the Maggid of Kozienice. The rabbi summoned her husband immediately. At first, he denied everything, but after the woman showed him the iron and sleeve he agreed to free her and give her a divorce.

On her way home the "shortening of the way" did not operate. A long time passed before she returned home, the bill of divorce in her hand and the wonders of the tzaddik on her lips.

How Rav Shimon Ashkenazi Became a Hasid

Rabbi Shimon Deutsch–Ashkenazi, the rav of Zelechow, was a fervent misnaged, and his heart was far from hasidism. He once became mortally ill, and on Friday, the eve of the Sabbath, his soul passed from his body. He was not buried because of the approach of the Sabbath.

[Page 113]

After Shabbes the khevra kaddisha came to purify the corpse. Suddenly? one of them noticed a light tremor on the dead man's face. They returned him to his bed return to him and imagine their astonishment when they saw life gradually return to him.

After arising from his "sleep" Rav Shimon told the people surrounding him the story of what had happened. "I went up to heaven late on Friday. The heavenly household was preparing to receive the Sabbath. They fixed up a separate room for me. As I went in, I heard a sound of noise and tumult, and angels running and shouting, 'The holy Maggid of Kozienice is going to greet the Sabbath!"

"I wanted to push my way through and enter the crowd of angels, but they did not allow me to approach. 'Whoever did not see the Maggid while alive has no permission to look upon his face!"

"Shabbes morning, the noise in heaven recurred: 'The Maggid of Kozienice is going to shakhris!' I ran with all my might, and this time the angels let me .approach the holy Maggid. 'Gut Shabbes,' I said to him. He wrapped his face in his tallis and said nothing."

"I wept bitter tears. Could it be that I would not merit to see the face of the Maggid? The angels took pity on me and advised me to go to the shaleshides, where I might be able to see him. When I approached him at the shaleshides, he hid his face again and said, 'Shimon, you are still young. Go back down! 'He took me by the ear and threw me to the ground, and that is how I was revived."

After he had finished his story, Rav Shimon said, "Let's rent a wagon right away," and at the first light of dawn he went to Kozienice. When he arrived, the Maggid ran to meet him and said, "I am here". From that time on, Rav Shimon was a hasid devoted to his teachers, the Maggid of Kozienice and the Seer of Lublin.

The Deceased Fiancée

From a certain man, an intimate of the Maggid of Kozienice, a hasid who lived in the fear of heaven, the Lord withheld the blessing of children.

The man and his wife suffered great anxiety on this account, and from time to time they journeyed to Kozienice to ask the Maggid to pray for them to have children. The Maggid put off their request for many years.

Once the woman belaboured her husband, telling him to go to Kozienice and not to budge until the Maggid promised him a child that would live. The hasid went to Kozienice and tearfully implored the Maggid to have mercy on him, for his life was worthless without children. The Maggid replied, saying, "go to the Seer in Lublin, and tell him that I have sent you."

The Seer told him to wait a while in Lublin, until he should show him what to do. One day he was called to the Seer, who said, "In your youth you were engaged to a girl whom you dropped after several years, and took yourself a different wife, prettier than she was. Heaven has therefore punished you by not allowing you children until you appease this woman and she forgives you for your great sin. Two months from now there will be a fair in the town of Balta. Go there and seek your former fiancée among the people at the fair, and ask her forgiveness."

[Page 114]

The man went to Balta, a great distance from Lublin.

In the meantime, his money ran out.

When he got to Balta he wandered among the streets and markets for many days, but did not find his fiancée.

One day a heavy rain broke out, and he went into a nearby store to take shelter. A beautiful woman, bejeweled and finely dressed, who had also gone into the store to escape the rain, stood beside him. When the hasid saw her, he drew back for reasons of modesty. "Did you see him?" said the woman to her companions. "He jilted me when we were young, and he runs away from me even now."

When the hasid heard this, he approached her and began to weep, begging her to forgive his betrayal. He added that he had been sent to her by the two leading tzaddikim of the time, the Maggid of Kozienice and the Seer of Lublin.

On hearing this last, the woman agreed to forgive him, provided he went to her brother, a poor scholar, in Subalk, and gave him two hundred gulden as dowry money for his daughter.

The hasid was very glad, and he went to Subalk. He inquired about until he found the woman's brother. As soon as he entered the house, he sensed its great poverty.

The brother spoke from his heart: he had promised his daughter's fiancée a dowry, but there was not a cent in the house. When he heard this, the hasid took out the two hundred gulden and told him that his sister, Shifra, the hasid's erstwhile fiancée, had sent him to atone for his betrayal with this act of charity.

The brother was terrified, and cried out, "But my sister Shifra died fifteen years ago, and I buried her myself!" However, the hasid, whose faith in his rebbi'im was rooted in his heart, explained that she had come back from the dead at the behest of the two tzaddikim in order to be appeased by the hasid's charity and his mitzva of supplying the dowry of a bride.

The brother took the money from the hasid, with the blessing that the words of the Seer and Maggid come to pass.

And so they did. The hasid was blessed with children and grandchildren, scholars and hasidim all.

Principle and Interest

When the Maggid was studying the Talmudic saying (Pesakhim, 87b), "God drove the Jews into exile only so that proselytes might be added to them," he raised his eyes to heaven and said, "Master of the Universe, what do you need with interest? Raise up the principle, be satisfied with its redemption and don't wait for any interest".

[Page 115]

A Tale of a Prince and a Dog

The Maggid of Kozienice used to lead the prayer on Yom Kippur. Once before Kol Nidre, he went up to the amud wrapped in his tallis and kittel,but was unable to open his mouth to pray because of the greatness of his sorrow. He merely wept without surcease. A couple of hours passed, and the Maggid had still not started to pray, but .was melting in his incessant weeping. Suddenly he turned to the congregation and asked, "Who here is from the town of Pilow?" The man answered that he did. "And do you know the dog of the prince?"

"Oh yes, that dog's very important to the prince," continued the villager, to the delight of the Maggid. "lt's as big as a cow. The prince paid eighteen hundred pieces of gold for it, and built it a special house. Every day he feeds it the finest food, and drink. The dog committed a transgression recently: it snatched the meat from its master's hand without permission. The prince punished it and banished it from his sight."

After hearing this story, the Maggid turned toward the amud and began to pray Kol Nidre with joy and ardour.

After the holiday the hasidim asked him to explain this. He told them, "On erev Yom Kippur a great accusation went out in heaven against the Jews, because of a work of charity performed by Prince Czartoryski. A poor Jew from the town of Mikow, near Cracow, was travelling from town to town in Poland to collect money for his daughter's dowry. He was a bashful man, and collected little money, barely enough to pay his expenses. Once as he was going along, he sighed and wept over the bitterness of his fate: a grown daughter at home, and poverty and want on the road. And behold, Prince Czartoryski was coming towards him in a coach harnessed with strong horses. He saw the wretched Jew and asked, 'Why are you weeping, Jew?'"

The Jew told him of his poverty and troubles. The prince took pity on the Jew, and took a note for a hundred gold ducats from his pocket and gave it to the Jew as a dowry for his daughter."

At once, an accusation went out in heaven against the Jews of Poland, all of whom together had not given one tenth of what Czartoryski had. The Maggid wanted to use the villager's story to soften the accusation, for Czartoryski also spent great sums of money on big dogs: "As far as Czartoryski goes, money is meaningless; the Jews of Poland are wretchedly poor, broken down, swept from place to place, and every cent is more important to them than a hundred of the prince's pieces of gold." After showing why Israel should receive grace, the Maggid was able to begin Kol Nidre.

Why Do You Want to Abandon Us in Exile?

A woman complained to the Maggid that her husband had taken a dislike to her, and wan ted to marry someone better looking.

"Why has he grown tired of you?" asked the Maggid.

"He says I'm not pretty."

[Page 116]

"And maybe, said the Maggid, maybe you really aren't pretty."

"What, wasn't I pretty enough f or him under the khupe? So how com s I'm no good now?"

The holy Maggid began to weep. "Master of the Universe! Why have you abandoned your people Israel? Maybe we're not pretty enough for you. True we have sinned, but remember your words, I remember the devotion of your youth, your love as a bride. When we were under the khupe on the day of our betrothal, at the time of the giving of the Torah when we said we will obey and hear, we were pretty enough in your eyes, so why do you want to abandon us in the darkness of exile?"

One Must Not Go To Kozienice

The Maggid heard of a great wonder: A misnaged had a son of thirty years after his wedding. The Maggid said, "Heaven wished to show the world that one must not go to Kozienice or Lublin for such things. The Lord hears the prayers of the childless, too."

The Kugel of Domestic Harmony

A couple came to the Maggid for a divorce. The husband complained of his wife: "When I come home from shul on Shabbes, I really want to eat. My very soul Longs especially for a kugel. My wife sets the table and starts serving fish, meat, and other fine dishes, but when she gets to the kugel I'm already full and have on appetite for it."

His wife answered, "It is a tradition in my family to eat the kugel at the close of the meal. A tradition is like the Torah, and I won't betray it even if it means divorce."

"From now no," ruled the Maggid, "make two kugels on Shabbes, one for before the meal, and the other for its end, so that you can fulfill your obligations to both your husband and the custom."

From that time until this, it has been a custom to eat the "kugel of domestic harmony" as an appetizer on Shabbes.

Woe Unto Him Who Disturbs Them

Some Kozienicer hasidim once met Rabbi Meshullam Zalman Ashkenazi, later rav of Lublin, in an inn. He was a misnaged, and the hasidim failed to treat him with the respect due him as a scholar. Rav Meshullam–Zalman's father–in–law, the magnate Reb Yusefa of Kuzmir, complained to the Maggid that his hasidim were belittling his son–in–law.

The Maggid said, "I will answer you with a fable. A lion was teaching his son the rules of hunting. 'Remember one major rule. You're the king of beasts, so don't be afraid of anybody except man.'"

[Page 117]

"While they were talking, an old man leaning on a stick went by. 'Is that him,' asked the son. 'No,' his father taught him. "He used to be a man, but now he's a dotard."

"After this, a child went by. 'Is that him?' asked the little cub. 'No, not him, either,' said the lion. 'One day he will be a man.'"

"Suddenly, a hunter with a rifle on his shoulder went by. 'That's him!' shouted the lion. Just then the hunter shot, and the lion fell dead."

"Hasidim are the same way. They are neither old men from the past nor men of the future. They are the men of today, young, strong, and holding their weapons in their hands. Woe unto him who disturbs them."

The First Yakhsn

The Maggid of Kozienice came from a family with no pedigree whatsoever. He once met a rabbi who did not stop talking about his yikhus (pedigree). When the rabbi had left, the Maggid said, "the difference between us is that he is the last yakhsn (one who has yikhus) in his family, and I'm the first in mine."

Why Should the Rich Man Eat Roast Chicken?

A rich miser once came to the Maggid. The Maggid asked him, "What do you eat every day?"

"I am satisfied with little; a piece of bread with water is enough for me."

"that's no good," said the Maggid, "you should enjoy your life. You should eat roast chicken, drink good wine, and take pleasure in every meal."

The miser promised to fulfill the Maggid's command.

After he had left, the hasidim asked the Maggid why he had issued such a command. "If he eats roast chicken," answered the Maggid, "he'll understand that the poor should at least have bread, but if he himself is satisfied with dry bread, he will undoubtedly think that the poor should be satisfied with stones."

[Page 118]

The Paidyom Melody

by Dr. Sh.Z. Cahana, Tel–Aviv

Hasidim going up Mount Zion on the intermediate days of Passover sing a special melody called Paidyom which, they say, originates with the Maggid of Kozienice. Despite his frailty and ill–health, the Maggid .was filled with fervor and ardour in the service of the Creator, especially in those matters having to do, with the Redemption.

The Maggid worked hard for the Redemption, and ran ardently and fervently to greet the Messiah with a special tune which Kozienicer hasidim still call by the name Paidyom, which means "Come on! Let's go!" in Russian. They tell a wonderful story about this tune.

The Maggid's seders were regal and splendid. Everything shone and glittered with silver and porcelain. The table was covered in royal fashion with silver cups, the golden one of the prophet Elijah shining out among them.

A Guest at the Seder

The mood was one of messianic expectation. They were all dressed for the holiday in velvet capotes, the Maggid sitting on the snow–white cushions of the Passover seat in his white <u>kittel</u>. When the crowd was standing about the long, wide table waiting for the Maggid to make <u>kiddush</u>, the Maggid arose, holding the cup in his hand as if it were the cup of salvation. "I will lift up a cup of salvation."

At that moment, the door was flung open savagely, and a guest entered, an uncouth, filthy fellow, a conscripted Jewish soldier with long mustaches and a torn caftan, his face a mass of wounds and scars. The <u>rebbetzin</u> was frightened by him; he did not suit the festive table. She had spent weeks making it shine, making it clean and beautiful, and in he comes with his dirty boots and filthy caftan where was she going to put him? .

The soldier did not wait for an answer; he took his sack and went to the head of the table, by the Maggid, and put his filthy sack on the spotless tablecloth near the Passover seat.

This deed called forth anger and chagrin on the part of the hasidim. They had wanted to seat him elsewhere, somewhere at the end of the table, far from the Maggid, but he would not permit this. He wanted to sit at the head of the table near the Czar, the Maggid. Since he had been in the army for twenty–five years (the term for which Jewish children were conscripted), he naturally wanted to drink a lot.

[Page 119]

The <u>rebbetzin</u>, who was very concerned about the beauty of her pesakh table wanted to take his filthy sack off of the tablecloth, but he would not let her. "When she asked him what kind of treasure he had in the sack, that he watched over it so closely, he answered madly and impertinently that it contained his entire exile—everything, from the day of his conscription until the present."

As he said this, the Maggid trembled; he glimpsed the whole crude exile on <u>pesakh</u> night, and looked on the soldier with wonder. They smiled at each other mysteriously.

The guest spent the entire <u>seder</u> leaning on his sack as if it were a Passover seat and snoring, evidently very tired from his long journey.

Paidyom le–Tzion

When the cup of Elijah had been poured, and the door opened for <u>Shfoykh Khamaskha</u>, the guest leapt from his place, grabbed Elijah' s cup, and began dancing with it, singing <u>Khasal Siddur Pesakh Ke–Hilkhasoy</u>.

The guest sang and danced, and the Maggid with him, until they had reached the open door. They stood there for a while, looking outside, and suddenly the guest began to sing again, "<u>Khasal Siddur Pesakh!</u>" When he came to the words <u>piduyim le–tzion be–rina</u> (joyously redeemed unto Zion),he corrupted and distorted them into Russian, and sang in the Maggid's ear, "<u>Paidyom le–tzion</u>," "Come on, let's go to Zion."

Hasidim said that the Maggid then heard a call: "Go outside! Go to meet him! Why do you open the door and wait for him to come to you? <u>Paidyom</u>, go to him!" He grabbed the guest by the hand and they both went out to meet him, singing and dancing with fervour and ardour: "<u>Paidyom le–tzion be–rina</u>."

This melody stayed with the Maggid for the rest of his life, accompanying him in his mystical labours to urge on the appointed time and bring the Redemption nearer.

The <u>Paidyom</u> march is the march of pilgrims to Mount Zion, the watchpost of the Temple, and the Western Wall, and will be so until the General Redemption.

The Heritage Of The Dynasty Of Kozienice

by Yissokhor Lederman, Rio de Janeiro

Kozienice was not a great city, but the reputation of the Kozienicer Maggid, the Kozienicer rebbi'im, and Kozienicer hasidism extended throughout Poland. We Kozienicer, though scattered throughout the world, take pride in our heritage and sanctify it.

It is already [1969] thirty–five years since we began to immigrate to various countries on account of unemployment, hunger, want, the boycotts and antisemitism of the Poles, Grabski's taxes, and the faithlessness of the government and its Jew–politics. And, more than all of these, the last great Destruction.

Although we have been dispersed for so many years, the longing for our home .town, where we lived through all of life's joys and sorrows, still lies rooted deep in our hearts.

I consider it a sacred obligation to pass on the heritage of our Kozienice to future generations. This heritage is bound up with the holy Maggid of Kozienice, the rebbi'im of Kozienice, and Kozienice hasidism, which have all been treated by various writers, myself included. In my youth, I lived and experienced Kozienicer hasidism with all its legends and tales, and I wish to immortalize it all in our memorial book.

The Maggid's Tomb in Kozienice- standing- the Cantor Hersh Ickhok – sititing two women beggars

A World That Is No More The sanctity of the Maggid

There was once a town, a Jewish town with traditions of hasidism bearing witness to two hundred years of hasidism in Kozienice: the Maggid of Kozienice, the Maggid's street, the Maggid' s shul and bes–medresh, his mikve, the houses of the rebbi'im and the Maggid's shtibl, sanctified by Jews and Christians, in which for 150 years there stood his tester, table and chair,an ark with sefer torahs, a tin chandelier with candelabra, a small kerosene lamp and a candlestick, a small cabinet containing a pen, a staff , a shofar, a withered esrog, a pair of tefillin, a white cloak and a white yarmaluke, as well as a siddur and makhzor which the Kozienicer rebbi'im used twice a year—on Shavuos for Akdamus and the reading of the Torah, on the Days of Awe for Kol Nidre and Ne'ila.

The rebbi' im used to go into the shtibl for the reception of the Sabbath and for havdole. They played and sang Ha–Mavdil there. The shtibl was closed the rest of the week, save for such emergencies as difficult births or grave illness, when candles were lit and Psalms recited.

[Page 121]

A monument after of the Maggid's pupils

The Cemetery of Kozienice

The cemetery, too, is sanctified. There stood the Maggid's tomb, in which six generations of tzaddikim were laid to rest: the Maggid, Reb Moishele, Reb Eliezer, Reb Yekhiel, Reb Yerakhmiel–Moishele, and Reb Asher–Elimelekh the last Kozienicer Rebbe, who is still remembered by everyone from Kozienice. He passed away two years before Hitler, may his name be blotted out, annihilated Poland, but his family was killed together with the rest of the Jewish community.

In the first room of the tomb, near the entrance, lay two rebbi'im of another dynasty, Rebbe Reb Zelig–Loser Shapiro, a son of the Blendower Rebbe, and Rebbe Reb Yissokhor, a son–in–law of Rebbe Moishele.

Around –the tomb lay the Maggid s students, great hasidim scholars rabbis, judges, and slaughterers from Kozienice and the neighbouring towns who had left wills directing that they be interred in the cemetery of Kozienice.

The rebbetzins lay to the side of the tomb. Their graves were surmounted by brick chests and tombstones, which were not permitted on the other graves. Only women of great piety and rebbi'ish line lay near them.

The cemetery before World War II

The Rebbetzin Perele

Legend has it that the Rebbetzin Perele, daughter of the Maggid, and the Rebbetzin Tzipoyrele, wife of Rebbe Moishele, belonged to that circle of holy women who gained renown for their piety and wonder–working. While still a child, Perele went along with her father to the Rebbe Reb Elimelekh of Lizensk. She wore <u>tzitzis</u> and dipped herself in the <u>mikve</u> every day before <u>davening</u>. She wrapped herself in a large <u>tallis</u> to <u>daven</u>, laid <u>tefillin</u>, and, while <u>davening</u>, wept bitterly for the Redemption to come for the community of Israel and for the Jews to be delivered from their exile.

She fasted on Mondays and Thursdays. She also wore a silken capote tied with a silken belt. The Maggid told his hasidim to pay attention to her, for she had a great soul.

There was also a legend circulating that the famous legal authority, Rav Yoysef Te'umim, author of <u>Pri Meggadim</u>, who wrote digests of sections of the <u>Shulkhan Arukh</u>—viz., the <u>Qyrakh Khaim</u> and the <u>Yoyre Deah</u>—besides other works, passed through Kozienice in the eighteenth century, fell ill, and died there. His grave was not far from the Maggid's tomb, but the stone sank into the earth, leaving no precise indication of the grave's location. The affair had, however, been noted down in the register of the Kozienice community, which was kept in the Maggid's <u>shul</u>.

Elderly Jews who still remembered the Rebbe Reb Moishele said that they had heard the story of the <u>Pri Meggadim</u> from their parents. A circle within which no one was allowed to be buried was made around the site of his grave. During the month of Elul, people used to light candles and leave kvitelekh on the grave.

[Page 122]

In discussing the cemetery, it is important to mention that it had no fence and was open on all sides, save for two hills on either side of the entrance. The other three sides were low–lying and open.

On one side there ran a river called the Hammer; a road to Radom with great forests around it ran along the second side; and on the third side were the houses of poor Christian workers and peasants. As the cemetery had no fence, the Christians used to pasture their animals on its grass; even pigs roamed there, often committing profanations. They would dig up new–made graves.

A question arises: Where was the congregation, where the <u>rebbi'im</u>? How could they have permitted such profanation of the Name and shaming of the dead? Yet there was an excuse in the form of a legend going back to the old days which was inscribed in the city register.

The cemetery was presented to the congregation in the days of the Maggid by a nobleman who was among his non–Jewish admirers. There was also, at that time, an old cemetery by the <u>shul</u>. Jewish law prohibits the fencing–off of

an old cemetery from a new one, in order not to shame those lying in the old
one. The legend has it that some years back the congregation wanted to put
up a fence. It was put up during the day, but fell down at night. Guards were
posted at night–they fell asleep, and when they woke up, the fence had fallen
down. They ran away in fright. It was ruled that no more fences were to be
made.

There was no fence up until the time of my departure from Kozienice.
Landsmen have reported that a fence was put up on three sides in the last
years before the war, but the fourth, towards the river, remained open.
Whether this fence is still there–that I do not know.

The Maggid's Street

The Maggid's house was a low, wooden building roofed with shingles and
enclosed by two high walled houses which were called the rebbi'ish houses of
Rebbe Reb Shmelke. A few steps further stood the bes–medreshand the shul,
which was called the Maggid's shul, for he had built it two hundred years
earlier. From the outside, it looked like a fortress, high and stout–walled.

It is said that the Maggid went around collecting money for the shul, and
that whoever gave him a donation was blessed with the life to come.

The house of Rebbe Reb Zelig Shapiro stood on the other side of the bes–
medresh and shul. The same road led to the cemetery, and was called mica
Magitowa, the Maggid's street.

On this street and the smaller streets around it lived all the clergy, rabbis,
judges, scribes, beadles, as well as people plain and simple. The houses had
all been Jewish for generations. On Shavuos and the Days of Awe the streets
were filled with thousands of hasidim from all over Poland.

[Page 123]

The Fire

I remember the great fire which broke out when I was nine years old.
Almost half the city burned, including the shul and bes–medresh, as well as
the Maggid's kloyz. The walls of the shul remained unscathed. The shul and
bes–medresh were later rebuilt. It is interesting that the houses around the
Maggid's house, as well as the Maggid's house itself, remained unscathed by
the fire.

A legend made the rounds that during the fire white doves flew like faithful
guardians around the Maggid's and the neighbouring houses, driving off the
fire with their wings. This legend convinced every believing Jew that something
holy rested in the house where the Maggid sat day and night studying the
concealed and revealed teachings.

The Legend of the General

My grandfather, Itche–Meyer Lederman, told me the following legend. At the time of Rebbe Reb Eliezer, there passed through Kozienice in the month of Elul an elderly Russian general of distinguished family and with many medals on his breast. He went straight to the house of the Maggid in his coach. At the threshold, he took off his shoes and hat, and put on a <u>yarmulke</u> which he had ready in his pocket. He entered the house respectfully, and with tears in his eyes he examined everything but dared touch nothing.

On his way out, he sighed and took out a bag of gold pieces which he gave to Reb Eliezer, the gabbai, saying in a broken Yiddish, "Take this."

Finally, he ordered that the money be used to fix the walls and roof, and to pave the entrance to the house.

It was told afterwards that the general was descended from Jews, from the Russian Cantonists.

Who Was The Maggid?

The Maggid of Kozienice, Reb Yisroel Hoffstein, was one of the greatest scholars and <u>rebbi'im</u> in the Poland of his day. He was a student of the Maggid of Mezritch, Rebbe Shmelke of Nickolsburg, and Rebbe Levi–Yitzkhok of Berdichev. He was one of the few <u>ge'onim</u> of his generation and it was he who disseminated hasidism in Poland. His name was intertwined and bound up with a large number of tales and legends.

He wrote many books, among them <u>Tehillat Yisrael</u>, <u>Avodat Yisrael</u>, <u>Ner Yisrael</u>, and <u>Or Yisrael</u>.

Just as Rebbe Levi–Yitzkhok of Berdichev did, so the Maggid chatted with God in Yiddish. On Yom Kippur he went forth as an intercessor for the Jews.

[Page 124]

The Maggid devoted a great deal of thought to the lot of the Jews. On the one hand, he realized that the Jews were the teachers of the nations; on the other, that the nations made the Jews to suffer. He cried out, "Master of the Universe, deliver the Jews from the <u>goyim</u>, and if you can't do that, deliver the <u>goyim</u> from the Jews" (<u>Megillat Polin</u>).

A great many tales and legends about the Maggid and his immense greatness and devotion to the people were current among the Jews as a whole.

He was small, weak, and thin from continual fasting. He was confined to his bed, and could barely stand up; nothing more than a bag of bones. Yet when he prayed or <u>davened</u> before the <u>amud</u> his tongue became flaming fire–

On Yom Kippur, he stood before the <u>amud</u> and <u>davened</u> the entire service. <u>Tzaddikim</u> said that he tore down heavens with his prayers.

He received his way of <u>khasidus</u> from the Maggid of Mezritch and Rebbe Elimelekh of Lizensk. The Maggid said that before he went to Mezritch, he had learned eight hundred books of kabbala.

He was sparing of speech in day–to–day affairs, but when it came to helping the Jews, he sacrificed himself completely.

Legends

Many tales are told of his longing for the Messiah, among them that of the three great Polish <u>rebbi'im</u> who locked themselves up in a room and made a solemn pact not to rest until they had brought the Messiah down by force. The three were the Lubliner, the Kozienicer, and Rebbe Mendel of Rimanov.

This happened on Sukkos, 1815. All three passed away that same year.

The Rebbe Reb Naphtali of Ropschitz, a student of Rebbe Mendel of Rimanov, once heard an oracular voice saying that he who did not see the Maggid of Kozienice would not be found worthy to see the fact of the Messiah. Hearing this, he put his sack on his shoulders, his stick in his hand, and ran breathlessly to Kozienice to look upon the Maggid, lest, God forbid, he tarry a minute and the Messiah come in the meantime.

Many legends and tales of the Maggid's longing for the Messiah are found in hasidic books.

Polish aristocratic circles also used to tell each other about the Maggid's wonders. The noblemen used to bow their heads respectfully before the Maggid and ask for his blessing and advice. He blessed these highly placed noblemen and princes on the condition that they show favour to the Jews, and they promised to do so.

When the Maggid built the <u>shul</u> and <u>bes–medresh</u>, the noblemen supplied all the wood and bricks for their construction.

[Page 125]

The nobleman Czartoryski of Pulaw was childless; he turned to the Maggid with a fervent request that he persuade heaven to give him a son, in return for which he would exempt his two Jewish leases from five years' rent on their inns. The Maggid raised his eyes to heaven and said, "Master of the Universe, you have so many <u>goyim</u> in the world, one more won't hurt."

Within a year, the duke from Pulaw had become a father in his old age, and he kept the promise about his leases.

Another Polish Nobleman also came to the Kozienicer, this time through a Jewish lessee, and asked him to give his mute son the power of speech. The nobleman said that in return for this he would give his tenant the inn. He brought his son to the Maggid, who cried out, "Master of the Universe, there are so many <u>goyim</u> in the world who speak that another one won't hurt." He then struck the mute <u>shaygetz</u>, who winced and suddenly cried out in Polish, "Father, the Jew is beating me." From that time on, the mute boy regained his ability to speak, and, in fact, talked a blue streak.

Napoleon, You Will Surely Fall!

There are still other such tales and legends in circulation, recorded in the books of the hasidim.

It is told that on Purim the Maggid read the <u>Megilla</u> and shouted out, "Napoleon, you will surely fall!"

Napoleon himself came to the Maggid and asked him why he was opposed to him, when he (Napoleon) had so great a guardian angel who wanted to give him the rulership of the world.

The Maggid answered that the guardian of the world was greater than Napoleon's and wanted to save mankind from wicked men who shed innocent blood in order to conquer the world.

Napoleon left the Maggid's in a rage.

I heard this from Yisroel–Yankele Zeigermacher and Pinkhas the <u>frum</u>, the oldest table–companions of Rebbe Yerakhmiel–Moishele.

It is likely that the Polish defense minister, Josef Poniatowski, was one of the Maggid's Polish adherents, and thanks to this succeeded in annulling many decrees which the nobility imposed upon the Jewish population.

The Maggid of Kozienice, Reb Yisroel Hopstein, was the son of a simple bookbinder named Shabsi. He was born in 1737 and passed away in 1815.

There are legends concerning the place of his birth. Some have indicated that he was born in Apt and later came to Kozienice as a preacher, and then revealed himself. However, his descendants, the later <u>rebbi'im</u>, have attested that he was born in Kozienice and that even Reb Shabsi the bookbinder lies in the Kozienice cemetery, where a structure has been erected over his grave.

[Page 126]

His descendants base their claim upon a legend passed down in the book <u>Shivkhei Ha–Besht</u>. One pitch dark Saturday night, the Besht came <u>into Kozienice and made straight for the home of Reb Shabsi</u>. After a long conversation, the Besht revealed that because of Shabsi's great faith in God, he would finally have a son who would illuminate the world and spread hasidism in Poland. The Besht stipulated that when the child was born, he was to be its godfather and hold it at the <u>bris</u>.

When the child was born, it was named Yisroel.

By virtue of this legend, the Maggid's descendants had no doubt that he had been born in Kozienice and gone out into the world as a child to study.

When he returned to Kozienice, he was already a giant in Torah, and was crowned with the title of Kozienicer Maggid.

The Story of the Khidushei Ha–Rim

It is an honour for us Kozienicers to record in our memorial book that the first Gerer Rebbe, the Khidushei Ha-Rim, Rav Yitzkhok-Meir Alter, grew up and was educated in Kozienice. His father was rav of the town Magniszow in the district of Kozienice, eight versts from Kozienice itself.

Hasidim tell that when his mother became pregnant with him, she went to the Maggid on foot to ask for a blessing that her son be a pious man and a scholar. The Maggid promised her that her son would adorn the world with Torah and righteousness, and would not remain a mere Kozienicer hasid, but would himself become a rebbe of hasidim.

Yitzkhok-Meir's mother died when he was three years old. Before her death she left a will stipulating that her child be given to the Maggid to be brought up. His father then went to Ger, remarried, and became the town's rav.

The boy grew up in the house of the Maggid, and the Maggid himself learned with him every day. He prophesied that the child would grow up to be an outstanding figure. Yitzkhok-Meir's sharpness of mind, proficiency in learning, and good qualities of character aroused love in the Kozienicer environment.

After the Maggid's death, the Khidushei Ha-Rim became a hasid of his son, Reb Moishele, who had taken over his father's position, and he was married at Reb Moishele's in Warsaw.

The young Yitzkhok-Meir Alter was renowned for his learning and acuity, and he was known as the ilui, or prodigy, of Warsaw and Kozienice. He demonstrated his genius in the writing of responsa, as well as in pilpul, and people from many lands turned to him with difficult halakhic questions–even the misnagdim proclaimed him a genius. He was crowned the premiere rebbe of Poland with the title Khidushei Ha-Rim, The Novellae of Rav Yitzkhok-Meir, after one of his books.

[Page 127]

Kozienice Before World War I

Until the first World War, our town was supported by the merit of the holy Maggid and the six generations of rebbi'im who spun the holy chain of hasidism. Three times a year, thousands of hasidim from all over Poland would come to Kozienice: Shavuos, the Days of Awe, and the twelfth of Elul, for the yorzeit of the Maggid's son, Reb Moishele. At such times Kozienice was transformed into a giant hotel for the Jews who had come to the Maggid's grave to plead for a good year for themselves and for all Israel. This was the major source of livelihood for many Jews in Kozienice.

Three Courts

It must also be noted that before World War I there were three rebbi'im in our town: the previously mentioned Reb Yerakhmiel-Moishele Hopstein, a descendant of the Maggid who had thousands of hasidim throughout Poland; Rav Zelig-Eliezer Shapiro, son of Rav Yaakov Blendower and author of Kehillat Yaakov, a commentary on the Torah. He considered himself one of the elders of the Polish rebbi'im, and was renowned in the hasidic world for his healing powers and amulets. Wealthy hasidim, scholars from Warsaw and other towns, used to come to him.

The third rebbe was Reb Shmelke Rokeach, a Galician from the Belzer dynasty and a son–in–law of a descendant of the Maggid. He was called the women's rebbe because he had no hasidim. Simple Jews, craftsmen, shoemakers, tailors, butchers, and peddlers came to this table. They were called Reb Shmelke's would–be hasidim.

In Elul, people from all Poland came to Kozienice to pray for a good year. All three courts were filled with hasidim and women, all of them running from one rebbe to the next with kvitelekh. Many rebbi'im, hasidim, and rabbis from nearby villages used to come for the Maggid's yorzeit on erev Sukkos, some of them staying for the holiday.

The Rebbe's Daughters

The rebbe's daughters, who furthered the progress of culture in our town, must also be mentioned and commemorated.

The Rebbe Reb Yerakhmiel-Moishele had four daughters, famed for their beauty, wisdom and intelligence. They took secret lessons in Yiddish, Hebrew, and Russian from the educated soldiers serving in the Smolensker regiment in our town. They also had connections with the "enlightened" students in the bes–medresh and helped found the town's first clandestine library in 1905 in the home of the town maskil (follower of the Enlightenment) Yitzkhok Krishpel, who ran a food shop near the rebbe's house.

Every night, with the shutters of the maskil's single, cramped room drawn shut, we–bes–medresh students, a few craftsmen, and the rebbe's daughters– would read Peretz and Mapu, study Nakhman Krochmal and A.H. Weiss and discuss such matters as socialism and Zionism which had a bearing on Jewish life in that turbulent epoch.

[Page 128]

Of course, there was no lack of indignities and outrages from the side of the Jewish clergy, but the more our work expanded, the more readers and listeners it attracted among hasidic circles and young artisans.

All the daughters married in accordance with their station, but only one, Khavele, the middle daughter, became a rebbetzin. Her husband was the Piaseczener rav. The other three and their husbands went to Israel after World War I and led the lives of pioneers. A few months before the outbreak of World War II, the eldest daughter, Khanele, returned to Poland to visit her family and was unable to get out. She shared the fate of Polish Jewry.

Rabbi R'Ahrele Hopstein, one the last Rabbis, a great-grandson of the Maggid

The Last Kozienicer Rebbe

The last Kozienicer Rebbe, the sixth generation from the Maggid, was Reb Aharon–Yekhiel, a son of Rebbe Yerakhmiel–Moishele Hopstein. On becoming rebbe, he initiated a new path of khasidus: he drove the old adherents from his table, gave no respect to wealthy and learned hasidim, took no kvitelekh or pidyoynes from women, and surrounded himself with common people, tailors, cobblers, porters, wagon–drivers, market–traders, and messengers. He devoted himself chiefly to the young, and carried on his tables with them. He left the court's headquarters in Kozienice and divorced his wife, with whom he had no children.

For a time he was a partner in a linen warehouse in Lodz, but the business went bankrupt after a short time because the customers were poor shopkeepers who did not pay.

The funeral in Kozienice of Rabbi R'Elimelekh Hopstein – great-grandson of the Maggid in 1935

After this, he went to Warsaw, travelling through different towns and carrying on in his new path. From time to time, he came to Kozienice, and each time he did so he threw the town into turmoil. Fistfights almost broke out between his hasidim and those of his brother Elimelekh, who died two years before Hitler annihilated Poland.

I cite the Yiddish writer S.L. Schneiderman, who describes the Kozienicer Rebbe, Reb Arele, as follows: The Kozienicer has taken as his constituents wagon–drivers, porters, and the merchants of the Warsaw markets, who see to it that his table lacks neither carp nor fat geese.

The wagon–drivers take the rebbe for long drives in their coaches, for which he blesses their horses with long life and usability.

The Kozienicer Rebbe is a descendant of the holy Maggid, Reb Yisroel Hopstein, who foresaw the fall of Napoleon, as well as the great world war after which the Messiah had to come: (Literarishe Bleter, Warsaw, 1934).

In the memorial book of Korev, a hasid writes thus of Rebbe Aharon Hopstein: There was a Kozienicer shtibl in Korev in which common folk, for the most part, prayed. They did not go to Rebbe Aharon, but he came to them.

[Page 129]

The rebbe was a good fiddler, and would not move without a fiddle. He davened minkha late at night, and mayriv just before daybreak. He distanced himself from scholars and the pious, while befriending violators of the Sabbath and plain Jews who scarcely knew how to daven. These sat at his table; with these did he go walking; and it was these whom he returned to the proper path.

"Seventy of his hasidim were registered in the town, the majority of them artisans. The Kozienicer shtibl was at Hersch YosseFs on the hill. The rebbe called him "colonel", and Abba the gabbai, Shashi's son, he called "adjutant". When the rebbe came to town, everything went topsy-turvy."

Reb Arele was in Zelechow at the outbreak of World War II, and he shared the fate of all Jews. His death made a great impression in Poland. His death and funeral are described in the Zelechow memorial book: "The Kozienicer Rebbe had been sent from Warsaw to Zelechow by his hasidim. At the time, many Jews believed that Zelechow would be saved, because the cruelties of the Germans there had been small in comparison with other towns."

"The Kozienicer Rebbe brought a certain hominess to the town. Crowds came to his table, which he observed after his own fashion. Although travel-passes were hard to come by, many hasidim yet came to the rebbe."

"On erev Rosh Ha–Shana, 1941, the rebbe became ill with typhus. He asked that everybody daven at his place. They did so both days of Rosh Ha-Shana, and recited Psalms in his house."

"His condition worsened all the time. He would lose consciousness frequently. His hasidim in Warsaw were notified at once, and even though the Warsaw Ghetto was then closed, they did everything they could to get to him, and brought two eminent doctors. Every possible remedy was applied, but to no avail: the rebbe passed away."

"They began to consider where the rebbe should be buried. Some thought that he should be taken to Kozienice where his ancestors were buried, but the householders of Zelechow protested and demanded that he not be given up. A rabbinical court was convened, and it was decided that the rebbe be buried in Zelechow."

"Almost all the Jews then living in Zelechow took part in the funeral."

*****

Thus ends the chapter–two hundred years of the Maggid and his dynasty, six generations of rebbi–im.

The last branches of the dynasty are in Israel and America. Reb Yisroel–Eliezer Hopstein, the youngest son of Rebbe Yerakhmiel–Moishe, has established his court in Brooklyn, New York.

[Page 130]

The Rebbetzin Perele Davens in a Talus

by Menashe Unger

In the history of hasidism, there have been women who were canonized, as it were, by hasidim. The first of these was the Baal Shem Tov's daughter, Hodel. Various courts had <u>rebbetzins</u> who accepted <u>kvitelekh</u> and functioned as <u>rebbi'im</u>. The Maid of Ludomir is famed in hasidic history: she was, for all intents and purposes, a <u>rebbe</u> with hasidim and gabbaim.

The <u>rebbetzin</u> Perele, eldest daughter of the Kozienicer Maggid, was well-known in Poland. She was married to the pious and eminent rabbi Aviezer-Zelig Shapiro, the rav of Grajec, who is quoted by the Maggid of Kozienice in his book <u>Beit Yisrael</u>, in which the Maggid describes him as "my son-in-law, our teacher Aviezer-Zelig, head of the rabbinical court of the holy congregation of Grajec". The Maggid's son, Reb Moishe-Elyakim, likewise quotes him in his book <u>Da'at Moshe</u>, in which he writes, "These are the words of my brother-in-law the rabbi, my teacher, Aviezer-Zelig Shapiro, may his light shine on".

Hasidim Gave Her Kvitelekh

It is Perele, however, and not her husband who has been commemorated in hasidic history. She was famed for her learning, and behaved like a man, <u>davening</u> in a <u>tallis</u>, a <u>gartel</u> wound about her dress, and fasting every Monday and Thursday.

The Maggid held her in great esteem, and he used to send hasidim to her with <u>kvitelekh</u> so that she could pray for them. Hasidim referred to her as they would to a tzaddik, and used to come to her with <u>pidyoynes</u>, asking her to pray for them.

She had many children, but they died young. Only one survived, Khaim-Meir-Yekhiel, known in the hasidic world as the Seraph of Mogielnica.

The Maggid, renowned as a wonder-worker himself, took his daughter with him to rebbi'im to be blessed with children who would live.

Moishele had the Soul of Moses

Hasidim say that before she gave birth to the Seraph, Perele had another child, Moishele. This Moishele was a prodigy, a <u>wunderkind</u>, but lived only seven years.

On the Sabbath of <u>parshas khukas</u> little Moishele was sitting at his grandfather's table at the <u>shaleshides</u>. The Maggid was giving <u>toyre</u>, and he mentioned the waters of Meribah on account of which Moses smote the stone, which episode was found in that week's Torah portion.

The seven year old Moishele stood up and said, "Zeide, I can solve the question of why Moses smote the stone." He then began to give toyre, and the Maggid took great pleasure in his grandson's words.

[Page 131]

Three days later, on Tuesday morning, little Moishele spent a long time over the silent shmone–esrei. When he had finished, his grandfather asked him why he had taken so long. Hasidim say that the child whispered into the Maggid's ear that while he was davening, he heard an oracular voice proclaiming that he was going to die; he then began to weep before his grandfather to be allowed to live.

Moishele Passes Away

As soon as Moishele got home from the bes–medresh, he complained to his mother of a headache. He was put straight to bed– He developed a fever. A doctor was sent for, but he said he could find no cause for the illness, and the child died two days later.

After Moishele's death, the Maggid said that his grandson had the soul of Moses, and had come down to the world solely to solve the question asked about Moses: Why had he smitten the stone? This answered, Moishele needed redress nothing more in the world, so he passed on.

In speaking of Moishele, his brother, the Seraph, used always to call him, "My dear brother, Moishe rabbenu" (Moses our teacher).

Hasidim have said further that since the Rebbe Reb Elimelekh of Lizensk, author of No'am Elimelekh, had blessed Perele with a child–Moishele–the child would be able to live only so long as Rebbe Elimelekh did, and that when the No'am Elimelekh passed away in 1805, the child, too, died shortly thereafter.

The Maggid's Advice

The story continues that Perele wept bitterly after the death of her son. The Maggid came to her and said, "My daughter, if you seen the great joy in heaven when your son went in, you wouldn't cry!"

Perele had no wish to be consoled, and she told her father that her only consolation would be his promise that she have a child who would live.

"Know, my daughter," said the Maggid, "that you have great thoughts, and that at the time of your coupling you bring down exalted souls which cannot endure our world. You must put on a silk dress in the latest style so that people will talk about you in town and say that you are impudent and dissolute. Then you will be able to bring a less exalted soul down, and it will be able to stay alive."

Perele did so, and afterward gave birth to her son Khaim–Meir–Yekhiel, the Seraph.

[Page 132]

The Seraph himself used to tell this story. His mother had a silk dress with twelve silver buttons made, according to the style of the day, "and then she gave birth to me...She had brought down an impudent soul. So am I not impudent then, when I stand myself up to pray for Jews? Isn't this really khutspe?"

The rebbetzin Perele mourned her son Moishele a long while.

Mama, Don't Cry!

Hasidim say that a day before she gave birth to the Seraph, Perele dreamt that she was led into a great palace in which her son Moishele sat at the head of a table of elderly Jews with beards and payes. At her entrance, Moishele stood up, and the old Jews after him. She wanted to go up to him and give him a kiss, but he said, "Mama, I beg you. Do not approach me and do not touch me."

She began to lament that she had not merited to bring him up on earth. He said, "Mama, don't cry! I promise you that tomorrow you will give birth to a son whom you will raise and who will be long–lived and illuminate all the worlds with his righteousness!"

She gave birth to the Seraph on the next day.

All the rebbi'im of her day used to say that Perele had the spiritual level of a rebbe. Her son, the Seraph, said, "My mother is a woman of exalted spiritual level who has merited a revelation of the souls of the righteous in Eden."

It Is Told By Hasidim

The hasidim say that one morning during the shakhris service, Perele, wrapped in her tallis and ringed with her gartel, asked the hasidim if that day were the yorzeit of such–and–such a rebbe.

They investigated the matter and discovered that Perele was right, it was indeed that rebbe's yorzeit. "Do you know how I knew it?" she said. "Today while davening I saw the rebbe, so I understood that it was his yorzeit."

She often used to go to pray at the graves of tzaddikim. Once she was going to Lizensk to pray at the grave of Rebbe Elimelekh. On the way, she stopped at the home of the Ma'or Va–Shemesh in Neustadt. He dissuaded her from continuing her journey, but the next day he told her that he had seen Rebbe Elimelekh in a dream, and that the <u>rebbe</u> had reproached him for not letting Perele journey to his grave. The <u>Ma'or Va–Shemesh</u> therefore asked her to go to Lizensk quickly, and he himself endeavoured to get her a horse and wagon.

Hasidim say that her son, the Seraph, was brought up by his grandfather, the Maggid, who once said to Perele, "You should know, Perele, that your son will be greater and better than I."

[Page 133]

"If he were only like you–that's all I ask."

"No, I tell you that he will be greater and better than I," reiterated the Maggid.

The Maggid died in 1815, and his daughter thought that her husband would assume his position, but it went instead to her brother, Reb Moishe–Elyakim.

I Am Crying for the Sake of Mitzves

Perele's son, the Seraph, thought very highly of his mother. It is said that when she became sick and was about to die, the Seraph found her crying, and said to her, "Of course you know what the <u>Gemore</u> says: 'If one dies with laughter, it is a good sign; with tears, a bad one.' So why are you crying?"

"My son," she replied, "You must certainly recall that the <u>Gemore</u> says (Kesubos, 103) that when Rabi was sick, Rav Khiya came in and found him weeping. He asked him, 'Why are you crying, Master?'"

"Rabi replied that he was crying for the sake of Torah and <u>mitzves</u>."

Speaking thus, she died. It was the winter of 1849.

The Seraph delivered a eulogy at her funeral and wept greatly.

The Hasidim Try Out Reb Moishe of Kozienice

The Rebbe Reb Moishe–Elyakim Beriah was the Maggid's second son, and was born about 1757 and died on the twelfth of Elul, 1828. The name Beriah is unusual among Jews, but it is found in the Torah (Gen. 46:17) as the name of one of the sons of Asher.

Moishe–Elyakim was Beloved by the Maggid

The Maggid's elder son, Mottel, passed away during the Maggid's lifetime, and so his second son, Moishe–Elyakim was particularly dear to him. The Maggid took the boy into his bed every night so they could sleep together, and he used his cap to cover the sleeping child's head.

Reb Moishe fell ill in his youth, and the doctors gave up on him. Hasidim say that he was rescued by the prayers of Rebbe Levi–Yitzkhok of Berdichev.

This is the story: The Maggid was very worried because his only son was so dangerously ill, but when he stood up to pray, he wanted to forget about the child, in order to be able to pray with devotion. "It is written," he said, "'And she cast the child under one of the bushes [sikhim]' (Gen. 21:15). One can interpret the si'akh [singular of sikhim, bushes] as having to do with prayer [si'akh can also mean talk or conversation], what is, that it is worthwhile to abandon the child for the sake of one word of davening."

[Page 134]

The Berdichever, who was a close friend of the Maggid's, sensed his feelings on this matter. He went straight to the mikve, saying that he had thus prevailed over the Maggid. The Maggid's child would not distract him from his prayers, for he, Rebbe Levi–Yitzkhok, would pray for the boy. This is the fashion in which the child was saved.

Reb Moishe in Onipol

When Reb Moishe–Elyakim had grown up a bit, he married the daughter of the kabbalist Yehuda–Leib Ha–Cohen of Onipol, the author of Or Ha–Ganuz and a student of the great Maggid of Mezritch. He was among the best–known tzaddikim of his generation, and is mentioned in many books. In the laudatory introduction to Or Ha–Ganuz Rebbe Mottele of Czernobyl writes that his father, Rebbe Nakhum of Czernobyl, was a close friend of Rav Yehuda–Leib Ha–Cohen, and that when they used to meet "righteousness and peace kissed each other."

After the wedding, Reb Moishe–Elyakim boarded with his father–in–law in Onipol. At the time, the Rebbe Reb Zishe, a friend of the Kozienicer Maggid's, was living there, and the Maggid asked him to watch over his son and guide him in khasidus.

Reb Moishe–Elyakim had always been gaunt and emaciated. The Rebbe Reb Zishe used to say, "Moishele! Stick a feather on you and your weight goes up. What will I tell your father?"

Reb Moishe learned his way of <u>khasidus</u> from Reb Zishe, and he includes what he heard from Reb Zishe in his books.

After Reb Moishe had completed the boarding period of his father–in–law's, his father, the Maggid, came to Onipol to fetch him and to thank Rebbe Reb Zishe for his guidance. As they were saying good–bye, Reb Zishe asked the Maggid, "What will you say about your son? He is on a higher rung than he was when he came here to board." The Maggid agreed that his son was on a higher level than he had been before.

A misfortune befell Rebbe Moishe–Elyakim when his young <u>rebbetzin</u> died, leaving him with a son named Yissokhor. Reb Moishe remarried a while later. His wife was the daughter of Rebbe Elazar of Lizensk, who was a son of the Rebbe Reb Elimelekh. Rebbe Moishe makes frequent mention of both of them in his books.

How Reb Moishe Became Rebbe

Reb Moishe studied with his father, the Maggid. He was very modest, and none of the hasidim knew of his greatness. When the Maggid passed away on <u>erev</u> Sukkos, 1814, the hasidim wanted to elect his son–in–law, Rav Zelig–Aviezer of Grajec, as <u>rebbe</u>, and make Reb Moishe, who had a fine voice, <u>khazan</u>, and put him in charge of the bathhouse. There were also hasidim who held that after the death of the Maggid they would begin to go to the Seer of Lublin.

[Page 135]

When these important hasidim arrived in Lublin, they found the Seer lying in bed. He was sick after "the great fall" on Simkhas–Toyre of 1814. When the hasidim came in to greet him, the Seer quoted to them from his sick–bed, "And when the ark set out, Moses said".

The hasidim understood that the Seer meant that after the ark–the Maggid–had "set out", the time had come for Moses to say <u>toy re</u>, to be the leader.

When his sister, Perele, came with her husband, Rav Zelig–Aviezer, to Kozienice, she went into the room where her brother Moishe was sitting, and said, "I see my father sitting at his side, as if he were alive. This is a sign that he should be our father's heir."

The hasidim, however, were still not agreed that Reb Moishe should become <u>rebbe</u>, so they gathered together a group of aged hasidim, who were to find out whether Moishe was worthy to be their leader.

As soon as the hasidim came in to him, Reb Moishe got up from his chair and said, "It is written: 'For though the Lord is high, he regards the lowly; but the haughty he knows from afar' (Psalm 138:6). This means that the Lord is very high, and whoever considers himself lowly and seeks no raising up–him will God regard; but 'haughty', whoever thinks he's big and seeks raising up–to him God says, 'he knows from afar,' I will regard him only from a distance."

When he had finished, he reached out his hand to welcome the hasidim and asked them, "Did you hear what I said?"

"Yes, we heard," they replied, "and we are your hasidim." And Reb Moishe became the rebbe of the Kozienicer hasidim.

His Path of Hasidism

The greatest men of the time, among them the Khidushei Ha–Rim who had spent seventeen years with the Maggid and was a member of his household, began to come to Rebbe Moishe.

Rebbe Moishe's path of hasidism was that of the perfection of humility. He himself was a very humble man.

Hasidim say that one of his hasidim was once engaged to the daughter of the scholar, Rav Shmuel Landau, a son of the Noyda Bi–Yehuda. Many rabbis and giants of Torah, misnagdim among them, were invited to the wedding, as well as Rebbe Moishe. Several of the rabbis agreed to ask Rebbe Moishe a difficult Rambam, in order to shame him when he proved unable to solve the problem.

When the rabbis had reached Rebbe Moishe's place and put the difficult Rambam to him, the Khidushei Ha–Rim suddenly appeared near them and said, "You come to the rebbe with such a little question? I, who am the least of his hasidim, can answer such an easy question," and he proceeded to do so.

[Page 136]

The hasidim also tell that Rebbe Moishe was once giving toyre full of kabbala and gematria. He afterwards asked one of the hasidim to work out the gematrias to see if they were right. It turned out ninety short. Now, the letter tzaddik has a numerical value of ninety, and the Khidushei Ha–Rim said, "There's a tzaddik missing. If we include the rebbe, there'll be a tzaddik."

The rebbe was very pleased with the Rim's statement, and he kissed him on the forehead and cried out, "You have delighted me!"

Nevertheless, the young genius Itche–Meir left Kozienice. "I don't need a rebbe who pets me **and** kisses me; I need a rebbe who will porge my veins" [i.e., make him kosher], he said. He was punished for this: thirteen of his children died because he abandoned Rebbe Moishe, but the Khidushei Ha-Rim would not stray from Rebbe Moishe's way. When Be'er Moshe was published in 1858, thirty years after Rebbe Moishe's death, the Rim never took the book from his table, and he consulted it constantly.

Rebbe Moishe Preached Humility

Rebbe Moishe used various means to express the quality of humility. He interpreted the verse, "and his mother made for him a little robe" (1 Sam., 2:19), as meaning that his mother made him a garment of the quality of humility, so that he would not have a high opinion of himself. Rebbe Moishe credits this insight to his father (Be'er Moshe, p.58).

He likewise brings forth an interpretation of Numbers 19:2: "in which there is no blemish, and upon which a yoke has never come," credited to his father. He who considers himself a person of importance and thinks that he has no faults and is completely holy and pure, gives a sign that he has not yet attained the level of taking the yoke of the kingdom of heaven upon himself.

Rebbe Moishe–Elyakim Beriah also inherited his father's great love for the land of Israel.

The Kozienicer Rebbe Rebbe Yerakhmiel–Moishe became rebbe at the age of twenty–six. At the beginning, he did not want the position, but his grandfather, Rebbe Elimelekh of Grodzisk, influenced him to accept it.

Rabbi Yerakhmiel–Moishe Travels to Czortkow

Even after he had become rebbe, Rebbe Yerakhmiel–Moishe was in the habit of going to other rebbi'im.

When he went to Rebbe Dovid–Moishe of Czortkow for the first time, he did not go to the mikve. He said that a mikve served to cover things, and that when one came to such a tzaddik as the Czortkower Rebbe, one should not disguise himself; and when one had shaken hands with the tzaddik, he naturally could not go to the mikve afterwards.

[Page 137]

The Czortkower wanted to find out what sort of a man the Kozienicer was, so he asked him who his friends were. The Kozienicer replied that he was particularly friendly with the children of Rebbe Nossen–Dovid of Szidlowca, the rebbi'im Yaakov–Yitzkhok of Biala, and his brother Pinkhas of Konsk, and also with Rebbe Simkhe–Yair of Bialobzeg, a grandson of the Yid of Pshiskhe.

"A fine circle of friends," said the Czortkower Rebbe.

Rebbe Yerakhmiel–Moishe Guarded Against a Lie

The rebbe guarded himself against lying. When writing a letter, he would but sign it, leaving his title to be added by the gabbai lest he give himself a title he did not really hold.

For the same reason, he never wanted to eat with silver–covered utensils if he was not certain that they were really pure silver. If they were made of some metal that merely shone like silver, he would be deceiving people.

He was not in the habit of saying toyre at his table. Instead, he told stories of his ancestors in the Kozienicer line, of his step–grandfather, Rebbe Aharon of Stolin, and of Rebbe Asherl of Stolin, his step–father.

One of his hasidim and his children*s melamed, Reb Elazar Dov ben Reb Aharon, recorded the rebbe's stories, publishing them in \9\f– in a book called Safran Shel Tzaddikim (Librarian of Tzaddikim).

Although the rebbe did not give toyre at his table, he did give brief and acute toyre at home.

He Hated Scoffing

Rebbe Yerakhmiel–Moishe hated scoffing, and he used to say that, "A scoffer will never return in repentance, for even if he does repent, the penance itself is a type of scoffing."

The rebbe was always happy, and he brooked no gloom. Thus he interpreted the verse, "I shall not die, but live" (Psalm 118:17): When I am living, let me not be a dead man.

The Rebbe Plays the Song of Elijah the Prophet

The rebbe knew how to play the fiddle and the flute. The flute had been present from his step–grandfather, Rebbe Aharon of Stolin.

Every Saturday night after havdole, he would go into the Maggid's chamber with a crowd of hasidim and play the song of Elijah the prophet for them. When he came to the words, "As it is written, Behold I send you the prophet Elijah before the advent of the great and terrible day," he would put down the fiddle and begin to play the flute.

[Page 138]

The melody was known as The Melody of Elijah the Prophet. The rebbe had it from Rebbe Aharon of Stolin.

The Rebbe Befriended Hasidim

The rebbe befriended every Jew, and even hasidim who had already been infected by the Enlightenment movement.

He also followed the path of Stoliner hasidism which held that the most important thing was not to fall into sadness.

Once, a hasid came to him and revealed that he had committed a transgression and was very worried and unable to repent. The rebbe said to him, "When a man has committed a transgression and then feels remorse, he must see that he does not fall into sadness, for sadness does not let one repent."

He believed that one should love every Jew. By "All Israel are arevim for one another" is meant not that they are responsible [arevim] for one another, but–arevim coming from orvah la–Ha–Shem [sweet unto the Lord]–that they are sweet. That is, each Jew makes his fellow sweet.

A Man's Got To Do What A Man's Got To Do

The rebbe often used to make use of sayings he had heard from his step–grandfather, the Stoliner Rebbe. Rabbi A.Y. Bromberg mentions in his book Beit Kozienice (p. 160), that the elderly hasid, Reb Avner, told him that he (i.e., Avner) once went to ask the rebbe's advice.

The rebbe said, "I will tell you a story about my step–grandfather, the Beit Aharon. A hasid once came to him and asked him to draw up an agenda of how he should conduct himself every day."

"The rebbe asked him, 'Is every day the same, then? There are days when you have to eat, and days when you have to fast. But you want to behave according to one rule: A man's gotta do what a man's gotta do, and what he ain't gotta do–he better not.'"

Rebbe Yerakhmiel–Moishe indicated the Beit Aharon's meaning: What you have to do–what the Torah commands; what you must not do–a matter of volition–that you cannot do.

His Love for the Jews

The Kozienicer Rebbe also told of his step–grandfather's love for the people of Israel. When his step–grandfather recited the Shema and came to the verse, "And the anger of the Lord will be kindled against you, and he will shut up the heavens, and there will be no rain, and the land will yield no fruit," he would divide the words thus: "And the anger of the Lord will be kindled against you, and he will shut up the heavens, and there will be no. It will yield its fruit," so that nothing but blessings came out.

[Page 139]

Rebbe Yerakhmiel–Moishe inherited this quality of his step–grandfather's. He used to say, "If one of my hasidim is sick, it is as if my own child were ill. The difference is one of distance only: the child is at home, and the hasid somewhere far away."

The Kozienicer Rebbe also worried about the prosperity of his hasidim. According to him, the saying of the sages that, "This is the way of the Torah: you will eat your bread with salt, drink a little water, sleep on the ground, and live a life of sorrow,: applied only until one has come to the Torah. Thus it is until one does so; but if one fulfils the Torah, he should lead a life of prosperity."

The <u>rebbe</u> used to say, "There are two verses in the Psalms which appear to contradict each other, but which are in truth bound up together. It is written: 'I keep the Lord always before me' (Psalm 16:8). One thing depends upon the other: when a Jew keeps the Lord always before his eyes, he then has some redress from the fact that he sees sin always before his eyes, and he will not commit the sin."

His Mother Sarah–Dvoire

The <u>rebbe</u> accorded his mother, Sarah–Dvoire, great respect. She came to live in Kozienice after she left Stolin in 1884.

The <u>rebbe's</u> wife, Brokhe, always used to wait meals for her, and whenever the <u>rebbe</u> heard his mother's footsteps, he stood up from his chair and waited until she had come in. Even if he were sitting among a group of hasidim, he would show his mother this respect.

On Friday nights after his table, the <u>rebbe</u> would go into the women's room where his mother and his wife and children would be sitting. He would sit down with his mother at the head of the table and distribute fruit to everybody.

The old <u>rebbetzin</u> would tell stories of <u>tzaddikim</u>, and the <u>rebbe</u> would listen like any other hasid.

Every Friday, the rebbe would go in to his mother, kiss her hand, and say, "<u>Gut Shabbes</u>". Afterwards, he would go into the Maggid's room with dainty steps, approach the Maggid's chair, say something softly, and walk out backwards, bowing as if he were leaving a king's chamber, and saying, "Gut Shabbes" at the door.

His Love for the Land of Israel

The rebbe had a great longing for the land of Israel. There was always an Eretz–Yisrael pushke on his table, and any hasid coming to give the rebbe a pidyen had also to throw a coin into the pushke. If he neglected to do so, the rebbe would put the pidyen into it.

[Page 140]

The rebbe used to make kiddush on Israeli wine, and bentsh with an Israeli esrog. Everything which came from the land of Israel was holy to him.

He once received a letter from Israel. The envelope fell to the floor, and the rebbe ordered that it be picked up, saying, "It's from Eretz–Yisrael, you know."

When he became sick, his hasidim wanted him to go to a doctor in Germany, but the rebbe would not hear of it. He said, "Germany is an impure country, the air there is impure."

When his sister, the Parczewer rebbetzin, went to Germany for medical treatment, he did not want to visit her. He said, "I will not cross the borders of that impure land."

The Rebbe's Death

At the end of the summer of 1909 the rebbe went to Krinic, Galicia, for treatment, but it did him no good. He then went to a hasid of his grandfather's in Kszanow, but he did not succeed in returning home, and passed away on the thirteenth of Elul.

Hasidim say that before his death he said, "I am God's and God is mine."

Hasidim had difficulty in obtaining a permit from the Austro–Hungarian government to take the body back to Poland. Permission was finally granted, and the coffin was brought in a sealed car to the railway station in Garbatka. Thousands of hasidim awaited it. They carried the coffin the fifteen kilometres to Kozienice and interred the rebbe in the Maggid's tomb.

Rebbe Yerakhmiel–Moishe was survived by three sons and four daughters.

The Kozienicer Rebbe in the Warsaw Ghetto

Rebbe Aharon–Yekhiel Hoffstein, who lived in Otwock in the last years before World War II, followed a unique path of hasidism. He was affectionately called by the pet name, Reb Arele.

Reb Arele Settles in Otwock

At first, Reb Arele lived in Kozienice, where he ran his court in regal fashion. Suddenly, he changed his mode of being: he left the town and began wandering from place to place; he no longer befriended respected citizens, but the masses instead. He began to befriend simple people, and he finally settled in Otwock, where he conducted this court.

Reb Arele was born in 1889, and named for his grandfathers, Rebbe Aharon of Karlin and Rebbe Yekhiel–Yaakov of Kozienice. He was a son of Rebbe Yerakhmiel–Moishe of Kozienice.

[Page 141]

A few months after Reb Arele's birth, Rebbe Elimelekh of Grodzisk passed away, and Arele's father became rebbe in Kozienice. The old hasidic town of Kozienice was resurrected by the hundreds of hasidim who used to come to the rebbe on Shabbes and yontif.

After the death of Rebbe Yerakhmiel–Moishe, there was a split among the hasidim of Kozienice, some of them taking Reb Arele as their rebbe, and some Reb Kalonymus Kalman of Piaseczna, Rebbe Yerakhmiel–Moishe's son–in–law.

After a few years, Rebbe Aharon–Yekhiel began to go his own way. He drove away the old hasidim, the scholars, the good Jews and wealthy men, and began to befriend simple people, artisans and labourers. He left Kozienice and settled in Lodz, then Warsaw, and finally in Otwock, where he established a court.

Reb Arele Befriends the Vulgar

The Kozienicer Rebbe's court was a place of refuge for the poor and sick. Every pauper knew that he could find a hot meal and a warm bed at the Kozienicer's.

I remember being at the rebbe's in Otwock in the early thirties along with Menakhem Kipnis of the Haynt, with whom I had gone to Otwock to collect hasidic melodies. We went in to the rebbe. It was Purim, and the bes–medresh was packed with porters from Warsaw and a large number of paupers. The rebbe sat at his table and ordered a hasid, a simple Jew, to sing Shoshanas Ya'akov. The crowd backed him up, the rebbe threw Yiddish sayings into the song, and a merry time was had by all.

Many Kozienicer hasidim could not abide the rebbe's strange path and began to go to other rebbi'im.

Reb Arele divorced his wife, and remained a childless divorce.

Hasidim told of Reb Arele's bizarre miracles, and of how he used his path to attract the vulgar and make them repent.

In Warsaw

When Reb Arele had been <u>rebbe</u> for thirty years, the Nazis marched into Poland, and he went from Otwock to Warsaw.

When it was already dangerous to go outside, the <u>rebbe</u> used to run about the streets of Warsaw under a hail of bullets looking for food for poor 3ews. He did not want for money, for rich Jews gave him as much as he needed.

As the book <u>Eleh Ezkera</u> (vol.3, p.81) mentions, the <u>rebbe</u> used to go <u>hungry, but he worried that the Jews should have a bit to eat.</u>

When our curses began, the rebbe changed his way completely. He sat learning in the <u>bes–medresh</u> day and night.

[Page 142]

Once, while sitting over his open gemore, he said, "I don't want any more." At that moment, his soul left him. This was the day before <u>erev</u> Yom Kippur, 1943, after the Nazis had already begun their slaughter of the Jews of Warsaw.

His devoted hasidim, who did not leave him for a minute, hurried to bury him in sanctified ground. He was buried clandestinely in the middle of the night in the Warsaw Jewish cemetery.

Where Did the Kozienicer Rebbe, Reb Arele, Die?

To the Editor of <u>Unser Vort</u>:

In <u>Unser Vort</u> of September 5, I read an article by a certain Dr. Orenstein concerning the death of the Kozienicer Rebbe, Reb Arele. He writes that he died in Otwock.

He also writes that a certain Moishe Borochovitch of New York states in the Zelechow memorial book that the rebbe passed away in Zelechow; but he does not mention Reb Arele's name.

He writes also that there was another Kozienicer Rebbe called Kalonymus Kalman, and that Reb Arele would have died in Otwock, and the other in Zelechow.

As one who both knew Reb Arele well and lived in Zelechow after the twenties, I confirm the statement of Moishe Borochovitch.

I saw Reb Arele when he was ill, and I was at his funeral. He lived in the same house as the Zelechower rav. He died there, and was taken from there to the cemetery. It is true that he had a white beard, and that almost the whole town attended his funeral. If possible, send my testimony to Dr. Orenstein, in order to release him from his error.

It is possible that there was a Kalonymus Kalman. I knew no such person. It is possible that he died in Otwock.

Respectfully,

Y.Y. Bialobroda

* * * * *

Editor's note: We would be glad if others who were personally acquainted with the Kozienicer Rebbe would speak out on this question, in order to establish whether the rebbe passed away in Otwock or in Zelechow.

[Page 143]

Still Greater In Death

In memory of the Kozienicer Rebbe, Reb Arele

(A prose translation)

by Yitzkhok Gochnarg, Sao Paolo

I see him before me as he used to be, pensive at the head of the table in his kloyz on Saturday nights. The rebbe's eyes immerse themselves in pure springs, as if nothing were hidden from them, nothing concealed. Consumed, he beholds dark tomorrows, so he drives off the gloomy storm clouds which hover above with faith in the Creator – they, too, will be lived through.

The rebbe's path is joy and song – the music brings him closer, unites him with the shekhina. He conjures up notes with bows upon strings – wordless teachings, exotic and fair.

Reclining at his table, plain working–class Jews – fishermen and smiths from Kuzmir and Pshiskhe, carters from Konsk, butchers from Stila, without shtreimelakh, without satin, without even velvet. At the rebbe's observances no pidyoynos are paid, no remnants of his food eaten at his table. He makes no matches, bestows no prosperity, but introduces a new melody.

Bows vibrate ecstatically on strings. A minyan of fiddlers accompanies the rebbe. The notes float up to the gates of heaven, and the Cherubim take up a new song.

So acted the <u>rebbe</u> for years, until Poland was invaded by bloody executioners; until their hordes brought violent death to the Jews.

In a small room on Gzibow Street in Warsaw the <u>rebbe</u> keeps a vigil together with the congregation. He cheers and consoles, allows no despair. The blessed Lord will help – despair is ugly.

Until once the heavenly sounds reached the ears of the Nazi serpents. They gnash their teeth – Jew impudence! They won't allow <u>this</u> in the ghetto. With skulls on their caps, their uniforms black, the S.S. – destroying–demons – march into the ghetto, forever to silence the Jewish sounds, to warn the <u>rebbe</u> that their turn has come.

The <u>rebbe</u> doesn't bat an eye. He mocks the destroyers with loud, bitter laughter. No power on earth can get in his way, nothing stops him from serving the Creator.

The hangmen continue to mock the <u>rebbe</u>. They order him to play a "Jewish" <u>freilakh</u> – "Take up the fiddle more quickly so we can hear a Jewish song!" The crowd stands frozen, the demons wait. The <u>rebbe</u> reaches his hands out dreamily, strokes the fiddle a long time with his delicate fingers, as if he were waving good–bye to a group of children.

Soon his glance becomes brilliantly sharp. Out of it shines, like a flash of thought, his courage, his tempted pride. His word is sharp as a sword with hate: "No!" He will not desecrate the sacred notes; rather smash the fiddle to pieces. He rips out the strings with tears in his eyes. He smashes the fiddle, he smashes the bow.

[Page 144]

At dawn, two horses hitched to a wagon drift through the streets like chattering winds. The <u>rebbe</u> is drawn after, lashed to the wheels. His body crushed. Blood pours from his wounds.

The streets are stained with the blood of the martyr. The sun rises red, <u>and a heavenly voice drifts through the world: "He was great in his life,</u> still greater in death."

The House of Rebbe Yekhiel–Moishe

The <u>rebbe tzin</u> Sarah–Dvoirele, the mother of Rebbe Yerakhmiel–Moishe of Kozienice, was distinguished for her fine qualities of character and good deeds, in addition to which the Lord had granted her wisdom and vitality. She was known as the estate–owning <u>rebbe tzin</u>, and rightly so, for she not only put her hand to business, but even purchased a large estate called Kolodna in Russia, sold it and bought another one, called Strikowic, near Kozienice.

She Sells the Estate

Naturally, she hired managers and overseers for the estate, but she herself supervised and managed all its affairs with great intelligence.

She had connections with the largest estates in Poland in matters of marketing produce, buying and selling livestock, and the marketing of fish from her fertile ponds, but the hasidim of her father, Rebbe Elimelekh of Grodzisk, as well as the hasidim of Kozienice, did not approve of her business. They claimed that it was not fitting for a rebbe tzin to engage in commerce as gentile landowners did. The hasidim not only disapproved, they beset her, forcing her to sell the estate.

This sorrow did not leave her heart or the hearts of her children and grandchildren for a long time.

With great wisdom and refinement, her daughter–in–law, the rebbe tzin Brokhele, gave all the administration of the house of Kozienice over to her, in order to take the pain from her heart. Brokhele was a good daughter to her.

These two great women exerted themselves to ease the suffering of the town's poor. They established a benevolent fund, and gave loans to small merchants who could not afford merchandise. Many were helped by these loans. When the fund was depleted, the two women would give to the needy from their own pockets.

Rebbe Yekhiel–Moishe Gave his Salary Away

Rebbe Yekhiel–Moishe, the fifth generation of the dynasty, was both rabbi and preacher. The Maggid's aptitude for preaching had been passed down from one generation to the next. As with his predecessors, hasidim flocked to him from all over Poland. Rebbe Yekhiel–Moishe distributed his salary among the slaughterers: he claimed that a shoykhet should be provided with a good living, in order not to have to worry about his needs and to be able to keep his mind on his work.

[Page 145]

The rebbe derived no pleasure from his salary, but gave it away for charitable purposes.

During the fire which levelled Kozienice, the rebbe's house was also burnt. The hasidim collected money to build him a new mansion. The hasid Reb Yankel Heschels, who was in charge of the construction, said that the rebbe gave the building materials to the poor to fix up their houses, rather than to the synagogue, which remained in its burnt–out frame. When Reb Yankelprotested this, the rebbe replied that so long as the town's poor remained in poverty and want, he did not want a mansion.

Ten years were spent in building the rebbe's court, during which time the rebbe because sick and died at the age of forty–some years. The rebbe was a great scholar, upright and just, a lover of the people and the land of Israel

Rebbe Yekhiel–Moishe's Children

His wife Brokhele was a righteous woman, learned and intelligent. They had three sons and four daughters, all of them holy and pure, great in Torah and secular knowledge.

Their eldest daughter, Khane–Golda, combined Torah and secular knowledge. She was among the first settlers of Avodat Yisrael – Kfar Hasidim. In the early years of the settlement, when its residents were visited with illnesses, she ran about among the sick and was a help and support to them all. Afterwards, she became one of the first female students at the Hebrew University in Jerusalem.

She did not succeed in returning from her visit to Poland, for the German invasion of 1939 was imminent, and she was killed along with the thousands of Jews of Warsaw on a rash and bitter day. May the Lord avenge her blood.

The eldest son, Rebbe Aharon–Yekhiel, was great in Torah, great in reputation. He used to give money to the poor; he took no pleasure in this world and sacrificed himself for the sake of every Jew. When the slaughter began in Warsaw, he went into his house and sat upon in his chair, slumbering in purity and holiness.

Rokhel–Khaye–Miriam, their second daughter and the wife of the rav of Piasczenca, may the Lord avenge his blood, excelled in learning and good deeds. She distributed her wealth to the poor of Warsaw, and ran the kitchen in her husband's yeshiva. Her door was open to all the suffering and wretched. She and her husband bought land in Israel but were not fortunate enough to see it. They were killed together with their children in the Holocaust. May the Lord avenge their blood.

The second son, the Admor and maggid of Rika (Lublin), Reb Asher–Elimelekh, was upright and just. The love of Israel and the land of Israel burned like a fever in his heart. He died following a serious illness while still young.

His wife Khaye was killed with their children in the Holocaust. May the Lord avenge their blood.

[Page 146]

Those Who Survived

The third daughter, the rebbetzin and well–known author Malka, was one of the first settlers in Kfar Hasidim. She is a highly cultured woman, and is married to the Admor from Grodzisk. Their house is open to all the needy.

The fourth daughter, Khave Shapira, was among the founders of Avodat Yisrael. She is well educated in both Torah and secular learning. She was in charge of the settlement's social welfare program, and provided clothing for new arrivals. She is married to Rav Shalom–Yoysef of the dynasty of Sadagora, a scholar, a lover of the land of Israel and of mankincd Their house is open to all the suffering and wretched.

The third and youngest son, Rebbe Yisroel–Elazar, is the founder of Avodat Yisrael, now Kfar Hasidim. He is great in Torah and wisdom, loves mankind, and is loved in return. He distributed all his wealth to the settlement's poor and sacrificed himself for the sake of the land of Israel. <u>He is married to the daughter of the rebbe of Zlotopola, who is known for her charity and philanthropy</u>.

Our Dear Brother,
Rav Yisroel–Elazar Hopstein
by Khave Shapira, Kfar Hasidim

Almost a year has passed [she is writing in 1967] since our dear brother, Rav Yisrael Hopstein, was taken from us. We both were born and educated at the home of our parents in Kozienice. We walked hand in hand in our youth, our devoted nurse, Sarah, at our side.

Rabbi Isroel Eliezer Hopstein – a great-grandson of the Maggid of Kozienice

There was a year and a half between us. My hair and eyes were black; he had golden hair and blue eyes. I loved his curls, for they resembled the rays of the sun; I loved his eyes, for they were as the brightness of the firmament in their purity. He was lean and straight as a cedar in childhood and adulthood alike.

He passed through difficult times. He aged very early. His health weakened, but his eyes shone, his stature remained straight, and his appealing smile never left his delicate, lovely face. He was always upright with God and with man.

He dove into the sea of the Talmud at a tender age, and his wisdom and sharpness brought forth many treasures from his mental storehouse, as his many manuscripts attest.

While young, he devoted himself with all the ardour of youth to the Avodat Yisrael organization in Kozienice, and to the establishment of the Kfar Hasidim settlement in Israel. In his concern for the settlers, he took upon himself the task of draining the swamps, in order to give them the chance to earn a livelihood.

My brother conferred with the engineer, Ettinger. Together, they worked out a program for draining the swamps, in order to prepare the land which had lain desolate two thousand years. The work was hard; the settlers were forced to work in the burning sun, mosquitoes stinging them unmercifully. Yet they stood the test. They accepted their sufferings gladly, aware of the benefits that would accrue for themselves and the people of Israel.

It happened more than once that my brother, the nasi (president) of Avodat Yisrael, as he was called by everyone, would appear suddenly among the drainers of the swamps while he was weeding. He found no rest except when participating in the settlers' physical labour.

Our sages taught that the merciful are among those whose lives are not lives, and the nasi was merciful and loved humanity with his heart and soul. He brought redemption and deliverance to others, but was unconcerned for himself. His heart grew weak, and the doctors told him to leave Israel. He did so, but continued to return, and each time he returned, he fell ill.

[Page 148]

After a number of years, he decided to settle in Israel, despite all the obstacles, and never to leave it again. But God's will was otherwise. To the sorrow of his admirers, who were bound to him with cords of love, his residence in Israel was not a long one. He passed away in Elul, 1966, and was buried in the cemetery in Sanhedria in Jerusalem in the place where, forty-three years before, he had signed the contract for the purchase of the land for Kfar Hasidim.

May his passing protect us; because of his merits the Lord remembered His people and healed the blemish in Jerusalem after two thousand years of desolation. Our heart sickens for the precious youth, the mighty men of their people, who have fallen for the sake of their land. The sorrow of their families is the sorrow of all Israel! May they be consoled – with the consolation of Jerusalem and Zion and with the General Redemption, speedily and in our day.

[Page 149]

Rav Yisroel–Eliezer Hopstein

by Naphtali Kirshenbaum

He is gone from us. He is gone from the hasidim of Kozienice. He, the glory of Israel, the founder of Kfar Hasidim, Rebbe Yisroel–Eliezer, the fifth generation after the Maggid of Kozienice.

The rebbe excelled in all the qualities of the house of Kozienice: he was modest, loved Israel and the land of Israel, and worshipped the Lord in holiness and purity.

His goodness of heart drew multitudes from ail classes to him. Whoever came into contact with him developed a fondness for him that is hard to describe. His facial features made a deep impression, for all the lineaments of the Maggid were engraved thereupon.

From time to time we heard toyre from him, all of it inculcating love of Israel, all of it afire with elevation of spirit.

It is worthwhile to mention the great event which took place over fifty years ago which changed the whole order of daily life in the house of Kozienice and breathed new life into the hearts of the town's inhabitants and all its hasidim.

Rebbe Yisroel–Eliezer took every opportunity to inflame the hearts of his congregants on behalf of the land of Israel. He called upon them to abandon the diaspora and go to Israel, but his words were as the voice of one crying in the wilderness. Yet at the close of the Sabbath on the seventeenth of Elul, 1924, when the rebbe was speaking in his usual fiery fashion about the land of Israel, something happened. His suggestions suddenly struck a responsive chord in the hearts of all his listeners, and they answered in unison, "We will do and obey–wherever you lead us, we shall go!"

That same evening the outline of an agreement was signed, and a board chosen on the spot, with Rav Yisroel–Eliezer, its founder, as president. The organization was called Avodat Yisrael, after the Maggid's first book.

From that day forth Kozienice was as if drugged. On all sides, the cry was heard: "We are going up to the land of Israel."

The land was acquired by the rebbe with the help of the hasidim of Jablona. The initial intention was for an agricultural settlement, but for economic and security reasons, it later passed into the hands of the Keren Kayemet, resulting in the foundation of Kfar Hasidim.

The rebbe, who was known as the nasi, or president, bore the settlers' burdens upon his own shoulders. He worried abut each one of them, and also about their spiritual lives, lest they be eaten up by their work. Before dawn every day he held a meeting in the bes–medresh, taught a chapter of Mishna, a page of Gemore, and finished with congregational prayer. Afterwards, the hasidim would go to work with a song on their lips.

[Page 150]

It is worthwhile to mention the words of Rav Kook, who said, "The holy Maggid created Avodat Yisrael in theory, and his hasidim are creating it in fact."

The rebbe was constrained to leave Israel on account of his health, but his vision of settling there had taken root in his heart.

He was chosen chief rabbi of Paris, and served in this capacity until the outbreak of the war. The day before the German invasion, he shut up his house and departed from Paris, leaving his rich library and the precious ritual objects inherited from his forefathers behind him. He took only a few books.

While boarding the train, he was arrested by the French police and taken, with all the Jews on the train, to a French detention camp. When the police realized who he was, they decided to release him at once, but the rebbe said he would agree to his release only if all the Jews in the camp were freed with him. They acceded to his request, and the Jews, with the rebbe at their head, were transferred to Nice, on the Mediterranean coast.

In Nice, the rebbe was elected head of the organization of French rabbis. He distributed his rations to others in equal portions, he himself almost starving.

In the meantime, the rebbe's name came to the attention of Washington, and the American government sent a demand for him and the rest of the Jewish clergy. The rebbe arrived in New York, in 1948, and was received with great honour.

His admirers fixed up an apartment for him in a religious neighborhood. He neither rested nor lessened his efforts to obtain visas for those Jews still in France, and he thus saved many.

After the war, we, the Kozienicer hasidim in Israel, turned to him and took him as our rebbe, in order to continue the dynasty of the Maggid. He visited Israel in 1954, at which time we established ourselves officially. In 1959, we discovered that he planned to settle in Israel with his family, in order to preserve the dynasty.

He visited again in 1966, after we told him that as we had gotten him a fine apartment with a bes–medresh in northern Tel–Aviv, but great difficulties resulting from various factors piled up and he returned to the U.S. to liquidate his affairs, and then come back to Israel to continue his work and establish a synagogue called Avodat-Yisrael, after the Maggid. But the angels triumphed, and his soul departed in purity.

With this article, I appeal to his intimates, his hasidim, his friends, to work with all their might in the name of his ambition to found a centre of Kozienicer hasidism under the name of Avodat Yisrael, in Israel. This will give pleasure to the <u>rebbe</u> in heaven, so that he will intercede for us until the coming of the Messiah and we merit complete redemption.

[Page 151]

The Baking of Matzah–Shmure
at the House of the Kozienicer Rebbe

by Khave Shapira, Kfar Hasidim

The odour of Pesakh was already felt in all the houses and courtyards of Rebbe Yerakhmiel–Moishe of Kozienice. From that day forth, the words "bread" and "khametz" ceased to be heard – all thought was given over to the baking of matza.

The members of the household waited impatiently for the seder, which the rebbe conducted with elevation of spirit and in magnificent splendour. Outsiders were not allowed at the first seder, for according to the heavenly commandment, each man must be master in his own house on that night.

Extensive Preparation

Great preparation was made for the baking of the matza–shmure. Boards were laid across the breadth of the old shul, which was in the Maggid's house. There was also a gigantic oven in one of the walls, built for the baking of matza. Sacks of flour stood in the corridor at the entrance to the Maggid's chamber.

In a corner by the door stood "our water", which the rebbe, his sons, and a congregation of hasidim had drawn from the river and brought home with a special tune used only on this occasion. A few days before the baking was to begin, everything stood guarded and covered lest it came into contact with anything bearing even a hint of khametz.

The walls of the shul were whitewashed for the third time, and were whitewashed again after every baking. The smell of the fresh whitewash was pleasant. The floors of the shul were covered with dried skins that looked like furs, because there was not time to clean the floors between the last baking and the beginning of the festival.

My father himself supervised everything. Reb Aharon, Reb Elimelekh, and Yisroel–Elazar watched over the baking. Hasidim and prominent members of the community stood humbly ready, waiting for orders from the rebbe's holy mouth. The hasidim hitched up the sleeves of their capotes with string, and held their tools in their hands.

The Boards Were Changed After Each Baking

The young kohanim stood outside the shul, some holding pumps to barrels of water, others holding wipers. After each baking, the boards, the shovels, and the rest of the tools were changed, and the workers came out to wash their hands. The young kohanim poured water over their hands and gave each man a towel.

And so it was after every baking.

[Page 152]

In the women's room of the shul there were my grandmother, the rebbetzin Sarah–Dvoire, the wise and upright; my mother, the rebbetzin Brokhele, wise and fair among women, and by her side, her daughters, Khane–Golda and Malke, both of them beautiful and gifted with wisdom and culture, with me, the youngest, by their side.

Even the maids, who considered themselves members of the family, all stood ready and waiting.

And the Window Frames Rattled

When the oven was ready, Malke, the elder boys' nurse who lived in my parents' house all her life, poured the flour into a wooden bowl. She covered her face with a white kerchief, and piously muttered a prayer the whole time.

Her son, Reb Shloime, poured "our water" onto the flour, and a certain hasid, a proofreader of sefer toyres and intimate of our family, kneaded the dough with the zeal of purity, from time to time changing with the hasidim Reb Yissokhor–Ber and Reb Itche Feigenbaum, a faithful friend of my father's house.

The rebbe took the dough from them and gave it to the hasid, Reb Leizer–Itche Rubinstein, who distributed portions of it to all those working in the courtyard.

As soon as the rebbe's voice was heard, hallel began. All those present answered "Hallelujah" with elevation of spirit.

And the window frames rattled.

Their cries were answered by the rustle and knocking of those who were rolling the matzas.

Their industry was amazing – as if this were the Exodus from Egypt itself. The baking of the matza–shmure concluded with song, thanksgiving and praise to the Lord, and with the blessing, "next year in Jerusalem." Tears of longing and endless yearning would appear in the rebbe's eyes. After this, the congregation would disperse.

Our devoted nurse, Sarah, took my brother Yisrael–Elazar and me to our quarters, to change us into new holiday clothes in honour of the seder. While we were crossing the courtyard, we ran into the congregation coming out of the shul, each one of them with a package of matza–shmure in his hand.

My attention was seized by our family's faithful friend, the hasid Reb Itche Feigenbaum, who walked joyfully, accompanied by his eldest son, the young married man and scholar Reb Aharon–Berish. I was particularly taken by Reb Itche's shining new capote, his well–combed beard descending on his chest as a sign of his virtues, and his radiant, patriarchal features. In his hand, a package of matza–shmure wrapped in white cloth was held close to his heart.

[Page 153]

He held onto the package as if all the happiness in the world were hidden in it – for was it nothing that he had attained to the most exalted of duties in the baking of the matza? He even received the matzas directly from the hand of the venerable rebbe himself, in all his glory! Who was like him, and who his equal?

Reb Itche's feet barely touched the ground; he walked as if springing through the air. All his worries had passed away from him – and good for him! When he placed this matza on the seder table it would lift him to an upper level, so that, during the recitation of the Haggada, he would feel as if he himself had gone forth from Egypt.

Despite the fact that I was but a girl then, I saw in my mind's eye the happiness of Reb Itche's wife at the time when her adored husband should bring this gift home.

His wife, Tziviye, was known in the town as a woman of valour who practised charity and loving kindness, a help meet for her husband. She worked in house and store from dawn until late at night, thus freeing her husband from the yoke of earning a living and enabling him to pass his time in study. She also worked with him for the education of their children in Torah and fear of heaven. He would share his portion in paradise with her nokh hundert un tzvantzik yor.

As they were passing by, Reb Itche's eyes fell upon us. He approached us, freeing his hand from the package in order to pet my brother's curls, and said, This boy will be a giant in Israel one day, like his pure and holy brothers. With this, he went on his way.

This encounter has remained engraved in my memory until this day. I offer it here as a memorial to the hasid, Reb Itche, the son of the family's shoykhet, Reb Mordekhai–Notte, a God–fearing man who used to lead the prayers in the Maggid's shul on festivals, sweetening our town's congregation with his song.

May their memory be blessed!

[Page 154]

The Slaughterer is Obliged
to Support the Butchers Widow

by Z.M. Rabinowitz

In the days of the Maggid, there lived in Kozienice a certain butcher, Itzik by name. Itzik was simple and upright, supported himself with the labour of his hands and walked in the ways of the Lord. But he had somehow acquired a bad reputation in his youth.

After a short time, he fell mortally ill and died leaving a widow and children behind.

After his widow had stood up from the shiva, she was besieged by creditors demanding satisfaction of her husband's debts. She grieved greatly, for her husband had not even left her food for a single meal. She went to the cemetery and prostrated herself upon his grave, weeping bitter tears over the husband who had left her only orphans and sighs.

After a few days, the widow was called to the Maggid of Kozienice. He interrogated her as to the debts she owed as well as her weekly and monthly expenses. The woman panicked, thinking that the Maggid had summoned her to demand her husband's debts, but the Maggid calmed her, adding that from that day forth all her debts would be repaid and she would receive a monthly stipend for her household. To her question as to why she had merited this, the Maggid did not reply. The story came out only after the death of the <u>shoykhet</u> of Kozienice.

Several weeks after the death of the butcher, he appeared to the<u>shoykhet</u> in a dream, demanding a <u>din–toyre</u> from him. The first time, the <u>shoykhet</u> thought it a coincidence, that there is nought but vanity in dreams. When the dream recurred, he went to the Maggid for advice. The Maggid told him that should the dream recur again he was to agree to go for a <u>din–toyre</u> in the Maggid's rabbinical court.

And so it was the next night. The dream recurred, and the <u>shoykhet</u> agreed to the <u>din–toyre</u>.

A special messenger was dispatched to the cemetery. He knocked once, twice, thrice – on the butcher's grave, and summoned him to the <u>din–toyre</u>. The next day, the Maggid and the judges convened. The <u>shoykhet</u> was present, and the pained voice of the plaintiff butcher was heard in the room.

"You, the <u>shoykhet</u>, are guilty of my death and of the hunger in which my wife and children find themselves. You were severe about the laws of <u>treyfos</u>; the better part of the animals I slaughtered you pronounced <u>treyf</u>. And so my money dwindled away and I became a debtor. Sickened with the greatness of my sorrow and sufferings, I fell ill and departed this world. It is therefore incumbent upon you to repay my debts and support my household!"

The Maggid considered the case and ruled that the <u>shoykhet</u> was to pay off the debts and support the widow.

[Page 155]

When the <u>shoykhet</u> had left, the Maggid asked the deceased butcher, "Tell me, Itzik, why is it that you have turned your attention to matters of money? Your judgement in heaven was obviously for the good, so tell me how you were received there."

"When I came to the upper world," he answered, "the angels of destruction wished to cart me into the pit of corruption, for my sins were very heavy and I could not raise my head. Sins, violations, and transgressions weighed down the scales, and I was almost condemned to hell, only at the last minute an angel came and spoke in my praise, telling that once in my youth, when I was a wagon–driver, I was driving a wagon full of scholars engaged in words of Torah, when a band of armed thieves fell upon us, practically killing them all. I had no weapon, but quick as lightning I grabbed the pole of the wagon and began to strike on all sides – I wounded some, and the rest scattered as chaff before the wind. This act of heroism, the saving of several lives, tipped the balance in my favour, and I was admitted into paradise. Only one sin remained – my unpaid debts. I therefore summoned the strict <u>shoykhet</u> to the <u>din–toyre</u>, from which he emerged obliged to support my widow and children."

[Page 156]

In the Court of the Maggid of Kozienice

by Malke Shapira, Jerusalem

The winds rustle through courtyards swathed with dusk, wrapped in cloaks of mystery veiling the awe of hasidim hurrying to hear the blessing over the Khanuka candles from Rebbe Yerakhmiel–Moishe. The rooms in the open-ended courtyard and the old bes–medresh, now empty of people, are drawn noiselessly after the groups of running hasidim. The air of the courtyard is wet with snow which lies piled in white heaps.

Malka Shapiro, Great granddaughter of the Maggid of Kozienice

The platform before the entrance door is covered with linen cloth, the ladder at its back, reaching to the roof of the horses' straw bin in the attic, covered with a white shawl. The thickets of hunched trees remaining in the frozen orchard next to the straw–bin alternately shrink and bend, dip and roll in the snow. The flame of the lantern sitting timid and fearful atop the modest lectern flickers and winks, absorbing blows from the trees, and, like a hidden eye, winks and blinks from the depths of antiquity into the air of the painted courtyard, winking at the ancient cellar's iron door which peeks out from the brick building and has grown green with age.

My grandmother, Rebbetzin Sara–Dvoirele, turned to the women, and, in the course of the walk across the courtyard, said, "Master of the Worlds, enough of sorrows on Israel, for the sake of our holy fathers". My mother, the righteous rebbetzin Brokhele also sighed frequently, her face growing very pale.

Bas–Tzion recalled the stories of the very old:

In this vaulted cellar the Maggid built a secret hiding–place for persecuted and tormented Jews who were running away from the oppressor at the time of the Kosciuszko rebellion when the elders and youth of Israel were tied to the tails of maddened noblemen's mighty horses and dragged through city streets.

The officers of the Russian army likewise executed terrible judgements upon them.

The cellar door guarded the hidden sighs of the persecuted children of Israel. Sighing in his old age under the weight of his patched cap, the Maggid sat in his small room which stood and watched and raised up the prayers for a tormented and persecuted people which he prayed with a mighty cry of pain.

Sadness had enveloped Bas–Tzion as she was seized by these reflections. The sled reminded her of walks through the paths of the pine forests. When she awoke and felt the snow wetting her hair and falling softly on her face, she felt pleasure. Behold now, they have been walking long since in sanctity to the lighting of the Khanuka candles.

The locked courtyard is absorbed in a silent listening. A strong, invisible wind brings snowflakes from the clouds on the other side of the horizon, where they have accumulated for thousands of years and solidified as the result of an inflexible judgement.

[Page 157]

As emissaries of mercy, the stars tear the clouds and peep at the clock winking out from the centre of the shut–up courtyard. The clouds run back and forth in the heavens, one chasing another, while the snow falls and melts.

Hasidim crowd together and go into the rebbe's old apartment and peek between the cracks of the shutters of the screened door at the tzaddik. He is standing on the threshold between the lintels of the inner doorway, a turbaned cap on his head, glory and majesty on his face, which glows with the light of faith even while it pales from the heroic efforts of his longing for victory.

The rebbe bows and lights the Khanuka candle in the old silver menorah with the wax candle in his hand. The blessing is sung as a dirge: "Who performed miracles for our fathers in those days in this season." The blessing is drawn out with longing in the dead silence. It stretches out and goes its way, breaks into the dimness of mystery in the courtyard, dies and is gone with the wind to the heights of heaven.

Bas–Tzion had stood quietly, but she was now flooded with emotion. She bent to her little brother, Yisroel–Elazarl, who was standing stock still, his blue eyes fixed on the Khanuka candle, and kissed one of his curling payes, which was soft as silk. Startled and agitated, the boy looked on her with angry eyes. He could not utter a sound, lest he profane the blessing by interrupting it, but his angry look rebuked her, while his hand adjusted his gold–embroidered cap.

As a storm seizes the silence, so did awakening seize Bas–Tzion, when she entered the cooking area adjoining the old bes–medresh. There was great agitation in the area where the meat dishes were being prepared. Sparks flew, tongues of fire shot out of the open door of the oven, licking the moist vapours rising and curling from the pots boiling on the oven. From the midst of all this labour, the merry voices of the labouring women rang out, breaking out of the foggy space. Girls in aprons smeared the patterned rolls with a solution of egg yolks, while old women in hairnets kneaded dough in triangles and fried latkes on the stove. The poor widow Khaye–Sarah asks to take part in the work in honour of Khanuka. Her little son, Shmerek, his eyes half closed in a pleasant nap, clutches the train of her dress. The rebbetzins, too, are burdened with work going frequently in and out of the dining room adjoining the kitchen.

Families wait to have their portions doled out. The rebbe tzins supervise the work, labour themselves, and help the workers.

A pungent odour of garlic from geese whose skin had been removed for Pesakh shmaltz and which were to be roasted after the khalas had been taken from the oven, entered Bas–Tzion's nose. "Goose is a crude sort of food," she reflected deliberately, in order to drive away the appetite awakened by the odour. "Father doesn't eat goose," she said to herself, "not even at the Khanuka meal, and it's hardly ever found at the women's meals, either."?

[Page 158]

"Come and eat a fresh raisin cake." Sarah, the old governess, a pan of soft, filled cakes, already baked and crusted in brown in her hand, turned to Bas–Tzion who had stumbled upon her on the way while she was carrying the cakes. The old woman took the cakes to the room where she was preparing the dairy dishes and boiling aromatic coffee for the household and hasidim.

Bas–Tzion sat eating the cakes which her governess had brought to the table, her little sister, Khavele, beside her on the wide, planed bench. The cake was pleasant to her taste, and she realized that her hunger had been real. She jokingly pinched her sister's full, tanned cheek, and embraced the thin old woman about the neck.

"I don't have time to play with you," said the governess, escaping from her grasp.

Bas–Tzion sat in her place, a dizziness in her head. Tranquility was spread through the warm, quiet room. Shloime, the young attendant, went in and out of the dimly lit room which drowsed in the light of a small kerosene lamp, pouring cups of boiling tea from the samovar and coffee from the pitchers for the sheine yiden in the bes–medresh.

The horses' groom happened in likewise, wearing a high linen cap which covered his forehead and ears. He was covered with snow. His whip was in his hand, his feet he stamped together. The sight of him reminded Bas–Tzion again of her trips in the sled, and she left the room in a cheerful frame of mind.

Conversations roll silently about in the warm hollow of the dining room which is sprinkled with light filtering through the pink, glass ball atop the kerosene lamp attached to a porcelain stand. The ancient walls, covered with embroidered wallpaper, absorb the constant ticking of the antique wall–clock; they listen to the shadows in silence, and return their echo to the room. The spreading scent of the tea steaming in shining glasses before the guests rise from the old, square table, covered with a shining oilcloth, in a curling vapour.

The rebbetzin Brokhele rises from the couch at the head of the table, bends to the porcelain lamp, adjusts the flame higher, and turns to the favoured hasidim drinking tea and telling tales of tzaddikim and hasidim, and says, "Let there be light for Israel, as in the days of Matisyahu ben Yokhanan, the high priest of the Hasmonean line."

"There is light in the settlements of Israel in every generation, when the tzaddikim reveal themselves," enthuses the hasid Reb Elimelekh ben Reb Pinkhas, wiping the sweat from his brow with the sleeve of his black robe.

"But where are the righteous women who bring deliverance to Israel, as dudith did in her day?" asks the rebbetzin with concern, and, turning to her daughters, who are playing dreidel at the end of the table with the household's apprentice girls and the daughters of respected families, adds, "And so, my daughters, be women of valour and the redemption will come through you."

[Page 159]

"Such as Judith were as angels, but we, rebbetzin, are as the children of men." Reb Elimelekh turned to the girls, who smiled and whispered embarrassedly among themselves. And when Khanele, the eldest daughter, rose to answer her mother, her shining face turning pink from the joy of the holiday, the rebbetzin added, "Your words are not fitting, Elimelekh. I knew women in the court of my grandfather, the tzaddik of Czernobyl, who were great in wisdom and fear of heaven. The works of Aunt Khane–Khaye were praised in the gates. The miracle which took place on account of a righteous woman is still well–known, and even you, my precious daughters, have undoubtedly heard of it from your elders."

The rebbetzin began the tale, her black velvet dress intensifying the expression of sadness on her face. The black muslin scarf covering her embroidered hairnet imparted the grace of modesty to her.

The story was like this: After the Maggid had died, the goyim hatched a plot against Israel, to come on the night of Yom Kippur to destroy them and lay them waste, from young to old, women and babes.

The sun was setting, Kol Nidre night was approaching, and the goyim gathered around the city, the Jews went to hide, their souls almost departed. Then arose Perele, the daughter of the Maggid, and summoned the daughters of Kozienice: "Let us go to the synagogues and pour out our hearts on this holy night, and let us not upset the sanctity of the holyday." They all paid heed to her words, and filled up the shuls and batei–medroshim.

A great cry went up during the praying of <u>Kol Nidre</u>, which put the fear of the Jews into the <u>goyim</u>, who ran off in every direction, screaming and crying for help. "Mercy! Save us! The Jews are upon us!"

The aged supervisress who brought the <u>shmaltz</u>-fried <u>latkes</u> waited for the <u>rebbetzin</u> to finish, then put a plateful of <u>latkes</u> on the table. They bubbled and blistered from the <u>shmaltz</u>, and perfumed the whole room with its scent. The hasidim turned themselves to them, praising their appearance and taste.

Reb Elimelekh was also pleased, and his clever eyes were smiling. He went wild with praising them. The old woman leaning back in her chair got up silently, sighed with the pleasure of fear of heaven, for her <u>latkes</u> were to the taste of the hasidim. A solemn smile hovered likewise on the <u>rebbetzin's</u> face.

The outer door opened, and in came the <u>rebbe</u> with his attendants and the Israeli.

"Are you playing <u>dreidel</u>?" he asked, with an affectionate smile. "If a man compasses his deeds with good and just intentions, the components of a life of charity and tranquility are compassed for him in the height of heights."

He spoke briefly, and went into his mother's adjoining room.

[Page 160]

The dining room was emptied of people – they had gone group by group to the old <u>rebbetzin's</u> room – and it wondered at the empty space covering the echoes of the conversations. The local girls kept their place by the kitchen door; Bas–Tzion, hugging the warm oven in her grandmother's warm room, listened to the sounds of the conversations in the two adjoining rooms, and to the whisper of silence in the pauses.

The <u>rebbe</u> blessed his mother, who had risen to receive him. The whole crowd, as well as the hasid, the rav Reb Hershele, rose also.

"How pale your face is, my son. You are throwing away your health," said his mother reproachfully. "You turn night into day. Look – the eyes of Israel are upon you, what is the point of such conduct?"

"The point is … the end, and the end is the beginning of the good," he said with a smile which had something of the suppression of pain in it, and fell silent.

His mother also fell silent. Worry darkened her face, her long lashes descended to cover her blue eyes, and deep concaves stood out by the arches of her thick brows. Quietly she let out, "Go on your way, my precious son. May heaven give you strength and the ability to continue."

The elderly Rav Hershele, a veteran and favourite hasid, stood in silence, sighing frequently. The light which was scattered and filtered through the patterned glass ball of the nickel lamp cloaked the silence. The panes of the double windows barred the outer noise like mightly gates to a kingdom. Even the tall acacia trees banging against the windowpanes as if they wanted to break into the room remained wrapped in white, remained in the frozen orchard on the other side of the windows. Here, in the warm, reflective space melting in whispering silence, here was the point and purpose of the universe.

Standing quietly by the warm oven, Bas–Tzion began to feel tired. The Israeli woman beside her, who had risen when the rebbe entered the room, reproached her with a glance, not to let her eyes close.

Their friend Khaiml came into the room, intending to cheer her up. When the rebbe had left the room, he told a tale of wonders, of what danger had befallen him while travelling, in the nearly gentile village. Miracles were commonplace for him when he travelled for business reasons in the cold of winter and the heat of summer, whenever his need was great.

The hymns began in the Maggid's old bes–medresh which was full of veteran hasidim. The rebbe had lit the candle in the menora, adjusted the wick with antique silver tongs, and begun praising the Lord. The hasidim responded with song and praise, and the wick from the Holy Land, made with holy unifications, burst into flame from the refined oil. The bes–medresh was seized by a flame of song, the flames of the candles in their silver sticks went up. The room was agitated, trembled; its sounds poured into and enveloped the sleep–shrouded courtyard from its foundations, at the time when the cock crows at midnight.

[Page 161]

"O give thanks to the Lord, for he is good; for his steadfast love endures forever."

"I will extol thee, O Lord, for thou hast drawn me up, and hast not let my foes rejoice over me."

The verses come out of the rebbe's mouth in tones as pure as the embroidered gold threads which go up with the rising of the sun, warming and shining upon the silence.

The bes–medresh, shining with an ancient light, shines in the spirits of the hasidim, who stand crowded, listening, breaking in and responding to the changing of the verses.

And the holy work continues and goes on.

The rebbe begins to play his fiddle clearly and in the old style. The notes quiver and tremble, flood and flow, break through the sluice gates, wrap and cover the space which is uniting in longing for the sacred.

A song breaks forth from the heart of the hasidim as if the agitated space itself were singing: "A song on the Dedication of the Temple."

And the holy work continues and goes on.

The notes became integrated with the stamping feet, the hasidim joined hands and began to dance with stormy souls. The dancers went round, hands in sashes and on shoulders. Their eyes were closed, only their spirits were watching.

The rebbe stopped playing his fiddle. He adjusted the menora's flame with the silver tongs. He began to dance, prancing, and his mouth did not cease from song. The shadows of the hasidim dance on the worn walls and tell of wonders from days gone by.

Bas–Tzion was already worn out with excitement. Her young brain imagined her an eagle soaring in the sky, then became a fish riding the stormy waves of the ocean which brought her, weak and pale, back to the girls' dormitory.

[Page 162]

In Memory of My Sister, Khane–Golda Hopstein

by Malke Shapira, Jerusalem

Chana Golda Hopstein, A great granddaughter of the Maggid of Kozienice

It is not in my power to weep for our sacrifices – the sources of my tears have dried up, for the calamity of my people in Europe was great. And those who had left the diaspora – why did they return to the valley of slaughter?

My sister spent years packed with suffering in our land. While she was visiting her relatives in Warsaw, she was stricken by the explosion of evil.

She went to Israel in 1925, imbued with a love of the land after the tradition of the house of Rebbe Yerakhmiel–Moishe of Kozienice and of my mother Brokhe–Tzippoire of the house of Czernobyl.

In the same year, she joined my brother, Rabbi Y.E. Hopstein, who had come as president of the <u>Avodat Yisrael</u> society. Together, they went up to what is now Kfar Hasidim.

In this fever–ridden desolation she marshalled all her powers in order to look after those with the eye diseases from which many, especially children, were suffering.

While in Jerusalem, she was engaged in the copying of ancient Hebrew manuscripts, and devoted most of her time to the suffering and wretched.

She was a rare personality, both in her talents and her suffering. May the Lord avenge her blood, and that of all our pure brothers. The enemy lifted his hand and killed, showing no mercy to dotard or babe. May the Lord give them their due, as it is written, "He takes vengeance on his adversaries, and makes expiation for the land of his people."

Rabbi Avraham–Elimelekh Shapiro

Rabbi Elimelekh Shapiro, Last Admor of Grudzisk, Son-in-Law and Nephew of Rabbi Yerachmiel Mosze Son of the Maggid

Rabbi Avraham–Elimelekh Shapiro, the last <u>admor</u> of Grodzisk, was both son–in–law and nephew (daughter of a sister) of Rebbe Yerakhmiel–Moishe of Kozienice, himself the son of Rebbe Yisroel of Grodzisk, a descendant of the Maggid Kozienice, the Seraph of Mogielnica, Rebbe Asher of Stolin, and the Holy grandfather of Rizhin.

After his marriage to the daughter of Rebbe Yerakhmiel–Moishe, the <u>rebbetzin</u> and author Malke Shapiro, he became a pillar of the <u>rebbe's</u> table and was bound to him with cords of love. A great part of his love for the land of Israel was received from him.

[Page 163]

In his introduction to the book <u>Mishnat Khakhamim</u>, a collection of the sayings of the heads of the Karlin–Stolin dynasty which he published during his residence in Jerusalem, he writes: "I received this manuscript in the summer of 1908 from my father–in–law, Rabbi Yerakhmiel–Moishe of Kozienice, who was educated by the <u>Beit Aharon</u> in Stolin. The Lord has favoured me with the printing of these holy words in the holy city of Jerusalem, and there is a certain condignity to this, for the thoughts of my father–in–law were always tied to the Holy Land. His desire to settle here was very great, and he distributed almost all his money to settlers on the holy ground."

Rav Avraham–Elimelekh was a great man in every sense, great in Torah, khasidus, and good deeds. He did not cease from learning. From dawn, after he had already risen and gone to the <u>mikve</u> while it was yet dark, he was always sitting in his <u>bes–medresh</u> occupied with Torah, gemore, <u>poyskim</u> and kabbala.

He was distinguished for his good deeds of charity and philanthropy. Charity in public; even more, in secret.

His humility is found in the same place as his greatness. His modesty and humility were boundless. He was imbued with the love of Israel. His conversation was wondrous and many came to his house for counsel and advice. He knew how to attract the young, and brought many of them back in repentance. He laboured daily to establish peace between man and wife, and man and his fellow.

Where the father–in–law was not favoured, there the son–in–law finally was: he and his family came to Israel in 1926 at the beginning of the <u>aliya</u> of Polish hasidim.

After the horrors of the Holocaust, many of his father's hasidim concentrated themselves about him in Jerusalem and Tel–Aviv. His house and <u>bes–medresh</u> in the <u>Zikhron–Moshe</u> neighbourhood of Jerusalem were turned into a tabernacle of Torah and <u>khasidus</u>, love of the people and the land of Israel.

[Page 164]

We have Gone Up to the Land of Israel

by Shalom Shapiro

Rabbi R'Shalom Shapiro, son-in-law of Rabbi Yerakmiel Moshe, son of the Maggid

After I had been ordained in 1909 by the gaon of Brod, A.D. Steinberg, I married a daughter of Rebbe Yerakhmiel–Moishe of Kozienice. I left my parents – my father, the admor of Gabozic, Rav Yitzhok–Mordekhai, and my mother, Tzippoire, daughter of Rebbe Yisroel of Sadagora – and settled in Warsaw, where I engaged in commerce, since I refused to serve as a rabbi.

My interest was in settling in Israel. Together, a group of us founded a society called Avodat Yisrael–Varsha, after the book by the Maggid. After the society had purchased some land in Israel at Kfar Atta, we left Poland in 1925. We did not go to Kfar Atta, but settled at what is now Kfar Hasidim, which was founded by Rebbe Yisroel–Elazar Hopstein of Kozienice.

[Page 165]

The Toyre of Khaim the Porter

by Henekh Kohn

I admittedly have no need to tell you this story, as you don't believe in miracles, and especially not in miraculous signs. So, what should I do, then? I simply want this to be recorded for the memory of later generations.

In independent Poland, at the time of Pilsudski, Jews were persecuted in the smaller towns. The enemies of Israel were unable to bear a lot of Jews travelling together [i.e., to their rebbi'iml for shabbes and yontef. The danger grew greater and greater, and the religious leaders decided to flee and settle in the larger cities.

In Otwock

During this period, the Kozienicer Rebbe, the Ostrowtzer Rebbe, and the Modzicer Rebbe all settled in Otwock, near Warsaw. Although Otwock was also a small town, its goyim were not antisemitic, for the more Jews came to town, the greater the prosperity for Jews and goyim alike.

Many rebbi'im did not understand the Kozienicer Rebbe's system of thought, so is it any wonder that simple hasidim who went to other rebbi'im made fun of him? They said that all his hasidim were rude, labouring types, that at his court one saw mainly porters, shoemakers, tailors, and tinsmiths. Even on shabbes, they sat at the table with their capotes hitched up with string.

By nature, the rebbe hated the rich. Should a rich man occasionally turn up and ask the rebbe for something, he was made to suffer.

The Kozienicer conducted his table in the same way as all rebbi'im, but the toyre he used to say was incomprehensible. At first sight, it seemed as if he digressed all over the place: one word somehow didn't go with another. But, when one paid attention and considered what he said, then one sensed his meaning. There were thoughts there, the mysteries of exalted ideas.

The rebbe took great pleasure if his poor hasidim ate a good meal at least once a week. He therefore demanded that people give of their finest and their best for his shabbes table.

Mendel Sarver

The Kozienicer's beadle was called Mendel Sarver [i.e., waiter or server]. He was a strange person, and his manner of dress was very queer. He always wore a broad, silk cap and a jacket with a slash in the back. As a frock coat, the garment was too short; as a regular jacket, too long. He also wore a thick, silk belt and big cowhide boots.

[Page 166]

In truth, it was Mendel Sarver, a Jew with a round, black beard, a sizable belly, and clever eyes, who ran the whole court. He understood the <u>rebbe</u> at a glance. The Kozienicer had but to look at him, and he immediately understood what was being asked for.

Khaim the Porter Tells a Story

Once, at the <u>shabbes</u> table, the Kozienicer said to one of his hasidim, "Khaim Treger, say <u>toyre</u> today!"

"<u>Oy, vay iz mir</u>, how do I come to say <u>toyre</u> before the holy <u>rebbe</u>?"

"Khaim, I'm ordering. Do you hear? Tell the people what happened to you on Friday."

Khaim the porter's hands and feet were trembling. He pondered, and said, "On Friday, I was at the station waiting for the freight train which was supposed to arrive from Warsaw. It was already getting late, and I still didn't have for <u>shabbes</u>. I was seized by pity for my wife, who was waiting at home. The poor woman was waiting for me to bring her a couple of zlotys, and meanwhile, I hadn't earned a groschen yet."

"Suddenly, some guy appears – he looks like a provincial nobleman – and says to me, 'Khaimke, I've got a heavy crate in my storeroom which has to be loaded, but the railway car's at the third gate. I'll give you five zlotys, but I don't know if you'll be able to <u>shlep</u> it.'"

"Sure, panie dear. To get for shabbes, I'd carry the biggest burden."

"I go up into the storeroom and give a look. <u>Oy, vay iz mir</u> – a crate, I can't even move it ... I spit on my palms and say to the lord, 'Dear Lord, give me a hand to get the crate on my back."

"I start going down the stairs from the storeroom. I can feel that I'm collapsing under the load, that I'm going to burst a blood vessel. I felt like the world was coming to an end."

"'Master of the Universe, a Jew must have strength to bear the heavy yoke of Torah on himself; so should I not be able to <u>shlep</u> this crate, then? God in heaven, help me – I'm doing this in honour of <u>shabbes</u>.'"

"Suddenly, a miracle occurred. The crate on my back became as light as a feather. I started running. You know, Jews, how far it is from the storeroom to the third gate? A couple of minutes later, I was already through it, loaded the crate into the railway car, and that's all."

"'You're a clever fellow, Khaimke. Here; here's a <u>fin</u>, and half a zloty extra."

[Page 167]

"I ran straight home to my wife, gave her the five and a half zlotys, and said, 'Khaye, quick! Run and shop for shabbes.'"

"Jews," said the rebbe, "have you understood the profound toyre that Khaim the porter has said before you here? Listen you, Berel Blaicher, have you understood the mystery of this story?"

If So, It's the Captive of the Jews

They say that a few weeks ago, the Kozienicer, while being beaten by the Germans, said that if the shofar should blow, the Germans would become a hare.

The Kozienicer asked if there were any Jews in Holland. He was told that there were. "If that's the case, then it's the Jews' captive, of course."

from Emmanuel Ringelblum, Notitzen fin Varshever Getto.

Warsaw, 1952, p. 46?

[Page 168]

Kozienice Elects a Rabbi

by Nekhe Katz–Goldberg, Holon

I don't remember exactly when it happened, in any case in 1933 On a hot summer day, dews from throughout Poland came to the Rebbe Reb Arele, who was running for the office of rav.

The other candidate was his brother Elimelekh, who had come from Cracow with his wife and children.

Jews from all over the country came quite early to campaign for our Reb Arele to be let in.

Rebbe Elimelekh's hasidim were householders, merchants and petty tradesmen.

Vote for Reb Arele

A very wealthy Jew from Mila in Warsaw had come. He was short and stout, with a little beard, and was called Yakele. He lavished money on every side. He was very clever: he dressed himself up as a stork, took a big horn, went up to the second floor of Dovid Yid's on Lubliner Street, and shouted as loudly as he could through the horn: "Jews of Kozienice, vote for the jewel of your city! All as one, vote for the Rebbe Reb Arele."

People did not go to sleep until late at night. The result was that Reb Arele was in. The rebbe was carried about in a torchlight parade. They sang and danced all night.

The next morning – turmoil and tumult. What should be done? Rebbe Elimelekh has a wife and children, he needs a living. They began to scream that the elections were fixed, that Yakele had bribed people to vote for Reb Arele.

The whole town ran after Reb Arele and his hasidim with Yakele at their head. They were running in tallis and tefillin to swear in the palace, in court, that nobody had been bribed.

Rebbe Elimelekh's hasidim were running, too, and Moishe Kestenberg (Moishe Gott) was with them. His wife tagged after him on his capote, and wouldn't let him swear.

She was screaming, "I don't want it! I'm afraid! I have small children – you will not swear!"

The conclusion was that nobody swore.

The elections were held over again, and the Rebbe Reb Elimelekh became rav of Kozienice.

[Page 169]

Kozienicer Bes–Medreshniks

by Yaakov Epstein, Montreal

My family and I left Kozienice for Warsaw in 1933, but we did not sever the thread binding us to Kozienice. We lived in Warsaw, but our hearts were drawn back to our beloved hometown with our families and our friends, almost all of whom were, alas, killed.

Kozienice was Famed for its Bes–Medreshniks

As I left Kozienice when I was learning in bes–medresh, I wish to cite the history of the Kozienicer bes–medreshniks who, with a few exceptions, were killed for the Sanctification of the Name.

Kozienice was famed for its bes–medreshniks, who would sit and learn in the bes–medresh from before dawn until late at night. On winter Thursdays, they would stay up all night and learn. You would hear the chant of Torah as soon as you entered the Maggid's street.

Whoever had the desire to learn found a place in the bes–medresh There were no class distinctions – rich or poor, hasidim or the children of artisans. Bokhurim who were Gerer, Porisower, Kolibieler, Piaseczner, Lubliner, and Kozienicer hasidim all learned there. We were bound together as one family.

Of course, hasidim from different courts would quarrel amongst themselves, as is usual, but while learning in the bes–medresh all was forgotten. A Gerer bokhur would learn with a Porisower. No one was ashamed, and anybody who wanted to learn received help.

An older bokhur would learn with a younger. The younger would learn by himself, asking the elder about what he did not understand, and the elder would explain it to him.

An evening class was initiated for bokhurim who worked during the day but had time to learn at night. An older bokhur learned with them. Moishe-Loser, Hillel the rav's, Moishe Shmuel's and others devoted themselves to this.

Book Repairs and Yorzeit Candles

Aside from learning, money was needed to repair torn books or to buy new ones. There was always a gabbai, one of the older bokhurim. He would send two younger bokhurim through the town to collect money to repair the books.

The bes–medreshniks had another task as well. Before the rebbe's yorzeit they would go through the town collecting yorzeit candles. When all the candles had been lit, the bes–medresh shone with thousands of burning lights.

I will here present a list of the bes–medreshniks whom I remember, so that they might be cited among the martyrs of Kozienice.

[Page 170]

The following were gabbaim in my time: Moishe Bornstein, Khaim–Dovid Henekhs, Herschel Weinberg, Aharon–Shmuel Korman (killed), Yaakov–Mottel Mandel, Hillel the rav's, Yankel–Shmuel Korman (living in Toronto), Moishe

Shmueles, Itche Freilakh, – a rabbi, still living – Khaim–Shmuel Korman (living in Toronto), Mordekhai–Shmuel Korman (killed), Mottel–Loser Menashes, Menashe–Yitzkhok Loser–Menashes, Notte–Moishe Yekhezkel Shoikhets, Avrum–Moishe Yekhezkel Shoikhets, Moishe Aaron–Berishes, Shmuelke Reisman (still living), Moishe dablonka (deceased), Khaim Salzberg, Borukh Salzberg, Yekhiel Khaim–Meirs (shot as a partisan), Moishe Katz, Alters, Shmuel Schwartzberg (Shmerls), Khaim Flamenbaum (living in Israel), Shmerel Ovenstern (still living), Yankel Epstein (living in Montreal), Moishe–Berel Sheners, *Moishe* Notteles, Herschel Scharfharz, Yoisef Mattes, Borukh Rosen, Ben–Tzion Freilakh, Moishe Notte Kovals, Shloime Wildenberg, Yankel Shapiro, Avrum Weinberg, Moishele from the sands, Shmelke Spiegelman (living in Montreal) Yitzkhok from Kalik.

My Grandfather

My grandfather, Yekhiel–Eliezer Kestenberg, may the Lord avenge his blood, was among the most prominent of the Kozienicer hasidim, and sat always at the rebbe's table: he never failed to go to one of Rebbe Elimelekh's tables.

Despite the fact that my father was a Porisower hasid, I loved to go to Rebbe Elimelekh's table with my grandfather, because of its good cheer and because the rebbe used to befriend everybody.

The rebbe would receive a guest hasid royally. A hasid from outside would eat the best food, and the old rebbetzin, Brokhele, made sure that all the hasidim had enough of all the shabbes delicacies.

And the spirituality, the ardour of saying Shalom Aleikhem to the Kozienice melody ... And how the rebbe made kiddush – with what sweetness! And after that, the tish and the distribution of bits of food (shirayim) which the rebbe used to give my grandfather.

And the zmiros? How Elimelekh Pinkhases or Aharon–Berish used to sing, with the whole crowd helping them.

After bentshing, we danced with such ardour as only Kozienicer hasidim can.

This was truly a pleasure to one's spirit.

Pesakh

Especially when Pesakh came. I remember baking matzos on erev Pesakh. The rebbe himself was present, and he would sing Psalms and Hal lei.

[Page 171]

That night, the seder – I will never forget it. Rebbe Elimelekh, in a white kittel, sat in stately fashion, his brother, Yisroel–Elazar, his brother–in–law,

Reb Shloimeke, and the old rebbetzin near him, and the crowd singing and dancing.

I remember how Shakhne Soifer and Moishe Yossel–Heschels danced She–Hoytzianu Mi–Mitzrayim for maybe two hours. At Ve–Hi She–Amda and Khasal Sidur Pesakh with Le–Shana Ha–6a'ah there was again singing and dancing.

The Twelfth of Elul

On Rebbe Yerakhmeil–Moishele's yorzeit on the twelfth of Elul, Kozienice appeared different from usual. Hasidim used to come from Warsaw, Lublin, Radom, and other towns.

The Piaseczner Rebbe used to make a point of coming for the yorzeit, and he would stay over for shabbes. He used to stay with my grandfather or with us. When he had a tish (table) all the Piaseczner hasidim would come, as well as prominent householders such as Reb Ben–Tzion Moyre–Hoyra'ah (Ben–Tzion Freilakh) and Elimelekh Pinkhases.

The 3ews prepared themselves devoutly for the Days of Awe, especially the prayer leaders and their choristers. The rebbe davened in the shut. Itche Berd davened the p'sukei de–zimra, and Aharon–Berish, who davened shakhris, would sing Ha–Shem Melekh, to the accompaniment of the choir. Later, Reb Elimelekh Pinkhases would say kaddish with the Kozienice melody, and his children and grandchildren would help a little. To me, this was the most beautiful music.

I remember how my grandfather used to stand by the ark all day – he had the claim on opening and closing it. As a small boy, I loved to sit on the high steps by the ark, from which I was able to see everything.

Sukkos in the Maggid's Shtibl

On Sukkos, the rebbe held his tish (table) in the Maggid's shtibl. As far as I was concerned, this was the biggest celebration of all. I waited all year for this day, because the rebbe used to show special honour to everyone who had the name of one of the ushpizin (the heavenly "guests" who visit the sukka).

The third day of Sukkos was mine – I was a real big shot. They gave me shirayim and wine, and also allowed me gelila.

The real festivity was Simkhas Toyre. I remember that my grandfather used to come with a group of out–of–town hasidim. Their arrival, its singing and dancing, could be heard from far off. Although they were admittedly a little tipsy already, my grandfather would nevertheless order that a punch of 96% alcohol, spices, hot water and other ingredients be made.

[Page 172]

My mother was a specialist in preparing the punch. After a shot and a bite, the hasidim became merry and Simkhas Toyredik; they danced on the tables and sang Ashreikhem Yisrael and other tunes.

All the sefer–toyres in the shul, about 100, would be brought out for the hakofes, which were led by the rebbe.

The whole town, young and old, men, women and children, turned out. They stood on the tables and benches. Each hakofe went on maybe half an hour.

The lightness and festivity, the singing at the hakofes, the children with their flags, the apples and burning candles – it is all before my eyes today. I will never forget it .

Parties and Institutions

Bnos-Zion Organization of Kozienice 1919

Betar Organization of Kozienice 1932

SECTION 3 - Parties and Institutions

The Zionist Organization to 1933

by Zvi Madanes, Tel–Aviv

On Warsaw Street was a big house owned by Yisroel Zifferman, on the ground floor of which was located the Zionist organization's meeting hall, consisting of a large hall with a dais, in the centre of which was a picture of Dr. Herzl. The dais is where the organization's governing body, headed by Pinkhas Freilakh and Alter Bornstein, sat. Alter Bornstein was head of the Zionist organization until the establishment of Betar.

The meeting hall was adorned with Hebrew slogans: – "If you want it, it is not a legend"; "If I am not for myself, who is for me?"; "Redeem the Lord" – and pictures of the land of Israel.

There was a small room with bookcases at the side of the hall which served as the library. It was open twice a week.

The Zionist organization carried on wide–ranging, many–branched activities in all areas of Zionism.

Zvi Madanes

Miriam Kirshenblatt Worked for the Keren Kayemet

In my time, Miriam Kirshenblatt was in charge of Keren Kayemet activities. Every month she decided who would empty the pushkes.

It is worth mentioning that the young members so chosen received particular satisfaction on going to Khayele Freilakh or Tova Mandel, from the Mintzberg family, who is now in Israel. Their blue and white pushkes were overflowing with money.

Or else take Mendel Zemach. He was a little out of the way, but it paid to make the trip. He received the young members amiably, and the Zemach family was among the first with their money.

As I recall, Zelig Shabbason from the sawmill was also among the major contributors to the Keren Kayemet.

Many people used to come in the summer to enjoy the fine air of the beautiful Kozienice forests. At that time we would arrange flower days for the benefit of the Keren Kayemet.

The Cultured Youth

Our Zionist youth in Kozienice was cultured and conscious of its merits.

We would often arrange symposia rich in content and well–attended by the membership.

[Page 174]

Hebrew was taught intensively, and many members attained a perfect mastery of the language.

The Zionist organization used to put out a Hebrew broadside, edited by Mordekhai Donnerstein, now in Israel, Frisch and Buchner.

The drama group led by Bezalel Madanes also formed part of the organization's cultural activity. He was known in the town for his great dramatic talents, and, as leader of the group, he always played the leading role.

It is also worthwhile to mention the services of Mendel Zemach (Moniek). He was a youth of great education, intelligence, and Jewish pride. He organized the Maccabee sports organization with the instructor Yosef Lichtenstein at its head.

When I recall all these names, their persons – the symbol of refinement, the pearls of the city – stand before my eyes as if alive.

Alter Bornstein, The Dynamic Force

The dynamic force of the Zionist organization was Alter Bornstein, a Zionist patriot and a fine speaker. He was the founder of Betar in Kozienice. This was the first Zionist youth organization to have a standard uniform, a splendid blue and white flag and a menora. Our marches through the Jewish streets awakened joy and envy.

The Kozienice Betar arranged meetings in neighbouring towns and carried on wide ranging activities. When Dr. Ben–Shem (Dr. Feldszu) and his retinue used to visit the Kozienice Betar, it seemed to the town that Jewish generals had arrived.

I should like here to mention our member Shmuel Gelberg, who is now living in Tel–Aviv at Nakhlat Binyamin 130. He distinguished himself with his devoted labour, thanks to which many young Jewish men saved their lives.

The Wizo Activities

Wizo, the Zionist women's organization, organized lotteries and bazaars, the profits of which were used for Zionist purposes. The head of the Wizo organization was the wife of Dr. Abramovitch. The publications of the Tarbut school were also covered by Wizo.

I recall the beautiful summer evenings when we would set up the benches from the meeting hall in the woods, and all together sing splendid songs of longing for our land. The notes floated through the depths of the forest till late at night.

A group of Zionists say farewell to their Hebrew teacher upon her departure to Palestine

[Page 175]

Alas It is All No More

Alas, it is all no more. As all Jewish communities, the community of Kozienice was exterminated.

Millions of Jews were taken to their death, and the world stood silently by. The Nazi murderers were able to do everything dictated by their animal instincts, for "Jews can be killed."

Alas, the Zionist leaders and instructors of Kozienice did not live to see the fruit of our work, the realization of our dreams, the liberation of our land and the Zionist flag flying high and proud.

[Page 176]

Haszomer Ha–Tzair in Kozienice

by Yaakov Lahat, Ein Ha–Mifratz

A cell of Haszomer Ha–Tzair was founded in Kozienice at the beginning of the thirties in the following manner. In the summer of 1931, the Rutman family arrived in Kozienice from Radom. One of the sons, Zvi Rutman, a dynamic young man of 16 or 17, at the time a student of the Tarbut high school in Radom and an instructor in the Shomer group there, decided to establish a cell in his new place of residence, Kozienice.

He decided, and he did it. Thanks to his talent for leadership, his knowledge of sports and scoutcraft, he succeeded in concentrating a number of youths about him.

During the summer, the meetings were held in the woods by the town, and with the onset of winter we received a room in the quarters of the Zionist organization, which was then housed in the brickworks, di tzegelnye.

Three "Tribes" in 1932

More youngsters joined the movement during the winter, and in the 1932 Lag–B Oymer parade there were three "tribes" of the "Sons of the Desert", the youngest class of membership, for children from 11–13. Each "tribe" had from eight to ten members.

In the early years, Zvi was the only instructor. He devoted every night of the week to the organization, and conducted activities with each group twice a week. On Friday nights and Saturdays there was a common activity for the entire cell.

Every year, new "tribes" were added in.

In 1934 Khaytshe Bornstein, Khane Karpman, and Khavele Rosenzweig took the leadership of the younger group upon themselves, and Zvi turned to intensive activity among the "scouts" (the second class of members) and to local leadership.

The cell's activity was great and diverse. It began with sports and scoutcraft, and finished with seminars on political economy, Darwin, and Gregor Mendel. Of course, the history of Zionism, Jewish history, study of Eretz Yisrael, and the learning of Hebrew were not neglected. And above all these, education for the realization of our independence in Eretz–Yisrael and the kibbutz.

Our Own Headquarters

Beginning in 1934, the organization rented a room with an entrance porch. Although it was in a wretched house at the edge of town, the room was always decorated and clean, several beds of flowers and vegetables, symbols of agriculture, were planted in the courtyard.

[Page 177]

There were many trips to the neighbouring forests, those in the summer very early on Saturday morning, those in the winter lasting until dark.

We would often meet with other Shomer groups from the area, such as those of Radom, Pszitik, and Zwolin.

So far, we have mentioned the achievements, but problems and failures were not lacking. Zvi Rutman left the city for family reasons, and the local instructors failed to carry the burden of the cell. The upshot was that the cell broke up and ceased to exist at the beginning of 1937. A small portion of the membership went over to other organizations, but the majority remained unaffiliated.

1939 – Re–establishment

At the end of 1938, several members of the "scouts" who had grown up in the meantime convened and decided to renew the activity of the cell. We were surrounded by misgivings as to our success, and thus, before the announcement of the official opening, we organized youth groups, collected money for quarters, and, at the beginning of 1939, we used this momentum to activate the cell at quarters on Lubelska street, across from the water tap.

On Tu Bi–Shvat we collected the largest sum for the Keren Kayemet from the sale of sacks of dried fruit from Israel. Every winter there were regular activities and the drafting of new members.

On Pesakh the adult members went to a conference in Kielce, at which the establishment of a new training kibbutz near Bialystock was announced.

After Pesakh, Khytshe Bornstein and Ephraim Kreizberg went for training. We also began preparations for going to summer colonies.

In the summer of the same year we had a joint colony for the youngest members ("Sons of the Desert") with the group from Zwolin, and one member was sent to the central leaders' colony.

A group of members of "HaShomer HaTzair" in the Ghetto of Kozienice

The Outbreak of the War

At the end of the summer, there was great activity in the organization. We received a visit from a member of the Shomer leadership in Galilee, and the question of their going to Bialystock for training was discussed among the adults. Many of them intended to do so, but the war broke out first.

At the outbreak of the war, some of the adults went to Russia, others joined the Polish army. The rest, as well as those who had returned to the town, attempted to reorganize. The youngest group no longer met, but the Scouts and the adults used to meet in private homes.

[Page 178]

Difficulties increased with the establishment of the ghetto. Ghetto housing was crowded, and most of the members were forced to work hard in order to support their families. Nevertheless, the adults succeeded in meeting every Saturday over a prolonged period.

The Visit of Mordekhai Anilewicz

Towards evening one day in the summer of 1941, a boy from the younger members appeared beside me and whispered that a messenger was waiting for me with the wagon driver who went to Radom (Per Garbatker).

I ran there immediately, and was very surprised to meet Mordekhai. He kissed and embraced me as if we were relatives, and loudly gave me regards from my aunt. While doing so, he drew me outside and asked me to keep his identity and his visit a secret. This was my first lesson in conspiracy.

I went home with him, and he asked that even there I present him as a friend from the colony. The next day, about fifteen people from the adult membership met at the home of Khaytshe and Yissokhor, and listened tensely to Mordekhai's words. They included:

    a. A report on the situation in Israel.

    b. Notice of a national council in Warsaw.

    c. A proposal to continue the Shomer activities in the ghetto and underground.

    d. A proposal to obtain pistols and grenades, and to practise with them.

    e. A mutual aid organization.

We separated from Mordekhai, who continued with his trip in the neighbouring towns, encouraging the members and giving them the movement's decrees.

After his visit, activity and mutual aid among members of the cell intensified, but the difficulties increased from day to day. Some members were sent to work camps and concentration camps, while others toiled to support their families. And thus, the activity of the cell approached an end

But in any event, not one adult member of the cell was persuaded to serve as a policeman or functionary for the Germans.

Of the 70–80 members of the cell most were killed with their families in the Holocaust.

Members Who Survived

Shalom Cohen (U.S.A.), Khavale Rosenzweig, (Washington U.S.A.), Yaffa Medallion (U.S.A.), Zelig Erlichman (Belgium), Yaakov Likverman (now Lahat) and Zvi Avenstern (Israel), survived in concentration camps. Ephraim Kreizberg (Brazil), fled to the Soviet Union. Two are now in Israel. Yaakov Lahat (Likverman) in Ein Ha–Mifratz and Zvi Avin (Avenstern) in Nir Yitzkhak.

[Page 179]

The Names of the Adults and Workers Who Were Killed

Shabtai Oboge, Khaytshe Bornstein, Yerachmiel Bergman, Yitzhak Greenspan, Khaim Weisbrod, Yissokhor Salzberg, Yoisef Salzman, Dov Karpman, Khane Karpman, Dov Kreizberg, Yissokhor Resenzweig, Zvi Rutman.

May their memory be blessed!

[Page 180]

Betar in Kozienice

by Ephraim Horowitz, Brazil

Ephraim Horowitz

As one of the co–founders of Betar in Kozienice, I consider it my sacred duty to recall my friends with whom I struggled for an idea.

Before proceeding to the matter at hand, I would like to open a page of memories of my youth, when Betar was our only hope for solving the Jewish national question.

It was in the years following the First World War. Parties were being organized in the town: the Volkspartei, the Bund, Agudas Yisroel, the Zionist organization, the Left Professional Society, Left and Right Po'alei Zion. Each party strove to enlist the youth in its ranks.

A large portion of upper and even middle–class youth joined the Zionist organization, and bound their belief to the Zionist ideal. We young people did not understand the difference between Betar and mainstream Zionism. Everything connected with Zionism was dear to us.

As has already been indicated, our town was famous throughout Poland for shoe manufacturing. The greater part of the youth employed in this industry, as well as poor artisans, joined the labour unions, in order to improve their economic condition.

At that time Betar developed throughout Poland with lightning speed. Middle–class youth, especially those educated in high schools, was engulfed by an immense enthusiasm.

The young people felt enthusiastic about the Zionist idea and the belief in the rapid establishment of a Jewish state. The blue and white insignia, the marching through the streets like proper, trained soldiers called forth joy and hope among the youth. In Betar they saw the future Jewish army of the land of Israel, the liberators of the Jewish people.

The name of Ze'ev Jabotinsky, the leader of Betar, became very popular and beloved among the young. Splendid heroic legends formed around his name. The young saw Judah Maccabee in him, and would go to hell and back at his command.

We Dream of a Jewish State

We dreamt of a Jewish state on both sides of the Jordan. We greeted one another enthusiastically with the words, "Tel–khai". 1928.

The enthusiasm in our town embraced a number of young people: Alter Bomstein, Mania Zemach, Yoyne Reisman, Moishe Fligelman, Popelnik, Rochman, and the writer of these lines. The Kozienice Betar was formed with great ardour and enthusiasm.

From time to time instructors from the larger towns came to give us instruction about the Betar movement.?

The founders of Beitar organization in Kozienice with delegates from Warsaw, Dadom and Keltz

[Page 181]

Masses of young people from other parties, as well as older people, used to attend our lectures. They would carry on discussions, and sometimes interrupt the speaker.

Executive of the Zionist Revisionist Party 1933

Although we were a small group, we were very active, and were an important factor in local Jewish cultural life.

Boys and girls, students from mercantile and hasidic circles, and also the children of craftsmen and the middle–class joined our ranks. Comradeship ruled in Betar, and we felt like one family. This, incidentally, led to persecution from religious, hasidic circles.

With pride and honour we wore the Betar blouse and marched through the streets of the city like real soldiers.

We turned Betar into a school. Every evening, Hebrew lessons and lectures on various topics were held in our hall. We strove to make Betar into a second home for the young. Alter Bornstein, Nakhum Teitelbaum, and others who were instructors in the Kozienice Betar, dedicated great effort to the organization in Kozienice.

[Page 182]

Ozrot Ha–Aretz in Kozienice

by Khave Shapira, Kfar Hasidim

Many girls sought my friendship, perhaps because I was the daughter of the rebbe, perhaps because I treated them with gentleness and delicacy. In any event, they were all desirous of my friendship.

I rejoiced to greet my friends and, greeting me, they did likewise. We were a happy and merry group, resembling the children of the land of Israel whose exultant voices fill the air of our land.

My Two Friends

Things were different as I grew older. I chose myself two friends like to myself, Golda, the rabbi's daughter, who was older than I, and Khayele, daughter of the sharp and clever hasid Reb Elimelekh, who was younger.

We three were bound by bonds of faithful friendship. I appeared to them as if I were the urim and thummim on the breastplate of Aaron. And why? Perhaps I really did have a pure heart in which love of mankind dwelt, according as my parents planted this virtue in the hearts of all their children; and perhaps I also had a healthy commonsense, my tender years notwithstanding. Therefore, my words always found an echo in their hearts, according to the rule, "Heart speaketh unto heart."

Khave, daughter of Hassia Honigstock   Kvahe Shapira

We Would Read and Study Together

Such was the nature of our connection. Everytime we met we would read and learn together, one of us reproving the others. In this way, we passed our time pleasantly, and each meeting turned into an experience.

I tried to bring them near to Torah, our homeland, and the treasures of Judaism. With them I read Ahavat Tzion, Zikhronot le–Beit David, Emek Ha Arazim, and so on. I imparted to them my love for the land of our fathers, which had always been a lamp unto the feet of my father's house.

Before any child born to my father's house learned to utter a single syllable, our parents taught him to say Eretz Yisrael. The bond between them and our land was that strong. These are the qualities I implanted in the hearts of my good friends Golda and Khayele.

Holding Hands is Not Enough

But I was not satisfied with this. I said, we can't stop at holding hands – we have to begin working among the girls of the town. A sacred duty is imposed upon religious girls to educate the daughters of both pious and assimilationist homes. They must be roused from their slumber; their eyes must be opened.

[Page 183]

At night I turned up on my bed, spinning various plans to attract these girls to my circle. We expected trouble when their parents learned that we were going to influence their kosher daughters, take them beyond the portals of their houses in order to teach them Torah or love of the homeland. We knew that we would be judged severely.

The religious zealots believed that "Everyone who teaches his daughter Torah, it is as if he taught her foolishness." The assimilationists believed that they had to walk in the ways of the gentiles which they preferred.

Indeed, we knew that we would bring trouble upon our parents, who were dearer to us than our very lives, but the fire of love of our land burnt within us, until its flame burnt out.

Thus Do Free People Live

One summer day in 1922 I sat with Golda and Khayele at the foot of the mountain which abutted the lake known as Jezore. The sun was spending its last rays, which reddened the water of the lake. The birds leapt from bush to bush, raising their voices in song. On the other side of the lake, families of farmers were harvesting the golden–brown wheat. Their white clothes, made of simple cloth and handknitted by their wives, grew whiter as the day sank towards evening.

When their work was done, the men collected their tools and put their scythes on their shoulders. Their wives loaded the infants onto their backs and went singing to their small, peaceful houses.

We sat as if fixed to our places. Jealousy burned in our young hearts. We gazed into one another's eyes without speaking, and a sigh burst from my heart, accompanied by the cry, "My dear friends! This is how free men live on their own land! Do you see their tranquility of spirit? And what have we?"

At that very moment we decided neither to rest or to keep silent, but to begin concrete activities. Even if our flesh were torn by scorpions, we would work, we would devote our lives to our people and our land.

That same evening we went down to the tunnel. By word of mouth we summoned ten or so girls to a meeting. By some miracle, hordes of girls began to stream to us. We worked together in joy and understanding. We did not have many funds at our disposal; therefore, I taught Tanakh, and my friends taught other subjects.

Hebrew was taught by a teacher who was the only male in our organization.

Moishele the Teacher

Moishele the teacher was short and thin, with sparkling blue eyes. A light laughter was spread over his face, and signs of suffering could be seen on him.
[Page 184]

He as an ardent Zionist; the fire of love for the homeland flamed in his heart. Moishele was born to poor parents who lived in a dilapidated wooden house behind the bath–house in the poorest part of town.

He lost his father while still a boy, and his mother was left destitute. Despite his great suffering, Moishele was very diligent and excelled in his studies. He sat bent over a gemore in the bes–medresh, and was known as a masmid. On nights when there was a moon, he studied outdoors by its light; on dark nights, he studied by the light of a candle obtained from his friends. In this fashion, he perfected his knowledge of four languages, all of which he knew perfectly. He was outstanding as a grammarian, even unto the details of the soul.

I recall the time he appeared in a new suit, the first of his life. He was then about twenty–five. There was no end to his joy. He did not wear the suitcoat, but hung it over his shoulders like a collar, in order not to spoil it. Woe to whomever dared touch the hem of this coat! But not from evil–heartedness, for he was gentle and good–hearted by nature, and would never harm a fly.

His students loved to joke, feeling the fabric and examining its quality. How much pain we caused him! We were too young to understand how much toil and sweat had been invested in this suit, how much he suffered to save the sum required to buy it and to get rid of the rag he had worn all his life.

Let all of us who knew him extol his memory. He gave his body and soul for the sanctity of every word, every letter of our language, and he taught its laws to many in our town.

We Hope to Make It Bear Fruit

We bore the yoke of the organization with our own strength. We called it Ozrot Ha–Aretz (Helpers of the Land). We cultivated it and hoped to make it fruitful. We contacted the Mizrahi in Warsaw and asked them for help, but we did not really receive any. What we did get were Shekels – membership certificates – which we were supposed to distribute. We fulfilled our task faithfully.

Perhaps the Mizrahi was also short of funds at that time. We therefore worked with our own forces. With great labour we piled one layer of bricks upon another, until the structure was completed. Were it not for the incident which revealed our activities to the townspeople, we would have continued until we attained to the realization of our ambitions, the emigration of religious pioneer girls from Kozienice to Israel.

I wrote a play entitled The War Between Sisera and Deborah the Prophetess. I did not know at the time that I, too, was prophesying the future, for several years later the Kozienicer Rebbe purchased Harosheth–ha–goyim, now Kfar Hasidim, for purposes of settlement. I wrote out the parts and read them to my friends, who became quite enthusiastic. We collected some money, which barely covered the expenses involved, and prepared energetically to mount the play. It was presented with great splendour, and its success exceeded all expectations. Its praise was the word of the day.

[Page 185]

The Secret Revealed, The Troubles Begin

The secret seeped through the walls of our organization, marking the beginning of our troubles. When word of our activities, which were not to their liking anyhow, reached the parents of the girls, especially the very religious and the assimilationists, they forbade the girls to participate in the organization.

Thus the first structure of its type – of religious Zionist girls in Poland – crumbled, despite the fact that the rav of Gombin, Ha–Rav Avida, who was known for his love of every manifestation of religious Zionism, praised us at one of the congresses.

"Among the women present," he said, "there is a unique representative who has been sent by an organization of religious girls founded by the daughter of the Kozienicer Rebbe. A revolution has broken out among the pure women of Israel, and the girl who brought this revolution about is called Khave."

"May all the daughters of Israel walk in her path. Let them work together with us in order to educate a generation faithful to our people and our land ... Let us help them in this exalted task, let us hold their hands with all our might."

The Candle Goes Out

His voice was that of one crying in the wilderness, for his call did not lead to action. The persecutions on the one hand, the help we failed to get on the other, weakened us and caused our hands to shake.

The candle lit by girls devoted to their people and religion in the great darkness prevailing in Poland went slowly out. The destroyer mounted the wonderful structure erected by me and my enlightened and active friends.

I am sorry for my dear friends Golda and Khaye, and for the rest of the girls destroyed by the terrible cruelty of the enemy.

My heart sickens that you did not attain to live in our liberated homeland, for which you sacrificed the best part of your youth.

Your memory will not leave our hearts forever.

A Zionist Revisionist organization – Brit HaChaial in Kozienice 1933

Left: Three comrades from the revisionist organization. Polish law did not permit them to carry weapons, only sticks.

A group of Zionists say farewell to Leon Szabason upon his departure for "Hachszerai"

Zionists say farewell to Zvi Madanes upon his departure to Palestine 1933

גדוד, בית"ר בקאזניץ.

The Zionist – Revisionist Young members organization called Beitar in
Kozienice going through military training

לזכר נסעת החבר ישעיהו מונאי לצבא סניף "החלוץ" בקאזניץ, שלום ! 1935

Members of HaChalutz say farewell to Veshayahu Munay before his departure
for military service 1935

Left: the first Hebrew teacher in Kozienice 1932. Right: A group of Zionist woman in the early 1930s

A group of the Hachalutz Zionist organication in Kozienice

Left: A group of the Tarbut Zionist organication in Kozienice

Right: A group of Zionist, 1928. All perished in the Nazi concentration camps

[Page 186]

The First Two Khalutzim Make Aliyah

by Elimelekh Feigenbaum, Ramat–Gan

Elimelekch Feigenbaum

In March, 1921, I left Kozienice and went to my brother Moishe–Hersch in Warsaw.

In July, 1922, I found myself in Radom with my father. He told me that Itche Blatman and a young man from Radom named Goldberg were preparing to go to Israel illegally.

We Fantasized About Israel

As is well–known, our family was inclined to Zionism. As early as 1917, at the time of the Austrian occupation, a branch of the Mizrahi organization was formed in Kozienice. Its meeting hall was not far from Magitowa Street.

We young men who were learning in the bes–medresh went over to the Mizrahi hall with our gemoras in our hands; but there was a great distance between being a Zionist in Poland and actually going to Israel. We always talked a lot about Israel, sang Zionist songs, and fantasized about the country, but none of us thought of making aliyah.

We were bourgeois children. We never thought about work – our parents had already thought about it for us. We dreamed of rich matches and a couple of years of free study paid for by our fathers–in–law; of opening a store after a while, like all good Jews.

We had heard that there were pogroms in the Ukraine and that Jews were fleeing to Israel. This we could understand – those Jews had to go to Israel; we, the Jews of Poland, still had time. But all of a sudden, the question was put to me: there is a chance to go to Israel. There is no time to think – you have to decide right now. So we met with Itche Blatman and decided to go. But how was it to be done?

We Go

Goldberg from Radom proposed that we should go to a good acquaintance of his in Bielica and consult with him.

So we went to Bielica. There, we were introduced to a woman who had connections with the police, and who was going to supply us with passes and visas for Czechoslovakia.

[Page 187]

We let ourselves be talked into it. We gave her our pictures and a sum of money, and she promised us that we would receive the passes within a week. After ten days had passed with no sign of passes or visas, we realized that we had been cheated. We no longer had any choice – we would go on and try our luck.

In Szczecin

So we left our money behind and went to Czechoslovakia. The border between Poland and Czechoslovakia was found in Szczecin.

We arrived in Szczecin at evening and went straight to the bes–medresh, where we found 14– and 15 year old boys sitting and learning gemora. They received us cordially, and began to ask us where we were from. We told them we were from Congress Poland, and they asked, "From Russia?" for until 1915, we were in Russia and they were in Austria.

One boy said that his father was also from Russia, and I asked him from where in Russia. "From Grica." His father was a shoykhet, and he told me his name. I told him that I had known his grandfather and that we were related, and he immediately invited me home with him.

How Can It Be?

When I got to his place, I met his father's mother from Grica there. When I told her who I was, she told me that she knew my father, for my sister–in–law, Tzippoire, was a sister of her son–in–law, Yehoshua Werzheizer.

Needless to say, I was well received. I was invited to eat and sleep with them, but when I told them that I was on my way to Israel, the shoykhet became another person. How can it be that Itche Mordekhai Notte's son is going to the Zionists, sinners, the goyim in Israel? I explained to him that I paid no attention to such matters and that my father had agreed to my going, and he calmed down.

The big Feigenbaum Family

My Relative Did Not Want to Help Zionists

Szczecin was divided between Poland and Czechoslovakia. A small river spanned by a bridge flowed through the middle of the town. If one crossed the bridge, one was in Czechoslovakia. All the Jews living in Szczecin had passes and were able to cross the border.

Of course, my relative the shoykhet could have taken me across the border without any trouble, but to my great disappointment he did not want to help me cross it because he did not want to help the Zionists and he did not want me to become a goy at their hands. No matter how much his mother pleaded with him not to talk foolishness and to help me, it did no good. He did, however, promise to put us in touch with a man who would take us across the border for money.

[Page 188]

Crossing the Border

Since we had no choice, we agreed. We remained in Szczecin for a week. Sunday afternoon, Itche Blatman and I went out of the town with a <u>sheigetz</u>, into a small grove where Christians went strolling. The river which served as the border was not far from this grove – its other side was already Czechoslovakia. We wanted to cross it, but how? Among the strollers there were policemen who made sure that nobody crossed the river.

The smuggler told us to walk around with everybody else, and to follow when we saw him go into the water. When it had grown a little dark, we followed him into the water and crossed the border with no trouble.

It was already quite dark when we reached the other side. The smuggler led us into a dark room. On awakening next morning, we saw that we were with a Jewish family. They received us hospitably, taking an interest in our trip.

We stayed with them all day. That evening, we went with the daughter to the train. She bought us tickets, we got on, and we were in Pressburg the next morning.

Levy Feigenbaum z"l

In Pressburg

In Pressburg, we turned to the Mizrahi and the Agudas Yisroel because we had letters to them saying they should help us get to Vienna.

There was a Jew named Greenwald at the Agudas Yisroel who promised to help us, but that it would take a few days.

We stayed in Pressburg for a week. All the Zionists there belonged to the Mizrahi because they were all religious, but not as in Poland: they wore short jackets and had, almost all of them, been Germanized – they had shaved their beards.

We found a yeshiva where bokhurim were learning, all in short coats and Germanized. This was something new for me; clean–shaven yeshiva boys.

After a week, Herr Greenwald from Agudas Yisroel went with us to the police in Pressburg, who sent us out of Czechoslovakia, but to Austria, not Poland, and gave us safe–conducts.

How to get Into Austria?

The safe–conducts would take us to the Czech border and allow us out of that country, but how were we to get into Austria?

We got in touch with a Jew who introduced us to some Christian smugglers who would take us across the border into Austria. We gave the Jew a sum of money to be paid to the smugglers when they brought him a note saying we had crossed the border safely.

[Page 189]

Very early on Friday, all four of us went out of the city and into a forest. We proceeded quietly until we came upon the border guard who was sitting behind a tree and holding a rifle.

The two smugglers took off. The soldier shot, but missed. Blatman and I stayed where we were, and he arrested us, but when we showed him our safe–conducts, he freed us at once and let us go.

We didn't know where to go, so we went back to the soldier and told him that we were on our way to Palestine and wanted to go to Vienna and proceed from there, but that we didn't know the way. We asked him to show us where to go.

The soldier understood and told us to go out of the forest to the Danube. If anyone was to ask us who we were, we were to say that we were out for a walk.

We Go To Vienna

We did as he told us. When we got to the Danube, we saw a mill with two men beside it in the distance. We went up to the men and asked them where the Austrian border was. They laughed at us – we were already in Austrian territory and had nothing more to fear.

We told them our whole story, that we wanted to go to Vienna, and from there to Palestine, but we didn't know the way and we had no Austrian money.

The elder Christian told the younger to take us to the train and buy us tickets to Vienna with his money. He bought us the tickets and warned us not to go into the station but to wait downstairs. We should go up only when we saw the train approaching. He waited with us until it arrived. An hour later we were already in Vienna.

Where Do You Sleep in Vienna?

When we arrived in Vienna, we began to look for Yekhiel Littman from Kozienice, whose address we had. We found him after great effort, and he was delighted to see us, but immediately began to think about a place for us to spend the night. In a big city, you have to show a passport to obtain lodgings, and we had no passports.

This was on Friday. It is worth pointing out that times were hard in Austria then. After World War I there was a great deal of inflation, unemployment, and hunger. There were Polish Jews from Galicia in Vienna, and the swastikaniks so agitated against them that every Jew was afraid to give shelter to an illegal Jew.

Yekhiel ran around looking for a place for us to sleep. Having no other choice, he had to take us into his room.

[Page 190]

I Learn Carpentry

On Sunday we went to the Palestine office and told them that we had come from Poland and wanted to go to Israel. After great trouble and influence we were taken into Bet Ha–khalutzim.

This was an Austrian military barracks in which khalutzim who wanted to go to Israel and were waiting for certificates were housed. We finally had a place to sleep – but what now?

My friend Blatman left for Israel after two weeks. He had been assigned to a family ... I didn't know what to do.

I had already met returning <u>khalutzim</u> in Vienna who told me that things were very hard in Israel. There was no work, and inasmuch as I had no trade, I should stay in Vienna, learn a trade, and then go to Israel. I let myself be persuaded, and stayed in Vienna learning carpentry for almost two years.

I Go To Israel

In May, 1924 I departed for Israel. During the two years in which I was in Vienna, I heard a good deal about what was happening in Israel and how hard the life there was. Many <u>khalutzim</u> who had gone to Israel, many of them suffering from malaria, were returning to Poland by way of Vienna. They cautioned me not to go, because I would not be able to endure the difficult conditions, but I was firmly resolved to go to Israel.

I arrived in Haifa a week before Shavuos. There were men standing in the port, laughing at us and yelling out, "Fresh victims!"

We Plant Tobacco

From Haifa we were sent to Rosh Pina, which has been founded by Rumanian Jews in 1883. There were forty colonists living there, and each one had Arabs working for them. The arabs received ten pounds a year, and used to work ten to twelve hours a day. They went barefoot and lived like animals.

We began planting tobacco in partnership with the colonists. They supplied soil and water, we supplied the labour. We received seven groschen a day, not in cash but in notes from <u>Ha–Masbir</u>. We bought things with these notes, but of course the merchants gave us whatever merchandise they wished to – rotten tomatoes and stale bread.

I spent an entire year in Rosh Pina and was married there.

In May, 1926 we went to Haifa because there was no longer any work for a Jewish worker in Rosh Pina.

[Page 191]

Kozienicers in Haifa

In Haifa, I ran across the first Kozienicer Jews who had come to Israel with Rebbe Yisroel–Eliezer in order to settle the colony which the <u>rebbe</u> wished to found near Haifa under the name of <u>Avodat Yisrael</u> in memory of the Kozienicer Maggid.

As I had no work, and as my parents and brother, Aharon–Berish, had bought plots in the colony, the <u>rebbe</u> suggested that I go with them.

At the River Kishon

We came together one fine afternoon, about twenty Jews from Kozienice. We had rented a truck, and we took some produce and some boards with us.

When we reached the historic river Kishon, we all got out of the truck and the rebbe gave a fiery speech. He compared us with the Jews who came into Israel thousands of years ago under the leadership of Joshua. This day we were crossing the Kishon in order to found a colony of Kozienicer Jews and perpetuate the name of the holy Maggid.

In the distance we saw hills with old, broken–down cabins on them. It was explained that Arabs lived there. At once we began to prepare ourselves for night. First and foremost, we had to think about security, lest we be set upon at night.

One Big Swamp

Rebbe Yisroel–Eliezer was the commandant. He was responsible for security and decreed that each of us must stand watch for two hours. Our first night in the new colony was spent sleeping under the stars.

In the morning we got up and went to work. We had to put up barracks to live in, for in the meantime our families were still in Haifa, and some even in Poland.

We bought a horse and wagon to bring water and foodstuffs.

We started to look around, and saw that the whole terrain around the hills where we found ourselves was one big swamp created from springs of water and the winter rains. The swamps were home to malaria–carrying mosquitoes, and one of our members indeed became ill with it.

We built barracks, and our families came to the new colony. My wife did not wish to stay there, so we went to Haifa.

Difficult Conditions

The conditions in the colony were very hard. There was no money available with which to continue our work. The money brought from Poland had been spent and no new money was coming in.

[Page 192]

They stopped sending money from Poland. The thought was that the Jews who had come to Israel first would prepare the site for those who would come later, but conditions were very difficult. The people were not accustomed to the harsh climate and the work in the fields.

Naturally, this was all sent back to Poland. This made a bad impression there, and the members stopped sending money. And so, thoughts of going to Israel were entirely forgotten.

Many people in the colony were dissatisfied, and several went back to Kozienice.

The Colony Builds Itself Up

But the colony built itself up. The Jewish National Fund came to the rescue: it helped drain the swamps and sent new people.

Kfar Hasidim stands there today. Beautiful houses have been built on all the fields and a big yeshiva and other institutions have been founded.

For all of this, we have to thank the fantasists, the "foolish Zionists" who dreamt of the land of Israel and whom the smart–alecks of Kozienice used to laugh at and ridicule.

Truly, it was at the cost of many sacrifices. I, too, offered up a sacrifice: my eldest son, Levi, was 23 years old when he fell along with thousands of other Jewish boys in the 1948 War of Independence. But all those who did not want to suffer and went back to Poland were, unfortunately, killed by the German murderers.

I have come to the end of my writing, and I hope that I have helped to immortalize our town and all its precious Jews whom the German killers so murderously destroyed.

[Page 193]

The Shul and the Bes–Medresh

by Yissokhor Lederman, Rio de Janeiro

Yissokhor Lederman

In the memorial books published since the Holocaust, the two religious institutions of the shul and bes–medresh have been described and sung with love and respect. These institutions also occupy an honoured place in Yiddish and Hebrew literature.

It seems impossible to commemorate a Kozienice without the shul and the bes–medresh, for they occupied an honoured place in the life of the town.

I consider it my sacred duty to immortalize our bes–medresh as we remember it from the days of our childhood.

Every Jew – merchant and artisan, the poor craftsman and the worker – spent some of his time between minkha and maariv in the shul or bes–medresh. These two holy, religious institutions, located close to each other, were mentioned in the same breath. But what a difference between them.

The Shul was Tall and Made of Brick

The shul was tall and made of brick, with high, wide windows which were built two hundred years ago by the Maggid, and looked like a fortress from the outside.

There was a wide iron door at the entrance, which led to a large, wide, and dark anteroom. To the side of the anteroom was a dark, windowless chamber in which the stretcher for corpses, purification board, and utensils for washing corpses were kept.

Two large iron hooks were stuck on the side of the anteroom near the entrance. Old Jews said that years before a great iron chain in which great sinners were locked up had been welded to the hooks. This threw fear into children and adults alike.

A modern building- three stories- was erected where the synagogue of Kozniece had stood.

Tales and Legends

Many stories were told in Kozienice about demons, spirits, and dead people who davened in the shul at night.

It was said that a Jew named Moishe–Mekhel was going by the shul in the middle of the night when he heard himself called to the Torah. He ran with great fear and trembling to the Rebbe Reb Moishele. The rebbe called the shamas, put the Maggid's cane into the Jew's hand, and said, "Knock on the door with the cane and go straight up to the table on the platform where the Torah is read. Without looking around, make the blessing for the Torah and go out backwards. But remember one thing: Don't let the cane out of your hand, and the shammas is not to go in with you."

[Page 194]

Fear to Pass By the Shul

Fear would prey upon those who had to go past the shul at night. Even those Jews whose houses were near the shul avoided the way by the shul, and used to go either from the side of Rebbe Reb Zelig Loser's or else from the side of the bes–medresh.

On this latter side, stairs led to the women's gallery of the shul in which there were half–moon windows from which the women could look down into the shul, hear the davening, throw nuts and candies at an ofruf, and on Simkhas Toyre throw down flags with red apples for the children. This was an old custom.

Everyone who visited the shul was taken with its beauty and suffused with awe.

The Shul was Famed for its Artistic Style

Before the great fire, the Kozienice shul had a reputation in Poland for the artistic style in which the Maggid had built it.

I recall how the old shul used to look in my childhood. On the eastern wall, in the middle of the ceiling, there were painted pictures representing the moon, stars, constellations, the Western Wall, and various animals. The pictures of these last were accompanied by biblical verses, for instance, under the deer, "Run like a deer, " under the lion, "And mighty as a lion," and the like.

Stairs led to the lovely platform from which the Torah was read. The chair of Elijah the prophet, used by the sandak (the godfather, who holds the baby) at a bris, stood near the table for reading the Torah.

On both sides of the amud and also by the ark were two large brick chests full of sand. They were used for the foreskins from the brisses, as well as for yorzeit and Yom Kippur candles.

Several chandeliers of varying sizes hung on long chains from the ceiling. Iron lamps and candlesticks were riveted to the walls. There were also round brick holes in which tallow and oil lamps were put on Yom Kippur.

The shul was so lit up on Rosh Ha–Shana and Yom Kippur as to throw fear and terror into people.

On Yom Kippur, generals and high Russian officials used to come into the shul for Kol Nidre.

A copper flag was found in the wreckages of the burned synagogue. This flag was on the tope of the synagogue. It said that the date when the synagogue was built and showed the direction of the wind.

Rebbe Yerakhmeil – Moishe Rebuilt the Shul

After the old shul burnt down, only the walls were left. Rebbe Yerakhmiel–Moishele rebuilt it, but without its former beauty, and even without the fear and terror of the tales and legends of the dead who came to daven and seek reparation for their souls in the middle of the night.

[Page 195]

In accordance with Jewish law, the shul had no mezuza on its entrance, and no stove for heat.

The shul was almost closed in the winter, being open only for shabbes and yontef both in the morning and for minkha – mayriv. The crowd was small, only simple Jews who considered it a mitzva to daven in the shul in winter. The khazan and Torah–reader were also simple Jews.

I myself was a Torah–reader for a certain time after my bar–mitzva when I was learning in the bes–medresh.

On shabbes, the rebbe learned in the shuL Of course, we always drank a le–khaim after the davening to warm ourselves up.

There were two siddurim and two makhzoyrim – a metre in length! – for the rebbe and khazan on the Torah–reading platform, as well as a register in which improvements to the shul were inscribed.

In summer, during the counting of the oymer, the shul was open in the morning and for minkha–mayriv.

On Shavuos and the Days of Awe, the shul was full to bursting with local worshippers and hasidim from all over Poland who had come to the Kozienicer Rebbe, Reb Yerakhmiel–Moishe.

The women's gallery was also full. They all came to hear how the rebbe said Akdamas or blew the shofar.

The Soldiers' Shul

Before World War I, the shul also contained a smaller shul for Jewish soldiers serving in the Smolensky regiment which was stationed in our town. They davened there on shabbes and yontef, and celebrated the Pesakh seders and yontef meals. This was supported by the congregational treasury. The soldiers had their own khazahim (cantors), a Torah–reader, and two sefer toyres.

The shul was filled with women and girls for the hakofes on Simkhas Toyre. They went to see how Jewish soldiers made hakofes and sang Yiddish and Hebrew songs. Many of them fell in love with and married Jewish girls, and remained in Kozienice, where they established their families, as for example, the Tabachnik, Zamoiski, and Spiro families.

The Two Shamosim were Absolute Masters

The two shamosim Oyzer and Khaim Frisch were the absolute masters of the shul. Khaim Shammes was a great wag who loved a drop of the stuff. He used to say that he was not afraid of the dead. True, he heard voices when he went to open the door of the shul, and these were certainly the voices of the dead; but before he knocked three times on the door, he took a good, stiff drink and went in spiritedly.

[Page 196]

Thus did the old brick shul, Kozienice's holy of holies set, in its solitude and mysticism, apart from the daily bustle, act and serve as a ray of light in the life of the town.

Weddings were held only in front of the shul.

The Bes–Medresh was a Second Home

The bes–medresh influenced the entire life of a Kozienicer Jew from his birth until the last day of his life. The bes–medresh served every Jew as a second home; it could be said that it was the general committee in which every shade of spiritual and religious life was concentrated.

Everyone had his place in the bes–medresh, whether in the east, not far from the rav, as a fine, rich Jew; on or near the Torah–reading platform, or else by the western wall near the washstand where people washed their hands.

The bes–medresh was there for old and poor Jews, locals and visitors to warm themselves by the hot stove on cold winter days. Whoever had a cold house and a broken oven, whomever the poor life had chased from his house, went to the bes–medresh.

Zalman–Borukh Gives the News

Between minkha and mayriv, Jews from all classes used to meet in the bes–medresh to hear the world news from old Zalman–Borukh who read Ha-Tzfira and knew every minister or enemy of the Jews by name. He used to tell wonderful tales of far–off America, where they ate khalla during the week, and explain his hypothesis that the ten lost tribes had once lived there and that the river Sambatyan was certainly, located there.

People would listen and groan. A dear land, but what was the outlook for yidishkayt there?

Even Yoysef the judge would lend an ear and listen to all the news, and then brush it off. "A goyish land, America. Even the stones there are treyf."

Elderly Jewish householders used to come to the bes–medresh to read a page of gemore or a chapter of mishna.

All year round, Jews would drop into the bes–medresh in the middle of the day to say a chapter of Psalms or look into a book of ethics.

On shabbes and yontef, a rabbi would learn khumash and medresh with the simple crowd. As payment, they supplied him with a living, with meat and fish for shabbes and yontef.

A group of young religious scholars with their teacher in the center of Kozienice. Members of Agudat Israel.

[Page 197]

The Students Played the Most Important Role

The young students supported by their fathers–in–law played the most important role in the bes–medresh. Every father – even craftsmen – who but had the opportunity did all he could so that his son might learn with the rav or a good teacher in the bes–medresh.

The boys felt free from all constraints in the bes–medresh. They could come and go as they pleased, learn, or play cards with their friends to pass the time.

In the last years before World War I, the bes–medresh boys began to look at life through the eyes of secular books which they would read under their gemores. More than one scandal took place in which a boy was caught with a secular book. Slaps fell like rain. Nevertheless, the life, the nationalist and revolutionary movements of the Jewish street called the bes–medresh boy to help build and create a new spiritual life, to found libraries, learn a trade, and study in the big cities.

Two Maskilim

Bes–medreshniks were found on every level of political life. The bridge leading them to community life was Itche Krishpel and Simkha–Nossen Kestenberg.

Before World War I, Itche Krishpel had a food shop not far from the bes–medresh; the first library was established in his house. There, with the shutters drawn tight, he learned Yiddish and Hebrew with bes–medresh boys and workers.

Simkha–Nossen Kestenberg had been one of the hasidic youth around the rebbe, and even sang Menukha Ve–Simkha at the shabbes table. He later became one of the most devoted maskilim (enlightened ones) in town.

He rented an apartment back of the town in which bes–medresh boys and girls from religious families used to meet clandestinely. Simkha–Nossen gave them Hebrew lessons, ardently studied the philosophy of Nakhman Krochmal and Jewish history with them, and led discussions of religious and political questions.

Naturally, this made an impression in town, and more than one scandal broke out between parents and children.

Simkha–Nossen left Kozienice for Drilz, divorced his pious wife, and got married to the daughter of a wealthy man who came from Kozienice.

He founded a volkshule in Drilz, and his wife became a teacher of Polish. Someone from Drilz told me that he and his wife had two well–educated sons who were killed in the Spanish Civil War. Simkha–Nossen himself shared the fate of all Jews. In Treblinka.

[Page 198]

The shul and bes–medresh gave us all this. They raised generations of Jews in Torah and wisdom: scholars, rabbis, maskilim, heretics, nationalists, revolutionaries, and plain, ordinary Jews who built in all areas of Jewish life.

An evil storm–wind has torn it all up by the roots.

O for those who are gone and cannot be replaced.

[Page 199]

Orthodox Kozienice

by Shmuel Reisman, New York

The history of Jewish Kozienice cannot emerge without reference to the activities of its Orthodox residents.

I will attempt to devote some few lines to the Orthodox Kozienice of the 1930's insofar as my memory does not lead me astray.

As is known, Kozienice gained a reputation in the hasidic world in the first years after the foundation of hasidism. One of the central pillars of the hasidic world was Rabbi Yisroel Hopstein, a student of Rebbe Ber of Mezritch, who became famous as the Maggid of Kozienice.

Jews from every corner of the world flocked to the town to take shelter in the rebbe's shadow and to ask for his help in times of need and distress.

Hasidic Communities

As in every city in Poland, there were different hasidic communities in Kozienice, each bound to its own rebbe, customs, and manner of prayer.

Hasidic life was organized around shtiblekh where the hasidim used to pray on shabbes and yontef, each community according to its fashion and melodies. Hasidim also went to the shtiblekh to learn Torah together, to listen to conversations and hasidic tales, to sing zmiros until late at night, and to take a morsel at the shaleshides.

On Saturday nights, especially in the winter, they prepared special, traditional food: potatoes with beet borscht and salted fish. At melave malkes they sang, made blessings, and rejoiced communally until the wee hours. The song Ish Hasid Hoyo was especially dear to them.

Similarly, the hasidim would go to the shtibel on the rebbe's yorzeit to rejoice their souls with a drink for the raising up of the rebbe's soul.

Particularly worthy of mention are the Gerer hasidim and their shtibel, which took in a large number of worshippers. It was first in the house of Pinye the builder, next door to the great prodigy, Reb Eliezer Reichappel (Eliezer Menashes), and later in the house of the gov Mlastek on Lublin Street.

Reb Moishe–Leib Dua was the gabbai. Among the worshippers were such acute and learned scholars as Reb Eliezer Reichappel, Shmuel–Moishe Korman, Yoyel Weinberg.

[Page 200]

Porisower Hasidim

The Porisower hasidim must be singled out from the other hasidic communities. Their gabbai was Eliezer Bornstein. They used to come together on shabbes and yontef to pray and study Torah, and, according to their custom, on shabbes morning they would drink coffee together, learn Torah, and speak of hasidic ideas.

Their shtibel was in the courtyard of Reb Naftoli Rubinstein, who was outstanding in his expertise in Torah, gemore, and toysefos. Among the hasidim of Porisow I recall the prodigy Reb Yitzkhakl Pinczover.

A group of students in the religious school Beth Yacov in Kozienice.

Other Hasidic Communities

Aside from these two communities, there were also Kolibel and Piaseczna hasidim in Kozienice, as well as Rebbe Yankele's hasidim.

Even the Kozienicer hasidim were divided into two camps, the hasidim of Rebbe Arele, and those of his younger brother, Rebbe Elimelekh.

There were also societies for studying the mishna before davening. In the house of the rav from Czepelow, they also used to gather on shabbes and yontef – to pray.

On shabbes and yontef there were also minyanim in private houses, at Berel Rochman's, Bezalel Khlivner's, Nossen Flamenbaum's, and Pikolek the butcher, but by far the greater number was absorbed by the shul and bes-medresh.

There is No Forgetting Elul 12 and 13

Can any Kozienicer forget the days of Elul, and especially the twelfth and thirteenth, the yorzeit of the Kozienicer rebbe? Thousands of Jews flocked to the cemetery to pray and beg for deliverance. The Maggid's street was full of Jews in shtreimelakh, their silken capotes flapping in the wind.

Who is able to forget the Days of Awe at the time when Rebbe Arele and Rebbe Elimelekh lived in Kozienice? Or the way to tashlikh on Rosh–Ha–Shana with its singing and dancing, when the rebbe and his intimates walked at the lead of the procession, with almost the whole town behind them?

There were also bes–medresh students who studied day and night, among them authorized teachers such as Khaim–dovid Fruman, Moishe Katz, Herschel Weinberg, Moishe Bornstein (Alter Bornstein's younger brother), and Hillel Mintzberg, the son of the rav.

[Page 201]

A younger group studied with the teacher Reb Bainish. Outstanding among them: Yoysef Gottlieb, Avrum Weinberg, Yoyne Gelberg, Shmuel Schwartzberg, Moishe Wildenberg, Avrum Katz, Mordekhai Korman, and left alive, Shmuel Reisman and Khaim Flamenbaum.

On occasion, Reb Bainish would take his students to the slaughterhouse to teach them when animals were kosher and when treyf.

The Activities of Agudas Yisroel

The vast majority of hasidic Jews belonged to Agudas Yisroel, which conducted extensive political activity. It invited lecturers, took part in elections to the Polish Sejm and the congregational board. Its representative in Kozienice was Moishe Goldzweig. It had been started by Yoyel Weinberg, the chairman, and his deputy, Leibish Reisman.

Michael Lenga and his two sons in 1926

A Girls' School

With their initiative, the Bes Ya'akov girls' school was established, with Leibish Reisman, Yitzkhok Korngold, and Pinkhas Danziger at its head. The school was located in the house of Herschel Berman on Koscielna Street.

A teacher with a diploma from the Bais Ya'akov teachers' seminary in Cracow taught the religious and non–religious girls to read and write Yiddish, Bible, prayer, Jewish history, and modest behaviour.

The school ran cultural activities: plays and field–trips, and from time to time a presentation in the cinema. For these, religious mothers would put on their wigs and holiday clothes, and go to shep nakhes from their daughters. The plays I can recall are: Hannah and her Seven Sons, Judith and Holofernes, the Cantonists, Haman and Ahasuerus.

The religious girls revealed extraordinary artistic talent. Among those who stood out in this respect I recall Khane and Khaye Zuckerman (the granddaughters of Itche Leibishes), Yokheved Gozyczainski, Sarah Popielnik, Rokhel Brandschaft, Gittel Katz, Tzimel Zidenwerm, and others.

The school was on a high level thanks to the devotion of the administration and of the chairman of Agudas Yisroel, Reb Yoyel Weinberg, who neglected his own interests and devoted himself solely to those of the school. With state support lacking, the school based itself on contributions from its organizers, and especially from the Gerer hasidim, and attained a very high level.

The older girls were organized into the Bnos Agudas Yisroel, under the guidance of the teacher from Bais Ya'akov. They participated in all the political activities of the Aguda, established a library, and also sent girls to the vocational school for religious girls in Lodz, among them Mindel Medallion.

[Page 202]

Tze'irei Agudas Yisroel

Male religious youth were attached to Tze'irei Agudas Yisroel, led by Yitzkhok Kestenberg and Herschel Weinberg. They conducted extensive political activities, such as gathering funds for Keren Ha–Yishuv, the distribution of the newspapers Togblatt and the Hebrew Darkenu, as well as the weekly Bais Ya'akov. They sent members to be trained in preparation for their emigration to Israel. Among them I recall Herschel Weinberg, Shmuel Reisman, and Nettel Goldberg (now Natan Gilboa of Tel–Aviv).

Moishe Katz was sent to the Agudas Yisroel teachers' seminary.

Tze'irei Agudas Yisroel ran a small yeshiva of 35 to VG students, with the famous scholar, Reb Yoysef Nashelski, as rosh yeshiva.

Mutual Aid

The care for one's own extended by Tze'irei Agudas Yisroel during the illnesses of Moishe Erlich (son of Nossen the blacksmith) and Moishe Goldberg (Natan Gilboa's brother) is worthy of note. Such aid also expressed itself financially.

In 1941, an epidemic of typhus broke out in Kozienice. The writer of these lines also fell ill with the disease. My parents gave way under the strain, but the members did not tire of helping me. Members both young and old sat at my bedside twenty–four hours a day, looked after me, and helped, me. Worthy of note among those who devoted themselves to saving me were Reb Moishe–Leib Dua, Reb Shmuel–Moishe Korman, and the younger, and older members of Agudas Yisroel. For weeks they did not leave my bedside. With the help of God, and thanks to the devotion of my friends, I recovered, and was fortunate enough to go to Israel and establish a family there.

There were also disagreements among the hasidim, in particular the political dispute between Ger and Porisow. The latter were opposed to the political ideas of Ger. According to the Porisowers, a religious Jew was forbidden to belong to a political party, and Agudas Yisroel was, in the opinion, an obviously political organization.

Reb Moishe–Leib Dua

I should like to take this opportunity to devote a few words to the activities and devotion to others of Reb Moishe–Leib Dua. Even in distant exile in Siberia, I was unable to forget him. He constituted the hospitality committee of Kozienice. Every Friday, the poor of the city visited his house, and he, in his patience, listened long to their cries, worried about arrangements for shabbes and Friday night, and put many of them up in his own house.

[Page 203]

He also specialized in medical help. His signature was famous. He ran around every day, sometimes late into the night, in order to extend aid to the needy. And he did so with no thought of reward.

He was also the town moyel. Eighty percent of the circumcisions in Kozienice were performed by him.

He also served as gabbai of the Khevra–Kaddisha, and tended to each corpse with his own hands in order to fulfil the mitzva of "the loving kindness of truth". Reb Moishe–Leib accompanied the Kozienice Jew from cradle to grave with help and devotion. Even when the Polish government nationalized the tobacco trade and Reb Moishe–Leib's fortunes declined, he did not leave off his holy work. He extended help and advice in silence and in secret.

Jewish life in Kozienice flowed thus in its accustomed channels until the outbreak of the war when the Germans – may their name be wiped out – conquered Poland and destroyed the effervescent life of Jewish Kozienice, which was completely destroyed and wiped off the face of the earth.

We, who have survived, are obliged to remember. As it is written: "Remember what Amalek did unto you."

Let us remember our brothers and sisters, our parents, our elderly and our babes who were slaughtered and burnt for the Sanctification of the Name because of their one sin – they were Jews.

May their memory be blessed.

I Have No Grandfather
(A prose translation)
by Bilha Rochman (the daughter of Moishe Rochman)

On a night in Nissan or Av, I thought who, o who is my grandfather?

I have read legends and stories of Elijah, the greatest of the prophets, who had a long white beard and leaned upon a staff.

Great is my astonishment that I have no grandfather; great my astonishment that I have not seen his face – For my grandfather, uncle, cousin and family are not alive – there, in the death camp of Treblinka, they were killed by the Nazis.

They were deported from Kozienice to slaughter and strangulation, there, in the distant death camp Treblinka. They were shot, strangled, slaughtered, and burnt while still alive, mother and child, the old, the young, women and men, because they were Jews.

And thus thousands of Jews were slaughtered each day, six million of them in all sorts of death camps, among them my uncle, my cousin, my grandfather and grandmother, may their memory be blessed, all of them victims of Hitler, in the days of the dissolution of the Kozienice ghetto.

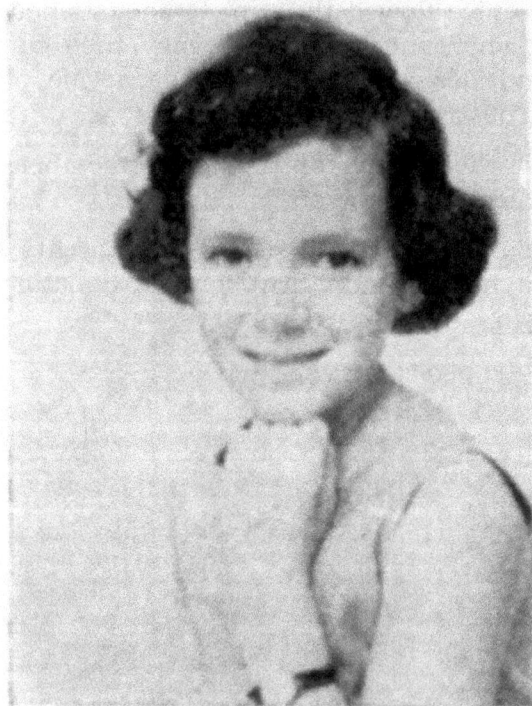

Bilah Rochman

[Page 205]

The Jewish Folkspartei

by Yissokhor Lederman, Rio de Janeiro

After the First World War, the old rebbi'ish and hasidic way of life lost its lustre. The town passed over to a new way of life.

1916 In that year the first culture club, in the name of Y.L. Peretz, was founded in the nicest meeting hall in town, which belonged to the Weinberg Family.

A group of bes–medresh boys and older people had founded a library as early as 1906 in the home of Yitzkhok Krishpel, the town maskil. A sports–club and drama group had also been founded and were directed by Khaim Berman, Tobe Berman, Melekh Avenstern, Yitzkhok Postasznik, Yisroel–Dovid Domb, Mottel Goldstein, Yoyne Weinberg, Shimon Berman, Yissokhor Lederman, Yitzkhok Krishpel (prompter), Yankel Ring, and others.

Every shabbes, there were concerts, discussions and lectures by Yitzkhok Weinberg, Yissokhor Lederman, Yitzkhok Krishpel, and Yankel Ring.

Party–life was developing greatly at the time. Each party naturally wanted to expand its influence, and this led to a fragmentation of the town's cultural forces.

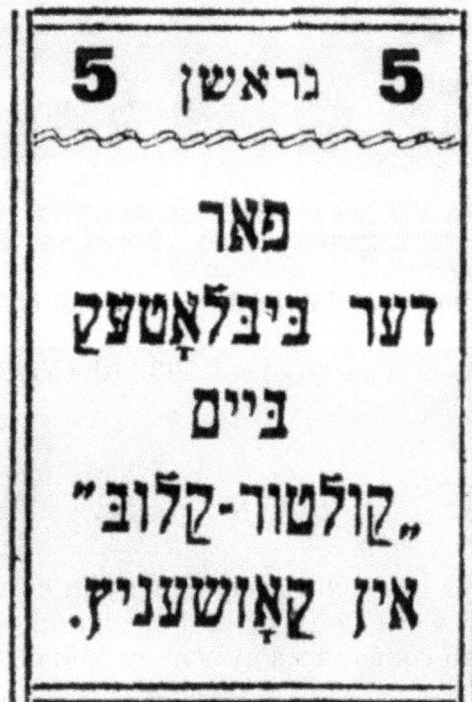

Stamp issued to indicate donation to the Library in the Cultural Club in Kozniece

The Party Was Founded in 1918

In 1918, the greater part of the membership left the club, and founded a cultural society called Di Yidishe Folkspartei (the Jewish People's Party). This took place in the Mintzbergs' meeting hall, in the same building as the residences and offices of the high Russian officials, as well as of the city hall.

The Folkspartei embraced almost the entire middle–class, artisans and merchants, as well as a large segment of the young.

The party conducted intensive cultural and community work. The most eminent of its leaders, writers and poets appeared and lectured, thus lending the town a certain prominence. Even Noah Prilucki came to Kozienice twice before the elections.

The Folkspartei and the artisans put three representatives into the town council, Khaim Berman, Z. Halputter, and Yitzkhok–Eli Korman. Their representatives on the Jewish council were Khaim Berman, Yissokhor Lederman, Leizer–Itche Silverberg, Moishe Wasserman, and Itche Kestenberg.

Left: A group of members of the "Folks Party" (the Yiddish caption appears to list names)
Right: A group of Folkists at a party – Year 1930 (the Yiddish caption appears to list names)

[Page 206]

All the representatives evinced a lively activity in every field of Jewish life: they gave help with their word, counsel, and deed, and sent representatives to all the Folkist and artisan conferences in Warsaw and elsewhere.

At that time we also formed a relief committee for the pogrom victims in Russia under the management of the Folkspartei.

Until my departure from Poland in 1928, the Yidishe Folkspartei was the representative and defender of the entire middle class.

Dr. Kruk visiting the cultural club in Kozienice

The activists of the Jewish "Folks Party" in Kozienice in 1922 – with Lacki Bertoldi

[Page 207]

The Trade Union Movement in Kozienice

by Yerakhmiel Sirota, Paris

There were no trade unions in Kozienice before World War I. There were also no large factories. The majority of workers worked for their parents.

Those who lacked the ability to employ their children looked for work in the larger cities. Many could not do so because of family matters or material considerations, and they were obliged to adjust to any condition–

Wages were very low then. After a week's work a number of workers were forced to go from house to house on Friday afternoon to make a couple of groschen. This was not a rare event.

The family of Yankel Birmbaum

Sixteen and Seventeen Hour Days

The work–day was sixteen or seventeen hours, and before yontef people would work all night. Hence, the exploitation was complete: there was never any talk of a strike.

The majority of the town's skilled workers consisted of shoemakers, tailors, carpenters, blacksmiths, stitchers of linen, shinglemakers, capmakers, and watchmakers – everything a city needs for its use.

The Stitchers Embroiderers Worked for Pennies

The stitching was concentrated in small workshops. This trade employed women, girls, and children of eight to ten years.

The bosses made a living. The work was brought from Warsaw and other cities for pennies. No machines were necessary; everything was hand–stitched.

There was a further advantage for the boss: he did not have to have all the workers in the workshop. Many of them worked at home due to lack of space in the shop. At home, the workers had no fixed hours, and one got the impression that the work went on twenty–four hours a day.

Yankel Birnbaum Opens a Shoe Factory

A little later, Yankel Birnbaum opened our first mechanized shoe factory. It employed twenty workers, and marked the beginning of the proletariat in Kozienice. The wages were dictated by the boss.

The entire production was directed to the Russian market, which gladly bought Kozienicer shoes.

[Page 208]

Once, Yankel hit the road before yontef with a lot of merchandise. Just then, conditions were good: there was a great demand for shoes, the designs were very nice, and the work was good, so the merchandise was sold quickly and Yankel took a lot of orders.

Things didn't always go so quickly. There were times when Yankel would be on the road for a couple of weeks. This time, he sold his merchandise quickly and brought back good things from Russia.

The Ball and the Strike

On his return, he threw a ball for his workers. There was every sort of good thing at the ball, and the crowd ate it all up with relish. What a shock, then, was visited upon the boss the next day when the workers presented him with a demand for increased salaries, told him that a ball would not satisfy the economic needs of their families, and then shut down work.

The strike didn't last long. The boss was forced to give in to his workers' demands.

This was the first strike in Kozienice before World War I.

With no greater events in the offing, the usual way of life continued until the outbreak of the war in 1914, except for the period of the 1905 rebellion when our town distinguished itself with demonstrations against the despotic Czar.

The Front was Close

Our town suffered greatly in the First World War. On several occasions, the front was close to us, and we were forced to abandon the town, carrying our necessities on our backs.

Many families, having nowhere to lay their heads, wandered through the fields.

Our parents' despair was great. After a few days of suffering and torment, we returned to town, for the Russians had succeeded in stopping the Germans for a while. To our great misfortune, half the houses in town had been burnt down. It was impossible to recognize the place where we had lived.

Everyone settled down somehow. Many left town and went to larger cities like Radom and Warsaw. Others suffered with several families in a single room.

Hunger and Want

After this, we underwent the Austrian occupation, accompanied by a terrible famine. The population did not suffer greatly at the hands of the occupiers; on the contrary, we felt freer, for the Russian Cossacks had caused us terrible suffering. They plundered, and we had to hide our girls.

[Page 209]

Thus, we did not – terribly regret the end of Russian rule. But the hunger was great, shortages and the black market were constant visitors.

There was no work. Everything was disorganized, and a terrible confusion reigned.

Slightly later, the Austrians began to repair the roads which had been damaged by the cannons and trenches. A considerable number of workers was employed in this, and it somewhat alleviated the want in many poor houses.

A New Page

Poland attained independence after the war, thus opening a new page in its history. Political parties and trade unions began to form immediately. In Kozienice, a great deal of activity in this area was established in a short time.

The Jewish shoemakers were under the influence of the Bund, the tailors under that of the Po'alei Tzion. The Polish shoemakers were under the influence of the P.P.S. The Wiedza Robotnicza was directed by the Communists, with Dr. Gruszczinski, the director of the gymnasium and a great friend of the Jews, at its head. They were all thrown into jail a short time later.

The Union Movement Develops

Skilled labour began to develop greatly. Large and small factories began to increase. A new market – Galicia – was added. Circumstances were looking all right.

After the war, people were empowered. The workers began to earn some money, strikes occurred more often, and prices were set by the unions.

The bosses also organized themselves into an artisans' union under the influence of the Folkspartei. Naturally, it sometimes happened that they would fight for several days during a strike.

Thus, the workers gradually became a fighting element.

Regrettably, there were no properly trained cadres at the time, but they remained in permanent contact with the headquarters, and representatives came to lecture from time to time. Workers' journals, pamphlets, and literature began to appear. And so, workers who took the administration of the unions upon themselves began gradually to appear upon the scene.

The Makers of Ornamentally Studded Shoes Go On Strike

First of all, order was introduced – work was to begin and end at fixed times. We proceeded to organize all the trades, for example, the makers of ornamentally studded shoes.

[Page 210]

Several people were employed in this trade, and it was not easy to call the first strike. They hung together: it did not last long, and we won. Then the workers understood that the union was a necessity and needed to be protected as if it were an eye, for it was their livelihood.

The Linen–Stitchers Strike

Next came the linen–stitchers' turn. They were not so hard to organize because they were just young girls. We organized them well.

Our first impression was that we were in a grade school. The first strike was not easy because the work was divided haphazardly. Until then, there had been no fixed wages, but we gradually shaped the girls into an exemplary trade.

We Organize the Porters

The moment when we called upon the porters to demonstrate unity and solidarity is characteristic. This was the first time, for up until then they had been ruled by fear, in both their work and their relations with their bosses.

They had never been paid according to the value of their work. In the greatest frosts and snows when it was impossible to make out a human face, they froze, waiting in the street, beard and mustache hung with ice, in case someone should call them. Many days could go by without their earning a groschen.

At the first meeting, we explained what was going on in simple language. The porters were very comfortable with me, because my father was a porter, too.

All the householders respected my father. They called him Colonel Moishe-Eli, but why, I don't know. I gave them to understand that if they were united, the bosses would have less chutzpah and their earnings would increase.

They understood that we wanted their good, and they all agreed that Moishe's son was indeed right. A three–man committee was selected at once.

The next day at a meeting of the elected committee with us, we worked out a schedule of fees: so much for a sack of flour, so much for a crate. Their work was off to a good start.

Some time later, I succeeded in organizing them into a partnership. My father was elected treasurer. They raised their fees so that their living conditions improved significantly. The bosses' treatment of them changed as well.

In this way we raised the morale of the porters.

[Page 211]

The Tailors Were Well Organized

The tailors' section was not large, but it was well organized. If an employer needed a worker, he had to go to the union; if he wanted to fire one, he had also to go.

A special commission to deal with all social conflicts was created in each section. The administration of all the sections was burdened with work. Thanks to their activity and devotion, their work became exemplary.

It is natural that the political parties were watchful that the work of the unions bear a class–conscious character, and moreover, they gradually began to recruit members, each for his own party.

Political discussion began to develop in the unions, the clubs, and the street, often in a very heated atmosphere. One tried to convince the other that his idea was more beautiful, better, and better adapted to the requirements of human life. It was simply a pleasure to observe the struggle among the parties.

The 1920 War

This lasted until 1920 and the outbreak of the Russo–Polish war, which brought great disorder to the work.

A number of active members were called up by the military. The Polish government didn't fail to show its stinking antisemetic face – many Jewish soldiers were confined in the concentration camp at Jablona under the pretext of giving military secrets to the Bolsheviks.

But the war did not last long. After the Polish defeat at Kiev, after the Bolsheviks chased them as far as Warsaw and Lublin, the Polish government was forced to make peace.

After the war, normal life gradually began to be established. All the military personnel were demobilized and they went back to their community work.

Many Threw Themselves Into Shoemaking

It can be said that the work of the various organizations bloomed and began to bear fruit. Economic circumstances were good. Shoe factories began to grow like mushrooms after a rain. Everyone threw himself into this trade. Even the hasidim began to open shoe factories.

Everyone in town wanted to be a specialty shoemaker, but the trade commission resolved not to let just anybody learn the trade and thus create a surplus of labour. One didn't need any great qualifications to become a specialty shoemaker: four weeks was enough to learn the trade perfectly.

[Page 212]

We Struggle for Influence

In 1921, a new page was opened in the history of the world workers' movement with the establishment of the Comintern. All the workers' parties suffered splits which created the secret Communist party, the vast majority of which consisted of the better element of the Kozienice working class.

A violent struggle for control of the unions began all over again. It was not easy.

We had a difficult struggle for endurance because of the police, who persecuted us at every turn. Yet despite all the difficulties, we gradually began to win the sympathy of many workers.

The town intelligentsia also began to join our ranks. We can say with pride that we had the nicest cadre in our town. It wasn't long before we controlled the work in the unions.

Our work in the political sector went on with the same momentum. Nothing was neglected. The struggle against Polish fascism and antisemitism occupied first place for us. We were not scared off by any sacrifices.

Our activities continued thus until Hitler's march into Poland. The work of all the parties, unions, artisans* clubs, youth organizations, drama groups, and libraries which was established with so much self–sacrificing devotion came to a halt.

Eternal glory to the fighters and martyrs of Kozienice.

We Continue Our Work

After eating, if it was nice out, you used to sit yourself down by the door and have a chat with your neighbour. We didn't have much pleasure, because we were all suffering for the sake of a piece of bread.

The town's surroundings were glorious. Thick woods, fields, several rivers and lakes. Summer was very pleasant. Boys and girls went out walking and sang songs. All in secret – their parents shouldn't know.

Many of us still remember the Beilis trial well. We lived in daily terror of pogroms. The Czarist government had a good chance to stir up antisemitism, and the Poles exploited it well. Jews were afraid to show themselves in the street; people yelled "Beilis"** after them.

Fights broke out between Jewish and Polish children. The Polish nobility and wealthy classes exploited this for their own ends.

[Page 213]

A Newspaper A Rare Event

In those days a newspaper was a rare event in town. There was nowhere to get any news, except from a purveyor who had gone to Warsaw for a little merchandise and came back with a little news. A Yiddish book could not be found.

A little later, before World War I, Yiddish books began to turn up secretly. Nasheleki was the pioneer. He recruited his readers, few and clandestine, from the bes–medresh boys. If any of the religious Jews had found out that Itche was leading the youth astray, he would have been placed under the ban.

There were the first sprouts, the first rays of light to begin shining upon our town.

A Lack of Cadres

After World War I, Poland became independent, with a provisional left–wing government, and people began to breathe a little more freely. Political parties, trade unions, and cultural organizations began to form immediately. Of course, cadres were lacking.

This made a particular impact on the ranks of the workers. The bourgeois parties did have some intelligence, but they did not understand that something must be given to those who had nothing. They felt like bourgeois aristocrats.

At the age of 16, I joined the Po'alei Tzion. I threw myself into its work with the fervour and energy of youth. Soon a workers' youth organization had been formed. After this, all the other parties imitated this example.

I was elected to the cultural commission. This was a great honour for me. My work was not easy; I had to distribute newspapers, books, and pamphlets which we received from headquarters. Regrettably, many workers and artisans, and the greater part of the youth were unable to read and write: This did not, however, scare us off. We organized evening courses in Yiddish and

Polish, and before long had attained good results. This gave us courage, and we continued our work more fervently.

In a short time, our town became unrecognizable. All the parties were active, each in its own realm. Lectures, readings, and "box–evenings" were arranged. Gradually, a class–conscious and mature working class started to crystallize.

There was also a gymnasium (Hi School) in Kozienice. Naturally, it was attended only by the children of well–to–do parents. Later, when the illegal Communist party had been formed, we had a great many sympathizers among these students. They were very active, especially in the field of culture. We formed a splendid library and a drama group, and put on a presentation with no outside help.

[Page 214]

At the same time, we went to organize workers in the neighbouring towns. There was a wide field for political activity. We also conducted a strong propaganda campaign on the street in order to combat antisemitism and fascism. At the time, the Polish jails were overflowing with political prisoners.

The May Day Demonstration in 1926

On May 1, 1926, we organized a united demonstration of all the workers' parties, Jewish and Polish alike. The demonstration was very impressive; in fact, Kozienice had never seen a May Day demonstration before. The local authorities mobilized the police from the whole vicinity. Representatives of all the parties gave speeches, and the demonstration broke up peacefully, each party with its flag. We carried the union flag.

Next day, the searches and arrests began. Twenty–six comrades were transported to the prison in Radom. This brought about my departure from Poland.

Despite the persecution, the work did not stop. Those who remained in Kozienice continued it with more courage and obstinacy.

Help From Paris

Coming to Paris, we organized a campaign for the benefit of those arrested in Kozienice. All the landsleit responded warmly, and we sent a considerable bit of money home.

Before the war, we formed a society embracing all the Kozienicers in Paris. In 1936, we organized a large fund–raising campaign for the sake of the needy in our hometown. All the Kozienicers in Paris took part in the campaign. We thus demonstrated our solidarity with our families who were a couple of thousand kilometres away.

Soon after the great catastrophe which befell our people, we the surviving Kozienicers, organized a committee for the benefit of our landsleit.

We raised money and brought it to needy houses. With love and devotion we gave support to all those passing through who stood in need thereof.

We have continued our work up until today. This is the greatest tribute we can pay to our parents, brothers, and sisters who were killed by the Nazi barbarians.

To their glorious memory.

[Page 215]

The Trade Union in Kozienice

by Yissokhor Lederman, Rio de Janeiro

The truth is that I am neither close to the union nor terribly familiar with its activities. Nevertheless, I cannot complete my work without mentioning the activities of the union, which conducted a self–sacrificing struggle for a better and more beautiful future.

When was the trade union formed in Kozienice?

It took place soon after the First World War, when Poland had become independent and the shoe factories and other workshops which had been shut down during the war began to organize themselves.

Jewish party–life revived. There was a need at this time for a workers' body which would stand guard over the workers' lives and protect their rights in every area.

True, the Bund, which had set the protection of the Jewish worker as its goal, was already in existence at this time, but the new winds of freedom from the Soviet Union helped to organize and strengthen the ranks of the so–called "Left Workers' Union", which represented a stratum of the town's labour movement.

The Union's Leaders

At the head of the union stood workers and intellectuals: Rosen, Brandspiegel, Sirota, Tennenbaum, Greenstein, Zucker, Shabsi Korman, Zeitfinger, and Rechthand.

The last three were girls who defended the rights of the seamstresses and stitchers. They conducted an intensive activity, and together with Polish workers organized strikes in order to raise wages, and also fought for an eight-hour day in the factories, where the workers were still labouring twelve hours a day.

At that time, this was a great achievement for the workers in Kozienice.

Together with the Polish workers, they conducted a fight during the elections to the Sejm and the city council. They carried on fine cultural work, were interested in Yiddish literature, and organized night courses in Polish and Yiddish for poor workers* children. They also had their dramatic group.

The Authorities Shut the Union Down

Regrettably, their activity did not last long. The reactionary Polish government cast an eye on the union, began to persecute its leaders, confined them to prison, and finally shut the union down and tortured its leaders.

[Page 216]

If I am not mistaken, young Rechthand died in the Radom jail. Some came out of prison with broken fingers, others with tuberculosis. Still others fled the country.

All these troubles and misfortunes were caused by a Polish provocateur who was shot in 1927 by comrades from the Warsaw Central Committee with the assistance of Greenstein, who fled to Russia during the night.

This is how the Kozienicer trade union was liquidated at that time. It wrote a beautiful chapter in the book of our town's workers' movement.

Later, I went to Brazil. Whether a union still existed after that is not known to me.

[Page 217]

The Story of a Red Flag

by Yissokhor Lederman, Rio de Janeiro

The story I'm going to tell here took place in 1901. I was then studying with Berele melamed, a gemore teacher, a very angry man, a kohen. He enjoyed thrashing the children on their naked bodies or on their heads. – it was a miracle that they weren't crippled. But this is not what I intend to tell.

Coming home from kheder on a certain evening, I met two strange men in our house, along with two Kozienicers whom I knew well. One of them was a shoemaker named Shayele Katter, who worked for my father as an apprentice.

Shayele Katter was the only son of Aharon melamed, a Gerer hasid. His mother, Reizel, sold cooked lima beans in winter and fresh water in summer.

The second Kozienicer was a baker named Ickowicz, a son of Yidel the bastard.

What Were they Doing at Our Place?

My sister, Khantshe, was a seamstress and a good stitcher. The men had brought her a red canvas with a big piece of paper on which was written in Yiddish and Polish, "Workers of the world, unite!" and "Long live the first of May!" They promised my sister three rubles if she embroidered these inscriptions in gold on the canvas.

Naturally, neither my father nor my mother understood the danger threatening their daughter, nor did they comprehend the significance of the words.

My sister sat at the work all night. Incidentally, it came out very well.

For her part, my sister was satisfied, too. She had earned three rubles for a night's work.

Turmoil in Town

Three days later the town was in turmoil. A group of Jewish and gentile strikers had come from Radom. Marching with them were groups of shoemakers, tailors, and other workers, with Shayele Katter and Ickowicz in front. They were carrying red flags with inscriptions, and went straight to the bes–medresh to hold speeches.

The streets were lively. Jews ran home, closed their shops. Women wrung their hands – a calamity for the town, the Cossacks would soon come and destroy the bes–medresh, and make a pogrom on the Jews.

[Page 218]

We kheder–boys ran after the strikers into the bes–medresh. Our mothers looked around for us and chased us home.

Although I was but a boy of eleven, I went into the bes–medresh. The strikers had stood their flags up opposite the ark, and were singing Yiddish and Polish songs.

I didn't understand the speeches but the strikers would often shout out, "Down!" and "Viva!", and I shouted along. A man with white–grey hair – I don't remember if he was a Jew or a Pole – yelled out, "Down with the Kaiser! Down with the pogromchicks!" and shot into the air.

There was a bit of a stir. The crowd began to march out of the bes–medresh, singing, and shouting "Down!"

With the flags in front, they marched through all the streets, until they reached the bridge.

The Police Mix In

After Lublin Street there were already soldiers and police. The mayor, Kozlow, asked that the demonstration disperse; if not, he would shoot.

Naturally, there was a commotion in the crowd. They did not wish to resist even though some of the Radomer group were armed. Due to the great number of women and children following them, they avoided bloodshed, and the crowd went singing back to town.

The same night, Shayele Katter, Ickowicz, and several Polish workers, were taken from their beds and sent straight off to Radom in shackles.

Afraid lest someone inform on her, my sister Khantshe went to my uncle Shmuel in Warsaw. She stayed there working until her marriage to Moishe Wasserman.

The end of the two Jews: in 1905 they were hung in the Warsaw prison along with other fighters.

[Page 219]

The Labour Movement in Kozienice

by Avrum Tennenbaum, Warsaw

My reminiscences will embrace almost exclusively the years from 1923 to 1929, as well as certain isolated incidents from my childhood.

The time I wish to describe was one of very far–reaching political-communal and cultural activity on the part of the progressive Jewish population of Kozienice. It was also the time of my own community activity.

If the years from 1918 to 1922 can be characterized as a time of establishment of political–communal groups and party organizations in Kozienice, the years from 1922 on can be considered as a time when all the Jewish workers of Kozienice were organized into the political organizations then in existence.

A significant portion of the workers belonged to the Communist party and its youth organization. The Bund was also popular among Jewish workers, and the Left Po'alei–Tzion had its adherents, too. There were also workers who belonged to the Zionist organization.

All workers, without exception, were organized into unions. The tailors' and stitchers' union was exclusively Jewish. On the other hand, the leather–workers' union numbered around four hundred Jewish and Polish workers, and was a strongly class–conscious organization, a strong support for the political work of the Communists, the Bund, and the P.P.S. This union was the chief organizing force of a large number of economic and political actions.

The First May Day Demonstration

The memory of Kozienice's first May Day demonstration in 1926 is engraved deeply in the memory of all surviving Kozienicers. Over a thousand workers with their wives and children demonstrated in the streets under red flags, and ended the demonstration with a great meeting, at which Jonas Weinberg, Rembalski and Yerakhmiel Sirota spoke.

The demonstration was the greatest political event in the town's history.

Among the prominent figures in the leather–workers' union were Meir–Shalom Tennenbaum, Yoysef Flamenbaum, or Yoysef Senate, as he was called, Waszita, Rembalski, Itche Weizberg, and others.

The stitchers of Kozienice, who numbered over 150 persons, also carried on a wide–ranging community activity. The Communist party had a great influence upon them.

[Page 220]

The Youth Was Very Active

The working–class youth of Kozienice was very active in political–community life. It can be stated that at certain times the role of the youth was decisive. It was very active everywhere. It is no exaggeration to say that a youth so ebullient, so full of life and a deep belief in a happy future as the youth of Kozienice was, was seldom found anywhere.

The bright figures of the Kozienice Jewish youth of my time would require a separate and comprehensive description. The youth – a separate, heroic chapter in the history of the Jews of Kozienice.

The political–communal life of the Jews of Kozienice had a reputation extending far beyond the town itself. We recall how many active leaders from the central authorities in Warsaw gladly used to spend days and weeks in the summertime among the people and woods of Kozienice.

The activities of Shloime Brandspiegel were also well known. Together with the great humanist Stephania Gruszczinska, they represented the interests of the workers – in the name of the Left Workers' Movement – on the Kozienice city council.

What, though really states the fact that the Jews of Kozienice were heavily engaged in community life?

Kozienice Lived From Work

First of all, the vast majority of the Jewish population of Kozienice was comprised of workers. Two–thirds of the Jewish population lived from salaried labour and labour in general, and with the arrival of summer, almost the entire population, young and old, was enlisted to make canvas slippers.

Despite the legal requirement of an eight hour day, the workers laboured ten and twelve hours, the bosses eighteen and twenty.

In winter, many people worked hard in the leather industry, but for significantly small wages.

Just how popular the summer season was can be seen from the fact that only shoemakers and those in related trades were said to be able to indulge themselves with fancy baked goods.

Another group of shoemakers, the so–called shpilkove, or makers of ornamentally studded shoes, occupied themselves with the production of shoes and boots for the fairs. Linen production was almost exclusively designed for export to Galicia.

There were proportionally fewer retailers in Kozienice then in other towns at the time.

[Page 221]

A New Age

This is the soil from which a wide–ranging, radical community movement grew, but external factors were also of no small significance.

I know that the reverberations of the victorious October Revolution reached the progressive Jewish population of Kozienice quickly. The workers felt and understood by instinct that a new age had dawned, and that no power would prop up outmoded social forms.

As is known, Jews the world over placed great hope in the October Revolution, which, among other things, set itself the task of up–rooting every form of racism and making an end of wild antisemitism.

We believed that the victorious October Revolution meant that dreadful antisemitc persecutions and pogroms had become a thing of the unhappy past, and that Jews would now be able to live on an equal footing with everyone else.

These new ideas had an even stronger influence on Jewish youth.

[Page 222]

The Communist Party in Kozienice

by Yerakhmiel Sirota, Paris

Among the other parties in Kozienice, a many–branched Communist party was also active. It embraced extensive circles of the youth, had a beautiful library, and a drama group which played in the neighbouring towns.

The party had five founders: Yoysef–Hersch Rosen, Avrum Kestenberg, Moishe Shapiro, Yoysef Flamenbaum, and Yerakhmiel Sirota.

It is worth mentioning that all the comrades who struggled self–sacrificingly for a free tomorrow and a beautiful future for all mankind were killed in the gas–chambers and crematoria, like all the Jews of Poland.

I will list several of them: Yoysef–Hersch Rosen, Yoysef Flamenbaum, Shmuel Huberman, Moishe Shapiro, Yissokhor Shapiro, Shmuel Weinberg, Itche Wizberg, Meir–Shalom Tennenbaum, Shmuel–Leib Goldman, Benzya Greenstein, Khane Orentstern, Leibel Rechthand, Yekhiel Silverberg, Ratze Silverberg, Pesya Krishpel, Beile Friedman, Feige Wizberg, Khane Rechthand, Pearl–Dina Potasznik, Avrum Kestenberg, as well as the youth which performed splendid work in the Movement until the Hitlerite murderers entered the town, and, along with the five thousand Jews of Kozienice, also killed the glorious figures of the Communist party.

We honour the memory of the unfortunate victims.

We, the survivors, are duty–bound not to forget them.

[Page 223]

The Bund in Kozienice

by Yissokhor Lederman, Rio de Janeiro

At the same time as the formation of the Folkspartei, the Jewish workers' party, the Bund, was also formed. Its leaders were Yoyne Weinberg, Dr. Schwartzbaum, Leibel Zaterman, Yoyel Weintraub, Kissel Roiseman, Binyamin Frish, Ya–akov Korman, Nossen Flamenbaum, and others.

They conducted an intensive activity among the poorer classes, such as small home–manufacturers and workers, organized strikes among the leather–workers when such were necessary, and took part in all May Day demonstrations and other actions with the Polish workers.

The "Zvkunft" a branch of the "Bund" for younger members – together with their leaders

A Wide–Ranging Activity

They also conducted fine cultural activities: they founded their own library, a school, a relief fund, and a sports section for the youth.

The central committee in Warsaw sometimes sent lecturers and propagandists to help develop the Bund's work.

They were at their most active during the elections to the Sejm, or city council, and kehilla. Although they were not a large group, they nevertheless got their representatives onto the city council and the kehilla: Yoyne Weinberg, Dr. Schwarzbaum, Yoyel Weintraub, and Leibel Zaterman.

In later years, younger forces distinguished themselves; Pola Luxenburg, the Weinberg brothers, and others whose names are not known to me.

In general, we must admit that the Kozienice Bund had a dynamic youth in its ranks, as well as older members, who energetically carried on its professional, political, community, and cultural work.

The founder of the Bund, Yoyne Weinberg, died of a heart attack when the Nazis occupied Poland. The other leaders and members shared the fate of the entire Jewish community of Kozienice.

[Page 224]

Left: A group of Bundist activists in Kozienice
Right: A group of Bundists say farewell to Ezra Arbeitman
(sitting-center) upon his departure to Paris – Year 1932

The Bund in Kozienice

by Leibele Fishstein, Ramat–Gan

In 1922, the economic life of Kozienice revived. There was not a single house in which a small canvas–shoe factory was not operating. The entire production was directed to Russia.

Such shops were opened not only by shoemakers, but wood–dealers, khazanim, and merchants took up this line of work. Whoever had enough money for a set of iron lasts and a little canvas became a manufacturer, hired workers, and made shoes from cardboard, canvas, and leather.

The manufacturers contracted their workers for an entire year, in order to make sure they would not go work for someone else.

Medem branch of the Bund in Kozienice

Activists of the Bund in nearby town Radom visiting their comrades in Kozienice – The leader Jonas Weinberg – Center

District committee of the Bund in Kozniece in 1931
Row 1, R. To L.: Yonah Vineberg, a leader from Radom, Sarah Arbeitman, Kisel
Roizman

Bottom Left: A group of Bund members in Kozniece in 1932.
Seated R. To l.: Avraham Kahn, Moshe Kahn, Pola Luxemburg, and Bunim Proveizer.
Standing: Haim Rakhman, Miriam Veisbord, Yankel Salzberg and Overshtern.

Bottom Right: Bund activists in Kozniece are on an outing to the village of Kuzmir.
Lying r. To l. Peretz Gelberg, Haim Rakhman
Row 1: Avraham Kahn, a Kuzmirer, Noah Safran (from Warsaw), a Kuzmirer, Pessach
Arbeitman, Leibush Zaterman
Row 2: Moshe Rubenstein, Yankel Salzberg, Ezra Arbeitman, Moshe Kahn, a Kuzmirer

Right: Shimon, son of Yunes and Rachel Vineberg
Left: House of Yunes Vineberg, leader of the Bund in Kozniece

Bund activists are saying good-bye to their colleague Peretz Gelberg prior to his making Aliyah.
Seated: Sarah Arbeitman, Peretz Gelberg, Hannah Gelberg
Standing: Moshe Rubenstein, Malka Mandel, Rachel Vineberg, Overshtern, Pessach Arbeitman

An End to the Long Work Day

The workers did not make bad money, but they worked sixteen hours a day, and all night before yontef.

Among the workers were several leftists who read a left–wing newspaper and who decided to put an end to the long work day.

They met at a secret meeting at which two items were dealt with: setting up a meeting hall for the society, and the institution of an eight–hour work day. The originators of the idea were Binyomin Frisch, Aharon Sherman, Yerakhmiel Sirota, Shalom Tennenbaum, Loser Lampa, and Kissel Roiseman.

In a short time, a sufficient sum of money had been collected, and a large hall was rented in Mintzberg's house. Yoyne Weinberg, a student, was engaged as secretary, and the society was opened.

At the first general meeting of all the workers, two new faces were noticed. They were emissaries from Warsaw, the one a Bundist, and the other a Communist.

The Bundist speaker clarified the importance of the eight–hour day, for which the Bund was fighting. Here, too, it was important to establish the party which fought to improve the condition of the workers as well as for national and cultural autonomy.

After the meeting, about seventy percent of those present registered in the party. Yoyne Weinberg took it upon himself to organize and run the party.

Party activities soon began in the hall. The Reds and Po'alei Tzion were not agreeable to the Bundist hegemony in the labour union, but they remained a minority.

[Page 225]

In a few years, the number of members had increased, and the party rented a whole house from Moishe Medallion.

The party conducted political and cultural work, and formed a youth Bund called Zukunft (Future), with the energetic Paula Luxemburg in command.

Paula Luxemburg

She came from a very religious family, and because of her activity in the Bund had a difficult life at home. But she came into her own. Day and night, body and soul, she was absorbed in the work of the party. Besides being chairman of the youth organization, she was also the leader of "Skif".

Her deputies, Yisroel and Khaim Rochman, were always prepared to sacrifice themselves for the sake of the Bundist ideal. They contributed a lot for the cultural development of the youth.

A New Hall

A very wide–ranging activity began when the Bund moved into the house with the tall chimney. It had a large hall in which lectures used to be held, and where heated discussions developed more than once with members of other parties who had come to oppose the speakers from Warsaw.

Those who came most often were the party leaders Erlich, Victor Alter, Ya'akov Pat, Himmelfarb, Shetmer, and others. When Kozienice saw a poster that a Bundist leader from Warsaw was coming to lecture, half the town went to hear him.

"Box" and recitation–evenings, entertainments, and one–act presenta- tions used to take place in the hall. There were smaller rooms around it: a library, a night school in which Yiddish, mathematics, history, geography, and natural science were taught. The teachers were the popular Yoyel Weintraub and Avrum Kohn.

Aside from this, there were "circles" which studied Bogdanow's political economy, and the philosophy of Spinoza and Kant.

There was also a dramatic circle which staged various plays in the cinema.

The party also had two cooperatives, a shoe factory and a consumers' co-op.

Yoine Weinberg was the Bundist representative on the city council, the leader and organizer of Bundist activity in Kozienice. He was very popular, not only among the workers, but among the entire population. He was a merchant and had a confectionery business.

[Page 226]

Economic Life in Kozienice

by Yissokhor Lederman, Rio De Janeiro

My work is based upon the economic life of Kozienice before World War I. I emphasize that memory is the major source of my work, because there are no documents which I could utilize at my disposal.

My *landsleit,* as well as plain readers of this book will forgive me any inaccuracies.

Maskilim Left the Town

Regrettably, our town is seldom mentioned in the history of the Jews in Poland. The reason could be that hasidic life had too strong a hold on the town, and the worldly segment of the Jewish population generated no great cultural forces.

Those who began to think differently had to leave the town. Among such were Khaim–Yekhiel Bornstein, to whom Nahum Sokolow pays great tribute in his memoirs, Simkha–Nossen Kestenberg, the Greenberg brothers who were teachers in the Warsaw region, the <u>maskil</u> Reuven Lichtenstein, Weinberg, the Yiddish teacher, and still others whom the life of the town drove away.

Although Kozienice had a Russian school, it never happened that a Jewish child attended it. As Pinye Katz tells in his memoirs, the rich Jewish families engaged private tutors for their children. The Jewish artisans taught their children neither general subjects nor foreign languages; the <u>kheder</u> and <u>bes-medresh</u> were their educational institutions.

Outside cultural forces who visited Kozienice from time to time have left notes on the life there. We have drawn some information from these sources.

In Yiddish and Hebrew literature our town was noted by Nakhum Sokolow, Khaim–Yekhiel Bornstein, Pinye Katz, Yitzkhok Shipper, Sh. Stupnicki, Lazar Kahan, Leo Finkelstein, Ya'akov Pat, A. Litvak, D. Reisen, and others as a town distinguished for two traits: hasidism and shoemaking.

Hasidim A Means of Livelihood

And it's no exaggeration. Fifty to sixty percent of the Jews in Kozienice made their living from these two sources. Three or four times a year thousands of Jews, hasidim and simple folk alike, visited the Maggid's tomb in Kozienice. On Shavuos, the Days of Awe and <u>shabbasim</u>, the Jewish inns were filled with hasidim from all Poland. Hundreds of Jewish families lived off the town's three rebbi'ish courts.

[Page 227]

Shoemaking

The second source of livelihood was shoemaking. This trade lay exclusively in Jewish hands, although there were also some gentile shoemakers who sold their wares at fairs and markets.

It is worth noting that neither the bosses nor the workers were organized, but shoemaking was yet a source of livelihood for hundreds of Jewish and non–Jewish families.

Shoemaking was divided into three categories: larger factories, which called themselves specialty shoemakers, in which hundreds of workers were employed: beaters, shiners, <u>rakhtevers</u>, upper–makers, button–sewers, box-makers, packers, buyers, and clerks.

Aside from these there were also merchants who supplied leather, boards, linen, tacks, laces, buttons, heels, and other materials for the factories.

Merchants came from Radom to sell leather, for Radom was famed for its tanneries. They sold the leather on their own and the customers' notes.

The second category was the workshops for ornamentally studded shoes, in which childrens' shoes and boots were made. Five to six workers were employed in the shops. Each workshop had its own upper maker who made boo tings for it.

The third category consisted of home–manufacturers. They worked along with their children, and sold their merchandise in the town itself and at fairs in the neighbouring towns. They didn't make much money. They always wanted for _shabbes_, but as we Jews say, "Make a living honourably and don't go looking for handouts".

It is worth recording that as soon as a Jewish worker got married, he started looking for a way to become his own boss rather than somebody else's employee.

Kozienicer shoes and boots were renowned throughout most of Russia. The manufacturers would take their merchandise to the farthest–flung spots in Russia two or three times a year, and come home with big orders. They also went to the yearly fairs in Lenczne, Lublin, Smolensk, and Nizhni–Novogrod.

Other Means of Living

Other trades in Kozienice remained in Jewish hands such as the tailors, capmakers, furriers, shingle–makers, soap–makers, pulp–makers, and carpenters. They all lived from the town fair and from fairs in the smaller towns around Kozienice.

Peasants used to come to Kozienice with their agricultural products, and the Jews would buy them up. The peasants would then buy shoes, boots, clothes, salt, candles, matches, and several metres of fabric from the Jews, and drink the rest of their money away in Jewish taverns.

[Page 228]

Although Jews numbered only fifty or sixty percent of the population of Kozienice, they comprised eighty to ninety percent of that town's wood, iron, brick, paint, garment, egg, fowl, fish, orchard, cattle, and horse dealers.

True, the Polish priests and estate–holders formed cooperatives in order to wrest the commerce from Jewish hands, but they were not successful. The peasant and urban worker had no faith in the pans and their clerks, before whom they were obliged to take off their hats and even to bow down.

The peasant felt more comfortable with the Jewish shopkeeper; he could buy more cheaply and was able to haggle. Deals were concluded with a handshake. In winter, he would warm himself by the oven and drink a glass of tea.

Kozienice also had a credit union run by Jews and Christians which supported the Jewish artisans and shopkeepers with low–interest loans. Shalom Mintzberg's son, Yoine, also ran a private bank which discounted checks.

It is important to mention that the Smolensk regiment, which was stationed in Kozienice until World War I, was also an important source of Jewish prosperity.

Nevertheless, the poverty was great. The majority of the common people lived in a section of Lublin Street: water–carriers, porters, messengers, carters, poor artisans, and plain Jews of every type who would go from house to house on Fridays – or even in the middle of the week – to beg for alms or a little bread for their ailing wives and children.

Thus did Jewish life appear before World War I.

[Page 229]

Only Ashes are Left of My Town

by Shmelke Spiegelman

(A prose translation)

Where are my father and mother, my sisters and brothers, and good little Shloimele? Where are you, all our children?

Where are you, good Jews of Kozienice, the beautiful, morally pure youth who worked and hoped for peace? Where are my near one's remains?

By the river bank in the valley, I see the moss–covered stones; many a time I have thought that the bones lie under them –

The bones of my nearest and dearest who were and are no more. I was not at their funeral, did not shed a tear.

Sometime from the mysterious wood, perhaps, from the muted green mountain, perhaps I will hear a voice, perhaps a sign will appear.

Or perhaps from the river in the valley, which noisily falls from the mountain, perhaps sometime it will tell how my town was turned into ashes.

[Page 230]

Jewish Livelihood in Kozienice

by Itche Blatman, Paris

The Jews of Kozienice engaged in all trades but agriculture.

The artisans employed no workers, but laboured by themselves from sun–up to sundown. Nearly all of them lived in one room in which they worked, ate, slept, and kept five or six children. Shoemakers, tailors, capmakers, tinsmiths, carpenters, and shopkeepers lived in such conditions.

There were two classes of merchants – small and smaller. No living could be made from trade because the competition was so great. People killed themselves to get a customer, and yet they married off their children and supported their sons–in–law for a year or two.

They all took their merchandise on credit. After each wedding, the large merchants went broke, while the smaller ones simply didn't pay, because they didn't have the money. After the years of support had run out, the sons–in–law became Hebrew teachers, or else their wives opened small shops, because the husbands knew no Polish.

The Zionist Ladies of Kozniece invite you to a Dance

My Melamdim Lived in One Room

There were many melamdim (Hebrew teachers). No matter how many I studied with, they all lived in one room in which they slept and cooked with fifteen or twenty students and three or four children of their own.

Although the mothers considered it a great mitzva to pay the melamed every week, all my melamdim went hungry. They were full only on shabbes, for their earnings sufficed only for shabbes. It was also a mitzva to eat on shabbes.

They were also butchers, peddlers, orchard keepers (sadovnikes), grain-dealers, and flour–dealers in town who had enough to eat because they dealt with the villagers. But their houses were cold and dark.

The Regiment Leaves Town

In Kozienice there was a regiment, that is, three to four thousand soldiers, from whom people made some money.

The regiment left Kozienice in 1911. The great fair, which had drawn peasants from the entire surrounding area, also fell apart. The whole town groaned; it was now impossible to support oneself. The elderly and religious began to emigrate to Belgium, England, and America, the young to France.

[Page 231]

A New Bunch of Sorrows

With the outbreak of the war in 1914, a new bunch of sorrows swept down onto the Jews of Kozienice. The authorities chased all the Jews from the town. They rode, they went by foot, without knowing where to, because such was the Czarist government's will.

Finally, the Austrians came into Kozienice, and with them prosperity. Men, women, and children became smugglers. They lugged packs on their backs, on their bellies, under aprons and capotes, and anywhere else they could. They had to guard themselves carefully from secret agents, Jewish and gentile alike. If you weren't caught the first or second time, you were caught the third time, and nothing was left of all your earnings.

Many became ill with T.B. from terror or physical exhaustion. The typhus which struck first visited the exhausted smugglers, many of whom died.

When Poland became independent, more troubles: "pure" Polish businesses, and propaganda were not to buy from Jews. The Jews of Kozienice groaned and hoped for better times.

Sheyne Yidn

There were Jews in Kozienice who were called sheyne yidn. They could learn well, had great pedigrees, and were greatly destitute. They had letters of pedigree, and went from town to town giving sermons and saying toyre, and made their living from this.

On Pesakh, they came home to their wives and children. Until then, the wives and children went hungry.

The Wealthy

There lived four great rich men in Kozienice, timber–merchants, the Justmans and the Mintzbergs. They conducted their lives in a fashion befitting their wealth. They engaged teachers and melamdim for their children; their wives and daughters went abroad to visit the baths. They went to the big cities to marry off their daughters, never to Kozienice.

They went their own way in Kozienice, and did not mix into community matters. In other towns, the rich would either raise or spend money for charitable, cultural or religious institutions, but in Kozienice the wealthy were no philanthropists.

Where Will the Money to Fix the Mikve Come From?

There was a mikve in Kozienice said to be several hundred years old, dating from the time of the Maggid. It had been closed down by the government several times because it was on the verge of collapsing from age. The community, however, had no money to build a new one. It always happened that, before his death, the rich man would go to Radom, and Kozienice would be stuck with the old mikve.

[Page 232]

The Fenceless Cemetery

The cemetery in Kozienice was not fenced in. All sorts of unclean creatures naturally hung around it, because it was completely open.

The community never had the money to build a fence. They always counted on one thing: when the rich man died, the khevra–kaddisha would get money for a fence from his heirs.

All four rich men had already left town prior to my departure from Kozienice and the cemetery remained unfenced.

Two Jews Import a Little Culture

Two Jews opened a crack to allow a little light to shine onto Jewish life in Kozienice. These two Jews began to import a little culture and some enlightenment.

A change in the spiritual life of the town began to be noticed. We have no documents bearing witness to the appearance of Jewish life in Kozienice one or two hundred years ago. Therefore, I begin at 1900 with what I myself have seen and heard.

A Hasidic Life

The Jews of Kozienice lived a hasidic life. There were three rebbi'im and three rabonim in town. Hasidim came from nearly all of Poland. Jews from Kozienice also traveled to other rebbi'im. Religious Jews founded Psalm–societies and Mishna–societies, and had teachers who learned with them every shabbes.

The bes–medresh was always full of boys learning. The entire spiritual life consisted of learning Torah, khasidus, and piety. No spark of enlightenment was to be discerned.

People sang and danced on Purim and Simkhas–Toyre. It was all very cozy, even though their poverty was great; yet they lived in the hope of better days.

It was 1909 or 1910. Jews used to come over to chat with my father, drink a glass of tea, and tell of boys in the bes–medresh who were reading the heretical Peretz.

At the same time, the rebbe married one of his daughters to the son of a rebbe from Galicia. It was said that the son–in–law also read such books ... The conclusion was that he was forced to divorce the rebbe's daughter.

About fifteen bokhurim left the bes–medresh at this time. Some went to the big cities, others became professionals. Eliezer the White became a poet, a writer; others got married and looked for a livelihood.

I recall several bokhurim: Eliezer the White, Khaim Berman, Yissokhor Lederman, Yankel–Eliezer Isaacs, Shayele Herschel Kokhniks.

[Page 233]

Itche Krishpel Founds a Library

Maskilim gradually began to appear openly in town. Something in the Jewish life of Kozienice had changed.

The first two heralds of spiritual change were Yankel Zeigermacher and Itche (Nashelski) Krishpel. Itche was a dear person with heart and soul and a great deal of culture. The first, clandestinely–read secular books in Kozienice came from Itche Nashelski. He had a small, secret library. The bes–medresh boys who secretly read secular books got them from Itche Nashelski. He later had an "above–ground" library. Many boys and girls began to read his books. Thus was the first library established in Kozienice.

Discussions at Yankel Ring's

The second person who helped with the enlightenment was Yankel Zeigermacher Ring. He was also a dear person, steeped in Jewish lore and widely read in Yiddish literature. He was a maskil, very emancipated according to the standards of Kozienice at the time.

Elder and younger maskilim used to come to his shop to discuss literature, philosophy, the theatre, and politics. Yankel Ring later set up lectures about Peretz, Shalom Asch, and others.

The Youth Yearns for Culture

So far as I remember, Jewish life in Kozienice began to change thanks to these two dear persons. The youth formed a self–education circle.

As we know, ninety percent of the Jews in Kozienice knew no Polish. There was a school in which Russian and a bit of Polish were taught, but no Jewish children attended it because the students were not allowed to wear caps.

I recall several girls who attended this school. They were daughters of the three rich men and of older maskilim.

I remember a teacher who taught Russian and Yiddish. He did not make a living from it, and he left Kozienice.

There was also a teacher called Tabachnik who ran a kheder where he taught writing and davening. He was also very poor, because he had no students.

At this same time, many boys went to Warsaw to work or learn a trade. They used to come home for Pesakh, bringing books and newspapers from the big cities, and would discuss literature and the theatre. A youth apart from the bes–medresh bokhurim was beginning to appear.

[Page 234]

The war broke out in 1914, bringing great troubles in its wake. Things were even worse in the big cities, and many, whose parents were still there, returned to their shtetlekh. They also brought something of the big city with them.

The First Steps of the Bund and Folkspartei

Parties were organized in Kozienice. Jonas Weinberg organized the first one, the Bund, which developed very nicely and attracted artisans and workers from the shoe–trade.

The second party was the Folkspartei, led by Kahim Berman and Yissokhor Lederman. This party, too, developed very nicely. It had a club in which members, especially Yankel Zeigermacher, often gave lectures. Yiddish writers would also lecture on occasion.

A drama group, which successfully put on plays by Shalom Aleichem, Ansky, and others, was formed.

The Zionist Organization

After the Balfour Declaration in 1917, the Zionist organization along with its women's organizations and children's groups, was formed. Every party had a children's group. The leader of the Zionists was a certain Erlich. He came from Warsaw, but was the son of wealthy Kozienicer timber merchants.

To write the history of the Zionist movement in our town would be very difficult. Nevertheless, I consider it an act of homage to mention those who helped disseminate the idea of political Zionism in Kozienice even before the First World War.

Forbidden by the Czarist Authorities

They, of course, had no organization, and, for various reasons, could have none. Firstly, the Czarist authorities did not allow any Zionist activity. Second, religious, hasidic circles persecuted the Zionists severely. They considered them dangerous heretics who did not believe in the Messiah and were leading the youth astray from the true path of Judaism.

Still, the Zionists secretly disseminated Zionist appeals among bes–medresh bokhurim, and read Ha–Tzefira and secular Hebrew books.

After the shabbes meal on Friday night, they would conduct discussions of the Zionist congresses and their leaders, sing Hebrew and Yiddish songs, collect for Keren Kayemet, sell membership certificates, and empty Eretz–Yisroel pushkes at home.

[Page 235]

The Active Zionists

This lasted until World War I. We will respectfully mention the names of the active Zionists: Re wen Lichtenstein, Shloime–Zalman Grabler, Mottel Potasznik, Ya'akov–Loser Weintraub, Itche Krishpel, Yitzkhok Milgroym, Shmelke Bornstein, Yitzkhok–Meir Silverstein, Avrum Rosenberg, Zelig Shabbason, and Moishe Avenshtern.

After their fifth year, young bes–medreshniks joined them: Yisroel Honikstock, Khaim Berman, Loser Weifer, Yissaskhor Lederman, Shmuel Karpman, Hillel Luxemburg, Avrum–Yankel Freilich, Shmuel Hirschenhorn, Notte Lipmann, Yankel Papieroshnik, and Yankel Ring, who came to Kozienice at that time.

This is the group which established the library at Yitzkhok Krishpel's.

After World War I, several events which made a great impression transpired in the town.

The Rebbe's Children Go to Israel

Rebbe Yerakhmiel – Moishele's daughters – Khanele, Malkele, Khavele – and their brother Yisroel–Loser departed for Israel with their families immediately after the Balfour Declaration.

Several merchants and artisans went with them. They bought large tracts of land and helped found the Kfar Hasidim colony. A portion of them returned and left their land ownerless, but the rebbe's children remained in Israel, lived through the holocaust there, and lived to see the Jewish redemption.

After the holocaust, several families who had survived returned to Israel and settled on their land.

And now, a few words about the Zionist organization in Kozienice.

A Society With its Own Hall

After the First World War, a Zionist organization with its own hall was formed, led by elder and younger Zionists: Yisroel Honikstock, Shmuel Karpman, Pinkhas Freilikh, Avrum–Yankel Freilikh, Zelig Shabbason, Y. Zeman, Kuropatwa, Yekhiel Salzberg, and others. They conducted Zionist cultural work among merchants and youth.

From time to time, they brought in great figures in the Zionist movement. They conducted a heavy propaganda drive for emigration to Israel, and thanks to them, several families did indeed emigrate.

They also elected representatives to the city council and kehilla. In civic matters, they were always hand–in–glove with the Folkspartei and tradesmen.

[Page 236]

A Cultural Development Appeared

Party lecturers and writers often came to Kozienice to lecture. In this way, a cultural development became noticeable.

When Poland became independent, a gymnasium (Hi School) with about forty Jewish boys and girls as its students was opened.

When I left my hometown in 1921, Kozienice had changed. A cultured, progressive youth which used Polish and enjoyed a secular education had developed.

The Change in Community Life

As we know, community life was run by overseers who were appointed, not elected. At the time of the Polish regime, the government demanded that a leadership be elected for the Jewish community.

The elections used to take place in the bes–medresh. There were two blocs: The "progressives" encompassed the Zionists, Folkists, and Bundists, and was led by Khaim Berman and the lame Berish Kronengold. The second bloc consisted of all the religious Jews, headed up by the rabbis.

The elections were held in the following manner: the religious stood on the eastern side, the "progressives" to the west of the oven, and representatives of the government counted them. The struggle was grim; the "progressives" won by a great majority.

The first change in community life in Kozienice took place then. The kehilla became more democratic up until such time as the Nazis destroyed everyone, religious and progressive alike.

The Shtarke Get Even With The Farmhands

There was a palace in Kozienice called Per Hoyf (the court) in which the nobleman Larski lived. The scenery behind the palace was gorgeous: green lawns, long fields of rye, beautiful lanes, and a narrow river meandering round and round. It was pleasant and enchanting, a veritable Garden of Eden.

When our parents used to lie down and relax on shabbes afternoons, we youth would sit out behind the palace in order to enjoy the beautiful scenery. Boys and girls would stroll, sing, discuss, and make love in poetic fashion.

The administrator of the palace didn't like this, and he used to send out the farmhands, who would beat up the Jewish girls and boys.

There was a group of Jewish workers in Kozienice called Di Shtarke (The Tough Guys). One shabbes afternoon, they went out behind the palace to teach the farmworkers a lesson. As soon as they showed themselves and began to interrupt the promenade, the Shtarke got even with them, as they well knew how.

[Page 237]

The Shtarke were no scholars, they did not sit and study day and night, but Jewish honour was dear to them. From that shabbes forth, the farmworkers never showed themselves again.

This is how we lived until the bestial Nazis tragically killed the Shtarke, as well as the romantic souls of the boys and girls of Kozienice.

The Jewish Artisan in Kozienice
by Issokhor Lederman, Rio de Janeiro

This article is not a history. I don't know how much it will interest the general reader, but the desire not to let anything connected with our town be forgotten obliges us Kozienicers to make mention of the Jewish artisan, who lived, struggled, and experienced all the joys and sorrows of Jewish life, and who exists no more. I therefore consider it my duty to revive, in so far as memory permits, certain memories of the life of the Jewish artisan in Kozienice.

I do not claim to describe everything which took place and was created in the years during which I lived among and was active in their ranks. It is a long time ago. As the son of a Jewish artisan and shoemaker, I experienced all their hardships, sorrows, and joys. I will only report what I remember of that time before the First World War.

Before World War I Jewish artisans and craftsmen constituted a neglected group. Their poverty was great. A very small portion of them was considered upper class. They had no organization for political and economic protection.

In the Cobbler Shop of Efraim Diamant are the workers: Moshe Gutmakher (5), Israel Rakhman (6), Simcha Vasserman (7) and Mandel Weitzman

The Artisan was a Tool

In the smaller towns, the bes–medresh was their organization. Between minkha and maariv, one would tell another in friendly fashion of his poverty, sorrows, and joys.

They took no part in community or kehilla life. The Jewish artisan was always a tool in the hands of the sheyne yidn – the influential people and clergy – who looked down upon him and were ashamed of him. This was the case until the First World War.

And now, to the matter at hand. As has already been indicated, our town had a reputation for shoemaking. Avrum Reisen's song was sung from every house: "Hammer, hammer, clap!"

Since Kozienice lived from this trade, it is important to report which Jews developed it even before World War I.

Let us mention their names respectfully: Ya'akov Birnbaum, Yankel Breitman, and David Huberman. They were ordinary people, not from the upper classes, but they had a feel for business.

Kozienicer shoes could be found in the farthest–flung towns across the length and breadth of Russia. Hundreds of Jews and Christians made a living from this trade.

[Page 239]

Ya'akov Birnbaum Was the Biggest Tradesman

Ya'akov Birnbaum was the biggest tradesman. He raised shoe–manufacturing to so high a level that shoes bearing his imprint were found throughout the length and breadth of Russia.

He himself could not even write. As an ex–Russian soldier, he spoke Russian well. He was a powerful person and had the bearing of a Russian gentleman, which helped him greatly in business.

Twice a year, he would travel to the farthest corners of Russia. Ya'akov Birnbaum even traveled to places where a Jew had never set foot, and took orders for his shoes. The police at every station already knew the Jew and his gifts of money. When he returned from his trip, he came with two suitcases, one full of golden five–ruble pieces, the other of commercial notes.

The greatest merchants and leather manufacturers in Radom were interested in dealing with Birnbaum, because the notes which he brought back were a hundred percent, and there was no doubt that they would get the unpaid ones back.

I am his son–in–law, but all Kozienicers who knew Ya'akov Birnbaum will admit that he was open–handed in support of scholars and poor people, and that he ran his house with liberality: "Let everyone who is hungry come in and eat", Jews and Christians alike respected him.

In 1932 he and his entire family went to Brazil, and there he lived out his years with respect.

Smaller Concerns

There were other, smaller manufacturers of shoes and boots who worked with a few apprentices, such as Meltzer, Fleischer, Huberman, Korman, and Lederman. They took their merchandise to the annual fairs in Lentshe, Lublin, and other places.

There were also small home–manufacturers who worked with their children and sold their merchandise at fairs and in small towns.

The shoe trade continued thus until the First World War.

In the Turmoil of Polish Life

The World War, revolution, and civil war cut deeply into the Jewish organism, cut up and divided countries and states, and brought about a change in Jewish life in the new Poland.

Parties began to crystallize, Jewish youth went out to the surface of life and founded party–organizations, unions, libraries, and sportsclubs of every hue. Jewish daily life awoke to a new political and cultural life.

[Page 240]

The Jewish craftsman, the simple, believing Jew, who formed the greater part of the Jewish community had wandered in chaos far from the life of society due to poverty and political oppression. Thanks to the youth, he was pulled into the turmoil and momentum of events.

The healthy senses of the simple Jew picked up the spurt in his environment, and he began to demand a place in the political and social struggle. The rise of independent Poland opened up new perspectives.

The Folkspartei Organized the Artisans

The economy was almost completely disorganized due to the war. What was needed was a strong and resolute organization to place the Jewish artisan in a new position in life and revive the shoe industry. Thus the artisans' union was formed under the influence of the Jewish Folkspartei.

The task of the new party was to ensure the Jewish artisan's existence in every field of life. Its leaders were Yitzkhok–Eli Korman, Yisroel Spiegel, Itche Kestenberg, Moishe Wasserman, Leizer–Itche Silberberg, Bezalel Kreizberg, and others.

The artisan progressed socially and culturally, he took part in all the artisans' conventions which took place in Warsaw at that time.

Against Old Leaders

The Jewish artisan began to conduct an organized struggle against the old community leaders who had spoken in his name for years. With his own power, and with the help of the headquarters in Warsaw, he secured his cultural and economic position. He put all Warsaw's resolutions into effect.

He also elected his representatives to the city council, the kehilla, and other economic, social, and cultural institutions. We must admit that at the time of my departure from Poland in 1927 the artisans' union and Folkspartei in fact ran all the social and cultural work in town.

Kozienice Produces Canvas Shoes

The artisan sought a remedy for his problems, and developed the production of canvas and leather shoes, which was a new source of livelihood for the town. It even attracted bes–medresh boys, and gave Kozienice a country–wide reputation for shoe–manufacturing.

Kozienice was the only place besides Warsaw (where there were also Kozienicer manufacturers) producing canvas shoes.

Hundreds of workers, Jews and Christians, were employed in this trade. Naturally, it brought new life to the town.

The labour unions and artisans began to conduct a lively activity. Each tried to bring in the best speaker.

[Page 241]

Yontef In Town

It was yontef when a speaker – a party leader, writer or poet came to town. The youth from the neighbouring towns came out to hear the speakers.

And which of the leaders of every party did not come to Kozienice?

Every shabbes and yontef our town was filled with youthful laughter, joy, song, dance, and life. The older generation was carried away with the new life. The halls were full when a speaker came to town. Heated arguments and discussions took place after every speech.

Together with the Grabski persecutions which raged on the street and made Jewish life in Poland more difficult every day, the stream of middle class Jewish emigrants was growing.

[Page 242]

These With Fiddle and These With Trumpet

by Khave Shapira, Kfar Hasidim

Our town's orchestra consisted of several members: Nekhemye, Itzik, Meir–Shakhna, Yisroel, and others. Each one played a different instrument: fiddle, bass, trumpet, flute. As far as I remember, this orchestra was the best in Poland and stood on a high level. The Christians of Kozienice and its environs also invited it to their weddings and balls.

Among the musicians Reb Yisroel, the trumpeter, stood out most, perhaps because from his shoulders upward he was the tallest, perhaps because the trumpet is the loudest instrument.

He was as careful about minor sins as about major. In order not to be corrupted by unkosher food, he refused to taste any of the delicacies served where he played.

The Wedding of Liuba Shpigler

The Book of Psalms was a lamp unto his feet. He stood straight in prayer, to the fullness of his height, the book or siddur resting on the palm of his left hand, opposite his face, praying ardently and with a sweet melody.

The Orchestra was the Focus of the Wedding

Just as the orchestra was always the focus of the wedding, so too, were the words of the khazan and badkhan Reb Eliezer, who succeeded in inflaming the hearts of his listeners. His words were as the drops of Jew which give life to the thirsting plants of the forest – they comforted and rejoiced the hearts of the mekhitonim.

Particularly exalted were the moments when the shamosim of the synagogue, Reb Khaim and Reb Matis, whose holy work was performed in faithfulness (even though their living was meagre), announced the procession of bride and groom in their hoarse voices. The orchestra polished its instruments, and broke out in the well–known march of the Maggid. The crowd made way for the groom and his attendants, the bride and hers behind them. They all turned to the courtyard of the great synagogue where all the weddings took place.

The ceremony at the khupe completed, the righteous women Rivkele, Sarale, Grine, and Hendel danced before the couple, a giant khalla in their hands. They danced with great ardour and stood out in the crowd, for they were tall. The flowers in their hairnets swayed in the air, their faces shone from the greatness of their joy. They felt and believed with a perfect faith that they were fulfilling the mitzva of making the bride and groom happy.

[Page 243]

Itzik the Fiddler

Itzik, the orchestra's violinist and music teacher to the rebbe's children, remains in my memory. He was distinguished for his expertise, and was strict that the notes be proper and pure. He was especially strict when he went over Beethoven's sonatas or Brahms' symphonies with his students. He would sit very tense, paying great attention with his left ear lest, God forbid, something wrong should sound from the violin's strings.

Should the student make an error, or his tone be impure, Itzik would gnash his teeth, stamp his feet, and emit a strange groan from his heart, "Nu, this. Deeper! Cleaner!"

At whatever time of rage or gladness, we were always waiting for his "Nu" and "Deeper".

May they all be remembered for the good in our town's memorial book.

[Page 244]

The Embroiderers of Kozienice

by Sarah–Mindel Kestenberg, Haifa

I became acquainted with the embroidering trade in our town at the age of fourteen. Other girls began to work even earlier.

Embroidering was an important branch of work for us. About 150 girls were employed in the trade, not counting several men, the contractors, known as *shpiliters*.

The merchant Haim Samakhad and his son

The Contractors Brought the Work

The contractors brought the work from Warsaw. The work consisted of stitching monograms, embroidery, and other trimmings onto blouses, blanket covers, pillow cases, and curtains. The materials were fine white linen, marquisette, and tulle – but the wages were even finer: five to ten zlotys a week for a ten to twelve hour day.

The girls of Kozienice gladly went into stitching because it was considered a refined trade and one was paid immediately. The work was merry – large groups of four, five, up to twelve girls in one room. The room was not only a workshop, it was also the dining hall, kitchen, and bedroom. In some places, they even ran a kheder in the same room.

Black Ettel

It was thus by Aharon–Leib. He taught the children in one half of the room, while his daughter, Black Ettel, ran her undertaking in the other. Black Ettel was a stern taskmaster. She did not yield to us, as her father did to the boys, and she watched over us to make sure that we were always working.

There were times when we wanted to laugh at the pranks the boys played on the rebbe, for which he paid them back with slaps and screams. Black Ettel was added to the chorus of screams, screaming at us, H"One, two, three, sew faster. Don't laugh!"

Our Lunch was Brought

We worked a whole day without any breaks and did not go home for lunch. Our lunch would be brought to work. We would share the tastier morsels.

We used to go home with the kheder boys. The boys had paper lanterns with candles inside them. These lighted the way so that we would not fall into any of the deep puddles which were not lacking in our town.

The greatest number of stitchers was employed by Miriam Flamm, Black Ettel, Khamele Samokhod, and Beila Auerbach.

[Page 245]

Our Own Section in the Union

We joined the trade union and had our own section, which was managed by the leftists. The chief organizer who brought us into the union was Yerakmiel Sirota. Most of the stitchers were the children of workers.

We received low wages for our work, so we decided to demand a pay hike. However we could not get one without striking.

The strikes were stormy affairs, with strikebreakers. We used to douse the work of the strikebreakers with kerosene. This happened to Khamele Samokhod when she refused to strike with us.

This is a small segment from the life of the young proletariat in Kozienice in the early twenties.

I was one of them.

[Page 246]

Bikkur–Khoylim and Linas Ha–Tzedek – Help For the Sick in Kozienice

by Yissokhor Lederman, Rio de Janeiro

It is worthwhile for us to mention an important institution which existed in our town after World War I. It was called Bikkur–Khoylim and Linas Ha–Tzedek.

Great Hardship

It was a very important institution at that time. Each one of us remembers the great poverty. Medical help was on a very low level. There was no hospital in town, and of course there were no doctors. In the last years there was a hospital of sorts run by nuns.

The town had one Christian doctor, Zadszinski, who served the entire region of Kozienice with all its towns and villages.

There were also three barber–surgeons, one Christian and two Jews, Khaim and Yiddele.

If a rich man became ill, a doctor was brought down from Radom, or else he was taken to doctors in Warsaw.

If, God forbid, a poor man became ill, he had to sell or pawn his candlesticks so that he would have money for a doctor or be able to buy medicine. There were cases of people dying for want of medical help.

Helping the Sick

The society was formed by craftsmen and plain Jews in order to provide help for poor people who needed it: visiting the sick person, staying over at his house during the nights of his illness, helping with doctors and medicine. Their task also involved getting a Jewish doctor and a Jewish dentist.

The basis of the society was its monthly dues. Rich people at whose houses people had stayed over had to pay five rubles in order to cover the expenditures for the poor.

The kehilla paid the society a ruble a month.

Every year on the last day of Khanuka, the society held a big banquet in the women's section of the bes–medresh. Everyone who had paid in half a ruble had the right to take part. The poor did not have to pay.

The society lasted until the First World War. I have forgotten the reasons for its dissolution, but if I'm not wrong, they were quarrels and ambitions.

[Page 247]

The Leaders of the Society

I consider it my duty to mention the leaders and founders of the society. Their register was kept by my father, so I can remember almost all of them by name: Arish Zaterman, Pesakh Mandel, Leizer Lederman, Zalman Hurwitz, Reuven Fleischer, Ya'akov Ziterman, the judges Reb Aharon Rechtand, Ben-Tzion Freilakh, Yehuda–Leib Feierberg, and the two barber–surgeons Khaim and Yidl.

The society was still in existence in the last years before World War I, but it had lost the lustre of the first years of its foundation.

Its last leaders were Moishe–Leib Dua, Leibish Reisman, Itche Ickowitz, Itche Haberman, Shloime Weinberg, and others whose names escape me.

This has been a brief history of the society, which did a great deal for the poorer population of our town.

Despite conflicts of party and religious issues, there were still dear people among us who sacrificed themselves one for the other. If someone needed help, no one asked or looked at who he was – they helped him.

[Page 248]

The Linas Ha–Tzedek Society in Kozienice

by Moishe Rochman, Pardes–Khana

On Khol hamoyed Sukkos, 1931, our neighbour, Shmerel Pinkhas Soyfers, informed me that at the general meeting of Linas Ha–Tzedek which had taken place in the great hall where Rebbe Aharon Hopstein used to receive his hasidim, it had been decided to accept me as secretary and bookkeeper of the society.

As is known, Linas Ha–Tzedek provided morale and medical help for the Jewish population of the town.

It turns out that Linas Ha–Tzedek had already existed in Kozienice for a couple of years, but with a small scope.

The only person who actively occupied himself with Linas Ha–Tzedek from the beginning was Reb Avrum–Khaim Freilikh. Every week, the collector used to bring him the money he had collected, and Avrum–Khaim would use it to pay the pharmacist for the prescriptions he used to sign for the poor Jewish sick who used to turn to him.

"Our Home" in Kozniece- a charitable organization
Row 1: Pinkhas Birenboim, Shlomo Itzkovich, Yaakov Shmeisser, Matityahu Fishbeoim
Last row: the leaders Arthur Bornstein and Shlomo Tabachnik

The Work Gains Scope

From 1931, the work of Linas Ha–Tzedek began to gain scope. First of all, the society had officially to be legalized with the authorities to whom an exact annual report of the year's activities had to be submitted.

An extensive managing committee and auditing committee were elected. The chairman was the baker Yisroel Ziterman; the treasurer, Meir Unger, Rebbe Yankele's son–in–law. Elected members were Avrum–Khaim Freilikh, Shmerel Schwarzberg, Shmuel Erlichman, Leibel Fleischer, Borukh Borenstein, and, as acting secretary, Yoysef Lichtenstein.

Despite the fact that I was very busy at that time with my studies in the Hi School and with other communal work, I did not turn down the position, and, together with the new management, organized a fine activity for Linas Ha–Tzedek in Kozienice.

Our income came wholly from the weekly membership dues. Moishe Zucker worked as collector. I organized a secretariat with propter bookkeeping. We bought a great member of medical instruments which we used to lend to the poor population.

We made a special agreement with the old pharmacist, Janeczek, that prescriptions signed by Linas Ha–Tzedek would enjoy a fifteen to twenty percent discount. Every case requiring medical aid was considered by two members of the administration: there were cases in which the indigent sick received help of from forty to eighty percent, and cases in which they received a hundred percent of the cost.

[Page 249]

Members of the Kozniece Municipal committee prior to the outbreak of World War II
Leaders of the Folk School, Marek, Haim Berman, Moshe Vasserman, Yonah Vineberg, Zelig Berman, Katzperek, Moshe Goldtzweig, Pinkhas Freilikh, Rembalski, Berel Salzberg
Seated: Mlastek, Itche Gradavotchik, Klimatchuk, Mayor Jan Shitkovski, Pokashinski

The poor would pay the pharmacist the sum recorded on the prescription by Linas Ha–Tzedek, and at the end of the month the pharmacist would submit a bill to Linas Ha–Tzedek, which then paid the remainder, with a discount of fifteen to twenty percent from the normal price.

These were cases in which Linas Ha–Tzedek paid doctors for their visits to the indigent sick. In each case, the requirements and material abilities of the patient were specially considered. Special cases requiring immediate help received it. There were also cases in which duty nurses were sent to stay with the patient at night.

Meetings of the management took place almost every week in the home of Rebbe Yankele in which his son–in–law, Moishe Unger, lived. Linas Ha–Tzedek became one of the most important philanthropic institutions in Kozienice.

A general meeting was held every year on Khol hamoyed Sukkos. Everybody worked for free except the collector, who received a small fee.

The managing members Avrum–Khaim Freilakh, Yisroel Ziterman, and, until World War II, Meir Unger and Shmerel Schwarzberg, worked with especial devotion.

More than once I wondered how I came to the society and how the management could tolerate my collaboration, knowing that I was not terribly religious, that I studied in the Polish Hi School, and that I did not occupy myself with any religious party work. Yet, I always felt respect and sympathy in the rebbe's house, in which I was a daily guest for years. It appears that the institution's aims, for which the entire membership worked so devotedly, had an effect upon the mutual relations of all the members. To our great sorrow and pain, our Linas Ha–Tzedek and its devoted members was destroyed along with the entire Jewish population of Kozienice on the second day of Khol–hamoyed Sukkos, 1942.

May their memory be blessed by us and our future generations.

[Page 250]

The Free Loan Society in Kozienice

by Khaim–Meir Salzberg, Toronto

It is quite possible that many Kozienicers do not know of the existence of such an institution in our town. It had no halls, signs, or advertisements, but it was popular among the poor merchants of Radom and Lublin Streets, and also among the artisans of Koscielna and Magitowa Streets.

When a note matured there was somewhere to turn for a loan.

The founder and first president of the free loan society was Menashe Shapiro, known as Menashkele because of his short stature. He had a mercantile mind, a good heart, and a feel for community work.

He was born and raised in Demblin, twenty–seven kilometres from Kozienice, and married Khaye, the youngest daughter of Khaim–Meir the baker. After the marriage, they opened a food store at 63 Radom Street, which they ran until the German invasion. They had two children, Yehudis and Yankel. The Germans killed all of them.

In the summer of 1936, Menashe called several distinguished householders to his house: Itche–Meir Silverstein, Hersch–Mordekhai (whose surname I have forgotten) and Yoysef Salzberg. He presented his plan to found a free loan society in town. He also informed them how such a society is run without interest, and that the loans would be distributed in small installments. "I am precisely informed as to how to run such a society," he said later, "because my brother was active in such an institution in Demblin."

The assembled persons listened to him with great interest and expressed their readiness to work with him.

Author: Haim Meir Salzberg, Toronto   Menachem Shapiro

The General Meeting

A couple of weeks later, the founding meeting took place at Menashe's house. Both rooms were packed, with people standing because there was no place to sit.

The first word was Menashe's – he explained how such an institution worked. Yossel Salzberg indicated the usefulness of such an institution. Itche–Meir Silverstein also spoke. Almost all those present signed declarations and paid in five zlotys.

This was the beginning of a very important community activity in Jewish Kozienice. The motivating group was elected as the management: Menashe Shapiro, president; Yoysef Salzberg, secretary; Hersch–Mordekhai, treasurer; and Itche–Meir Silverstein.

The good news was borne about quickly. The number of members grew from day to day, thus also increasing the base capital.

[Page 251]

The management decided to put a one hundred zloty ceiling on the loans. The sums grew with time as the capital increased. Shortly before the war the loans had reached the sum of 500 zlotys.

The society developed and progressed so quickly that the office became too small. The secretary was heavily burdened with work. At the suggestion of Itche–Meir Silverstein, the society moved to his house, where there was more space.

Moishe Fuchs, who worked with great diligence, was engaged as secretary.

At the annual general meeting, after the secretary's and treasurer's report, elections for the managing committee were held. As a token of appreciation, the same members were elected with only a small change: Menashe Shapiro, honourary president; Yoysef Silberberg, president; Itche–Meir Silverstein, secretary; Hersch–Mordekhai, treasurer.

The founders and members of the sport club "Macabi." 1928 in Kozienice.

Members of the hand ball sport club "Macabi."

A Benefit Show

The founding group sought means to increase the institution's capital. It was suggested at one of the meetings that a Yiddish play be put on and the receipts be dedicated to the society.

The presidium went to a group of amateurs, who agreed to their proposal. M. Fershtand agreed to direct the play, Dos Pintele Yid. He accepted the suggestion of the play, and began to prepare a group of amateurs which consisted of Zalka Madanes, Elye Huberman, Ber Silberberg, Zalka Karpik, M. Wasserman, Yekhiel Kohn, and Reizel Branspiegel.

After two months of intensive rehearsal, the group was ready to stage the play. The society had rented the largest hall in town, the Shope, or the Kino (cinema) as it was called, the only hall in town which was owned by Zelig Bermam

Athletic club in Kozienice with their instructors.

Athletic club in Kozienice. The younger generation.

The night of the show finally arrived. An expression of satisfaction could be seen on the faces of the management when the hall filled up within a short time: its financial success was guaranteed. The presentation began on time, a rare event in itself. The crowd sat and enjoyed it. In a word, the undertaking was a success.

Intensive work continued. The society grew, more members joined, and the amount of the loans was increased.

This activity continued until the outbreak of the Second World War. The German murderers destroyed Kozienice Jewry, which was an honoured link in the golden chain called Polish Jewry.

[Page 252]

The Khevra–Kaddisha in Kozienice

by Yissokhor Lederman, Rio de Janeiro

As I have already indicated, there were many Khevras (societies) in Kozienice, among them a khevra for Mishna study, one for the Psalms, for bridal dowries, a Khevra shoymrei shabbas, and the khevra–kaddisha.

The khevra–kaddisha was the most powerful, best organized and most eminent. It had power and had its say in all community matters: choosing officials, distributing Pesakh flour, accepting a judge or shoykheE it was complete master over people in life and after death.

The khevra consisted of two classes, plain and educated Jews. The plain Jews were the stretcher–bearers, diggers, and buriers. The educated Jews performed the purification and delivered eulogies.

The leader of the educated Jews was Faivel Margolies (Tshwok), a man who had neither worked nor engaged in trade in his life. He lived from interest and a little rent. Moreover, he was a little scholar and a big drinker. He was the terror of all his surroundings. He decided how much to charge and where to bury. He took care that there was plenty of whisky at every purification.

On the fifteenth of Av, the khevra had a big banquet, with fat geese, white rolls, kegs of beer, and plenty of whisky, in the gabbai Yoine Silverstein's house. None of the general public was allowed in, except for dayanim (judges) and shammasim. They sang, danced, and whooped it up for a night and a day.

The biggest celebration was on Simkhas–Toyre, which was the merriest time for the khevra–kaddisha. Feivele Tschwok was the chief of the drinkers. He danced on the table, and spoke jests and idle words.

Afterwards, the gabbai was taken into the shul for the hakofes with song and dance. They drank a le–khaim after every hakofe, and there was joy and merriment in the town.

Thus did the Jews of Kozienice live and conduct themselves, despite bad times and bitter troubles.

They had the sky over their heads and the ground under their feet, and therefore they lived with faith in better times in both worlds, and especially in the next.

[Page 253]

The Sports Society in Kozienice

by Zelig Berman, Bat–Yam

My friend Ya'akov Krishpel and I organized a Jewish gymnastics and sports society in Kozienice. The first youth meeting took place on Targowa Street, at Shimon Schwartzberg's school.

Every <u>shabbes</u>, boys and girls used to meet there for lectures. We were concerned that the youth should also develop itself physically and not be disabled.

The Jewish sports society in Kozienice was formed. Youth from every class signed up, an administration composed of the following was elected: Zelig Berman, Ya'akov Krishpel, Notte Levi, Polly Domb, and Sarah Orbach. Berman was elected chairman and Krishpel secretary.

The provisional meeting hall in the school was too small. The administration went to the artisans' union and Folkspartei, which had a beautiful hall, and asked their permission to use it. OUr request was granted, and we began an extensive activity in the fields of sport and physical education. Several older members who helped us get organized were attracted: Shimon Berman, Yoine Weinberg, Pinkhas Gisser, Khaim Berman.

An instructor, Shimon Berman educated the youth in the spirit of sports.

The chairman of the artisans' union and Folkspartei, Khaim Berman, did everything to organize a drama group, which played not only in Kozienice but also in the neighbouring towns.

At that time, we wanted to put on a Purim play, The Selling of Joseph. We had no text, so we invited Binyomih Frisch (the shammas of the shul), who knew the whole play by heart, to sing it while we wrote it down.

And so, on Purim we presented The Selling of Joseph with great success in the artisans' hall. We also played twice in neighbouring towns with the participation of the amateurs Z. Berman, Y. Krishpel, Sh. Goldman, Y. Rochman, Khlivner, Notte Levi, M. Weinberg, and others.

The income from the play was detailed for uniforms for our members – white caps with blue stripes and special blouses.

The members used to meet almost every day to do gymnastics. There were also several girls' groups.

Jewish Athletic club. Founded by the Folks Party in Kozienice in 1919.

We Celebrate Lag–B'Oymer

The administration and instructors decided to demonstrate solemnly on Lag–B'Oymer. I remember as if it were today that Lag–B'Oymer came out on a Sunday. The sports society assembled in its holiday best – its caps and blouses – and, led by Instructor Sh. Berman, marched with music and song over Radom Street. There were over two hundred of us, in rows of four. The Jewish population greeted the Jewish children joyfully, and applauded.

Teachers of the high school (Gimnazia) together with members of the city council in Kozienice.

Children of the elementary school – the fourth and the fifth from the left are two Jewish religion teachers – husband and wife.

SECTION 4 –
Rabbis Community Figures

and Simple People

R' Yosef Yehuda Minzburg   R' Elimelekh Freilich

The Tzaddikim and Rabbis of Kozienice

by Rabbi Avraham–Abba Zuckerman, Haifa

I have responded to the request of the Kozienice Organization to write a few words in order to immortalize this town, but there is no beginning to write about Kozienice without first mentioning the holy Maggid.

It is said in his name: "Were it not that I lived in Kozienice, no one would know of its existence."

Were I gifted as a writer, I could still not succeed in capturing the Maggid's holiness on the page. He was the pillar of the town and of the Maggid's street ... The Maggid's street – thus was the street known during the rule of all the nations who ruled Poland.

Thousands of pages and books without number have been written on the glory of his holiness and that of this town. To our sorrow, it ascended the pyre together with all of exiled Israel at the hands of the Germans, may their name be wiped out.

May God avenge their blood before our eyes, speedily and in our day.

Only Descendants of the Maggid Bore the Title Rav

As is known, no one in this town ever bore the title of <u>Rav</u> or <u>Bes Din</u> except members of the golden chain of descent from the Maggid. His descendants were endowed with the title of <u>Rav</u> of the town until the office passed to Rebbe Yisrael Eliezer Hoffstein, the founder of and worker at Kfar Hasidim. Every judge or chief rabbi who served in Kozienice was called simply chief rabbi (<u>Moyre tzedek</u>) or authorized teacher (<u>Moyre hoyra'ah</u>). I mention their names here in order to immortalize them until the coming of our redeemer. Naturally, this list extends only to 1927, when I left for Israel.

Rabbi Ben–Tzion, born in Kozienice, served in high style as rabbi of his native town after his father, Rabbi Pinkhas; until he left Kozienice and settled in Worka where he served as rav and <u>bes din</u>.

Rabbi Yoysef, born in Kozienice, the son of Rabbi Zelig Eliezer, descended from one of the honoured friends of the Maggid.

These two rabbis were killed in the Holocaust.

May the Lord avenge their blood.

[Page 257]

Rabbi Yoysef–Yehuda Mintzberg

Rabbi Yoysef–Yehuda Mintzberg was born in Ostrowca, the son of Rabbi Shmuel of Ostrowca. Torah and greatness were united in him. His great and righteous teacher, the Genius of Ostrowca, said of him that he knew how to decide legal questions properly.

Rabbi Mintzberg served as rav and <u>bes din</u> in the town of Czepelow before coming to Kozienice.

As a well–educated young married man, I was naturally in contact with all the rabbis in town, but in Rabbi Mintzberg's house I was one of the family, not – God Forbid – for political reasons, as was usual in Polish towns – <u>mayn rebbe</u>, <u>dayn rebbe</u>, etc. – but simply because of the vineyard of the Lord, the wealth of learning and piety which I found there.

His big room was filled to overflowing with legal books and responsa, books of pilpul, and the like.

It is no wonder that his library was so rich. He was the son of a wealthy scholar who left him this library, and whoever had not seen the library of Rabbi Y.Y. Mintzberg had never seen a library in his life. The margins of his books were filled with notes, variant readings, and discussions of Torah, all in his handwriting, which resembled print.

He was, as it were, a basket full of books. His acuity was boundless. Again, it is not to be marvelled at that at the time of his bar–mitzva he had completed the entire Talmud with toysfos and all the commentaries, for he grew up in a household of such acuity that there was none greater, viz, the house of the Genius of Ostrowca. Therefore, I was able to clarify and explain every obscure matter. Over such as he one can truly bless, "Blessed is He who hath given of his wisdom to those who fear him."

We Established Torah Institutions

Aside from his devotion to scholarship, his thoughts were also occupied with humanity: " he loved Israel and brought them near to Torah with all his heart and soul. When he returned from Russia after World War I after being held hostage along with his friend Rabbi Ben–Tzion", he said to me, "Reb Avraham–Abba, if the verse, "And Jacob came safely," is to be fulfilled in me, something must be fixed." He did not leave me until I had promised him to work to correct a certain matter in our town."

I fulfilled my promise with the help of God: in a very short time, a talmud–torah, secondary–school yeshiva, and Tikkun Eruvin society had been founded in our town. Naturally, this was all done with the help of the community and distinguished householders, several of whom I mention here in order to immortalize them: Reb Levi Mandel, Reb Tevye Mandel, Reb Yoyel Weinberg, Reb Shloime–Pinkhas Leibishes, and others.

[Page 258]

Evening Classes for Adults

Since one mitzva engenders another, the tzaddik, foundation of the world, Rebbe Arele, came to me, saying that he was about to establish evening classes for adults, and asked me to be the principal and lecturer. Having no choice – one cannot refuse the great – I promised to do so, and with the help of God I fulfilled my promise properly all the while that the Rebbe stood at the head of the institution.

It is fitting to end on a happy note. I pray to Him who hears every prayer that the merit of the righteous and holy men mentioned here will defend us and all of Israel until the coming of the Redeemer, speedily and in our day, Amen and Amen!

[Page 259]

My Father Rabbi Yoysef Yehuda Mintzberg

by Tova Mandel, Tel–Aviv

I was fifteen years old when I was orphaned from my father, Rabbi Yoysef–Yehuda Mintzberg. How can I remember him?

Nevertheless, an image of my father made up of memories and stories I have heard sketches itself before my eyes.

Left: Hillel Mintzberg, son of Rabbi R'Yoseph Yehudi Mintzberg
Right: The Rebetzin Malka, the wife of Rabbi R'Yoseph Yehudi Mintzberg

In my mind's eye I see the glory of his face and the nobility of his spirit. His tall figure is before me, his warm glance still caresses me.

Father loved us, and we loved him. How happy we were when father devoted his attention to us; we did not want for his warm and loving gaze.

Until our happiness came to an end one cloudless morning. Father passed away. He was forty–seven.

At so early an age, and in so sudden a manner, he parted from us forever.

An oppressive grief descended upon our house.

Joy and happiness were taken from me.

And I was fifteen at the time.

I will attempt to sketch a general outline of my father's image from fragments of memories.

My father was born about 1880 in the town of Ostrowca, near Kielc.

His father served as rabbi of the town.

My father studied in the yeshiva of Rabbi Yekhiel, the Genius of Ostrowca. He distinguished himself with his quick grasp and breadth of knowledge. He was thirteen when Rabbi Yekhiel ordained him to the rabbinate.

As was the custom in those days, my father married at a very early age. At the age of fourteen, he married my mother, Malke Levin, the daughter of Reb Meir Levin of Macziow, in Wohlin, who was of the same age.

Mother used to tell us that after the wedding she would take off her wig and play with it. It delighted her.

[Page 260]

Melekh Freilich playing chess with a friend

Rabbi R' Benzion Freilich

My father lived with and was supported by his father–in–law in Macziow for several years.

He did not touch the dowry he received from his father–in–law, but took the entire 10,000 rubles and gave it to the Rebbe of Porisow.

At about the age of twenty, my father assumed the rabbinical chair in Czepelow near Zwolin.

He served as rabbi there for ten years.

My two sisters, my brother, and I were all born there.

About 1910, my father became rabbi in Kozienice through the efforts of the Porisower hasidim and with the agreement of the influential Zemach and Mintzberg families.

The Gerer hasidim opposed the choice of my father, but over the course of time he endeared himself to the wider public and was chosen chief rabbi of Kozienice.

At the outbreak of World War I, my father was sent to Russia at the command of the military government, and was held hostage for three years in a jail in Moscow.

My mother and the children went to live with her father in Ostrowca until the days of rage had passed.

Israel Moshe Mintzberg at the grave of his father Rabbi Yoseph Yehudi Mintzberg

Scarcely any impressions of our residence at my grandfather's stayed with me and those which remained have been forgotten with the years.

My father was freed at the end of the war, and we returned to Kozienice.

My father inclined to Zionism all his life. All the town's Zionists prayed in his shul, but he never dared to demonstrate his Zionism in public.

I remember very little of his community activities.

I know that he was very active in this field – he devoted years of his time to the yeshiva in Lublin.

In 1928, my father fell ill with appendicitis.

The doctors in Kozienice and its environs failed to diagnose his illness, and it was thus neglected.

When it intensified, my father was taken to the hospital of Dr. Soloveitchick in Warsaw, where he died at the age of forty–seven.

[Page 261]

An oppressive grief descended upon our house.

The town of Kozienice trembled at the dreary news.

Rabbis and eminent scholars from the entire district attended my father's funeral.

Stores, workshops, and businesses were closed.

All the residents of the town went to pay their respects to my late father, and to bewail his sudden death.

As a token of appreciation for my father and his work on behalf of the town, the community officials decided to pay my mother his full salary for the rest of her life.

And so, the officials kept their promise until the outbreak of World War II, and my mother enjoyed my father's full salary.

I went to Israel in 1933. Before leaving, I married my husband, Levi. I parted from my mother, my brothers Hillel and Moishe, and my sisters, Hadassa and Rokhel.

I did not realize that this was my last good–bye even though my heart was pinched.

The survivors who lived through the war told me that my mother was shipped to Treblinka and killed. My brother, Hillel, who distinguished himself by his help to all the needy at the time of the Holocaust, refused to be parted from her, and they were killed together.

May their memory be blessed!

The same bitter fate visited my sister, Hadassa, her husband, Mordekhai Bornstein, and their two children, Roizele and Itchele; my sister, Rokhel, who lived in Ostrowca with her husband, Nossen Lieberman and their three children.

Of our extensive family, only my brother, Moishe Mintzberg, and I survived. During the war, he fled to the Soviet Union, where he passed the seven levels of hell, and in 1964, after much wandering succeeded in reaching Israel, and has lived in Ramat–Gan ever since.

The heart is pinched with anguish and does not wish to be consoled.

How have we been left alone?

May their memory be blessed!

[Page 262]

How Great The Calamity

by Tzvi Madanes, Tel–Aviv

Would that my head were all of water, and my eyes a fount of tears, day and night would I weep the defilement of the daughter of my people.

Your sons are all fallen in captivity, flames of fire have consumed your houses of study. Your heart is torn to pieces for the glory of Israel and its defiled Torah.

Pyres of fire consumed the Torah scrolls, and they forced us to dance around them. Enemy guards surrounded us. "Where is your God?" they asked with scorn.

The head of the congregation, Reb Yoysef Dayan, was hitched to a plow, and a Jew beat him with a whip. Blood and sweat soaked his clothes, and his soul departed with the Sh'ma.

This was on the Day of Judgement. They toiled as of yore. Reb Moishe Donnerstein arose in prayer and supplication, and the enemy clove his temples.

Khaneche Danziger and Khayele bas Reb Melekh were not parted in life or death. They lay without breath of life, their blood mingled in a puddle.

In talis and tefillin, Reb Herschel Popilnik, scholar and man of action poured out his heart. He did not finish his confession, and his blood was spilled like water.

Feige Shabbason – the enemy called her out, the Jewess. She, charming and modest, tarried. A shot was heard in the house. The children lost their sister, and thus fate turned bitter toward them.

Here lie scattered bodies, little children slaughtered like fowl ... This is Torah, this its reward? How great the calamity, and how great the sorrow.

The destruction of an entire house. The children and their mother lie without breath of life. As a bird spreading its wings over it young, thus was Alter Bornstein's wife with her children.

The family of Dr. Abramowitz fell like heroes. Before the murderers came to destroy them, their father gave each one a pill, and thus these bold ones found their death.

Reb Elimelekh Freilakh, of the elders of the town, walks with the congregation. He holds his grandson to his body, their hearts beating to Kiddush Ha–Shem. Thus the congregation of Kozienice was ended and completed.

[Page 263]

Rabbi Ben Tzion–Freilakh

by Leibele Fishstein, Tel–Aviv

The bes–medresh was packed with worshippers in tallis and tefillin, but no one had yet approached the amud.

"Shakhna! Why don't you go to the amud?"

At that moment, three mighty blows on the bima rent the silence.

"Raboysay! There will be a big celebration in town today. Rav Ben–Tzion Freilakh, freed from Siberia, is coming on the second train. We're all going out to welcome him."

Nobody davened with the minyan anymore. Everyone davened by himself, in order to be among the first to bear the news.

At one p.m. the street leading to the station was filled with people, Jews and goyim, waiting for the great rav.

The station was about two km. from town. Droshkys with specially invited guests and distinguished householders went to the station. On the way back they stopped at the bridge by the town's entrance, their occupants got out, and went into town on foot. The escort wore their holiday best, and Ben–Tziele walked at their head.

He was a tall man with long bright yellow points to his beard, payes hanging to his shoulders like tubes, and a high, brown shtreimel on his head. His fur coat was unbuttoned, allowing his tzitzis to show.

He walked with dignified steps. With a smile on his face, he greeted the crowd on all sides.

Ben–Tziele was the master of the bes–medresh. Shabbes afternoons he would teach the week's Torah portion to the crowd in the bes–medresh, explaining and illuminating every verse in Yiddish.

On Friday night the <u>davening</u> did not start until Ben–Tziele arrived. The <u>khazan</u> did not begin the <u>Shmone Esrei</u> until Ben–Tzion gave him the word.

On Rosh Ha–Shana his brother, Avrum–Khaim, had the right to <u>daven shakhris</u> on the first day and <u>musaf</u> on the second. The same on Yom Kippur. The rest of the <u>davening</u> belonged to Ben–Tziele.

His quiet, murmuring lament <u>Al Da'as ha–mvkom ve'al Da'as ha–Hakuhol</u> froze everyone in their tracks, and nothing was heard but his lament and the crackling of the candle flames.

[Page 264]

Blowing Shofar on Rosh–Ha–Shana

With Ben–Tzion standing on the <u>bima</u> with the <u>shofar</u> in his hand and his <u>tallis</u> over his head, it seemed as if every sound from the <u>shofar</u> hit the ceiling, seeking a path to heaven.

At the amud, he used to dance in time to his singing. Everyone around would sway back and forth and beat time with their hands. He also used to cry so that I took pity on him. I would think that the world was about to end, and that he and his lamentation had to save it.

The women were delighted by his davening: "You hear a word, a song, a dance. There is a power in his very marrow."

His brother, Melekh Reb Pinkhasl's, was another sort entirely: of middle height, rotund, with a short blond beard, wore a <u>shtreimel</u> on <u>shabbes</u> and <u>yontef</u>. Twisted fringes of hair hung down from his <u>shtreimel</u>. He was a merchant, owned a mill, and employed a score of workers, some of them Jewish. His hoarse voice did not prevent him from standing at the <u>amud</u> and <u>davening</u> from beginning to end on Rosh Ha–Shana and Yom Kippur, and not allowing anyone else to approach.

The third brother, Avrum–Khaim, was tall and broad shouldered. The skirts of his garments were always undone. He was always in a hurry, as if he had scores of businesses. Even his <u>davening</u> at the <u>amud</u> was always at such a pace that the women couldn't catch up to him.

The Czepelower Rav R'Yoseph Yehudi Mintzberg

The Czepelower Rav was popular among a large section of the population of Kozienice who were his admirers (Czepelower hasidim). He was renowned as a great scholar and sage. He was tall, with beautiful, clever eyes and genteel noble features. <u>Din–toyres</u> and conversations on societal, communal, and political matters among distinguished householders often took place in his house.

His celebrations on Simkhas–Toyre, Khanuka, and Purim were very merry. On Purim, the Czepelower hasidim prepared a special program. Every year, Ya'akov Ring (Yankel Zeigermacher) used to put together a selection of humorous poems and Purim songs; he played his fiddle, and the whole crowd sang along, danced, laughed, and had a good time. Many hasidim would get dressed up and make merry.

Whoever frequented the Czepelower Rav, <u>noshed</u> on many good and clever words. For example, he used to say that "a rav is not a person," because the night before, he had conducted a <u>din–toyre</u> until midnight. Finally, the litigants said, "You know what, Rebbe, we're going to go to the people." This means that a rav is not a person.

[Page 265]

The Czepelower Rav was a son of the Ostrowcer. His wife came from a rabbinic family, and ran a nice, warm household. Every guest was received cordially, and treated to a cup of tea and citrus preserves.

The rav had two sons, Hillel and Yisroel–Moishe, and three daughters, Hadas, Rokhel, and Tove.

In 1928, he suddenly fell ill. His family and friends did all they could to save the beloved rav. They brought doctors in from outside, then sent him to a specialist in Warsaw. But it didn't help, and the rav passed away.

The whole town mourned and lamented the loss of a great sage.

Almost the entire Mintzberg family was killed by the Nazi murderers during the last world war. His daughter, Tove Mintzberg, now Mandel, survived because she and her husband had emigrated to Israel in 1933.

His son, Yisroel–Moishe, is also living. He saved himself by a miracle in Russia, and like his sister, lives in Israel today.

The Czepelower Rav made no use of the <u>shul</u> and <u>bes–medresh</u>. He kept aloof. Everything was in his apartment: a courtroom, a large hall for <u>davening</u>, and his dwelling. A separate kingdom, in a word.

The only other rav was Reb Yoysef, a man who did nothing but study, a batlan. He was small and stooped, with a high back. He was always studying. You wouldn't go to him with a <u>din–toyre</u>, but he was an expert on women's questions: a needle in the gizzard or a swollen liver on a fowl, not to mention exorcising the evil eye.

What he lived on, God only knows.

Rebbe Yekele Shapira

Rebbe Yekele Shapira was the only <u>rebbe</u> in town. He was Reb Yoysef's brother, and had a genteel, delicate, pallid face. He was always sick, broken, his soul barely sustaining itself within him. He observed his <u>rabbanus</u> in a detached wooden house.

A good bit of yeast, so the <u>shabbes khalles</u> would come out well, could be bought only from Reb Yekele's wife. On this account, religious women bought their yeast nowhere else, because the <u>khalles</u> turned out well with the <u>rebbetzin's</u> yeast.

His hasidim were picked men: calm and quiet paupers.

[Page 266]

Two Brothers, Two Rebbi'im

Across from the bes–medresh stood a large, long house of brown brick. It looked unfinished, although it was already several score years old.

Two brothers lived in this house. They were conducting a war between themselves as to who should be rebbe number one and who number two.

They were the descendants of the Kozienicer Maggid. There were two kingdoms in the house: in one half lived Reb Melekhl and his sister Brokhele (she lives in Kfar Hasidim); in the other half, his elder brother, Reb Arele. Reb Melekhl with his pious, bearded hasidim, and Reb Arele with beardless, clean–shaven, non–religious hasidim.

Hundreds of hasidim from throughout Poland flocked to Reb Arele's table. Magitowa Street was filled with people. On yontef, all the tables were overflowing, not to mention all the people who couldn't find a place at the table.

Reb Arele used to disappear from the table in the middle of the evening, go into his private chamber, and take a nap. After his nap, he would appear before his hasidim and ask whomever he ran into to show him his tzitzis. Woe unto him who was not wearing them. The rebbe took him by the ear into another room, took a towel, moistened it in water, twisted it double, ordered him to lie down on a long bench, and he – the rebbe himself – spanked him in the tukhes.

As he got up, the rebbe said to him, "You know what that was? I gave you a pledge (as in a pawnshop)."

Happy was he who had the luck to receive a "pledge" from the rebbe's hand.

"Dance!" the rebbe suddenly commanded. They all embraced one another. The mass of people swung in a circle. The rest crawled onto the benches and tables, singing, and clapping their hands in time.

Ya'akov Did Not Give Up His Socialism

In the midst of the dancing, a young man burst in crying, "Rebbe, give me a remedy for my child. Things are very bad with him."

The mass of dancers froze in astonishment.

The rebbe approached the young man and gave him his hand. "What's your name?

[Page 267]

"Ya'akov."

The rebbe tilted his head back and put his hands over his eyes. He stood like this for a long time. The crowd was mute and still.

Suddenly, he snapped out of his trance and shouted, "Ya'akov, dance!"

The rebbe left the hall and soon came back with a bowl of oranges. Slowly he climbed onto the table and threw the oranges over the heads of the dancers. All those standing on the tables and benches dashed after the oranges. The crunch was immense, and the rebbe kept yelling, "Ya'akov, grab an orange!"

Ya'akov had scarcely managed to make his way to an orange when the rebbe yelled, "Ya'akov! Go home quickly and give your child a bit of the orange."

Ya'akov Bondol – for so he was called – was clean shaven, short–coated, and a bit of a socialist. His wife had forced him to go to the rebbe for a cure.

When the child regained its health, Ya'akov became a fervent hasid of the rebbe's, but he did not renounce his socialism.

Let the Goyim Platz

On Lag–B'Oymer there was an assembly of all the hasidim in the great square near the rebbe's house. They marched through the main streets in rows of three, the rebbe at their side, counting like an officer, "One, two, three, four" only counting in Hebrew.

" Goyim? What goyim? Which goyim? Who's asking them? Let them look and platz!"

On Purim, the antryroom of the shul was turned into a theatre. At the rebbe's command, a stage was put up. Binyomin–Khaim Yagges and Vadyalle Kokos and other such "artistes" performed Joseph and His Brothers after the reading of the megilla.

From the same stage, Avrum–Abba (now a rav in Haifa) used to teach the weekly portion every shabbes afternoon. Avrum–Abba was the rebbe's chief adviser.

Reb Velvel Klein of Lodz, the shammas, was the rebbe's administrator and chief of supply. He used to store the tens of cases of wine which rich merchants sent the rebbe before every yontef in a special supply room.

[Page 268]

The Story of a Pinch

During the Shmone–Esrei on Simkhas–Toyre Shabsi Katz took advantage of the opportunity of standing behind Velvel Klein. He pinched him. When Velvel turned around from the Shmone–Esrei to see who had pinched him, Shabsi was already standing in another corner. Velvel looked everybody in the eye in order to find the guilty party, but alas...

After davening, Velvel told the rebbe, took his golden watch from his vest pocket, pressed the rim, and opened the cover. "I'm giving you five minutes. If the culprit doesn't come forward, he's going to regret it."

The five minutes were long past, and the guilty party had still not presented himself.

Shabsi's Wife Gets Well

Shabsi Katz's wife was in great danger. There was faint hope of her recovery. Desperate, Shabsi decided to make an end of the secret which had been boring through his heart the whole time. Thinking that he had sinned against the rebbe, he decided to confess that it was he who had pinched Velvel.

When Shabsi had told the whole story, the rebbe burst out laughing and left Shabsi alone in the room.

"What can this mean? Instead of becoming angry with me, the rebbe dismissed the whole thing and disappeared," complained Shabsi to himself. Standing in the large room, he felt as if his knees were buckling beneath him.

He stood like this for a long time, not knowing what to do. Should he leave the room and go home with nothing? Or wait here until the rebbe's return?

Fatigued, he started looking for a place to sit, but there was only one armchair in the room – the rebbe's – and he did not dare sit down on it.

Suddenly, the door was flung open and the rebbe rushed in, crying, "A hundred bottles of wine for the table!"

"Rebbe," cried Shabsi in a trembling voice, "my wife is very ill. The doctors have taken everything from me. All my possessions would not be enough for so much wine."

[Page 269]

"Pawn your wife's jewelery and get a hundred bottles of wine!" Then God will give your wife a complete recovery."

His wife regained her health. The jewelery was redeemed, and Shabsi became the <u>rebbe's</u> devoted hasid.

Ulica Magitowa

After the Maggid's death, the gentile city council hung a sign on the street where he had lived: <u>Ulica Magitowa</u> the Maggid's Street.

The thick–walled <u>shul</u> stood on this street. Although it had been built

130 years before, it looked unfinished. Inside, there was no ceiling.

When the <u>khazan</u> was singing during the <u>davening</u>, the birds under the roof would chirp along, making it seem as if they, too, had come into the <u>shul</u> to pray.

It was most beautiful when a bridegroom was "showered" with sweets (a <u>bavarfns</u>). The birds would swoop down very low over the people's heads in order to catch the nuts.

From the <u>shul</u> to the river behind the town, not a single <u>goy</u> lived on Magitowa Street. Yet, the panes in all the windows were broken: <u>shkutzim</u> who used to pass late at night would amuse themselves by tossing a stone through a Jewish window.

The <u>shul</u> was closed, except on <u>shabbes</u> and <u>yontef</u>.

When the <u>shammas</u> opened the <u>shul</u> on Friday evening, he would first knock three times on the door.

All kinds of legends were told about these three knocks. For example, that demons prayed in the <u>shul</u> at night. If you went past the <u>shul</u> after midnight, you imagined hearing how those passing by were called to the Torah.

The Bes–Medresh

Near the <u>shul</u> stood the great <u>bes–medresh</u>, which rested neither day or night. People sat learning in the entrance, let alone in the <u>bes–medresh</u> proper in which every table was occupied.

At one table, someone sits bent over a big <u>gemore</u>, learning; at the next, a whole group quibbles loudly; they're saying Psalms at a third.

Two tile stoves stood at the western wall. Crazy Bezalel slept on the bench by one of them. During the day he carried water from the market pump or the tap for housewives doing their laundry; they used to get their own water for cooking.

[Page 270]

Gavriel slept by the second stove. All day long he went from house to house with <u>makhzoyrim</u>, story–books, letter–writing guides, fringed undergarments, and the fringes themselves. At night he went home to sleep on his bench by the tile stove.

The long tables and benches stood by the walls. The centre, around the <u>bima</u> was empty. On <u>erev</u> Rosh Ha–Shana and at <u>Kol Nidre</u>, the empty area was completely filled.

At the right–hand corner of the eastern wall a brass khanuka <u>menora</u> was nailed to the wall. When the <u>shammas</u>, Avrum–Moishe, made the blessing, "to light the khanuka candle," snowballs prepared by pranksters flew over his head. It was a sort of custom. A miracle would have taken place here, too, if the <u>shammas</u> had not been hit by a snowball.

The greatest miracle took place this Khanuka, for there was not yet any snow.

The Maggid's House

Motke Weinberg

Behind the houses fronting the street, not far from the <u>bes–medresh</u>, stood a wooden house so low as to seem half–sunk into the ground.

From without, it looked like a cell. The two six–paned windows started from ground level. The house was bent away to one side, had a dutch–door at the entrance, and in the corridor, a floor of pressed clay. In the room, a table, an armchair, and a cane with a bent handle hanging on the chair. Also a canopied bed and several bookshelves.

Every Saturday night, Rebbe Eliezer would recite <u>Ha–Mavdil</u> there, and afterwards pass fragrant spices around.

The Crown Rabbi

Rabbi Ya'akov–Hirsch Weinberg, the government–appointed rabbi, was the most interesting character in town. His bearing and attire were appropriate to his office. He was a born aristocrat, a pedant: neatly dressed in black with a collar and tie. He knew several languages and was involved with all the government officials.

Jewish children who wanted to leave the country or go to the big city for work and who had no passes, had to go to the crown rabbi for a birth certificate.

The rabbi went to the city hall, took a thick book from the shelf, went over to an official seated at a small table and said to him, "Here, in this place write Moishe–Dovid Stein, born twenty years ago. You know how to fill out the rest. Make a birth certificate and a pass right away."

[Page 271]

Melamdim

The noise of children was heard from a window looking out of a roof on a side–street. This was the <u>kheder</u> of the <u>melamed</u> of the youngest children, Yisroel–Mendele.

He was small, round as a tub, and high shouldered. His head rested upon his shoulders as if he had no neck. His feet could not be seen when he walked, for his capote reached the ground. It seemed that he was not walking but gliding forward in the air.

Rabbi Jakob Hersh Weinberg and his wife Toba

He never walked through the streets alone, but was always seen with tens of children, some with their visors cocked to the side, some with the flaps open at the back of their pants and their shirts sticking out. Some of the children had two types of shoes: two right or two left, one black and one brown. He went with the children from one woman in childbirth to another to read the Shma.

This was his privilege. He had taken it over from his father, and no other melamed took it away from him.

When there happened to be two or more readings of the Shma on the same day, the children were happy. Their pockets were stuffed with nuts and cookies which they divided up among their brothers and sisters at home.

Moshe Weinberg son of Rabbi Jacob Hirsh, the only Jewish officer in the Polish army from Kozienice

When it got dark outside, Yisroel–Mendele himself lit the little candles which he himself had made from tallow which he took from dripped–down <u>yorzeit</u> candles in the <u>bes–medresh</u>. He put a candle in each child's paper lantern, which he had likewise made.

The children set out merrily through the streets on their way home. He turned the table over to his wife, Khave, and went to the <u>bes–medresh</u> to <u>daven</u> <u>mayriv</u>.

Khave resembled her husband. Following his example, she always wore a dress which practically swept the floor. It seems that her long dress was calculated to conceal the difference in the length of her legs. One was shorter than the other and her body inclined sharply to the left. Her only adornment was the calico bonnet on her head.

Every evening, when Yisroel–Mendele was in the <u>bes–medresh</u>, his place was occupied by Khave. That of the little boys was occupied by marriageable girls whom Khave taught to <u>bentsh likht</u>, <u>bentsh</u> the new moon, and to make a blessing when removing a piece of dough for burning.

When Yisroel–Mendele returned from the <u>bes–medresh</u> Khave was already through with the lessons, and had covered part of the table with a towel and placed the evening meal atop it: a salt–cellar with salt, a bread, near it a knife, a glass of tea, and a spoon on which lay two saccharin tablets.

In the market in Kozienice

[Page 272]

Yoysef Hanover Ran A Modern Kheder

In a basement room across from the <u>bes–medresh</u> there was a <u>kheder</u>, or rather, a school. The children called the <u>melamed</u> "teacher", not "rebbe". His name was Yoysef Hanover; the local householders called him Yoysef Singer because the <u>kheder</u> had been modernized and all the lessons were taught to a tune.

From the entrance–door to the window, which stood between the ceiling and the level of the ground, stood a long table with benches. To the right was a proper school–bench with a lectern with holes cut out for inkwells. Children learning khumash and Rashi sat at the table, bar–mitzva boys at the lectern bench.

The teacher, Yoysef, was short and thin, with broad shoulders. He had a long black beard, a large forehead, and a yarmulke so small that it barely covered his bald head. His hands were always wrapped in bandages from finger to sleeve. He suffered from chronic eczema, a curse visited upon him because of his beatings.

Every morning before sitting down at the head of the table, he used to take the military belt with a Russian crown on its brass buckle from his pants and place it near him on the table.

Lying on the table, the belt excited different fantasies in every boy: Now I'm lying over the whipping–bench and the belt jumps over my back; now I'm hiding under the table because I didn't want to lie on the bench, and the teacher's chasing after me with the belt. I get a blow with the brass buckle, a lump forms, or else a hole with blood running out.

Once, when the teacher had kept up his beating from morning until it was time to go home, a feeling of vengeance awoke in the children. On the way home, they all stopped for a while.

"Boys, we're going into the bes–medresh. We can't talk here."

They went into the bes–medresh, secluded themselves in a corner, and decided to liquidate the belt. They drew lots on the spot to see who should take the belt outside. The lot fell to little Leibele.

Leibele didn't sleep all night. He lay in bed with his eyes shut, making plans for spiriting the belt away without the teacher's knowing....

And what to do with the belt? Dig a hole and cover it? Maybe throw it into the river? Yes, that's the best – into the river with it. It'll swim far away. If someone bathing in the river should find it, he won't know that it's our belt.

The execution was carried out the next day. The river carried the belt far away.

[Page 273]

The following day, the children looked at the place where the belt always lay. They looked at the teacher. He was silent. Who knows what will happen today? Maybe he thinks he lost it somewhere.

A few days later, a mat made of leather shoelaces twisted together lay in the belt's accustomed place.

In the mornings, they davened with a minyan. Every day a different boy davened as khazan at the amud. The davening was sung with a merry tune from beginning to end.

The studies took place exactly as in a public school: a brass bell rang every hour, a five–minute recess followed, then the bell rang again.

Yoysef's wife, Blume, was always complaining about her luck in having to share a basement room with a kheder and go mad from the noise. Fortunately, the room was the size of a barn, so she sectioned it off with a partition made of blankets hung from iron rings. On her side of the "wall" there was a dining-room to the left by the window, and a bedroom to the right.

They had three sons. The eldest, Zelig, was a quilter. He worked for a Warsaw–ite who, heaven preserve us, had no children and who treated Zelig as if he were his own son.

The second, Binem was a shoemaker and the third, Herschele, would also not be a melamed when he grew up, concerning which his mother, Blume, was already concerned.

Borukh Melamed

A small, narrow little room. The table and two long benches were squeezed in between both walls. The table, by the window. On the other side of the window, outdoors, was a large pump with a long iron stock. In summertime, there was always mud around it; in winter, glossy ice, like a mirror. The pump was covered with straw in the winter to keep it from freezing.

There was a fair in town on Thursdays. Peasant carts were lined up the length of the street on both sides, one beside another.

The window had to be shut all summer, because of both the noise and the stench caused by the horses.

[Page 274]

On the days of the fair, the entrance–door to the kheder was left open to let in a little air.

Across from the door in the long corridor was Loser's old clothes shop. Peasants went in and out of it, one with trousers thrown over his shoulder, another with a jacket in his hand.

The studying out loud resounded down the length of the corridor. The goyim going by used to stop and look into the kheder. Some laughed mockingly, others put their caps on out of respect and stood looking for a long time. Borukh was already so accustomed to this that he didn't even turn his head to the door.

His wife, Feigele, had a small shop near the window. It seems that she had divided the room in two, one half for the kheder, the other for the shop. A barrel of axle–grease, a barrel of kerosene, a bag of salt, a barrel of herring, and blotting papers for rolling cigarettes were all she had to sell.

Borukh was calm, meek, and shy, and she – his wife – was always agitated. "A <u>melamed</u> wanted me," she used to scream every Friday night, "Some bargain I got. You sit and teach the children all week, and on Friday I don't have what to make <u>shabbes</u> with. If it wasn't for the couple of groschen I take in from the shop, I'd really be well off."

The Public School

The compulsory education law called forth anxiety among many Jews. The children would have to sit in school bareheaded. The very religious did not send their children to school: "What will be, will be."

Moishele Berishes was an exception. He was a pious and deeply learned Jew. He had a hardware and shoemakers' accessory store. When you went into his store to buy something, he was always sitting behind the counter with a book in his hand. He would kiss the book, close it, and put it aside.

His boy was named Melekh. He was the only boy in the school to wear a hard, round black cap and to hide his <u>payes</u> behind his ears.

The <u>shkutzim</u> at school would sneak up behind him and throw his <u>payes</u> from behind his ears so that they were in front of them. Melekh hid them again. Did he have any choice? If he were to go and tell the teacher, the teacher might order him to cut them off.

Once, on the way home, a strong wind flung the cap from his head, and it rolled away so quickly that it was impossible for Melekh to catch it. The <u>shkutzim</u> saw this and gasped with laughter, and it seemed to Melekh that Janek or Antek had stood behind him and flung the cap so that the wind would carry it away.

[Page 275]

The next day, Melekh reported them to the teacher. The teacher called both <u>shkutzim</u> and wanted to punish them, but they denied it absolutely. They didn't do it, they claimed, the wind did it. They broke out laughing so hard that the teacher joined in. Then he said to Melekh, "You should tell your father to buy you another cap, a soft one that won't be able to roll away."

Jewish children amounted to fifteen percent of the boys' public school, but double that in the girls'.

The House With the Red Chimney

Behind the town, at the end of Warsaw Street, there was a forest on one side in which a colony for the children and teachers of the Medem Sanatorim in Warsaw was set up every summer. A large, one–storey, red–brick house stood on the other side of the highway. Although it was already old, the house looked unfinished, or else like a factory building, for a tall, round eight–storey chimney stood by the building. The house contained large rooms in which five parties were located: the Zionists, the Po'alei–Tzion, the Revisionists, the Bund, and the Communists.

Aside from small rooms, every party also had a large hall for readings and lectures with specially engaged lecturers from Warsaw. Every Saturday night, one of the parties held a lecture with a speaker from Warsaw. The hall was always overflowing. Opponents from other parties presented themselves after the lecture, and lively discussions developed.

Melekh Ravitch came very often with his literary–philosophical lectures, as well as Ya'akov Pat, Victor Alter, Henryk Erlich, Noah Prilutzki, and others.

Every party had its own library, and young people could be seen in the evening, going back and forth from "The Red Chimney" with books under their arms.

Every party had a drama group. These put plays on quite often in the kino. Their gifted directors Khaim Berman (who worked in his photo studio by day) and Paula Kirshenblatt (she worked in his quilting workshop) were busy with rehearsals every evening.

Every party had night courses for adults and night schools for the young. The Zionist organization's Hebrew courses were organized at a high level. A large number of the students who survived the war and went to Israel learned fluent Hebrew in these courses.

The Bund had a first–rate school and evening courses under the direction of the beloved teachers Yoyel Weintraub and Moishe Kohn. Their devotion to and love for educational work deserves to be honoured in the warmest words.

[Page 276]

The first of May was celebrated on the scale of a large city. All the Jewish and non¬Jewish socialist parties demonstrated with flags in the street.

There were twenty–four city–councilmen, twelve of them Jews, who played an important role in the town's economy.

Radom Street was the main street. All the businesses there were Jewish; even in the market all the storekeepers were Jewish. Only a few butchers were gentile.

On Thursdays, the whole area was occupied by Jewish stalls. On every side, one saw peasants bargaining and shaking hands with the storekeepers.

Shabbes in Kozienice

The marketplace had a different aspect on Fridays. All the tables were filled with fish, fruit, and vegetables. The customers were Jewish women who went home loaded down with baskets for shabbes.

On Friday afternoon, Jews with bundles of clean clothes under their arms went to the bathhouse. Aharon–Leib, the attendant, stood by the entrance collecting the admission fees. He and his family had worked all week to prepare the bath and the mikve: they drew out the old water, let fresh water in, chopped wood to make a fire in the boiler, tied small brooms for beating, and set hoops in the collapsed buckets.

It was scarcely dark when one saw the same Jews dressed for shabbes, walking slowly with siddurim in their hands to the shul and bes–medresh.

Shabbes candles sparkled in every window.

After the Friday night meal, the young people went to their organizations for "box–evenings". It was a sort of custom that every organization had a "box–evening" on Friday night. During the week, people put questions into the box hanging on the wall. These were answered on Friday night.

Those young people who belonged to no organization went strolling back and forth in the darkness. Young couples in love clung to each other.

On shabbes afternoons in winter, our parents lay down to sleep, resting up from a week's work. In summer, people went to the forest to lie on the soft grass.

The religious went to the bes–medresh to hear Ben–Tziele teach the week's Torah portion. The non–religious youth went on excursions and to sports work–outs.

[Page 277]

Kozienice Sews Shoes

Kozienice came back to life in 1922. Shoe merchants in Russia placed huge orders for canvas shoes. Seventy percent of the town threw themselves into this trade. Even those who were not professionals went to Warsaw, bought a set of iron lasts, and began sewing canvas shoes.

No house was without one or two shoe factories. Going by on the street, one heard the beating of hammers on all sides.

Loser, the khazan in the shul, set himself up a small shoe factory in which his two daughters stood at the worktable with hammer, pliers, and knife and made the shoes themselves. Binyomin, the son of Khaim Yagge the shammas, cut the hard leather. Itche Tokasz, Rivele Tokasz, Shmerel Holtzhendler, Avreimele Shabbason, and Moishe Spiegel also set up large shoe factories.

The greater part of the youth, whose parents were tailors, carpenters, and bakers, became makers of canvas shoes.

The notions–dealers became contractors. They brought uppers and lowers, tacks, nails, needles, and yarn from Warsaw.

The biggest contractor was Avrum–Abba, today a rav in Haifa. There was also a scribe, Shakhna, among the suppliers of soles. He had a large storeroom for leather, and nearby a small room to write <u>sifrei–toyres</u> and <u>mezuzah</u>.

New trades arose. Bookbinders became box–makers, carpenters heelŒmakers. Shingle makers made chips and boards. Mechanics brought in modern machines to sew the soles.

Boys used to take shoes to be sewn from all the factories and deliver them to the sewers. All the stitchers and seamstresses became shoe–finishers.

A union, to which all shoe workers belonged, was established in the finest house in the centre of town. Its leader was Binyomin Khaim–Yqgges, its general–secretary, the Bundist councilman Yoyne Weinberg.

The union had its own laws and its own court. Whoever worked more than eight hours was punished. Employers who committed offenses were also punished.

Everyone employed in shoe–production made a good living, and thus other lines of work came to life.

Canvas shoes later went out of style, and Russia no longer asked for them. Leather shoes began to be made. Until the outbreak of World War II, Kozienice flooded all Poland with its shoes.

[Page 278]

Faivel Qger (i.e. Faivel Stallion)

Faivel made his living from a small cart half the size of a normal peasant's cart: four wheels and a shaft. A thick rope was tied to the shaft. He himself was the horse. He would lay the string on his left shoulder and hold the shaft in his right hand.

The cart always stood at the intersection of Lublin and Koshcielna Streets, near Leshish's Christian restaurant and the Bundist consumers' cooperative. One side of the cart was always empty, and Faivel always sat in the cart as if reclining in an armchair.

He held the lunch, which was brought him in a small pail by his wife, between his knees, and ate it with such appetite from his wooden spoon, that you would have thought the grits or scorched soup the finest delicacy.

When the cart was heavily loaded, he bent over. He did not feel that children were hanging on from behind. When the cart got stuck in the mud or sand, passers–by would push it out and children would scream, "Giddy–up, giddy–up."

If someone was moving, no one could compete with Faivel's price for carting his things.

On Fridays, he brought kegs of beer from Yoyne Zemach's brewery to the restaurants; a box of siphons from Yoyel Weinberg's soda water factory; collected cholents and took them to the baker. On other days – a sack of sugar, a sack of flour, and what–not. It all paid him.

He had no need of a stall for his horse. He also needed no oats. He worked half–free. But he always managed to make a living.

In summer, he needed no shoes except to go to shul on shabbes.

His wife helped him make a living. She did laundry for rich Jews.

This was called the romantic tree in the forest near the city of Kozienice

Binyomin and his Father, Khaim Yagge

Sara–Rivke was going fast; her hernia slipped out. Calling a doctor never entered her mind. What could a doctor do to it? Nothing. He'd order her to the hospital. Binyomin Khaim–Yaigge must be called. He was an expert in the field. With him, a few minutes go by, and bang! The fallen organ's back in place.

But what happens if Binyomin doesn't agree to come? In such cases he goes only to men. She tells them to ask the rebbe. If the rebbe commands it, Binyomin will come.

[Page 279]

The rebbe commanded and Binyomin came. Before ten minutes had passed, Sara–Rivke was out of bed and healthy.

Binyomin was neither a doctor nor a barber–surgeon. He was a leather–cutter, a shammas in the shul, a badkhan at weddings, and also a big shot in the Bund. He inherited his specialization in collapsed hernias and being a shammas from his father.

His father, Khaim, was very smart and had a great mastery of stores. In his old age, when he could no longer get out of bed, Noah Prilutzki came to Kozienice especially to see him, and take down several stories and anecdotes which Kahim Yagge told.

Prilutzki asked him with what he could thank him for his stories. The old man answered, "The only thing which would be cheap for you and good for me is a bottle of vodka."

"Where did you get such an idea, Reb Khaim?" wondered Prilutzki. "It seems to me that at a time like this vodka would be poison for you."

On hearing the word "poison", Khaim sat up, took a bottle of vodka from under his pillow, and, pointing to the bottle, said, "Thanks to this, I've lived to be an old man."

Yissokhor Shoykhet

A quick glance testified that he was a shoykhet: a small, dried–up fellow with long hands, a small face, a few long hairs at the tip of his chin. Even his payes were sparse. His head was bent forward, so that his back looked high and rounded.

He tucked his pants into white socks which reached his knees. In the summer, he wore a buttonless cloth robe. His belt held it closed. It was always unhooked in the front, and his yellowish, woolen tzitzis would peek out.

He was so wrapped up in his own thoughts that he never noticed anybody, neither in the bes–medresh, where he stood without looking around for the whole davening, nor when shekhting – he took the birds, slaughtered them, and threw them away. He didn't even know who had given it to him; all he saw was a hand holding out money.

On erev Yom Kippur, my mother awakened me at four in the morning and gave me a few kapores to take to the shoykhet. I got into line and watched how skillfully and quickly he worked. This time, his son, Moishe, took the money.

[Page 280]

The Band

Itzik had three sons. He himself played the fiddle, but his eldest son, Shloimele, played all instruments. Besides playing in his father's band, he was also leader of the firemen's band. This band played on every national holiday and at visits from highly–placed personalities. Shloimele marched in front with his baton and brass hat. Every couple of minutes, he turned towards the band, turned back, and waved his baton in time.

The second son, Yakel, had his own barber shop and also played in the band.

The third son, Meir, was still a boy of about twelve. He played his small fiddle and didn't miss any of the weddings.

There was another fiddler called Nekhemye Klezmer (musician). He merely strummed tunelessly to the beat. Although he could read music, his function was simple: to strum to the beat on his fiddle or the big bass which stood on the ground and produced low notes. He also had his own barber shop in the centre of town.

Tall Yisroel played two instruments, which he changed every couple of minutes: a trumpet and a long trombone. Besides playing in the band, he had an old clothes shop in his home and a stall in the market. His boy, Leizer, played the drum and cymbal.

Old, broad–shouldered Meir-Shakhna used to play the clarinet. He played no other instruments.

Nekhemye used to accompany the badkhan with a sad tune when the latter was singing of the bride. He was just a strummer, and his fiddle used to weep mournfully. When the bride was led to the khupe, tall Yisroel's trumpet drowned out everyone else.

The Doctor of the Poor

by Itche Blatman, Paris

I remember many dear and nice Jews in Kozienice, but I will only mention two.

He was called only Moishe–Leib, and that was enough. Small children and the elderly knew who Moishe–Leib was: A Gerer hasid, a great scholar, an official of the Khevra–Kaddisha, a Jew who was always looking to do good deeds.

He was not wealthy, but he made a living. He, Moishe–Leib the expert, was the doctor of the poor.

Poor people rarely called a doctor or a barber–surgeon because it cost money. Moishe–Leib was indeed busy with sick poor people day and night. They would awaken him in the middle of the night; he would get dressed quickly and run to the patient.

I remember once I was at his place on business. Suddenly, a very mournful woman came in. Moishe–Leib recognized at once why she had come, and, leaving me there to wait, went off with the woman to a patient. Often, he would also leave a couple of groschen to buy a prescription.

His wife was a dear woman, modest, saintly. If someone came in to call her husband and he was not at home, she would give them a place to sit and wait for him – he was with a patient. Meanwhile, she comforted them – God would help. Moishe–Leib came home, she sent him to the sick man right away. In this way she helped him with his holy work.

This is the sort of dear people they were, Moishe–Leib and his wife.

[Page 283]

Kozienice the Exalted

by Rabbi Yitzchok Freilakh

During the generations, giants of Torah imparted their glory to the cities in which they chose to live. Such towns as Vilna, Volozhin, Mir, Slabodka, in the world of yeshivas; Medzibozh, Mezritch, Berditchev, Lublin, in the hasidic world, did not become famous because of their material wealth, but thanks 'instead' to the giants of Torah and saintly persons who pitched their tents there.

The town of Kozienice merited the designation "city and mother in Israel" because one of the lights of hasidism lived and worked there in his time – the tzaddik Reb Yisroel, famous the world over as the holy Maggid of Kozienice. This saintly figure left several generations of famous tzaddikim behind him.

They enlightened all Israel with their teachings and righteousness until the enemy came and put out the ember which had warmed thousands of the leaders of Israel.

The Maggid's House

In the heart of the city was a street which served as a stronghold for thousands and tens of thousands of Jews from every corner of Poland. The street was called Magitowa, after the Maggid. Among the low houses on this street fluttered a tiny, two–room house in which the Maggid housed his name, in his day and for generations thereafter. In the first room, which appears to have served as an anteroom, there were two armchairs and other expensive furniture. In the door at the entrance to the Maggid's chamber there was a peephole through which, according to hasidic legend, Rebbe Levi–Yitzkhok of Berdichev looked into the Maggid's dwelling and saw the house filled with light.

In the second room stood the Maggid's bed and chair, the amud of his grandson, Reb Elezar, and the armchair of Rebbe Yerakhmiel–Moishele Hopstein, the offspring of a dynasty of jewels, the fifth generation in uninterrupted succession from the Maggid.

In the last years before the murderous war, the chair of Rebbe Asher–Elimelekh, a son and the heir to the throne of Rebbe Yerakhmiel–Moishele, was also moved into the room.

On shabbes and yontef, the rebbi'im went there immediately after davening to bless a good shabbes. At the end of shabbes they returned accompanied by their hasidim in order to play Eliyahu Ha–Navi on the fiddle to the Maggid's tune, known as Per Heiliger Niggun.

The Maggid's chamber also served as a sukka for him and his descendants.

Behind the house, a twisting path led to a low mountain on the way to the town mikve called Starszik's barg, after the goy who lived nearby. Elderly hasidim said that Rebbe Levi–Yitckhok of Berdichev rolled down this mountain on his way to the mikve.

[Page 284]

The Rebbe's House

Across from the Maggid's house stood a splendid stone house which served as the court of the palace of the Kozienicer rebbi'im in Poland, a brilliant and many–hued personality. In addition to his duties as rebbe, he also served as head of the Kozienice rabbinical court and as preacher in Rika, a village near Kozienice. Thousands of hasidim from every corner of Poland flocked to him.

For several years the rebbetzin Brokhele lived there, and from time to time, heirs to the throne served there. Rebbe Aharon–Yekhiel Hopstein, among the most famous rebbi of his generation, who was endowed with his father's chair. Over the course of years he pitched his tent in Otwock.

His brother, Reb Asher–Elimelekh, also among the great rabbis, lived in Lublin for several years, and returned to his father's house in the last years before the war. He served there permanently. His sanctity shone out to thousands of hasidim from there.

The society Avodat Yisrael was also founded in the rebbe's house by his third son, socio rum junior, Yisroel–Elazar, now living in Brooklyn. During the twenties, the young rav influenced several Kozienicer hasidim to liquidate their residence in the diaspora and join him in going to Israel to show pity to the land and build their future in the land of the patriarchs.

The president from the house of Kozienice went up at the head of several families, set his tent–pegs in land of the Keren Kayemet, and built Kfar Hasidim. His sister, the rebbe tzin and authoress, Malka, the wife of the Admor Elimelekh of Grodzisk, the Rebbetzin Khanele, may the Lord avenge her blood, and the Rebbetzin Khavtche, the wife of Rabbi Shalomke Shapiro, went up together with their great brother and opened a new page in emigration of hasidim to the holy land.

In this house – remember it? – the tables were arranged from year to year by the Admor Kalonymos Kalmish Shapiro of Piaseczna – son–in–law of the Kozienicer Rebbe, and the late–born son of Rebbe Elimelekh of Grodzisk – who went to prostrate himself on the grave of his ancestor, Rebbe Moishe–Elyakim Beriah, the Maggid's only son, and the grave of his father–in–law, Rebbe Yerakhmiel–Moishele, on the thirteenth of Elul.

The Bes–Medresh and the Shul

Across from the rebbe's house stood two splendid and up–to–date buildings, the bes–medresh and the shul. The Jews of the town flowed into the bes–medresh day and night in order to pour out their prayers to their creator.

[Page 285]

I spent many days and years in this bes–medresh. I was among the scholars who sat around the table or stood by the platform and learned gemore, poyskim, and toysfos regularly. There I merited to pour water on the hands of several of the town's scholars. I learned together with young men who excelled in Torah and superior moral qualities. I took part in the work of repairing books, at the head of which stood the most distinguished of the fellowship, Reb Avi Ezra Zelig Eliezer, the only son of the rabbinical judge, Rabbi Yoysef Shapiro, of a dynasty of jewels, a diligent Torah scholar. When he married the daughter of his uncle, Rebbe Elimelekh of Garvolin–Warsaw, he assumed the post of rabbi in one of the Polish towns.

His position as head of the book–repair committee was filled by Moishe Borenstein, the son of Reb Eliezer, known as Elazar FoygeL He was likewise among the prize students, urged on the repair of the Porisower shtibl, and stood at the head of the Reb Meir Ba'al Ha–Nais society.

His elder brother, Alter, was chairman of the Revisionist organization. At this time I was learning together with my cousin, also among the better scholars, the learned and sharp Yerakhmiel–Moishe Freilakh. He influenced my father to send me to learn – together with him – at the yeshiva Da'as Moishe, founded and supervised by the Piaseczner Rebbe.

The shul was open only on shabbes and yontef. From time to time, public meetings, at which civic or community leaders addressed issues of the day, were held there.

Shtibelekh

The majority of the adult congregation were hasidim. There were practically no misnagdim of the Lithuanian type, which is not to say that the Jews of Kozienice did not oppose hasidism. Absolutely not!

As good Jews, they well knew the "law of opposition"; they were not opposed to Ba'al Shemian hasidism, but to anyone else's rebbe: the Gerer hasidim opposed the Porisower and vice versa, while the Kozienicer hasidim opposed them both.

In addition to the rebbe's, where the Kozienicer hasidim prayed, there was also a Piaseczner shtibl not far from the Maggid's, a Gerer shtibl, and a Porisower shtibl, both on Lubelska Street. There were also isolated hasidim of the rebbi'im of Radzin, Kolubiel, Garvolin, Lublin, etc. In the neighbourhood of the bes–medresh, Reb Yakele Shapiro, heir to Reb Zelig–Eliezer and a descendant of the Maggid, also served as rebbe. Several tens of his followers prayed in his bes–medresh.

The Zionist organization also had a regular m in van on shabbes and yontef. The Zionists, their sympathizers, and some of the Zionist youth prayed there. Their shtibl was in Beit Ha–Tarbut on Radom Street.

[Page 286]

My Grandfather

While speaking of holy places and synagogues, I will recall the house of my grandfather, Reb Elimelekh–Eliezer Freilakh. He was a lion in the hasidic world; his name spread far beyond this city and his residence in the palaces of the greatest rebbi'im was firm.

When I parted with him for the last time – during the days of wrath, in fact – he was broken and crushed from the blows of time. The enemy ruled in the fullness of his cruelty, but my grandfather did not despair. On the contrary, their torments increased his faith that the Lord would not abandon his people.

I recall the last time I saw him. 1 went to him in the early hours of the evening in order to bid him farewell before leaving my birthplace and my father's house. He lay in bed already, his lips murmuring his credo. Every Friday night before the kiddush, he was accustomed to repeat the credo he had composed, which encompassed far more than the thirteen principles of Maimonides. With tears dripping onto his long beard, he began: "I believe with a perfect faith that the Creator, blessed be his name, is the creator and leader of all creation," continuing until he had completed the thirteen principle points, and thence with his own composition.

"I believe with perfect faith that our father Abraham was true, I believe that our father Isaac was true," continuing and including all the choice of the patriarchs, the twelve tribes, Moses, Aaron and his children, Joshua and all who came after him, David, Solomon, the Tanniam, the Amoroim, the rabbis who compiled the Babylonian Talmud, the geonim, the Baal Shem Tov and his descendants, and the greatest of the admoyrim up until his last rebbe, Rebbe Yerakhmiel–Moishele Hopstein.

On the evening when I went to him for his blessing, my father's sister, Khayele, said to me, "Go to father's bed and listen closely to what he is muttering."

I approached to where he lay in the dark room, muttering to himself "I believe that the holy Rabbi Akiva was true. I believe that the holy Rabbi Khanina ben Teradion was true," and so on. I stood at his bedside for an hour listening to the speech from his lips and burst into tears. I left the room. Next morning, I took my leave of him, and he blessed me with, "Let him appoint his angels to guard you in all your ways."

I saw him no more, for he went up on the pyre during the storm.

He was very old at this time, but he was still awake and alert to all that took place in his town and the world. He took an interest in all the events of that terrible epoch, and tried with all his might to justify the law and "tell that the Lord is upright".

[Page 287]

It was said that he was born to greatness. He was gifted with the power of understanding and a wonderful intelligence and also with excellent abilities. From the dawn of his youth, he learned in the house of his father, Reb Pinkhas Freilakh, the town rabbi, until in the course of time he was proficient in the Talmud and poyskim, and dove into the sea of the Talmud like one of the giants. Here he also acquired his self–sacrificing devotion to everything sanctified, to the needs of the congregation, and especially to being bound with bonds of love and fear together to his rebbi'im, the enlighteners of the eyes of Israel in his and the coming generations.

In his youth, my grandfather went to Rebbe Elimelekh of Grodzisk. Despite his tender years, he bound himself to the rebbe until he became one of his favourites. At the rebbe's he was called by his second name, Eliezer, out of respect for the rebbe.

After the Grodzisker's passing and Rebbe Yerakhmiel–Moishele Hopstein's coronation with the rebbi'ish crown, my grandfather clung to the latter with all the threads of his soul. He never referred to him but as "mayn heliger rebbe", and to his children, two of whom became distinguished rabbis in their own right, as "mayn heligen rebbi's kinder".

My grandfather was his father's eldest son. His brothers were Reb Avrum–Khaim; Reb Pinkhas; Reb Shmuel, who became Pinkhas' son–in–law by marrying his daughter, Yutele; and Reb Ben–Tzion, who inherited the rabbinical chair from his father. They were all sharp–witted scholars whose fear of heaven preceded their wisdom.

His sisters were Sorele and Rivkele who, with the passage of time, became famous figures of charity. In their father's house, they learned how to answer many questions concerning what is forbidden and what permitted.

Reb Elimelekh's wife, my grandmother Khanele, was the daughter of the generous hasid Reb Yitzkhok Schwarzbard, one of the leading Vorker hasidim. Like her husband, she was graced with superior moral qualities and became a genuine woman of valour. All her life, her husband was her only happiness, she was a help mate to him and a merciful mother to all the needy.

My grandfather preferred business to the rabbinate. Therefore, while he was still with his father–in–law, he rented a mill in the village of Koszlek near Kozienice, and, when it succeeded, he added others, closer to town. With the passage of time – and with financial help from my father who was very wealthy in those days – he built a mill in the town itself. He supported himself from it, as well as others, and became known as one of the wealthy men of the town.

My grandfather merited to see an upright generation. His sons, his daughters, and their children were all scholars, well–educated in secular matters, too, faithful and devoted to their people and to Zion. My grandfather had four sons: Reb Shmuel–Elya, the eldest; my father and teacher, Reb Avrum–Ya'akov; Reb Pinkhas, and Reb Aharon who died during his father's lifetime.

[Page 288]

After his marriage, Reb Shmuel–Elye settled in Kaluszin, where he became president of the congregation and director of the local bank.

My father and teacher, Reb Avrum–Ya'akov, married the most beautiful of women, Roizel–Dvoire, daughter of the generous hasid Reb Naphtali–Tzvi

Boorstein, one of the leading Vorker hasidim in Radom. His first steps in business were crowned with success. This was at the time of the First World War. He became very rich and was liberal in his donations to charity, for he was in the habit of enriching those who enriched him. In order to remove any shadow of doubts to whether he was giving the poor a fifth or a tenth (the rule of liberality specifies not to give more than a fifth), he used to thrust his hand into his wallet, and the sum that he came up with was what he distributed to the poor and to charity. When his fortunes declined during World War II, he was especially sorry that he could not afford to support the poor, as he had done before. Both my parents were the best of the best with respect to their charitable qualities.

At the outbreak of the murderous war, Reb Pinkhas was head of the congregation, president of the Zionist organization, and a member of the Kozienice town council.

His daughter, Yutele, married her uncle, Reb Shmuel, a great scholar and great in fear of heaven. His second daughter, Khane–Pearl, married Yitzkhok–Meir Madanes, likewise a scholar, a hasid who lived in the fear of heaven. At the outbreak of the war, his third daughter, Khayele, married a distinguished young man of great piety who was plucked up in his prime.

My grandfather attained the splendour of paterfamilias of a well–known and many–branched family. He delighted to amuse himself in discussing Torah and secular matters with his sons, daughters, sons–in–law, and grandchildren. They all treated him with great respect, and he loved them with a great paternal love.

My grandfather's family was many branched, bearing sweet fruit nourished by the great tree, that same man great in piety and excellence, Reb Elimelekh–Eliezer Freilakh. When the enemy led him out to ascend the pyre for the Sanctification of the Blessed Name, he was accompanied by his sons and daughters, his brothers and sisters and their spouses, and their children: Pinkhas and Yerakhmiel–Moishe, Altele, her husband, and children; the sons and daughters of Yutele; my sister, Tzippoire–Gittel and her husband Elye–Pinkhas; their children, Shulamis–Ruth, and a girl baby of a year; my brother Yishaye–Yekhezkel; my younger brother Naphtali–Tzvi; Bezalel Madanes, his wife and children; Ya'akov and Khanyele, the children of Yitzkhok–Meir and Sarah–Pearl Madanes; Pinkhas Warezki, Sara–Pearl's son by her first husband, and his children.

The rest of my grandfather's family was taken in captivity, and the Lord, father of mercies, had mercy on some of them and left them as a remnant.

[Page 289]

The City–Fathers, the Rabbis

Today, when one writes of the city–fathers, the reference is to the mayor and his advisors. In the days before the terrible Holocaust, the city fathers were the rabbi and his court. The spiritual leader was the central personality; individuals and groups turned to him in all their dealings and all their needs. The rav was like a father and protector to his congregation; he rejoiced with them in their happiness and was pained when they were sad.

Before the Holocaust, there were three such "fathers" in Kozienice all called either local judges or authorized teachers. As mentioned above, the rebbe also served as head of the rabbinical court. As a sign of love and esteem for their venerable rebbe, the Jews of Kozienice signed a document making him chief rabbi and gave it to him, knowing in advance that he would have not time to devote to the day–to–day needs of the congregation, for all his time was dedicated to the service of the Lord. Thus the yoke of the congregation was placed, for all practical purposes upon the shoulders of the dayanim (judges).

There were three of these to mediate disputes in my time in Kozienice. My uncle, Rabbi Ben–Tzion Freilakh, inherited the chain of the rabbinate from his father, who had it from his father, Rabbi Aharon, who had it from his father, Rabbi Yitzkhok, a student of the Maggid, lovingly called Reb Itchele by the Jews of Kozienice.

Ben Tzion received his post at the age of sixteen when his father passed away. At the same time, he was ordained to the rabbinate by the genius and famous tzaddik Rav Meir–Yekhiel Halevi of Ostrowca.

Over the years he gained renown as one of the greatest rabbis in Poland.

His fellows in this exalted service were Rabbi Yoysef Shapiro, one of the four sons of the admor Zelig–Eliezer, a descendant of the Maggid, and Rabbi Yoysef Mintzberg, who served in the town of Czepelow before coming to Kozienice, and was deferentially called the Czepelower Rav by the Jews of Kozienice.

These rabbis sometimes worked together as one group in the supervision of shekhita and butcher–shops, of the mikve and eruv, and the like.

There was an old established custom in Kozienice for the rav or dayan of the town to be present at the slaughterhouse during the slaughtering of cattle and fowl, in order to provide khalakhic instruction for any question which might arise. Therefore, the rabbis set up a roster, each one of them being in the slaughterhouse once or twice a week.

[Page 290]

There were also several fields in which each one worked by himself. For example, Pinehas Freilakh preached in the great bes–medresh on two shabbosim a year (the shabbes before Pesakh and the one between Rosh Ha–

Shana and Yom Kippur). He was also the chief speaker on national holidays, prayed regularly in the bes–medresh, where he sat to the right of the ark and was the regular Torah reader, and was given the sixth aliya every shabbes. He also inherited his father*s right to daven musaf on the Days of Awe. In the bes–medresh, his brother Avrum–Khaim davened shakhris, and in the shul, where the rebbi'im prayed on the Days of Awe, the right to musaf was my grandfather's.

Rabbi Yoysef–Yehuda Mintzberg prayed shabbes and yontef, except for the Days of Awe, in the shul. He heard the reading of the Torah and then went home to daven musaf in the company of several of his adherents who prayed at his house. He also appeared occasionally on national holidays; he was learned, an excellent speaker, and a commanding personality.

Rabbi Shapiro prayed shabbes and yontef in the bes–medresh of his elder brother, the admor Reb Yakele, and in the bes–medresh during the week.

These three rabbis instructed on questions of permission and prohibition and ruled at din–toyres between two opposing parties.

As is the Jewish custom, there were also groups in Kozienice who supported and preferred their own rabbi to the exclusion of any others, but in general all three rabbis were accepted by the community, which drank of their waters and accepted and fulfilled their instruction.

During the time between World War I and the beginning of the nine teen–thirties, there was also – in addition to the rabbis just mentioned – an "appointed rabbi" who bore the title with respect to the civil authorities. He registered the congregation's marriages and births. The office was held honourably by Reb Moishe Weinberg, a refined man, pleasant in his bearing and accepted by the congregation. His children were active Zionists. One of his daughters, Dvoire, went to Israel and settled in Tel–Aviv with her family. After Rabbi Weinberg's death, the registration of births passed to Rabbi Freilakh, and the congregation had to hold elections for city rabbi.

In the meantime, Rabbi Freilakh was chosen head of the rabbinical court in Worka, and Rabbi Mintzberg passed away. A young rabbi was chosen, the son–in–law and heir to the throne of Rebbe Asher–Elimelekh Hopstein, the son of the admor of Stolin, Rabbi Nakhum–Shloime Perlov.

Rabbi Perlov was an outstanding scholar, a man of parts and superior qualities. He returned the position of the rebbe's house to its earlier glory. The house of the admor was once again a stronghold, and everyone predicted a glorious future for him, until the brutal German soldiers came in their S.S. uniforms and destroyed, and performed abominations, and trampled everything holy under the foot of pride.

[Page 291]

Rabbi Perlov and his wife together with his mother–in–law and his young brother–in–law Moishe were forced to leave the town in disappointment. When they departed "its glory departed, its brightness departed, its splendour departed," until the entire congregation was destroyed.

The Congregation and its Leaders

As in all the cities of Europe, "The Jewish Community of Kozienice" (the kehilla) was the chief institution of the town's Jews. All the Jews living in the city and its environs belonged to it– There was a president at its head, and an administration chosen once every few years in democratic elections.

I recall two community leaders from the last years before the war.

Moishe Wasserman, a sensitive man, a tailor, was elected to office by the anti–Zionists on the administration. He represented the Folkists. My uncle, Pinkhas Freilakh, represented the Zionist movement in all its branches. He was a refined man, active, a well–to–do merchant by the standards of the town, and a fervent Zionist who also served on the town council.

The secretary of the kehilla was Reb Moishe Goldzweig, a pious Jew with a long beard, dressed in a long elegant coat without stains. On shabbes and yontef he wore a shtreimel and silk clothes. Although he had never studied in a Polish school, he knew Polish perfectly and used it freely in speech and writing. He was also a member of the city council and was respected by the Christians.

The heads of the kehilla changed, one going and one coming, but Moishe Goldzweig was attached to his office.

I knew the Jewish youth of Kozienice in the years before the war. Most of them were precious pearls, always ready to sacrifice themselves on the altar of the land of Israel and for the sake of their people.

I well remember the youth in the Betar uniforms, the members of He-khalutz and Ha–Shomer Ha–Tzair, the youth who took part in the Betar training in Kozienice, the Zionists, the Revisionists, Brit Ha–Khayil in their uniforms, Ha–Shakhar and Maccabee, Tze'irei Mizrahi, the religious Shomer organization, Tze'irei Agudat Yisroel They all studied and knew Hebrew; several of them were extremely cultured, and the characteristic common to them all was that they thirsted to learn and to know.

The Freilakh Family

(Note: Except for the following list of names, everything in this section has already been mentioned earlier in this article).

[Page 292]

In order to set up a monument to the pure and holy members of the Freilakh family, along with their children, I will record their names in the register of the martyrs of Kozienice insofar as I can recall them today, twenty-two years after the Holocaust.

Reb Elimelekh–Elazar ben ha–Rav Pinkhas Freilakh
Reb Shmuel–Elye ben Reb Elimelekh–Elazar Reb Avrum
Ya'akov ben Reb Elimelekh–Elazar
His wife, Roizele bas Reb Naphtali–Tzvi Burstin
Their daughter, Tzippoire–Gittel
Their son, Naphtali–Tzvi
Reb Pinkhas ben Reb Elimelekh–Elazar Freilakh, and his wife, Frieda
Yutele bas Reb Elimelekh–Elazar Freilakh
Her daughter, Alte bas Reb Shmuel Freilakh
His son, Pinkhas ben Reb Shmuel Freilakh
His son, Yerakhmiel ben Reb Shmuel Freilakh
Sarah–Pearl bas Reb Elimelekh–Elazar Freilakh
Her husband, Reb Yitzkhok–Meir Madanes
Their son, Bezalel ben Reb Yitzkhok–Meir Madanes
Their son, Ya'akov ben Reb Yitzkhok–Meir Madanes
Khayele bas Reb Elimelekh–Elazar Freilakh
Reb Avrum–Khayim ben ha–Rav Pinkhas Freilakh
Ha–Rav Ben Tzion ben ha–Rav Pinkhas Freilakh
Sorele bas ha–Rav Pinkhas Freilakh
Rivkele bas ha–Rav Pinkhas Freilakh

A group of Jewish students in Kozienice

[Page 293]

The Household of R'elimelech Freilich

by Zvi Madanes, Tel–Aviv

Rav Elimelech Freilich, the first born of R' Pinchas, was known in our town as a sharp, intelligent scholar. In his youth it was foreseen that he would become the Rabbi of our town. But he did not get that position since his younger brother was cantor and judge. He understood the soul of every human being, saw to the awakening of all aspects of life in the city, and knew how to treat his fellow man. Thanks to this, he won for himself the respect of the Jewish community of Kozienice.

After morning prayers, he learned a few pages of Gemarah, his daily chapter of Kabbalah and his daily amount of Zohar. He would then take the newspaper "Hyant", which was considered to be Zionist and read it through, without skipping a single line. He wanted to know about his fellow Jews in the rest of the world, but the more pious Jews in the community criticized him for reading such an "unkosher" newspaper. Grandfather never used to pay attention to this criticism because he always looked for, and found, some good in every Jew.

I will never forget grandfather's singing "next year in Jerusalem" at the Seder table, to the tune of the Rebbe of Kozienice. All of us grandchildren would sing for an hour in voices that pierced the heavens: Next year in Jerusalem! And each one of us felt in our hearts that next year we would really be in Jerusalem.

Abraham Freilich   Ickhok Freilich, son of Abraham Freilich

Welcoming the Sabbath by grandfather was also something special. On Friday, even before candle lighting, you could feel the Sabbath approaching. On the table was spread a white tablecloth. The two challahs were covered, and beside them lay a special knife with the words "Holy Sabbath" engraved on it. The stoves in the kitchen were closed, and the pleasing odor of the Sabbath fish filled the whole house. Grandfather arrived from dipping in the ritual bath, and put on his special Sabbath clothes: A white shirt, a long robe made of black silk, a silk belt and a fur trimmed round hat.

My grandmother, Hannah, of blessed memory, inserted a few coins into the blue box of the Jewish National Fund, and went to light the Sabbath candles. The house was filled with light and calm.

Grandfather combs his beard with his hand and goes off to the house of the Rebbe for the prayers welcoming the Sabbath. It is filled with worshippers and when they see R'Elimelech they begin. At the end of the service they greet each other with Gut Shabbes and head for home. Grandfather walks out slowly because going to synagogue one must hurry, but coming from synagogue you walk slowly, especially on Friday night, when every Jew is accompanied by two angels. As he walks home he hums a Sabbath tune.

[Page 294]

Khana, wife of R'Elimelech Freilich   R 'Elimelekh Freilich

From windows and doorways of houses, the glow of the Sabbath candles shine like the stars in the sky. Grandfather approaches and enters, saying Gut Shabbes. As he goes to the head of the table he recites prayer sections from the Zohar dealing with the holiness of the Sabbath. Tears flow from his eyes and the light of the candles accompanies the path of his tears. In his prayers he never forgets his relatives and friends. He also mentioned a certain Mr. X, and for the merit of the Sabbath candles, he prays that the light of Israel not be extinguished, God forbid. When he finished his prayers, he said the blessing over the wind. Each word was uttered with intent and in complete holiness.

Neighbors, who had already finished their meals and said the grace, came over to grandfather's house. He had a musical talent. Every year he would compose new tunes for the additional service of Rosh Hashanah and Yom Kippur. We, the grandchildren, could recognize by his facial expressions and the humming, that we were supposed to catch the new tune. He would open his eyes under his bushy eyebrows, and turn to my brother, of blessed memory, who was the head composer in the synagogue, and say: "Nu Betzalel, will you be able to repeat the new tune for the prayer " "Remember Us For Life?" "Yes grandfather," my brother would answer. Then all the people at the table would start singing the new tune for that prayer.

This would happen on every Sabbath. We sat together as one big family, children and grandchildren, and sang together the songs of the Sabbath.

Before the Kol Nidre Prayer

The sun is setting. Mother is lighting the candles as well as the Memorial candles. Each one of us goes to mother and father and wishes them a Happy New Year. Mother, trying to hold back her tears, blesses us and cries over us.

The whole town is on its way to the synagogue. In the synagogue, Jews are already standing wrapped in their prayer shawls ready for the prayer before Kol Nidre. On each side of the Holy Ark memorial candles are burning; big candles made of wax, whose light blends in with the light from the hanging chandeliers. The quiet spreads. Only from the women's section, the sound of wailing can be heard. Mothers are sobbing for the well–being of their offspring and households. A knock on the table signals the opening of the Ark as we say: "Open the gates of Heaven to our prayers".

Rabbi Elimelech, in his white robe and white socks, circles the platform and repeats the verse: "light shines for the righteous and joy for the upright." The crowd repeats this after him, and from the women's section a heart rending sigh is sounded. The scroll of law is returned to the Holy Ark, and R'Elimelech begins the Kol Nidre. The entire congregation hums the melody softly with intensity and awe.

[Page 295]

That synagogue was ruined. The Holy Scrolls were burned and the entire congregation was led to their deaths. O' Congregation of Kozienice, you are holy to us, and your last groans we hear to this day. Together with you we turn to God and pray to him to pour out his anger on the murderers for their destruction of the House of Jacob.

[Page 296]

Pinchas Freilich, May the Lord Avenge His Blood

by Yaakov Leib Eisemman–Bogata

Our first meeting was accidental, during a visit which I made to one of my family who married a Kozienicer young man. I think he was also from the Freilich family. Over a glass of tea, my relative introduced me to a blond young man who had come into the house. He was a lovable youth with a sympathetic smile, which added a special charm to his appealing demeanor. We discussed the problems of our times, and discovered that we both belonged to the Zionist Org., which bound our acquaintance even more.

My new friend, Pinchas Freilich was the son of the worthy and well–known Chasidic patriarch, R' Elimelech Freilich, the first adviser of the Maggid's dynasty, a Jew of stature, with a clever head. R' Elimelech was the most important member of the Freilich clan, the outstanding family in Kozienice, or as they joked, "The Czarist family". We can say that half of the town were members of the family, among whom were counted the Rabbi's family. It is understandable that they controlled the religious and communal life of the town.

But, at a time, when all family members dressed in traditional Jewish garb on the Sabbath – long coats and round fur hats; one broke away. This was my friend and comrade, Pinchas. He appeared on the streets in European garb and a felt hat. He also conducted his family life in a more modern fashion. In this he was helped by his wife, who came from a modern Jewish home in Galicia. His free time was dedicated to his lifetime ideal – Zionism. He threw himself into the work of creating a Zionist Org. on a large scale. He constantly came to me with plans on how to draw the youth into the movement. We worked together to establish a Yiddish and Hebrew library. He engaged in this work even though his family considered him a transgressor and free–thinker, who was leading astray the upright Chasidic sons and daughters. He often neglected his business for the sake of the movement. Disputes arose between him and his father, but he ignored them and continued his path. When it was time for elections to the Polish Senate the Zionist Land–Organization shook the world. They sent out circulars and propaganda materials, as well as speakers in order to elect more deputies from the Zionist Party. We were drawn into party squabbles, especially my friend Pinchas, of blessed memory. He didn't rest, but used his influence among the Jewish populace, that they vote for the Zionist list. With the help of the well organized youth we were victorious. In 1931 I left Poland forever. For a while we corresponded, but for various reasons we stopped. He is fresh in my memory to this day. May his memory be blessed!

[Page 297]

My Father Pinchas Freilich

by Cesia Freilich–Luxemburg, Stockholm

My father was born in Kozienice in 1898. He was descended from a strict religious family. In his twenties, he came up with the idea to organize a branch of the Zionist Org., which would struggle for a Jewish homeland in Eretz Yisroel, which was then under British mandate. At the time, my father married my mother, Frieda, of the Kirschenbaum family, which had come to Kozienice in 1918. My mother was born in Novi–borek, near Tarnow. After the wedding both my parents were active in Zionist institutions. My mother was especially active in WITZO. She collected money and thereby saw to it that our home was open to friends.

Pinkhas, Frieda and Meyer Freilich

For a long time my father was active in community affairs. He was chosen chairman of the Zionist Org. and held the position until 1939. In about 1933 father founded the Tarbut School and a kindergarten. I remember that one of the teachers in the school was Zvi Semiatizky, who now lives in Israel.

My friend, Sarah Rothman–Mandel, who lives in Israel, and who had studied Hebrew with Zvi Semiatizky, writes that her daughter now has the same teacher. Such coincidences occur in life – that a mother and daughter have the same Hebrew teacher many years apart.

My father was also Chairman of the Jewish National Fund and one of the co–founders of Hechalutz. He often traveled to Warsaw for conferences and saw to it that our town was visited by leaders of the Zionist Org. My father was also chosen as a board member of the Jewish Community Council.

After the Outbreak of War

September 1, 1939 was the start of World War II. On September 8, our town was occupied by the Germans. The difficult days began for us. I was witness to the murderers cutting off the beard of my grandfather, Elimelech Freilich. The Nazis waited for his outcry, but not a sound came from his lips. He stood quietly as if nothing were happening. They used large shears to cut off half his beard and only then did they leave him alone.

My father was especially hunted by the Nazis because of his position in the Zionist Org. and the Jewish Community Council. Several days after the occupation, the S.S. came to my father's mill and demanded payments. With difficulty the sum was accumulated since we were a poor town. My father understood what was in store for the Jews and did not want the leadership role. He suffered a great deal and grew old and gray so quickly that he couldn't be recognized. Afterwards the Germans liquidated our mill, and my father and his brother went to do forest work.

[Page 298]

The bread cards which each Jew received were insufficient and so hunger became a regular guest in our house. When the Jewish Militia was organized, good friends suggested that my brother should join, and in that way alleviate our need. My father rejected the suggestion because he didn't want our family to serve the interests of the Hitlerite murderers. Better to suffer hunger, with a clear conscience, than to help the Nazis.

After the Destruction

After the Ghetto was destroyed, my father and mother went to work in the Kozienice area. My brother worked in Pionki. There he became ill with inflamed lungs. In November 1942, the Gestapo came from Radom and took away 17 young men from the hospital. Among them were some 14- year olds, my 17 year old brother, Marcel and his friend Genzel. In the same month all Jewish work places in Kozienice were liquidated. Some of the people were sent to Treblinka and the others to other concentration camps. My father was sent to Volanov, where he suffered physically and morally. From there he was sent to Blizshin and then to Auschwitz.

My mother worked as an Aryan in the munitions factory in Pionki. She was a brave woman. She used to bring food to Volanov and Skarshisko and saved some Jews from camps by bringing them by train, at night, to Pionki. This was heroic because she risked her life to save others. Once, on the way to work, she was betrayed by a Christian named Tomashevski. This was at the close of 194–3. She denied the charge, saved herself, she was interned in Krushetz, from where in July, 1944, she was sent to Auschwitz.

In Auschwitz

In Auschwitz my mother met my father. Through the electrified fence they carried on a conversation. My mother didn't survive. She broke down both physically and mentally, and passed away at the beginning of 1945 at age 47. My father was sent to Mathausen in Austria, where he broke down. Two days before the liberation, at age 47, he died of hunger and illness.

I write of their tragic fate, and want their suffering memorialized in The Book of Kozienice. I hope that future generations will read this and not have to ever suffer such indignities. I also wish to memorialize the Genzel family, none of whom survived. Adele and Eva were shot in Kozienice; Rozalia and Yuzek died in Bialostok. Mauritzy Genzel, our religious teacher, died of hunger even before the transportation of the Ghetto Jews.

[Page 299]

Images From the Depths of Forgetfulness

by Malka Shapiro, Jerusalem

An old–time Hasid was R' Melech, the son of R' Pinchas. He was both a sharp scholar and merciful father to his children. What can a Jew do, who is engaged in many business ventures, and even after buying the flour mill in the town of Kotzlik, cannot make a living. His worries about running the mill came up in his prayers when he poured out all of his sorrows before the almighty. Since he is the cantor quite often in the synagogue of the Maggid the holy preacher from Kozienice. Beside him stands the righteous R'Yerachmiel Moshe, of blessed memory, the heir to the seat of his grandfather, the holy preacher. The cantor's prayer, which comes from his entire body bursts forth from his heart and enters the hearts of all the congregation. They pour all of their sorrows before the almighty with the words "from our distress we call upon you." Who could forget such a prayer? Who can forget R' Melech, the cantor of the beautiful voice and troubled heart who beseeches God to grant the Children of Israel a good and happy year. There were times when R' Melech forgot his troubles during prayer and danced like a schoolboy before holier prayers to a march tune, which the holy Maggid of Kozienice had heard from the Angels of God. At that time the Maggid led the Jew, Shmuel Zbitkover to the Garden of Eden. And by what merit did this simple, assimilated Jew, the husband of the righteous Tamril did he reach the exalted state of admittance into the Garden of Eden? When the Cossaks attacked the Jews in the city of Praga on the banks of the Vistula River which cuts through the capital, Warsaw. At the height of the pogrom, when the Cossaks were looting and slaughtering, Shmuel Zbitkover stood with a barrel full of gold coins in the square and announced: "He who brings a live Jew will receive two gold coins, and he who brings a dead Jew will receive one gold coin." The pogrom ended, and the martyrs were buried. The living were saved from the murderous Cossaks. It was after this event that the melody of the march was revealed to grandfather, the holy preacher. I remember well, the dancing of the cantor during his prayers, to the tune of this march.

The Small House of Study

Not only on the High Holy Days but also on Friday night in the small, ancient study house, R'Melech sang with feeling the tune to: "Come let us go forth to welcome the bride, the Sabbath queen." He was accompanied loudly by all.

The congregation was composed of Jews from all walks of life. All were Hasidim, dressed in long coats, good and upright Jews. Simple folk, like Shlomo Berl's, who served the scholars who sat and learned in the house of study, and Eliezer Itche, of blessed memory who ran his small store, together with his wife, honestly so that even non–Jews came and knew that they would not be cheated.

[Page 300]

R'Zundel, the miller, with his bass voice, would provide the flour from which the Shmurah Matzah was baked on the eve of the Passover. Many others were also present. On the Sabbath eves, the faces of the Jews of the city, which were troubled all week, took on a look of Sabbath joy. The Sabbath melodies of my family, of blessed memory, entered the soul, as my younger brothers, may their memories be blessed, sang them. R* Arele and R' Asher Elimelech, together with their families were slaughtered for their Jewish martyrdom in the Nazi Holocaust.

The crowded space of the ancient study house would seem to spread and enlarge on those Sabbath eves, when the candles sparkled in the silver candelabra, and in all the surrounding homes. This was after the great fire which had damaged many homes and the study house. All was rebuilt.

At times, on Sabbath eves, I feel as if I'm still in the company of the wife of the Maggid, of blessed memory in the women's section, which was the connecting room between the study house and the Maggid's quarters. It seems that I am also with my sister, Chana Goldele, may God avenge her blood, who came on Aliya to the valley of Zevulun in 1924. Today it is known as Kfar Hasidim. When she came on a visit to Poland in 1939, the war broke out. She was shot by a German after she had brought my wounded nephew to a hospital. And I also feel the presence of my sister, the righteous Rachel Chaya Miriam, of blessed memory, the wife of the Rebbe of Piasetshna who together with their children perished in the Holocaust.

I also find myself standing besides grandmother, Sarah Dvorale, of blessed memory who sighed as she prayed and my righteous mother, Brachale, may her memory be a blessing. All of the women I remember; the wife and daughters of R'Melech, the cantor; his sisters, Rivkele, Sarale and Gruna and their mother Ruchama, all of them tall, who seemed to me like the daughters of Tselafchod in the desert, in the time of Moses.

Also at the conclusion of the Sabbath R'Melech would sing at the final feast for bidding the Sabbath farewell. Those melodies could be heard until the wee hours of the morning. The melodies from the house of the preacher were so beautiful that they would even influence the non-Jews to act more friendly to Jews.

With the beginning of the work week, R'Melech would return to his flour mill in Kotzlik. Besides the obligation to support his family, because he had to worry about each and every one of his sons and daughters, each with his or her individual needs, he not only worked hard at the mill, but found time for study, especially on long winter nights, after the Rebbe had distributed volumes of the Talmud to each of his Hasidim. Full days of learning took place on the 18th and 19th of Kislev, the "Yahrzeits" of Rebbe Baruch'l and the Great Maggid, R' Dov of Mezritch. In spite of his preoccupation R' Melech always smiled. A heartfelt smile appeared on his broad-bearded face even after he would get angry at someone. Non-Jews were friendly with him and his workers knew that they must treat his horses who pulled his wagons, kindly.

[Page 301]

Once when bandits fell upon one of his wagons and the wagoneer tried to save the horses, he was shot in the head. The non-Jewish farmers then started to protect the wagons, even in the winter when travel on the roads was most difficult. Survivors of the town of Shivia tell, with feeling, of an incident at the end of winter when the horses could barely pull the wagon because of the icy conditions. At that moment a non-Jewish farmer rushed out of his house near Kotzlik, with his accordion and began to play. The playing of the music calmed the horses and they continued on their way.

A special fondness was displayed towards R'Melech also by the Austrians in World War I, after they had conquered Kozienice and its nearby fortress. The military governor called him the wise Melech, and enjoyed his intelligent conversations. By the way, not a single Jew was either killed or wounded during the bombardment of the city by heavy cannons. We were witness to a miracle thanks to the merit of the Maggid of Kozienice. Unfortunately, this cannot be said of the Holocaust, but our martyrs, may God avenge their blood, live on in our hearts. But R'Melech stands before our eyes, as if he were alive, to this day. We see him walking to the study house to pray, to the stores with the flour he brought from his mill and to his home on the street that bordered the home of the Maggid. His merciful way with his children had a soothing influence on all.

Even after the great fire, when the Maggid was accompanied to his temporary home by his Hasidim, and among them R'Melech, we felt safe and secure. In kindness I remember how soothingly he spoke to members of the family of Rebbe Elimelech of Grodzysk when, shortly after the Rebbe had passed away, his daughter-in-law gave birth to a girl and not to a boy as they had all expected. He influenced others to say that there was nothing to be upset about, and as she grew older, he would often go to see the child as she grew.

And now, after the Holocaust that the Nazis brought upon us, his image appears before my eyes among all of the martyrs, may their memory be blessed, those who were beloved and pleasant in their lifetimes, and in their deaths were not parted. That R'Melech, just like in his lifetime he was filled with feelings for others and faith, so also, on this last day as survivors tell it, he was taken by the Nazis on his last journey, holding his grandson to his chest. This was the son of his daughter who had been born to him when he was well along in years. Speaking words of comfort to the child, the Nazis killed both of them. Only our Father in Heaven can avenge this innocent blood, and he is faithful to the remnant of Israel, and will reward us with a complete redemption, materially and spiritually, speedily in our own days.

[Page 302]

Jews Who Built Kozienice

by Isaachar Lederman, Rio de Janeiro

As I've already indicated, right before the outbreak of World War II, about 5,000 Jews lived in Kozienice, who were engaged mainly in making canvas and leather shoes of all kinds, which were sold in the east and Galicia. Small merchants and businessmen were but a small percentage of the Jewish population, and their activities were also tied to the shoe industry. Even Rabbis and religious judges were involved in it

Eliezer Lederman

Besides these, there was in the city a brewery, two flour mills and 2 sawmills which belonged to Jews. One of these was Israel Honigshtok, a school chum of mine. He and his children were killed by the Hitler murderers. His wife, Hese, came to Brazil after the war, and died here five years ago.

Before WWI, there was also in town a large factory "Hammer", which produced copper sheets. The owners were Gerer Hasidim, scholars, who carried on a rich, observant Jewish life and participated in all facets of Jewish life. The factory was destroyed by the Russians and the owners went to Warsaw and never returned. The Poles confiscated the factory property, because it had been Russian, but it was never rebuilt.

Rachel Mintzberg daughter of Rabbi Yoseph Yehudi Mintzberg with her three children

The Larski Courtyard

A large palace was called the Larski Courtyard. It covered a very large area, surrounded by tall buildings and walls. In the center stood a beautiful palace with orchards, field, water and woods. There were also walking paths for young couples and sport areas. In the courtyard lived hundreds of workers, laborers, and shepherds with their families, who were engaged in various occupations. Jews had regular access to the courtyard. They provided everything for the inhabitants. Jews bought the grain, the fish from the ponds and the milk from the cows.

The milk and cheese industry was in the hands of a Jew named Moshe Getzels. The whole thing was run by a Russian with the help of Jews and Poles. The owners of the courtyard had palaces in Warsaw, Petersburg and Moscow. Once a year they came with their entire staff to do the accounts for the entire year. After WWI, the courtyard was confiscated by the Polish government. A Polish nobleman and his officials settled there and became the owners. Understandably, access to Jews became almost forbidden. All was taken over by Poles, even the milk and cheese industry. The orchards were no longer leased to Jews. A Pole, who invested nothing, always had to be a partner.

[Page 303]

Kozienice Was Nicely Built

There were nice markets, woods, gardens, entertainment centers and places for swimming and bathing. In the summer they came from Warsaw and Radom. The streets were broad and mostly paved. Many streets, such as Lubliner, Warshaver, Bzhuska, Radomer, Kostchelna and Magitova were inhabited by Jews. Poles lived all around the city. Only on Warshaver Street were there Christian establishments.

The Mintzberg Family

There were a number of high–rise houses, of which, almost all belonged to Jews. The nicest houses, which covered a large area, with many rooms and salons, belonged to the notable and wealthy Mintzberg and Weinberg families from before WWI. The Mintzberg's were the MRothchildsH of the town, and well known throughout Poland. They were lumber merchants. Yerachmiel Mintzberg was a scholar with a beautiful long white beard. In his old age, he sat and learned day and night. He had a large beautiful library with both religious and secular books. He read the Hebrew periodicals "Hatzfirah" and "Hazman", and conducted himself in an upright and honest manner. He did not chase honors. On the Sabbath he prayed in the House of Study. He raised his children to be religious and worldly. He had good teachers for them – learned Jewish soldiers who served in the area.

The great writer, Pinya Katz, was also one of their teachers. Grandchildren studied in Warsaw, Radom and Keltz, and some even studied in foreign countries. During WWI, when all Jews were driven out of Kozienice, the Mintzberg family went to Radom. The old man died there and the family didn't return. They rented their houses and even sold some of them to other Jews and Christians.

Only one son–in–law, Yona Tzemach, and a grandchild, a son of Shlomo Mintzberg, remained. The former had a beer brewery and the latter a bank. They provided credit to merchants and landworkers until WWII. The family perished in the Holocaust in Warsaw, Radom and Kozienice. Only a daughter of Yona Tzemach survived and is now in Israel.

It is important to mention how the Mintzberg's acquired their great fortune. It had once belonged to a Russian general who was stationed in Kozienice. He had no family. Yerachmiel Mintzberg was well acquainted with the general. He would lend him money and advise him. When the general fell ill in his old age, Yerachmiel and his wife did not leave his bedside and served him faithfully till the final moment of his life. Before he passed away, he gave Yerachmiel a signed paper indicating that his entire fortune, houses, gardens and forest were willed to Yerachmiel and his descendants forever. Old people told this story which they remembered. It was obviously a true story since the family never denied it.

[Page 304]

Rabbi Yosef–Yehuda Mintzberg

Before WWI our town appointed him as Rabbi in place of R'Rechthand, who had passed on. He was a big scholar of the same Mintzberg family – the Ostrovzer Mintzbergs, who were also very wealthy and the largest iron-mongers in the city. When WWI broke out, the Russians took the Rabbi hostage. He was in Russia till the October Revolution. When he came back from Russia there was joy and happiness in the city. He died in Warsaw in 1929 of a serious illness.

The Weinberg Family

The second family, Weinberg, as I mentioned above, was descended from R' Lipa Yona, a vigorous follower of the Kozienice Maggid. He was a prominent wine merchant, who traveled occasionally to Leipzig and Danzig, and was connected with nobles and foreign merchants. He was the wealthiest Jew in the Radomer area and a great philanthropist. After his death, his son, R'Gedalia, followed in his father's footsteps. He raised his children to be religious and worldly. Some were learned, and in town were called wild non-believers. The oldest son, Heshel, who came from Warsaw, founded a Yiddish school (in which I was a student) and secretly the "Bund" Org. of Workers. In 1905, he organized a large meeting in the House of Study, with the participation of delegates from Radom. That same night he had to flee the city, because of informers, and his end was: Siberia.

Another member of the family, who lived in Warsaw, (I don't remember his name) was among the few scholars who participated in the revolutionary movement. He was also sent to Siberia. When he was later freed by the October Revolution, he became the director of the large National Library in Moscow. One of the family members was director of a Polish school.

Yona, the son of Yitzhak Weinberg, who came after WWI from Radom, took over the inheritance of his grandfather and was very active in the community. He founded the Bund and the Youth Bund, a sports organization, and a Jewish school for poor children. His wife, Rachel, and 2 children, survived the Holocaust and came to Brazil, where she had 3 brothers–in–law. Two years ago she died here.

This is the family tree of the two wealthy families, about whom you can say that Torah and Wisdom went hand–in–hand. They built and perpetuated Jewish life in Kozienice. I also consider it my obligation not to minimize, God forbid, the entire Jewish community – rich and poor, merchants, small storekeepers, handworkers, workers, butchers, delivery men, wagon–drivers, porters, fishermen and market–place hawkers – all of those beautiful Jews, together with their wives and children, the people of Kozienice, who were cruelly murdered by the Hitler murderers – may their names be forever blotted out.

[Page 305]

By The River

by Chaim Dimant, Paris

I stand at the river and remind myself of my childhood years
All have passed, but everything lives in memory.
The sun sends her warm rays,
Almost all the walls of the houses were white.

I couldn't control myself and ran to the river.
I looked and saw how the sun sparkled like diamonds.
The beauty and warmth I greeted with a smile.

It was hot.
Under a tree I waited for a breeze.
The leaves murmured. The grass bent
Back and forth as you rock a child.

I fell asleep because of tiredness and heat.
A sweet dream greeted me on a hill,
Until I climbed to its summit.
I saw my river, and I became overjoyed.
We engaged in conversation.

The water shimmered with a smile.
It cannot speak otherwise, because it is, alas, a river.
But we understand one another.
Because we were often together.
I ran there quickly,
As soon as I could free myself from my mother.

My mother sang, the children under her wings.
I imagined that she rocked me in a cradle.
The sun went down, and night fell.
I arose, tired. I was faint.

[Page 306]

A Memorial to My Many – Branched Family

by Elimelech Feigenboim, Ramat Gan

I am fulfilling by this a holy obligation to establish a memorial to my large family. My late father, Yitzhak David Feigenboim, was called in our city, R' Itshe Notis, the Ritual Slaughterer. He devoted all of his life to the household of the Rebbe, R'Yerachmiel Moshe, of blessed memory, and after he passed away, his son to the Rebbe R' Arele, of blessed memory. My father would neglect his own affairs and his family in caring for the Rebbes' households. After the death of Rebbe R' Yerachmiel Moshe his three single daughters and two sons were orphaned. Before each and everyone of their weddings, father would travel to all of the towns in Poland to collect money from Kozienicer Hasidim.

My late mother was short and thin, with a prayerbook always in her hand. The yoke of making a living fell upon her, since father spent his time in the Rebbe's household. In spite of the worries of a livelihood, she always found time for communal activities. My mother and our neighbor, Shaindel Dina, collected money for the sick and for poor brides. The material world did not interest her at all. One needs to care only about the world–to–come. Every Monday and Thursday she fasted. The Ninth day of Ab (Tisha B'Av) was a day of mourning in the full sense of the word in our town. The townsfolk sat in darkness and waited for a miracle, that the Messiah should come and redeem Israel from its bitter exile. This was the only hope for these pious Jews.

There were seven children in our family, five sons and two daughters. We received a traditional education. The girls did not learn in a school. My oldest brother, Aaron Berish, had a candy and cookie factory. He would send his products to the surrounding towns. He had a beautiful house on Lubelska Street. He was a well respected Hasid, who would lead the services on Rosh Hashanah and Yom Kippur. He was pleasant to all, helpful and a pillar of the community. His son and three daughters, all married, perished in the Holocaust. My second brother, Moshe Hirsh, an enlightened man, fought together with other young men, such as Avraham Freilich, Shmuel Karpman, Pinchas Freilich and Isaachar Lederman, to change the way of life in Kozienice. Before WWI, Moshe went to live in Warsaw. My sister, Nehama Leah, lived in a town near Kozienice. She was married to Moshe Chmilnitzki and they had a number of sons and daughters all of who perished in the Holocaust, except for a son and daughter who now live in Israel. My second sister, Raisel, who was married to Avraham Zucker, lived in Kozienice, had four children and they all perished. My late mother Tzivia Esther of the Rozen family, was the daughter of Yaakov Rozen. He was a respected cloth merchant from Radomska Street. His wife Rivke was called Grandma Rivkele, because they had many grandchildren and great-grandchildren.

Rokhma Feigenbaum   Rachel Feigenbaum

[Page 307]

My grandfather had six sons and two daughters as follows: R' Shimon Rozen, an observant, respected and important cloth merchant. At dawn he would rush to the synagogue for the first minyan, summer and winter. His large family included sons and daughters, grandchildren and great-grandchildren, all of whom perished, except for two grand–daughters, who live in the United States.

R'Moti Rozen, an observant, modest cloth merchant, whose very large family perished, except for two daughters and a grandson. R' Ezra Rozen, a clever, observant Jew, father and grandfather of many. His final years he lived in Lodz. All of his family perished. R' Moshe Rozen was the youngest in the family. His wife, Feige, was the daughter of Uncle Shimon. He was called Moshe di Bobes, because there was another Moshe in the family. He was a cloth merchant on Radomska Street, and observant. His four children perished. Aunt Chaya Leahtses, whose husband died in his youth, remained a widow with five children, three daughters and two sons. One son was called crippled Berish, because at age three he contracted Polio, and could only crawl on his backside with the aid of his hands. She, my aunt, had one of the largest cloth stores in the city and was clever and respected. All of her children married well. Of the whole family only five grandchildren remained alive; two in Israel and three in Canada.

R' Fishel Rozen, an observant wool merchant, and his wife Pesia, lived in Radom. They had two daughters, Chanele and Tzivia, who perished. Eliezer Rozen and his wife, Leah, lived in Kazimiez. They had three sons. One, Shlomo, was an observant rich fur merchant who went to Israel before WWII and died there. My grandfather, R' Chaim Yaakov Rozen, a cloth merchant and father of the large Rozen clan was a tall Jew with a white beard, who smoked a pipe and was respected by both Jews and gentiles. My grandmother was short. She had fifteen children, eight of whom remained alive. Understandably, my grandfather was observant, but did not incline towards Hasidism. Both reached a ripe old age. Grandpa died in 1916 and Grandma in 1917. They established a large family that was called the Rozen Clan. My parents had a cloth store on Rodomska Street. We were never rich, but we never lacked food or clothing. We were considered middle–class, even though life was not easy.

Left: A group from the Feigenbaum family at the cemetery
Right: Fishel and Khana Feigenbaum

My Teachers in Kozienice

I and my brother Fishel were the youngest. We received a "modern" education. From age 3 to 6 the Melamed, R' Yisroel Mendele taught us. My deceased mother used to tell us that he was called to come to our house, where he was paid the sum of 50 ruble for a period of three years, on condition that he take the boys in the morning and return with them in the evening. There were –0 children who learned in his Heder. It consisted of the teacher's family room and kitchen. Understandably, we knew everything that went on in his family. In the 3 years we began to learn aleph–beis (alphabet), the prayers and Chumash.

[Page 308]

We played more than we learned. He had an assistant, who helped with the discipline. We had no games, so we played outside in the sand or with stones. He had a whip which he used when necessary, but only on the poor children. For the recital of the "Sh'ma" prayer in the home of a woman who had given birth to a boy, we received bags of candy for the seven day period until the circumcision. We would also help the teacher's wife and take care of his children. After him, we had Rebbe Moishe Tuter. Here we learned Torah with Rashi's commentary. At age 9 we went to the yellow Moti, who had a red beard. Only 12 students learned Talmud with the commentaries. In the summer we learned from morning till evening, and in the winter until 9:00 p.m. At night we returned home carrying a paper lantern with a lighted candle in it. This Rebbe raised geese, and his wife sold them in the marketplace. We learned all the details of the business, and he was more concerned with it than he was with our learning. On sabbaths in the winter we would come to learn, and in the summer we would learn Ethics of the Fathers. On sabbaths the Rebbe would visit at the homes of his students to test them. Woe to the Rebbe if the student did not pass the test. At age 13 there weren't any teachers for us, so we went to Shedlitzer Yeshiva. Every day we ate somewhere else on Sabbath by relatives. With the outbreak of WWI the Yeshiva closed and we returned home.

[Page 309]

Chaim Berman, The Community Leader

by Issachar Lederman, Rio de Janeiro

I thought that Zelick Berman, who lives in Israel, would write about his brother, Chaim, and eternalize his memory, as he well deserved. I was sure that he would tell what happened to Chaim at the time of the destruction of the Kozienice ghetto, how he perished as a martyr in a Pole's cellar, where he had been hidden; and how, after the liberation the survivors of Kozienice together with Zelick took his remains from the cellar and gave him a Jewish burial.

Unfortunately, Zelick did not do it. Instead he wrote to his brother–in–law, Berish Shabason and asked that I write about Chaim. I firmly believe in the rule that "in a place where there is no other ..." it is my duty to write about a chaver, who earned the eternalization of his memory in our Yizkor Book.

Chaim Berman was a very intelligent person, and perhaps the only one in our shtetl who combined To rah learning, wisdom and labor. He stemmed from simple parents (his father was a photographer) but they knew very well how to raise children.

We learned together under the tutelage of the best teachers (melamdim). From age 12 to 15, we were taught by the great scholar, Lozer Karpman, who was Mendl Alter's only son, a Lubliner Hasid. Chaim's parents sent him to good Polish teachers at the time he was learning in Bais Medrash. My parents couldn't afford this luxury for me.

At age 15 we both left for the Makover Yeshiva. We studied there for 2 years. When we left Kozienice we had been strictly religious, but upon our return from the Yeshiva we were both free–thinkers. We were already well acquainted with both Hebrew and Yiddish secular literature and viewed life from a different perspective. Kozienice Hasidism and the Bais Medrash.

Chaim learned his father's trade and later went to an uncle in Lodz, where he worked and came home only for the holidays. I, on the other hand, stayed on in the four walls of the Bais Medrash.

During Choi Hamoed the Passover of 1907 we, together with a group of Bais Medrash students; Shmuel Karpman, the White Lozer, Avraham–Yekl Freilich, Yisroel Honigshtok, Moshke Tepper, Hillel Luxemburg and a few more students, together with a few elderly Maskilim and the Kozienice Rabbi's daughter, founded the first Jewish library in town in Yitzhok Krishpel's chamber, under the eyes of the Rebbe and his disciples.

In–between we married – and fortunately, we, excluding the White Lozer, remained in town. Then the first World War broke out and the old Hasidic life in "shtetl" disappeared. In 1918, we openly, and not in a closed chamber, founded the first Jewish folks–club in town. Chaim became chairman and I, vice–chairman.

[Page 310]

It was time for the elections to the town council and we joined the Jewish Folk–Party, and brought into town Noah Prilutsky, Latsky–Bertoldi, Leo Finklestein, S. Stupnitsky, Lazar Kahan, H.D. Nomberg, S. Beeber and others. We also organized the Jewish handworkers. Chaim was a good leader, speaker and organizer who was perfectly fluent in Polish. Other parties respected him and paid attention to what he said. He was elected with a large majority to the town council and his list pulled in two other councilmen; Zygmunt Halputer and Yitzhok–Ely Korman. Chaim was also chosen as Alderman by the Magistrate.

Communal elections are held. Chaim Berman and his group of folklorists and handworkers: Issachar Lederman, Moshe Vasserman, Leyzer–Itche Zilberberg, and Yitzhok–Ely Korman were elected.

When the Folks–Club founded the first drama circle in town, Chaim Berman became the actual leader of the circle. The "Children of Berman" as they were called in town; Chaim, Shimon, Tobe and Zelick always had hits. Even Hasidic Jews went to see their performance of The Dybbuk. They even came from the surrounding small towns to see The Dybbuk.

Briefly then, from "Heder" and until I left Poland in 1928, Chaim Berman and I were true Chaverim, who together had built up the Yiddish culture of our town.

May my words serve as a fitting memorial for my chaver, Chaim Berman, of blessed memory, who died a martyr and did not stain his good name with any deed or act which could have been of any help to our murderers.

[Page 311]

Chaim Berman, The Community Leader and Folkist

by Levi Resnick, Bogata

It was the last Sunday in the month of March, 1941. The time was 11:30 and the Kovno–Moscow express pulled into the Vilna station. We had almost a half–hour, so we went out of our sleeping car to look, maybe for the last time, at "Jerusalem" of Lithuania (as Vilna was fondly called by Jews).

Be Well

And there was much to see! Not far from the tracks waited Herman Kruck, Chaim Yaakov Bjustovski, Israel Raban, Paulina Prelutzki and others, whose names I no longer remember. They had all come to bid farewell to the group of Jewish journalists and writers who had the good fortune to leave Lithuania, the 13th Soviet Socialist Republic. The "farewell" was a sad one, with tears which appeared involuntarily on everyone's cheeks. Each one of us thought: "Who knows if we're not seeing each other for the last time?" Because, as we mentioned at the time, our group was permitted by the Soviets to leave their territory for effective dollars that were paid for us in America.

At a distance from the group, standing all alone, due to fear, it seems, of being identified with counter–revolutionaries, was Noah Prelutzki – may God avenge his blood. He who loved companionship, avoided us because at the time, he was the head of the Yiddish Language Department at Vilna University. All of his life he had hoped and striven for this opportunity, which was so dear to him and for which he was willing to sacrifice his life. The Jewish Communists knew of this weakness of his and as soon as Lithuania became the 13th Republic they offered him the position which he couldn't decline. So he stood at a distance, his head buried in the collar of his coat, and his eyes filled with tears. Maybe he already regretted his decision? Who knows? He was certainly a sacrifice to the dear mother tongue – Yiddish! It didn't take long! Three months later on June 22, 1941, Nazi Germany attacked Russia and all of our colleagues, who didn't have the good fortune to leave, were, together with all of Vilna's Jews, subjected to a martyr's death. We honor their memory!

Chana and Chaim Berman

Noah Prelutzki and Chaim Berman

I remember, as if it were today, during my visit to Kozienice in 1937, that I met Chaim Berman by accident. In fact, it wasn't an accident. I was invited to dine with him. I was already acquainted with his "credo". Although I was a Zionist, his personality impressed me due to his enthusiasm and down to earth attitude, about which, we will write later.

[Page 312]

When I returned from Kozienice to Warsaw, I told Noah Prelutzki of my impressions of my trip to Kozienice, and especially about his fellow party member, Chaim Berman. I remember it as if it was today, that the conversation about Chaim lasted several hours. He praised his "disciple" as he called Chaim, and to me he said: "You're really a capable member of the Poale–Zion movement and party, but since you've been in Chaim's home, You're worth something, as far as I'm concerned!"

Kozienice's Folks–Party Members

The Jewish Folks–Party was founded in Russia in 1906 by Professors Simon Dubnow, Yefroikin and Kreinin. The party platform stated that since Jews are spread among the nations, and will remain in those countries, which are not to be considered exile, but homelands, they will increase and obtain national, cultural and community autonomy, consisting of communal unity, with their own languages and schools.

The Folks–Party in Poland in 1916 had grown under the leadership of H. D. Nomberg, Noah Prilutzki, Shmuel Hirschhorn, Leo Finklestein and others. The Party proclaimed Yiddish as the national language. It established Yiddish schools, participated in the political life, was successful in some elections to the Polish parliament, and city councils, and published their own organ, "Dos Folk" (the People). Since 1926 the party was splintered and lost its influence among Jews. There were various reasons for this decline. Even though the Folks–Party lost its former influence among Jews, Kozienice remained perhaps the only remaining stronghold of the Party. This was thanks to Chaim Berman, who tried until the last moment of his life, to keep the contact between the Party and the handworkers of Kozienice, thanks to the encouragement of his mentor, Noah Prilutzky.

Not only the Folks–Party was active in Kozienice, but also other parties, with which our Jewish lives in Poland were blessed: Zionists with their leaders, Yosef Lichtenstein, Motl Goldstein and others. The "Bund" had a group of activists, with Jonah Weinberg and others. At the head of the Poale–Zion stood Shmuel Sharber. There was also a large group of Agudas Yisroel. But the Folks–Party had the largest number of members, maybe because the majority of workingmen were shoemakers, who belonged to the Party. The success of the Party was mainly due to Chaim Berman.

The Secret of Chaim's Success

We often write disparagingly of the Jewish Shtetl. We would make fun of the little town, but the truth is that Jewish life in the small communities was different from life in the big city, and not only statistically. Fewer Jews lived in these towns, but this was an advantage since in the big city people did not know each other, whereas to the shtetl everyone knew everyone else, and could even trace their ancestry way back. The quality of life was different. Parents could feel secure believing that their children were safe under the protection of the Kozienicer Maggid.

[Page 313]

One had to have tact and community experience to deal with the mass of handworkers, who were far from the religious influence which blew from the Maggid's street. Chaim's success enabled him to stand for many years at the head of the Folks–Party, and fill other and different positions. The fact that he had had to go to work at a young age enabled him to accomplish this. He had also attended the Yeshiva at Lodz for a few years where he ate each day in different homes. Also his work as a photographer there helped him a great deal in his later dealings with people of all sorts. A good photographer can set his camera for just the right moment, when the person who is being photographed, changes his appearance. This means that even though he's a bitter person, with a sour outlook all his life, he must smile and appear as a pleasant and often lovable person to others in his photograph.

If the photographer is not able to improve the character of the sour face, there is another solution, retouch the photograph. Lines of mouth and lips can be arranged to make it seem that the subject is smiling. In other words, photography means that a photographer can be God's partner so that the person photographed will truly be in the image of God.

What was Chaim's greatness, that he was able to hold on to, for 20 years, the same community posts? We all know of the insults and criticism that is heaped upon community leaders. How could he hold on to these political posts, in spite of opposition from within his own party, the Zionists, the Agudah, and the Bund, how was he able to overcome his political opponents? Let us leave the questions for a while and give some biographical details about him, which will clarify and answer to the questions.

His Youth

He was born in Kozienice to Kalman and Sara–Malka (his father was called Kalman Toibes). At home there were three other brothers and a sister. His father was a photographer. They were fairly well–off. He went to Heder and learned in the House of Study till his Bar Mitzvah. He then left home for the Lomzer Yeshiva, where he learned for a few years, ate "days" (every day somewhere else) just like other Yeshiva boys. There he got the urge to leave and go out to the wide world to see how the other half lived. He was very capable with a good head and an excellent memory. He remembered everything he read in Peretz, Mendele and Sholom Aleichem. From their heroes he learned about the poor masses of workers.

In Lodz

Chaim ran away from the Lomzer Yeshiva to the industrial city of Lodz, where there were many workers. There he learned his father's profession, photography. He also learned of the oppression of the Jewish worker, who wasn't admitted into the large factories, but had to go to small factory owners who exploited them, not merely for the sake of exploitation, but because the small owners themselves barely made a living.

[Page 314]

With his keen sense of observation, Chaim saw how on Friday afternoons, there would be a rush to bring the finished woven goods to the Jewish factory owners, and to receive from them the raw materials for the next week's work. They would also be paid so that they in their turn could pay the shopkeepers, butchers and coal–mongers in order to renew their credit for the following week.

Chaim saw in Lodz, which was ripe with new ideas, the need and enslavement of the handworkers. They worked from dawn to late at night. Their homes consisted of one large room which served as living room, kitchen, bedroom and workroom. He saw that even on the Sabbath they were so tired that they couldn't catch their breath. He also saw that the sackmakers and bootmakers, the most widespread Jewish occupations, in the large industrial city (Lodz) did not live any better or more comfortably. Handworkers needed work–cards, which they had difficulty getting because of language difficulties and a lack of proper education.

Chaim wandered through the streets, and saw the poverty which reigned everywhere. He heard the sigh of the masses, and saw how children begged for bread, which could not be given, even though their fathers worked 20 hours a day. His heart ached especially because these workers could not get into the large factories only because they were Jews. After a few years of work in Lodz, during which he thoroughly mastered photography, he went to Warsaw, where he practiced for two years, and then returned to Kozienice.

But this wasn't the same Chaim, who had left to learn in the Lomzer Yeshiva. He was entirely different; not only his clothing, but his ideas and ideals. He was determined to improve the lot of the Jewish handworkers, and obtain for them the same rights which their neighbors, the gentiles have.

Chaim Berman and His Handworkers

When he arrived he found a broad field to work in. Yisroel Domb, Motl Goldstein and others had formed a group which they called "Brotherly Love." The aim of the group was cultural. They would gather every evening, discuss a specific topic, discuss and read a Yiddish book.

[Page 315]

They also had a Torah Scroll so they could pray together on the Sabbath. Every Sabbath our friend, Itshe Nashelsker taught Bible. This went on for a while, Chaim became interested in the group, but he was interested in political activity as well as culture. Two things happened which hastened the establishment of the Folks–Party. First, Chaim was thrown out of the Study

House. When he came to pray and already had his phylacteries on, he was pelted with towels as a protest against his having discarded the long coat and traditional Jewish headgear. Also the group "Brotherly Love" did not have any better luck. Avraham Chaim Freilich went into the group's meeting place, and together with the beadle of the synagogue, took back the Torah Scroll. That put an end to the group. Chaim Roth organized a group which included Yisroel David Domb, Yitzhak Potachnik, Melech Avenshtern, Shmuel Ziterman and others. He invited Noah Prilutzky to come to Kozienice, and the Folks–Party was founded in collaboration with the Handworkers Organization. First he organized the shoe workers, who were the majority in Kozienice.

The leaders of the Handworkers were, besides Chaim Berman, Yitzhak Eliyahu Korman, Isaachar Lederman, Itshe Kestenberg, Yaakov David Kestenberg and others. Chaim devoted himself completely to the work. He ran and intervened for the benefit of different handworkers. He was all over, yelling, doing and helping. When the government closed down the local branch of the Party, they came running to Chaim and he in turn called upon Noah and together they would get the local branch reopened.

Chaim was not only the leader of the Folks–Party, but he was also chosen as Elderman in the city council, and inspector in the community (for a given time he was also presiding officer). As is known, an alderman was paid for his work. Chaim donated this money for the upkeep of his institutions. He also conducted literary readings on literature and politics. He established a dramatic circle group which presented The Dybbuk, The Slaughter, The Kreutzer Sonata and other presentations.

From Where Did Chaim Get His Strength

As we see, he had the energy to hold a number of positions that were not similar, but demanded different approaches. He also had his own family that he had to support. Where did he get the resources to do all this? Where did he get the spiritual strength in one and the same evening to deal with entirely different themes? In the Folks–Party, with the handworkers, to deal with economic matters relating to raw materials for making shoes; and later to run to his drama circle to direct the productions, or to stand up himself and do an entire role from memory? His knowledge came from the Kozienicer House of Study together with the Hasidic enthusiasm of Kotzk, Ger, Sochachev, Aleksander and Modzhitz, and from the dry misnagdim (opposed to Hasidism) but extremely sharp methodology of the lomzer Yeshiva. Both of these methodologies influenced Chaim's approach to his party work and to economic and cultural matters.

[Page 316]

With Hasidic enthusiasm, but with the cold logic of a Litvak he analyzed everything that there was to see and to learn in a city like Lodz in those days. In Lodz he witnessed the founding of the two religious workers parties, the

Hapoel Hamizrachi and the Poale Agudas Yisroel. Who can forget how they were ridiculed, "new workers with their tephillin bags under their arms!"

Today it is quite normal to see a scholar from the Etz Chaim Yeshiva in Jerusalem, who is also a tank commander in the Israeli army, but in those days it created quite a stir. It caused many tragedies when the student son–in–law left his father–in–law to go out to make a living on his own. Bundists and Poale Zion members would sneer at the new proletarians with beards and sidelocks.

Chaim observed this odd occurrence on the Jewish street. He ran to every gathering of the old parties and also of the new ones. He heard all the speakers: Yisroel Lichtenstein of the Bund; Leizer Levine of the Poale Zion; Moshe Limon of the Zionists; Avraham Levinson of the Hitachdut and also Yitzhak Rivkind and Yitzhak Piltz of Hapoel Hamizrachi and certainly Benjamin Mintz, A. G. Fridenson and David Zilberstein of Poale Agudas Yisroel. These were divinely inspired orators, who filled auditoriums with listeners, who swallowed each word and thought. He himself learned in Lodz, not only how to be an orator but also the method of how to conduct himself on stage, modulate his voice, how to gesture and basically how to win over an audience. And he also learned the theater in Lodz.

Lodz had not only the nicest theater building in all Poland on Constantine Street, but also the greatest actors performed there. The critics who wrote at the time included Dr. Mokdoni, Isaiah Unger, Moshe Broderson, Zalman Zylbertzveig, and the poet Yitzhak Katzenelson. Choruses were conducted by Glatstein. From there stems Chaim's later triumphs in Kozienice as a speaker, political activist, and disseminater of culture. To hold on to, for so many years, to so many communal positions one needed an iron will and steel patience.

Chaim Was Never Tired

Chaim was the typical activist, who never liked to rest on his laurels. He was never tired when he had to deal with intervening on behalf of a fellow Jew. He was always ready to run, to oppose an edict, and there were plenty of edicts in Poland. The authorities always had edicts in their arsenal which gave them the right to close down a workers club. Chaim did not tire of running from one official to another in order to nullify one edict after another. In the final years when the antisemitism reached its height and got worse from day to day, it was impossible for Jewish leaders to breathe. Jewish representatives in government positions found the antisemitism endemic. In the small towns it was even worse than in the bigger cities. In the cities there was at least a Jewish senator or deputy, who was able to try to nullify an edict.

[Page 317]

In a small town like ours only Chaim could do it. He had to be aggressive and display "Chutzpah" in order to accomplish anything. Even the biggest antisemites would listen to him in the council room. He did not try to please the gentiles in his speeches, but sought to present the Jewish case. He was also very modest. He would not talk down to people, but tried to lift them to their level. His Jewish knowledge was well rounded, well thought out and presented. He did not speak from the top of his head and his thoughts were well prepared. In this way Chaim led his handworkers for many years. He advised them to be not only capable workers, but also proud Jews, who are not afraid of every goy. The Kozienice shoemakers, not only knew their trade well, but they could read books, be involved with world politics and know what was going on in the Jewish world. Chaim's language was humane without frills. He spoke right to the matter at hand, calling a spade a spade. He learned this directness from his teacher, Noah Prilutzky. He wasn't afraid to grab the bull by the horns, to see the great danger that is facing the handworkers. He was successful more than once in postponing the carrying out of some order that would have harmed the handworkers.

Chaim Loved the Individual as Well as the Community

It made no difference to him if he had to run for an individual or a group. He always possessed a few new thoughts which would prove to the goy that he was wrong. And the goyim had an unusual respect for Chaim. For him they had open ears. They didn't consider him the typical Jew, but a proud Jew, who speaks their language, with a pure accent, and giving them the feeling that he is speaking to equals. This approach caused a favorable response on the part of the officials involved. One could not refuse Chaim. The goyim respected him. They knew that when he intervenes, it is not on his own interest, but for the community, and therefore they also loved him. They knew that before them stands a Jew of stature who is worthwhile listening to. They knew that they couldn't get rid of him with a simple response. They must hear him out and grant his request, and if not, he would unleash his entire arsenal of words in the city council. They also knew that it wasn't advisable to be his enemy, but much better to be his friend, and not bother the Jews whose cause he was defending.

September 1, 1939

This is how it was until September 1, 1939, a Friday morning, when the radio announced that the German armies had crossed the Polish border. There was confusion in the town. People fled from their homes into the streets and back not knowing what to do.

The shoemakers worked all week and on Friday they would finish quickly, so they could run to the bakery of Yisroel Yitzhak Frisch to buy a large "tacks" cake. (It was a simple butter cake but was so called because the money for the cake came from banging tacks into shoes). Whoever banged faster earned more, and could therefore buy a bigger cake. The children counted the days until Friday, awaiting father's coming home with the cake. This Friday the shoemakers forgot to buy the cake, and the children, although they knew what war means, instinctively felt that today is different and it's pointless to await father's coming with the cake.

[Page 318]

Without Chaim

Chaim's house was filled with people. They came to ask advice, and what to do. All had forgotten that there was no point to asking because Chaim was no longer the former Chaim Berman. He no longer had a say. His good friends, the goyim, hearing the German military march, understood that it would be better not to befriend the Jews, and even though it wasn't said openly, it would be better to put some distance between themselves and the Jews. The Poles learned Hitler's hatred of Jews very well. Till now it had been hidden, since we were after all neighbors for so many years, and weren't there advantages for them, such as borrowing money, etc. But now with the German armies marching so quickly on Polish soil, and the Polish army retreating, it wouldn't be long before they'd be in Kozienice.

Chaim made out as if he didn't see the change in his good goyish friends. He knew what was happening. He began to liquidate papers, lists of names of activists, in order to eliminate any sign of those who had cooperated with him. He knew well that there was no place to run. As a folkist he would be just as unwelcome among the Russians as among the Nazis. He decided to place his life and that of his family in the hands of fate. What will be will be!

The Nazis, may their name be obliterated, quickly began to persecute Jews. They were helped in this by the former "good goyim", who were not only neighbors, but could even speak a good Yiddish. The goyim knew exactly what each Jew had, how much money, how much merchandise, and if someone had hidden something, they the "dear neighbors", knew exactly where it was. Previously they had spoken nicely, but each one of them had made the reckoning of how much he would get, if this or that Jew had to flee or was driven out by the Nazis.

Chaim No Longer Intervened

He engaged in his profession. He realized that if he intervened, he would willingly or unwillingly, be drawn into the Judenrat. And the new "leaders", when they came to ask his advice, he had one answer for them, "I am no longer Chaim Berman. I know nothing, and don't want to know about anything." Since he knew that he was the best photographer in town, he hoped that in some way this would help him survive this evil time. "I want", he would answer, "to keep my good name. Whatever happens, I won't change my mind." He didn't change his mind, and turned everyone away. They begged him not to be stubborn and to help lead in the conduct of Jewish life. Also the Nazis wanted him to assume the leadership of the Judenrat, but he managed to avoid them. His being such a good photographer helped him do this. They came to him for photos which they would send home to their wives and brides in Germany.

[Page 319]

Chaim really thought that he could survive the evil times. Other Jews thought the same. I must note that at the beginning, as long as the town was occupied by the regular German army, Jews were able to breathe. At least there was hope for survival. Even the biggest pessimist could not predict what was to come. It wasn't long before the Gestapo arrived in town. They spread out over the whole town like a pestilence, and every day there were new decrees. We Jews felt it. There was talk of sending Jews to work camps. In every home people began to pack up their belongings. Everyone looked for his best goyish neighbor in order to give him things to keep until this was over. I need not mention what eventually happened to these things. We all know! Day by day things got worse. They began to send Jews to work camps. Among them were Chaim, his wife Ghana, and their two sons, Amos and David. They were sent to Volanov. They managed to stay together until the end of 1941, when Chana and David were shot by the beasts. It's not difficult to imagine what Chaim went through. He also wanted to be shot, but the murderers didn't want to do him that "favor". He remained in the camp together with his son, Amos.

Death in the Cellar

Afterwards, his brother Zelick, who had hidden himself in the cellar of a Christian, sent false papers with someone in order to smuggle Chaim and his son out of the camp. The person came back, but without Chaim. Afterwards, Zelick once again sent a Christian woman, who succeeded in smuggling out Chaim and his son. They were hidden in the same cellar.

In the early months of 1942, Chaim became ill with typhus. Conditions in the cellar weren't sanitary. There weren't any medicines to relieve Chaim, who suffered. Chaim's screams were so piercing that the goy, who's basement it was; chased Zelick and Amos up into his house. What he did to Chaim has remained a secret, which Chaim carried to his grave. When Zelick and Amos returned to the cellar, they no longer heard Chaim's screams for he was dead. His brother and son wrapped his body in a sheet, dug a grave in the basement and buried him there. Later Zelick got sick with typhus, and lay on the grave of his brother until he was smuggled out of the cellar. Amos went to Warsaw. He wanted to reach acquaintances, but he was recognized by goyim, who turned him over to Germans, who shot him.

Burial on the Kozienice Cemetary

In the latter half of 1945 the war was over. A few Kozienice Jews returned from the camps. They asked about everyone and discovered that Chaim was buried in the cellar. They exhumed the body. They included Hese Honickstock, of blessed memory, who died in Rio De Janeiro, Paula Luxemburg, Balvina Kohn, Mindele Domb, Gershon Borenstein, Yehudit and Sarah Hershenhorn, and others. The corpse was brought to the cemetery, of which no sign remained. They dug a grave and buried the one who gave so much of his life to the benefit of Kozienice.

The Berman family at the grave of their mother Sara Malka

Toba and Emus Berman

[Page 320]

The Prophet Amos

Having been in Chaim Berman's home, the writer of these lines heard how
Chaim named his son for the prophet Amos. I wondered how come a Jew, a
Folkist like Chaim, was naming his first–born for one of the twelve minor
prophets, Amos, and Chaim replied: "It was not a capricious act." Since my
days in Yeshiva, Amos' simple words of rebuke from a shepherd's mouth ring
in my ears. He was not an aristocrat, but a simple person, like my Jews, the
handworkers. I gave my oldest son his name hoping that in his life he will
symbolize the personality of the prophet Amos. Let us here say, in memory of
Chaim Berman, who esteemed Amos, that the prophet criticized the rich for
their treatment of the poor. He prophesied the earthquake and the destruction
of the kingdom of Israel. Only at the end of his book do we find his words of
redemption: Behold the days are coming when the ploughman overtakes the
reaper – when the hills are aflow with the juice of grapes – and I will bring
about the restoration of my people Israel. Chaim, may God avenge his blood,
more than once warned the Polish city fathers that a day would come when
they would be punished for their previous crimes against Jews.

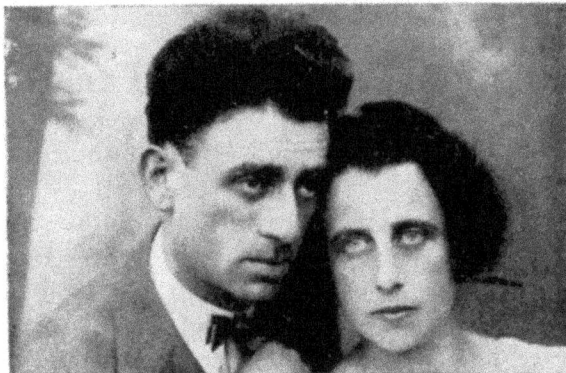

Shimon Berman and his wife

[Page 321]

The Korman and Shpiegel Families

by Feige Gunik, Kiryat Chaim

At 27 Bzhuska Street stood a beautiful house, built of red brick. The house was divided into two equal parts with a few steps. The house was built before the war by two brothers–in–law: Yitzhak Eli Korman and Yisroel Shpiegel. Both had shoe making establishments. They were well–off and conducted themselves as observant and upright Jews. Both engaged in community tasks, and were members of the directorate of the Handworkers Org., and were also members of the Folks–Party. Yitzhak Eli Korman was also elected to the city council as the representative of the Handworkers Org.

The two families lived together peacefully. Yisroel Shpiegel's family consisted of six people: Yisroel, Gitele, his wife, and four children. The Korman family also consisted of six people: Yitzhak, his wife, Altele and four children. The Shpiegel children studied in the Folkshul. Their son, Arele, studied medicine and married Shifra Kohn. The children of the Korman family also studied. The oldest, Z'ev (Velvel), finished Gymnasia (High School), and moved to his uncle, Yisroelke Korman, in Columbia. When the war broke out, both families became impoverished. Their finished shoes and leather were confiscated. Now the two had to work for others, but even then they still gave to others, who were poorer, as much as they were able to.

Dr. Arele Shpiegel and his wife Shifra died while working in a hospital in Russia. The other members of the family died in Treblinka. Only a daughter, Felly Shpiegel, who was married to David Goldman, remained alive. They live in Brussels, Belgium.

The Korman family also perished in Treblinka. Only Wolf Korman, who lives in Columbia, remained alive, and Yisraelik Korman in New York, and Avraham Korman, the youngest, in Paris.

[Page 322]

Chaim Yehiel Bornstein, The Writer

by Issachar Lederman, Rio De Janeiro

In the gallery of personalities of Nachum Sokolow, we find a note about our fellow townsman, Chaim Yehiel Bornstein, the Hebrew author and chronologer, who was unique in his generation. He was born in Kozienice in 1845. His mother was from Warsaw, an enlightened woman of a fine family. She was widowed at an early age. When he was quite young his teachers said that he would grow up to be a genius and a great man.

Chaim Yekhiel Borenstein, writer and poet

He studied in the House of Study in town. At age 13 he was knowledgeable in Talmud and its commentaries; immersed himself in astronomy, and studied foreign languages. At age 18 he married a Hasidic girl from Mogilnitz. His father–in–law said that he had been deceived because he took a rabbi for a son–in–law, and ended up with an accountant.

Chaim Yehiel returned to Kozienice and worked as a bookkeeper in a sugar factory which belonged to the wealthy Bornstein in the village of Menishev. His mother who helped in his development, wanted him to go to Warsaw, but he loved the quiet place where he could study in peace. From time to time his mother came to visit. She had two other sons there, Asher and Shmelke, who were in the liquor business. They had two active families who were involved in all aspects of Jewish life. His mother was the first woman in town to wear a wig that was decorated with her own hair. It's to be understood that this was frowned upon by the other mothers. He lost his job in Menishev and went to Warsaw, where he made the acquaintance of the great scholar, Ch. Z. Slonimsky.

Nachum Sokolow relates that the young Hasid from Kozienice was more expert in ancient Alexandrian tablets from Egypt, than Slonimsky, the scholar and mathematician, who enriched our literature with the treasures of his wisdom. Chaim Yehiel was the secretary of the Tlomatzke Synagogue in Warsaw. He occupied himself, especially with the chronology of the Jewish calendar. His heart was open for all sorts of problems and his soul was tied to his people and its culture.

From his prolific works, the best known are: The Debate Between R'Saadiah Gaon and Ben Meir.

The Development of Chronology in Israel, and Dates in Israel

He also translated Shekspirs Hamlet into Hebrew. His books and translations made an impression on Hebrew literature. Nachum Sokolow wrote an article about Bornstein's life and accomplishments in the 1927 issue of the annual "Hatekufah". In old age he became blind, and his wife and children died while he was still alive. He continued creating and dictated to his secretary who entered it into the record book of the synagogue and submitted it for publication in "Hatekufah". We Honor His Memory!

In 1906 a group of Kozienice's young men, who learned in the Study House, founded in Yitzhak Krishpels' house a library and a Drama Circle!?

[Page 323]

Issachar Lederman 70 Years Old

by Dr. M. Nisker, Rio De Janeiro

Who of us doesn't know Issachar Lederman! We see him everywhere where Yiddishkeit lives. We hear him everywhere where a Jewish problem arrives. Thousands of Jews heard his lectures on Jewish writers and poets, or about Jewish martyrdom. Also the Jewish community leaders in Sao Paulo, Bella Horizonta, Curitiva, Porto Alegre and other places know our Issachar. Not once did he appear on their lecture platforms spreading Jewish culture successfully. On the occasion of his 70th birthday 1 want to tell about his communal activities in the old home, Kozienice, where he was born in 1890, in a poor but proper home.

Rebeka, wife of Isoskhor Lederman

His father, a shoemaker, tried to give his son a religious upbringing, and while he was still young, sent him away to the Makover Yeshiva, where, in a period of two years he absorbed Jewish tradition and Talmudic knowledge. The young man strived for other things. He quickly became the secretary of the Handworkers Org. and in 1918 he took part in the first Polish Handworkers Convention. As a member of the Ortiker Community, he was a candidate for the city council. He took part in all the conferences of the Folks–Party in Poland, as chairman of the party in his birthplace.

In Rio De Janeiro

Due to well known reasons, Issachar was among the emigrants, who, after WWI looked for new homes. He brought his cultural baggage to Brazil. In his new home in Rio, during the first few months, he became an active communal worker. He was chosen as chairman of the Y. L. Peretz Club, a position he held responsibly until 1930, when the Club disbanded. Later he was chosen for the Executive of the Farband of Polish Jews, which was founded to replace the Peretz Club. Thanks to his worker background and social and national consciousness, our friend understood how to build up organized Jewish life wherever he lived, so that new Jewish immigrants would have a place to go for communal and cultural activities.

His Activity in Leopoldine

He was one of the most active communal workers in the suburb. In that neighborhood of Rio he was co–founder of the Library, which took the name of Simon Dubnow, because Issachar was one of his most ardent admirers. He got a letter from the great historian, thanking him for the honor. The letter has been kept to this day in the archives. In 1937 and 1938, when reactionary winds blew in our land, our friend Lederman did not get frightened but stood ready to defend the synagogue which was the center of our suburb. In 1945, he joined the more progressive elements, where he found his proper place.

[Page 324]

After long years of activity in the suburb, where he was chairman, and to this day honorary chairman, he joined the "Ikuf", where he is to this day on the executive board of the Central Committee. Tens of times he has represented the Institution. Besides Ikuf, you can meet him in the Sholom Aleichem Library, where he is vice–chairman of the Board. He is Secretary of the Board in the Farband of Polish Jews. He is an active co–editor of the beautiful and traditional publication "The Polish Jew", where he is represented by a weekly column. His fellow townsmen chose him as Chairman of the Association of Kozienice Jews in Rio.

Lederman at 70

This communal worker, who can be found everywhere, turned 70 in November, 1960. It was mentioned in the columns of the newspaper "Unzer Shtime" (Our Voice), the only progressive Yiddish periodical in Brazil, where Lederman works since the early years of its founding and is represented in it by more than 170 different articles. In his articles which contain both Jewish and progressive themes, he urges a new lifestyle, which will bring contentment not only to Jews but to all nations in the world. He calls for world peace, which would also guarantee peace on Israel's borders. With pen and words this "young" 70 year old fights for ideals with youthful pathos to achieve his mission in life. It is difficult to list everything that he has accomplished in progressive circles. We hope that his inexhaustible spirit will continue to help us build Jewish community life in Brazil for many years to come.

[Page 325]

My Mother Devorah Blotman of Blessed Memory

by Itshe Blotman, Paris

I remember when my father died. My mother had a nice gravestone set up for him. For you mother we cannot set up a gravestone, to our great sorrow we do not know where your grave is. I remember Friday at noon, you would begin to prepare for Shabbat. How you prepared the white tablecloth, and set the brass candlesticks. Before the sun set, you would light the candles, circling them with your white hands and saying the blessing. When father came from the Study House and made Kiddush (the benediction over the wine) you listened religiously and said Amen.

I remember Shabbat morning when I would carry your special prayer book for you because on the Sabbath it was forbidden to carry on the street. I remember the afternoon, when father would lie down to rest and you would read the weekly Torah portion from the Tzena Urena, the special Yiddish version of the Five Books of Moses for women. When the sun started to set you would escort the Holy Sabbath with the special farewell prayer "God of Abraham Isaac and Jacob". I remember when Shabbat ended, after the Melave Malka (escorting the Sabbath bride), you immediately began to worry about your children and grandchildren. You, mother, knew that we your children were not observant, but you never punished us for that. Never was a bad word said with you, because your good mother's heart and virtuous modesty would not let you cause your children grief. I remember how a few days before my Aiiya to Eretz Yisrael, you were depressed you had other children, but each one was dear to you as if he was an only child. Your consolation was that I was going to the land of your dreams. Every Friday, before candle lighting you would throw in a few groshen into the coin box of R' Meir Baal Hanes and say that the money is for Eretz Yisrael, the land of our forefathers. I remember how you accompanied me to the train. It was a gray, rainy day, and in my heart I felt your grief and sadness. You embraced me, kissed me and cried.

Although many years have passed since then, I can still see the tears in your eyes. Your memory, mother, is holy to us. Your charitable deeds and righteousness will remain in our memories forever.

Some Biographical Highlights About Franz Kreitzberg

He is the Painter, who on the "Bienal" in Sao Paulo, was honored as the best Brazilian painter. Franz (Ephraim) Kreitzberg was born in Kozienice in 1921 to poor parents. His father was a shoemaker. He studied in Heder, just like all Jewish children in he small towns. His parents couldn't give him any better education, so at age 12 they sent him away to an uncle in Tschenstochov. There he finished a folkshule and learned how to paint landscapes, portraits, figures and animals.

[Page 326]

In 1939, when Hitler invaded Poland, Franz fled to the Soviet Union, where he arrived at the Leningrad Academy and studied painting there. In 194–1, when Hitler invaded the Soviet Union, Franz enlisted in the Red Army and marched from Stalingrad to Berlin. After the war he continued his studies in Germany with the great artist, Boimeister. In 1949 he came to Brazil. For a few months he lived in Rio. For various reasons, he couldn't establish himself and lived in great poverty and almost starved. The Farband of Polish Jews bought his first painting for 5,000 Cruzeros. It was called "The Ghetto is Burning" and portrayed Mordecai Anilewitz. The painting is displayed annually at the ghetto memorial. He then lectured to the writer's circle of the Ikuf on the topic; Expressionism and Abstractionism, which was well attended.

In 1951 he went to Sao Paulo. Also there he wasn't helped much by the Jewish community. He had a few exhibits in the Folk House and other locations, but the community failed to understand his painting. For a while he worked as a designer for the Klabin firm, but the work was not satisfying. He wanted to gain entrance into the Brazilian artists family. With struggle, work and after great effort he reached his goal. Four of his paintings appeared in Sao Paulo's "Bienal". An international jury acknowledged him as the best painter in Brazil and he got first prize, consisting of 100,000 Cruzeros. Kreitzberg was greeted by the President of Brazil, His Excellency Zuselina Kubitchek, and other exalted personalities. His picture and reproductions of his paintings continue to appear in Brazilian newspapers and journals. He is praised by the greatest critics. His paintings have been sold for very high prices. It is an honor for the entire Jewish community in Brazil and for his fellow Kozienice townsmen.

Organization of Kozienice Rio – Sao Paulo We Greet Our Fellow Townsman Franz Kreitzberg

We greet our fellow townsman, Franz (Ephraim) Kreitzberg on the great success in his career as painter which came on the occasion of his exhibit at the International Exhibition in Sao Paulo (Bienal), where he received first prize as the best painter in Brazil. We wish him even greater successes in his career.

The Board

Fires in Kozienice

In 1778 – The synagogue, House of Study the Rabbi's house and other Jewish homes burned.

In 1782 – All of Kozienice burned.

[Page 327]

Kozienice Personalities and Figures

by Issachar Lederman, Rio De Janeiro

When we record for eternity in our Yizkor book everything and everyone that existed and lived in Kozienice, then there appear before my eyes our homely folk–Jews who memorialized themselves forever with their good deeds in our wretched life. I want to mention a few interesting personalities of our town, and may words serve as a memorial stone for generations to come.

R' Yeshayahu Shabason

A beautiful Jew, distinguished looking, with a white beard. He was always spotlessly dressed. He made his living from a pub on Radomer Street. He saved hundreds of children from an illness which was called the "fungus–disease" and appeared in the throats of new–boms. In those days there wasn't any childrens doctor in town. The old–time barber–surgeon served as doctor, but for this childhood disease he had no cure, so many children died.

Then Yeshayahu went to Warsaw to a famous pediatrician, and the doctor showed him how to eliminate the fungus. Thanks to him hundreds of children, Jewish and non–Jewish in the whole Kozienice region were saved from this terrible scourge. He wouldn't take any money for his help. He considered it a privilege to save children. Doctors said that if Shabason had studied medicine, he would have become a great physician. He conducted his life in a fine, upright Jewish manner, raised children and grandchildren, and died after WWI at a ripe old age.

The family of Shaja Shabason

R' Yonah Zilberstein

He was a Kolebieler Hasid, a Torah scholar, distinguished looking with the high forehead of a scholar, tall and beautiful, with a long white beard; a lively and happy Jew. He was the gabbai (beadle) of the burial society (Chevra Kadisha). He would walk slowly, step by step, and a bit stooped. In the morning he walked to the study house with a big tallis sack under his arm, in which he had a large turkish tallis, with a silver neckpiece, two pairs of tfillin (phylacteries) a Beth Yaakov prayer book and a silver snuff box.

Everyone respected this Jew. He lived in a wealthy manner, in his own large house, with a flour and grain shop on Magitover Street. His wife, Riva, ran the shop. All day she sat in the shop and recited the Psalms, so that the grain and flour would go up in price by a groschen per pound. And what Jewish woman wouldn't buy her flour for the Sabbath challahs from Riva? If a poor Jewish woman came to buy, Riva knew it by the way she walked and how she said "good morning". She knew the woman didn't have the money, so she would quickly say: "Don't be embarrassed. You'll pay me after the Sabbath. Go home and bake your beautiful challas for shabbes." Yona and Riva lived out their years honorably and lived to see grandchildren.

[Page 333]

His daughters were members of the library. This is how he lived out his years, and died after World War I. His family perished, except for his daughter Yocheved, who is in Israel since before World War II.

R' Avraham Rosenberg (Soda Water Factory Owner)

He was among the old enlightened ones in town, a clever Jew, who could tell a good joke or a tasteful story, and above all a Jew who knew everything. What his eyes could see, his hands could make; all sorts of woodcuts and bone carvings; a builder of houses; a fixer of furniture; an upholsterer, and an engraver of tombstones– In short, if this man had ever finished his schooling, he would have become a great inventor. But his greatest virtue was his modesty.

He read many Yiddish and Polish books, lived a respectable family life, never became rich and never wanted to. He loved communal activities, and helped to found the first Jewish library at Yitzhak Krishpel's. Many of the books he himself bound. When WWI broke out he went with his family to Warsaw and remained there. Only from time to time did he come to Kozienice to see his old friends, and spend some time with them, especially with Yekl Shipper. He was an old man when he perished in the Warsaw Ghetto.

Itzik Klezmer (Nodelman)

Itzik Klezmer and his sons were well known in town and in the surrounding towns. . He was first fiddle, and conductor of the ensemble, most of whom were relatives or close friends. Old Shmerl and his bass, Meier-Schachne with his clarinet, the tall Yisroel with his long trumpet, and Chemya with his fiddle. The drummer was tall Yisroel's son, Elale. They played at weddings and other joyous occasions for Jews and Polish nobles, in other towns, villages and rural areas. They were the only musicians in the area.

When Itzik bent his head down on the fiddle and began to play, the women cried openly and even the men shook their heads and wiped away the tears. He was truly a violin virtuoso! Here are some words of a folk song:

Itzik with the fiddle and Shmerl with the bass, Play for me a song, in the middle of the street.

About his son Shlomo, we heard from the Kozienicer refugee, Shimon Bobtshe, who during the Holocaust worked at one of the gas chambers in Treblinka. At the door of the ovens, the Nazis set up a band to play music. Shlomo played in this band. Suddenly he saw his only, nine year old son. He begged the Nazi officer to remove his son from the queue. The officer laughed and punched him in the stomach. At that moment Shlomo hit the S. S. man with his fiddle, and marched with his son into the gas chamber. We honor his memory!

[Page 334]

Motl Vadie's

This name was well known in all of Kozienice region as a Badchan (humorous performer at weddings and other celebrations). He would even entertain Rabbis and scholars. ' Together with the musical ensemble he entertained, making bride and groom joyous with his singing and jokes, which he made up on the spot. How much he gave of himself depended upon the importance of the participants. In his youth he had been a tailor. While working with needle and thread he would sing so well that it was a joy to hear him, and he would create rhymes as he talked.

When he got older his eyesight weakened, and he became a "badchan" (Humorous story teller) and became famous. He used to tell folk tales, and very juicy jokes. He was a humane Jew with talent, who didn't even know how to write. His son–in–law, the crippled Lozer, a teacher, used to write down everything that his father–in–law sang and recited, and there came to Kozienice young men, who wanted to become "badchanim" so they bought the notes cheaply.

Motl's wife used to bake honey cake for Shabbat and the holidays, and sell it. All of the Jewish organizations and synagogues, large and small would order honey cakes for Simchat Torah, weddings and circumcisions. When Motl got old, he taught his grandson, Vadie Kokos to be a "badchan", and sent him out to weddings. Vadie Kokos was also a bit of a jester with talent, but not quite up to his grandfather. He perished together with all the Jews in the death camps.

R' Pinchas Schvartzberg

R' Pinchas was a scribe, descended from a long line of scribes. He considered himself a privileged character because of his vocation, even though he barely made a living from it. Every few years he would write a Sefer Torah for a rich man. There were five scribes in town, but each of them had some sideline in order to support wife and children. Pinchas was a clever Jew, lively, joyful and the father of a large family. Besides the scrib's work he looked for other sources of livelihood. He pickled barrels of cucumbers to sell. On the high holy days this home became a boarding house for rich Hasidim, who came to the Rebbe. He also sold Mezuzos, Tephillin, Tzitzis, Machzorim and Siddurim, and from all of these he and his family were impoverished. His four sons did not become scribes. Two became merchants and two bootmakers, but he did have a son–in–law who was a scribe. He lived out his years honorably, had "nachas" from his children and grandchildren, until the Hitler gangsters fell upon Kozienice. He was shot in the street as he was coming from the

House of Study. May his memory be blessed! A fraction of his grandchildren, the three sons of Shmerl Schvartzberg, saved themselves by a miracle. Two are in North America, and the youngest, Chaim Yekl is in Brazil, where he leads a very nice family life.

[Page 335]

R' Chaim–Yekl Hirshenhorn

He was a well educated, clever Jew who was not a Hasid, but an interesting personality. He owned several houses and an oil press in which he would press oil from seeds the peasants would sell to him. The houses were not far from the river, where he had an orchard. His sons took care of it. Jews and Christians would buy the fruits. We also would go every evening to buy a pound of apples or pears. On the sabbaths the orchard was filled with young people who stayed there all day. The old Chaim–Yekl did not interfere in the running of the orchard. He made his living from the press and rents.

He had five sons. One studied in the Moscow Yeshiva. The others were merchants. Some of his grandchildren became skilled workers. After WWI the press and orchard were destroyed, and the children couldn't make a living from the houses. Chaim–Yekl and his wife passed away. Of the entire family, only a grandson survived, who had been named for his grandfather. He is in Brazil. After the Holocaust he married the daughter of Benjamin Krishpel. The grandson of Yitzhak Krishpel is active in our Kozienice Society, and helped with this Yizkor Book.

R' Yidl Grodniak and His Wife Chavele Tzorn

The world says: "God sits up above and rides down below", but luck is essential in family life. This was true for this couple.

He and she were two different types in life. Yidl was a clever Jew, and played the role of a merchant, a wealthy Jew, and even a bit of a Hasid, a follower of Rabbi R' Zelik–Eliezer Shapiro of Kozienice. He had a dyeing plant on Koshtshelne Street in the center of town. He was a Jew who loved life and wanted to get the most out of it. But unfortunately his life was not a life! It wasn't a decent home; there were no children who would understand him, and above all, an evil wife. His wife, Chavele Tzorn was the exact opposite of her husband. She was not good for him or for others. She had a small, hard, sunken head. Instead of a wig, she wore a cap with fringes on all sides, which looked like sidelocks by the ears. Her face was constantly smeared with rouge and powder. Her dress was dirty and half torn, with two big mannish boots on her feet, winter and summer. Her pale lips and small mouth steadily spat out curses. As soon as she would see Yidl, she looked him in the eye and looked for crumbs in his beard, to make sure he hadn't had a snack or had eaten at

Yaakov Shipper or Isaachar Shabason's pub, and fondled his girls and "shikses". Woe is him if she found anything. "Yidl, Yidl, may the worms eat you already!" "Chavele, be quiet, don't yell, so people won't hear. It's a crying shame! The whole town can hear you." But here it only began.

[Page 336]

"You should be seized and torn to shreds. Your mother should have miscarried you, before I married you. A crying shame you and your girls, eating and drinking with them at my expense." Their son Leyzer Bozer was just like his mdther. He stood at the door, scratched himself and laughed. Dirtied with the stains of the dyes he looked just like a jester. "Yes, yes, father, mother already told me that my bride is coming. I'm going to get married, and mother told me exactly what to do on the first night after the wedding." In the meantime there gathered a large circle of people, and it became lively because of Leyzer's words. Another joker, a young man runs over to him and pulls his hat over his eyes. His mother continues to shout: "Why have you gathered here?" She grabs a broom, and Leyzer runs after her adding to the confusion. Yidl stands aside, thinking about his misfortune, the mother and the son, and shakes his head. "Lord of the universe, of what use is my life? For whom am I slaving away? I thank you God for the favor, for this wife and son!"

Chavele jumps from her skin at these words and yells even louder. "You don't like it? Jews have an alternative! Let's go to the Rabbi and get a divorce!" "Don't you think I want to?" answers Yidl.

"Fooey Chavele" a neighbor tries to interfere. "This can lead to serious consequences. Forget about a divorce. You think my husband is any better. But let God grant us that we live out our years together!"

Chavele begins to cry and scream, "Mine, yours, all the same. Mine will drive me to an early grave!" Yidl runs out. He curses the day of his birth. No wife, no children! "Mother, mother" shouts Leyzer, "a child wants to buy 10 pounds of lime and a package of dye". "You should perish with your father! Where has he run off to? To the grave, hopefully!"

With troubles and suffering, not living and not dying, Yidl Grodniak and Chavele ended their years together in the gas–chambers.

Feivele Qger

Jewish legends tell about reincarnation. When we mention the name of Feivele Oger, we can truly say that this Jew was reincarnated. From early morning until late at night, he was harnassed, like a horse to a wagon on four wheels. He was bent over from pulling the cart and the name Oger (stallion) suited him. Whatever he came upon, he would carry off and from this he was able to support a wife, seven children, and an old father from whom he inherited the cart.

[Page 337]

He lived with his family on the street of the bathouse in a wooden shack. In order to enter the house, one had to bend in half. When Feivele would pull the cart, we children used to run after him and shout: "Feivele, stallion! "He wouldn't even turn around to the children. "Let them shout", he would say. He wouldn't even harm a fly on the wall. But if a sheygetz (a non-Jewish boy) would run after him and try to hold back the cart, or to make fun of him, he would hit him, hard enough so he would remember. Not one did he have to hit, and he would continue pulling his cart and murmur: "He won't bother me anymore."

All year you wouldn't see this Jew (Feivele) in the House of Study, not even on the Sabbath. Only on the High Holidays, Rosh Hashanah and Yom Kippur, would Feivele and his old father, drag themselves, bent over as if they were pulling the cart, to the study house. They would each carry a stool to sit on. Not far from the door, in the foyer, they would sit, not speaking to anyone, wrapped in their Talesim, and open their old Machzorim (High Holiday prayer books), which they had inherited from their grandfather, who had been in charge of the baths and the Ritual Bathouse of the Maggid. They didn't know how to pray, so they didn't bother to look into the Machzorim. Jesters used to say that they saw how they held their Machzorim upside down. When the Beadle banged on the table, they would both stand up at attention like soldiers. They would be the first to come and the last to leave. In this way this Jew, in dire poverty, worked hard without complaining, to earn his piece of bread.

Hersh–Leib Bozer, Water Carrier

Since I mentioned Feivele Oger as a reincarnation, Hersh–Leib was the second reincarnation in town. In Kozienice, there were other water carriers who carried water into Jewish homes, and from it they made a living. As far as I can remember, this occupation was exclusively Jewish. There was Isaacel and his sons, the blind Shammai and his brother, the gravedigger, and Yankele Polkovnik and his sons. Also women were water carriers; Zlatkele, Dobrele and Yonele and his wife. "At one time" water cost three coins. The housewives, who lived near the pumps, would carry their own water or paid less; three coins for two pails.

To this day Hersh–Leib is engraved in my memory, because he was the only water carrier for Rabbi Yerachmeil-Moishele. There, at the Rabbi's, he was a personality. All of the maids and the Rabbi's beadles dealt with him. He would bring the water, carry out the dirty water, helped lift the heavy filled cooking pots, clean the pots, sweep the courtyard and do the heaviest work in the Rabbi's study house for the hundreds of Hasidim who came to the Rabbi for the Sabbath and Holidays. On the High Holidays he would run around like crazy. He was the type of person who would not let himself be forgotten. He was the eternal slave. He just barely knew how to pray, but was religious. His water carrying made him one of the Rabbi's assistants. On the Sabbath he wore a high hat and a shiny long, belted coat. He had a small beard, and looked like a Purim–play performer. If anyone insulted him, or called him a name, he would hit him. He was quick to anger and had complaints against the whole world.

[Page 338]

After World War I, when the Rabbi's court declined, Hersh–Leib was water carrier for other Hasidim, but he wasn't pleased with this, and he would curse the housewives with the bitterest curses for the slightest thing. But this Hersh–Leib had two fine children, a son and a daughter. The son studied in a Warsaw Yeshiva, and ate on different days at the homes of Kozienicer Hasidim, and married a Hasidic girl from Shedletz. His daughter was a good seamstress. A year before World War II, she married Yitzhak Weinberg's son Yoske. After the wedding, Yoske Weinberg went to Brazil, where he had a sister and brother. Unfortunately, he was unable to take his wife to Brazil. The war broke out, and she perished, together with her father, mother, brother and all of the Kozienicer community.

Rachele Tsholok

I consider it an obligation to mention, with a few words, a female reincarnation in our town, whose name was Rachele Tsholok, who was Abba, the coachman's daughter, from his first wife. Rachele was nine years old when she was orphaned. From that time on, she knew every household in town and all of the housewives knew her. Wherever she went she would carry "cholent" to the baker, scrub pots and empty dirty water basins for a piece of bread and soup. As she got older her work became harder and more bitter. She was never in the same place for a night and a day. Almost barefoot, alone with swollen hands and feet, winter and summer, she would wash other people's clothes, and carry them for rinsing to the river. In the winter she would return frozen, with her teeth chattering, crying and cursing. She would throw herself down by the oven and without even eating, would fall asleep. Her price for a weeks work was 30 coins. She would wrap the money in rags. There were even some "nice" housewives, who would take the coins from her.

On Rosh Hashanah and Yom Kippur there were some goodhearted souls like Chavele, who took her along to the women's section of the synagogue. "Let her at least pray for a good new year, poor soul!" All day Rachele would sit in shul near the door and counted the windowpanes. Women looked pityingly at her, shook their heads, and let a tear drop from their eyes. It was after all, Judgement Day. On the way home the women wished her a good year, and she would answer, smiling and shaking her head, "You too!"

But there were days when she became sad, and didn't want any work. She would sit on the hard floor by the oven, crossed her legs, put her head down, wouldn't eat and sighed, cried, cursed and sang a song. Tbe words and melody of the song were sung to me by my daughter Feigele. She had heard Rachele sing it at her grandmother's house.

> Strolling,
> strolling,
> We both went
> Among thick
> leaves
> Rachel life,
> Rachel life,

[Page 339]

> Let us travel to
> uncle. Rachel–
> life, Rachel–
> life,
> Groom yourself
> nicely.
> Rachel–life,
> Rachel–life,
> Let us go on a
> journey.

That is how she would sing the song several times, until she fell asleep. Children and young girls would sing the song. Older women said that a Dyubbuk sang from Rachele. She died of hunger in the Ghetto.

Jews in the Kozienice Area

In 1897 the Jewish population was as follows in these towns in the Kozienice area:

Glovatshov	1109 Jews
Greynitz	1213 Jews
Gnievashov	523 Jews
Zvolin	3242 Jews
Yanovietz	308 Jews
Magnushev	771 Jews
Ritshivol	492 Jews
Shetshechov	125 Jews

Our Father, R' Moshe Goldtsveig, of Blessed Memory

by Nechama Goldtsveig–Mendelevitch and Gittel Goldtsveig–Stavsky

Before our eyes there appears the image of a wonderful Jew, with a long, gray beard, dressed in a beautiful, pressed kapote (long coat). Burning eyes, filled with wisdom and all of the beautiful Jewish characteristics, which he had. Can this figure disappear from our eyes? This is indeed our beloved father.

He was born in Zshelichov, and married young, barely 19 years old. Later he moved from his birthplace to Kozienice with his entire family, and spent almost his whole lifetime there. Like the majority of our good Jews in Poland, he led a religious life. It's interesting to note, that in addition to his religious lifestyle, he was gifted with worldly culture; an exception among Jews of Poland at that time. He spoke and wrote fluent Polish. Our grandmother used to tell how her son learned the Polish language. Every morning, before leaving home to go to Heder, his mother would give him a few groschen, so he could buy himself something to eat. It seems that he didn't spend the money, but saved it, and at the end of the month he would pay a private tutor for teaching him how to speak and write Polish. From childhood on, it was noticeable that he was a child prodigy, and this proved to be the case.

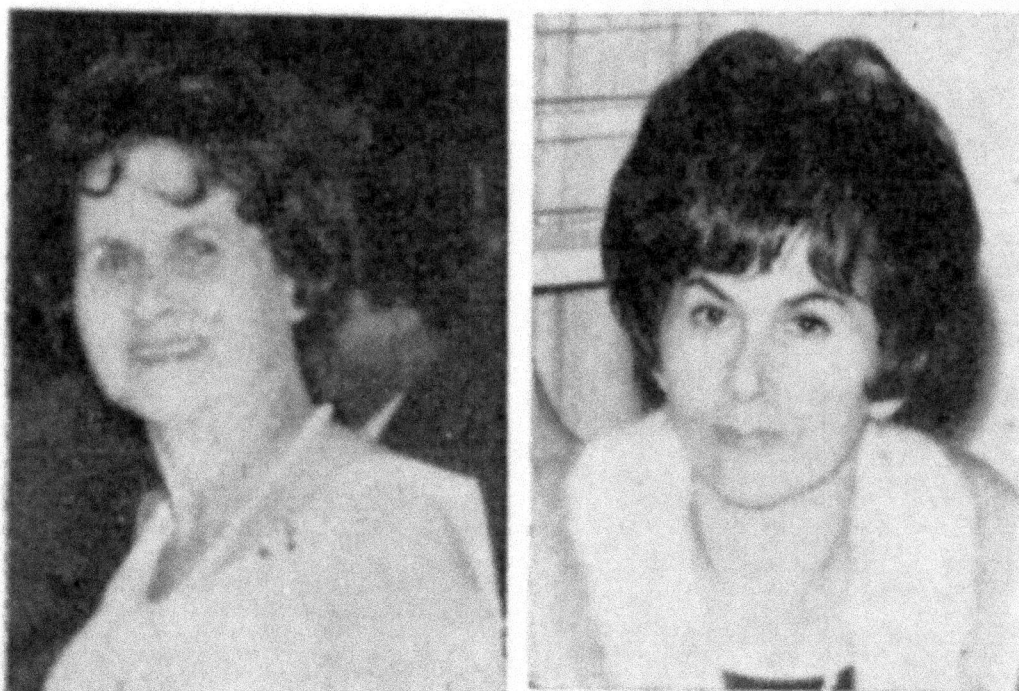

Nechama and Gitla Goldzweig

The doors of the highest spheres were not closed to him, in order for him to carry out whatever he was determined to do. He was the secretary of the Jewish Community, a member of the magistrate, where he worked wholeheartedly for his Jewish brethren. He would advise people, give help to the needy and from these activities drew his greatest satisfaction. Jews and non–Jews admired his worthwhile activity. Once when the President of Poland visited Kozienice, (his name was Ignacy Moshtzitzki) our father was chosen as chairman of the delegation that greeted the President.

[Page 341]

Don't Forget!

by Meir Zaltzman, Montreal Translated From Yiddish

From my place in the valley
My gaze heavenward sunken in thought,
Lime–ovens, many times
I thought I see.
Set up by devils hands,
Who want to destroy the world,
Day and night they burn and burn,
They can never cool down.

In order to rule the world,
In order that Germans be satisfied,
The first thing to do, which is missing: You must kill all the Jews!

And once, it seems at eventide,
When the sun set aflame,
Many Kozienice Jews, it seems to me,
And among them, also my good mother.

And the good Shloimele, the small one,
On his chest a yellow patch,
And there with him another Jew,
It was, it seems, my father.

And from the clouds, like wool,
And from the matte heaven,
I heard a voice,

My father's will and testament:
The innocent, pure blood that was shed,
Is not to be forgotten, never to be forgiven,
It is a will and testament for your children,
Therefore you remained alive!

[Page 342]

I Can Find No Answer

by Shmuel Reisman, New York

When I was 3 years old I began to study in Yisroel–Mendel's Heder. The Heder was on the street of the bath–house, Brovarne, in a large uncompleted house, with low benches against the walls. R' Yisroel Mendele was an old, good–natured Jew, who lived with his daughter, an old maid. With her loud and screechy voice, she helped him in his teaching duties. I remember, when one of my feet froze and I couldn't walk, the rebbe came and carried me on his shoulders to Heder– My second teacher was Berele, short, sick Jew with a short scraggly beard, with a pair of broken eyeglasses, tied with a string to his ear. He lived n a small house, near the Maggid's synagogue. In this Heder, I began to learn the Five Books of Moses.

I remember how my mother, may she rest in peace, would come to the Heder with sweets for the Heder boys, and when I stood on the table, the rebbe (teacher) would ask: "And what does a young boy learn?" And I answered: "Vayikrah (Leviticus, the 3rd of the Five Books of Moses)". "And what does Vayikrah mean?" "And he called". And so on and so forth, as was the custom in those days. The Heder's neighbor was Shachna, the scribe. When he would prepare the parchment, we would help him in his holy work, and for long hours sit and watch him write Torahs, Tephillin, and Mezuzos.

My Third Heder

The third Heder made a lasting and different impression on me, especially the rebbe, Baruch Shvartzberg, and his family. The difficulties of going to Heder, were unimaginable. We lived at the time in the Rebbe's old house, which stood on Brudne Alley. The Heder was on Koshtshelne, near the water pump. Near the pump, on the way to Heder, I had to pass Yechiel Koshkis' place. He had an angry rooster, who used to attack me daily, bite me and take away my piece of bread, which I used to carry with me. My mother, may she rest in peace, wanted to speak to the owner about tying up the rooster in order to make him harmless, but my father prevented it and said, "Why start up with him and quarrel? He won't do it, anyway." Father advised me to go to Heder a different way, even though it was two blocks longer, but I wouldn't have the trouble with the rooster. And so it was. That became my way to go to Heder, until I was notified that the hen was slaughtered.

Learning in the Heder was no pleasure either! If you did something wrong, or you didn't know the lesson, he would punish with the rod on your bare backside. If you unfastened and lowered your trousers yourself, you were hit four times, but if the rebbe had to do it, he would add a few extra!

[Page 343]

For good behavior and diligence in learning, the rebbe would allow you to rock his child in the cradle in the darkened alcove, especially on Thursday, which was market day and the rebbe's wife, Feigele, was busy selling. The summer months had a special significance. The courtyard of the Heder was rife with flies from the surrounding buildings. Besides teaching, the rebbe had several other sources of income. On the High Holidays he would be the cantor in a nearby community. A month before he would already be busy preparing his voice and practicing the blowing of the shofar, and his wife ran the Heder like a tyrant. The other Heders weren't any different, or any better. The Heder, the kitchen and the bedrooms were in the same room, and more than once the rebbe would quarrel with members of his family, and for us it was a holiday. The rebbes knew nothing about pedagogy or child–rearing. He who was a ne'er–do–well at everything else, became a teacher. This was our education, and this was how we spent our best childhood years. More than once I wonder how from such an education, there grew up such fine young men, who took part in all of the political and community institutions on the Jewish Street. I Can Find No Answer!

[Page 344]

A Few Personalities and Figures

by Elimelech Feigenbaum, Ramat–Gan

The cripple, Berish Kronengold, as he was named, was the son of Chaya–Leahtshe Kronengold. She had a manufacturing business on Radomer Street, and was the daughter of Chaim–Yakl and Rivke Rosen, manufacturing merchants on Radomer Street. She was left a widow with five children: three daughters and two sons. When her husband died, she was only 22 years old. One of her sons was the cripple, Berish, whose feet were paralysed. At age 3, he had contracted polio, and that's how he lived out his years. His hands served as feet.

I remember that when he was a small boy, and learned in Heder, we his relatives, would carry him on our shoulders to Heder. He would remain there all week, and for Shabbat we would bring him home. This is how it was during the winter, but during the summer he would move himself, without anyone's help. When he was full–grown, he married a poor girl from Radom. Her name was Leah. She was from an impoverished family, and very primitive. She couldn't speak Polish, and of course, couldn't write. He divorced her and married a second wife, but they never had any children.

He was truly a scholar, who knew several languages. He taught himself Polish and German, and was the Chairman of the Zionist Org. People would consult with him on various matters. According to some, he became religious in his old age. The Nazi murderers did not give him any special consideration, and he was killed together with all of Kozienicer's Jews.

Moti Karpman

R' Motl Alter's was dressed like all Jews, in a long kapote, with Jewish headgear. He had a white beard and was a Jew filled with wisdom. He had a bake shop on Radomer Street. His son was the well–known Shmuel Karpman, who had a beautiful, sweet voice, and was full of life. R' Motl was not foolish. He did not preach to anyone to mend their ways, even though he was a religious Jew, who went to pray three times a day. He understood the younger generation, read a newspaper, and understood world politics. You shouldn't forget that in my time in Kozienice, a newspaper was never brought into a religious home.

I remember an event that occurred in 1917. The Austrians occupied Kozienice. Suddenly Polish legionnaires, under the command of General Haller arrived. They were antisemites par excellence, and also hooligans. They would catch Jews and cut off their beards. R' Motl was caught by them, on his way to Warsaw, and half of his beard was shorn. He was depressed. He was ashamed to appear on the street. If they had taken away his entire fortune, it would not hurt him as much. He couldn't calm himself. My family lived in the same house. We were two brothers, young men.

[Page 345]

Our parents were very strict. We weren't allowed out to meet boyfriends, much less girls. We would sit and learn constantly in the study house. R' Motl would say to my mother: "Let the boys live, and go out for some fresh air. They're still young, and have plenty of time to learn. You have to understand the younger generation. Let them enjoy the world." It was a pleasure to speak to this Jew, because he was filled with humor and joie de vivre. Let us set up a memorial for our dear friend, his wife and two sons: Hershl and Shmuel and their families, whom the Nazi murderers killed together with all the Jews of Kozienice.

[Page 346]

Yekl Ring, the Watchmaker

by Yissachar Lederman, Rio De Janeiro

I was tired of sitting at home. It was after the season. The trade in cloth shoes was slow. Merchants didn't go out to peddle leather shoes, it was still too early. Merchants would give long term notes, and traders would extract a percentage and so would Yonah Mintzberg at the bank, so that sometimes only half of the sum would remain. Other merchants would not accept the notes because of the long term.

It's Not Good

In short, it was not good. Wherever you turned you were faced with the same eternal dilemma, how to make a living? I wander at home amongst my wife and children. I hear the wife ask "What are you doing at home? What will become of us? Go do something!" Times are hard, maybe you'll meet a merchant who has come to buy shoes? Or maybe you should travel around or go to Lemberg?

In Yakl Ring's Shop

With clamped lips I drop in on Yakl Ring. Here I'm free. I meet acquaintances, Chaim Berman, Kalman Berman, Yitzhak Weinberg, Halputer, Yitzhak Milgrom, Bendler, Itshe Mandl and his brother, and a few others, whom poverty drives out of their homes. We talk about politics. Poland has become antisemitic. Grabski will impoverish the Jewish masses. Wages are too high, and the Jewish handworker and small merchant should only be able to pay. A discussion develops about the Bund speaker, who spoke out this past Shabbat against Zionism and Hebrew. I bury myself in a corner and listen to a Bundist, a shoemaker, rise against those who criticized the speaker. Unfortunately, the entire discussion doesn't interest me. I'm worried about making a living, which is more difficult than the splitting of the Red Sea. Times are bitter and winter is approaching. I move to Yakl's corner, where he sits bent over his table, with his nose almost touching the watch that he is working on. His small round beard rolls on the table, and from his creased forehead there sticks out his magnifying eyepiece, like a black chimney. With two fingers he manipulates a small fork. The table is overflowing so that a slight blowing would overturn everything. The shop is small and narrow. The people who stand around his table, or at the sides make it sticky and the small window which illuminates the shop and is part of the wooden door is overhung with a few old–fashioned watches. On the table are wheels, gears, covers, springs, crystals, etc. Everything thrown about and spread out. For Yakl every piece is a treasure. He watches with his eye in his head. We knew that we mustn't touch.

[Page 347]

Be Happy, Jews!

Yakl's face can't be seen, but from time to time he hums a melody, for a passage which he alone made up and played on Purim at the Rebbe's feast. He lifts his head, smiles and says: "Bundism, Zionism, Hebrew, Yiddish; everything is unimportant. Do you know what the best politics is? A good plate of noodle soup. My wife, may she enjoy long life with me, told me to come home a bit earlier. She's prepared a good meal for me. Let it be like Shabbes, a bad Shabbes but a good weekday."

Everyone starts to laugh. Yakl takes his fiddle from the wall, plays and sings the Purim song Shoshanas Yaakov. "Be joyful, Jews! Hainan wanted to do away with us, and we hanged him. Be joyful, Jews! May the antisemites and Germans have a bitter end!"

Yakl Ring knew his freewheelers, who worry about the world's problems, but in their own homes it's dark. A dried up potato with a piece of bread on a holiday – therefore he cheered up the crowd with his fiddle. In the midst of his playing he remembered that his wife and five daughters are waiting for him at home. They do not go out for they are ashamed of their impoverished appearance. Even though the housework is minimal, his wife must do everything: repair or sew up a dress or a shirt, and prepare food for the children who are returning from school.

His Only Son Doesn't Want to Learn Watchmaking

His only son sits dispirited, because his father wants him to learn watchmaking and he has no desire to. "What do I need it for, father? Can't I see how little you have been able to earn from it?" He lifts his head from the table and looks at the small window. Outside stand young people, who do nothing and live it up: They eat, promenade, are nicely clothed, have pockets filled with money, and flirt with the young girls. "You see, father, people have luck. Their children don't work and have everything."

Yakl Ring glances at his son "Why are you looking there like a clay Golem, you fool. Do you envy them? Their fathers slave away. They don't sleep at night, runaround all day like poisoned mice in order to provide their wives and children with luxuries, and worry about dying too soon. Your father, my son, doesn't run, doesn't sweat, doesn't cheat with bankruptcy proceedings, and earns his piece of bread honorably. Better to look at the watch. You'll spoil it. It's time to learn the skill. Wherever life will drive you, you'll have a skill and not die from hunger. Work is a kingdom from which you don't have to depend on others."

[Page 348]

Noodles and Soup are More Important Than All

Even before Yakl finishes his lecture, his wife sticks in her head, and begins to shout: "Again with your son, Yakl. Enough of a lecture. It's time to go home to eat something. Who knows how late it is already? You must surely be hungry!"

"Nu, what do you say about my wife? May she live to a ripe old age!" Yakl licks his chops with joy. "Surely, my wife, there'll be the Sabbath treat today: noodles and soup!" He bends himself even closer to the table, gathers together the scattered watches and their parts and says to his son: "Come home, since you don't give a damn for the watches anyway. Eating noodles and soup is more important than everything. If the stomach is full, the heart is overjoyed. A man is not an angel. You must eat in this world, Jews; only in this world! There, there is nothing! As long as the soul is within him, says the commentary. With a full stomach it's even good in the other world. Even there they respect a pot belly. Ask the rich, Shlomo Mintzberg, if he hungers? Or Moshele and his children if they hunger? Jews, go home, because even burnt soup is a treat. Your wives are waiting for you."

We laugh at his jokes and words of wisdom. We go home to our wives and children or to the small stores, where the wives sit and wait for buyers. In the evening, when Yakl Ring closes his shop, he runs up to R' Mintzberg, to hear what's new in town. Or he goes to the Folkist Club, entertains with his jokes and folksy words. That's how Yekl lived out his years as a happy pauper.

Yakl Marries Off His Oldest Daughter

He married his eldest daughter to Nuta, the wagon driver, the son of Lazar Bondol's, who considered it a fitting match. Yakl didn't give any dowry, not even the wedding expenses. After the wedding, the couple went to France. Later on they sent for the other daughters and son and brought them to France. If they survived Hitlerism, I don't know. Yakl Ring and his wife died before World War II, with a good name. May their names be eternalized in our Yizkor Book!

[Page 349]

Yechiel Eliezer Zaltzberg,
the Community Activist

The children of the Zalcberg family at the grave of their father

Yechiel, better known as Yechiel Chaim Meir's, was born in Kozienice, where he lived all of his life. He got his education in Heder and the House of Study, like most young men at that time. And even so he spoke a fluent Polish, which came in handy in his public capacity. He was a tall, strong man with a serious countenance, a dark brown beard and clever blue eyes. He was married young to a daughter of a prominent family in Warsaw, Simcha–Itshe Reichman's, with whom he had six children: Mirl, Yekl Bruchale, Tsima Baruch and Chaim–Meir. He was a religious, progressive person, and as such, he was elected chairman of the Jewish Community. He held this position for two terms. The Community had insufficient funds so that its activities were limited. In spite of this, Yechiel considered it a holy obligation to build a fence around the cemetery, which was outside the city, where hooligans would damage and deface the tombstones. As an only son, he inherited his parent's bakery, from which he made a living for his family. In Kozienice there were 12 Jewish bakeries, and four non–Jewish. Unanimously, Yechiel was chosen chairman of the bakers. Often he would confer with the officials about bread prices and other matters. He was also a member of the city council. At age 41, he became seriously ill. They took him to Warsaw to the Tshiste–Hospital, where he lay for almost a year. He came back to Kozienice, but never regained his strength. After a short while he died.

[Page 349]

The Writer, Yitzhak Weinberg

He was born in Kozienice in 1878. He finished the Gymnasia (High School) in Radom, and from 1899 studied at Warsaw University, Berlin University, Breslau University and the University of Paris. He first studied the German language, and afterwards Semitic languages, and even the modern dialects of Abyssinian. He was in prison from 1907 to 1911 for his membership in the Polish Socialist Party. At first he was sentenced to hard–labor, but when he was found to be ill, it was changed. He is the author of great scientific works in Russian, Polish and German. He also authored popular scientific brochures in Polish and other languages, and translated the stories of Oscar Wilde into Yiddish. From 1902, he wrote scholarly articles in the Yiddish "Folkszeitung", which was edited by H. D. Horwitz and M. Spector; the Warsaw "Letzte Nayes", in the New York "Forverts", in "Tzukunft", and in a Yiddish library. In 1925 he was director of a private Polish–Yiddish Gymnasia in Vilna. He also signed the first call to found the YIVO (Yiddish Scientific Institute, which is today called the YIVO Institute for Jewish Research).

[Page 350]

The Teacher, Shlomo Tabachnick

by Tzvi Madanes, Tel Aviv

He was not born in Kozienice. He came to us during WW I, as a Russian soldier. After the war he decided to remain in Kozienice. He met here his lifelong companion, and together they built a Jewish home. Materially, he was not too well situated. He was a Jew who commanded respect. His outward appearance was impressive: A straight figure, who walked with an aristocratic walking stick in his hand, with decorated gold eyeglasses, which shone. His beard was trimmed and cared for. His promptness was legendary, and symbolized the Jew of the Enlightenment Era, who adhered to the principle: Be a Jew at home, and a Jew outside your home. Even at that time he was an ardent Zionist, starting with the Lovers of Zion Movement. He participated in many of the Zionist Congresses.

Left: Moshe and Rachel Tabatchnik
Right: Shlomo Tabatchnik, his wife, son, daugher-in-law and grandchild

He quickly became beloved by all of the groups in the city. He became the teacher of Kozienice's children, and founded the first modern Heder in the city. The very religious criticized his Heder and wanted to ostracize him and his Heder. The other teachers felt uncomfortable when compared to this aristocrat. Every morning, before the start of class, every child was checked for tidiness and cleanliness. He would start his classes with ethical and moral teachings, and taught beautiful Yiddish penmanship. Among other things, he also taught grammar. With his work, he laid the foundation for the Tarbut (Culture) Schools.

He realized his ideal and sent his oldest son, Hershel to the Holy Land, with the hope that eventually the entire family would join him. This was in the twenties, and a year later he and his wife journeyed to Eretz Yisroel, where he continued his pedagogic work. Later, when the bloody WWII broke out and the Hitlerites exterminated the Jews in the gas–chambers, he became weak with longing for his two sons who had remained in Kozienice. Our society members in Israel often visited him, and made him feel that he's not alone, right up to the last moment of his life.

We honor his memory!

[Page 351]

The Business Man, R' Yitzhak Milgrom, of Blessed Memory

by Yaakov Leibush Eisenman, Bogata

In my memory there lies the image of my father–in–law, R' Yitzhak. He was always dressed fine and clean. This was unusual in Polish towns of that time. He wore a dark kapote, a good cloth hat and fine and snug boots. His dark satin beard well combed, with a hard collar and black tie. That's how I remember him during the twenties of this century. He was, of blessed memory, a strict Jewish counselor for 30 years in Kozienice. Everything that took place, or would take place had to get his approval. His word carried weight, and respectfully people listened to him. He would not bow before any man, was always strict, almost cruelly so, and got his way in life. Even at home he was strict. His word was law. Nothing was done without his knowledge.

Ickhok, Khana and Sara Milgrom

He was the father of six daughters, each one smaller than the other. I never saw an expression of worry on his Jewish, aristocratic face. He had no appetite for money, as I would notice among other Jews. He never served the clientele of his book and paper business. The children took care of them always. Even for the buying of merchandise, one of his children would travel to Radom. His life and time were devoted to the public and community affairs. He was elected Alderman, and defended, with courage and national pride, the Jewish interests. He opposed the so–called Christian city–fathers, who wanted to exploit the already robbed and poor Jewish workers. With honor he carries forward the Jewish banner, and doesn't let it be lowered. This arouses Kozienice's antisemites. They search for ways to remove him from the council.

If thou seekest, ye shall find! Thanks to a cunning combination, with the help of the religious Jesuit Burgermeister (Mayor), they found an edict saying that an alderman must have an academic background, and since this "Jew", Itzik, doesn't have it, he must be removed from office. The protests of the entire Jewish populace were of no avail, and neither was the intervention of a high official from Radom. I recall the first months of 1920, when the Joint Distribution Committee, sent to Poland, to the impoverished Jewish towns, hundreds of wagons of flour, rice, sugar and medical supplies. How devoted and faithful R' Yitzhak Milgrom worked for the benefit of all of the Jewish population. His home became the head office for distribution of the items among the poor and needy.

Being, by nature so strict, he had few friends, but all had to acknowledge his honesty and virtue in the distribution of the products. He had the support of the Yiddish, as well as part of the Polish press.

Every Sabbath morning, his best friends came through the front door of his store to visit him. They were Yaakov Zifferman, with his gray–white beard, Yisroel Yitzhak Frisch, Itshe Noshelski, the town philosopher, and others. At covered tables, they read the newspaper "Heint" (Today) and drank black chicory. According to reports that I received from the Ghetto, my father–in–law conducted himself properly during the German occupation, as suits such a Jew. May God avenge his innocent blood!

[Page 352]

The Lifestyle of Tovah Berman, of Blessed Memory

Let us with pleasure relate the beautiful, noble deeds, which our fellow townsman, the righteous convert Leon Kenzsherski, who possesses the Jewish virtue of generosity, was able to do for our Jewish institutions, in memory of his wife, Tovah Berman–Kenzsherski, of blessed memory, on the first anniversary of her death. With this he eternalized her and his name. Donations for the following institutions:

For the Jewish Help Association and Polyclinic – after 120 years (my death) they shall possess forever the beautiful building, with the large business and 2 apartments at 1217 Uranas Street in Leopolddina.

For the Jewish Women's Association and Parents' Home – 200,000Cruz.

For the Children's Home – 200,000 Cruz.

For the Mendele Mocher Sephorim Jewish School in Leopolddina – 200,000 Cruz.

For the synagogue "Ahavas Shalom" in Leopolddina – a large crystal chandelier.

For Jewish National Fund trees in Israel – in Tovah's name and the name of her mother Sarah Malkah, of blessed memory, – 200,000 Cruz.

We consider it our obligation to tell briefly about Tovah's life: She was born in Kozienice in 1888, to respected parents, Kalman and Sarah Berman. Even at that time her parents understood that it was necessary to give their children a Jewish–national and worldly education. Tovah finished a Russian–Polish School in Radom, with a diploma as a midwife. With a Jewish teacher she studied Yiddish and Hebrew, impressed all with her beauty, cleverness and intelligence, and was well versed in Yiddish and Polish literature.

Her Communal Activities

During WWI, Tovah Berman, together with her brother, Chaim, of blessed memory, took part in the organization of the first Jewish Folks Club, which had a drama circle and sports section, which was directed by her brother Shimon Berman, of blessed memory. The drama circle was actually conducted by Tovah and her three brothers, and became well known because of its presentations in surrounding communities.

[Page 353]

During WWI, she also participated in organizing the Kitchen for Needy Children, and in the Aid Committee for Jewish Refugees, who came to Kozienice after the Petlura Pogroms. In 1921, Tovah Berman went to Brazil. Her leaving made a deep impression in town.

Leon Kenzsherski Converts

He was an upper class Pole who held a government position and fell in love with the beautiful Tovah. She accepted his declaration of love on condition that he become a Jew. He agreed, left his home, his Christian faith and his career, and the two left for Brazil, where he underwent conversion according to the Jewish Halacha. Also in Brazil, Tovah displayed her love for the Yiddish Theater. Several times she acted with Lubeltshik's Troupe in Rio and Sao Paulo, with great success. The proof we have of this are the critical writings, which are in our possession.

Because of the economic situation in Brazil in 1929, Tovah and her husband left for Belgium. They were there and survived the Holocaust. Since Leon still had his Polish passport, and Polish name, he was able to save himself, his wife and a number of acquaintances from the Hitler murderers. In 1951, they came back to Brazil, where her two brothers lived. Shimon, who was active in the community died in Rio in 1955, and the second one, may he live long, Zelik Berman, was saved from the Holocaust and came to Brazil with his wife in 1949. They had lost two children in the Holocaust. He is active in our town Society.

On December 24, 1960, Tovah died, without leaving any children. The beautiful deed of her husband, the righteous convert, has eternalized the two of them in the above mentioned institutions, forever!

We Honor Her Memory!

[Page 354]

In Heder by Baruch the Teacher

by Ber Zilberberg, Tel Aviv

As a Heder boy, I learned with the teacher, Baruch. He was one of the best teachers in Kozienice. In his Heder stood two large tables with benches. At one table sat the teacher at the head, and each time he would call one of the boys, and teach him while all the others listened. Every Sabbath, he would go to some boy's home, to test him and teach him a portion of the Torah, so that the parents should see what the boy knows already. The parents would honor him with some refreshments. He would often be accompanied by his own little boy, Avrahamele.

R' Baruch Knew Everything

He stemmed from a prominent family, who for generations had been scribes. He was very talented. Besides pedagogy, he knew how to prepare parchment, write Mezuzos and the portions that are inserted in Tephillin, the Tephillin boxes themselves, he could also make from leather. He knew how to scrape a horn so it would become a Shofar. He could wind the Tzisis and insert them in a Tallis, and carve Chanukah Dreidles (spinning tops) from a block of wood. He would turn away an evil eye and recite the formula to release people from their vows. He blew the Shofar. Besides which, he knew other things.

Money Becomes Shards

Once he discovered that his wife, Feigele had accumulated some money, tied it in her kerchief, and hidden it in the mattress of her bed. When she went out of the house, he ran over to the bed and began searching. He overturned the bed and there fell out the tied kerchief. Quickly he untied it took out the money, and replaced it with the shards of a broken plate. He retied the kerchief and replaced it, straightened the bed, and again resumed his teaching. Feigele, his wife, returned and he continued to teach in an even louder voice: The Gemara (Talmud) says: "That if a wife hides away money without her husband's knowledge, it will turn into shards". The children repeated what the teacher said again and again. When she heard what the children were learning, a fright seized her and she inched over to the bed and withdrew the kerchief. She untied it, looked, and was shocked. No money, only shards, dust as they had been learning. She burst out crying: "Oh, woe is me! What a misfortune has befallen me!" Hearing her wailing the teacher ran over to ask what had happened. She showed him the kerchief and said: "I had money in here and it has turned into shards, just as you've taught the children, and I can see that the Gemara tells the truth."

[Page 355]

The Children Respected the Teacher

They had great respect for him even when he would occasionally hit a boy with a cat–o–nine tails. When that happened his wife, Feigele would shout at him: "Baruch, you mustn't hit strange children!" In the short winter days we would learn until after it got dark. Some of the children made for themselves paper lanterns, in which they inserted candles. More than once, the wind blew the candle and the lantern burned up. Moshe, the teacher's oldest son would escort the children home at night.

On holidays the teacher would travel to the neighboring towns, where he would conduct the prayer services. He would take a Torah scroll with him, a shofar, and his eldest son, Moshe to help him sing the melodies of the prayers. When Moshe got older, he didn't want to help his father anymore. He opened a food shop and became a business man. On Thursdays, when the peasants came to market, and stood in front of Moshe's shop, he would announce in Polish, what he had for sale: "Naphta, candy and other goodies, etc."

The Teacher's Wife Gave Birth to Twins

One morning, I came to Heder, and as soon as I opened the door the teacher said to me:

"Ber, today we're not learning! Go home and tell your parents that my wife Feigele has given birth to twins, a boy and a girl." With joy I ran home! Wasn't it something, a day off from school. Free as a bird! To be able to go swimming in the river, or run into the forest, which was on the road to Warsaw, near the tall chimney. If you climbed to the top of the chimney, you could see the entire area.

The next morning I came to the Heder. As we sat down to learn, the neighbor, Hershele, the tailor, came in and said to the teacher: "R' Baruch, do you know that you have to register the new born children?" The teacher dressed himself in his Sabbath clothes, from head to toe, tied his special belt (gartel) around him and left. As soon as we saw the teacher leave, we began to live it up. We began to play all sorts of games, using buttons in place of money. A bone button was worth twice as much as others.

[Page 356]

The Teacher Goes to Register the Twins

Meanwhile my teacher is walking the streets and thinking: How do 1 tell them in Polish that my wife has given birth to twins, and I want to register them. He is already standing at the door of Police Headquarters on Varshaver Street. He takes his hat off and wearing his yarmulke, he quickly enters the building. The police officer on duty looks at him and asks him jokingly: "What happened?" The other policemen laughed and my teacher was frightened. He began to speak in Polish: "I want to report that my wife found a gun!" (He meant to say "gave birth to twins"). Hearing that his wife had found a gun, two policemen took their guns and ammunition, lowered the straps of their caps and tied them under their chins and then placed the teacher between them. "Come, show us the gun."

The Policemen Laughed Heartily

That's how Baruch, the teacher, was escorted through the streets of the city, by two policemen. Immediately, people began to run and create a commotion. "What's happened? Two policemen with guns are escorting Baruch, the teacher!" It didn't even occur to anyone that it was Baruch who was leading the police! They came into the Heder. The children got scared and shrunk away in fright, when they saw the teacher and the police. The teacher led the police to the bed, where his wife was lying with the twins, and pointed "Here lies the gun!" At that moment, the neighbor, Hershele came in and made it clear to the police that all the teacher wanted was to register the birth of the children and by mistake went to the police instead of the town hall. The police laughed heartily and then left.

[Page 357]

Reuben Rozenboim,
the Barber–Surgeon

by Shaindl Baron

He was called Reuben, the barber–surgeon. He had a barber shop and was a devoted Zionist. All of his life he strived to go to Eretz Yisrael, but unfortunately he didn't live to accomplish it. He perished at the hands of the Hitler murderers Kozienice loved him for his fine character and Jewish heart, which could never refuse anyone who requested a favor. He often visited the Rebbe's Court and was beloved by the Rebbe and his Hasidim.

He didn't have any children, but he did a great deal for me. I was his sister's child. My father died when I was three years old. Until this day I miss him, my second father, who raised me with great love, which only a father can give. I am now in America, and I would very much appreciate it if you would publish my few words about Reuben Rozenboim in the Yizkor book of Kozienice.

[Page 358]

My Mother's Candle Lighting

by Berish Shabason

Berish Shabason

With reverence and a holy shiver of pain and grief, I'd like to perpetuate the holy memory of my mother, my dear and beloved mother, of blessed memory, Liebe–Matl, or as she was called in town, Liebele. She was martyred in Treblinka together with all the other mothers, and shared the bitter fate of death in holiness and purity, may God avenge her blood. Deep in my memory there is engraved the deaths of generations of Jews who lived and wove Jewish life in my birthplace, Kozienice.

Like One Big Family

Dear, cordial Jews, poor and rich. Who can forget the Jewish Sabbaths and Holidays, Jewish sufferings and joys. Merchants, small dealers, handworkers and skilled workers lived together like one big family. Worked hard and bitter to lead a decent life, and hoped for better times. But instead, unfortunately, came the Hitler–flood, which erased everything, and drove to the doors of the Treblinka gas–chambers our dear and beloved ones and extinguished their lives, like the lights in holiness and sanctity.

Her Door Was Always Open For the Needy

Among all of the holy figures whose resting places we do not even know, I see the figure of my cordial mother, of blessed memory, who lived a truly righteous and religious life, not only for herself and her children, but also for those who needed her help. Her door was always open to the needy. Our mother always carried the yoke of the housewife. She was, as the expression goes, the head of the household, and helped support the family. She spread her wings over the children, like an eagle over its young ones. She prayed to God for us, the children, that we shouldn't become wanderers, God forbid, that we shouldn't lose our way on strange paths. Not one teardrop fell from her eyes when she prayed or lit the candles.

Shabbat at Candle–Lighting

When she covered her eyes to light the candles and said the blessing: "to kindle the Sabbath Light", we children heard her sighs filled with entreaties. It was quiet, no one said a word, in order not to interrupt mother's candle-lighting, in honor of the Sabbath.

[Page 359]

On the morning of the Sabbath, while the children were still lying in bed, wrapped in their covers, and dreaming their youthful dreams, my mother would tiptoe through the childrens' room with a light step, in order not to disturb our sleep. She would carry her thick prayer book, with the worn yellowed pages, and covered herself with the beautifully colored Turkish shawl, which she had inherited from her mother, Esther–Bayle, who had acquired it as an inheritance from her grandmother. And that way treading lightly, she would go summer and winter to pray in the House of Study. When she stepped over the threshold of the study house, she sat at her place religiously, which her father, Godl Dimant, had bought, when they had built the new House of Study, after the big fire, when almost half of the town, together with the synagogue and House of Study were destroyed.

Saturday evening, when the sun was setting, it was my biggest pleasure to hear how my mother bade farewell to the Holy Sabbath:

The beloved week should come,

With health, life, a livelihood and luck,

With peace and good tidings,

And everything good,

And let us say: "Amen and Amen!"

When she finished her entreaties, she cried out in great joy: "A good week, a good week children!" She kissed the little ones, and requested of the bigger ones to open the doors of our establishment.

Yom Kippur Eve

Most of all there is engraved upon my memory, my mother's candle-lighting on Yom Kippur eve before Kol Nidre. In those moments there was an awesome stillness in the house. No one spoke a word. We only looked into each other's eyes. Father stood sunken in thought, and everyone's attention was riveted on mother, who was preparing in awe and fear for the Day of Judgement, with the lighting of the Yom Kippur candles. We watched as she put four candles in the candelabra, a separate candle for each child, and lights the wicks, which this time seem to be different than at other times. Then her hands were waved around the holy lights, covered her face with them, and in a beseeching tone said the blessing for the lighting of the Yom Kippur candles.

At that moment she asked the Lord of the Universe, that he should have mercy on her husband and children, even if they should transgress; and that he shouldn't judge them harshly, but as a father judges his children. When she finished the candle–lighting, she called us to her, and gave us her blessing. I felt her tears upon my face. After the blessings, all of us, together with father, went to the study house, or to the Maggid's Synagogue.

[Page 360]

My Mother's Eyes Accompanied Me

It is already 25 years since Poland was destroyed. With my own eyes, I witnessed the destruction of Warsaw. I lived through years of torture and sufferings, wandered for two and a half years among goyim with a false Polish passport, listened to the murderous pronouncements of the Poles, and the words of the "good" Poles, which tore my pained heart. Often, I sought a place to spend the night, and often sought a place in which to hide my sister and brother at moments when they already had vials of poison in their mouth. At the time of the Polish uprising in Warsaw, I wandered from cellar to bunker and suffered hunger and drank drain water. Every day and every minute, I could see the Angel of Death before my eyes. I also saw eyes filled with murder and evil that followed my every step and movement. And always on the verge of death, I would see my mother, and I was saved from the hands of the murderers. Only by her merit did I and a few others of her children and grandchildren remain alive. How come? We ourselves don't know. A miracle, miracles!

Mother, With Honor I Bear Your Memory

In the last few years, when Yom Kippur comes, before Kol Nidre, I remember my mother's candle–lighting and I hear her prayers, her broken voice, and I see the flickering candles of the Yom Kippur lights. I am sure that in the last moments, in the Treblinka gas–chamber, my mother shed tears, and accompanied her last steps with prayers for her children: "Let my sacrifice atone for my children, and may they be saved to outlive this bitter decree!" Mother, dear! With honor and pride I'll carry your shining memory!

How Many Jews Lived In Kozienice

In 1611 – There lived in Kozienice 5 Jewish families in their own homes and 10 Jewish families in rented houses.

In 1726 – There were 630 Jewish souls living in Kozienice.

[Page 361]

Jewish Barber–Surgeons in Kozienice

by Yissachar Lederman, Rio De Janeiro

From my childhood, I remember three barber–surgeons in Kozienice: Chaim Feldsher, Yidele Zembel and Aaron Bendler. There was also a Polish barber–surgeon, named Pockshevinski, and an old doctor, named Zarzinski. It is understandable that when Jews got sick, they called a Jewish one. The custom was, not to run immediately to the local doctor, or to call upon the doctor from Radom, when one didn't feel well First all home remedies were tried: a wet towel for a headache; quinine for nausea; an enema for belly–ache; garlic and pepper for a toothache; incantations to ward off an evil eye and sugar candy for a bad cough or sore throat. When, after all of these remedies didn't work, we would call upon a barber–surgeon to bang away at varicosities, or place heated cupping glasses upon the affected area. And if the ill person did not recover, the women would run to the cemetery to beg the departed to intercede. They would run to the Rebbe to get an amulet or to the House of Study to implore before the open ark a complete recovery for the sick one. Or candles would be lit which the Beadle would extinguish almost immediately, so that he could use them for memorial candles. If all of this didn't help, a rich Jew would call the local doctor or the doctor from Radom. The life of the poor would be extinguished like a candle. This is how it was until WWI.

Now a few words about the last barber–surgeon, Aaron Bendler. He came to Kozienice after WWI. He learned his profession in the Jewish Hospital of Warsaw. He served in the Russian Army, and practiced as an assistant to the military doctors. The Jewish inhabitants trusted him more than they did the

Polish barber–surgeons or doctor. He was also a hairdresser. By nature he was a quiet man, who tended towards cultural community activities. His children participated in Jewish cultural life. He very often helped the sick poor, wouldn't take the money from them and loved to tell a joke. He and his family perished in the Holocaust. Only one daughter and a child saved themselves.

[Page 362]

In Memory of Missing Parents and Brothers

by Yitzhak Maydan, Kiryat–Chaim

Our family was many–branched, consisting of five brothers and two sisters, but only two of us, brothers, remained alive.

I want to tell about the family that disappeared and is no longer among the living. In 1941–1942 we lived in the Ghetto in Magnishev. From there we were driven to Kozienice, and from Kozienice to a forced–labor camp. My parents and sisters were sent to an extermination camp and since then were never heard of again. My parents were Shalom and Pesia; my sisters: Bella and Leah, and one brother, Moshe, lived in Warsaw and disappeared in 1941. We were two brothers in one camp and the other two brothers in another camp. I went through all the camps with my brother, Leib. For me he was not only a brother, but a caring father. We hoped that when the hell would be over, we would remain alive. But fate was cruel to us and my brother died in Bergen–Belsen, on April 16, 1945, one day after the liberation. Leib had been the one at home who cared for the family and we all loved him. He was a gentle soul. Of my two brothers, who were in a different camp, Yitzhak remained alive, and Koppel died in 1944 on a transport from Pionek to Auschwitz. Koppel was interested in everything, and wanted to know everything. He had golden hands, and he knew how to do many things in good taste and with charm. The following are the ages of my parents, brothers and sisters:

My father, Shalom	60
My mother, Pesia	55
My sister, Bella	35
My sister, Leah	25
My brother, Leib	33
My brother, Moshe	31
My brother, Koppel	27

May Their Memory Be Blessed!

[Page 363]

Story of a Stingy Man

by Issachar Lederman, Rio de Janeiro

In our town there was an ancient custom – from the time of the Maggid – that at dawn, and on Fridays at candle lighting time, the beadle of our synagogue would knock 3 times with a wooden hammer on every Jewish door, to awaken Jews to come to the synagogue for services. If there was a corpse in town, he would knock only twice so that the Jews would know that on that day there would be a funeral. It so happened that in town there was a scholarly Jew named Leibush Weinberg (Getz), who was a wealthy Gerer Hasid, but extremely stingy. He would literally skin poor shopkeepers and laborers. He had chests filled with pawn securities and a great deal of rent money, but would never give a contribution. He wouldn't even support needy worthy institutions. He never socialized except on the Sabbath, at services, in the Gerer Shul (Shtibl).

As I've already indicated, the Yeshiva students had established a fund for repairing holy books. Every Friday, two students, carrying collection boxes, went out to collect funds, which were used for repairing and rebinding damaged volumes, and to buy new books from the booksellers who came to town. Understandably, every Jew considered it a good deed to support this worthy project. But this miser, Leibush Weinberg, would not give, even when his wife requested it, under any circumstances.

Teaching Him a Lesson

Even his fellow Gerer Hasidim couldn't move him. "I'm not giving!" he shouted. "They don't want to learn, but only to play cards, and eat lima beans at Leibush Kesil's!" The students were disappointed. He not only didn't give anything but also insulted them. They decided that he must be taught a lesson that he would remember all of his life. On Thursday night the students held a meeting concerning Leibush Weinberg. What could be done to such a Jew! Moshe Rabi, who wore long sidelocks, a large ritual belt and was also scholarly and clever, said: "I have a suggestion. In the foyer of the synagogue there stand all of the utensils needed for preparing a corpse for burial. Between the afternoon and evening services, one of us will leave the latch of the foyer door open and at midnight a few of us will take the burial utensils and the box for the corpse and place them at the door of Liebush Weinberg's home. One of us will knock on the door of the beadle, Ozer, and tell him that Leibush died during the night, so that in the morning he will knock twice on every door." We all agreed to this plan. The youngsters, among whom I was one, were told to go home and not tell anyone about the plan.

[Page 364]

If You Don't Give While Alive...

In the morning, Ozer, the beadle, knocked twice on every door. "Who died?" "Leibush Weinberg!" "Who?" Jews asked, "That so and so?" "The burial society will not gain much from this one. He had sacks of gold and never gave anything." People began running from every direction to Leibush's house. The street filled. The burial society came running. People stood from afar and laughed, because Leibl had opened his window. He became bitter and sour. People guffawed! "Leibush – have you already returned from the other world? Do they charge interest there also?"

Two students, including Moshe, went to his window and said to him: "Reb Leibush, if you don't give while alive – then you must give after you die. If you won't give 100 Rubles to buy a new set of Talmud these burial utensils will stand at your door until you die!" Leibush ran through his house like a madman. He began to tear his hair from his head, and began to bargain, but to no avail. He paid the 100 Rubles and groaned as he did so. Tears poured from his eyes, but he didn't utter a word. The burial society was extremely pleased by the whole thing. The students collected the burial utensils, marched through the streets with them, singing and blessing Leibush, to whom they gave an additional name – Getz. My pen is not capable of recording what went on in town at that time. My memory also fails me a bit. This all happened 65 years ago. But I'll try to record the end of the story.

Leibl's wife Chaik'l, was a dear, pious Jewess. She was the exact opposite of her husband. She gave charity, without his knowledge, and suffered in his hell! The townspeople knew about this, but since she was so fine, she suffered in silence. After the above event, she said to the Rabbi: "I want to divorce him. As far as I am concerned, he's dead. I can't endure him any more!" They were divorced. Her only son, Mottel, she sent to the Gerer Yeshiva in Warsaw. He married a rich Hasidic girl. When he came back to Kozienice, he opened a sewing supply store on Radom Street. Mottel Weinberg was the father of Shlomo and Yoel. He died in middle age before WWI. Both his sons were Gerer Hasidim, businessmen, and leaders of the Agudas Israel movement. They were representatives of the Jewish community, and perished together with all of Kozienice's Jews, even though they were members of the Judenraat.

A few words about their grandmother, Chaik'l. She died of old age with an untarnished reputation. She supported the indigent sick. She would take food to the sick and chicken soup to poor children.

After the above incident, Leibush himself fell into a deep depression. His fortune evaporated. His wife and son took over the debts and the house and had nothing to do with him. Even after he passed away, they wouldn't mention his name. He died alone in a windowless shack, belonging to Nehamale the bagel baker. As the students had said: "If you don't give while alive – you'll give after you die!"

[Page 365]

The Rise and Death of Chana Rechthant

by Feige Gunik

Chana was born in 1902, into a poor and needy home of 6 children. At age 9, she left home to go to relatives in Warsaw, where she worked hard for her upkeep. She was separated from her home, but never complained. She was always even–tempered, but her eyes reflected her despair. At 16 she returned home and began to learn needle–work, a popular occupation for girls in Kozienice.

Chana Organizes the Needle–Workers

In 1922–23, the workers1 movement in Kozienice was organized. Chana joined and became active. She advanced quickly, was elected a committee member, and afterwards elected to chair the Needle–Workers section. She helped organize the trade, and it wasn't an easy task. When, after a huge effort it was more or less organized, the first strike was proclaimed. In those days the needle–workers worked from dawn to late at night in very unsanitary conditions. The employers called a lockout. The committee was organized, and we decided to establish a cooperative. A delegation was chosen, with Chana at the head, to go to Warsaw in order to bring back work. The women workers were temporarily employed. I want to note that, at the time, we found ourselves in a private home, and there we worked until victory. But Chana wasn't satisfied. She organized a youth group, and worked actively in it. She read a great deal of literature and held private readings for the youth. They honored and respected her. Her outward appearance aroused trust and all loved her.

Chana Flees to Russia

At the outbreak of WWII, Chana lived in Lodz. When the persecutions and selections began, she decided to flee to Russia. It was a difficult journey, and for weeks she wandered. Finally she succeeded in crossing the border to Russia. There she was sent to a labor camp, where she worked under difficult circumstances. She suffered hunger, lost her husband, and became ill and broken. In 1945 she returned with all of the repatriates to Poland. Kozienice had become Judenrein, and the Jewish repatriates were brought to Shtshetshin. That's where Chana lived. She couldn't make peace with the loss of her family and friends. Her heart ached! Walking on the street one day, she lost consciousness fell and died. Strangers picked her up and carried her home. This is how her pure soul left her body on July 6, 1946, on a Polish street!

[Page 366]

My Brother, Meir Shalom Tennenboim

by Esther Midan–Tennenboim, Kiryat Chaim, Israel

A few words about my dear brother, Meir–Shalom. He was a communal man of action who was connected with the professional associations. For a longer period of time, he was chairman of the association. In 1925 a strike of shoe–workers broke out. It was a bitter struggle between workers and management. One day his boss came to him and proposed that he should secretly lower the demands for the increase and then they could sign the agreement which would settle the strike. My brother answered that he, as chairman of the association, would not break ranks with the strikers, especially after so many months of hunger and sufferings. Afterwards, the bosses signed an agreement ending the strike, but they all boycotted my brother. Another worker was hired to replace him.

My brother was unemployed for months, until he was forced to sell his apartment and its contents and left for Paris. His wife remained with us for two years, until he established himself, and then he sent for her. For twenty years, my brother lived in Paris, with his wife and grown daughter, until the time of the Nazi occupation. He hid then in a cellar. His wife and daughter were taken by the Nazis during the selection process. They were beaten and the Nazis demanded that they reveal my brother's hiding place. They cried bitterly and loudly. My brother heard their outcry. He came out of his hiding place and showed up for the selection. This is how my brother ended his tragic life together with his family. The others, who had been hiding in the cellar with him, survived. This has been written by his grieving sister.

[Page 367]

In Memory of the Yona Tzemach Family, of Blessed Memory

by Malka Tzemach, Tel Aviv

Hinda Shwarzbaum, Deborah Weisberg and Nina Lerner

The many–branched and prolific Tzemach family originated in Spain. This fact was mentioned in the Family History Book which Shlomo Tzemach possessed, and which had been handed down by the Gaon Tzemach of Lublin. Grandfather, Avigdor Tzemach, was a resident of Radom. His son, Yona (Jonas), born in 1871, married a daughter of the Mintzberg family of Kozienice, a family of prominence. After an attempt to manage holdings in the vicinity of Radom, which did not succeed, the family settled in Kozienice, and together with my uncle, Shlomo Mintzberg, bought a beer factory, which supported them until the outbreak of WWII. The children of Yona were Sarah, Chana, Devorah, Hinde, Mendel, Nina and myself, Malka, the writer of these lines. The Tzemach family was known and respected in the entire area. The head of the family was counted among the followers of the Rebbe of Gur, and his righteous wife, Libe, contributed a great deal to the communal life of Kozienice. The family house was hidden among the trees of the forest in a suburb, surrounded by a large landholding and factory, which from 1929 was in the sole possession of my father.

My father, of blessed memory, was a member of the City Council, on the school committee, and employed many clerks and workers. The family was alert to the needs of the public and contributed a great deal to the needy and the poor. My brother, Mendel, was among the founders of the Zionist Organization and "Macabee". His aspiration and dream was to go an Aliyah to Israel. To our great misfortune, the health of my parents deteriorated, and the death of mother at an early age in 1929, put an end to his hope for Aliyah. The oldest daughter, Sarah, was married in 1912 to Moshe Ortshtein, and lived in Warsaw with her children: Avigdor, Chaim and Malka. A second daughter, Hinde, wife of the dentist, Michael Shvartzboim, lived in Kozienice. With the outbreak of the war, father was confined to his bed with a fractured leg. In this condition, he and his daughters, Hinde and Chana, left their home and fled eastward. When they heard that all of Poland had fallen to Germans, they returned home. Only Michael and his son remained in Russia.

When they returned home, they found all of their possessions had been looted, and their landholdings in the hands of Christians. Destitute, the family moved in with their daughter, Nina, in Warsaw, and from there to Kreshnik. In May of 194–2 the Germans removed the Jews of Kreshnik, and Chana Mondshein, and Hinde Shvartzboim with their children were sent to a death camp. Also, the husband of Devorah, Bernard Weisberg, died in a death camp. In October of 194Z, Yona Tzemach, old and sick, died in the death camp. His daughter, Devorah, succeeded in hiding from the Nazis, and went to Warsaw, armed with forged Polish papers. After everything was stolen from her, she entered the Warsaw Ghetto penniless, where she died during the Ghetto Uprising.

[Page 368]

Also the youngest Tzemach sisters, Nina and Malka, lived in the Warsaw Ghetto. They went through the seven sections of hell, hunger, sickness and degradation. In April of 1942 the Nazis removed from the Ghetto, all those who were not employed in essential work. We were able to obtain work in "Shuf", and thanks to that we remained in the Ghetto. By a miracle we were saved from two Nazi "actions" in 1942 and 1943, and several days before the Uprising, we passed over to the Aryan side. At the end of the War in January of 1945, we returned to Kozienice, the last remnant of a prolific family. The factory and family home were destroyed. In 1946, Nina married Dr. Lerner Masnuk, who had also experienced the bitterness of the War and the Holocaust– In 1947, the Lerner family and their sister Malka went on Aliyah to Israel. Dr. Lerner was employed as a Kupat–Cholim doctor in Zamenhof in Tel–Aviv. In 1948, a son was born to the Lerner family – Jonathan. In 1957 Dr. Lerner died, and in 1965, after a prolonged illness, his wife, Nina died. There remains of the family – Malka Tzemach and Jonathan Lerner.

These I Remember Fondly
by Chava Shapiro, Kfar Hasidim

Every evening, Chava, the teacher, would return to her room, which was in the houses of the Maggid. She would be exhausted from running from house to house, where she taught poor Jewish girls the Aleph-Bet, how to read Hebrew and the meaning of the prayers. The walking was difficult for her because she limped, but in spite of it, an expression of charm and satisfaction always graced her face which was wrinkled before its time. She was devoted to her work with heart and soul, and felt great satisfaction in that she was able to impart of her learning to the daughters of Israel. Since it's impossible to live from satisfaction, my mother would secretly help her with support. At night I would steal behind her room so that I could hear her pure prayers that would be enunciated without mistakes. Also on the Sabbath and special seasons I would likewise listen to the weekly portion, chapters of the Mishne and the "Borchi Nafshi" prayer. I loved her expressiveness which reflected her solitude, because Chava was a lonely widow. Although I was very young then, I understood her broken heart, and remember that she was taller than the other women her age, and if I was privileged to be sent by my mother on an errand to her, my joy knew no bounds. It is incumbent upon us to recall among the people of our city, this pure and righteous woman, Chava, the teacher.

Hersh–Leib, the Water Carrier

He was a unique personality, a simple man who carried his burden of two buckets upon his shoulders, from dawn to dusk. His body bent more and more from the weight, but he paid little attention to his tired body. Happy and good–hearted, he joked with all who came into contact with him, and from time to time burst out with a wise saying or a joke. His buckets he filled faithfully to overflowing. If he spilled some on the road he wouldn't charge for it, and when mentioned to him, he would answer: "It is forbidden to fool people, God forbid!"

His wife was a virtuous woman who kept their narrow room clean. They ate modestly, and saved from food to send their only son to study Torah. He was an excellent student and advanced until they were able to send him to one of the better Yeshivot. During vacation time when he returned home, not only his parents but many in the city looked upon him proudly, as if he were city property. Wasn't he the son of the water carrier of all of them? On the Sabbaths, when he went to synagogue with his father, Hersh–Leib's body straightened, and he would walk proudly as if asking: "What do you think of the pride and good fortune that the Lord has granted me?" True! Many envied him! Who could imagine that the water–carrier, Hersh–Leib, would be privileged to see a son, a scholar, so fine and also good looking.

[Page 370]

R'Eliezer, the Teacher

He would dress meticulously, was modest in his ways, soft–spoken and every word of his mouth carefully thought out. He supervised his students to be diligent, and wise in the use of their time. He was a scholar and God-fearing. He exuded life, and loved to joke. His knowledge of the Talmud and its commentaries he had acquired by himself, because his father had died when he was young. His mother supported herself by baking a special kind of bread. He studied in the Heder, and loved learning. His mother's occupation did not attract him, so he was of no help to her, even though he loved her dearly. Years passed and he spent his time sitting in the synagogue and learning, until people took notice of him. A respected and prosperous family chose him to marry their only daughter. He began to teach, was extremely successful and produced outstanding students. Many envied him. His mother's joy knew no bounds. She had lived to see "nachas" from him. Besides his teaching ability, he distinguished himself by his moral characteristics: honoring his fellow-man, not speaking evil, nor displaying envy. We remember him as one of the martyr's of our city, who were cruelly destroyed by the unclean animals.

R'Fishel, the Tailor

He would sew silk garments for the people of the city. He was pure and holy. By day he was engrossed in his work, and his nights were spent in the House of Study of the Mishne Association, of which he was a founder. While he worked he wouldn't pay attention to anything else. The needle went up and down, his hands trembling and his eyes closed due to the effort. He produced little because he was so diligent. He prayed that the Lord protect him from cheating people, and that his work should be satisfactory. I remember when he came to measure the silk garments for the Rabbi's family, of blessed memory. With measured steps and humility he approached the door, and stepped back, as if sunken in thought. He feared that perhaps he would disturb the children of the Rabbi at their studies. How could he dare to go inside. Perhaps..., but he must take measurements!

Thoughts followed thoughts, until suddenly the door opened, and the rebbetzin found R'Fishele standing shamefaced, without uttering a word.

"Shalom R'Fishele" she greeted him pleasantly, "What brought you in the middle of the day to our house?" With difficulty the words came and he stuttered "To measure! I want to measure."

The rebbetzin, who understood his confusion, tried to calm him with words: "Come in, come in R'Fishele." He entered and began measuring. Everything went well. When asked by the rebbetzin if the clother would be ready for Pesach, he answered with lowered eyes and with emotion: "With God's help, if the Lord will help me." And then he was on his way. This precious Jew deserves to be remembered in the Memorial Book of our city.

[Page 371]

R'Asher

He was the watchman of the houses on the street of the Maggid of Kozienice, a simple man who loved his work. On the long winter nights, when all was covered with snow and frost, when the roofs of the houses groaned under the weight of the frost and snow, and when people were tucked into their beds, and sunken in deep sleep, only the steps of R'Asher's studded boots were heard, and his white form, with a long stick trudged from one end of the street to the other. He harkened to every sound, perhaps a burglar is attempting to steal into one of the houses on the street. When he heard suspicious barking of dogs, he placed his stick on his arm, ready for battle.

In this way he circled year after year, during the hot summer nights and the long, cold winter nights. In the morning he prayed with the conscientious early risers, said some of the Psalms, grabbed breakfast, and a short nap, and again returned to his tasks. He loved to chop trees, and wouldn't let a stranger approach this work, because from time to time, when the rebbitzin ordered Yuzef, the house Goy, to chop wood, R'Asher would become very angry. How could anyone dare to steal his work of lighting the ovens? He was a wonder! He loved his work, body and soul; never complained; on the contrary, he always spoke with joyful enthusiasm, and the gleam of satisfaction spread over his face. We will remember him for good in the Memorial Book of the Jews of Kozienice.

[Page 372]

This is Not the Year of Redemption

by Malka Shapiro

The rebbetzin, Sarah Devorale rose and turned to the elders in the group: "Perhaps you remember the story of the Sabbath on which the portion "Bo" is read?"

"Wasn't it on the portion of Bo that your father, the Tzaddik, R'Elimelech, used to come to Kozienice, from the house of Grodzisk, after he was appointed chief judge of the city rabbinical court" said the beadle, Issachar–Ber, a native of Grodzisk. "Indeed, so it was. My father, of blessed memory, would arrive on Thursday with his entourage, at a late hour, because the snow covered the roads, and the wagons were pulled blindly through the forest."

While the Hasidim were still hurrying to the lighted stove in the Study House, frozen from the cold, my father stood, may his soul be in Eden, wrapped in his fur coat with my grandfather's staff (Rabbi Elimelech of Liz'insk) on the threshold of the Study House, inquiring of the townspeople, who had come to welcome him: "Nu, how is Berele?" This question he asked annually, when he came to Kozienice. But this time he received a reply, because Berele was on his deathbed. My father commanded that Berele and his bed be brought. The messengers hurried and brought Berele to the entrance of the Study House. My father took him quickly to the Maggid's room and there he was closeted with him for a long hour. After Berele was returned to his home, my father came to his rooms and his face shone, but he was quiet and wouldn't answer the questions of those who approached.

On the morrow Berele died, and a large funeral was arranged, as if he were an important personage. And since my father and his Hasidim accompanied the coffin to the cemetery, all of the city's inhabitants came to his funeral. People even said that it appeared that Berele was one of the 36 secret righteous men for whose sake the world existed, because during the funeral clouds covered the sky and darkened the earth. Also a wailing was heard from all around the city and no one knew from whence it came. But my father would not talk of the matter any more, and no one dared to ask him about it.

And behold the year 5,620 rolled around, and all of the giants of the generation thought it would be a year of redemption, and in all of the diaspora there was an awakening in anticipation of the coming redemption. (The Hebrew letters signifying the year spelled the word crown.) Only then did I dare to ask my father about the meaning of his meeting with Berele, and whether because of it he knew the exact date of redemption. After a long period of silence, my father turned to me and said:

"Your intention is to know the truth my daughter, and supposedly Berele was to pass on the information to one of the sons of my holy father before he died. Therefore I would inquire after his health every year when I came to Kozienice, thinking that perhaps the time had come for him to tell me. When I heard that he was deathly ill I rushed to speak to him, and now that I have I can only tell you that this year, is not the year of redemption."

[Page 373]

These are My Family Members in Kozienice

by Roza Greenberg, Netanya

I was born in Kozienice into the Ankerman family. I lived at no. 28 Lublin Street, in the house of my grandmother, Tcharna–Devorah Mandel and my grandfather, Shlomo. My grandmother had four children, Chana–Feige, Henna–Tsirel my mother, Yaakov–Hirsh and a daughter of their old age, Raisel. All of them established families, but to my despair, almost no one remained to memorialize them, therefore I must be their spokesman. Chana–Feige, the eldest was married to Naftali. They established a family and five children were born to them: Aaron–Shlomo, Yisrael–David (who survived the Holocaust, but died 3 years ago in Israel of a serious illness), Feivel, Esther and Henakh.

My mother, Henna–Tsirel, married my father, Gedala–Tuvia and they had six children. The firstborn, Shlomo–David, was God–fearing, and followed in my father's footsteps, was diligent in his Torah studies, but had difficulty making a living. My father was God–fearing, was interested only in holy things, lived only for others, and did not strive for greatness. The second daughter, Rivke Roza, that's me, the third, my beautiful sister, Malkale, the fourth,

Moshe–Gedalya, and after him was born my brother, Yaakov, the last of the sons, and then my sister, Chaya–Sara.

The third brother, Yaakov–Hirsh, married, and his wife Chana gave birth to five children: Shabtai, Rivke, Sarah (Sonia), Yosef and a son of their old age: Shlomo. My youngest sister, Raisel, married Yaakov and they had four children: Sarah, Dina, Shlomo and Chanale. The oldest son of Chana–Feige, Aaron–Shlomo married Chava, and they had three children. After their marriage they left Kozienice. Yisrael–David and his first wife, Rachel (the daughter of Hershel Popelnik) had three children: the eldest, Shlomo, a daughter, Esther and one other. Brother Feivel married and left Kozienice after his wedding.

The daughter Esther, married Meir and they had two children. The youngest brother Henach remained a bachelor. The eldest son of Henna–Tsirel, Shlomo–David, married Chana, who gave birth to three children: Benjamin, Esther and a daughter of their old age, Rivke. I Rivke–Roza, and my husband live in Israel, and we remained in order to memorialize our family. In poland, we gave birth to a daughter, Sarah–Malka. During the war I handed her over to Christians, in order to save her, but we lost track of her during the war and to this day I don't know whether she is alive or dead. But in my heart she will remain alive until the end of my days.

The third sister, Malkale, married Shlomo. They had a daughter named Chana. The brother, Moshe–Gedalya married Rachel. They had a son named Leibele, and his mother–in–law's name was Chana Kestenberg. Near Kozienice was a small village named Sheczechow. There were about 300 Jewish families in the village before the war. My father–in–law was the Shochet (Ritual Slaughterer) there. His name was Mendel and his wife, Sarah–Malka. They had seven children: Bracha, Glika, Chana–Bella, Pinchas–Levi, Reisel, Yisrael, and my husband who survived, Moshe–Bunim.

[Page 374]

The eldest daughter, Bracha, married Moshe Valtman and they had three children: Joshua, Bracha and Reisele. The second daughter, Glika, married, and her husband Moshe Dorfman, who survived, lives today in the U.S.A. Three children were born from their marriage. The eldest lives with his father in the U.S.A. The second, Kalman, perished in the Holocaust, and also their sister Rachel perished. Chana–Bella married but she and her husband, Joshua didn't have any children. The brother, Pinchas–Levi, married Ita. They had three children; Joshua, Feige and Rachel. Reisel was married to the son of the Shochet of Shidlovsk Chaim. They had three children: Brendele, Sarah and Malka. The brother Yisrael married the daughter of the Shochet of Shidlovsk, Shaindel.

Now, I want to mention some members of my family, because almost no one else has remained to memorialize them. Therefore I will recall them. I had an aunt by the name of Tziral, and her husband, Shlomo Kugel. They had six children, two of whom went on Aliyah to Israel, and one who died in Israel.

The eldest daughter, Chaya, and the second daughter, Bracha now live in Tel Aviv. The son was Avishai, and the other daughters were Devorah, Tzima, and Tovah, who died in Israel. Another uncle was Yaakov Weintraub. He lived in Kozienice on Lublin Street, and had a leather store. His wife was Blumele. They had seven children: Miriam, Chaya, Puah, Frieda, Yoel, Meir and Bracha, who survived and today lives in Belgium. My grandmother, as I've already mentioned, had a big house and she would rent out rooms.

A few people left no one to memorialize them and I'll mention them. One was Hershel Kammer, the baker and his wife, Leah. Another neighbor was David Tzaitvingel and his wife Tovah.

[Page 375]

Leibush Pesach a Happy Folk–Type

by Leibele Fishtein, Ramat–Gan

He was always penniless. He lived by Yosl Didyes in a small house which contained five souls: Pesach and two sons, his wife Rechele, and a daughter. In the house there always stood cartons and baskets with childrens' shoes, which the shoe factories sent to be nailed with wooden spots. He sat at a shoemaker's bench and with an awl made holes in the soles, and his two sons would hammer the wooden nails into the holes. From all three breadwinners, there was never enough to finish the week. He was always so well organized that he wouldn't have to think about having enough to make the Sabbath. He was known throughout town as the one, who if he would play a trick on someone and would not succeed, he would worm his way out because everyone would say it was just a joke.

Yosl Didye's wife once met him going out of the cellar with a pot of her goose fat, which she had prepared for Pesach. "What are you carrying, R' Leibush Pesach?" "I'm carrying a pot of fat. I'm going to ask my wife if it's our fat." "But it's my fat" says Esther. "It's your fat? So here take it back, and let my wife go and take her own fat from the cellar!" On Friday, he took a pot with two handles (A cholent pot), filled it with water, covered it with paper, tied it with a string, carried it to the baker, and paid for having it cooked. On the Sabbath, after the services, the bakers used to take the pots of cholent out of the oven and set them on a shelf . Everyone who came to take his or her cholent knew their own pot. Leibush Pesach always came first. He carefully surveyed each pot, in order to make it appear that he is attempting to identify his own. The different cholents could always be identified as to where they came from – from the poor or the middle class, or the rich. Leibush knew how to recognize each. He always took home a cholent from which he would truly have a satisfying Sabbath. He would do this every Sabbath. When he was caught in the act, he would say that a man is not an angel and is bound to make a mistake occasionally. "What, I should bring back a cholent that I've opened? What's the difference? A cholent is a cholent."

On Fridays, on the way home from the Mikve (Ritual Bath), it was a custom by us to eat a carrot Tzimmes or baked Ferfel. Leibush already knew exactly who did and didn't observe this custom. He would tour several homes. When he would enter, he would say: "Shprintze, my life, Your excellent Tzimmes just melted in my mouth. I can taste it at this very moment." "R' Leibush Pesach, today I don't have a carrot Tzimmes. I made baked Ferfel, and it got completely burned. It's bitter and doesn't fit to eat. I wouldn't dare give you any." "O' Shprintze, dear life, you should only know how I love bitter Ferfel, and especially if it's burned a bit. You would certainly give me the entire batch. In that way you would not upset anyone who might eat it."

[Page 376]

There is a saying that kadochis is not an illness, and Purim is not a holiday. But as far as Leibush Pesach was concerned, Purim was, indeed the best holiday. All year he would gather and write down addresses, of those to whom he would send the traditional Purim treats (Shalach Manos). When Purim came, he would employ all three children in the carrying of three large plates, which were covered with clean napkins. Each plate contained only a written note: "To Yona Tzemach; to Yitzhak Milgrom; to Pinchas Freilich. For today's big holiday of Purim I am sending you as Shalach Manos: a blessing, that you and your entire family should be healthy and live till 120. He, who is in Heaven should make all of your undertakings successful?"

The rich who read this blessing and heartfelt wish did not stop to think too long, and filled each plate with Purim baked goodies and a coin. The child who had brought the plate, was also given something for carrying and bringing the plate. Even those who weren't rich would put in a small coin and cover it with Hamantaschen.

The Entire Family Perished in Treblinka!

[Page 377]

Where are the Gorgeous Souls?

by Abraham Tenenboim, Warsaw

Almost 40 years separate me from that time, when I lived together with the 5000 Jews of Kozienice, lived with them and among them. Even so, hundreds of them stand before my eyes, as if alive, Kozienicer Jews. Types and figures peculiar, exclusively Kozieniceites. Kozienicer butchers, blacksmiths, carriers, water carriers, shingle makers, carpenters and musicians. Here they stay in front of my eyes: Itzik with his fiddle, tall Yisrael with his trumpet. When Shlomo Itziks marched through the streets in military uniform, at the head of a military orchestra, he thought the whole world belonged to him, so proud was he in the role of conductor.

Tens of Jews has animal nicknames. For example: Feivel Oger (stallion). Harnessed like a horse, he pulls his heavy wagon, and we little chaps hold his wagon from the rear. When he feels us, and that it has become difficult, he turns around and begins to chase us away. Meanwhile, other chaps appear and pull his wagon into a side street.

Even greater troubles, created by us, were endured by the old water carrier. (I've forgotten his name. Let other Kozieniceites mention him). Often, when he was carrying two heavy buckets of water, we used to run behind him and throw stones or rubbish into the water. The old man would get angry and at the top of his voice scream: "Bastards!" But the truth of the matter is that it was he himself who was born before his mother's wedding. He would become so embittered, that tears would stream from his eyes, and we, 10 year old rascals, were overjoyed with our accomplishments.

Khanale, a blind beggar at the cemetery

The Kozienice "Tshortes"

For generations, legends were told about why they were called "Tshortes" (Devils, from the Russian word Tshort). For generations, the onion trade in Kozienice and the surrounding communities was exclusively in the hands of the Kozienicer "Devils". They were plain, good and hardworking people. A whole "tribe": Shmiel, Yisrael–Abraham, Luzer, Reuben, Naftali, Feivel and others. They all lived together or near each other. There were very friendly relations between them. It was a well–planned corporation. They would contract with the producers large plantations of onions, and would not have to occupy themselves with any of the details. Where are They, the Enlightened Figures?

It is true that these unconnected, detached thoughts cannot give a picture of the variegated life of thousands of Jews, who were either gassed or burned alive. The heart becomes clamped as I write. Where are they, the gorgeous souls, the Kozienicer Jews, the Jews of Poland and Europe?

[Page 378]

And once again the Fascist–Antisemitic beasts are preparing to do their deadly work. Fifty anti–semitic newspapers in Western Europe circulate millions of copies daily with poisonous attacks on Jews. I believe that publishing this book at a time like this is an extraordinary necessity, for the honor of the martyrs as well as for the on–going war against the bloodthirsty anti–semites. It would be good if every one of the survivors would mention at least a few of those who were murdered. In that way we would eternalize their names on the pages of the book for our children and for those who follow us.

Zalman–Baruch, The Politician

After the outbreak of WWI Kozienice Jews would impatiently wait each day for the blind one (on one eye) Zalman–Baruch. He, with his yellow–gray, long beard, was the greatest politician in Kozienice. He is among the few, who read the pages (of newspapers), therefore he is well informed as to all of the events in the world. Since when is Zalman–Baruch such a great authority and politician? From the moment that he won the Lottery. How many thousands of dollars it was, I don't remember, but people of the older generation remember this great event, when shortly before WWI he won the Lottery. Every day as soon as he settles himself in the Study House, he's surrounded by a mass of people. Each one wants to be as close as possible. He's proud of his task, and he expounds on causes of the war. Wanting his audience to understand how the war was being conducted he used to fill his hand with spittle, to signify the sea, and then he would show how Austria and Prussia (Germany) attacked Russia. Kozienicer Jews would listen attentively to all that Zalman–Baruch had to say.

As If Alive, They Stand Before My Eyes

And perhaps all of these Memorial Books will, in time, fall into the hands of historians, so that they will be able to work up a new history of the most unfortunate nation in the world. As if alive, they stand before my eyes: Shmiel Weinberg and his wife Rode; Shmuel–Leib Goldman and his wife Male; Feige Flamenboim–Reiss; Yisrael Rochman, their brother and partners; Yisrael Shpiegel; Gittel Rechthand; my three brothers, Yaakov and Hersh Shermeister and Yarachmiel Tenenboim, my mother Hendl, her three sisters; Abraham Kohn; Yakl Zaltzberg; Yisrael–Itche Dimenshtein (Briks); Eli Fleisher and his wife Gele; Chanale Avenshtern and her husband Shmiel; their children, Luzer the groats–maker and the Chlivners and tens of others; Hundreds of Jews: Communists, Bundists, Zionists, religious Jews and irreligious ones, young and old, mothers and children, all, who incorrectly perished only because they were Jews!

[Page 379]

Blind Chanale

Who in our town didn't know the blind Chanale? In my youth, Chanale was about 60. She was born blind in both eyes. When we knew her, that means in the nineteen–twenties, we knew that she was all alone. She didn't have a single relative, and never had her own home. She lived with the female milk carrier, near the river, in the neighborhood of Shmerl Falberg. She was thin, tall, dark–complexioned. Her blindness didn't keep her from knowing the entire city, she knew who was who and how much money he possessed; where everyone lived; who loved whom; who is traveling, and where; what maiden or woman is pregnant, and from whom! Blind Chanale would, with full confidence, predict whether the pregnant women would give birth to boys or girls, and if it happened that she was wrong in her prediction, she would not let it upset her, and wouldn't keep her from making further predictions. On the other hand, when she would predict correctly, her blind face would light up. Everywhere she went, she would proudly repeat: "You see! I said that Blume Moshe's would have a daughter!"

She got around without a walking stick. Instinctively, she knew each Jewish home, and even knew how many rooms there were in each house. She knew everyone by name. She would support herself from alms, that were given to her everywhere she went. She was always given food and a few groschen (pennies). She loved children, and because of it children loved her. She would often tell them stories, and children love nice stories. Before Pesach when all houses were whitewashed, Chana would know instinctively exactly which houses had already been done. She would be asked: "Chanale, how do you like the whitewash?" She would open her blind eyes widely and exclaim: "Beautiful, as if it were painted!"

Feivel Oger

Where he lived, I don't know! When I would awaken in the morning, he was already with his four wheeled hand wagon and two sons in front of Yankl Shipper's restaurant. That was his home base. Until late in the evening he would sit there with his family, his two sons. There he would eat his breakfast, lunch and supper. You could always meet him sitting on his wagon. It was his table, bed and workshop. In summer, when the sun was hot, he would sit on the large boulder which lay in front of Yankl Shipper's restaurant, at the intersection of Radom and Lublin Streets. He would sit and dream of the "good old days", when the shoemakers sent packages of shoes to Lemberg, Katovitz, Sosnovietz and other cities. In those days he would load up a high wagon with packages, harness himself to his wagon and drag it to the train station, about three kilometers distance. Then he would earn about 10 zloties a day.

[Page 380]

His two sons would help push the wagon and it provided a livelihood. Later a post was set up in the city, and they would take the packages with horse and wagon to the train. There he sits and waits, maybe someone will have a package he wants delivered. Why he was called Feivel Oger (Stallion), I don't know. Maybe because he would harness himself to his wagon, if one hadn't seen him but only heard his name, I mean his nickname, he would think that this Jew was a giant. But in actuality it wasn't so. He was a short, thin man, with a bronzed, sun–tanned face, and barefoot. He didn't believe in shaving himself, but he had no beard. A few stray hairs on his chin hung every which way. A goat has a thicker beard. Rarely would one hear him speak! What for? When he was given something to deliver, he already knew where to take it. He knew everything and everyone in the city. All one had to do was to shout out loud: "Feivel! "

[Page 381]

Searched For and Finally Found

by Chaim Dimant, Paris Translated from Yiddish

Everything is white, and cold as ice,
The lips burned, the fists clenched All is
spoiled, because who endured?
Why oh why did this happen?
People hanged, they wanted to destroy the
world, Children seized by force and ending as
smoke. Women raped and then choked.

Why oh why did they murder:
Fascism, banditry and Hitlerism
No, I must leave here for I die of fright.
The streets run with blood, all fields one grave.

I have no more courage – since I felt the rod.

A storm they brought on the world,
Because that is what they yearned for:
From the world – to make one wild animal,
And to make fun of this wild animal.
The world understood what these outlaws
thought up, To enslave Europe, torture her
with skill.

For freedom is our yearning,
And then the world came to its senses.
To free the world with force,
And again and again use force and power!
Freedom came,
The whole world rang,
To welcome freedom All sang out.
We are young, the world is open We sought
freedom, and finally met it!

[Page 382]

These Are the Kind of Jews That Lived in Kozienice

by Itshe Blatman

You can say, that the water–carriers were the most upright and honest Jews in town. One of them, Hersh–Leib, was not at all a lion (Leib). He was a small, weak, skinny Jew. He was also called Hersh–Leib Bozer. Bozer means a fool. But he was not at all a fool. He was more of a Bontshe Shveig (a silent one). He carried the buckets of water in the winter, in the worst cold, and in the summer – in the greatest heat, spoke little, did not complain about his fate and always seemed satisfied His only needs were a piece of bread and a verse of the Psalms. And even so, he often went hungry.

Hirsh Leib the water carrier

His kapote (long black coat) was always covered with patches, but he knew why he worked and suffered cold: Because he had an only son, who sat in the House of Study and learned day and night. I remember how he used to come into the House of Study. He used to stand near the furnace and warm himself while looking at his son, learning. He was fortunate, because it wasn't a small thing to have a son a scholar. He convinced himself that he was the richest man in town, because ordinarily, by such Jews as he was, their children usually went out to work at age 10, but Hersh–Leib supported his son, the scholar, until his wedding, and was well–rewarded for everything.

A fine Jew, a very wealthy man, came from another city and took the son as a son–in–law for his only daughter. In that way Hersh–Leib, the water-carrier, got a fine, rich Jew as an in–law. I want to tell about two other water-carriers. They didn't have the spiritual history that Hersh–Leib had, but thanks to them a great event occurred in town.

One, Shammai the blind, because he was very near–sighted. He had to use his hands, in order to see better. He carried the buckets of water and aged until he became an old bachelor. The second, "Shkanke, water–carrier" unfortunately died very young, and left a wife and daughter. His wife took over his occupation and the clientele of her husband. All day the mother carried water, in order to earn a piece of bread for herself and her small daughter.

Shamai the blind water carrier. His daughter helped him earn his livelihood

The Prominent Ladies Arrange a Wedding

The little girl lived in the street and grew up, like a wild creature of the forest. When she was a bit older, he mother gave her two buckets for carrying water. She was almost 18 years old, and this disturbed the prominent ladies in town: Henye–Yechel–Yelner's wife, and Yaakov Becker's mother, a dear and righteous Jewess. Day and night, on Sabbaths and Holidays, she was occupied helping the poor: Winter – with a bit of firewood, a warm cloak for a child or a pair of shoes. She also assembled challah to distribute for the Sabbath.

[Page 383]

Another prominent lady, Hodes, the wife of R' Yonah, the town cantor's wife. She was called the proof–reader, because her husband was also the proof–reader of scrolls of the Torah. She was also a dear lady, and very modest. She fasted on Mondays and Thursdays. She also occupied herself helping the poor, older ladies. She sold candles in front of the Maggid's tomb, and women would buy them and light them at the Maggid's grave. She also did everything to see to it that Shammai, the water–carrier, should be a Jew, equal to all other Jews. She saw to it that he had a prayer–shawl, and that Shkanke's daughter should not become an old maid.

With luck a match was arranged, and the prominent ladies began to prepare the wedding. They ordered new clothes for the bride and groom, and prepared all sorts of goodies for the feast. The wedding took place near the synagogue, where all weddings were held, and not at the cemetery, as was the custom for poor orphans in other small towns. In fact it was held at the Rebbe's large House of Study, and the whole town participated. The musicians played vigorously. Everyone ate everywhere and it was merry and joyful in town. Most of all, the prominent ladies were overjoyed; Henye and Hodes, and the rebbetzin, of blessed memory. A child was born. The father Shammai, unfortunately, later became completely blind. With his hands he patted the baby's head and was pleased, like all fathers. The German murderers put an end to them.

The First Contact with Eretz Yisrael

I remember, in 1910 or in 1911, there was an uproar in town: Moshe Berishes was going to Eretz Yisrael. He was a learned Jew, a scholar. He would teach a group of Jews, laborers, on Shabbat, although secretly he was a bit of a "Maskil" (enlightened). Therefore he dreamed of going to Eretz Yisrael. In the end he didn't go. They said in town that he had applied to Baron Rothchild in France, for financial help for his trip, and that the Baron did not reply. Therefore he remained in Kozienice. What happened to this Jew afterwards, I don't know.

In 1921 two young men from Kozienice left for Eretz Yisrael. One was a Mizrachi (religious Zionist) and the second, a Zionist. The first, Elimelech Feigenboim, was a son of Itshe Mordecai Nutes. The second, Itshe Blatman, from Staroviesh, was myself, the writer of these lines. It took us one year to reach Eretz Yisrael, but we arrived. A few years later other Kozienicer Jews arrived, but the first letters to reach Kozienice with stamps from Eretz Yisrael came from us two "Halutzim" (pioneers).

[Page 384]

In the Fight for Poland's Freedom

We lived on the sand dunes. "Na Piaskach", as the neighborhood was called. I remember, about eight men passed our shop. My father asked them where they were going, and they said that they are going to the copper factory to request money for an organization, which is fighting for Poland freedom from Czarist Russia. The delegation consisted of half Jews and half Poles. I remember a few of the names: Arish Schneider, Yisroel Zifferman, and Eliezer Friedman, all of them respectable Jews. The Poles were Pokzshevinski, the barber–surgeon, Mlastek and others. When they were coming back, my father asked them if they had gotten anything. They answered that they had gotten more than they had expected. The owners of the copper factory were Gerer Hasidim, very dear Jews, who were observant, educated aristocrats. When they went to prayer services on Friday evening, everyone knew that it was time to close up shop. In this way Gerer Hasidim and other respectable Jews in Kozienice helped the fight for Polish independence from the Czarist yoke of Imperial Russia.

Another Jew helped fight the Czar in his own way. This was in the year 1905, when the struggle against Czarism was aflame. The repressions were great, especially against Jews. The revolutionaries in Kozienice, at the time the P. P. S., were ready to demonstrate openly in the streets against Czarism. they needed a flag, which would express the character of the demonstration. There was a Jew, named Abraham Rosenberg. He was called "Abraham of the soda–water", because he manufactured soda–water. He was a respectable Jew, from a nice, prominent family, a Hasidic follower of R' Zelick. He knew how to print, and the ability to draw caricatures. He made the banner for free. It portrayed the Czar with a large whip in his hand, and a big pig next to him. The caricature was very expressive. The banner was carried at the head of the demonstration. Police and Cossaks beat and maimed on all sides. There were many wounded. But Abraham's banner was transferred from hand to hand and from one street to the next. Children and adults talked about the banner in the House of Study and in the synagogue. He had created a commotion in town. These are the kind of Jews that lived in Kozienice.

[Page 385]

Types and Curiousities of Kozienice

by Yerachmiel Sirota, Paris

Many of us very well remember Khaim Yage, the beadle of the synagogue, and old Jew, with a curly grey beard who was extremely wise. By nature he was very jolly and good–hearted. He would observe things and then pass them on to everyone in a joking manner. He didn't like some of the wealthy men because of their stinginess, and many Hasidim because of their hypocrisy. Whenever you would meet him, he would almost immediately make you laugh. Once, he told his good friends, that he had revenged himself on a stingy rich man. On the eve of Yom Kippur, the rich man came into the synagogue, and requested that I whip him, as was the custom then. So I whipped him a few times. Standing up, he said to me: "You didn't spare me. It must be good to be able to whip someone!" I answered: "You fall into my hands only once a year, and it was my intention to drive out your stinginess."

Left: A mentally disturbed man. His living place was in the synagogue. His name was Tzalol
Right: Berele Melamed an old Hebrew teacher

Each To His Own Trade

Once I met the town undertaker, Yankele Polkovnik, a short Jew. Jews were afraid of his good morning greeting, because you have to answer him "a good year!" I asked him: "How's your livelihood?" He answers: "Not good; in fact very poor. I haven't had a single job all week." He relates that in his youth he was a shoemaker, and worked with a Pole. "What can I tell you?" He spoke Yiddish like flowing water, and in the morning he even said the blessing with the children. When the boss went to the fair, he, banging the nails into the shoes, remarked about a boy who forgot to put on his cap while saying the blessing. Nu, you should have heard Michael Shaltz yell at his son "why he was saying the blessing without his cap on."

Once before the holidays, a bookseller came to town. He sold, near the Study House, prayer books, high–holiday prayer books, prayer–shawls, and even story books. The bargaining was intense and only with great bitterness was he able to sell something. He became very angry and pleaded; "O, Lord of the Universe, send me at least one non–Jewish customer!"

Once, going quite early to the first minyan (prayer service), I heard a scream. All of the neighbors from the surrounding streets came running, so I also ran. I asked: "What's that screaming?" A neighbor answered: "Hershel Becker's daughter doesn't feel good." So I asked the neighbor: "How old is she?" "19 years old." "It's almost 80 years that I don't feel good and I don't make such a fuss."

One winter during a cold spell, two cheder teachers were sitting in the Study House near the hot furnace and discussing their respective livelihoods. One says: "You know, if you were a minister in the government, you would have a fine livelihood!" "How so?" "You would still be able to continue teaching the children ABC!"

[Page 386]

Once Yankel Treger met me and pleaded: "All year I come to pray in the Study House, and I am never given the honor of being called up to the Torah. What have I done to deserve such treatment?" So I spoke to the Gabbai (the man in charge of distributing honors), and he told me that on the coming Sabbath he would give him the honor. And so it was. But instead of calling him to the reading of the Torah, he gave him the honor of lifting the Torah, after the reading had been completed. Yankel became very angry and yelled up to the Gabbai: "Keep it for yourself! All year I have the honor of lifting loads without you." (The name Treger was a nickname, because he worked as a porter, and Treger means carrier).

Abish Bontshe was a round (no Father no Mother) orphan. When he was still very young, he lost both parents, and was raised by his grandfather. At age 17 he was tall and fat without measure. He ate "days" (every day somewhere else), and was constantly hungry. Yankele Noreck, the shoe manufacturer, had pity on him and took him into his factory and provided him with room and board. His sleeping place was behind the workshop, and the mistress brought him his food in a large bowl. His table was the work bench. Once the mistress brought him soup. He began to search with his spoon, searched and didn't even find a single potato, only water, suddenly he threw off his jacket, and his shirt, and was at the point of removing his pants, when the owner asked him: "What are you doing, Abish?" "I might drown in the process, but I'm determined to find a potato!"

They Will Not Harm the Jews Kozienice, 15th of Tammuz, 5641 (1880–1881)

When the official of the city of Kozienice learned that most of the inhabitants of the villages are whispering against the Jews, and request to change market day from the weekdays to the Sabbath, the official ordered that market day be changed to the Sabbath, and that the Jews should turn over the keys of the pubs to Gentile women. On that specific Sabbath, hordes of farmers flocked to the city, except that without Jews there was no business. When there were no buyers for the produce that they had brought, and no store open for them to sell them food and supplies. Even in the pubs they couldn't quench their thirst, and trade was at a standstill. Towards the end of the day the city official went out on the street and asked the farmers about the business of the day. They replied: "How can there be a market day without Jews?" This was the official's opportunity to convince them how bad it would be if the Jews were driven out, because then there would be no trade at all and they wouldn't be able to sell their produce. He proved to them how essential the Jews were for their well–being. They scratched their heads and admitted how right he was, and promised that they wouldn't harm the Jews.

[Page 387]

Chaim Yage Tells About the Kozienicer Maggid

by Ber Zilberberg, Tel Aviv

Chaim Yage was a regular visitor to our home, besides his monopoly on every Friday and eve of a holiday. When he would come to us he would have a stiff drink, and this he loved very much. As soon as he came, my father, of blessed memory, poured him a drink. He would down it and began rubbing his hands. "Oh, now I've become a different person." My father knew already that the "different" person also had to have a drink. After the two glasses, R' Chaim was completely satisfied! I was only a small boy at the time, and I watched in wonderment how R* Chaim downed the burning liquor in one gulp. Afterwards I would request of him: R' Chaim, tell a story of days gone by, of what once happened!"

A Short Partnership

And so he began to tell: "Once, two Jews came to the Maggid; workmen, tailors, and requested that he draw up partnership papers for them. They wanted to set up a business to make and sell clothes at the fairs. One would put up money and the other his house for the work, and so on and so forth. The Maggid took a piece of paper and wrote the four letters: Aleph, Bet, Gimmel, Daled, (A.B.G.D. first letters of Hebrew alphabet) and gave them the paper. The Jews looked and saw that nothing was written about their partnership that they had discussed; but only the four letters of the alphabet. They said: "Rebbe, you didn't write anything about our partnership." So the Rebbe answered them: "This is enough for Jews who enter into a partnership." Aleph means "ernes" honest, which means that each of you will have a Beth (second letter B), which stands for Bracha, "a blessing." And if there should be between you a Gimmel (third letter), meaning "genavo," stealing one from the other, then you'll both come to Daled (fourth letter) which stands for "dalus", meaning poverty. Now you both know what each of the letters represents!"

A Gift For The Rebbe

When the Maggid was still a boy learning in Heder, there was a farm boy learning with the Maggid. His name was Asher–Zelik, and his father was an overseer for a Polish noble. Asher–Zelik was provided at the Heder with room and board. On Fridays he would go home to be with his parents for the Sabbath. Years passed. Yisroel became "the Kozienicer Maggid", and Asher–Zelik became the overseer in his father's stead. Once, Asher–Zelik said to his wife: "Rivke, you know the Rebbe, who lives in the city, was a classmate of mine in Heder." His wife said: "That must be one of your new dreams. You'll soon tell me that you are also a good Jew!" "Rivke, what are you talking about? Am I a bad Jew? Rivke, I want to bring him a gift."

[Page 388]

Asher–Zelik took a basket, put cheese, butter and eggs in it, and went off to the city to the Maggid. Asher–Zelik came to the Maggid's prayer house, looked in through the window, and saw that the Maggid is engrossed in learning from a huge tome of the Talmud that covered the entire table. "Good morning, Rebbe, shalom aleichem to you, Yisroel. Do you recognize me? It is I, Asher–Zelik, from the village of Yenikov, who learned together with you in the same Heder. I brought you a gift."

Asher–Zelik looks around the small prayer house and sees one bed. He bangs the Maggid on the shoulder and says: "Yisroel, you conduct yourself just like I do. In my house there also stands a pull–out bed!"

A group of young women in Kozniece in 1939-40
R. to L.: Manya and Sale Rozenboim, Tale Flas, Hayushe Luxemburg, Renya
Rozenboim.
Last on left: Tzvia Lipmann

R. To L.: Berish Shabsan, Mendel Tzemakh and Yankel Freilikh. The technical and
radio pioneers in Kozniece.

Leibl Hirshorn, killed by the Nazis in Camp Veizshevnik 1944 and Aaron Kramarski

L. to R.:Mekhel Grinstein, Volf Shpigelman and Yerakhmiel Sirota

Seated L. to R.: Elimelekh Vasserman, Eli Huberman, Shlomo Kestenberg, Ber Zilberberg, Hershel Rakhman

Standing, L. to R.:- Yerakhmiel Rakhman, Yaakov Zilberberg, Moshe Kestenberg

SECTION 5 - Memories

Holidays 1933- friends meet in Kozniece
Right to left: Yehiel Litman, Kh. Z. Silberstein, Velvel Potashnik, Israel
Burstein, Mordehai Donershtein, Yankel Mandeloim, Itamar Flamenboim, I. L.
Frisch

A group in Kozniece
Right to left: Issachar Frisch, Rivka Lerner, Salzberg, Yankel Mandeloim
(seated)

Kozienice in the Year 1903

by Pinie Katz, Buenos Aires

Pinie Katz

In autumn, 1903, I came home from Odessa, to my birthplace, Orgayev, in order to present myself for military conscription. There were rumors that the recruits would be given a short military preparation, and they would be immediately sent to the Japanese front.

They Convinced Me To Desert

My family began to talk me into deserting, as many others had done. I couldn't convince myself to do it. In their hearts every one wished that the Czar and his government would suffer a defeat because of the Kishinev and Homier pogroms, the slaughter of the Kiev students, for sill the decrees against Jews for the crowded prisons filled with political prisoners, and for Czarist rule in general. But I didn't do it and I didn't cross the Russian border. We, the recruits, were drafted as soon as we were declared fit for service.

Only in the evening were we able, for a few kopeks, to go wherever we pleased. That evening I went to a Bessarabian wedding and I saw our Bessarabian Jews dancing up such a storm that their slippers flew in the air. The second evening, I together with a couple of local recruits, were guests in a prominent home. Young men and girls held a philosophical discussion. They were showing off for me, the Odessaite, and I sat, looked at them, and didn't understand a word. Afterwards, we hired a carriage and rode from Orgayev to Kishinev to see the place where the pogrom had begun.

To the 25th Smolenski–Division in Kozienice

On the second day we already rode by train from Kishinev to Kozienice, to the 25th Smolenski–Regiment, where we were assigned to serve. Finally, we stopped off in the town of Rozdielne, where my father came to say goodbye to me. We also stopped off in a few larger cities: Berditshev, Dubne, Kovel and Brisk; crossed the Polish border cities: Lublin, Ivangrod and Radom. We ate Polish foods in restaurants and came to Kozienice, the city of the Kozienicer Maggid, who blessed our regiment, that as long as we were stationed in Kozienice, no Jewish soldier should die. We came to Kozienice on Friday morning. In the courtyard of the regimental headquarters the adjutant wrote with chalk on our jackets, the number of our company, and gave us leave. As he did so he shouted: "Go wherever you want to go, but in the evening you must be in the barracks." Jewish soldiers were already waiting for us, in order to acquaint us with the town. They took us to Jewish homes, where we were able to eat a kosher meal in honor of Shabbat. We could also receive letters at their address, and spend our free time on Shabbat and Holidays.?

[Page 390]

I Become Acquainted With Kozienice

In one home we became acquainted with nice, intelligent girls. That home was called the "Staff Headquarters". To that home used to come soldiers, craftsmen, tailors, shoemakers, and other skilled craftsmen, or sons of the wealthy who used to receive packages from home. From there I went to the Rebbe's shul, or as Jews used to call it "The Maggid's Shul".

A Very Large Shul

For the first time I attended a shul of Polish Jews. I stood like a stone by the entrance, like a stranger. Such a strange melody for welcoming the Sabbath I had never heard. Not at all like ours. A march tune was used for singing "Lecha Dodi", come my beloved. Boys in long kapotes, with thick sidelocks surrounded me. They looked at my sewn blue shirt over my pants with the strange belt, with the black lace and tassels, and they didn't know how to treat this "uncircumcised one" who stumbled into their shul. I understood that if I didn't say something, they would ask me to leave, so I remarked to one of them: "Young man, let me look into your siddur". He looked at me with suspicion and curiosity. I returned the siddur to him and went to the barracks of the fourth regiment, according to the number which the adjutant had written on the flap of my jacket.

I Became a Regimental Scribe

I took upon myself the strict barracks–discipline: to sleep on a hard straw sack, to do muster and gymnastics patiently, and I gained the respect of the authorities, in order to be on their level, and to be able to speak to them as an equal. I had presented myself upon registering for the regiment as not having been too well educated and trained.

But already by the morning of the second day, I betrayed myself. The commander of the regiment a "chochol" (nickname for someone from Little Russia) with a sense of humor, asked everyone where they were from, and posed several riddles which not everyone understood well enough to solve. I sat silently, since I had pretended not to know too much. But this officer, staff–captain Sadavski, comes to me and says: "And you, why are you quiet? A Jew must know!" This officer, I think to myself, is a bit more perceptive than the Jewish youngster who, yesterday, in shul saw in me a goy. You can't fool this one. Why shouldn't he see that a Jew does know everything? 1 figured everything out for him, that he had requested. From that day on I became the scribe and bookkeeper of the regiment. Every day I had to figure out how much meat had to be cooked for a whole batallion and how much groats and bread are needed.

[Page 391]

My Prestige at Staff Headquarters Grows

Because of my position, I was exempted from the early morning gymnastic drill. I would first go into the writing–room, and later leave. My greatest privilege was when I was assigned to guard duty at various posts in the city and on the outskirts. They started saying that the staff wanted to organize an evening school for the "unlettered" and that I should be the teacher. Nothing came of it. The high command decided that learning to write means too much of "liberalism". The only thing that did come of it was that my prestige rose a bit. My friendship was therefore sought not only by common soldiers who called me brother Katz and asked me to write letters home for them, but also among the noncommissioned officers. They used to invite me for a drink or a snack.

My prestige rose even higher, when the officer, Tzvietkov, the son–in–law of staff–captain Sadavski, used to converse with me about literature, and even got me to read the novels of Victor Hugo, Emile Zola and others. Also the officer, Zacharov, used to invite me at times to his office to discuss Jews, Zionism, and Socialism. But I kept my distance, I listened and didn't answer, as if I was not concerned with these matters. I told him that Jews believe in the Messiah, as he probably knows, and we don't want to know about any other Messiah. He left me a bit annoyed, because I didn't answer any of his questions. The soldiers, who were on duty and saw how much time we spent together in his office were amazed to see us speaking together as equals.

I Become a Hebrew Teacher

As I've already mentioned, I wasn't destined to become the teacher of Russian soldiers in the barracks. In spite of it, I became a teacher of Hebrew in the prominent Kozienice homes. I don't know how my fellow Jewish soldiers found out that I knew Hebrew, and that I was a "scholar". It's possible that my friends, with whom I traveled from my town to Kozienice, learned of it as a result of a conversation that I had with a student from Odessa, who was traveling to the border, and conversed with me in Hebrew. Maybe they had heard it in our town, where I had relatives, who boasted of their relationship to my father, the "Maskil" (enlightened one), and his talented son.

Once, a Jewish soldier of the Kiev group, by the name of Kovalsky, came into my barracks. He had already completed his service, but they kept him on because of the war. He said: "Katz, I want to propose a match for you with a beautiful and rich girl". This Kovalsky, if you could ignore his military garb, looked exactly like a born "Shadchan" (matchmaker). But I understood that he wasn't talking about a match, but that he was plotting something. "Tell me!" I said. "What's going on here?" "Do you want to have an interesting Jewish home to go to, and right here, a short distance away?"

[Page 392]

"Then listen: Not far from the barracks, there lives the contractor, Yustman, a very wealthy Jew." "He has two daughters and a son, and he is stuffing all sorts of knowledge into them; Russian and Polish, and they also converse in French and German and Hebrew." He writes in the Hebrew journal, "Hatzfirah". "He wants, and even more so, his daughter wants, that you should come to their home. In fact it was she who sent me to you. She has seen you pass by and wants to meet you."

I Teach the Yustman and Mintzberg Children

The very next day I became the teacher of the two girls and the boy. I received a pass to leave the barracks daily in the afternoon, from iny boss, who was proud of his secretary and bookkeeper. He would boast about me to his colleagues. My pupils were "open heads" (very bright). Especially the oldest one, a young lady about 18 years old, blond and rosy-cheeked. 1 taught the younger one the Prophets, and I would forget myself and chant the Heder melody, because of the beauty of the language and prophetic vision. I also taught them Hebrew grammar, in a special way, as if I was taking a gun apart, or a watch with its wheels and gears. They understood what I taught and learned it. The older girl read and understood Hebrew very well. With her I would read the daily political articles by Sokolov in the "Hatzfirah" under the title "Words of the Day" and his weekly reviews which were called: "From

Sabbath to Sabbath", which were filled with many words and expressions of the sages, and old and new Hebrew. Through Sokolov's Hebrew I was able to inculcate my intelligent student with the knowledge of where Sokolov had acquired his rich language knowledge, and his great erudition. I had acquired the reputation in the Kozienicer Jewish homes, as a good Hebrew teacher, and obtained a teaching position in a second prominent Kozienicer Jewish home, the Mintzberg's.

I Make the Acquaintance of the Kozienicer Rebbe's Daughter

I also began going to the home of the Kozienicer Rebbe, R'Yerachmiel–Moishele Hopstein. This was thanks to a second soldier, Nachum Twersky, who was one of the Rebbe's relatives from the Tshernobiler family, which had remained in Kozienice due to the war. I made the acquaintance of the Rebbe's daughters: beautiful, intelligent, well brought up. I secretly became their teacher. I brought them secular books, which my father sent me from time to time from home. I became so popular in Kozienice that I did almost nothing except teach. The owner of the Koziencer beer brewery, Yona Tzemach, who was Mintzberg's son–in–law, asked me to teach his children. He used to boast that he was descended from the great scholar "Tzemach–Tzedek", and therefore his name was Tzemach. He was a Vilna Jew, a fine man, hospitable, with a good Jewish heart.

[Page 393]

An Event Happened

An event occurred – it happened just at the time of the Christian Easter – my sergeant, a family man, who lived outside the barracks, induced me to commit a sin – I should record a few pounds of meat more, because he wants to invite guests to stay with him for the holiday.

The captain of the first company audited the books and discovered the theft. He came to the barracks, called me to him and asked me what the story was. I didn't want to implicate the sergeant, because he was, after all, a family man, so I pleaded guilty. As clerk, it is understood, I had to record my own punishment with my own hands – 10 days under arrest. I had to remove my belt and order two soldiers to accompany me to the guard–house. To my good fortune, after a day of confinement, they opened the door of my prison and ordered me back to the barracks. There I met the commander of the battalion, a strict German, and he began to reprimand me: "You, a Jew, a teacher, a secretary, should commit such a folly, and implicate yourself."

I remained quiet. He understood my silence and said: "So, nothing to say. We already know everything. Please be good enough to record 10 days of confinement for your sergeant." He immediately left the office and said: "Tell Miss Yustman that I fulfilled her request."

Of course, I immediately went to tell my student, that I'm a free man. But she already knew everything since Kovalsky had told all. She had then told it all to the captain, and asked him to set me free. According to all the rules of the novel, I should have taken my blond, 18 year old student, with the rosy cheeks into my arms and kiss her. And I must admit that I felt a strong desire to do so. And it was obvious that she was awaiting it. But what is the story of that "particular Hasid", who was beaten in the face by his hanging fringes, I simply extended my hand to my student and like a cavalier in uniform, I brought her hand up to my mouth and kissed it. From there I no longer returned to the fourth company, but went to a work company, and became a painter and a teacher of the children of the sergeant. From then on I had more free time and became almost exclusively a teacher.

Kozienice in 1905

Almost two years, my years of soldiering, were spent in Kozienice, with small interruptions, for shooting practice, somewhere near the town of Konsk, in the province of Radom. At the time, I also had the opportunity to become acquainted with a variety of Polish and Jewish towns between Kozienice and Konsk; their inns and stores. With their healthy young wagoners, and with their worthy, tender and enthusiastic daughters. When I returned at the end of the summer of 1905 from camp, I received a letter from my brother, Yosl, who worked at the time in Odessa. He wrote to me about the uprisings which were occurring in all of Russia.

[Page 394]

I read the letter to my friends in the work company. We looked at each other and asked the question: "What are we doing here?" Great events are taking place in Russia. Her very foundations are crumbling, and then I made the decision to return home. It wasn't difficult for me to convince my sergeant that he should place me at the head of the leave list. He helped me a great deal. I bade farewell to my fellow soldier friends, my students, and all of the Jewish homes that I had visited. On foot 1 went to the Garbatke station, because the railroad tracks in all of Russia hindered communication. For 25 days I was stuck in Lublin. While there I looked up the Lubliner Jewish Workers Movement, in a dark attic, occupied by a few sad young men, like the walls of the house. I had gotten the address from the Bund in Kozienice. They were overjoyed to see the soldier, who brought them such warm regards from the Kozienice shoemakers and from the Worker's Bund. My soldier's uniform opened for me a place on a fully packed wagon, which finally started its journey after 25 days of a strike. I arrived in Odessa on the 6th of November, 1905, only after all of my leave was up.

A Few Words About Kozienice

Kozienice was a town of shoemakers, with all of the details involved, and even in those years was already a stronghold of the Bund. The leader of the Bund was Yidl Weinberg, a Yiddish teacher, who conducted a school. He was a relative of the wealthy Yustman family.

His brother, a student who belonged to the P.P.S. came from Radom. Another brother studied in Paris, and in those years traveled with Prof. Feitlovitsh's expedition to Abyssinia, to determine the relationship between the Falashas (Black Jews) to the Queen of Sheba. The Weinbergs knew that I was a member of the Russian party, "Iskra", but we didn't have any party discussions, even though we would meet often. It was unnatural to me that Kozienice, a Hasidic, Jewish town, should be Bundist.

I would come into a shoemaker's home, and I enjoyed hearing how a boy, who worked for a different shoemaker, used to speak about Socialism and the workers' struggle. The Bundist theory of cultural autonomy did not concern him in the least. He had a dark complexioned charming sister, Reshke the dark–complexioned one, who used to tastefully sing the song "Oifen Pripetshik" (In the Fireplace Burns a Fire). And when she sang the words: "Whichever one of you will learn better – will receive a flag", she would smile coquettishly, so that it would pluck at the soul. Jewish soldiers were tied to and connected with the town. They had their Jewish homes and true friendship. Very dear folksy Jews and hospitable people were the Kozienicer Jews. Some of them attached themselves to Kozienicer permanently. Afterwards, when they completed their service, they got married, remained there as sons–in–laws, led fine family lives, and raised children and grandchildren with pleasure and joy.

[Page 395]

The Soldiers' Synagogue

Jewish soldiers had their own synagogue, separate from the large synagogue, on the side of the enter room. It had all of the holy articles and other necessary minuates. The synagogue had a large enter room, like all Jewish synagogues. In it stood the sink that was used for the ritual washing of the hands of the "kohanim" (priests) by the Levites with copper pitchers. This was done on the holidays before the kohanim blessed the congregation. Near the sink there hung a long wet towel for drying the hands. The enter room also served as the place where the overflow crowd and young people (who did not pray) congregated. On the day before Yom Kippur this was also the place where the collection plates were set up. On Simchat Torah this was the place where people were called for an Aliyah (calling up) to the Torah for everyone attending the services. The enter room was also the place where the youngsters would fool around and joke about the Rebbe and his followers who would come to him seeking advice and blessings.

On the side of the enter room the soldiers set up their synagogue, with their own officiators, cantors and readers (of the Torah). Passover they would conduct the Seder there. The Jewish community provided them with Matzah, meat, fish and wine for the "four" cups necessary for the Seder. Also, on the other holidays they would conduct the festive holiday feasts there. The Jewish towns of Russia would send their craftsmen, religious functionaries and also their Yiddish and Hebrew teachers to Kozienice. When the Kozienicer Rebbe married off a daughter, the Jewish soldiers were participants just like the other Jews. The drummer of the 8th company led the bride and bridegroom with his drum when they were escorted to the wedding canopy. On Simchat Torah when Jews carried the scrolls and danced with the Rebbe around the shul, we, a group of Jewish soldiers, stood a side and enjoyed their enthusiasm. At that time, I received a resounding slap from the Rebbe. I don't know if it was meant for his relative, the soldier, Nachum Twersky, who was very tall or for me as revenge for misleading his daughters by bringing them the secular books, which my father, the enlightened scholar would send to me from time to time. I accepted the slap with love, and hide it away in my memory, as a reminder of my feelings very much at home in the Polish town of Kozienice, where I spent the two years of my military service.

The Smolenski–Regiment

I consider it my duty to acquaint Kozieniceites with the Smolenski–Regiment.

After the partition of Poland between Russia, Austria and Germany, at the beginning of the 19th century, the russian government built the Ivangrod Fortress. In order to reinforce the fortress the government sent the 25th Smolenski–Regiment to Kozienice, because it was the center–point; 18 versts (a verst was the Russian measure of distance, about .66 of a mile) from the fortress and six versts from the River Vistula and a railroad fan from Kozienice to Radom and Kielce.

[Page 396]

The barracks were set up in three parts of the city: On Lubliner Street, across the bridge, in the village of Stara–Viesh stood the first barracks. On the Radomer rail–line, not far from the Jewish cemetery stood the second barracks. These barracks had a Jewish commander: Yosl Tzitrin. On Varshaver Street, not far from the forest, stood the third barracks. Not far from the barracks were Jewish shopkeepers, who drew their livelihood from the soldiers by buying and selling.

The important officers lived with their families in the beautiful homes on Varshaver Street, not far from Chrystian Church. There they had their military club, the chancellaries and the court. They also had their own Greek Orthodox Church with a priest, their own hospital with doctors and barber–surgeons and their own undertaker for Greek Orthodox. Jews were the contractors who provided food and merchandise of all sorts for the military. They became wealthy. Among them were the Yustman, Itzkovitsh, Avenshtern and Freilich families.

Four years before WWI in 1910, the 25th Smolenski–Regiment was sent out of Kozienice. The reason for the move was a military secret. When WWI broke out in 1914, the Jew–hater, Nikolai Nikolayevitsh, may his name be eradicated, issued a decree that all Jews be driven from the towns surrounding the fortress, including Kozienice, within 24 hours. It's understandable that everything was left in a mess. They .ran wherever their eyes led them, to the towns around Radom and Warsaw. When Germany drove the Russians from Poland, Kozienicer Jews returned to their homes and the youth began to build cultural institutions, which had not been tolerated during the rule of the Czar.

[Page 397]

There Was a Town Kozienice

by Sarale Hirshenhorn, Stockholm

Once there was a town, Kozienice
where the glory of God did dwell
Whosoever saw it even once,
would burst with pleasure.

There were the righteous of the highest degree
Craftsmen without limit
Yeshiva boys, with the flame of Torah,
Merchants, dealers – and few wealthy.

There was only one mill – Freilich's
And Yona Tzemach had a brewery,
Honikshtoks, Shabaszons – Saw Mill
And Leizer–Itshe's – biggest house.

Chaim Samochod – a deliverer
Shlomo – a porter, Nute – a blacksmith,
Moshele Gott – a peddler to the villages
And Moshe Goldtzveig – a scholar a Jew.

Aaron Leib – a bathhouse attendant,
Moshe–Leib – head of the burial society,
The Flakes dealt in orchards,
And in the synagogue a beadle – Tokazsh Itshe.

If I would mention all the names
Which as I write rhyme so nicely
And so that I shouldn't miss anyone,
We must begin with the Rebbe – and end with
the water–carrier, Shame.

Where do we get the time,
To describe what there was in town:
The singing of joy, the sadness of suffering
And everything that was heard and seen.

For eternity a curse on the lips,
For those who harmed our nearest and dearest
For destroying the beautiful figures and types.
For our little children, that they burned.

Let us cry aloud, and let tears fall,
Scream, demand and call
So that the whole world hears and God punishes the
murderers?

[Page 398]

The Military Conscription in Kozienice

by Yerachmiel Sirota, Paris

Kozienice was a centrally situated city and every year, right after the Succot holiday, the military draft would be held there. From all of the area, the towns and villages, the young peasants would come to Kozienice. During this period, the Jews of our town were fearful, because immediately afterwards the young peasants would drink up, and the local antisemites would use the opportunity to stir them up to attack Jews. This happened a number of times, until the young peasants were taught a lesson by our local Macabees, that they well remembered. On the Jewish side there arose a group of leaders who carried on the battle. Our group was armed with iron pipes, thick sticks, rocks and shoemaker knives. The strategy of our leaders was to fool the drunken peasants into coming into side streets, and there to beat their brains out. Many of them would return home crippled. The city would then resemble a battlefield. The Russian householders would side with the antisemites, and never worried about the defenseless Jewish population. Quite the contrary: Russian officials would arrest innocent Jews. But these officials never caught the members of our group, who were too fleet to be caught. And if our group was not around, the antisemites would attack and rob, even the poor women who sold a bit of fruit and sugar. We can be proud of our youth who with so much devotion defended the honor of Jewish craftsman, merchants, shopkeepers, and students.

Our Macabees have not disappeared from my mind: Gutman Meltzer, Itshe Hoffman, Shmuel Fleisher, Simcha Fleisher, Yankl Vasserman, Shlomo Lampe and his brother, Note Kovall, and many young butchers and porters. All of them would year in, year out, prepare themselves for the struggle. I also want to mention the sons of Leizer Kotter and Falye Bondol and his brother Chaim of the Veitzman family, and many others who unfortunately have slipped from my mind. From all of these workmen there was organized an army of defenders of Jewish honor in Kozienice.

Besides all of the troubles that we had to endure, the economic situation in many Jewish homes was tragic, because their sons had been conscripted and were sent to serve in the army for almost four years. The wailing of Jewish mothers can not be described. They knew that their children would be far away deep inside of Russia, near the Japanese border. They wouldn't know of Shabbat or holidays, and would eat non–kosher foods. And they would hear that their sons were serving in the cavalry, mounted on horses, then the tragedy of the Jewish mother would be unbearable, and their eyes swelled with tears. Young children would never see the world outside of Kozienice, and of course, never spoke Russian. Who would take care of them in the bitter cold? How often would the mother go down at night to see if the child was covered.

[Page 399]

Poor parents had only one hope – perhaps, with God's help, their sons would be exempt from military service, or receive a red or green ticket. In this matter the difference between rich and poor was immense. For 300 Rubles, an exemption could be bought. Every official, from the lowest to the highest could be bribed. Everything was done to escape the draft. Some would even cripple themselves for life – chop off the toe of a foot, pull out all the teeth, give oneself a hernia, redden the eyes, and even make oneself deaf – everything and anything to avoid serving in the Czar's army. The poor who didn't have money and didn't want to cripple themselves for life, had to go serve. This was no secret to anyone.

And the leaving for military service? The poor mother could no longer sleep at night. Till the parents survived the return of their son after four years of service, their eyes would pop out of their heads. And so the years passed one after another. Every year there were new troubles in many Jewish homes. And the moaning and tears of the mothers never ceased.

[Page 400]

The Russian High Command Seized Our House

by Chava Shapiro, Kfar–Hasidim

In 1916 the Austrians invaded Poland, and with the speed of lightning conquered the Demblin Fortress, and approached the gates of Kozienice. The Russian High Command seized our new house, and called it Port Arthur, like the well–known fortress in Russia, because the walls of the house were more than half a meter thick. It's possible that the enemy knew this, therefore they considered the house a strategic place and directed most of their artillery fire at it. Our family and all of the inhabitants of our city didn't move until the situation became impossible. On Simchat Torah, under a hail of bullets, grandmother, the rebbetzin Sarah Devorah, grabbed me in one hand, the boys, among whom was Yisroel Elazar, of blessed memory, in the other hand; my mother, rebbetzin Bracha with her big children and left the Houses of the Maggid.

All of the City's People Followed Us

When they saw the Rebbe's family go and leave, all of the city's people streamed after us. With devotion they loaded the sick and the pregnant women on vehicles. That picture will never be erased from my memory! Thousands left, in a fleeing moment, leaving their homes and possessions, dressed in holiday finery, and fleeing from the enemy gunfire. I remember that they persuaded grandmother and my mother to mount a carriage, but they wouldn't consent. Their concern, as always was for others. It was they who had founded the society for visiting the sick, a free–loan fund. They used to distribute loans to small business men to enable them to support their families. I also want to mention the respected and wise lady, Mrs. Haikl, of blessed memory, grandmother's friend, who faithfully helped her carry on her charitable work; Their palms they spread out to the poor, and their hands extended to the "poverty–stricken".

We Arrived In Radom

We walked about fifteen kilometers without turning around, and without resting for a moment, until we reached the village of Yedlna. There we rested until the holiday ended. And from there we turned our steps towards Radom. We got an apartment in the house of one of the Hasidim. For a long time our ties to Kozienice were severed and we didn't know what was going on there. Only after the Germans had conquered all of the territory and the cannons were silenced, did some individuals begin to seek ways to return home. The conqueror raised difficulties and didn't even permit passing from the German areas to the Austrian ones. But in spite of all, there were some people who risked their lives and crossed the border. Some returned to their homes and possessions with pure expectations, but others with dire thoughts. There were old people who were afraid, perhaps, God forbid, they would die in a strange place, and not in their own city. Among them was Mrs. Chana Miriam, of blessed memory.

[Page 401]

It was impossible to convince her to wait and not return to Kozienice. She returned. I'd like to mention something that I heard from her: When she came to Kozienice, she headed for the house of the Rebbe. At the entrance she saw an elegantly dressed man standing before the mirror with a fan (which one of our girls had left behind) in his hand, and another young man playing a violin. She turned to them and said in German: "Pure and righteous people live here. Watch everything, because this belongs to the Kozienice Maggid." One of them answered me very politely: "Yes, my name is Yoachim. I am one of the sons of Kaiser Wilhelm". And he promised me that he would guard the house, which belonged to important people. My dear mother thought that the story was a figment of Chana Miriam's imagination. But afterwards it turned out that it really was Prince Yoachim. Also our father's expensive violin disappeared.

The Conquerors Didn't Permit Us To Leave and Go To The City

A few weeks later, the people of our city began to return to their homes and businesses. The situation was difficult, but life began to return to normalcy.

The conquerors didn't allow us to leave or return to the city. It was impossible to send letters, since there was no mail. Travel required a special pass which could only be obtained with difficulty. Only two people began to come and go. They were R'Velvele and R'Chaiml. They would leave surreptitiously, for Warsaw, and cross the border. The German and Austrian sentries got used to them. The first had no children and the latter had many. They were both the kind of individuals who sought a livelihood, required little, and were very good–hearted. They got low prices for the goods that they brought in. They also performed charitable deeds for people, since they were the only ones going and coming. They buoyed the spirits of many with the news and messages which they conveyed from place to place. When they arrived from Warsaw, groups would gather around them on the streets of the city, to hear the news, because there were no newspapers at the time. The two of them were given the title: "News Vendors". We will remember them among the martyrs of our city, who perished in the Holocaust at the hands of the Nazi conquerors.

[Page 402]

Kozienice, a City and Mother in Israel

by Elimelech Feigenboim, Ramat–Gan

Kozienice was a typical Jewish town like all the towns in Poland. There were all kinds of Jews there: Rich, poor; merchants, workers and craftsmen; religious and free–thinkers. All of the various parties that existed than in Poland, could be found there: Starting with the Communists and ending with Agudas–lsrael; Hasidim of all kinds and also Mitnagdim (those opposed to Hassidism). Until 1914 all Jewish affairs were conducted by three prominent Jews, who represented us before the government and city fathers. The leader of the three was R'Abraham Chaim Freilich, of blessed memory, a Jew of pleasant outward appearance, tall, with a black beard, wealthy and acceptable to Jews and Gentiles. He devoted his entire life to the welfare of the community, freely, and everyone who had any dealings at all with the city or government would turn to him and he was always ready to help. The second was R'Yitzhak Milgroim, owner of a stationery store, more progressive in his thinking, but not any less devoted to the affairs of the community.

The Young People of the City Throw Off the Yoke

In this way were the affairs of the city conducted until the outbreak of WWI. In 1914– the war broke out. The front, which was at the Demblin Fortress, approached our city. One month after the outbreak of war, the order was given by the commandant of the Fortress, that all Jews leave within 24 hours. A delegation of Jews, with R'Freilich at its head, went out to the commandant to request that the decree be rescinded or postponed. But to our great sorrow the delegation didn't succeed, and all Jews had to leave to a distance of 12 kilometers from the city. The Jews panicked when they heard the decree, and they began to leave their homes. Everyone who was able to, took his possessions. The poor didn't have this opportunity, and the mayor promised that their possessions would be guarded. The Gentiles took advantage of the opportunity, and offered to help move Jewish possessions at inflated prices. They weren't ashamed to ask for 10 to 15 Rubles, for the 12 kilometer distance – a very high price in those days. After 2 days, permission was given to the Jews to return to their homes. The mayor had kept his word, and had guarded Jewish property. A month later the Germans approached the city and the Russians began a retreat through the city. It was during the Holiday of Succot, and all of the Jewish owned stores were closed. There wasn't enough food for the soldiers, and the Rabbis decreed that it was permissible to bake bread for the retreating army. Jews were afraid that the retreating Cossack army would make a pogrom and loot their homes, so they had one of the city's inhabitants, a reserve Russian General, by the name of Simyonov, go out in full–dress uniform, to prevent the Cossacks from looting the Jewish homes.

[Page 403]

Suddenly, a German patrol appeared, and almost captured the General, but the Jews managed to hide him. He changed out of his uniform and in this way was saved from the Germans. A few days later, the Germans and Austrians battled the Russians in the fortress. The Russians drove back the Germans, and the battle was conducted in the city. Part of the city was destroyed, and Jewish property went down the drain. A year later the Russians retreated and the Austrians ruled in Kozienice. Life returned to normalcy. As a result of the change, the young people threw off the yoke. Political parties were formed – from Zionists to Communists. A modern community was formed with a communal head. A cultural center was established where lectures were held, and also political debates. The most important was the activity of the workers' organization, the Socialist Bund, that fought for the improvement of workers' conditions. Most workers were engaged in the manufacture of shoes. The shoes of Kozienice were renowned throughout Poland.

Standing: Israel Feigenbaum, Melech Freilech, Shlomo Tabatchnik
Sitting: Sara Feigenbaum, Abraham Chaim Freilech and his wife, Nachma
Tabatchnik, Yakov Freilech

Kozienice, the City of the Holy Maggid

Kozienice was famed as the city of the Holy Maggid, R'Yisrael, who lived 150 years ago. A street in Kozienice bears his name. On this street were located the Synagogue, the House of Study, and the house of the Maggid. During the period with which we are dealing, the chair of the Maggid was occupied by R'Arele, of blessed memory, who was murdered by the Nazis, may their name be eradicated. He was a 6th generation descendant of the Holy Maggid, the son of R'Yerachmiel Moshele, who died in 1910. On the cemetery there was a special tomb (2 rooms) where the Holy Maggid and his five sons were interred. On the anniversary day of his death or of the death of one of his sons, thousands of Jews from all over Poland would come to pay their respects at the graves of the holy ones. At the time of R'Arele, the rebbetzin, Sarah Devorele, of blessed memory7, his grandmother, and also the rebbetzin, Brachale, of blessed memory, his mother, were still alive, and also brothers and sisters.

To the Rebbe of Kozienice, there flowed Hassidim from all of Poland. Especially on the High Holy Days. Then the Rebbe and his Hassidim would pray in the Synagogue, which had existed for hundreds of years. The walls were more than a meter thick. The doors were of brass, the Holy Ark was permanently set into the wall, and its doors were also of brass. In this Ark were to be found hundreds of Torah Scrolls from all generations.

On Rosh Hashanah, the Synagogue was full. The congregation would greet the Rebbe by rising en masse, with respect. The prayers were conducted with enthusiasm. My grandfather, of blessed memory, led the morning prayer, and we, his grandsons helped him. Thanks to this we were privileged to stand close to the Rebbe, of blessed memory.

[Page 404]

The Rebbe would be dressed in a white silk "robe" and a wide white silk belt, which he inherited from Rebbe Elimelech of Lizansk. The big event of the day was always the Rebbe's blowing of the shofar. The huge congregation waited for it impatiently. Silence pervaded the synagogue, before the uplifting of the spirit. TTie Musaf (additional service) was then led by R'Elimelech Freilich, of blessed memory. Barely were the townspeople able to grab a light meal before setting out for the river bank for the Tashlich Service (symbolic casting of sins into water on Rosh Hashanah afternoon). Men, women and children streamed to the small river which was outside the city limits. By the time they returned it was already dark, and the procession moved to the light of torches and the accompaniment of singing. On the Rebbe's street, dance circles formed as young and old danced together. The enthusiasm reached it's peak.

The family Feigenbaum in Kozienice

On Simchat Torah the Rebbe took part in the first Hakafah (circling of the shul holding a scroll of the Torah). It was the custom to do the Hakafot under a wedding canopy. After the first one, the Rebbe went with prominent Hassidim to Kiddush (a collation) at grandma, Sarah Devorah's house. After the Kiddush, at midnight, began the Hakafot in the Synagogue of the Rebbe, and continued almost all night. In the Rebbe's house there was a room, which the Holy Maggid lived 150 years ago. In this room stood the furniture of the Maggid: The table, chair and bed. This room was used only at the end of a holiday. The Rebbe would then enter the room, sit in the chair and play the well known melody of "Elijah the Prophet" on the violin, using the Holy Maggid's melody. All of the Hassidim would sing along with enthusiasm. At those moments of uplifting, they could forget their troubles. Near the Synagogue, stood the Study House, which was open all the hours of the day and night. This was used by the public at large. Besides prayer it was used by young men from Bar Mitzvah to their weddings, for study of Holy texts. Married young men, who were supported by in-laws, also used it for study. In the evenings it was a meeting place for all. In effect it was the place where all groups socialized, studied "Ayn-Yaakov" (a folklore and fable text), Mishnayot, or just engaged in secular conversation.

The Rebbe Bakes Matzot

In one of the villages of the area lived a Pole, from whom the Rebbe bought wheat before it was even ploughed and sown. It was agreed that this wheat was special for the Rebbe and his family, come the Passover. On the fast day, "Tisha-B'Av", the Hassidim went from the Rebbe's house to the village, harvested the wheat and brought it to the house of the Rebbe. During the winter the young men from the Study House would separate and choose the kernels of wheat. A month before Pesach they brought mill-stones to one of the rooms and ground the kernels into flour. In the Rebbe's house there was also a stove for the baking of the Matzot.

[Page 405]

This work was done only by the men. A carpenter was always present so he could smooth and polish the boards, so that the dough would not stick to them. Every year, on the eve of Pesach, the Hassidim would bake the Matza Shmura (guarded matza). Everyone would come with his own bag of flour, and they would cast lots to determine the order. During the baking the Hassidim recited Psalms of Praise (Hallel). A few select individuals were privileged to receive Matza Shmurah from the Rebbe for the first Seder night. The first Seder at the Rebbe was reserved for family only. His Hassidim participated in his second Seder, which would last all night. When they got to the passage: "Pour out thy wrath upon the nations..." the Rebbe himself would open the door of the Holy Maggid's room.

My Family

My family was one of the largest in Kozienice. My father, R' Ttcha son of R'Mordecai Natan, of blessed memory was a "shochet" (ritual slaughterer). My grandmother, of blessed memory, Tzivia daughter of Rivke, was the daughter

of R'Chaim Yaakov Rozen who was a merchant manufacturer on the main
street. He was a respected householder, and honest merchant. He had six
sons and two daughters. In our family there were 4 sons and 2 daughters.
Father was a follower of Rebbe Yerachmiel Moshele and his son, Rebbe Arele,
of blessed memory. He served them with all his soul. My brother, R' Aaron
Berish, the first–born, was a candy manufacturer. On the Days of Awe he
would lead the services at the Rebbe's. My second brother, Moshe Hersh led a
modern life in Warsaw. My sister, Nechama, of blessed memory, lived in the
village of Yedlnia near Kozienice, and my second sister, Raisel, the wife of
R'Abraham Zucker, the watchmaker, lived in my father's house in Kozienice.
My twin brother, Fishl, lived in Warsaw. I'd like to memorialize all of my
relatives, who were murdered by the Nazis.

Levi Feigenboim, Of Blessed Memory

My son, Levi, was born in April 1925 in Safed (Israel). He was educated in
elementary school in Haifa, where he was accepted in the "Camps for
Immigrants". From Haifa he went and finished school in Kiryat–Chaim. From
an early age he wanted to be a farmer, so he entered the district school in
Yagur. In 1942 he finished, was drafted into the Palmach, and stationed in
Upper Galilee. From there he went to Tel–Yosef, where he distinguished
himself with his courage and devotion. He loved sport. He was among the first
of a group of Palmach members in the lower Galilee. He guarded fields of a
kibbutz. He organized the library in the kibbutz, Beit–Keshet. He read a lot
and was the first father there. On 16 August 1948 he went out with 8
comrades on patrol and didn't return. He fell defending Beit–Keshet. May his
memory be blessed!.

[Page 406]

My Birthplace, Kozienice

by Pinchas Feigenboim, Moscow

It is more than 30 years since fate has driven me from my birthplace.
Ignoring the fact that I find myself far from my town, there they stand before
my eyes the superb, historical places, which were my daily companions: The
large Study House, the Synagogue, the Maggid's small prayer–house, the
palace, the river, the forest, nature, the beautiful spring nights and my
companions and friends.

It is Difficult to Forget

A person can forget many things, but that which he digested with his mother's milk, is difficult to forget. How can one forget the Heder years and their impressions? My teacher, Berele Melamed, whom I will not forget until my dying breath, and other teachers, who would beat me with their cat-of-nine tails whether you deserved it or not. How can one forget the mood on the eve of Rosh Hashanah, Yom Kippur, and other holidays? When I remind myself of those days, a shiver passes through my body.

No small thing – such days! Doctors, shoemakers, tailors – all, like one, would tremble on those days, like fish in water. It even seems as if the sun and the moon were in the holiday spirit, because all would serve those holy days. Weekday worries were cast away. Everyone attempted to forget the bad that he did and that was done to him. Those, who had the opportunity and means, would give charity, so that poor Jews, on the Holy Days, would feel as equals of everyone, and that on their tables there should be food and drinks. Comrades and friends used to meet and enjoy a glass of wine. And then there would be the Hakofot in Shul, which we prolonged until after midnight. Who doesn't remember how the Kozienicer Rebbe, R'Aaron Hopshtein and his brother Elimelech, would do their Hakofot. It was a pleasure!

Wise Jews

There were in our town many wise Jews, who knew how to learn (holy texts). For example: R'Elimelech Freilich, Abraham–Chaim Freilich, Ben–Zion Freilich, The Kozienicer Rabbi, the Tshepelever Rebbe, R'Yosef–Leib – an extremely clever and progressive man, Yaakov–Hersh Weinberg, Chaim Chmelnitzky, his son Moshe, Yitzhak Milgrom, Itshe Feigenberg, Yona Tzemach, Chaim Borenstein and many other talented and wise people, who earned for themselves the right not to be forgotten. The majority in our town were laborers. Jews were occupied with the daily worries of a livelihood. They weren't boors, the striving for knowledge was widespread.

Many Parties

There were many parties in our town, and each one had its local chapter. They would arrange discussions, readings, quiz evenings, and always there were many participants. Very often lecturers would come from Warsaw.
[Page 407]

We also had a very large library, and newspapers, so that the cultural life did not cease even for a moment. Now a few words about the parties, dust as it is customary among Jews, there were, thank God, many parties in Kozienice, who conducted ideological warfare among themselves. Fathers and children, sisters and brothers – each would defend his party. The orthodox fought fanatically. The progressive parties conducted their struggle with the help of ideological literature.

The warfare would heat up before elections. There were elections to the Siem (Polish Parliament), to the city council, to the Jewish Community Council and to other organizations. There was no bigger holiday than election day. Big and little would on that day participate in party propaganda. Nobody was neutral. Even old and sick women would be healthy on election day, and go to vote.

In our town there were people who loved to occupy themselves with theatre. They performed the "Dybbuk", Two Hundred Thousand" and many other plays, Jewish performers from other towns would also come.

Let's Not Forget the Mothers?

I want that in our book, we shouldn't forget our mothers, who did not have easy lives. We, children, did not feel the burden which they carried upon their shoulders. I remember, that after WWI, when we returned to our town, everything was burned and destroyed. But our mothers, with their own hand repaired and rebuilt everything. We won't forget our mothers, who wouldn't eat or sleep, but provided all for our development. Eternal honor to the memory of our mothers and fathers, who fell as a sacrifice of the Hitlerite bandits.

[Page 408]

Story of a Bottle of Chometz (Not For Passover) Whiskey

by Yissaachar Lederman, Rio de Janeiro

Maybe the story, which I tell here is known to all of you, and many of you remember it. It happened in 1927, before I left for Brazil. The purpose of my writing is to refresh our memories of days gone by. It is enough to recall a small episode, and I desire to record it, because that life will never again come to pass. That observant Jewish life has vanished, therefore we sanctify the memories. Now to the story:

A chometz bottle of whiskey led to a spoiled Pesach in town. People became enemies. The prayers and reading of the Torah were hindered and interrupted. Yosef, the judge, ran around like a crazy man. THIS IS HOW IT WAS... A Hassidic Jew, a merchant, named Shmerl Shvartzberg, forgot to sell his chometz on Passover eve. The truth is he didn't deal in chometz goods, but in leather. As he returned from Warsaw at nightfall on the eve of Pesach, he had no time and just forgot to sell his chometz. On the second day of Pesach, Shmerl went up to his attic and saw a bottle of Chometz whiskey. He became frightened – chometz in his home on Passover! It's a sin! No chometz is to be seen or found in a Jewish home on Pesach! What should he do? Not to tell is also a big sin! Immediately he ran to the religious judge, Yosef Shapiro, to ask what to do. There was no greater scholar then Yosef, therefore he was the judge. A joke about him circulated in town that he could only adjucate in matters concerning women. Yosef listened to Shmerl, took out various tomes, the Shulchan Aruch (Religious Laws) creased his forehead, and gave his opinion: to take a Goy to go up in the attic and throw down the bottle of whiskey, since it is forbidden to enjoy it. Shmerl didn't like it! What's this? Throw out a bottle of good whiskey? Why? He left Yosef very upset. A Gerer Hasid, a bit of a joker, approaches him and says: "Shmerl, what happened? So troubled on a holiday? You didn't sell your leather? You have to pay I. O. U.'s?" "No," answered Shmerl, and he tells him the whole story. So the Jew said to him: "Fool! Make out as if you know nothing and go ask the Rabbi what to do!"

Shmerl took the advice, ran up to the Rabbi, and asked the same thing. The Rabbi answered: "Shmerl go home! After Pesach bring the bottle to services and we will make a good L'Chaim over it, but also bring some Pesach goodies." Shmerl ran immediately to the Study House, and told the whole story– that Yosef had told him to break the bottle and that Rabbi Mintzberg told him to leave it till after Pesach. Nu! What happened then in the Study House! Two sides formed: For Yosef and for Rabbi Mintzberg. The Rabbi was also a great scholar, a pupil of the Ostrovtzer Rebbe, so he invited a few Gerer Hassidim, scholars, and showed them that the Rabbi of the town has permission to sell, on the eve of Pesach, all of the chometz in his community, and the bottle of whiskey is included in the general sale of chometz.

[Page 409]

What did Yosef the judge do? He didn't sleep either. He gathered about him a few Jews from among his supporters, and they surreptitiously went up to the attic, took the bottle, threw it out into the street and broke it.

Nu, it sure was lively in town after that! After the holiday, Shmerl sued Yosef before a rabbinical court (Din Torah). He demanded to be paid for the bottle of whiskey. Yosef said that the law was that one couldn't enjoy what had been chometz, once Pesach was over. The conclusion of the story was that the community council called Shmerl Shvartzberg and paid him for the bottle. This was what the Rabbi had ordered and the money was deducted from Yosef's salary.

But for months and years the story remained on the daily agenda in the Study House. Rabbi Mintzberg sent the problem to the Ostrovtzer Rebbe, and to the Brisker Rav, and both sent him an answer which concurred with his decision in the case!

[Page 410]

Memories of Our Town

by Yehiel Mandel, Pariso

Yehiel Mandel

With my writing, I want to recall, and relive in our memory, our town, which laughed, sang and, at times also cried. There were many houses in which people plainly hungered, but they would jest and tell stories. The plain folk of Kozienice were simple but sharp–minded.

Maksimenko Got It In His Hand

I recall the fact that in our town there was a chief of the police named Maksimenko, who ordered that all drain holes and chimneys be painted white. This caused a commotion. Jews took off their long kapotes and set to work, because it had to be completed in one day. On the next day the Russian officials with Maksimenko at their head came to the Jewish streets. Whoever had not completed the painting was given a fine of several Rubles or go to jail. When it had to take several days, Maksimenko was called in, a bribe placed in his hand and everything was OK. The Jews calmed down a bit!

Thursday Was Market Day In Town

Jews would stroll, touch every bag of grain, taste it, haggle over price, until the peasant agreed. The grain merchants would go around with a straw in their mouth, touch the bags of grain, and bargain a bit. And what about our old–clothes dealers, shoemakers, tailors and milliners. They would unpack their merchandise and wait for buyers. If a peasant would approach and want to buy, he would be kept so long that he wouldn't leave emptyhanded, and other merchants (competitors) would gaze upon them with envy.

I remind myself that I studied with a teacher, who was named Nachum Ezra's. I remember: A full house, packed with children. The teacher would go hungry ten times a day, so he undertook another job: exorcising evil–eyes. Women would actually come to have him exorcise the evil–eye, and the teacher would mumble and then sneeze, meaning that help was on its way!

Pese Sells Chestnuts

Pese, the chestnut vendor, gave pleasure to the young. When they saw her in the street, with her pot of chestnuts they would run after her: "Pese, give me a groschen worth of chestnuts!" She had a little measuring cup with which she would measure the amount and then add a few more chestnuts, so that all would know that she's giving a fair measure. She had another livelihood. She would bake honey cake. Whoever made a nice wedding, used to hire Pese to bake honey cake. The guests and in–laws would plainly lick their chops.

[Page 411]

Pinchas Sofer Sells Pickles. He would set up barrels full of cucumbers, and people would indeed run to him with quart jars, and carried home sour pickles with lots of pickle juice, which was very sour. And these were the Jewish livelihoods, of little or no consequence!

A Wedding in Town

When a wedding took place in town, the tall Yisrael went with his trumpet, and Meir Shachne with his clarinet, and Yitzhak Klezmer with his fiddle, and Nechemia Klezmer with his fiddle and escorted the bride to the wedding canopy at the Shul. In winter, late at night, teeth chattering with cold, townspeople, with candles in hand and children trailing behind. Often non–Jews, who knew the bride and groom, would come to see the entire ceremony. On the way back from the wedding, the mother–in–law, with a cake in her hand, would sing and dance: "Bridegroom, here is a cake, for life, so seek not another wife!"

On the Eve of Yom Kippur Even Fish in Water Tremble

"When the eve of Yom Kippur arrived even the fish in water trembled!" – This was the folk–saying. For every child, a hen, rooster or fish was bought for the Kapparot ceremony. (Expiation of sins) At the time of the afternoon service, they would run to the Study House for the traditional Malkos (whipping with a branch). I would see how Jews would lie on the ground, face down and with their right hands beating their hearts. At the shoulder stood a Jew with a whipping branch in his hand and he would whip the shoulders to drive out the sins. The person would then rise red–faced, and run home to eat the final meal before the fast. I remember the awe that seized everyone as they started to run to Kol Nidre. Every Jew exuded Holiness, so it would seem to me that I am seeing God and all of his seven heavens, with all of his ministering angels placing their stamp of approval on all sides. Yom Kippur and the fast would pass. I say fast because there was no alternative. Every move I made was watched.

The Night Ending Yom Kippur We Build the Succah

At the end of Yom Kippur, after eating, we went out with a spade and marked the spot for the Succah. The custom was that several neighbors would chip in. One would bring a bundle of s'chach (covering for the Succah), another some branches of pine trees, and together we would set up a Succah. When it came time to eat, after the prayers, rich and poor would eat together in the Succah. The rich would eat all sorts of delicacies, starting with braided challahs, gefilte fish, a good hen, and a good plate of soup with kreplach (meat wrapped in dough). Since the poor person was embarrassed, because he had nothing prepared for the holiday, he would arrange with his wife to ask him: "Do you want gefilte fish?" "No." "Do you want chicken?" "No." "A bit of compote?" "Yes!" The poor fellow would explain to his neighbors in the Succah that unfortunately, he had no appetite.

[Page 412]

On the Sands

By us in Kozienice there was a neighborhood that was called "On Sand". There, lived mostly poor laborers, carpenters and shoe polishers. The "On Sand" reminds me of unpleasant things. There we would escort the dead to the cemetery. There we would sink in the sands, almost unable to drag the feet. Before the High Holidays we would go there to visit the graves of our near and dear ones to request of them to beseech the Lord to give us a good year to come.

Recruits Promised Not To Bother Jews

I remember a fact. We received an alarm that the young recruits from around Kozienice, who have to report for military conscription, are going to engage in a pogrom against Jews. They didn't conduct a pogrom, but they seized Jews and beat them. They also fell upon and robbed Jewish shops. Nu, our Jewish youth got organized. In order to protect us they went out on the street and beat up on the hooligans, and broke their bones so that they would never bother Jews.

I want, with my writing, to awaken memories of my dear town, Kozienice, in order that they be engraved in the memory of young and old for generations to come. Kozienice was well–known in all of Poland for her impressive forests, and her Hassidism.

It Should Be Engraved In Memory

Who hasn't heard about the Kozienicer Maggid? And about R'Arele, who was founder of a Progressive Hassidism, in order to attract the youth, to keep them from the wrong path. In the entire area they spoke of it, and said that, God forbid, the Rebbe has abandoned his Rabbinical ways. I remind myself, that prior to the High Holidays, there used to come to our town Hassidim from all over Poland to go to the graves of the Maggid and other holy rabbis to request a good year. Our town was pleased to have such an influx. We would live it up, especially the merchants who sold prayer books, fringes and mezuzot. The scribes did a brisk business, and who even mentions the paupers of the entire area? They had a full day begging.

Three Quarters of the Jews Lived From the Shoe Industry

Almost 2000 Jewish families lived in our town. Seventy five percent of them lived from the shoe industry and spats making. The remainder were small merchants and shopkeepers plus a few grain merchants. All lived, I should say happily – but that would be a lie. But they were satisfied. They married off children, and grandchildren, and life went its merry way.

[Page 413]

A Fine Cultured Youth

We had a fine, cultured youth, a rich library containing the classics, a drama circle, a professional association where we would gather, discuss things and carry on strikes. A few of the communist influenced youth were imprisoned for 3 or 4 years for opposing the established order. There were also other organizations: Hashomer Hatzair, and the Folks–club, which arranged for lecturers and concerts. Our Kozienice folk were very active in everything and involved, each to the best of his ability.

Rabbinical Disputes

I also want to mention the dispute which broke out when a portion of our Jews were not happy with a specific Rabbi. They brought in another Rebbe, more modern, the Tshepelever. Things were hopping "on tables and on benches" as we used to say. People fought tooth and nail. If one of the rabbis said something was kosher the other said it was treyf. It was lively in town, until one of them capitulated, and fled with his family to another place, and only then did things calm down.

The Youth Searches For The Practical

A portion of the youth, especially the more progressive youth, did not see any future for themselves in town. So they left – some to Warsaw, some to other large cities in the province, and only came home for the holidays dressing in the latest big–city fashion. They would bring gifts for father, mother and their young siblings. They would also bring grapes for the recitation of the Sheecheyanu blessing. That's how life went by. Children grew. Some went out of the country looking for a purpose in life. They would send letters or a package with a few zlotys, in order to support the rest of the family, since help was always welcome in Kozienice. After receiving letters from abroad, parents would run to neighbors, to show off the letters and photos: this one with a wife and children already, and that one with a bride.

A Number of Types From Our Town

Feivl Oger was a tall, thin Jew, beardless. He was called Oger because he pulled a wagon, just like a horse. If someone had to move some rags, he would hire Feivl Oger. He was very honest, occupied all of his life, with never enough to eat for himself or his family.

Crazy Mendele didn't bother anyone. They used to throw him a piece of bread and an onion, and this would sustain him. Mordecai Hoke suddenly became angry, leaped onto the platform in the Study House and called out: "Jews, I'm leaving town. Get yourselves a different Mordecai Hoke."

[Page 414]

Shammai, the water–carrier slaved away all of his life. With his two pails of water hanging on his shoulders, he used to fill many utensils with water among the housewives, and barely earned a living.

Hersh–Leib Bozer knew why he was slaving away so hard and bitter: because he wanted that his son Moshe, should become a scholar. And so it was. His son actually became a scholar. He would sit day and night in the Study House and learned. People said that he was a genius. He went away to

Yeshiva, and there a very wealthy man chose him to be his son–in–law. All this until the accursed war broke out with its atrocities and Nazi hordes.

My Family

My father had the good fortune of dying in the ghetto, a few weeks before the selection, and he was buried on the Kozienice cemetery. A sister of mine and her four children were thrown into the ghetto. When they took my sister, Rachel to the gas–chambers, she could barely stand on her feet, her oldest daughter, Sarale, ran after her and cried: "Mama, I won't leave you alone." And she clung to her. As soon as the Nazi in charge of her group saw this he said to her: "Don't cry, Fraulein. You will go with your mother. You will go together." In this way they were both gassed and cremated and martyred. That was how our dear town of Kozienice burned together with her martyrs. Only a few Kozieniceites saved themselves. Some are in Paris. Together with those who had come earlier, we formed a society, and each year we visit family graves to weep. We also set up a memorial for our departed fellow townsmen, and in this way we have eternalized their holy names.

[Page 415]

Our Cursed and Beloved Kozienice

by Yerachmiel Kestenberg, Tel Aviv

I'll forever remember my birthplace, Kozienice. Til remember you in your prosperity and in your tragedy. In you flourishing and in your destruction. There, where I saw my first light, and where for the first time, I heard the word, "Jew". Kozienice – there where I went to Heder, and learned in school, and played with children. There I also received the first stone on my head, from the hand of a Goy.

Kozienice, where I wove my childhood dreams – how beautiful are your surroundings. Hardly anywhere such a panorama of mountains, woods, lakes and meadows, where sheep grazed and where children picked flowers and told wonderful tales. Everything looked so wonderfully beautiful and so cruelly destroyed by the German murderers. Kozienice, the city of righteous shoemakers – was also the city of cultural creativity. Kozienice, the city of the Holy Maggid, of Hassidism and religious belief, together with revolutionary pathos and Zionist activity.

But Kozienice was also the city which bathed itself in Jewish blood; where the German murders slaughtered Jewish children, women and men.

Cursed by your borders, Kozienice. For eternity may your name be erased, and may you never be mentioned because of the innocent Jewish blood that was shed. Kozienice, blessed be your remaining sons and daughters in the newly freed Jewish homeland, and everywhere else, wherever they may be, because faithfully and virtuously they carried Jewish honor. Kozienice, until my last breath, I won't forget you. I hate you so, and still I love you!

I want to mention my mother, Libe Rechthand, a granddaughter of R' Aaron, of blessed memory. R' Aaron was for 40 years the Rabbi of Kozienice. Because of it we were always referred to as the grandchildren of R' Aaron.

[Page 416]

A Bundle of Memories of Kozienice

by Teme Potashnik, Paris

The spiritual life of the Jews in Kozienice consisted of fanatical belief and Hassidism. My father, of blessed memory, had his own library. But, as is well known, books in those days were considered an abomination. Father's friend, named Kuropatve, a secret "Maskil" (enlightened one), told us that in the Study House they say that Itshe Krishpel will come to a bad end, because he is an Agnostic. This information reached the Russian superintendent, who spoke Yiddish. He was told that Itshe Krishpel possesses a library of revolutionary literature. Once, on a nice early morning, the police came and carried away the entire library, in a wagon, together with my father. They kept my father under arrest for half a day, and in that way checked all of the books. Finally, they freed my father and returned the books. It seems that Mendele, Peretz and Shalom Aleichem were not considered subversive.

If we remind ourselves of how our parents lived, it seems a bit strange. But in spite of all they were devoted Jews, even though fanatically religious. The beastly Germans killed the fanatics as well as the free thinkers, and all were dear Jews.

Faiga and Itche Krishpel

The Drama Circle

I remind myself of the superb youth that we had in Kozienice. We organized a dramatic section which performed the "Dybbuk" and other plays. Chaim Berman was director. His sister, Tobe Berman, his brother, Zelick Berman and another brother, Shimon Berman, took part in the presentations. My brothers, Yankl and Benjamin Krishpel, and my sister, Pesye Gutmacher, whom the Germans deported, also took part in the dramatic section. Others, who participated, were Yissachar Lederman, Aaron Potashnik, Sarah Hershhorn, Yisrael–Dov Domb, Yitzhak Potashnik, my husband, and other Kozienicers whose names I no longer remember. I acted the role of Leah in the "Dybbuk". We lived well in the town of Kozienice. We had a club where we danced, held gatherings, lectures and social affairs. I'll never forget my town of Kozienice, where I was born.

Vanyusha the Son of Yasha

Give me, here, Vanyusha, your drunken chin, and I'll kiss you, but what, unfortunately, did you have against the paupers? You should have beaten the wealthy, the rich speculators, who would skin us, and who spread themselves out in the palaces which I built. Oh brother! I tell you openly, my stone is for the Jewish nobleman. But he lives high, so it missed him and hit instead the pauper. And Vanyusha picked tip his stone and I read it: Ivan Chaskelevitsh, I'll ask only you, and nicely, you obedient cur. Did you bring from your home a fortune to me? You want to be called Ivan son of Yasha son of Kish you have a land, it seems, Palestine. Too hot for you there in your Canaan, so you came to cool yourself in my land in my cold Kursk, in my Astrachan.

[Page 417]

You came dressed in uniform. I don't need a partner. The eating of pork, and dancing of the Kamarski, I can do better without you. And you already want equal rights with me. To spread yourself out at the head in my senate, and that I should carry garbage and clean toilets. No, dear Tevye, my brother! And when all the baptized will be on the verge of death and the priest will sing over them, as loud as he will chant his church melody they'll still hear the mumbling of Kol Nidre in their heads. You may build railroads, and become manufacturers; one may be called a banker, another even Baron, as far as I'm concerned you're only wealth beggars, with imposing fronts, chins without beards, without a nation and without a people. If I revile you and beat you, what can you do to me you wealthy Jewish magnate. You'll complain to the government, but do you have a consulate to defend you? And wherever you'll be rich with sugar factories I don't have to approach a consulate to speak to you, I only have to send my gendarmes, and you are speechless, you Jewish banker. I will spit upon the beatings and drink a glass or two, and then give you such a beating that you will scream. Leave me alone, I'm leaving!

Yankel Krishpel in Paris

[Page 418]

A Guest For a While

by A. Zilberstein

In 1928, I visited Kozienice. After an operation, I used the opportunity to visit my brother–in–law, Shimon Likverman, the son of Aaron Pinchas, of blessed memory, and my sister–in–law, Yehudis Potashnik, daughter of Mo tele Potashnik, dear and heartfelt people. Without cares, I walked through the beautiful town, and heard the nice stories of the great Kozienicer Maggid. The town looked like a picture by Chagall. It hovered in the air as if pure spirit. Also the people looked to me as if they lack nothing and are seeking only to perform good deeds. It was a small town, but beautiful, filled with charm. You can walk through the whole town, its length and breadth in half an hour, and it bakes itself deep into your heart. I wasn't born in Kozienice, but thanks to my dear wife, I've written these few lines.

A group of cultural activists in Kozienice

[Page 419]

Old Kozienice

by K. H. Band

Among the nations, various scholars, especially historians, dig in various materials, which enlightened the life and work of this or that dead personality. They speculate and hypothesize over every iota which is connected with their lives, and it is all written up, and preserved in various museums. But by us, unfortunately, very little is done in this respect, especially when it concerns a great religious personality. Let's take as an example the Kozienicer Maggid, of blessed memory, who even occupies among Polish historians a very important place, but Jewish scholars, in this respect did not interest themselves in this great spiritual giant, one of the pillars of Hassidism, who lit up Poland.

The writer of these lines recently visited Kozienice. I found tremendous material there which cried use me and work with me! Let them see the role that I once played in Jewish religious life!! The first street on which the car stops is called Magitova, because on this street the Holy Maggid had lived. The street commemorated his name. It is also holy to' the Christian population, and many legends are woven around it. The town of Kozienice, like all other provincial Jewish towns exudes poverty from its windows. Shopkeepers stand at the doors of their shops looking for buyers, and wait. Bent houses, crowded in one next to the other, as if they were connected to protect their existence. Among the row of houses is found the house where the Maggid used to live.

Here the Maggid Lived

As soon as you enter the house you must bend down, in order not to bang it on the lentel. You pass through a narrow corridor until you come to the small dwelling where the Maggid lived. The manager of the Maggid's dwelling, R' Asher, a Jew from Vilna, goodnatured gives you a warm welcome and immediately begins to tell stories of the dwelling. And by the way, a few weeks ago, the dwelling was visited by a Polish professor from Kovel. The professor – R' Asher tells – stood awed at the entrance, and was afraid to enter, but only looked in. It is called the "Holy Dwelling", and consists of two small rooms, whitewashed, with small panes in the only window. Inside are found the Rebbe's "Heavenly Bed", his stool and low commode, which also served as his writing table, where he wrote his new Torah commentaries. On the ceiling hangs a metal chandelier with six branches. The walls are engraved with names of visitors and requests, and in general whosoever needs salvation would come to pray in the Rebbe's "Shtibel" (dwelling). Every nook and cranny has stories and legends about them. "Look" shows me R' Asher – "You see that small round window, which is cut out in the door? Once through the window, the Mogelnitzer Rebbe, the grandson of the Maggid, when he was a little boy – looked in and saw the Maggid occupied in earnest conversation with a strange, impressive looking Jew. Later the stranger suddenly disappeared, and the boy ran to the Maggid and cried out: 'Zayde, I've seen Elijah, the Prophet, because that stranger must certainly have been him.☐ 'No my child' answered the Maggid, 'That was the great Rabbi, R' Ber and the appearance of great righteous men is greater than the appearance of Elijah'."

[Page 420]

One is overcome with fear when they mention who lived here, what a great spiritual giant worked in this dwelling, what a light streamed from the small windows, which lit up half the world. The other rooms, where the Maggid had lived have been done over and locals live in them. There was no one to guard them, and the heart breaks to see how the house in which the Maggid and his children and grandchildren lived, until the last Maggid died, is today a bakery!

"Do you see that hill?" says the one accompanying me at a hill near the Mikve. "When the Berditshever Rebbe, was in Kozienice, and went on Shavuot to the Mikve, a great enthusiasm seized him, and with impetus rolled himself down the hill."

The cemetery gate in Kozienice

On the Cemetery

Approaching the cemetery, we met an old Jew, who thoughtfully examined the new fence around the cemetery, which the community had recently set up. "Huh, what a waste. Thrown out money! The fence won't last long!" "Why?" "Because whenever a fence was set up around the cemetery, it fell. There is a tradition that the Kozienice cemetery is much larger than is known, and therefore when it is set up, it soon falls." In the midst of the cemetery stands the Maggid's Mausoleum. Next to it are the Maggid, R' Yisrael, his son, Moshele and then one son after another, Eliezer, Yehiel, Yerachmiel Moshele. They all lie in a line, and partition circles the holy graves.

The eternal lamp flickers silently as it hangs over the graves. A holy shiver seizes one, when you think about the holy and pure who rest under the tombstones. The Jewish heart, which is always so bitter, and constantly filled with pain and sorrow – when one has such an opportunity, to pour out one's feelings, and lighten the burden a bit – the words come out by themselves as if from a fountain.

How Can You Rest So Peacefully

Holy, dear souls! How long do you think! How can you rest so peacefully, when your brothers and sisters, the entire community of Israel is in such catastrophic condition? In Germany, Jewish blood is flowing like water, 500,000 Jews in danger of being slaughtered by the Hitlerite bandits, God forbid. The 3 million community of Russian Jews in danger of assimilation, and God forbid, of apostasy. If you find a teacher teaching children, or a father who has circumcised his son, they are sent to Siberia. Thousands of Jews die of hunger and want. Also by us the economic situation is tragic. Jewish enterprises and livelihoods are daily broken. Jews are selling their last household possessions, in order to buy bread for hungry children. Jews don't have the money to pay tuition for the children and there is growing a neglected generation. Young men who want to study Torah, go through fearful trials and tribulations, suffer hunger, and want, and there is no one who interests himself in them. Who can enumerate the many troubles and sufferings. We are drowning in a sea of blood and tears!

[Page 421]

Storm the Heavens!

Holy and dear souls! In your lives you martyred yourselves for the community of Israel, and now you are even greater Tzaddikim than in your lifetimes. Storm all of the 7 heavens, so that the Lord, blessed be he, will have pity on us and send us complete redemption. Around the Mausoleum lie the Maggid's students, but unfortunately the tombstones are missing. We don't know exactly who is in the graves. On some of the tombstones the letters are erased and can not be read. On one gravestone there is indicated that here lies Noam Maggid, R'Eliezer Halevi Horvitz from Tarnogrod. He died in 1809. He used to travel to the Seer of Lublin and the Maggid of Kozienice. Once, while traveling from Lublin to Kozienice, passing the Kozienice cemetery – he called out: "How pleasant this place is, here I want to rest". A few weeks later he passed away, and was buried here, and was eulogized by the Maggid with a great eulogy. (From the newspaper "Yiddisher–Tageblat" – Warsaw).

[Page 422]

How Does the City Sit Deserted?

by Leibele Fishtein

Leib Fishtein in Ramat Gan

Does the house still stand there today,
Opposite and over the small garden?
Do the branches still reach far
And cast a shadow on my door?

Do the chestnut trees still stand,
As once they did before my time,
And stretch their green Hands
Over the broad unpaved road.

Is the city still encircled,
On two sides, by forests?
And does the shine from the South
Still gleam from the broad grown fields?
Does the hill, the silent one,

Behind Leizer, the stitchers home,
In the winter with slippery snow,
As children with sleds would sleigh.

Did my little boat sail off by itself
From the shore of the lake, as a seagull
May no more boats come,
Rocking themselves on him with my dear Eve.

I am driven from my dear town,
Far into Kazakhstan, exhausted.
Here I have my Bed of Exile,
I dream of coming to you again.

I know
That the German, may his name be eradicated,
Also from our town Made a waste and void.

Only from the hangman's hands torn away the ax
Did the Allied commander.
On my head I do not wear a sack,
But I ask: "How does the city sit so desolate?"

[Page 423]

From My Childhood Years in Kozienice

by Leibele Fishtein, Ramat–Gan

On the western side of the city, before the Radomer forest, there stood, in the form of an H, Yosl Tzitrin's house. The house was called "The barracks", because it occupied an area of 150 meters, and there lived almost 1,000 souls, Jews and Goyim – all of the impoverished of the town. In the courtyard stood a round artesian well with a bucket, attached with a chain which was wrapped around a wooden log. On the side was a handle for turning, in order to lower the empty bucket and pull it up filled with water.

It wasn't easy to obtain the bit of water, because it was about 20 meters deep and there was always a queue at the well. The house was built of wood, and the roof covered with shingles. In the same house the owner built an extension with a few rooms, where he lived.

Yosl Tzitrin Was an Upright Jew

He was also merciful. A few of the locals didn't even pay any rent at all, and he didn't bother them, because he well knew that they had nothing, unfortunately. He had a son Noah, and daughter, Miriam. The son had his father's admirable traits. The daughter was active in the community. Every Thursday, she would go out with two other old maids, collect money, and buy Challos, bread, fish and candles. On Friday morning she would distribute it among a few, poor families, so they would have a bit of the pleasure of Shabbat.

Kalman the Landlord and his Family

Kalman, the landlord was in his sixties. His long thick beard was already half grey, and he himself was a quiet man, upright? and well groomed. He was free of financial worries, because he had those upon whom he could depend. His wife, Chanele a very fine person, was quite alert and young looking. She, together with her two daughters, Chayale and Devorale ran the stationery and cigarette business. His son, Yosl, as I mentioned, was a lumber merchant. He was also a partner in the only bank in town, which belonged to Yontshe Mitzberg. Yosl was the only one of the family who survived. Today he lives in Natanya.

Orchard Keepers

During the intermediate days of Pesach, when the orchards bloomed, many Jews went out to the villages, where they dealt in orchards. They were able to determine exactly how much fruit each tree would yield. They also knew which orchard had been fruitful the previous year and whether it would or wouldn't be this year. They would bargain with the peasants about leasing the orchards for a year or two or even longer. Before Shavuot all of the family went out to the orchards. Each large orchard had a lean–to with a two–sided roof of straw and a place for sleeping. Outside was a kitchen, which consisted of cemented bricks, on which there lay two iron rods for holding pots. When a family leased a few orchards, they would assign a few children to each one, to watch that ruffians shouldn't steal from the trees. In Kozienice, there were about 20 orchard–keepers. All summer they would flood the market with fruit. Of them all I'm the only one who survived. All honor to those who so tragically perished!

[Page 430]

My Father's Will

by Shmelke Shpigelman

On the bank of the river, in the valley,
With my glance at heaven sunken in thought
Lime ovens, already many times That I see – so
I thought

Jews with their hands tied,
And with Sh'ma Yisrael on their lips,
Like flaming Scrolls of the Torah –
Are being burned on coals.

Mother–father, sons and daughters,
Sisters, brothers, all together,
Uniformed Germans laughingly –
Throw Jewish children into the flames.

Once, there at eventide,
As the sun sank aflame,
Between the clouds, it seemed to me,
That I see there: My mother.

I see the good Shlomole, the little one,
On his chest a yellow badge And another Jew –
one,
He was, it seems, my father.

And from the clouds, like wool,
And from the sky, the dull,
I heard a voice,
The will and testament of my father:

The destruction of Kozienice, and its Jews
You shouldn't forget, don't forget!
Hand this testament down to your children
Because for this: You were left alive!

[Page 431]

The Hassidic Serenade

by Yaakov Leibish Eisenman, Bogata

Already from early morning you could tell that this Tammuz–day was going to be a scorcher, because the first rays of the sun with their fine gold darts actually stabbed the eyes, as if with redhot needles. Such a heat there had never been. The business in my soda fountain reached a peak. We became exhausted from the difficult work of serving so many people. By my neighbors at the other side of the hedge, below, in their cellar apartment there lived great grandchildren of the Maggid. Among them some girls and one boy, Chaiml. It seems to me Chaiml Samochod's brother–in–law, very short, stout person with a black well–grown beard. There they sweated today, carried out their house furnishings, and in place of them set up tables and benches, because tonight Chaiml is getting married. That night I went to sleep very late: First because of business and secondly because I was so tired.

Loud Singing Awakened Me

How long I slept, I don't know. Loud singing awakened me. I am straining my memory to understand the significance of the singing. What sort of a holiday is it today for Jews? I fall back on my bed but I really want to recall! I try to fall back asleep, but the religious, mystic singing doesn't let up, quite the contrary – it gets even stronger, with more ecstasy. For such joy what does one do? I have no choice but to dress myself and go out to see what is taking place? I approach, slowly, the Rebbe's house and see a group of eight Hassidim in a half circle, right near a blanket hung well hammered window, which looks out from the cellar apartment almost level with the ground. The eight Hassidim are dressed in satin kapotes, with skull caps on their heads and with big talesim, with the wind blowing their tzitzes.

What Sort of Singing Is This?

The group is holding small books and continue singing. What sort of singing is this? And why so late at night? I didn't get an answer. But I don't leave it alone, because I want to uncover the secret. Bit by bit I obtained some information from one of them, and you can imagine how embarrassing it was. But listen and don't laugh. A half hour ago they accompanied the young couple to a special room, where our bridegroom, Chaiml, has to perform his third obligation, according to the Germara. These Hassidim are the closest in-laws. They stand here under the window of the special room.

They are singing chapters of the Psalms, and they are designed to insure that the cohabitation should be in holiness and purity and that the act performed be a Mitzvah. And who knows what else.

Maatel Luxemburg-Zucker Tsipa Luxemburg-Lichtenstein

A group of boys and girls meet on a weekend (top middle Avigdor Zylberknopf)

A group of friends from Kozienice on a hike

Beila and Hertz Bichman from Zvolin died in Treblinka

[Page 432]

Some Dates in the History of Kozienice

In the 12th and the 13th Centuries Kozienice belonged to an order of Norbetaner Mnishkes.

In 1300 the Mnishkes gave up the village of Kozienice and got for it a different village.

In 1400 a bridge was built over the Weisel (Vistula), which led to Kozienice.

In 1467 there was born in Kozienice the Polish King, Cazshimiezsh the First.

In 1549 the proprietor of the village of Kozienice, Piotr Firley, obtained the right to build a city, with an autonomous council, its own court and the right to arrange fairs.

SECTION 6

THE DESTRUCTION OF KOZIENICE

THE SHOAH

A memorial for 22 holy victims of Kozienice

Avraham Tenenboim using the shovel in the common grave

The Darkened Sky

by Sidney Lipman

On Friday, September L, 1939, Germany invaded Poland. At the time I was living in Kozienice with my family which consisted of my parents, five brothers and four sisters. I was two months past my twelfth birthday. I do not ever remember celebrating anyone's birthday including my own. There were too many children in our household to pay attention to such unimportant things as the date of birth. The date of birth was always recorded on the last page of the Book of Genesis. If you could not find it there, it surely was on the inside cover of the Machzor of Yom Kippur.

On the second day of the war, Saturday, I was in my married brother's house listening to his radio as we did not have one. The reporter was describing the approaching German aircraft crossing the border into Poland. His broadcast was interrupted by intermittent firing at the approaching aircraft. He candidly admitted that the enemy had crossed over the border unharmed.

The war was a continuing topic of conversation in our community. I was witness to one heated discussion between my father, Israel Frish and Itche Gradovtchik. By consensus the final conclusion of the three was that the war would last three weeks.

When France and England declared war on Germany there was a great deal of jubilation in our household, especially among my older sisters. My mother did not join in all this celebration. She had considerable doubt as to how long the war would last, who would win and which of her children might go off to war. She had vivid memories of World War I and was considerably worried about the outcome.

The next few days passed rather uneventfully. On Thursday we had a family discussion about the war, and a practical conclusion was that in war time it is desirable to have good walking shoes. Maybe we would have to leave town by foot. On Friday morning, September 8, at about 7 A.M., the three youngest boys (my older brother Jacob, a younger brother Fishel and myself) were sent to the home of my oldest brother Khiel who in turn took us to his father–in–law, Mr. Kestenberg, who made shoes. He gave each of us a new pair of brown shoes with wide toes and long shoe laces. We used to call these "ski shoes". The three of us proceeded home wearing the new shoes and carrying the old ones in the new boxes. As we arrived home, my father asked me to go to the Monopoly Store to buy tobacco for him. Rather reluctantly I left the house for the store which was on Radomska Street, one street away. As I stood in line outside the store I heard some engine noise. I looked up into the sky but could see nothing. In the street one could see only a few small groups of

Polish soldiers in twos and threes heading towards the Vistula River. Suddenly planes appeared very low overhead.

There was some intermittent firing and a very large explosion followed by several other explosions. I ran into the nearest place, the Zalcberg Bakery, and remained there for several minutes. As the noise subsided, conscious that I had not bought the tobacco, I decided to return home. I walked through the back of the bakery. As I emerged on Targowa Street, I found the street covered with a mixture of soot, dust and feathers and could not see across the street. Beginning to feel panic I ran towards my house. The house was no longer there. There was only a very large crater extending past the siJewalk into the street. In the bottom of the hole was a body. The only part of the house remaining was part of a wall of my uncle's apartment. Somebody walked me away from the crater, told me he had seen my family go towards the river, pointed me in that direction and told me to go look for them. I knew it was not the truth, yet I proceeded towards the river to look for them.

As I was running on Lubelska Street there was some additional firing and explosions. I ran into the nearest house. The place was full of people who sought to escape the confusion of the street. Somebody said that a bomb had fallen into the Lipman household and killed my entire family.

I ran towards home. My brothers Khiel and Moishe and some other people were digging in the rubble. They had already dug out my father who was injured and my sister Rifka who was barely breathing but who died that night. My youngest sister Ruchale had been thrown by the impact of the bomb into the Rabbi's yard and suffered only a broken leg. The bomb had killed my mother, three sisters, two brothers and two neighbors.

The war had begun for the people of Kozienice.

[Page 433]

Who is the Kozienicer, Who Writes About The Holocaust?

Ringelblum–Archive, No. 1 Registration 846

The four notebooks of an unknown Kozienice author were found after the War.

On the banks of the Vistula–waters, among forests of tall pine trees, on a side of the Radom–Lublin Railroad, lies the old, historic Jewish town of Kozienice. The question is well known, why Kozienice? Because it was there that the Kozienicer Maggid lived. And even though it is already more than 100 years since the large entourage of the Maggid lived there, till this day, when you come into the town you can still feel the influence. When you come into the town you feel it. You can see it in the historical buildings, in the conduct of the inhabitants, and also in their daily lives.

When an inhabitant encounters troubles, he goes to the Maggid's grave to pray. Women go to the Maggid's Mikve (ritual bath) – for it serves as an amulet. Merchants swear in the Maggid' s name, and even Christians accept such vows, because they also fear and respect his memory. Among the Christians, to this day, there are legends, which are passed down from generation to generation about the holiness of the Maggid. They know that the well–known, Polish Prince Yozef Poniatovski, visited the humble dwelling where the Maggid used to live, and that he inscribed his name on the wall like all visitors from every corner of Poland. Each one feels it is his obligation to inscribe his name on the day of his visit.

The majority of the inhabitants are Jewish, skilled workers in the shoe industry, who used to produce for the large cities, and earned their livelihoods in this way. In general – a town like all Jewish towns, with but one advantage over them – its "yichus" (proud ancestry). The historical places of Kozienice are: The Maggid's Shul, which he alone built and put 100 gold "rendlech" (coins) into the foundation (according to the town archive); the modest house where he was born and lived his entire life, and his Mausoleum on the cemetery. In Kozienice can also be found the large historic palace of the last Polish King, Zygmunt August Poniatovski, which tour excursions used to visit because of its historic value, its royal splendor and beauty, on which was engraved the seal of roominess and comfort of a Polish King. The Christian sector of the town consisted mainly of folk–Germans, and not far from the town was to be found the large German colony, Vilki. The Germans lived on very friendly and neighborly terms with the Jews. They would rent Jews their houses and gardens, sold their grain to Jews, and in general were very friendly. That's how everything looked until

The Maggid's tomb partly damaged after the first bombardment of Kozienice

[Page 434]

War Atmosphere

For a long time there hasn't been such a successful year – the peasants revealed to the Jews of the town. The Jews are pleased. They won't have to get angry at the vacationers, who arrive and cause everything to become more expensive by their buying up everything. If it's a plentiful harvest it will be good for all.

And strange, it doesn't occur to anyone–there's serious talk of war...the old are frightened...the young wager small bets on it: It isn't, it won't be... "He" only threatens the world... He's bluffing...He wants more concessions, but actually fight – he's afraid. They" are hungry" (this is specifically stated in "Moment"); the "boycott" has ruined them (it was clearly stated in "Radio")...They can't fight...They don't have the tools... (writes the "Hayntike Nayes" and all of the world press)...The recesses, between the afternoon and evening services, last longer due to intense discussion of politics...Knowledgeable ones said that the war is unavoidable. The few taverns in town, where there were radios, were besieged by people, who wanted to hear the news. The disquiet grows" from day to day. No one has the patience to work. Everything is disturbed, nervous and tense.

A great many military personnel drive through town, on the way to Demblin (an airport), and Pionek. This is disturbing. This irritates the situation even more. The point of culmination – is Wednesday, when the pink placards appeared on the streets, placards announcing general mobilization. The elderly tremble; their hands shake even more – to have lived to see another war; they thought they had had enough for even the generation of grandchildren, with the other war (WWI). Again blood, again tears, again destruction! The youth cries... Heartrending scenes occur. All stand and cry, when young Reizman, two weeks after his wedding, has to part from his wife and go to the front... The tragedy is even greater, because from the same family two other brothers and the father have been called up. They leave at home an old broken–up wife and mother. The men are transported to Demblin. The whole town escorts them. Among the escorters there are also a few who will have to leave on the morrow.

Women cry and wail. Polish police beat the women and children, who are clamoring among their husbands and fathers. The police exhort them with patriotism, because they cannot part from their loved ones. (The patriotism of the Polish police – is a chapter by itself...) In town it is tragically quiet. You can feel it with all the fibers of heart and soul. Crowds jam the grocery stores. They create emergencies. Everyone can feel the cloud which hangs overhead, and the storm, which is approaching.

Writings about Kozienice were found in the Ringleblum's archives hidden underground in milk cans.

[Page 435]

All the Germans to Bereze

Who in town didn't know the Yiddish speaking Goyim? "Folks–Deutschen" (Folk–Germans) – was already a later name. They lived peaceably with their Jewish neighbors. The Poles had a bundle of trouble from them. They would beat the Polish farm–hands, exploit Polish workers, and in general ignore the orders of the Polish government. They only obeyed their own "village–judges", and the judge knew that he is representing Berlin and not Warsaw. The Polish authorities tried to meet them half–way, but this had just the opposite effect. The more rights they were given, the more they demanded, and even further neglected their duties as Polish citizens. They were on friendly terms only with the Jews (mainly to anger the Poles), and when the Poles proclaimed a "boycott of the Jews" in town, the first "boycott breakers" were these Germans. Only during the last few weeks before the war, did they begin suddenly, as if by command, to hate their Jewish neighbors. They stopped coming, and didn't want to deal with Jews under any circumstances, and wouldn't even respond to a Jewish "good morning".

They also vigorously provoked the local Polish population. On a beautiful morning we noticed that all the chimneys of the German colony were painted red. Also the chimneys of the German houses in town were painted red. We realized that these were signals for the enemy, and by order of the Skladkovskin, all of the German men were sent to Bereze concentration camp. In automobiles they were transported through the town. The attitude of the Germans was brazen. They would cry insults at the Polish officials, screaming "Heil, Hitler!". Their attitude was so aggressive, that the Police, in self–defense, had to use rubber clubs. In sealed autos they were transported to Bereze. While they were still on the way, their German brothers appeared, not in automobiles, but in planes, and dropped bombs only on the houses whose chimneys were not painted red.

The Bombardment

The night before. We heard enthusiastic talks on the radio. The talks disturb the mood. "We will win, because we must win!". As soon as the megaphones are quiet, the heart gets this weird feeling. Maybe it's the fear of the night? The surrounding darkness? Because it is already dusk. We hear only the tread of the duty patrols. It happened on Friday, September 8, 1939, before dawn. The town was awakened by the sound of planes overhead. We heard frequent nearby explosions. The houses shook and windows fell out. We heard screams. We run to help, but the planes are directly overhead, and are dropping heavy bombs, on "Military–Targets" on the peaceful civilian population. From all over town come the terrible reports. Many streets are aflame, and the number of casualties grow from hour to hour. The bomb–shelters do not help; even there, destruction and casualties are great.

[Page 436]

The destroyer dominates every corner. The sky is clear. They can see very well where to drop the bombs and they bomb without let–up. People run around half deranged by fear, because there is nowhere to hide from a frightening death. Mothers run with their children in their arms seeking refuge. The ill are carried in their beds, but no one knows where to go. The streets are filled with people, screaming, crying and reciting the confessional before death.

Suddenly, as if by a command, all run to Radom Street which leads to the nearby forest. All at once, the entire town, women and children, grabbing food, run into the forest. But not all reached the forest. The planes chased after them with bombs, and the scene is gruesome as we see how R'Moshe, the Ritual Slaughterer, is carrying with him to the forest, the remains of his torn–asunder wife.

The Town Hides in the Forest

Friday, before sunset. The Jews are in the forest. In the same forest where they used to promenade in the evening leisurely and forget the workaday worries. In the calm sunset shadows of the trees they gathered, in the same beloved place, at the same hour...and with so much fear, and fright not knowing why or wherefore. They remain calm without being ordered to do so, because this is what the heart commands. Nobody knows the enemy's position, how far away he is from here. We see only those who are fleeing in panic, without any order, with arms and without arms, with shoes and barefoot, soldiers and officers of the Polish army. They cross the Vistula River in boats, and the planes target the moving boats. The unarmed soldiers, with screaming find their death on the River Vistula.

And new water flows, as if nothing has happened. The river runs again in it's quiet natural fashion. Night falls, darkness, pitch black. From near and from afar shooting can be heard. We lie on the ground. It gets cold. Every so often we see projectiles which light up heaven and earth, and in everyone's heart there is darkness. Every so often family members ask each other if they are still here and how they are. We can hear how Jews are softly reciting the Psalms from memory. From time to time the silence is rent by a moan and a voice: "Oh, Holy Maggid! Please intercede for us!" We hear a woman's voice: "Oh great God! Forgive us all, for a whole town of women did not kindle and bless the Sabbath candles today!"

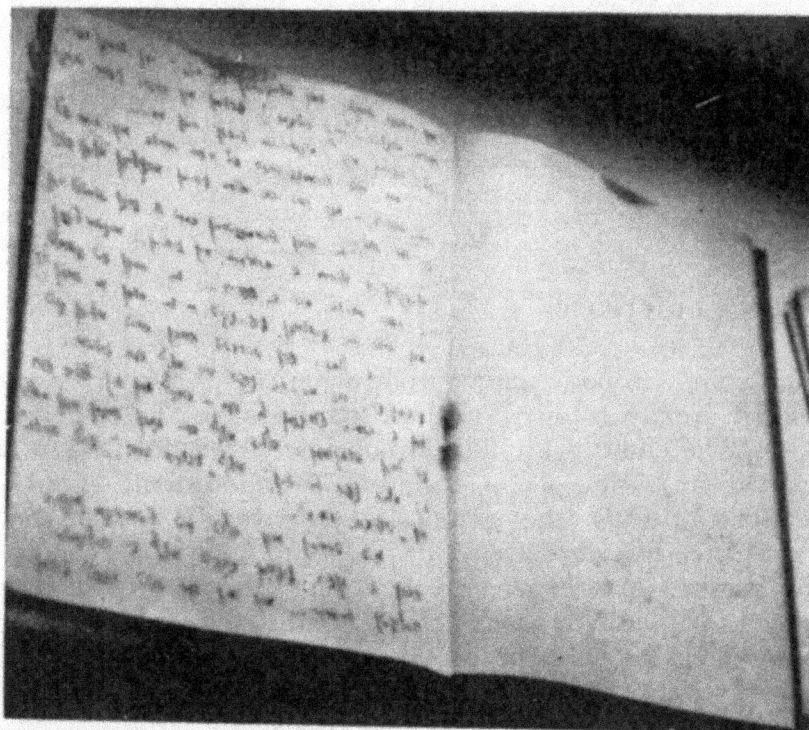

This is the handwriting about Kozienice in the Ringleblum archives

A quiet movement. All begin to murmur quietly. Nobody knows what, but everyone nearly has heart failure from fright. They say, that a figure is approaching. It appears to me a military man. What does he want here? Maybe he's come to tell us that the enemy has been driven back? That we are returning to the town? We want to get close to him, to hear from him alone, what he has to say, but we are told to remain seated where we are. The officer, in excited calm, said as follows to the Jews around him: "Our government has fled Warsaw already. The army has collapsed... He heard that the Jews of the town are in the forest. He was always a friend of Jews. He's from Vilna. He has a wife and mother there. He requests that his name be recorded, Jozef Dembski. Write to them and inform them that I've taken my own life?" He didn't finish his recital – a shot was heard. He falls. There is an indescribable commotion. We want to run. We fall to the ground, and we soon discover, what a great tragedy has been enacted here. He is dead. He was a patriot. He didn't want to become a prisoner of war! We are afraid that they might say that the Jews killed him. The elders say that we should immediately dig a grave, but we have nothing with what to dig. We find some branches and we also dig with our bare hands. We do it quickly and quietly. And when he was already buried, we Jews were able to breathe freely.

[Page 437]

After such a fearful night – day came. Jews didn't know what to pray for. Night – when the plane and bombs are silent, or day – since we want to know what is taking place in town, what happened to our homes and possessions. There is no food left to eat. But hearts pound, since it is day and who knows what the day has in store for us. But we are still under the influence of the night. The head is still in a daze, and Jews have to remind each other. "We have to remember: His name was Jozef Dembski from Vilna. As soon as we can – we shouldn't forget – to write."

The Sabbath Conference

Like lightening, nobody knew from where, the rumor spread that the Germans were already in town. But how is it possible? The whole war is only a week old – and already in Lublin? Impossible! Jews don't want to believe it. What does it mean? They? The Germans? We read our fill about their cruelty and persecution of Jews. They! They! Have arrived in town? What do we do? Go back to town? Turn ourselves over to the hangman? Maybe we should run for it – even further and deeper into the forest. And as if by itself a conference was organized. All. Old, young, religious, freethinkers, men, women, all people were beating their breasts, beseeching forgiveness. "This is" calls out one "because we used to read about the cruelty in Czechoslovakia. At lunch we would eat meat and for dessert, Jewish troubles."

"This came" says an old man "because we didn't observe Shabbat." "Why they came here is not important. What is important is that they are here, and we have to think about what we can do because with each passing moment we are in mortal danger." Jews cry and yummer. Women wring their hands. Young men tear their hair. "What do we do, what do we do?"

[Page 438]

The debate centers around a young man, who came running from the town, and says that he couldn't control himself, and before dawn he ran to the town to see what was taking place in his home. He met the Germans, and they asked him: "Where are the Jews?" He answered and told them that all of the Jews are in the forest, having fled the bombs. They told him to say that if by one o'clock the Jews don't return to the town, they'll shoot up the forest. Indescribable confusion reigned. Every one took sides. Some said that we should return, because we had already gotten a taste of. their bombs. We had already heard of their deeds, and their warnings are not just threats. Others said, and among them also the head of the community, that we should head for Lublin, through the forest, together with the retreating Polish army. A very small group decided to follow the head of the community, and parted from their relatives and went deeper into the forest in the direction of Lublin. The majority, with heavy hearts, decided to return to the town, trusting in God.

Back in the City

The scene of returning to the town is unforgettable. They arranged themselves in the following order: A train of 2000 people. First the elders; in the middle the youth, and the women completed the train, so that the youth could protect them. Each one was carrying a small package on his shoulders. They felt instinctively that the present return was not to their own homes, but to a new exile. They don't want to, but there is no alternative. Every little while they rested, not because of tiredness, but because they wanted the journey to be prolonged. They don't want to meet with "them" yet! And maybe a miracle will occur.

Nobody speaks. A whole community of Jews is on the move and nobody speaks due to the mute grief and sorrow. The elders tremble. The young cry. And it is worthwhile mentioning that it was the women and the mothers who calmed and consoled the others. We were already close to the town, and met a well–known peasant whom we asked: "What's happening in town?" Everyone encircles him and he says: "By the skin of my teeth I escaped the persecutors. They are beating everyone, and take them away in autos. The young break out in a spasmotic wailing. One, Michvel Horovitz, calls out to his father: "Father take a knife and slaughter me, as our grandfathers did during the Crusades, and don't hand me over to the hangmen." We feel that this is his youth speaking and a majority of the youth would heroically choose such a death, the death of martyrs rather than be demoralized by physical tortures. We can already see the first house of the town. We are passing the hospital, which we can hardly recognize. It has been destroyed." For two hours without letup it was bombed, even though the Red Cross flag could be seen from a distance. There were more than 60 casualties there, among them, two pregnant women.

[Page 439]

How is it possible not to be afraid of such barbarians, since life is so cheap to them? Nothing can stand up to them or in their way, and the most elementary ethical principles mean nothing to them. These sad thoughts are interrupted by the sound of a passing auto filled with soldiers, who with wild murderous shouts called out: "Death to Jews!" Jews wince and then calm each other as soon as the auto passes, but the calm lasts but a moment.

The Welcome From the New Owners

Like destructive–angels, there was suddenly heard the sound of flying autos filled with soldiers. The autos circled the entire train. Fully armed soldiers jump out. With their rifles and fists they began to beat murderously: men, women and children, whomsoever their guns or fists could reach. The men they grabbed by the beards and pulled and tore. Others began to cut the beards with their bayonets and also cut flesh in the process. The fear is indescribable...we feel as if we've been attacked by wild beasts. The soldiers yelled so wildly that they gave the impression that they were the ones being attacked. On the other hand the Jews were so disturbed, upset and lost that they almost didn't scream at all. In the midst of the beatings, they saw before them a young man, a "hunch–back", the son of Saul, the water–carrier. They removed him from the train and immediately shot him, before everyone's eyes...People turned to jelly at this atrocity. His mother began a frightful screaming and yammering. But suddenly a shouted command: "Quiet! Stand still! If not – everyone will be shot on the spot! We are going to search everyone, to make sure that you are not armed!" And right there, in the middle of the street, they searched everyone, and found the bit of money – zlotes and dollars – which all had taken with them as they fled. They confiscated all of it. Also the women were searched by the soldiers in a most brutal and hateful fashion. What could they, the helpless Jewish women, unfortunately, able to do for their shame, since they were left standing, half–naked, in the middle of the day. They simply looked upon them with disgust, and when they had stolen all of the Jewish "arms", and stashed it away, there came another order: "Forward march!" Surrounded as they were by the watchful soldiers, all, men, women, and children, were escorted into the town, into the church on the courtyard.

Kozienitzer Jews drying swamps by the Vulka

The Seven Departments of Hell

Broken and exhausted from the past few days, on Sabbath eve, September 9, 1939, they arrived in the church of the courtyard, and thought that they would be held there for a while and then sent home.

But, unfortunately, it was here that the real tortures began, consisting of humiliations and inquisition like tortures.

[Page 440]

To begin with, a soldier demanded: "All men to one side, and women to the other!" At that moment there began a wild chase of soldiers who are securing "order" by stamping with their feet. You could distinctly feel that they were lacking the limbs for beating Jews. When they were already separated, there was another strict search for "arms" – meaning Jewish possessions. And if, by chance, some money still remained in someone's possession, it was now, during this strict search, taken away. The sun set. Night falls. People are lying in the street shivering with cold, but we are pleased that they too, the evil ones, are going to sleep, so that we too, even on the street in the cold, will be able to catch a nap. It's already a few nights that we haven't slept.

All of a sudden – we hear, from inside the church, frightening shouts. All of the Jews sit up. "What happened?" We hear someone screaming inside. They are torturing somebody. At night in the dark, it is especially frightening to hear. "Gevalt! Gevalt! Oy! Oy! Oy!" We shudder from fear, and all ask: "Who? Who is missing?" But nobody knows. And maybe someone had remained in town? Again screams. We listen carefully. But suddenly it got quiet. Thank God! Perhaps the persecutors have ceased their Inquisition. The door of the church opens. We see soldiers carrying out a sanitary portable litter. They carry it over, light it up with flashlights, and oh...oh... there lies therein a "lump" of a person, his entire face bloodied, and his clothes. He is moaning quietly. Everyone wants to see, maybe he'll be recognized. But in vain. The soldiers say: "We will make all of you like this, you dogs!" They order room made among the Jews. They put down the cot. They take out several shovels, and order that a "grave" be dug. We hear him groan, and want to say that he is still alive, but are too frightened to say a word. The hands are trembling with fear. The soldiers are also very serious. They aren't beating anyone, but they shout: "Faster, faster!" The grave is ready. He groans. The soldiers call over a couple of Jews, and tell them to throw the body from the cot into the grave. The knees give way. They barely hold up and don't collapse. The Jews move their lips, as if asking his forgiveness. Revenge is God's. They throw him into the grave and we hear a loud "Oy!"

The flashlights light up the inside. They order the grave filled in. Again the order is carried out. The soldiers take the cot and reenter the church. Jews are aroused from their stupor. They cry softly. They run to the "undertakers". Perhaps they recognized the Jew? But they are upset and can't speak to anyone. They lie crouching on the ground. Their teeth are chattering. One asks for a drink. They rub his hands and feet to warm him. They move away from the grave of the "unknown martyr". They cuddle against each other like helpless lambs. Again it quiets down. Some fall asleep from weariness, and others lie awake and can't fall asleep out of fear. Again noise. Again Germans. Again shouts. They light up with flashlights and tear the coats off the men. Have these robbers suddenly found honesty? The women and children are cold and they must have the coats.

[Page 441]

The Hanging

It begins to dawn. The day of September 10, 1939. It's cold. We are broken. We feel that we haven't eaten for two days. "Get up! Get up, you lazy dogs!" They tell us to line up in four rows, old and young, but not the women. They are going to have a bit of sport now. Running! Faster, faster and whoever falls, is beaten with rubber hoses, murderous blows." Stand still! Stretch out on the ground!" We lift ourselves! Run! Fall! Run! The young hold fast, but the older ones fall and are beaten mercilessly. The "sport" lasted for an hour. Now we'll work. All must work. Carrying brooms and shovels, we're ordered to sweep the courtyard. Jews with beards are told to sweep the courtyard with their beards. A party of Jews are sent to clean the toilet facilities, but not with rags and brooms, but with their bare hands. They forced people to eat excrement. People vomited and fainted away.

12 noon. People became a bit happier since they expected lunch, for no strength is left. But the soldiers remarked cynically: "We are going to lunch, and you aren't getting any food. Jews wanted this war – let them die from hunger". After this kind of lunch came the order: "Women and children are being freed, and the men must remain here." The soldiers add: "They will all

be shot here, these enemies of the world." An indescribable wail rises up from the women... They don't want to leave the men. But they are "freed" from the courtyard with the stocks of the rifles. The farewells are tragic, frightening. Who knows if they'll ever see each other again? The women circle the fence and call through the cracks in the fence, in order to pass something to eat to the men. Everyone shares whatever they've obtained. But not much is obtained. They feel that after the pause something will arrive. A soldier comes out and announces: "The Jews must tell where Rabbi Perlov (the Rabbi of the town) is to be found. If not, they will all be hanged."

You can imagine the panic and the fear among the Jews. The Rabbi isn't here, because during the bombardment he left for Lublin. So they took the most prominent citizen, a great scholar and the richest man in town, Shmuel–Moshe Korman, led him to a tree, and hanged him in the sight of everyone. At the last moment, they cut the rope. He fell from the tree...And when he came back to himself, they hanged him again, and again cut the rope. Korman began to beg them to let him die, but this was the answer of the hangmen: "A dog is killed. But a Jew is worse than a dog. A Jew is tortured." The inquisition lasted for several hours. It's already the fifth time that he's been hanged. Every Jew that cries out in fear, is beaten. They will do the same to everyone here. Mrs Korman has found out what they're doing to her husband. She ran with one of the German folk to the commandant, and for fifty thousand zlotys, and other things, the hanging was ended.

[Page 442]

The Resurrection of 60 Jews

On Monday, September 11, 1939, we also slept in the courtyard...Again the wild awakening, again "sport" and again beatings. Life has already become unbearable. What will happen? Till when will we be tortured like this here? We feel as if the strength is simply fading away...We eat only that which is smuggled in through the fence. And the soldiers beat the women murderously when they catch them in the act. We are told to line up. An elder passes along and picks out 60 Jews. "Come along!" They give them shovels and order them to march. But to where? Nobody knows. They lead them into the nearest forest and they order them to gather up the scattered arms, which were thrown all over the forest, by the retreating soldiers. And they are warned that if they attempt to flee they'll be shot. They worked in this way until noon. The elder tells everyone to gather in one place. He speaks to them: "Since the Jews are the world's enemies, they and Chamberlain provoked this war, so they must dig for themselves a grave!" The Jews began to plead and to cry. They fell at his feet – but nothing availed. They must dig, and if not, they'll be shot on the spot immediately!

All is lost? Jews begin to recite the final confessional. They dig for themselves a large communal grave. They wet the ground with their bloody tears. They dig lazily, slowly since the shovels fall from their hands. Knees cave in. They fall with the shovel. They can't look each other in the eye. They don't know which one of the "four deaths" will take place here. They dug a large grave...He told them to lie one on top of the other in the grave. Jews fall on each other's necks; they say farewell to each other; beg forgiveness from each other, cry out the "Sh'ma Yisroel", and walk, alive, into the grave. He called over the soldiers to cover the grave. Jews lie spread out with their eyes closed. They can't open them due to fear. First they hear how one soldier calls out: "Carol! We don't need it!" And they hear again how the Dusseldorfer man-eater says to them: "Get up!" Two of the 60 Jews, Gozshetshansky and Baruch Manela went insane as a result of this incident. Two young men went out of the grave grey, as two white doves..The remainder barely returned to the church in the courtyard and informed the remaining Jews not to worry since Jews have a great God! If they were resurrected from the grave, then they'll certainly go out of the church. They took upon themselves, every year, on the same day, to celebrate it as a holiday, and to give charity for the miracle which occurred to them Jews in town say that the soldier, who had called out to save them, was not a soldier, but the spirit of the Holy Maggid.

Emptied Dwellings

All of the torture-acts took place in the church square, but into the church itself Jews were not allowed, with the excuse that the Jews, by their presence, will defile the place. But on the fifth day, September 13th, an order came: All Jews must enter the church. And there the Jews encountered a new disaster: A lack of air! The torturers had figured out that even though it was cold in the courtyard, by day the Jews have plenty of fresh air to breathe. So they took approximately 2000 people and stuffed them into one room, so that they would immediately choke for lack of air. People began to faint. R'Chaim Kleinboim, 65 years old, a prominent figure and great scholar, fell down. Jews wanted to save him, keep him alive; so they asked for water from the guards. They received a cynical answer: "All of your days here are numbered, so it doesn't matter if this Jew dies a day earlier!" They wouldn't let anyone out to take care of his physical needs. When Jews had to go, the "religious Protestants" designated a special place – by the Altar.

[Page 443]

You cannot imagine how odiferous and choking the air became. In addition, every little while, soldiers would come in and make a grand entrance, demanding that a wide aisle be made for them to pass through! They didn't want the dirty Jews to touch them. Jews choked, but the walls couldn't be stretched, and the bloodthirsty soldiers would beat them with rubber hoses till blood flowed. They tore wounded and opened holes in heads – only for the pleasure of seeing Jewish blood flow. The Jews felt as if they had fallen among hungry wolves. And here the tragedy became even greater, because inside the church no food could be obtained from the outside. Jews prayed: "O' Lord of the Universe, may death come from your hand, and not from these evil-doers!" We were in this Hell for a day and a night. On the sixth day, in the morning, an. order came that everyone leave the church. They lined them up, but they had become shadows of human beings – broken, tortured and starved. They ordered them to wait. It didn't take long, and they brought a transport of "Polish irregulars" who had been captured around Kozienice. We could recognize in these blackened, weakened and tattered soldiers, that they had really been Polish soldiers, who had looked so trim during maneuvers. They could see how the Jews looked and the Jews could see how they looked, and with silent glances these "brothers–in–sorrow" expressed their sympathy.

As soon as the soldiers saw how the Germans are beating Jews, their own Jew–hatred was aroused and they began to murmur: "We didn't want this war. They instigated this tragedy." With each passing moment the Jew–hatred grew. They forgot all about the common enemy. They indicated that they were barefoot, with torn feet, and that the Jews are still whole. The Germans permitted some of them to tear the boots, shoes and clothes off of Jews. They demonstrate their unused courage and bravery on the helpless Jews; with a fury they tear off shoes and clothes and let them stand naked and barefoot. The captured "heroes" in this way showed their depravity and inhumanity. The Jews, on the other hand, held fast and understood that the soldiers were being thrown a Jewish bone as a reward for their bravery. They were also immediately quartered in the stalls of the courtyard, and the Jews returned to the church. On the morrow, the seventh day, in the morning, everyone was again lined up in the courtyard, and Jews over 45 were beaten and thrown out of the courtyard.

[Page 444]

The younger ones, on the other hand, were told to remain. They felt that they were lost. They look at the older ones, who still hadn't gone home, but had remained standing in order to bid farewell, with pain and tears, to their children, whom the hangmen loaded into armored vehicles, in order to take them to an unknown destination (to Radom in a concentration camp).

They were old and grey as a result of the seven days. Broken and barely alive they returned to their homes (those that were still whole after the bombardment.). Many women don't even recognize their, own husbands...The men don't recognize their homes, because the Germans robbed and emptied them. But more important – they had removed the joy from the homes: They had removed the young men and children and husbands and carried them off to torture and extermination.

The New Order

When Jews had recovered, they began to think about how to earn a zloty for a livelihood. They wanted, bit by bit to return to commerce and skilled labor. But every day there were new proclamations and directives to produce order in the city. An order came that peasants must not sell food products to Jews. The death penalty was decreed for anyone who defied this order. With this there was sown in the region unrest and disorder. We are living human beings who must buy food, and the peasant wants to sell his produce to Jews, because in exchange he can get kerosene and salt; and so there began to be smuggling on a large scale. It involved attempts to catch the "offenders" and the passing of bribes. They, the German's, quickly learned to take bribes. The wheelers and dealers became known to familiar Germans, and these were the first steps of the "new order". Two weeks after the holiday of Succos, on a nice early morning, Gendarmes came and drove the Jews out of the two main streets, where prominent Jews lived: Radom Street and Warsaw Street. They didn't let them take anything, not even their household effects. They drove them into the narrow crowded streets, and their homes were occupied by poor families of folk–Germans. Jews stand by and see how their hard earned possessions are taken over by their former "good–neighbors".

The driving of all the Jews into one, crowded quarter, understandably worsened the sanitary conditions. The Germans said, that the Jews are spreading disease, and that it was really for that reason that they had to institute "The New Order". When Dr. Krueger, a folk–German would inform about a case of typhus, the soldiers used to come into the Jewish quarter and shoot the sick person as he was lying on his sick–bed. For this reason they shot the 10 year old, only Shapiro son (16 Church Street) as he was lying in his sick–bed, at the time when his mother was at the drugstore, having a prescription filled. The "New Order" also posted an announcement, that all women, as a "sign of shame" must cut off their hair; and the men their beards. They also requisitioned from the dirty Jews their quilts and blankets for their soldiers, and took from the "infested" homes furniture and beds for the officers. Jews would be thrown out of food stores and bakeries, and they were forbidden to go to the villages to buy food. Everything was forbidden to Jews. And as "payment" for this treatment, the New Order demanded of Jews – labor and to let themselves be tortured.

[Page 445]

Labor and Blows

On the day after Yom Kippur, the "Black Ones" (SS) came! They beat Jews viciously and grabbed them for forced labor. The invitation to forced labor came in the following manner: They "would come out in the street, and as soon as they would see someone who looked Jewish (it was still before the yellow star), they would with a blow on the head invite him to come to work. They would take them to clean highways and roads, but they would also have the Jews do special "work". They would order them to dig pits and then fill them in. They would have them gather rocks and later have them return the rocks to the place where they had found them." At work, they weren't fed. Vicious beatings till blood would flow, and verbal abuse of the foulest kind. This went on daily. It was of no use to attempt to hide, because the "Blacks" would from 7:00 a.m. go from house to house, search attics and cellars, and find those who attempted to hide, and shoot them on the spot. In spite of the fact that they were so abused at work, Jews stopped trying to avoid it by hiding. The weakest would be taken for the hardest work. And to top it off they would demand that the Jews sing while working.

They brought the equipment to photograph the "working" Jews. At such times they were ordered to laugh and smile, so that in the photos it would be obvious how "thankful" the Jews are for the work, and how pleased they are with the New Order. Once, on that "bloody Thursday" (that's what it was called in town), there was literally not a single Jew whose blood didn't flow. From early morning the Sturmfuehrer and about 100 "Blacks" (SS) invaded the town and made visits to Jewish homes. "He" would first tear the Mezuzos off the doorposts and stomp them with his feet. Every Jew that he met, either he or his accompanying henchman would beat mercilessly till blood flowed. When they would already see blood, they would calm down, leave the victim alone and continue further on their "chase". For "labor" they would especially take the "fatter ones" and those that were dressed elegantly. They met the assistant mayor, Dr. Gonsher. Our town did not consider him a Jew. He simply looked like a Jew. They stopped him and asked: "Are you a Jew?" It didn't take long till, calmly and with dignity, he answered: "Yes, I am a Jew!" He began immediately to feel the taste of a Jewish beating. They took him in among a whole group of Jews, who were disturbed not only from the beatings that they were receiving, but also from their new "brother in misery", the assistant mayor.

When the group was already in the courtyard, the SS leader came out with a Torah in his hands, carried it over to Dr. Gonsher, and told him to burn it...Jews turned to stone at this scene...They did not know how the "new Jew" would react...Dr. Gonsher became very pale and again answered calmly that he cannot do it...They fell upon him with rubber truncheons, and stomped him with their boots. "You must do it!" shouted the SS leader. And he hit him with his fists. But Dr. Gonsher categorically refuses to do it. The SS leader burst with anger and tells him that he won't leave here alive. It doesn't help. They beat him over the head. He falls covered with blood. Next to him lies the Torah, soaked with his blood, but whole...He orders that the dirty Jew be taken away. The Jews took him and with great effort, were able to keep him alive for a short while.

[Page 446]

The SS leader couldn't calm down, and runs again into the city. A young man, Yitzhak Ravitzky, passes him. He orders Yitzhak to stand. The young man tells him that he is running to fetch a doctor for his wife who is in labor. He beat Yitzhak, stomped him with his feet, and accuses him of knocking over a soldier as he was running. The young man begs for mercy, because his wife needs a doctor immediately, since her situation is desperate. The young man was sent off to a concentration camp! The unfortunate wife wrestles painfully with death. She sees that her husband hasn't re turned. She waits, she waits. But the child cannot wait. Due to her fear, she delivers a dead child. When she came back to herself, they told her that her husband was away with a work battalion.

Racial–Shame

It is worthwhile noting that, on the one hand, the evil–doers degrade the Jew; but, on the other hand, these very same degenerates, the officers, raped a Jewish daughter. It happened late at night. Two officers came to the home of Dr. Gonsher's wife, who herself was a dentist. (At the time she was sitting Shivah for her husband, whom the Germans had tortured to death). They had come, ostensibly to remove machines. She asks her daughter to go and bring them. The officers go along. The wife hears from the other room her daughter's terrible screams. She wants to run in, but the door is bolted, and the officers tell her that if she doesn't calm down, they will shoot both her and her daughter on the spot. It continues. The officers exit and tell the wife that if she reports this incident to the commandant, they'll set fire to the whole town. The mother goes into the daughter's room. They exchange silent glances. The daughter wants to drink ammonia, but the mother prevents it.

"My child. Because of these barbarians, we have lost your father and my husband. He died courageously. You, my child must stay alive. You are young, and must continue to live. The shame is not yours, but it is their shame!"

The Maggid's Shul in Flames

It was Simchat Torah. They were conducting the Hakkofos (carrying of the Torah Scrolls around the synagogue), but like mourners, without the joy; without singing, and foremost – everyone wanted that they should be over already. Everyone wanted to be in his own home already. When everyone had returned home already, and gone to bed – at about midnight – the entire town was rocked by a tremendous explosion...But no one knew what had occurred. No one is allowed out on the street. We hear a second, a third. We don't know what to do or what it means. And perhaps – there begins to stir a flicker of hope – maybe the British are bombing, and the Germans will have to flee. And if bombs are falling again, they can also hit the "unpainted chimneys".

[Page 447]

Jews again began to pack their few remaining possessions, the bedding, linens and household items. Suddenly, we see that the sky has turned red, and the town is lit up. We see that it's a huge fire, but we don't know where or what exactly has happened. Jews had noticed during the last few days, that taxis filled with German officers had come frequently to the Maggid's Shul. They would go inside, look around, take photographs, from every angle, and drive away. Others said that the German nation has a feeling for "historic buildings". It is an attraction for them to see a primitive but artistic work, such as the ancient gold–trimmed ark in the Shul. Others said that we shouldn't be naive – in the Berlin and Frankfurt synagogues there were also things to see, and these synagogues, together with their artistic vestments were burned.

It is necessary, therefore to remove, gradually, a little at a time, from the synagogue, whatever possible, and foremost the Torah Scrolls, holy books, and historic precious vestments, since we can expect unpleasant surprises.

The SS commander and some soldiers came on Simchat Torah, after midnight, and went into the Shul. They found there two Yeshiva Bachurim (young men) who were strangers, not from Kozienice, who had stayed because of the war, and would sleep in the Maggid's shul. They were, first of all, beaten and tortured, and not allowed out of the shul. Then the evil–doers poured blasting powder all around and set fire to it. The shul was immediately engulfed in flame. They awakened the nearby neighbors, men and women, told them that the shul is burning and ordered them to bring water to put out the fire. Everyone grabbed whatever could hold water, ran to the wells, filled the utensils with water and ran to extinguish the fire in the beloved Maggid's Shul. But when they approached the shul with the water the soldiers, with sadistic laughter, poured the water on them, soaking them from head to toe. Afterwards they brought the old Rabbi, R'Yosef Shapiro, to observe. They threw him into the flames, pulled him out and then threw him in again. His clothes began to burn and they pulled him out again until he fell into a faint. And then, when the Rabbi was lying faint, and from inside the shul could be heard the cries of the unfortunate Yeshiva Bachurim, and the entire shul was engulfed in flame, the soldiers encircled the building and with wild fanaticism began singing the song: "When Jewish blood spurts from the knife" (the Horst Vessel Song).

If the wild, barbaric tribes of the jungles would have come, on that night to this European town, they would certainly have said the following: "We also know this kind of work, but we use drums to drown out the cries of those we are torturing...But you do it even better – without drums, without musical instruments, but with song, with unabashed enthusiasm." On the same night, they also burned down the town's House of Study.

[Page 448]

Vandalism

On the morrow, Simchat Torah in the morning – the ruins of the Maggid's Shul are still smoldering, Jews pass, they don't stop. They glance at the ruins of their holy site in the town, shed a tear, and go on their way. But the vandals don't calm down. Their thirst for torture hasn't yet been sated. They go today from house to house and search for Torah scrolls, religious books, etc. and ordered them to be brought to the place where the Maggid's Shul had stood. Jews are disturbed! What does this mean? What will be done with the Torah scrolls at that place. Will they have Hakkofos there? And why the books? But they don't allow time for thoughts. They beat the Jews till blood flows and hurry them along – faster, faster! In one place, in a cellar, they found a hidden set of the Talmud, that had been published in Vilna. (20 large volumes). So they went to search all of the cellars in town. The scene was frightening: Jews carrying Torah scrolls, accompanied by soldiers. Women and children carrying holy books, and uniformed Germans guarding them. Many scrolls and holy books were gathered. They ordered that everything be placed on the ruins of the Shul. Almost the whole Jewish population of the town was driven together. They chose the oldest and most prominent and ordered them to set fire to the scrolls and the books. They refused. They were beaten and tortured. They must do it! The scholars of the town indicated that according to Jewish law, this is not a case where one must forfeit his life, rather than comply. In but three instances must a Jew martyr himself rather than comply: When forced to idol–worship, sexual excesses, or the spilling of blood. Otherwise he may comply in order to save his life. With tears and blood, and with trembling limbs, the elders poured kerosene on their holy possessions – and silently prayed that this would not be looked upon as sinning. And they were ordered to set them afire. Jewish scholars, who would sit day and night and learn a "page of Germara (Talmud)", Jews who's minds had been sharpened through their immersion in the holy books, and drew comfort and hope from them, now with their own hands had to set them afire. When all was already smoke and ashes, there came the order to dance!. Jews must dance around their burning holy books. They beat them and they danced. Again a command: "Sing!" Jews cried, danced, and sang around the ashes of the burned Maggid's Shul, and around the fire and smoke of the burning scrolls and books. And this is how it is to be entered in the new chronicles of Kozienice – that in the year, 1939, Jews celebrated their Simchat–Torah Hakkofos – two weeks after the Germans arrived in the town.

Also the Poniatovski Palace in Flames

They consider themselves above all races, more important than all, and from the conquered nations they will wipe out all traces of independence and freedom. Nothing will stand in the way of their holy mission – not art, antiquities or history! Since the human being has lost all meaning for them, then why his art or creativity?

This house was built in place of the beautiful Poniatovski Palace burned down by the Germans.

[Page 449]

And in this way, on the 17th of October they burned the historic Poniatovski Palace. And they did this right in the middle of the day. This was also done with blasting powder, with explosives, with noise and with laughter. And here also the Christians go with clenched fists, pale...This was something they didn't expect. Such splendor, such architecture, such an extensive library with antiques. Must this all go up in smoke? Why? They didn't understand, the Poles, that it begins with Jews, and the Germans, who can burn synagogues and scrolls of the Torah, can also destroy and burn magnificent works of art and thousands of precious books.

Crimes and Punishment

History will certainly remember to record that the German code of punishment began with – shooting! For them this was the smallest and most insignificant punishment. Not only for military offenses, but also for civilian crimes. Because officially it was declared, shortly before the occupation of Poland, that we were to have civilian rule in place of the military rule. There was no proclamation which did not end with the warning that if it would be defied – the offender would be shot. Whether it was for "black–marketeering", or the baking of white bread, or leaving the Ghetto without a pass, or falsifying questionnaires...for everything – shooting! And indeed, we knew full well that this was indeed the mildest punishment meted out by these cruel monsters, because how many thousands of Jews were not privileged to receive such a quick death. Their punishment was that they were allowed neither to live or to die, only to be tortured again and again...until these martyrs gave up their souls in agony.

We have reached the point where, before we can record an incident of a shooting, we must preface it with a justification, even though we know that their cruelty surpassed all bounds. But history must record every fact. The entire Jewish population of the town was crowded into three narrow, small streets (previously there had been fifteen). They took away bread and air. They were forbidden to go out to the village, and there was not contact whatsoever with any other city. What should Jews do? Perish? In spite of the anguish, Jews wanted to live. They hope that it will again be good, again a world. What do Jews do? They go out at midnight to the "cemetery" (a kilometer from town), at the risk of their lives, but what can they do? From there they go on foot, or in a peasants conveyance – to Radom. If caught in this offense – they are shot on the spot. Once there were eight victims in one day. They seized a vehicle with eight passengers, six Radomer Jews and two Kozienice Jews, but they did not shoot them on the spot. They brought them to headquarters, in the courtyard. The community exerted all of its influence on the folk–Germans, but to no avail. The bloodthirsty evil–doers want only blood! They were offered ransom money – but they wouldn't hear of it. They appealed to their "sense of honor" to release the women, at least, but the crime is so great that nothing will help, and they did indeed shoot them right there in the courtyard. They let them out again, but in sealed coffins. The two Kozienice victims were the two sisters: Chana and Freyda Tzucker, from Magitover Street, one 18 years old, and the other 20. The other six were Radomer. In this way, unfortunately, fell the martyrs one after another, for the crime of wanting to live.

[Page 450]

Here, again a horrifying fact occurs: The Jews were confined to a few streets, but at the beginning they were not fenced in, but only the boundaries were marked with the warning, that if. Then they would shoot! For the grownups that was enough of a warning – but what about the children? Were they to be kept under lock and key? The mothers thought: "What if they should sneak out? What would they do to the children?" They (the mothers) were, in fact, neglectful the first days, until...until the evil ones displayed their culture. In those first days they shot three –little children because they had stepped over their "limits" for no particular purpose or destination; but probably because one of their playtoys had rolled over.

Kozienicer girls wearing armbands with the Star of David

The Extraordinary Dr. Neuman

"Who was he?" was the big question asked by Jews. His name was beloved by Jews, but he, himself, was an enigma. Jews from Kozienice held the view that the Holy Maggid endeavored that they should have something unusual! In no other town was such a thing heard of! A uniformed German, an officer, should so greatly love Jews, and actually sacrifice his life for them! He is worthy of having his name historically inscribed – for a blessing! Dr. Neuman came from Berlin (his home town) and took over the management of Kozienice's military hospital. The Jews saw him for the first time at the ruins of the Maggid's Synagogue with photographic equipment. Not just that one time, but on several consecutive days. Already the Jews recognized him – he comes openly to show the world his sorrow! Children came to love the tall German, with his apparatus, and they became very friendly.

The German distributes sweets among them, converses with them, questions them as to where they live, how it is with them, what do their parents do, and what would they like to achieve? At first the children were

afraid to speak to a German about such things, but the kind eyes of the
German, and even more, the good sweets that were so generously distributed,
made the youngsters talkative. They tell him about their difficult and bitter life
and how Jews return day after day from laboring for the Germans, and that at
home there is no food. The children note that there are tears in the German's
eyes. What is this?! A German crying because of the suffering of Jews? And
herewith, 10 year–old Shmuel Prager stops the conversation and tells that his
father came home today with a swollen foot, as a result of being struck by a
soldier, and is now lying down and can't move. Dr. Neuman asks the boy
"Where do you live, little one?" The boy becomes fearful, and will not reveal
where he lives under any circumstances! Until Dr. Neuman takes him by the
hand and goes along with him. He accompanies him all along Magitova Street
until they reach number 26. A poor tailor – Prager lives in a basement. He lies
in bed with a swollen foot. He sees the German and becomes frightened – the
poor unfortunate tailor. Dr. Neuman approaches, examines him, prescribes a
salve, and orders him to remain in bed. But afterwards he goes to the
community and requests that they send a local doctor to Prager. Not so much
because of the prescription, but in order to get a statement from the doctor,
that he is unable to work for a few days.

[Page 451]

It was already then forbidden to German soldiers to visit Jewish homes.
Secretly, Dr. Neuman would daily bring medicine and bread for the poor family
– sometimes even fuel and sugar – until the ailing Prager was back on his feet.
Modestly, Dr. Neuman said: "You owe me no thanks. I am just fulfilling a
humane duty." (Remember that a German military doctor is speaking.) "When
you hear of a Jew who is ill, have your son come quickly to me in the hospital.
I will understand why, and I will come to you and you will take me to the sick
person." Understandably, such a story could not be kept secret, and it quickly
spread through the entire town. Dr. Neuman acquired a tremendous practice.
The sick and weak already knew that there was a free German doctor who also
dispenses medicine and even a little food gratis! And above all, he is so
courteous, so noble, that he gives courage and comfort, day after day!

Dr. Neuman Worries About the Head of the Yeshiva

With utmost devotion, he did everything possible for the greatest scholar in
town, the Kozienicer head of the Yeshiva, who had become critically ill. Dr.
Neuman examined him and told him that it was very serious, but he would do
whatever he was able to do. And he kept his word! This time too, you could see
his self–sacrificing courage on behalf of Jews. First, he brought special
medications from the hospital, and when that didn't help, he appealed to the
commander for permission to use the military hospital's x–ray machine for the
Head of the Yeshiva, with a special permit for him to come to the hospital

daily. The commander warned Dr. Neuman not to become too committed to Jews. But the warning went unheeded. Dr. Neuman continued to request the x–ray equipment, and insisted that it concerned his personal friend.

The commander is cognizant of his service as a military doctor, and his outstanding excellence as an officer! And so, he permits him to use the x–ray machine. If someone could have seen the joy and rays of happiness beaming from his face when he ran to the Rosh–Yeshiva and called out: "My friend, you will get well!", he would certainly have said that he is hearing the oracular voice of an idealistic humanitarian love! But the commander readied a surprise for him! That very same day he sent him away to Polav for a period of 10 days, to oversee improvements in Polav's military hospital. The Jews in Kozienice did not know where Dr. Neuman had disappeared. Immediately rumors spread that he had been arrested because of his contacts with Jews. The Jews became very despondent. They feared reprisals against them. And then, behold, in 10 days, Dr. Neuman again appears in town. He comes to the Rosh–Yeshiva in an agitated state, for he realizes that he was thus "repaid" for his friendship to Jews. He swallows the "bitter pill" and redoubles his efforts to help Jews.

Nurses in a temporary hospital in ghetto of Kozienice

[Page 452]

He advises the Rosh–Yeshiva to go to Warsaw, and gives him a letter for a doctor of his acquaintance, who administers the Radium Institute of the hospital in Warsaw. He requests that the doctor cure the patient with redium treatments to be administered free of charge. (The family is in possession of Dr. Neuman's letter, for it was never delivered.) Dr. Neuman also sends food products to Warsaw for him; for at that time, the first winter, food products were difficult to come by in Warsaw. When Dr. Neuman sees that it takes 6 weeks for news from the Rosh–Yeshiva, delivered by his personal courier to arrive, he announces to the family in Kozienice that he wants to visit the sick Rosh–Yeshiva personally. He asks for his address in Warsaw, and requests that the family write of his coming so that the family with whom the Rosh–Yeshiva is staying will not be frightened when he appears.

When the Rosh–Yeshiva returned in a deteriorated state and Dr. Neuman noted that the end was near, he came often to spend time with him, especially on Friday evenings. As the decree not to visit with Jews in their homes became stricter, and obtaining food became more difficult, Dr. Neuman would send bread with a young gentile boy for the ailing patient. When the Rosh–Yeshiva died, Dr. Neuman cried like a small child who lost a very dear friend. It would be extremely interesting to relate the themes of their intimate talks together. Many curious things about Dr. Neuman's life in Germany became known, but our space is limited. We will describe in brief, some of his interesting biography as it pertains to historical value, and his friendship for Jews.

Dr. Neuman was born in Berlin and received degrees in medicine, the humanities and philosophy. He always desired to be in the company of Jews. So much so, that, in school, he was called "Jude". Most of his friends were Jews. After Hitler's takeover, he spent much enjoyable time with Jews. He hid many Jews from the SS storm troopers. In Berlin the SS caught and beat Rabbi Ezra Funk. At that moment, Dr. Neuman came by and endangered himself in order to rescue Rabbi Funk. Afterwards, because of that incident, he had a duel with an SS officer and was left with a scar on his head. He loved Germany but hated the regime. He would say: "He who is an antisemite cannot be a friend of humanity." One time, in the midst of a conversation, he suddenly became quiet, his eyes hazy, and he spoke of a family tragedy. He relates, in a low voice: "I had a 14 year–old son. Against my will he became a member of the Hitler Youth. Now he is dead. Thank God! If he would have lived, I would have hated him because of the Jewish Question, and there would always have been conflicts between us! Better that he is dead!"

[Page 453]

Dr. Neuman had in the basement of his home in Berlin, a library of pro-Jewish books, which he would lend his acquaintances. This was actually high treason. He also supported the Yiddish cultural community and the German Aid Society with donations, as was evidenced by the receipts he had. Dr. Neuman turned, officially by letter, to the head of the Jewish community in

Kozienice, telling him that they must immediately, without hesitation, establish an infirmary for the poor Jewish sick. It should appear as if it were being done for sanitary reasons, but in actuality it was because it had become almost impossible for him to minister to the Jewish sick. Dr. Neuman contacted the town's Jewish doctor, Abramowitch, and requested him to spend several hours each day at the infirmary. He also appointed him as Director of the infirmary.

A group of Kozienicer women together with Dr Abramowitz (center) from an organization of help for the needy

It became apparent that nothing could even begin, because of a severe shortage of medications. The commandant would not even issue a travel permit to buy the medications in Warsaw. "Let the Jews die!" was his answer! But Dr. Neuman found a solution. For a very large sum of money (many thousands) he was able to obtain medications from the military hospital, and thanks to him, a beautiful Jewish infirmary was established. His second request was to set up a communal kitchen for the poor. And the third request was the crown of his achievements in Kozienice – The Orphanage! All of these were established with his wholehearted moral support. He visited all three institutions in an official capacity, and praised them all very highly. He constantly spoke about the Jewish creative spirit!

His work came to a halt with the military order that was conveyed to him – "To the front!" At the beginning of November, 1940, Dr. Neuman left for the front. In his home he left a picture of himself, on which were inscribed the words: "The suffering of the tortured – is my suffering!" It is our duty to inscribe the most worthy, Dr. Neuman in our Kozienice War Memorial Book. First, because he was indeed the only ray of light in the bleak and black stormy time when his fellow Germans were spilling Jewish blood in abundance, like water, and their greatest pleasure was to see "that Jewish blood spurts from the knife!" But one other thing made it incumbent upon us to eternalize his name – and that was the objectivity of the Jewish historians from ancient times to this very day. Among all the Hamans, we have also remembered to eternalize those non–Jews who have helped us in our most trying times – such as Charvonah, who is mentioned favorably in the Book of Esther – "May Charvonah be remembered for good!"

[Page 454]

Thoughts of a Survivor's Child

by Chana Teitelbaum, Daughter of Luba Frysz–Teitelbaum

My daughter's name is Rochel; my son's Feivel. With the birth of my third child, I rebelled. No longer would I give my newborn children names of dead relatives, unknown to me and my American born husband, people whose lives were clouded by abrupt, painful endings and who had passed fitfully into the statistics of a "Holocaust". No. This little baby girl would be Chava – life, her life, one that she had fought tenaciously to maintain, without the stigma of the past or burden for the future.

But it is not so easy to wipe the slate clean of burdens and memories, even second hand memories at that. I have heard the names of the streets of Kozienice and Demblin all my life. I have imagined in my mind those now middle–aged friends of my parents, strolling on a sunny afternoon, pausing to chat on a Shabbos, running to picnic in the fields behind the towns, or watching the young cadets strut throughout my father's town. I know their friends' maiden names. I see their faces in my mind's eye, and they are the same faces that stare shyly from the "Tarbut" portrait. The hair is long and braided, the smile whimsical, the eyes brown and deep–it is all there. The promise of youth, the gleam of idealism, the unrealistic and unattainable aspirations of vivid imaginations – it is all there. Their youth demands they grab the future with outstretched hands.

But the streets of Kozienice and Demblin are no more. Gone are the playing children, the nieces and nephews whose names and faces are so hard for me to piece together, the multi–colored shades of red and blond hair that distinguished them all as part of one large, tightly–knit band. And gone is the young niece with the piercing blue eyes upon whose unsteady shoulders the future hopes and aspirations of the family were placed. In its place are memories – hundreds of thousands of them crowding themselves into the day to day process of living. Crowding holidays with yahrzeits, crowding empty hours with reams of stories of the past, crowding me with love for two people who never said die.

So I have a daughter named Rochel and a son named Feivel. So they are named after two people whose lives ended abruptly, but who went fitfully to their deaths. So I wish I had five or ten or a hundred more children to name after them all. So instead, I had Chava.

[Page 455]

Kozienice Up Until the Selection

by Zelik Berman, Bat–Yam

Zelik Berman

1939. Suddenly, on a beautiful, clear day, German bombers attacked our city, Kozienice. They destroyed almost all of the roads, cut off all telephone communication and electricity. A few people were killed, and a few seriously wounded. Among them was Pese Krishpel, the wife of Moshe Gutmacher, who was wounded in her leg.

Everybody Runs

Many houses were damaged, collapsed and burned. The populace left everything, grabbed the children and ran to the forest, or to neighboring villages. Late at night they returned to their homes, leaving their families in the forest. Almost all of the roads were inundated with Polish soldiers who were hungry and thirsty. It was difficult to go from one side of a street to the other. The soldiers were in a hurry to cross the Vistula River. The German bombardiers did their job without pause. They destroyed all of the bridges over the river, and the blitzkreig rolled on. They were already at the gates of Radom.

In the Garden of the Church

Dawn. A patrol of German soldiers is already in Kozienice. The entire civilian population, Jews as well as non–Jews, are driven into the garden of the church, surrounded on all sides, and closely guarded by the Germans. In inhuman fashion the civilians are held in the garden. The beatings begin. They go on for two days. First the Poles are released from the garden, and afterwards the Jews. Immediately there begins a rush to work. Jews fill in the craters in the roads, and repair rail lines. As they work, they are beaten mercilessly. SS men appear with scissors and knives in their hands, and they beat Jews and cut off beards.

Jewish Community leaders during the Nazi occupation of Kozienice

God, Help Us!

In the evening the Germans drove over with a wagon loaded with straw and gasoline, and on Magitova Street they set fire to the Synagogue and House of Study. They took the Rabbis, R' Yosef Shapiro and his brother, R' Yakele Shapiro from their home and cut off their beards. Then they pushed them into the burning Synagogue. Afterwards they threw out the holy books of the Holy Maggid, tore them, cut them up and threw them into the flames. The entire Magitova Street was on fire, a veritable inferno. The inhabitants of the street, frightened to death, fled with their children and with packs on their backs to nearby streets. The German murderers shoot from all directions. A stifled cry for help is heard: "God, help us!" At the same time the Germans set fire on ail sides, to the historic Larski Palace.

[Page 456]

It was a dark night. Our town is burning. Not a person is seen, only the fire and the red sky. We heard the crackle of the dry wood and the rat–tat–tat of the machine guns. Everyone searched for a safe hiding place for themselves and their children. This was the welcome with which the occupiers greeted our city of Kozienice!

Abandoned!

On the morrow, in the morning, no one is to be seen. A bit later – the Polish neighbors relate – that the Germans are going to specific Jewish houses, removing the men for labor and beating them mercilessly. Jewish stores are opened, and the Germans throw the merchandise out on the street or distribute it among the Polish populace. The German killing and robbing of Jews pleases the Poles. They accompany the German murderers and show them where they can find the best Jewish merchandise, especially textiles. Even the peasants from neighboring villages come with sacks in their hands. With joy they fill their sacks with Jewish merchandise. A fearful chaos in the city! Jews are abandoned!

Hunger

The local commandant, a German officer, becomes the owner of the city. He rules temporarily from the city–hall. He holds life and death in his hands, and issues strict decrees in regard to Jews. Jews have no right to appeal to the commandant with their grievances. Hunger reigns in the city. There is no bread. The poor are starving to death. According to the commandant's orders, the bakeries may bake bread from the reserve supplies of flour which still remained. A line forms for the distribution of bread. One bread per family. When the turn of the Jew standing in line comes, a Wehrmacht soldier pulls him out, beats him and places him last in line, so that rarely is a Jew able to get a loaf of bread. All of the bread was distributed among the Polish population. It is worthwhile mentioning that there were a few Polish citizens, upright, who helped Jews with bread up to the limits of their ability.

The Germans Nominate a Judenraat

In the meantime, the District Commander of Radom appointed as Burgemeister of the city, the former Austrian officer and Director of Welfare, M. Trag. As his representative the folk–German, Miller, from Volke, was appointed. The Burgemeister immediately invited Jewish representatives and community activists, such as Zelik Shabason, Yisroel Honikshtok, Pinchas Freilich, Chaim Berman, Zelik Berman, Yonah Weinberg, Moshe Goldtzveig,

Zigmunt Halputter and others, to consider forming a Judenraat which would conduct Jewish affairs. All of those invited begged to be excused. The Burgemeister, M. Trag, willing to compromise, frees a few and appoints the following to the Judenraat: Yoel Weinberg, Moshe Goldtzveig, Hershel Popyelnik, Leibel Fleisher, Moshe Bronshtein and Zigmunt Halputter. Shortly afterwards, Hershi Perl was chosen as chairman and Moshe Bronshtein was put in charge of the labor division.

[Page 457]

All Must Work

The Judenraat immediately decreed that all men aged 15–60 must appear every day at 6:00 a.m. at the local headquarters of the labor exchange. If they don't show up on time, they will be severely punished. These men appeared promptly at the Judenraat headquarters, where they were given work assignments by Moshe Bronstein. The working classes quickly became accustomed to the work. After work, when they went home, they were given a piece of bread, which was scarce because hunger reigned. The plight of the handworkers, small business men and the middle class was worse. They were mostly older men, and the Judenraat burdened them with heavy levies which they were required to pay. The plight of the Jews worsened from day to day.

In compliance with a special decree of the Germans, the Judenraat organized a Jewish police force, which accompanied the workers to their work. All Jews had to wear on their left arms a white armband with a blue star of David on it. The city was divided in two: The Jewish quarter and an Aryan quarter. Jews weren't permitted to enter the Aryan quarter without a special permit. If they did enter and were caught without the armband, the penalty was death. As a result there were several deaths in the city.

A Barbaric Decree

And now, another barbaric decree. Every Jew must greet every German that he meets by removing his hat. This gave the Germans a pretext to beat Jews. When a Jew greeted a German, the German would beat him mercilessly. Why did he greet him? He's not his friend! And if he wouldn't greet the German he would also be beaten, because he had failed to obey the decree. The murderers would toy with Jews on the streets. They would cut off half a beard. They would order Jews to remove their trousers and dance naked in the middle of the market place. Polish children would gloat over the troubles of the Jews. Most of all the intelligentsia suffered. They would be recognized and would therefore be assigned the most difficult work, and beaten half to death.

Kozienitzer Jews regulating the water and drying swamps under the direction of engineer Gartchitski

Dr. Gonshor Commits Suicide

Before the war, there lived in our city the family of Dr. Gonshor, who worked as the government veterinarian in the Radom District. He was beloved by the Poles as well as the Jewish populace. He was a very upright person with a Jewish heart, as was the rest of his family. The German murderers heard about him, and gave him a great deal of trouble. They took him, undressed him and led him through the streets together with a horse. Afterwards they gave him a Torah scroll and ordered him to dance and sing naked and barefoot in the streets. Round about stood people who witnessed the degradation and shame of Dr. Gonshor. After this he went to the hospital, said he was ill, and there committed suicide. We honor his memory!

[Page 458]

The Judenraat Sucks Money

In front of the Judenraat headquarters, at the labor exchange, there always stood and waited all sorts of people, each with his or her bundle of troubles. Mostly they were laborers and the poor. Each day they were sent to work. At home they would leave a hungry wife and children, who. were simply dying for a piece of bread. At first protests didn't help, but later, when the workers were a bit organized and informed the work chairman that they would no longer go to work but remain at home to starve together with their wives and children, the Judenraat distributed bread to the families and also to the poor. The coffers of the Judenraat became filled with money for the rich, who didn't go to work, paid very well for the privilege. They would come, either by themselves, or brought by the police and were told that either they pay up or they would be sent out to work on the morrow. The upkeep of the Judenraat, and the payments for escaping labor had to be paid promptly. If not, police were sent to confiscate their money, and it also happened that those in arrears, would be awakened in the middle of the night and sent out to work. Everyone strove not to be torn away from his family in such trying times. The Judenraat took advantage of this situation and sucked money from all sources.

"Lapankes" and Labor–Camps

Besides the work in the city, there were established work places far from the city, under the supervision of Polish engineers, such as Gortshitzki, who employed Jews in Vilka to regulate the river, Jews were also sent to Pionki to work. Naturally, by arrangement with the Judenraat, Jews were poorly paid for their work. The Judenraat's labor department functioned perfectly. The supervisor knew everyone who hid and shirked his labor responsibility. If a worker came home to see his wife and children, the police were immediately informed. When the coffers of the Judenraat would empty a bit, they would bring a German civilian and in the middle of the day make a "Lapanka". They would seize Jews on the street, beat them, pack them into waiting trucks and haul them off to Pionki. During such a "Lapanka", I and Yosef Lichtenstein were sent away to work. As the truck, packed with workers was about to leave, there arose an outcry of wailing from wives and children, who had come to say farewell. The Burgemeister was someone we knew from before the war. He had pity on my wife and children, and ordered the work supervisor to bring me back from Pionki to Kozienice. My friend, Yosef Lichtenstein also benefited, and we were both freed from labor in Pionki.

[Page 459]

Jews Flee to the Other Bank of the Vistula River

After the "Lapanka" the Jewish populace was desperately frightened. The fear aroused a hatred for the supervisors of the Judenraat and the Labor Batallion. Everyone thought about how we could rid ourselves of the terrible occupying power, together with the Judenraat. Jews fled to the far bank of the Vistula, to Zshelichov and other towns, with the intention of fleeing to the Soviet Zone, in order to save their lives. With broken hearts men parted from their wives and children. A portion of Kozienice Jews, who were successful, with great difficulty, in smuggling themselves over to the Soviet Zone, remained alive, but the remainder perished!

Hunger, Pain and Typhus

This is how life looked in the Ghetto: Constantly getting worse and worse. Hunger, need, enslavement and Typhus – everywhere! The mortality rate – extremely high. The Burial Society in Kozienice consisted of the following people: Moshe–Leib Dua, Hershel Popielnik, Yisroel Blachazsh, Shafirstein, Hershl Kliger and Shmuel Moshe Korman. The chairman of the Society, the old community activist of the Agudah (ultra–Orthodox) Movement, Moshe Leib Dua, was an upright and honest Jew, beloved by the entire population. He used to go among the sick, and help them in any way he could. He worked intensively with his colleagues, day and night, in order to properly care for the dead. If there was a lack of money to buy shrouds for the dead, he alone, or together with Shmuel Moshe Korman would run daily to gather money for this purpose. He used to tell that Issachar Shabason and his son–in–law, David Sigelman, who perished, would help the Burial Society buy linen for shrouds.

The year 1941 arrives. Harsh decrees against Jews. The Ghetto is sealed off by a special commission, blockaded and encircled by barbed wire. A curfew is imposed. For leaving the Ghetto to go to the Aryan side, the death penalty is invoked. The situation in the closed–off Ghetto goes from bad to worse. Smuggling of life giving food and supplies is risky and difficult. These items become unbelievably expensive. Hunger reigns! Paying no attention to the sanctions, there are those who go secretly on a daily basis to the surrounding villages, to peasants with whom they are acquainted, for something to eat: A bit of groats, potato, or a piece of bread. Fortunate and satisfied, they quickly return home. At the entrance to the Ghetto the city's gendarmes wait. They are all shot on the spot, with their life–giving packages in their hands. Warnings do not help to stop people from attempting to reach the villages. Daily there are new victims, who have returned from the villages and are shot dead as they attempt to reenter the Ghetto.

The scenes are indescribably tragic at the daily funerals in the Ghetto, since these deaths are in addition to the normal deaths. They occupy the Burial Society full–time.

[Page 460]

A New Decree

A bit later – a new decree. All Jews must, during the coming 24 hours, give up to the Judenrat, their fur coats. For not giving them up, or for hiding them the penalty is death. All run quickly with their fur coats and bring them to the Judenrat. A tragic event took place in our city, and this was after giving up the furs. A Polish woman told the gendarmerie that she knows that two Jewish women had fur coats which they sold. The gendarmerie ordered the two women: Chayele Freilich and Ch. Danziger, Yerachmiel Danziger's wife, to appear before them. The Germans took them outside the city into the forest on the road to Glovatshov, and there they shot them.

The whole city trembled and deplored the two innocent victims.

Sadism On the Part of the Gendarmes

It is impossible to record in writing the sadism displayed by the bandit gendarmerie in Kozienice. Every day several of them would come to the gates of the Ghetto and call to several Jews who would be entering or leaving a house to speedily get inside. If this wasn't done quickly enough – they would enter the Ghetto and beat up the Jews that they were able to catch. If Jews would approach them upon being called, they would immediately shoot the victim. In this way was Chayele Bornshtein Rappaport, the wife of Moshe Rappaport, innocently shot. Such incidents occurred frequently by us in our city.

A Polish girl, whose name I do not remember, and who visited the gendarmerie frequently, informed them that she had seen with her own eyes and heard with her own ears, that Jews spoke against Hitler, may his name be blotted out. And she named: Berish Shabason, Menashe Frisch, Chanke Zeman and others whose names she did not know. Gestapo agents came from Radom, arrested those named, as well as others, beat them brutally, and took them to the jail in Radom, where they stayed a long time. Thanks to influence with the authorities they were finally freed.

Serious Troubles

At the orders of the German High Command all the Jews in the Kozienice District were brought into the Kozienice Ghetto. In bringing them to the Ghetto, the Germans caused them serious troubles. The situation in the Ghetto worsened from day to day. Fear, hunger, need and terribly crowded conditions caused a serious outbreak of Typhus, and a high mortality rate. In such circumstances did the Jews of Kozienice and those of the surrounding villages live during the occupation of the murderous Germans. This persisted until the deportation to the Concentration Camp, Treblinka, where they perished in the gas–chambers. We honor their memory. Tragic dates in Kozienice's destruction:

9. 9.1939 – Occupied by Hitler's army

9.13.1939 – Jews imprisoned in church courtyard

9.21.1942 – Jews sent to Treblinka.

[Page 461]

The School in the Ghetto Of Kozienice

by Rochama Chayut–Freilich, Kvutzat Yavne

Two pictures of the school, at which I worked in the Ghetto, and which had been kept by Paula Luxenburg, reached me. Memories that had been forgotten, due to the passage of years, were aroused anew, even though they were unclear. I'd like to bring up, whatever possible, about this special educational enterprise, even though I don't remember all of the facts. I certainly won't be exact with words and names as I convey the facts. In the spring of 1940, when it seemed to the Jews of Kozienice that those who had overcome the hunger and sickness, would also overcome the war, the teaching couple, Genzel, of blessed memory, decided to set up a private school in their home that was located in a district in which Jews were permitted to live. They invited me to help them with the teaching.

A kindergarten in ghetto of Kozienice

Many parents came with their children to register, even though there hadn't been a public announcement. The children were divided into classes, and there was even a 7th Grade. Studies began. The children learned with unusual diligence, but the happenings on the Jewish streets, the troubles and tragedies, the constant fear of the pounding hooves of the horses of the gendarmerie – took their toll on the nerves of the teaching couple. A few months after the founding of the school, there came a rumor that the street on which the house of the Genzel family stood, would be closed off to Jews. The Genzels ceased teaching, and the children were sent home.

A number of weeks later a few parents approached me. Among them, Mrs. Abramowitz, of blessed memory, (the wife of the doctor) and Mrs. Paula Luxenburg, and proposed to me to reopen the school. Thanks to the help of these two women and their encouragement, and especially thanks to the great help of my Aunt Chaya, of blessed memory, who was my right hand, I was successful in rounding up about 70 children, of all ages. The overcrowding in the Ghetto grew daily, because new streets became Judenrein. The community put at my disposal a small room, in the house of the Vilchik family on Lutelska Street. We set up a table, a closet and benches – and the children learned. From the 70 children I formed 3 or 4 classes, each one consisting of two grades. Every class learned about 2 hours daily. The language of instruction was Polish. I taught: mathematics, Polish, geography, and to special groups, also Hebrew. In the evening I would correct the notebooks, give out marks as was expected, and the children were happy with their good marks, like all children. At the proper times, we celebrated the Jewish holidays. I especially remember the Purim celebration, at which were present some parents, among them Paula Luxenburg.

A school for children in the ghetto. The teacher is Rochma Freilich.

[Page 462]

With the sealing off of the Ghetto, I lost the room in the Vilchik house, and found a place to continue in the room of my grandfather, R' Elimelech Freilich, of blessed memory. There I continued with slight interruptions, which were caused mainly by the conditions of the time, until the Germans filled the Ghetto with the Jews of the surrounding towns. The train appeared at the building of the Kozienice Station. As last stop, there was printed on the train the name Treblinka. The parents desired to assure their children's peace of mind, in order to instill in them the feeling that "such is the world and it's customs." There was nothing else to do. The children remained at home. Even I didn't have the strength to continue, and so passed days and weeks, and the day of the expulsion came. Only a few of these dear children survived. According to the testimony of Paula Luxenburg only four children of those in the picture, are still alive. Let us the living, please remember those who were plucked from us in their prime, and weren't privileged to survive. May their memory be blessed!

1) The kindergarten in the Ghetto of Kozienice. The survivors were: Ruth Luxenburg–Kalb and Medezia Bendler–Forshtand. Next to Ruth Luxenburg – Yaakov Pitkkowitz.

2) The school in the Ghetto of Kozience under the direction of the teacher, Ruchama Freilich.

In the 12th and the 13th Centuries
Kozienice belonged to an order of
Norbetaner Mnishkes.

In 1300 the Mnishkes gave up the village of
Kozienice and got for it a different village.

In 1400 a bridge was built over the Weisel
(Vistula), which led to Kozienice.

In 1467 there was born in Kozienice the
Polish King, Cazshimiezsh the First.

In 1549 the proprietor of the village of
Kozienice, Piotr Firley, obtained the right to
build a city, with an autonomous council, its
own court and the right to arrange fairs.

My Tragic Experiences
by Abraham Shabason, Tel Aviv

I believe that I am the oldest of the Kozieniceites. I and my family were well known in my birthplace, Kozienice. My father, of blessed memory was called Shaye Zelick's. Quite early, on the morning of September 25, 1939, there appeared on all the streets of the Jewish quarter, black figures with large death–heads on them. These were the SS gangs. They dragged women, men and children from the houses and were not sparing of their beatings. They robbed the Jewish storekeepers of their small bit of merchandise and drove everyone they met to forced labor.

Abraham Szabason

A High Command is Established

Later there appeared on the streets an officer of the SS, accompanied by several soldiers and went to the community's headquarters. The headquarters were empty. The chairman and his committee didn't want to show their faces. The Germans commanded that the elders of the community appear immediately. The householders of the city understood what was going on, so they organized a committee with a chairman at its head, to carry the responsibilities of the populace. The same week there came a representative of the city council who proposed the nomination of proper people, and not permit the election of unsuitable persons. A high command would be established with the most important members of the community, and Hershel Perl would be Chairman. The secretary would be the man who had held the post before the war, the honest, religious, Yiddishist, Moshe Goldtzveig.

Various committees and sub–committees were formed. A labor committee, a sanitation committee with the well known, religious Moshe–Leib Dua, of blessed memory, at it's head. There was also set up a finance committee to help the poor. Winter was coming. 75% of all Jews have lost their livelihoods. Hunger and cold become regular guests in town.

I Seek Connections

In the morning the Commandant and soldiers come to take Jews for labor. Distribution of work is handled by the labor committee of the community. But mostly the soldiers run around, catch and beat everyone who encounters them. At work everyone receives a portion of bread. The plundering by the SS gangs and the military does not cease. We begin to look for ways to become acquainted with the officers in order to modify their behavior towards Jews. In the morning, while it is still dark outside, I stand and count people and distribute bread. I begin to seek connections with the soldiers, until I'm successful in striking up a conversation with non–commissioned officers, and also with some commissioned officers, and convince them not to run through the streets. I'll see to it that all goes smoothly. It is to be understood that by doing this we had to pay off every one of the murderers. To put it plainly, it meant bribing them. In this way things became a bit quieter. Later, the head of the SS, for a very large amount of money, arranged that the Jews should appear for the labor detail on their own, and not be brought by force. Day by day we managed to push through the winter of 1940.

[Page 464]

I Become the Delegate to Warsaw

I was called to the community headquarters for an important session. It was springtime. The situation has become more difficult. Decrees and other annoyances were applied to Jews. Among them an order that all Jews, who live on the Polish streets, should move into the Ghetto. The chairman said to me as follows: "We've called you because we know who you are, and your family background. We are all condemned to the same fate. Help, us in a difficult and tragic task. Carry the burden of your brothers. At times like this, informers and underworld characters are active. The situation causes it. We want, therefore, that in our city, one brother should not lift his hand against the other. As much as we can we should prevent this. Your task will be to prevent this. Turn to the proper individuals who will help you in your work. You are therefore delegated to go to Warsaw, in the name of our city, in order to meet with the representatives of the Joint Distribution Committee, to get them to help us, because we are unable to satisfy our needs on our own. But remember, Abraham, first of all to uphold order, and help all who are in need."

Getting to Warsaw – was not one of the easiest things. First, because there weren't any communications. After a few days, I met with the representatives of the "Joint". I didn't get too much help from them, but I didn't return with completely empty hands.

The Situation Worsened

Meanwhile many Jews worked at the canal. This was a big help, because the Polish engineer used to pay something, from time to time for the work. And so passed the summer of 1940). In the winter of 1941 the situation worsened. First of all, because of winter, and secondly, because of the decrees. As long as the Ghetto was open, Jews were able to help themselves. This one could wheel and deal, another could run to the village and arrange something for himself. But with the arrival of 1941, the murderers issued a decree, that whoever would leave the Ghetto – would be shot! And they carried it out! Not once would someone come to me with a cry of despair that this one or that one had been caught. I would run to try to save them. At times I arrived in time to help deal with the murderers. They would break the Jew's bones, but then let him go. Very often, I would come too late! Then I would be beaten! "You've come again! Don't you know that there is a decree not to leave the Ghetto!" I would accept the beating and return empty handed!

Jewish community leaders meet in Warsaw. Year 1941.

[Page 465]

They Live With Us

by Gershon Bornstein

The hungry holiday was already prepared,
The SS, may their name be obliterated, surrounded the Ghetto,
Lakes of tears wet the night.
Resounding sirens reached the Jews and signaled them:
Out of your homes all together!

There remained dead, still walls,
All trembled and wrung their hands.
Tragic stillness remained in the homes,
Like on the cemetery the quiet covered graves.
Children cried, and cuddled close to their mothers,
Not knowing that they would be poisoned with gas.

Heaven and stars were witness,
As sheep to the slaughter they had to go.
The road was piled with the dead,
Seas of tears accompanied them,
In enclosed and sealed boxcars.
In the town remained those who had been shot.

Barefoot, without water, hungry and needy,
Brought to Treblinka to a gruesome death.
Each one counted the minutes and steps,
Knowing, that no road leads back.
In clouds of smoke their bones disappeared,
May their holy souls enter the Garden of Eden!

Revenge for us! – Was their last request.
Destroy the Nazis, they should cease to exist
In sorrow, with bowed heads,
We feel forever their fright and pain.
They live with us in holy spirit,
For each of us – that is our only comfort!

[Page 466]

In Place of a Tombstone

by Yaakov Shpigelman

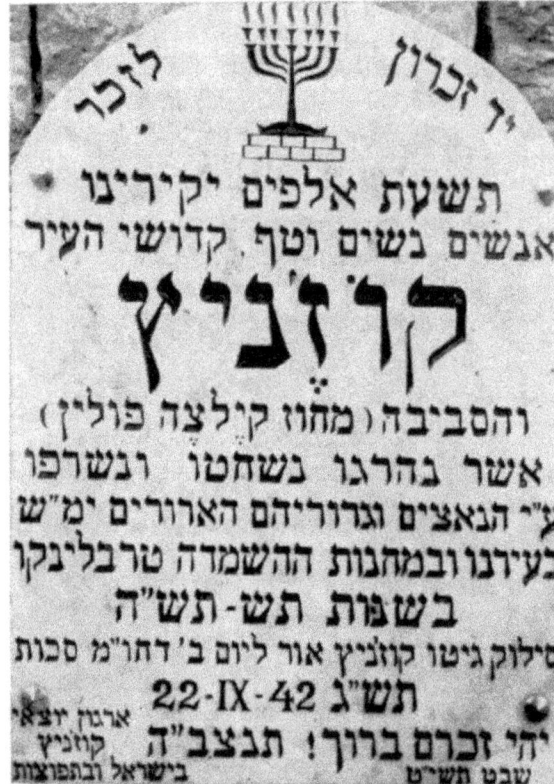

Memorial tablet for the martyrs of Kozienice on Mount Zion in Israel

Since nobody survived from the family of Abraham–Meir Alperman – I consider it my obligation to mention an episode that took place during the early days of the occupation of our town. First, a few words about who Abraham–Meir (Blachazsh) Alperman was. He was a Nikolaievsker veteran soldier, who was very strong and had received a medal for alone lifting a cannon. He came, with his wife Baile from Russia. If someone in town got sick, or suffered from a chill, and had no money for a doctor or barber surgeon – they would call Abraham–Meir, and he would set his big copper cups, which he alone had made. If someone had a toothache, and had no money for a dentist, they would go to Abraham–Meir, and he would seal the cavity with sour salt. He was a member of the burial society, and was the "general" of the Kozienice Rebbe, R' Arele. Since the Rebbe would call his Hassidim "soldiers", there had to be a "general". To do something for his fellow Jews, Abraham–Meir was always ready, day or night, even though he himself was a poor man.

When they drove most of the Jews into the church courtyard, which the Germans had made into a camp, a German officer gave an order for all Jews to line up immediately. Then he announced that because Jews had fired upon German soldiers, 25 Jews, the healthiest and handsomest, should willingly volunteer to be shot. Without waiting, he began to pull out of the line the healthiest and handsomest. 20 had already been chosen, and among them, my brother, Shmelke. But there were still 5 lacking, so the German ordered that 5 more should willingly volunteer. So the first to step forward was Abraham–Meir, and he stood next to my brother. They did not shoot them at that time. They only took them for field labor, cleaning stalls.

According to what I had heard from Meir Zaltzman, who had contact with the 25 until the deportation, they had decided not to let themselves be deported. They dug a bunker under the house in which they lived, at 18 Magitova Street, armed themselves with axes, iron bars, and other primitive weapons, and did not allow themselves to be deported. May these few words be a gravestone over their unknown graves.

Simchat Torah – 1939

The Hitlerites burned the Maggid's Shul, the city's House of Study and tortured the Kozienice Teacher R'Yosef Shapiro.

[Page 467]

The Ghetto in Kozienice

by Chaim Dimant, Paris

The first of September in 1939 fell on a Friday. At first, it seemed it would be a fair day. This one was rushing to work, another to pray, a third to his business. The children were either in school or in Heder (religious school).

Mobilization

Suddenly, the frightful word fell: MOBILIZATION. Whosoever heard the word became terribly upset. Mothers and women cried, for their husbands and sons who would have to go off to war. Many Jews fasted and recited the Psalms. But nobody thought then about the bitter fate which awaited our people. The Poles went to defend their country, and we Jews understood that we could not look forward to any good tidings. Immediately, in the morning the bombardment began. A large number of Jews ran off to the villages, thinking that only the cities would be bombed. Eight days later everyone who was able to, came home with his packs and bedding on his shoulders. Many of us were caught by the Hitlerites and imprisoned in the church courtyard. Our Jewish hats were removed and burned. Afterwards, they took us to Radom. At the same time Jews were seized for forced labor and beards were cut off.

A Shiver Went Through the Bones

I still remember as if it were today, when they took the old Shochet (Ritual Slaughterer), put his Talis on his shoulders, and harnessed him like a horse to a wagon, and made him pull the wagon through the entire city. As he was doing this, they beat him mercilessly and made fun of him. A shiver passed through the bones, because everyone knew that he can expect the same for himself. The seizure for forced labor became a daily occurrence. Jews hid themselves, because at work the Hitlerites beat them and broke their bones. The Hitlerites looked in every corner. When they found someone, he did not escape them alive. They took elderly Jews into horses' stalls, and ordered them to clean the horses. If the horses didn't break their bones, the Hitlerites did.

[Page 468]

The Synagogue Burns

At the same time there began to occur terrible things. Once, at night, the entire city lit up. We understood that it was burning. We weren't allowed to go out at night, but we understood that the synagogue was burning, Jews ran with water to put out the fire. Immediately we heard gunfire. Most ran home and hid themselves, because they were afraid. After the fire, the Germans requisitioned the homes, and drove the Jews into the Ghetto. It was forbidden to leave the Ghetto, and there was no work. People's bellies swelled from hunger. Whoever escaped from the Ghetto, in order to get a piece of bread, was shot and brought back into the Ghetto and buried. The Germans organized a Jewish Committee with Jewish Police, and made strict demands. Whoever wasn't able to pay, was sent to a Concentration Camp. To live long in a camp was impossible. If someone tried to escape, he was shot and buried. On the beautiful city of Kozienice, with her cultured youth, there fell a darkness.

A few families lived in one apartment. The people were unrecognizable and the young people had been sent to the camps. This is what happened until the Ghetto was liquidated.

A Memorial Tablet On Mount Zion in Jerusalem

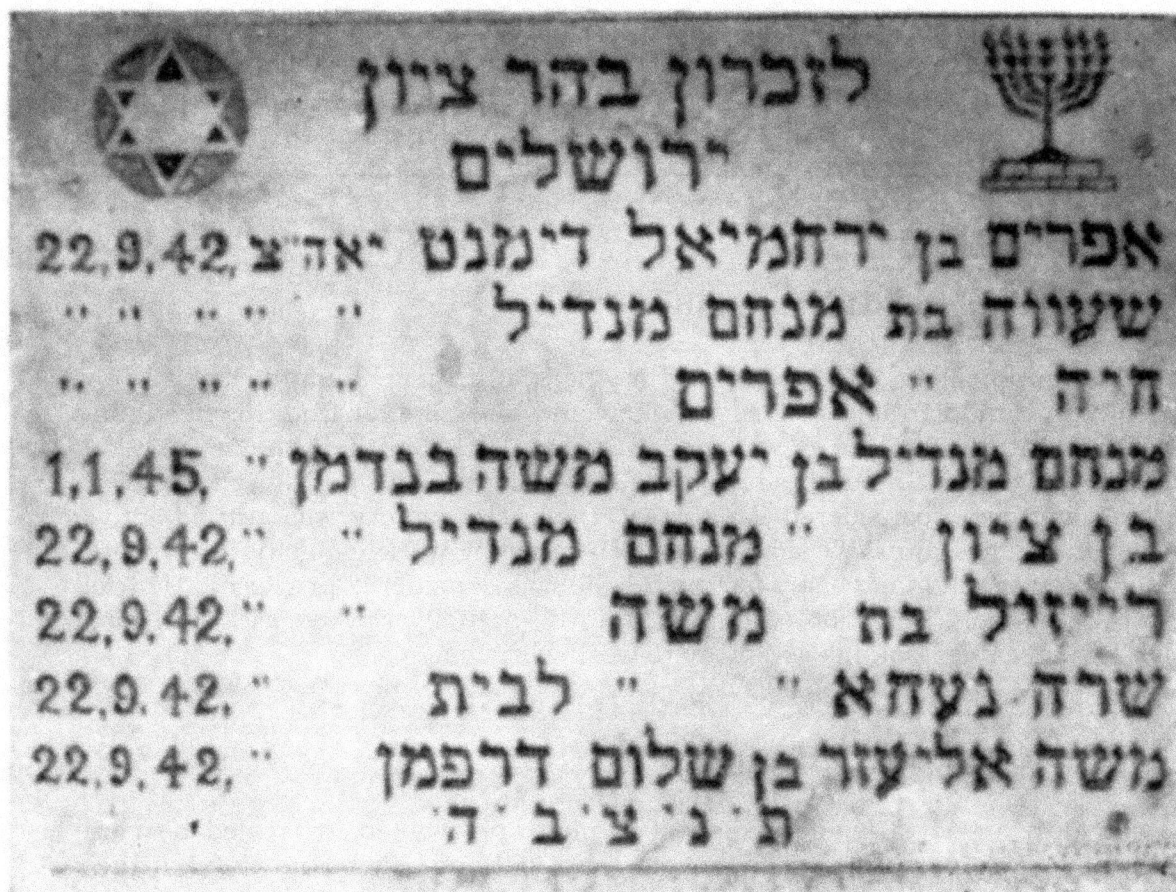

לזכרון בהר ציון
ירושלים
אפרים בן ירחמיאל דימנט יאה״צ 22.9.42,
שעווה בת מנחם מנדיל „ „ „ „
חיה „ אפרים „ „ „ „
מנחם מנדיל בן יעקב משה בנדמן „ 1.1.45,
בן ציון „ מנחם מנדיל „ 22.9.42,
רייזיל בה משה „ 22.9.42,
שרה נעחא „ לבית „ 22.9.42,
משה אליעזר בן שלום דרפמן „ 22.9.42,
ת׳ נ׳ צ׳ ב׳ ה׳

Some Kozienicer martyrs names mentioned on the tablet on Mount Zion

Emphraim son of Yerachmeil Dimant who died on September 22, 1942

Sheva daughter of Menachem Mendil who died on September 22, 1942

Chaya daughter of Ephraim who died on September 22, 1942

Menachem Mendil son of Yaakov Moshe Bandman who died on January 1, 1945

Ben Zion son of Menachem Mendil who died on September 22, 1942

Reisel daughter of Moshe Bandman who died on September 9, 1942

Sarah Neha daughter of Moshe Bandman who died on September 22, 1942

Moshe Eliezer son of Shalom Dorfman who died on September 22, 1942

May Their Souls Be Linked to the Chain of Life.

The Ghetto is Liquidated

When they liquidated the Pionker Ghetto, many Jewish young people already worked in the factory that manufactured the so–called war powder. 1942. Coming home from work, the ones who distributed the work notified us to take our things with us, because the Ghetto is being liquidated. Older men and women were stood to the side. Those who were capable of working were lined up.

[Page 469]

Mendl Bandman and His Family

It was appalling, the farewells of mothers and their children. I recall how Ben Zion Bandman fell upon his mother, and tore his hair from his head, and begged that they let him go with her to Zvolin. And from there they were taken to Treblinka. The SS bandits tore him away violently, and put him in line, with those who were considered capable of work. The factory was turned into a Concentration Camp. We could see each other at work, or going from work. Mendl Bandman made boots for the SS. He was considered privileged. He tried to take his son, Ben Zion, with him, and he actually worked with him for a while. Later they took his son away to work with coal.

Let There Be An End Already

In duly, 1944, a whole transport of men and women, in sealed boxcars, were sent to Auschwitz, without water and without being able to fulfill their bodily needs. All had already despaired of everything. Let there be an end already. How long can a human suffer so? After a few days and nights we were brought to Auschwitz. After going through the procedure of "left and right", we were left alive. In three more days they took a group of a few hundred Jews, and sent them away to Gana, Auschwitz Number 3. The work, at the beginning, was with cement. Later – with coal – and it was difficult. Mendl Bandman died on the first of January, 1945 from an inflammation of his lungs. His son, Ben–Zion said the Kaddish all eight days.

In Buchenwald

A few days later they took us away. At first on foot, and afterwards in open trucks, until we were all taken to Buchenwald. Right before the Liberation by the American Army, Ben–Zion Bandman was taken away on a transport, and nobody, to this day, knows what happened to him. May their names be memorialized and remain part of the history of our city.

All Died in Treblinka

I allow myself to add that I am a son of Ephraim Dimant, who was born and lived in Kozienice until the deportation to Treblinka, where he perished, together with our mother, Sheva, of the Rochman family, and with my young 11 year old sister, Chayale. The majority of our family: My uncle's sister, Reisel, her husband, Tepper and her son, Yerachmiel, perished in Buchenwald in March, 1945. My mother's sister, Eidel Golde, her husband, Gutmacher, her brothers: Moshe, Beryl, Leizer, Leibl, Yenkl and Abraham all perished with their wives and children in Treblinka after the liquidation of the Kozienicer Ghetto.

[Page 470]

Tomorrow – Our Lives End!

On the first day of Succos – 1942, Kozienice Jews knew that on the morrow their lives would end.

Parents bade farewell to their children, and children with their parents.

Crying they said to each other: Tomorrow our lives will end!

Ben-Zion Bondman

[Page 471]

Forgive Me, Dear Parents!

by Shmelke Shpigelman, Montreal

In the camp, which the Germans created from the church and it's garden, they drove the majority of the Jews. Among them, my father, of blessed memory, my brother, Yaakov, and me. My father, even though I tried to hide him from German eyes, with my shoulders, had his beard shorn together with pieces of skin from his face. This happened when they seized us to clean up the mess in the garden that had been left over from the prisoners of war who had been kept there. We had to clean the offal with our bare hands. Old Jews, who couldn't run fast with their hand full of the offal, were beaten mercilessly. These degrading scenes were repeated on a daily basis. Each day a German officer would announce, that if someone would oppose his orders, the entire camp would be shot to death. It is understandable that no one took it upon himself to protect his own honor at the expense of other's lives. A few days later the Germans freed from the camp the elderly and the sick, and on the 8th day there arrived transport trucks which carried away the young. They said that they were being sent to Radom.

We Free Ourselves From the Camp

We decided to flee, after we had seen what the Germans did to us during the first week of the occupation. We were able to imagine what awaited us in strange cities and in a real concentration camp. My sister's children used to come to the wall of the garden to bring food. Not once did they receive beatings from the clubs of the German soldiers. I told them that Yaakov and I were going to run away. If we were to die – then better here, in Kozienice. We hoped, that after we had loosened two of the wooden posts of the garden fence, we would be able to get to the other side of the church garden, and again be reunited with our family. When my sister, Rachele, heard this, she ran out to Dr. Abramovitsh, put down her jewelry, cried and begged that he should give her a certificate stating that we were ill. She knew that the church was surrounded by tanks and machine guns, and she was convinced that it was impossible to escape. The doctor gave her a paper, without charge, indicating that we were extremely ill, My sister came with the paper, fainted at the gate, and she succeeded in having us released.

We Seek a Way to the Other Side of the Bog River

We remained for another two months in Kozienice. We got a taste of forced labor and beatings. We saw the looting of Jewish houses, the shootings of those on bread lines. We heard the screams from Jewish homes, as German soldiers broke into them. We also witnessed the burning of the Synagogue and the House of Study in the middle of the night. Understandably, we couldn't forsee Hitler's plans for exterminating all Jews by all sorts of horrible deaths.

[Page 472]

But everything that we did see was enough for me to seek a way to get to a place where Jews weren't the exception. And this place was on the other side of the Bog River. We gathered together a small group: My brother-in-law, Rachele's husband, Nachum Qventshtern, my buddy, Simcha-Pesach Eisenmeser, my brother, Yaakov and myself. My cousin, Shalom Krishpel, and other acquaintances, had already gone away earlier. I left my old, good father, my dear faithful mother, my sister and her three children, buddies and friends, my beloved town – and went on the difficult journey to the Bog. After three rainy days, tired and thoroughly soaked, we finally arrived at the border, which separated Germany from Russia. That afternoon, I'll never forget. The sky on our side was overcast and dull, but on the other side of the border the sky was clear, and the sun warmed the wet trees and small houses of the fortunate village of Drogotshin. Fortunate – because it was on the other side, where Jews were the equals of all others. My brother-in-law's longing for his family was so strong, that at the border he turned back home, where he later perished.

On the Other Side of the Border

We hid among the reeds and waited. When night fell, the peasants of the village on the opposite side began their work of ferrying the refugees across the river. Understandably, they were well paid for their trouble. A few minutes later, we were already upon the blessed soil.

Free – But Not For Long

Immediately we were seized by Soviet border-guards, who took us to a place, not far from the river, where there were already, sitting on the ground, a few hundred refugees. A few stated that we would be sent back to the Germans. Others said that in Semiatitsh, a nearby village, there were many refugees who were free and being given support. We decided not to wait for them to send us back. Let's flee! I saw that it wasn't difficult to flee, because we were being guarded by only a few Soviet soldiers. I was also certain that Soviet soldiers would not fire upon refugees. It didn't take long before my thoughts were interrupted by a youngster: "What are we waiting for, Jews? To be sent back to the Germans? Let's flee!" A portion of those who were sitting began to flee and we were among them.

564 Kozienice Yizkor Book

In the forest we met a group of White Russian or Polish bandits. They held us and wanted to take us to the Militia. I told them that we are going no further, but remaining right there. They told us to speak softly. We thereby understood who they were. We assured them that we possessed nothing except that which we were wearing, and that they are losing time paying attention to us. They left us alone. We decided to go no further, in the dark, because who knows what sort of surprise awaited us.

[Page 473]

From Semiatitch to Brisk

We sat down to rest, until dawn, and then we went to Semiatitch. I was barely able to walk because my feet were frostbitten from sitting on the ground. In Semiatitch we met many refugees. We therefore went on to Brisk, where I spent two weeks in the hospital. My buddy, Simcha–Pesach, came to me in the hospital, and told me that he's going back, in order to bring his family and other buddies. "I now know the way" he said. I understood that his longing for my sister's daughter, Itke, whom he loved. He went away, stayed there, married Itke, and was later shot by the German bandits.

The Soviets Send Us Away

My brother Yaakov and I worked in a tailor shop in Brisk until an order came that refugees were to distance themselves 100 kilometers from the border. The Soviets, who expected the German attack, wanted to clear the border area of refugees. We did not want to accept Russian passports, because we were afraid that with Soviet passports we would be counted as Russian citizens, and that we wouldn't be able to leave Russia. Our dream was, after the war, to return home, and be together again. Therefore we attempted to remain close to the border, where we could from time to time receive regards from home, from someone who would take the risk to smuggle it. The Soviet authorities took all who had not accepted passports and shipped them to the far north. This act, by the way, saved our lives. If we had remained in the western zone, we would have perished together with all other Jews. In Siberia, we were interned for 15 months and then freed. From there we went to Middle Asia and lived for three and a half years in Uzbekistan.

Tovia Shpigelman and his son Volf

The War Ended

The war ended. We went home, but there was no longer any home. The German bandits eliminated my entire family: my good, quiet father, Tuviale, my faithful, observant mother, Chana–Tzime, my devoted sister, Rachele, her husband, Nachum, their three children: Ite, Leah and Tzirele, and the good, Shlomole, who went together with his grandfather to Treblinka. From my Kozienice family, there remained only my brother, Yaakov and myself, who saved ourselves in Russia. In Paris, the German murderers hands reached out to my dear sister, Tzirl, and her children. My idealistic brother, Wolf, his wife and children, except for one sister who saved herself and her children by a miracle in France.

[Page 474]

Forgive me, dear parents, sister, brothers, for not remaining with you. I know that your only revenge on the Germans is the fact that we were not with you, so that the murderous hands could not reach us. I know, dear mother, how you loved your youngest son, Yaakov. Yaakov and I are alive. We have families and we write about what happened to you. Generations will mention you and generations will remember what happened to their grandfathers and great grandfathers, grandmothers and great grandmothers. They will shed a tear for the town of Kozienice and for the memorial which this Yizkor Book will be for you. Cursed forever shall be the murderers of our people and of all our beloved and dear ones. WE HONOR YOUR HOLY MEMORY!

[Page 475]

And Your Life Shall Hang in Doubt Before You

by Rabbi Yitzhak Freilich

On Sabbath morning, the 8th of September, 1939, we looked – for the first time – upon the faces of the Germans and we were disturbed. Their expressions bore witness to the fact they are Amalekites. (The people who first attacked the Israelites, when they left Egypt). Their deeds confirmed that in murder there is no people like unto them in all the world. Before they came to Kozienice, they poured fire upon the town, without pity, for a number of days. From the 4th of September, they didn't cease to drop bombs on the city and surrounding area. The city emptied of it's inhabitants. A number of houses were destroyed, and there were casualties, and the chaos was great. Men, women and children fled without knowing where to turn. Friday eve the noise abated suddenly, and we understood that "they" are already in the city. In the morning, we were ordered to immediately return home, otherwise Jews were condemned to die. We said to ourselves: From this Ashmodai (Devil) there is no escape.

We passed through the patrols of the enemy who had encircled the city like a "ring" and we came into the city. We trembled with fear because the curse of the Torah had come to pass: "Outside – the sword reigned, and inside – fear!" The cruel enemy took advantage of the opportunity, and with German precision, began on that very day to slaughter Jews, and it increased from day to day, and month to month, until they completely eliminated all Kozienice Jews on the 2nd day of Succos in 1941. On that day, the persecutors took all Jews out on the street and burned the House of Study and Synagogue. With unbearable tortures they forced the aged R' Yosef Shapiro, may the memory of the righteous be a blessing, and may the Lord avenge his blood, and some of his neighbors, to throw with their own hands, the scrolls of the Torah into the flames. From that day on there began a period of five years of terror against the Jews of the city. A portion were killed by the sword, and the remainder were packed into boxcars that took them to the hell of Treblinka. There they perished, sanctifying the Holy name.

The "acquaintance" between the murderers and the Jews of the area was not long in coming. Firstly, they began to seize the men for forced labor. They searched and examined every room, attic and basement, every hole and crack, and when they found their victims, they beat them mercilessly. Their unclean hands stole and robbed and about Kozienice the dire words of the prophecy could be said: "And your life shall hang in doubt before you, and you shall dread day and night, and shall have no assurance of your life. In the morning you shall say 'If only it were evening; and at evening time you shall say' If only it were morning; for the fear in your heart which you shall fear, and for the sights which your eyes shall behold." (Book of Deuteronomy, Chapter 28, verses 66 through 67).

[Page 476]

Jews Have No Right To Live

by Zelick Berman, Bat–Yam

A day before the deportation of our Jews of Kozienice, there came to me my friend, the former Burgemeister of the city, V. Sab, and told me that there had arrived at the train station over 60 railroad cars. The supervisor of the railroad station told him that he didn't know what they were for.

We Don't Know!

With that information I went to the Director of the Judenraat and asked him if they knew about it. "We don't know about anything that is supposed to happen in the city." With that answer, I went away.

A Terrible Commotion

Early on the morrow we were alerted by sirens from the sawmills and electrical works. The whole town and the Ghetto were already surrounded and occupied on all sides by special SS units, Gestapo gendarmes, and Ukrainians. In the Ghetto police were scurrying, and also firemen, officials of the city council, and the Vice Burgemeister, Miller. Also the Poles were running around like crazy. The order came: All Jews, big and small, old and young, are to leave their houses with a small pack, and line up in a row, five abreast. Whoever doesn't leave his home will be shot! In this way began the deportation of Kozienice Jews to Treblinka in September, 1942.

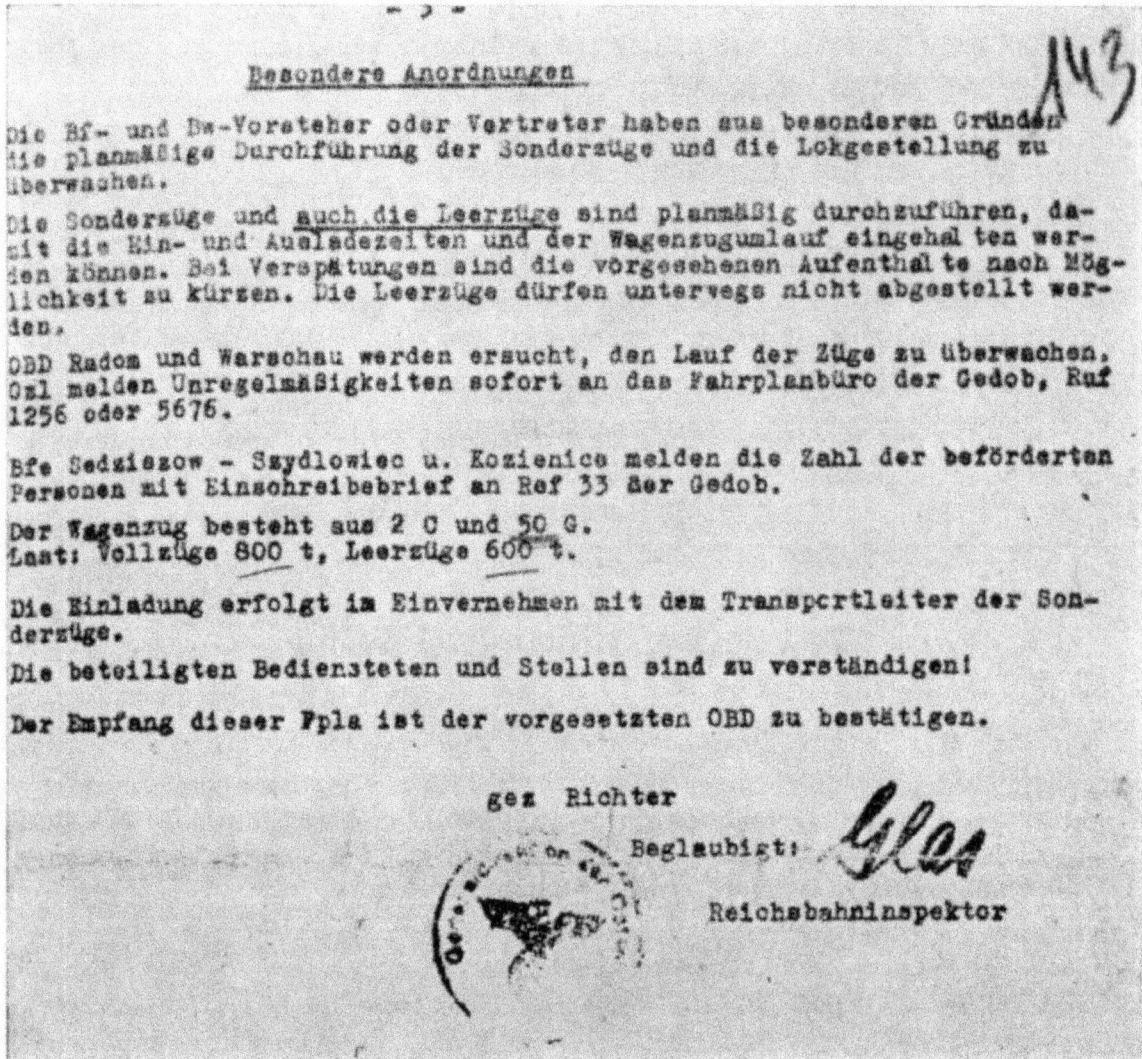

Besondere Anordnungen

Die Bf- und Bw-Vorsteher oder Vertreter haben aus besonderen Gründen
die planmäßige Durchführung der Sonderzüge und die Lokgestellung zu
überwachen.

Die Sonderzüge und auch die Leerzüge sind planmäßig durchzuführen, da-
mit die Ein- und Ausladezeiten und der Wagenzugumlauf eingehalten werden können. Bei Verspätungen sind die vorgesehenen Aufenthalte nach Mög-
lichkeit zu kürzen. Die Leerzüge dürfen unterwegs nicht abgestellt werden.

OBD Radom und Warschau werden ersucht, den Lauf der Züge zu überwachen.
Sie melden Unregelmäßigkeiten sofort an das Fahrplanbüro der Gedob, Ruf
1256 oder 5676.

Bfe Sedziszow - Szydlowiec u. Kozienice melden die Zahl der beförderten
Personen mit Einschreibebrief an Ref 33 der Gedob.

Der Wagenzug besteht aus 2 C und 50 G.
Last: Vollzüge 800 t, Leerzüge 600 t.

Die Einladung erfolgt im Einvernehmen mit dem Transportleiter der Sonderzüge.

Die beteiligten Bediensteten und Stellen sind zu verständigen!

Der Empfang dieser Fpla ist der vorgesetzten OBD zu bestätigen.

gez Richter

Beglaubigt:

Reichsbahninspektor

A special order of the train inspector for a special train for Kozienice

(The special order of the Railroad Inspector about the special railroad cars
for the Kozienice transport)

A terrible commotion. Children and grown–ups cry and scream. Children
search for their parents and parents search for their children. Shooting from
the Gestapo is heard. Small and big, young and old; all run. The sick, who
can't walk, drag themselves on all fours. Miller walks around among the Jews.
He helps with the evacuation, and spreads false rumors, that the Jews are
going to be taken to a special labor camp. Heart–rending scenes take place,
which are impossible to describe in writing: A son carries his old mother on
his shoulders and falls near the line, and so on.

[Page 477]

The Elderly Are Shot on the Spot

The old and the sick, among them Berish Krongold (the lame Berish), are herded together in a separate place. They are laid down together in a cart and in this way led to the slaughter. A few of the elderly are shot on the spot, and some on the way to the railroad. Also the old, Mendl Frish is shot. On Koshtshelne and Targove Streets stand our nearest and dearest five abreast, guarded by the Gestapo and beaten murderously and without pity by the Ukrainians. Chaim Klainboim's wife lies sick in bed and can't go out. She buys her life for a small sack of gold. The Gestapo takes away her fortune and promises her that she will remain alive, but she is soon shot by the bandits.

A Cat Has the Right To Live, But Not a Jew

At the order of the Gestapo, the death–march begins. All Kozienice Jews march to the railroad station by way of Lubliner Street, five abreast, and closely guarded on all sides by police Gestapo, gendarmes and Ukrainians, who beat mercilessly and shoot many. The Polish populace looks on at this terrible tragedy of Kozienice Jews. Not a shred of help for Jews from the Aryan side. There wander around in the Ghetto SS and Gestapo, and they say to a passing cat: "You have a right to live! You're not a Jew!"

All the workers, who remained in the Ghetto after the evacuation, approximately 70–brow–beaten and broken individuals, mourn their dearest and nearest, who were so murderously taken to Treblinka. Night falls, dark and black. No more Jews in Kozienice. The small Jewish fortune, together with the prepared holiday food remains at the entrances to the Jewish homes. A strong wind blows. The shutters of the windows bang back and forth. A picture of the aftermath of a terrible pogrom, which had no equal in Jewish history. The Angel of Death hovers over Jewish houses.

Kutsher Takes Revenge

Among the workers there was a well–built and bold young man from Glovatshov. He was called Kutsher. I don't remember his first name. We often spoke about organizing a partisan group, but we had no weapons. Kutsher said that we should give him money, and he would buy arms. On a specific day he went with the money to Gnievashov, but he didn't accomplish his mission. When he returned he said that he wouldn't deal with the German's any more. Once, at dusk, the Gendarme Zomer, took Kutsher to work and beat him mercilessly without notice. When he returned, bloody, from his labor, he told me that he must revenge himself on the bandit. And that is what he did. He told the murderer, that he saw in a cellar hidden merchandise. He took the bandit gendarme under the synagogue, where there actually was a cellar of a wrecked house. He went down with him to the cellar, grabbed him by the neck, beat him up, took away his revolver and ammunition and ran away. In the morning we all heard about this nice work. We were certain that we would all be shot, but because of shame the gendarme didn't even ask about Kutsher. According to what I heard, Kutsher was hidden with other Jews in a bunker, where he perished. We honor his memory!

[Page 478]

The Hangman, Zomer, Shoots a Jewish Girl

A Jewish family, it seems, had left on the "sand" (this was what we called the part of the city outside of the Ghetto) with some Polish people, a small, charming dark–complexioned little girl. After the evacuation the Polish family threw the girl out of the house and told the gendarmerie that there is a Jewish girl wandering around. On Sunday, the murderer, Zomer, came and ordered that the child be brought to the Jewish hospital. At the door of the hospital the child was shot. He immediately ordered that the body be brought to a different street. A terribly shocking scene, which has no equal, stands before my eyes even today. The child was taken in a small wagon to Lubliner Street. The child was still alive and gasping for breath on the wagon, and her innocent blood was flowing on the streets and sprinkling the road. Poles from surrounding villages, were just then coming out of church. They stopped, looked upon the scene and made fun. I worked with Yehudah Hoffman and with a student from Glovatshov, Albert. At a specific moment, there came over to us a gendarme and a Polish policeman from Radom. They called the student, Albert, away, and shot him before our eyes.

Beginning of December, 1942

After a specific amount of time, we were informed that all of the Jewish Ghetto laborers were to be transferred to a separate barracks on Radomer Street, near the electrical station. We have to be there early in the morning and take along our rucksacks. Immediately there appeared gendarmes and Polish police, and the oldest of the bandits said to us: "You're going from here to Radom. Whoever won't keep up or goes out of the line will be shot." I don't remember the date. It was winter. Snow was falling. I was walking together with Chanale Avenshtern, Shmuel Zavali's wife, who was leading by the hand her little boy, Zeveck. Close by me walked Yehudah Hoffman, Chaim Meckler, Me lech Orbach – approximately 70 men and women. I talked about saving my life by running away. But we are closely guarded, and we have no opportunity to escape. We continue walking!

I Run Away

Not far from Yedlnie, Chaim Meckler moves close to me and says: "Zelick, if we're to escape – now is the time, because I am well acquainted with the area. Later may be too late – for the thick forest comes to an end. Don't lose any time and save yourself!" At the moment there drove by a peasant with a tall load of lumber. I run past his wagon on the other side and into the forest. The police begin shooting. Following me, ran Melech Orbach, who was killed near me, and the little Kreitzberg. The police shoot and I run deep into the forest. I feel my boots fill with blood from the bullets which had hit my feet. I stuck myself into a hole in the ground. Late at night I came back to the city. Being close to the city, I asked myself: "Where does one go in such circumstances? Frightened, tired, bloodied and dirty."

[Page 479]

It's best for me to go to our close acquaintance, T. Parashinski." I knock on the door of their appetizing store." "Who's there?" I answer calmly: "Zelick Berman." "Can't be" is the sharp rejoinder, "They shot him yesterday on the way to Radom." It takes a few minutes. I stand at the door, I show them all the signs of life. They finally open the door, but don't let me in. He and his wife are very fearful. They're trembling. After a few moments they lead me to understand how frightened they are. Too many gendarmes are wandering around. In other words: I cannot remain there. My eyes darken!

Don't Be Afraid

I cried and begged that they allow me to remain until morning, because I have nowhere to go. I request that they tell my friend, Sabat, to come to me immediately. He came immediately, and greeted me heartily in front of them. I cried a great deal. "Don't cry", he said to me, "If you're still alive today, with God's help you'll live. I'll take you out of here and hide you in a safe place, which I've already prepared for you." At night, my good friend comes to me, takes hold of me under my arms, and leads me over the bridge in the direction of Stara Viesh.

Just at that moment, gendarmes passed. Scared stiff, I ceased talking and stood still. "Calm yourself", he told me. "My fate is now tied to your fate. If shooting is your fate, we'll both be shot. Come be bold and don't be afraid."

We go into the house of a teacher acquaintance from the Folkshule, where there had been readied for me a cellar; not a big one, with a few stairs.

- 2 -

4.) Rückleitung des Leerzuges:

Lp Kr 9231 (30.11) von Treblinka nach Szydlowiec am 24./25. Sept.

Treblinka	(11.24)/15.59	im Plan	Dg 91368 B	
Siedlce	17.56/18.42	" "	Dg 91445 B	
Lukow	19.36/20.37	" "	Dg 91266 B	
Deblin Gbf	22.34/23.36	" "	Dg 91266 B	
Radom	1.34/ 1.50	" "	Dg 91266 B	
Szydlowiec	3.08/(21.30)			

5.) P Kr 9232 (30.9) von Szydlowiec nach Treblinka am 25./26. Sept.

Szydlowiec	(3.08)/21.30	im Plan	Dg 91249 B	
Radom	22.49/ 0.13	" "	Dg 91255 B	
Deblin Gbf	2.00/ 3.10	" "	Dg 91257 B	
Lukow	5.17/ 6.08	" "	Dg 95402 B	
Siedlce	6.58/ 8.34	" "	Dg 91365 B	
Treblinka	11.24/(15.59)			

6.) Rückleitung des Leerzuges:

Lp Kr 9233 (30.11) von Treblinka nach Kozienice am 26./27. Sept.

Treblinka	(11.24)/15.59	im Plan	Dg 91368 B	
Siedlce	17.56/18.42	" "	Dg 91445 B	
Lukow	19.36/20.37	" "	Dg 91266 B	
Deblin Gbf	22.34/23.36	" "	Dg 91266 B	
Bakowiec	0.00/ 0.05	im Sonderplan (Kreuzung mit P		
Kozienice	0.35			

7.) P Kr 9234 (30.9) von Kozienice nach Treblinka am 27./28. Sept.

Kozienice	20.00			
Bakowiec	20.30/20.43	im Plan	Dg 91237 B	
Deblin	21.08/23.01	" "	Dg 91243 B	
Lukow	1.08/ 3.11	" "	Dg 91464 B	
Siedlce	4.01/ 5.08	" "	Dg 91359 B	
Treblinka	7.20/(15.59)			

8.) Rückleitung des Leerzuges:

Lp Kr 9235 (30.11) von Treblinka nach Tschenstochau am 28./29. S

Treblinka	(7.20)/15.59	im Plan	Dg 91368 B	
Siedlce	17.56/18.42	" "	Dg 91445 B	
Lukow	19.36/20.37	" "	Dg 91266 B	
Deblin Gbf	22.34/23.36	" "	Dg 91266 B	
Radom	1.34/ 1.50	" "	Dg 91266 B	
Skarzysko K.	3.51/ 4.44	" "	Dg 91266 B	
Kielce	6.41/ 7.40	" "	Dg 91106 B	
Tschenstochau	14.02			

Lok stellen: Bw Siedlce bis Skarzysko Kam., Bw Skarzysko K. bis
Deblin, Bw Deblin bis Lukow, Bw Lukow bis Siedlce, Bw
Siedlce bis Treblinka u. Lp zurück bis Lukow, Bw Deb
von Lukow bis Szydlowiec bezw. Kozienice u. Skarzysk
Bw Skarzysko K. bis Kielce, Bw Kielce bis Tschenstoch

Zub stellen: Bf Jedlnaow bis Skarzysko K, Bf Skarzysko K. bis Deb
lin, Bf Deblin bis Siedlce, Bf Siedlce bis Treblinka
Lp zurück bis Deblin, Bf Deblin bis Kozienice, Szydl
wiec u. Skarzysko K. Bf Skarzysko K. bis Kielce, Bf
Kielce bis Tschenstochau.

In Tschenstochau ist der Wagenzug vorübergehend abzustellen. An-
ordnung über Weiterverwendung folgt.

A German travel plan for the train from Treblinka to Kozienice. See #6 and
from Kozienice to Treblinka. See #7.

The First Night in the Cellar

All around me it was dark. The cellar isn't big. There is even a small window with bars, but it is blocked, so that no one should, heaven forbid, look in. The cellar there is a barrel with sauerkraut, old things, bottles and potatoes for the winter. I look in all four corners. Black darkness. The walls cry with me. Water is dripping from the bricks. I seat myself in a corner, and lean my head against the barrel of sauerkraut. And that's how I slept through the first night. Promptly in the morning, my new landlord came to me, converses with me briefly, but plainly and to the point. They give me breakfast. They will also bring me lunch in the cellar. And so it was ... It was more difficult with a place to sleep. They had no bedclothes, but my friend provided them for me.

[Page 480]

I Become Accustomed To It

I quickly became accustomed to the difficult circumstances. The family consisted of three people: a man, his wife and a little girl of seven. The wife was English, with a fine character. The landlord, a born Pole, did not despise the "bitter drop". The child resembled her mother. When the landlord wasn't home, the wife locked all the doors of the house, and opened the cellar door, so that I could get some air. As time passed they would call me up from the cellar, converse with me a bit and tell me the news. I would do all of the housework myself. I fixed the tile kitchen and the oven. I had plenty of time, and I was indeed fortunate to be out of the cellar. They were pleased with my work. They gave me some whiskey, which was considered a great gift. I became used to the family, and they became used to me. From time to time they displayed some pity and empathy towards me.

Homesickness Befalls Me

On a particular day, sitting in the cellar near the barrel of kraut, I reminded myself of a tragedy, I saw that there was no end to my troubles. I became homesick for my own, who were still alive. I looked at my situation and burst out crying. My landlady heard my crying. She came right down to the cellar and asked what happened, and why I'm crying so bitterly today. Maybe I'm hungry, or maybe I've been mistreated by them? "No?" I answered. I couldn't calm myself and cried again, until I burst out with the reason for my crying. I long for my wife, my son, and only brother. I told her of my tragedy. Together with me she shed many tears and said: I'll help you. I know the camp in Volanov. If I'll be able to, I'll go there and bring your brother, wife and son to us. But you must first ask my husband to agree to this, that I should go there, and that he should watch our child.

I waited for an opportunity, and poured out my bitter heart to the landlord. I told him and begged him to the best of my ability to allow his wife to travel to the camp in Volanov, and maybe succeed in bringing my brother, Chaim and his son, who remained alive after the selection. I talked and begged forcefully, and then cried. Our conversation lasted a while. I noted that his facial expression was changing to pity. He said to me: "Let her go to rescue your brother, Chaim. We knew you all well. Such upright people, as your brother, Chaim, who was beloved by all the inhabitants of the city, need to be helped. May no evil befall my wife, God forbid, and may she return home safely." It's unnecessary to write about my joy. It was a great day for me and the family. On the morrow, in the morning, my landlady rode off towards Volanov in the wagon. I lay in my cellar, not eating or drinking, only thinking and praying that the female savior would succeed to bring my brother and his son out of that hell!

[Page 481]

The Situation Becomes Serious

Three days passed. My landlord came from the street in a bad mood. He doesn't know what it means that his wife hasn't returned as yet. The situation in the household became serious. I defended as best I could, the delay in the return of his wife and attributed it to the sorry state of communication in the country, but tried to reassure him that she would return safely. This took five days. My landlord said to me, after drinking a glass of whiskey: "Listen! In my unfortunate circumstance of losing my wife and my child's mother, you are to blame. Too bad, but I'll finish you off today–Besides which, your friend and his family will also pay with his life..." I didn't know what to do with myself. The truth was that I was to blame. I was afraid to speak to him. I had nowhere to hide, and nothing with what to commit suicide. Meanwhile, he took his little daughter and went with her to the city. I was left alone, like always. I understood, that the danger is growing from minute to minute, because he was cleaning the house, so that no one would notice the slaughter as he carried out the murderous act against me.

What happened to me at the time, on that day, I don't know and don't remember. Either I was drugged or I fell asleep by myself? When I opened my eyes, there stood by me in the cellar, my friend, Sabat. He spoke to me, but what it was – I don't know. I answered him, as if from sleep: "I just saw my mother, may she rest in peace, who died a long time ago, and she brought me food and drink and asked me about Chaim and his son, Amos, and then you came and awakened me." "I know everything" – my friend answered me. "Today, I'll stay with your landlord all the time and watch that he does you no harm."

At 12 Midnight, Chaim and His Son Came

I remember, that it was Thursday. On the same day, late at night, about 12, there came from the railroad Pshilutzki with his coach, out of which there stepped my brother, Chaim, and his son, Amos, and the dear savior – the landlady herself. I became so excited that I didn't know what to do first, or what I was about. I took my dear guests, who were very dirty (as was to be expected, coming from a camp) to my cellar. In the cellar we were all together. Our joy was great. Each one told of his own troubles. My brother, Chaim, told about the tragic death of his wife, Angie, and his youngest son, Danek, in the Volanov Camp. We mourn our nearest and dearest, who died so tragically. Later my brother told me: "You see, Zelick. The fact that in these circumstances you were able to organize all of this, is a sign that maybe we will survive the war."

Emus, David and Marilka Berman murdered by the Nazis in Kozienice

[Page 482]

All three of us cried. A bit later, Chaim wrote a letter to his friend, the Judge Pakusinski, with whom he had left his entire fortune. My brother was full of hope, that the judge would help him. My brother wrote the letter in a very courteous form. He asked to meet with him. My brother, Chaim, got an answer from him on the same letter as follows: "Under the circumstances, our meeting is not possible." Reading the few words, my brother said to me: "I didn't expect this, that in such a troubled time, he should write to me in such a manner. Lately, I see that I've made a mistake. I don't know if there's a chance that we'll survive the war."

We had both been born and grew up in the city, and for many years had been councilmen on the City Council. My pension from it was signed over to worthy causes. After so many years of communal work, there is no one in the Polish populace who is ready to help save our lives. We weren't together in the cellar for a long time. Suddenly, my brother, Chaim, became ill with Typhus, and got a very high fever. I immediately contacted my friend, Sabat, and requested medical help. He brought me all kinds of medicines. Unfortunately, he was unable to provide the help of a doctor. My brother had terrible pain. He groaned and screamed with pain. In the meantime, his son, Amos, also came down with Typhus, and had a high temperature. After a few days, Amos recovered, but my brother became worse with each day. For the entire time I nursed the sick.

Your Brother is No Longer Alive

I remember as if it were today – it was Friday – my brother was in great pain and groaned vigorously. I couldn't relieve his pain, simply because I didn't have anything with what to do it. The landlord called me and Amos out of the cellar, and went to him himself. It wasn't long before he came out and said to me: "Your brother is no longer alive." How he murdered him, I don't know, because I didn't see it, but during the exhumation, which took place in Kozienice on the 11th of December, 1945, Mrs. Hese Honigshtok told me that the head had been severed from the body. From this it was obvious how my brother had been murdered. The murderer wanted to place the body in a sack and cast it into the Zagozdzshonka River. I sacrificed myself and Amos so that wouldn't happen. It cost money, strength and health, until we begged that he be buried in the cellar. We together dug a grave and buried him there in a white sheet. In this tragic way, the talented and beloved civil servant, my brother, Chaim Berman, perished. After he died, I remained with Amos in the cellar. It tore my heart to look upon the young man. We lay together upon his father's grave in the cellar, cuddled one against the other. We cry. Together we flood with our tears, the fresh grave and our resting place.

[Page 483]

Amos Flees to Warsaw

On the morrow, in the morning, my friend, Sabat, came to me. We come to the conclusion that we must seek a way to save the poor, orphaned, Amos. There is only one possibility: Send him to Warsaw. Because here it is terrible. I dressed Amos in his father's clothes, bought a ticket, gave him money, and with a broken heart sent the orphan to Warsaw. There he sought help from acquaintances, and relatives. According to what I was told, the Poles turned him over to the gendarmes and they shot him. We honor his memory!

Warning – Typhus!

After Amos' going away my landlady came down with Typhus and a very high temperature. I also got a temperature and couldn't walk around. The landlady was immediately taken to the hospital. I remained lying in the cellar, on my brother's grave. A few days later when my Typhus flared up, and I was lying in the cellar, without help and unconscious, a sanitary commission came, which consisted of a doctor, an assistant and representatives of the city council as well as gendarmes and Polish police. They came into the house, where I was hidden in the cellar. They disinfected the house, sealed it, and nailed a warning on the door: Warning – In this house there is Typhus!

Zelick, You Must Leave the Cellar

In this way I lay upon my brother's grave for a long time, all alone, until the day when my friend, Sabat, tore the warning off the door. He came to me in the cellar, looked around, stood still and could not speak, because I looked like a wild animal: bearded, dirty and almost unconscious. "Zelick" he said to me, "You must go out of the cellar. The situation is terrible. If you don't, we'll all perish." It was the Sabbath. With force he removed me from my brother's grave. I couldn't keep my head up. He said to me: I will change you, buy you a ticket, and tomorrow (Sunday) you travel to Warsaw.

I Travel to Demblin

On the morrow, he changed my clothes, cleaned me up, and brought me food, which I wasn't able to eat. At 6:00 p.m. they gave me a valise in my hand, in which they packed a few things. He went first and I followed. There was a great frost at the time. The earth was covered with snow. I approached the railroad, and I fall. I can't get up. I make a mighty effort and raise myself, so that passers–by will not recognize me. "Nu, come a bit faster", they shout to me from the distance. That way I went to the railroad station, sit down in a coach near a window and travel to Renkowitz. There I get up, go out and down the steps to the pump, and hide myself to keep from being recognized, and wait for the coach to Demblin. It doesn't take long and along comes a crowded coach. I push myself in among the passengers and we arrive in Demblin. The coach stops. All of the passengers get off. I remain for last. I can't get off with the valise. I don't have the strength. One of the passengers helped me. I stand in front of the station.

[Page 484]

A railroad official goes by. I approach him. I can barely utter a word. My feet are trembling. "Excuse me" I say. "Where is the waiting room for Poles." Meanwhile there comes a tall German official and asks him what I want. He answers him and tells him that I want to wait for the train to Warsaw. We all three together, go into the waiting room. The German goes in first, and we two remain. The railroad official takes me aside and asks me softly: "Are all of your documents in order?" "Why do you ask, sir?" – I say to him. The Polish official answers me quite calmly: "Yesterday was crazy. They killed a gendarme. Today many Gestapo people came and they are checking everyone's documents. On top of it all, you look awful." I don't hesitate too long and I say to him: "Sir, it's as you say. Please have pity on me and save my life. I'll pay you well. I have money with me." "But how?" he asks. "Hide me in a good spot until the train comes." "That I can't accomplish, but don't lose any time and come quickly with me. I'll show you where to wait until the coach comes."

The Coach To Warsaw Came

I sat that way on my valise and waited. It was a dark night. The great frost froze my hands to the valise. Two o'clock at night I heard footsteps. It's my savior, the conductor with his searchlight, tells me that the coach is already coming. "Come with me, I'll put you on the coach." We go together. He holds me under the arms, because he sees that I can't make it on my own, and leads me into the train. We say farewell to each other. I give him the money, but he doesn't want to take it. He tells me in a loud voice, so all can hear: "Have a safe trip. May God always protect you from evil!" The coach is filled with passengers – smugglers, who are carrying merchandise to Warsaw. I can't stand on my feet, and fall down. The passengers step on me. I shout and beg for mercy in the name of God: "Have pity on me. I'm sick." Until one of the passengers called out: "People, have God in your hearts. You're killing one of our sick people, on whom you are stepping. Move away from him a bit." The crowd moved away a bit, so that I was able to breathe freely. We rode to East Warsaw. There all the smugglers embarked. The coach emptied. I remained sitting with two elegant gentlemen, who asked me: "Where are you going?"

"To Warsaw", I answer. "You are already in Warsaw. Why don't you go out?" "I need the main station." I turn to the window and hide my face behind my scarf.

Stop You Are a Jew

At the main station in Warsaw, I take my valise, and go down. At the exit there are many Gestapo, gendarmes and Polish police. I go among the rows, give my ticket to the controller, and have safely passed through to the other side. My heart beats faster. I'm frightened of falling on the street. I go boldly, with my valise in my hand. Suddenly I'm seized by a Polish minor official from behind. "Stop, you're a Jew!" "What are you talking about? Me a Jew? You're mistaken" I tell him. "I'm sick, as you can see, and I came here to see Professor Pokzshevinski. I see that you want to earn some Zlotys. Take me to the doctor, and I'll pay you."

[Page 485]

But I wasn't able to get away from him, and on top of it he stuttered a bit, but I understood him perfectly well. He stated that for turning in a "Jew" he would get sugar from the Gestapo, plus a liter of whiskey and money. I gave him my money. I also gave him my valise and asked him to give it to my cousin, who lives nearby, at a false address. Looking at the valise, I got rid of him for a few minutes and used the opportunity and ran to Yerozolimske Alley, where acquaintances were hiding out.

I rang the bell and as soon as they opened the door for me, I fell and fainted away. I remained without any sign of life. The Polish family, as well as those who were hidden there, were very concerned: How will they dispose of my corpse. They therefore took care of me and I felt somewhat better. It didn't take long and the Polish family feuded with neighbors, who informed the Gestapo that they are hiding Jews and also a small, Jewish boy, Zigmunt. Unexpectedly the Gestapo came at night with Polish police. They undressed the Christian and checked to see that they weren't Jewish. A miracle occurred. They banged on all the walls but not on those where we were hidden. In this way, were five Jews and a child, who is today in Israel, saved from a certain death. From that area all Jews had to leave, so naturally I also had to seek a different hiding place.

Kalman Berman

I Meet My Wife

In 1942, when the situation in Warsaw, was very tense. At the hottest time, Mrs. Helena and her child traveled with me from the Viner train station to Vielkie Demby in the district of Minsk–Mazovyetzki. There I meet with my wife, who possesses Aryan documents, and my sister–in–law, Rachele and her four year old son, Avraham Tzigelman, who survived with his mother, and is in America as a practicing Psychiatrist. In Vielkie Dembi, by a Polish family, where the husband was a rail official, we stayed until the front approached Minsk–Mazoviyetzki. Then we went into the forest. The "Katyushas" banged from one side and the German military from the other side. I'm not in a situation to describe, how our liberation took place. Over 14 days we lay in the forest with the child, until we fell into the hands of the Russian Army, who protected us, and helped us with food until we came to Lublin. Holy be the memory of my children: Malka Chayale and Kalman Berman, my brother Chaim, wife Angie and two sons: Amos and Danek Berman. Also the family of Shaul, Rive, Tobe, Hershl, Yisroel, Sarale and Yehudis Rechtman.

[Page 486]

The Evacuation of the Kozienice Ghetto

by Shabbtai Bornstein, Ramat–Gan

The second of the Intermediate Days of the holiday of Succos, the 28th of September, 1942. Four o'clock in the morning the Ghetto was lit up. The sirens began to wail. This meant that we must prepare ourselves to leave our homes.

We Leave the Houses

SS murderers, Gestapo and Ukrainians with black uniforms and machine guns guarded the Ghetto. We received an order to leave our houses and go out on Targova Street, from Yisroel–Avraham Yoskovitsh's house up to Yisroel Shpigel's house, where the Ghetto ended. A Gestapo murderer ordered that we line up in a row, ten abreast, on one side of the street, near Yisroel Yitzhak Frish's house. With us we were able to take only what we could carry in our hands, up to 15 kilo (33 pounds). The outcry of the children and their parents cannot be described. They hold on to each other. They had talked it into us that we were being sent to forced labor, and that we wouldn't lack for anything. After we lined up by tens, the murderers began to choose from the line–up the healthy young men, and also skilled laborers such as shoemakers, tailors, bootmakers and other hand workers. Altogether they picked out about 120 people. Among them, my father, Moshe–Yitzhak Bornstein, the hat maker, who made caps for the German gendarmes. My father didn't want to remain with the 120, so he was beaten with a stick on the head and had no choice but to comply. We stood together, the whole family: my mother, my father, I and my two sisters. My–father. My father stepped out of line and took me along. I was 18 years old at the time.

The Evacuation Began

At nine o'clock in the morning, we began to leave the Ghetto. The way, along Lubliner Street, was long and hard. To the railroad it was about 2 kilometers. The murderers shot those who were unable to walk. Afterwards there came along some large wagons, and we put the old and the sick in them. By two o'clock in the afternoon, Kozienice was emptied of those nearest to us. The experiences of the 120, who remained, cannot be described with words. They left us to clean–up the Ghetto and carry out other work among the gendarmes and in the horse stalls. We would work daily until late at night. There were times when the Germans beat us soundly. In the meantime, Typhus broke out among the 120. The gendarmes got word of it, and ordered that a hospital be made of Mote Leibush Aaron's home. We brought the sick there, and at night the Germans came and shot them.

Rachel–Leah Vasserman was shot by the SS on the day of the evacuation to Treblinka, near the railroad. Her husband, Simcha, was shot by the Germans on the day of the Liberation.

[Page 487]

What Could We Accomplish?

We, the remaining 120 people, got an order to ride to the train and distribute water to the evacuees in the wagons. We were given a half–hour for this. What could we accomplish in a half–hour? A long train of wagons (cars). We handed up the water through the small windows. In the first cars they got water. Afterwards the murderers ordered us to halt the distribution. It was a hot day. They pushed the people into sealed cattle cars. Like animals they were pushed in. They took their shoes and baggage away. As soon as they closed the doors of the cars, there was a lack of air. After halting the water distribution, we returned to the Ghetto. They ordered us to move into a few houses situated between the houses of Issachar Shabazon and Veve Kdshemacher, on Targova Street.

Living Orphans

In the afternoon of the same day, the train traveled to Treblinka. We began to clean up the Ghetto. We went into the houses, carried out the furniture, bedding and other things, which people had accumulated over an entire lifetime. Poles came with wagons. The Germans permitted them to come into the Ghetto. Like robbers, they loaded everything onto the wagons. Our hearts cried for our huge destruction, which had befallen us. We remained in the Ghetto for two months, and worked for the German murderers, who wandered around and kept on looking, digging in the cellars and banging the walls. Every day they came to search in a different place. Poles sneaked into the Ghetto and searched on their own.

The End of December, 1942

We were almost finished with the work. We were notified by the gendarmerie that we were leaving the Ghetto. We went to Radom on foot. We were accompanied by Polish police from Kozienice. About 70 of us left Kozienice. A portion of this number were taken to the ammunition factory in Skarzshiska Kamienna.

The Bloody Road to Radom

The road to Radom was difficult and bloody. Our friend, Melech Urbach had bribed the police. 5 kilometers beyond Kozienice, after the Babya–Gura, he attempted to escape. A Polish policeman chased after him and shot him. Unfortunately, we had to bury him in the forest. We went on with trembling feet and pounding hearts. The distance is approximately 37 kilometers. To us it seemed a lot longer.

[Page 488]

In Shidlovtze

We slept in Radom overnight, and in the morning we were sent to Shidlovtze, where we found a new hell. Cold, hunger, a shortage of water, dirt and Typhus ruled there. People fell like flies, even though the Germans spread rumors that in Shidlovtze Ghetto Jews would be safe. We lived in a house together with other Kozieniceites. My father, Mo she–Yitzhak, and I were connected with an ammunition factory at Pionki, where our acquaintances and relatives worked, and we begged them to save us from the hell!

It Fell From Heaven

One day, two autos came from Pionki with Nachman Kaplan, and began choosing workers for the factory from among the few Kozieniceites. My father wanted me to go to Pionki, so a memory of our family would remain. I wanted my father to go with us. Unfortunately, he didn't want to go. He was a broken man. Finally I decided to go to Pionki. But they didn't want to take me. It was dusk, at the end of December, 1942. Cold and snow. The auto began to leave. I leaped up on the roof of the auto. I don't know from where I got so much courage and energy, at the time. On the roof, I got cold, so I tore open the canvas and fell inside. All became speechless. They thought that I had fallen from heaven. That was how I saved myself from the Shidlovtze hell, which two weeks later, in January, 1943, made Judenrein. At that time the remaining Jews from Kozienice, including my father, were sent to Treblinka. We also received information at the time that of the 120 Kozieniceites, no one remained alive.

In the Pionki ammunition factory, we Kozieniceites: Women, men, girls and boys, worked in construction work and unloading arms and ammunition. Conditions were not that good. We hoped that we would survive the evil time and be reunited with our nearest. We were there for a year and a half, until June 1944–, when the Russians approached the Vistula River, and we were sent to Auschwitz. In Auschwitz, I met my brother, Gershon, who had been sent there from Garbatka. From Auschwitz, I was sent to other death camps, until I was liberated by the Americans at Dachau on the 29th of April, 1945.

[Page 489]

Yosl Lederman and Yankl Fligelman

by Meir Zaltzman, Montreal

I take the opportunity to write about a tragic event concerning two Kozienice youngsters, who perished at the hands of the Nazi murderers. It is difficult for me to write, because, first of all, I'm not a writer, and secondly, while I write this I'm reliving it again. The whole scene appears before my eyes. During the somber evacuation, they took out of our city, a small portion of people and sent them to labor three miles from the city. A few weeks later they sent us to hard labor in Volanov. In the camp they sent me and 9 other Kozieniceites to work on barracks, which housed German soldiers. On a nice morning they ordered all ten of us to line up separately. They took us into the Inspector Robi, who commanded the German soldiers. He put his revolver on the table, and instead of asking us he promptly announced that since one barrack had burned down, while we were working on it, we will be shot during the next half hour. He called two policemen and ordered them to shoot us. While being led away to be shot, a miracle occurred. God didn't want us all to die, so the camp commander approached us. Before the war he had been a professional hangman (executioner). He asked the police where they were taking us. They told him everything.

He wanted to show the former murderer that he was boss, so he ordered us back to Robi. He came along with us and told Robi that he is not in charge of the Jews. He asked who of us had worked in the barracks that had burned. The two Kozienice heroes, Yosl Lederman and Yankl Fligelman stepped forward and said: "We were there alone, and no others." Their intention was to save the other eight of us. They were shot and we were chased to work. Their bodies lay a whole day unburied, for us to see. We looked upon the faces of our two dead friends. I'll never forget that scene.

May my words be a memorial, and may children and children's children remember our two quiet Kozienice heroes! We honor their memory!

[Page 490]

Frightful Days and Years

by Chaim–Meir Zaltzberg, Toronto

In 1938 the Polish Government began to regulate the Zagozdzshonka Stream, which flowed along the east side of the town and formed a natural boundary. On the opposite side, to the east, there no longer lived any Jews. There was the village, Staraviesh. As soon as it would get warm, and the snow and ice melted, the stream swelled its banks and flooded large areas.

The Huge Melyoratzie–Project

The bridge, which led to Demblin, became flooded, and many villages were cut off from the city. This flooding caused great damage to many people who lived near the stream. They had to leave their poor hovels and be put up with relatives. The situation changed when the regulatory work was done. The city no longer suffered from flooding. It meant that the project had been carried out, thanks to the efforts of the Seim (Polish Parliament), initiated by the Deputy from the Kozienice area. A similar project, but on a larger scale, was planned by the government in the area called "Povishle". Many years before the Vistula had flowed there. Surprisingly the largest river in Poland had changed it's course, leaving good fertile soil, and also large areas of swamps. The objective was to cut canals which would draw off the water, dry up the swamps and make the land fruitful. For this objective, outside laborers were brought in from an area of chronically high unemployment.

The few hundred workers, who were employed on this project, brought some life to the town. When the "Viplate" (payment) took place, they would appear on Radomer and Lubliner Streets, where they bought food and on Koshtshelne Street where they bought clothing, and Jews earned a livelihood from them.

In 1939, when the war broke out, the workers went home. In brief, the Polish Government also fell, and the work ceased. A larger number of German military settled in the city. The condition of Jews was poor. They knew what to expect from the so–called "Bearers of the Western culture." Jews were seized for all kinds of labor: Chopping wood, building barracks, grooming horses, etc. Jews were beaten very often. In spite of it, many had contacts with German soldiers, and they would daily come to work hoping to bring home a bread to their families. The majority of Jewish workers were unemployed and didn't have the means whereby to live. The production of shoes for export to Galicia ceased. Other industries, such as the manufacture of boards and glass works ceased to exist.

[Page 491]

The Two "Platzuvkes" (Work Places) at the Water

Nature was also cruel: It snowed a great deal, combined with sever frosts. In a word: 1940 was a severe winter for Kozienice Jews. The engineers from the two firms that had been carrying out the draining project, tried to convince the German authorities in Radom (the Germans didn't recognize the Kozienice authorities, and the district was administered from Radom) to authorize continuation of the project. Their attempt was crowned with success. The Jewish authorities received an order to provide workers. A notice was posted about the work, and the major condition: That an extra bread would be given! In spite of the low pay, many willingly volunteered. Every morning the workers would assemble, and a Jewish policeman would accompany them. This was the beginning of the two "platzuvkes" which was called by that name according to the engineers, who carried out the work: "Gortshitzki". I maintain that this gave a few hundred Kozienice Jews a chance to play the "lottery", whose big prize was surviving the war. For two years, a large number of Jews carried out the slave labor under horrible conditions: In water, hungry, fearful of the morrow. In the winter the work ceased for a few months.

The gendarmerie would make searches and take away a few potatoes, or a beet, etc. There were cases when they would shoot someone for no obvious offense. When I think of it there arises before me the puzzle: What interest did the Germans have in carrying out this project? It was only useful for the immediate region. Did they really believe that the area would remain a part of their imagined 1000 Year Reich, or was this but another way to torture Jews? In 1942, a few weeks before Succos the news spread that the end is near. Panic increased. People ran to sign up for labor. I was among them. A few days later the volunteers were assembled in the horse market, where about 20 horses and wagons were already waiting.

We Fool Ourselves

Representatives of the Jewish establishment and the German gendarmerie took us in the direction of the village of Vilke, where we were duped. Everything was carried out with German efficiency. Midway, two gendarmes ordered us to stand still. They had realized that they had let slip by the opportunity to rob a few Jews. They searched us thoroughly and whatsoever pleased them, they took. At dusk, we came to the place. It was an unfinished village schoolhouse, without windows, and doors, standing by itself. Here we had to accustom ourselves to a new life. It was already fall. When it did not rain, many of us slept out–of–doors. It was much worse when it rained: Everyone had to sleep on the floor, where there wasn't any room. After such a night, we would get up in the morning, barely managed to eat something, lined up, and marched a few kilometers to work. The overseers were a better class of gentiles. We were divided into groups of 10 and the work assigned accordingly. My group consisted of my relatives: My brother Yakl and cousins.

[Page 492]

Not once did we think to ourselves: This is how the Chalutzim worked in draining the Hula swamps (in Israel). I envied them. They had an objective, an ideal. My heart clamped with pain, that so many Jews are being forced to lend a hand in bettering the conditions of the Poles, who so readily cooperated with the Germans, in order to exterminate Jews. On Sundays the Polish overseers didn't work, so we also had a day off. Some would bathe; others made their beds, and some cooked outside.

The Terrifying News

Suddenly there was heard in the neighborhood the whistle of a locomotive. To Kozienice there ran a narrow track which existed thanks to the Jewish shoe workers, who had sent shoes to Galicia. On the morrow we found out that the deportation had taken place. A special train with many cars had carried away our dearest and most beloved to extermination, to Treblinka. That was on September 27, 1942. The second day of the Intermediate Days of Succos they perished. That was the tragic end of Kozienice's Jews. To this day the whistle of a locomotive and a train remains for me a nightmare. All were strongly affected by the horrifying news. Many collapsed. On the morrow all had to again get up, and march to work as "normal".

How I Saved Chantchele

A few days later, there came to us the rumor that in the women's camp there had been a selection and that those selected were to be sent away. Chanatchele, my sister's little daughter, was also among them. I, my brother, Yakl, and my cousins were beside ourselves. She was the only member of my eldest sister's family, Mirl and Yosef Zaltzberg, who had so far saved themselves. We decided that I should go see the architect, Taras. I told him, that I can't remain here, if they are going to send away my sister's child. He shrugged his shoulders. He cannot help at all. Then I offered him money.

He thought it over a while, and then he called out: "You know what, come in at 12 o'clock to the office. The cashier will be there." The cashier played the chief role in all transactions. I quickly ran back to my group and told them of the results of my interview. We worked on, pushing wheelbarrows full of mud, but our thoughts were concentrated on the bad news about the selection. The time passed very slowly. Finally the clock showed 11:45. My brother, Yakl, gave me a sign that it was time to go. All gave me encouragement.

[Page 493]

Soaking, I opened the door of the office, where there were to be found already the cashier and other officials, all Poles. I immediately announced why I had come. I was very surprised, when he told me that he knows. The architect, Taras, had told him about my money. I gave him the money, and he wrote out an order: "Chana Zaltzberg is immediately to be freed, and the Jewish police are to return her to the women's section". When he gave me the "document", he added: "See to it that this gets to the Jewish police, who are guarding the women, quickly." Encouraged by my success, I ran back to my group. I showed them the paper. We consulted about what to do next, and decided that I should take a shovel in my hand and remove my shirt, a sign that I work at the canal. All of the laborers worked almost nude, because we stood in water.

Armed with the "document", I ran swift as an arrow, along the canal, in the direction of the camp. It was approximately 4 kilometers. The entire way, I only thought about not being too late. I had no time to think about the danger that I myself was in, if a gendarme or some other German would meet me. Finally, I approached the camp. Here I met a boy named Shtecker. He worked in the kitchen. He told me that the gendarmerie is in the camp, in order to carry out the selection. I became fearful that maybe I was too late. With my heart pounding, I approached closer. I looked in and saw that there were no Germans. I went to the barracks where those who had been selected to be sent away were assembled. They were resigned to their fate. Unfortunately, I remember only a few names, which I want to enumerate: Gitele Zilberberg, Baile Korman, Esther Mandelboim, Angie Flam and her mother, Frimet Rappaport and others. I told my sister's little daughter, Chana, that I had come to take her out, and I went with her to the two Jewish policemen.

I showed them the note from the cashier. After reading it, they shook their heads and said that they couldn't free her, and they certainly can't take her back to the women's section. Meanwhile there came in a jeep, the camp commandant, Zolech, a Pole. I showed him the letter with the cashier's signature. He carefully read it and ordered: "Take her out of here!" We left hastily out of the camp and headed for the men's quarters. We were thoroughly afraid that some Germans might notice us. Finally we arrived. My brother and cousins were overjoyed to see that we had returned safely in the evening when we returned from labor, they didn't let us into the camp. They told us to wait outside the gate. We discovered that the gendarmerie were there, in order to remove women and men, who had been selected to be sent away.

[Page 494]

A Father with a Great Deal of Courage

Not far from us there was a former neighbor. He had been one of the wealthiest Jews in the city: Eliezer Itshe Zilberberg. He had heard that his little daughter, Gitele was among those who were to be sent away. Suddenly he said: "No, I won't allow my child to go out in the world alone!" Quickly he went to the headquarters of the camp and requested that he go along. His act made a strong impression on me. When I recall the incident, I come to the conclusion, that he was not only an outstandingly good father, but also a man of great courage!

In a few days we found out that all of the people, including the Jewish policemen who guarded them, had been sent to Zvolin.

We Are Taken to Skarzshiska

On a nice autumn day, the sun reflected brightly from the fluids which we drank. The warm weather revived us. The surrounding fields were already bare. The peasants had already harvested their grain. A light wind blew the falling leaves from the trees, which remained bare. The entire surrounding panorama bore witness to the fact that winter was coming. Suddenly our eyes darkened. A gendarme approached us and ordered to cease our labor and line up in a row. Yisroel Tenenboim's little boy did not line up quickly enough, so the representative of the "master–race" beat him mercilessly. His eyes glazed and he began to faint – this partially stilled his cries.

At the order of the gendarme, we went to the camp. On the way the gendarme noticed how a Jew was leaving the home of a peasant. He probably had been buying some food from the peasant. He drew his revolver and immediately shot the Jew for his terrible "crime". The one who was shot was Fritz Rozen, the husband of Dina, the son–in–law of Issachar Shabason from

Kuzmir. During the war, he and his family had come to Kozienice. In the courtyard of the camp they lined us up and again counted us. Suddenly a Jew stepped backwards and began running. The gendarmes and their helpers chased him. In a few moments they disappeared among the trees. A few shots were heard, and the Jew fell dead. He was a son of Mote Shvartzberg.

They gave us 10 minutes to take our possessions. In our great hurry and excitement we left more than half. A few months later, we would become aware of the fact that an undershirt or some other piece of clothing was an unreachable fortune.

[Page 495]

In four rows they led us to the main road, which was pitted, and there waited for us large transport trucks. During the two kilometer march to the main road, we were guarded by the Polish overseers. Many used this opportunity to flee. I remember a few of them: Yerachmiel Tepper Shalom Vasserman and others. The Polish overseers were helpless. They shouted: "Ya poviem!" which means: "I'll tell on you!" You can ask: "Where was there to run?" We were surrounded by enemies. Those, who ran away,.were afterwards, together with all the women, and a few tens of Jews who worked for the firm "Tsharnota", were taken to the Skarzshiska Concentration Camp. We passed through our city. This was a last chance to catch a glimpse of the place where we and also our parents, and grandparents had been born. With great longing and sorrow we looked at the Jewish houses and places of business, that stood empty and orphaned.

The Camp Volanov, A Second Babi–Yar

The camp was located about 10 kilometers from Radom and a few kilometers from Volanov. Here the Germans had confiscated from the peasants a very large area, and had set up a city of barracks for the military. A few kilometers further along was located the camp for Jews. At the entrance we saw a few large mass graves of Russian prisoners. They had died of hunger, or were shot for bringing a bit of water. In the camp itself, there was no water, even though there were wells at the surrounding homes of the peasants. For the guards it was sufficient excuse to shoot, when someone approached the fence. I want to answer the critics who ask: "Why didn't the Jews put up any resistance?" My answer is a typically Jewish one: "Why didn't the Russian prisoners put up any resistance?" They were actually starving to death. They were also only young military men. They would have also gotten more sympathy and help from the surrounding Polish population than we Jews. The Commandant of the camp was a German named Bartman – a murderer in the full sense of the word. He had a characteristic figure: very tall, with two cross eyes – one never knew where he was looking. He was dressed in civilian clothes, I would say Tyrol style. At all shootings and mass murders he played the leading role. At the head of the Jewish camp administration stood

Zygmunt Immerglick. With his strictness and use of force, he could be compared to the SS. He came from Radom. The Radomites said that he was actually from Cracow. He and his chief helper wore on their hats three and two stars.

A professional policeman wore a special hat with a red stripe and a pair of better boots. Their sidearms consisted of a rubber hose, which they often used. The official language was Polish. I wondered: "Why Polish?" Because the highest posts were held by the so–called Jewish "Intelligentsia", whose fathers were a bit wealthier and they were able to obtain more education. Or, maybe because the Polish language is so rich in banalities, which flowed so lightly from their tongues.

[Page 496]

Not once did I grit my teeth, when such a person would "sing out" about an upright Jewish woman, who had not lined up fast enough, or for being tardy in coming out of her barracks. I must say that we are an exceptional people, "chosen by You." In all the countries the Germans arrested the intellectuals, because they knew that the intellectuals are the kernel of resistance. Among us Jews, exactly the opposite: the intellectuals were the first to collaborate. In the Volanov Camp there were Jews from Volanov, Radom, Shidlovtze, and Kozienice. We lived in the worst barracks, worked at the most difficult labor. The firm "Vunderveter" was a very bad place to work. There they poured cement. The German overseers were a gang of criminals. They would beat us mercilessly. After a difficult day's work, when we returned to the camp, we had to line up in front of the kitchen and wait, because our privileged "goodhearted" Jewish women, who worked in the kitchen had not managed to have every thing cooked in time.

In 1943, there broke out an epidemic of Typhus in the Camp, and almost all Kozieniceites "danced at the wedding" (meaning they came down with the disease). We were afraid to inform that we were ill, because there had been a case, when all of the sick in the infirmary had been shot. Every morning, when they chased us out to work, the rows were filled with sick who had temperature, and could barely stand on their feet. I once worked next to Yakele Shpigel. He was burning up with fever, probably about 104– degrees, and was shoveling snow. A few other Kozieniceites died in the camp of natural causes. Among them were: Yoachil Huberman, Velvel Zaltzberg and Shmelke Rozentzveig. Half, about 60 men, died in the various executions.

A Frequent Appearance

Slaughters were a common occurrence in the camp, and were carried out in the camp itself. It was not so common in other camps. The first shooting which we experienced, was carried out against the patients of the so–called hospital. They told the sick to go out. The murderers stood at the door and shot. A few Kozieniceites were among those shot. Unfortunately, I remember the name of only one: Rachel Leah Vasserman. The second shooting that we experienced, was carried out against Jews who were removed from the small Ghetto at Shidlovtze, and had come to Volanov. The Germans employed a ruse. They proclaimed a few towns as Jewish towns, in order to fool Jews into leaving their hiding places. The Jews that were left in each town after the evacuations, to clean up the Jewish homes, saw in this a spark of hope that maybe they would allow this small remnant of Jews to remain there. Unfortunately, the disillusionment soon followed: All were led away to extinction. One of these towns was Shidlovtze. Twelve Jews, who had escaped the small Ghetto there, came to the camp, and among them were a few Kozieniceites, who went daily to labor. They didn't have any ration cards because they weren't registered. In this way they lived illegally for a few weeks.

The mass murders were carried out by a special group from Radom, which consisted of Ukrainians, may their names be blotted out!

[Page 497]

Two Kozienice Victims

There is a suspicion that one of our Jewish helpers reported to the authorities and I maintain that as a result, he is responsible for the deaths of Yakl Fligelman and Yoske Lederman, both from Kozienice, who were the victims of a false accusation that they had set fire to barracks number 117. Ten of us from Kozienice, and I among them worked on the "Plaza". We helped the bricklayers, who set up the clay kilns. So that the clay shouldn't freeze we heated small iron stoves. It often happened that a stove with live coals was brought into a second room. When we went to work and saw that a fire had broken out, we felt a bang on our hearts. Before we had a chance to turn back Bartman appeared and ordered us to follow him. He was our judge. In just a few moments he decreed the death penalty for Yakl Fligelman and Yoske Lederman: shooting for sabotage.

My brother, Yakl, and Meir Shalom Luxenburg, intervened with the Jewish authorities, thinking that perhaps they could do something to repeal the decree. The condemned were put in a wooden prison far from the sentry who guarded the camp. We would converse with them and comfort them. They knew that this was their end. The next day, as soon as we came back from work, we went immediately to see them. Unfortunately the chamber was empty.

In the autumn the largest mass murder took place. All was prepared in accordance with German efficiency. At two o'clock we were ordered to stop work and return to camp. We were lined up in rows. The murderer, Bartman, accompanied by the boorish Pole, Banak, made the selection. Those to whom he pointed with his finger, were separated. Some others went over to that group, because they didn't want to be separated from their brothers. I remember such a case with the Halbershtat brothers.

They ordered us to run into the barracks. The Ukrainian murderers, who had sprung up from the earth, opened fire on the second group, until all had fallen. The murderers ran among the victims, woorie that none should remain alive. The camp yard looked like a battlefield. Unfortunately I only remember the following names of those who were massacred: Chaim Berman's wife, Chana, and her young son; Moshe Goldtzveig; Issachar Frish; Moshe Fuks; Yoel Weinberg; Itshe–Meir and Hershl Weinberg; Eliezer and Hershl Halbershtat, Yisroel Lichtenshtein and many others.

A Miracle Took Place

Even so a miracle occurred – three Kozieniceites were saved from the Angel of Death's hands: Gedalya Lichtenshtein and M. Rappaport, two young men, who hid behind the barrels. Gedalya lives in Belgium and M. Rappaport in Israel. It cannot be understood how come the children didn't die of fright. The third one was Itzik Fuks. When the shooting started, he fell, and on top of him some of the dead. As soon as the murderers rode away, the Jewish police counted the dead. Suddenly they heard Itzik Fuks' voice. They asked him if he was alive. They helped him get up and brought him to the barracks. He wasn't even wounded, but covered with blood. With a weak voice he called out: "This must not be forgiven!" This scene I'll never forget. Unfortunately, he perished later in a different camp.

[Page 498]

How Mrs. Berman Perished

I want to mention an event which happened to the woman, Chana Berman. She was working once with other women shoveling snow, not far from "Yunakan–Camp". This was a work camp of young Poles, only men. They would wear uniforms and go home on leave. They were treated a lot better than were Jews. Their commandant was a Pole, named Banak, who went around dressed up as if he were a general. This boorish character would pass through when the Jewish women were working. He stopped and turned to Mrs. Berman, and with his boorish tongue said: "Come, I will have sexual intercourse with you!" She looked at him and said that she hadn't come here for that. At the big selection, this vile one pointed to Mrs. Berman and the murderer, Bartman, placed her on the left side. This meant annihilation.

Guests Visit Us

In spite of the intense week, we had a few guests from the "Aryan side". Tzeche Frilich came to see her father, Pinchas. She told us what was happening on the Goyish side. She had dyed her hair blond and obtained Aryan papers. I admired her for her courage and daring. Reizele Shvartzberg also came to see her father, Mote, and helped him a bit. Every word, which came out of her mouth we held on to with great eagerness. Another woman, Sarah–Leah, a sister of the woman, Starovshtshik, came to see her brothers, Yisroel and David Rozen, from Glovatshav, who were friends of my brother Yekl. We wondered how a woman with Semitic features could hide her identity with Aryan papers. She came to give regards to the Rozen brothers from five members of their family, who were in hiding. They were: Yakl Rozen, their father, and the brothers, Yehoshua, Yoel, Meir and the wife of Yisroel, Rachel. Also four members of the Eliezer Starovieshtshik family, his wife and her sister, Sarah–Leah.

Yakl Rozen knew a forest ranger, Tomashevski. He dealt with him. When the situation became unbearable, the family made an agreement with the forest ranger, and with his consent they came to the forest. He made a cave for them among thick woods and provided them with food. Understandably, the Goy was well paid. These Jews slowly settled in, and hoped to survive the war. After a few visits to the camp, Sarah-Leah went back to the cave. She related how the situation was in the camp.

The Horrible Death of the Rozens

A number of months passed, since the brothers Rozen last received regards from their hidden families. With great effort they located a Christian woman whom they trusted. They wrote a letter and sent it to the forest ranger. She was supposed to bring back a letter. Understandably, for her effort she was well paid. Days went by. The Rozens were very impatient. Each day seemed like a year. Finally the woman returned and brought tragic news. With tears in her eyes she told how one time, at night the forest ranger and his sons had placed straw on the door of the cave and set fire to it. They stood with guns so that no one could escape. One brother, Meir, succeeded in crawling out of the burning cave and ran.

[Page 499]

They chased him and shot him in the leg, but he escaped. He maintained himself in a neighboring village and healed his wound. A few days later peasants caught him and brought him to Soltis. He locked him in a chamber, and went to call the German gendarmerie. When the murderers came, they found him dead. He had cut his veins with a razor. Thus, alas, the prominent two families came to a tragic end. The Rozen brothers in our camp collapsed. We were also besides ourselves, because of the bitter news.

We Arrive At Strachovietz

In 1943, the building of the barrack came to an end. The liquidation of the camp began. The first group was sent to Radom, in the "Vitvurnie" (ammunition factory). That is how I parted from my brother Yakl. I never saw him again. He perished in Germany, in the Alach Camp, a branch of Dachau. A few months later the second group was removed. I was among them. We came to Strachovietz, where we worked at heavy industry. People told us that we had arrived in a Paradise, in comparison to what it had been previously. The commandant was a bandit, Altaf. He used to shoot Jews in the courtyard and the barracks. For him this was some kind of sport. The total of Kozienice people was about 20. Here we were called Volanover, because we had come from that camp. A few months later they took the remaining ones out of the Volanov Camp and ordered them to march. On the way they were driven along and beaten. They came to the Blizshin Camp where they were employed in a stone quarry. Life in Strachovietz Camp was like in all other camps.

They Shot Me in My Foot

I will here tell about an unusual accident which befell me. A Ukrainian shot me in my left leg. It happened while going home from the second shift in the factory. Because it was already dark they would take us back by truck. Since everyone could not be taken at one time, the truck would make a second trip to take the remainder. I saw how people were shoving to get into the truck quickly. The guards were "having a fling"; shouting and beating with the butts of their rifles. A friend remarked to me: "Chaim, we'll go on the second trip." We stepped aside. All of a sudden we heard a shot. The Jewish policeman came running and asked who had been hit. I wanted to take a step and felt heat in my leg. I was brought to the camp hospital. My cousin, Yakl Shapiro, and my good friends, the three Lenga brothers, were awaiting me. For eight weeks, I lay in the hospital. Too much medical help, I didn't get, but I didn't go to work, and the food was a bit better. The head of the hospital was a Jewish doctor from Starachovitz, a good, upright person. Unfortunately, I can't say this about the hospital aides. They were a privileged group, who had bought their positions for money.

[Page 500]

A Selection in the Hospital

One time, in the morning, I heard a commotion outside. When I looked out through the window, I saw that we were surrounded by armed Ukrainians. A bit later, the German administrator of the camp came in and a selection began. All of the sick people were driven out of the barracks and ordered to run. In the middle stood the boor. To whomever he pointed with his finger, his fate was sealed. The Ukrainians would immediately push him onto the truck. This procedure took place in each barrack separately. Then the fat German entered the hospital and commanded: "Everyone out!" The camp administrator questioned me, since I was first in the line of the sick, while the doctor and other hospital personnel were lined up on the other side. I yelled out: "I'm healthy!" And with that I stretched myself out like a string. He immediately went to the second one and made a motion with his hand; then to the third, and so on. In short, I was left all alone. The murderers had pushed all of the rest onto the truck. Among those from Kozienice, was one in particular called Huberman. He had injured a finger and went around with his hand bandaged, that's why he was in the hospital. He asked me to watch over his things. That same day, the murderers brought back the clothing of the victims to the camp warehouse. As to the question: "Why was I left behind?" I can give but one answer: "A miracle!"

I Flee to the Partisans

At the beginning of the summer of 1944, I, together with a group of Jews, escaped. Our goal was to join the Partisans. We were under the impression that all those who were fighting against Hitler were our friends. Without mishap we entered the forest and began making contacts. Alas! We discovered that here, too, we are Jews...no one wants us, and our lives are in danger even from the Partisans. We had experience with the A.K. (a Polish Partisan group) which was large and armed with British Sten guns. They were supported by the Polish Government–in–Exile in London, and possessed English pounds. The Poles were more occupied with killing Jews than with fighting the Germans. A second group, the N.S.Z., were also armed with British weapons. They collaborated with the Germans. Their main task was the killing of Jews. We succeeded in making contact with the so–called "friendly" group, B.C.H.A., a peasant party that was supported by Russia. Their leader heard us out and his answer was: "We don't take in Jews!" We were the oldest inhabitants in Starachovitzer Forest. Our numbers increased. Every Jew that we found in the forest and in the surrounding villages we took in. Larger Partisan groups would not remain for long in one place. We would intervene with every Partisan group to take us in. The answer was always a negative one. In the area was a Russian intelligence group. Among them was a pair of Jewish youths from the Lublin area. They were sincere Jews, who came to us, bringing news, and also giving us instruction. Once we became very excited. An armed messenger came to tell us that we were being summoned to headquarters where they will give us 10 weapons. Very cautiously, we followed the Goy.

[Page 501]

General Motshar Gives Us Ten Guns

Finally, we came to a large Partisan camp. Everyone wore Polish uniforms. These were units of A.L. (Armia Lyudova) also supported by Russia. A tall Pole came out, whose name was Motshar; the present well–known General in Warsaw. He spoke briefly to us, and then we were given ten rifles with two rounds of ammunition. Among us was a Galician Jew, a certain Meizlitsh, who had been an officer in the Austrian Army, and he became our military leader. He quickly organized a military drill for the Pole, in order to express gratitude. We marched past him and saluted. The bystanders accompanied us with shouts: "Moishy! Moishy!" We parted and went away to carry on with our own "kingdom". At the time we were overwhelmed by the noble treatment that we had received from the "staff." Later on we understood their intentions: We were stationed a few kilometers away from them. They gave us the weapons, so that we could serve as their advance–post. If the Germans attack, they'll hear the shooting and be able to flee in time. But there is a Jewish God in this world, and exactly the opposite occurred: The forest was surrounded and attacked from the other side, where the large Polish Partisan camp was located. Later we were attached to a different group of Partisans.

We Want to Cross Over to the Russians

The winter began, and the neighboring villages were inhabited by the German military. Survival in the forest became very difficult. The leadership decided that we should steal across to the other side which had been liberated by the combined Russian–Polish military forces. Not far from Sandomiezsh–Tzuzmir the Russians had crossed the Vistula River and occupied a small bridgehead. It was our goal to reach that point. We were separated from the front by 70 kilometers. For two nights we traveled in snow and cold. Finally we reached the German trenches. Because of a misunderstanding we failed.

The Germans opened fire on us. The Russians heard the shooting and thought that the Germans were going to attack, so they also began shooting, and we found ourselves in the middle. We quickly withdrew, suffering casualities. We wandered for a few days until we reached the forest. Two weeks later we again attempted to penetrate the front; this time led by a Georgian, Hatshek. We strayed, and when we reached the trenches, dawn was already beginning to break. We were uncertain, and didn't know what to do. Hatshek gave the order to advance, but he and his helpers, stayed behind.

[Page 502]

Understandably, no one moved from his place. We, the handful of Jews, took counsel about what to do, since we very well understood our situation. We decided to reach the nearest village where there lived a civilian population.

We went on our way. We noticed a large stand of straw in the middle of a field. I suggested that we hide ourselves in the straw, because it was risky to proceed during daylight. A few people agreed, and we went into the straw. The others went on their way. It just so happened that the snow covered our tracks.

A whole day military trucks passed to and from. This was actually at the front, and we were literally "in the lion's mouth". Suddenly, a wagon stopped. Somebody pushed aside a bit of straw. I noticed a woman. Seeing us, she also became frightened and said: "O la boga!" She went away, and we heard as she said to the Germans: "No, no potatoes!" Apparently, they were looking for potatoes. As soon as it got dark, we again set out in the direction of the forest. On the way, we learned that there had been a "hunt" (search) in the first village. Our fellow Jews and other Partisans fell into German hands, and all perished!

We tried a third time to cross the front. This time we were better organized. A portion of the underground leadership was also with us. We also had better information about the way, yet there was no lack of excitement. As dawn began to break, we already found ourselves on the other side. We sent out a reconnaissance patrol They returned with two Russian officers. Yakl Binshtok, from Shidlovtze, fell upon me and we kissed each other. "Chaim, we are free, free!" he said. We put aside our arms, and remained a few days with the army. They permitted us to use their bath, and we felt actually revived. A Polish officer arrived with a truck, and he took with him all Polish citizens to Lublin.

A Meeting In Lublin

The truck stopped on a beautiful, wide street. The officer entered an office to take care of the formalities. We were cold so we descended to warm ourselves. We eyed the passers–by with curiosity. Many looked like they were Jewish. I didn't have the boldness to stop anyone. Suddenly an elderly person approached. He was carrying a small package under his arm. He remained standing and looked at us. I screwed up my courage and asked if he were a Jew. "Yes," he answered and we began to converse. When he found out that I was from Kozienice, he pointed to the package, and said that he was bringing Kosher meat to Kozienice. "I don't remember his name, but I know that he had a movie theater in town," he said. "Oy, Zelick Berman!" I shouted. I asked him for a pencil and paper, and I wrote a few words to Zelick.

They conscripted all of us into the Polish Army, which was still fighting. After two weeks of intensive searching in various military units, Zelick Berman found me. I was besides myself with joy. I believe that the lines that I have written, will shed some light on that terrifying epoch, that Jews had lived through, during Hitler's occupation of Poland, and will serve as material for future historians.

ON OCTOBER 17, 1939, THE HITLERITE MURDERERS BURNED THE PONIATOVSKI PALACE IN KOZIENICE.

[Page 503]

The Seven Degrees of Hell Passed Over Me

by Yaakov Lahat (Likorman) Kibbutz Ein–Hamifratz

Jacob Lahat (Likerman)

When the Germans smashed through the Polish border, and advanced with lightning speed, I heard that a regiment of volunteers was forming in the Polish Army. This regiment was preparing to cross to the other side of the Visla River. Together with two other members of the "Hashomer Hatzair" (Leftist Zionist Youth Movement) we showed–up in the military camp, and received rifles and uniforms. With this army we retreated to the city of Kovel, and there the high command informed us that the war was over, and that we could return home. On the way home, at every place that we got to we heard: The Germans were here but they've retreated. This was a tactical retreat to the Visla River, in order not to meet up with the Red Army that had started advancing. After these difficulties, when I reached home, exhausted after three weeks, I had no desire to return again, meaning, to flee to Russia, as did many of the young people of our city.

The Conquest of the City by the Germans

As soon as they entered the city, the Germans rounded up all of the men (Jews and Poles) in the courtyard of the church, and there they detained them for a week. A month after the conquest they burned the two synagogues that were in the city, and shot at the Jews who wanted to save the Scrolls of the Torah. The seizures for forced labor also began immediately. The head of the community, a Zionist, fled to the Soviet Union. The new head, who volunteered for this job was: Moshe Bronshtein, a bachelor, who was also an active Zionist. It is possible that he volunteered to be the "Jewish–Elder", in order to make amends for the fleeing of the former chairman, and it is also possible that his motive from the start was a pure one. He reached an agreement with the local commander, and with the commander of the local gendarmerie, that the community provide 200 workers on a daily basis.

The Jewish–Elder informed the populace (5000 Jews), that each adult would work two days a week (the arrangement was according to streets). The Jews accepted this arrangement, and the "seizures" of workers ceased. And what did the labor consist of? Mostly it was degrading work for army units. Each unit received 10–20 Jews for "labor". There were units that used the Jews to clean up their area, to help in the kitchen or in the stables. But there were also units that abused the Jews: Had them carry piles of stones while running, or digging pits, etc. Understandably, sweeping of the streets in the summer, and snow removal in the winter were Jewish labors, and the payment – nothing! This was forced labor without pay, but there were military units that distributed work–clothes. It did happen that some workers made good connections, remained for an extended period, at his job, and succeeded in providing for his family. In the meantime the Judenraat issued work–cards on which were listed the complete labor obligations. As time passed, arrangements became such that the rich didn't go to work, and the poor labored in exchange (for them) for 2 kilo of bread.

[Page 504]

The Jewish Police

The Jewish police was organized at the instructions of the Germans. They were organized by the Judenraat, partly – from the youngsters "from good homes", a few burly fellows, and one – an informer, who was recommended by the German gendarmerie. A total of 12 men.

The Judenraat

At the outset the Judenraat was comprised of three men: "The Elder of the Jews" – Moshe Bronshtein, the secretary, who worked in the office and the Shamas (the Beadle). At the start the Judenraat did not interfere when, in place of a rich Jew, there appeared for labor a "hired worker" who had been paid. But, in time, they came to the conclusion that here was a source of income for the Judenraat, and they prohibited the substitutions. In other words: Either you appear for labor twice a week, by yourself, or else you pay the Judenraat, and they will send someone in your stead, because they know who needs the support. As time passed, this money was not enough, and the Judenraat began to levy taxes. At the beginning only a small amount from those who could afford, but they found a "patent" how to soak money. They sent the Shamas with a note which read as follows: "You are to appear on the following date (usually about a week later) with a shoulder pack and eating utensils," and the Shamas would add secretly: "Looks like you're being sent to camp."

Understandably, each one who could afford it, ran quickly to the Judenraat to request not to be sent, and this, in exchange for a large amount of money, with someone else sent to replace them. In some cases, no one else was sent and this became a clever way of extracting money. In such a case, when I would receive a notice "to appear with my backpack", I appeared, but most of the time I was sent back home or sent out to the "regular" labor. Once I was also in prison, because my father didn't pay the tax. They didn't replace the Elder of the Jews in our city. The Jews couldn't change him, and the gendarmes were pleased with him. The Jews didn't consider those active in the Judenraat as collaborators who oppressed us, but as a link between the inhabitants and the German rulers, who did their best to lighten the burden of "the evil decree". Once a new "type" appeared at the Judenraat. This was a German Jew who had arrived in our city. At first he supported himself by forced labor, but speedily, he became acquainted with the gendarmes, and became active in the Judenraat. The relations between him and the other members of the Judenraat were strained.

[Page 505]

The Ghetto

At the beginning of 1940 the Ghetto was enclosed, partly with a wall and partly with boards and wire. Understandably, the Jews who lived on streets not included in the Ghetto, were ordered to leave their dwellings and move to the Ghetto. My family moved to my aunt's house. Twice a week, I worked at forced labor, and four days I would go out of the Ghetto. I learned dental technology. There was no strict guarding of the Ghetto as yet, and it wasn't sealed hermetically. People would cross the boundary, but there was always an aspect of danger, that passing gendarmes would catch you. If a Jew was caught outside the Ghetto, he was ransomed with money. (The price always increased.) This matter would be dealt with by the Elder, since he was the only one who had contact with the German commandant.

All cultural and educational activities ceased. It was forbidden, and there was no auditorium in the Ghetto for such activities. As want increased the Judenraat set up a kitchen for the needy. The money for this was raised by increasing the tax on the rations permitted to Jews by the Germans. An incident occurred whereby a German soldier fell in love with a Jewish girl, and helped her and her family. Also a gendarme who was courting a Jewish girl, did not interfere with the slaughterhouse that had been set up in her home. A few Jews also became wealthy. Jews who succeeded in hiding merchandise, lived well. The peasants of the area needed clothing, shoes and even furniture, and the Jews needed food. For all sorts of merchandise, the peasants paid with food. Most of the inhabitants of the city became impoverished, but until the summer of 1942, when the Germans began to settle the Jews of the surrounding towns and villages in the Ghetto, there wasn't a case of death by starvation.

A Meeting with Mordecai Anelewitz

Before the war, there was in the city, a branch of the Hashomer Hatzair, consisting of about 70 members. In 1939 there was a summer camp of "Sons of the Desert", together with a branch from the south. I was one of the counselors in the camp, and when it ended I went to the "Central Camp for Counselors" in the Carpathians. Tusia Altman was a counselor, and Yosef Shamir lectured there. With the outbreak of the war, a portion of the adults fled to Russia, and a portion supported their families by smuggling skins from Radom. We would hold meetings from time to time and decided to continue to meet. We were about 10 seniors in the movement. Difficulties increased. One day (about a month before the convention in Warsaw), I was informed that a guest from the movement had arrived. This was Mordecai Anilewitz. I met him at the wagon driver who brought travelers from Kozienice to Radom and back (travel was illegal). He spoke to me as if he were my uncle and asked about my family. He told me to be careful.

[Page 506]

On the morrow we arranged a meeting of the senior group. Ten members appeared. Mordecai gave us news of what was happening in Palestine. He spoke lovingly of the Soviet Union, and gave us news of the progress of the war. At that time we still thought that the laborers would remain alive. He spoke about the establishment of two training farms, and suggested that we hoard arms. The purpose of his visit was to establish a bond with our branch of the movement, and to choose representatives to the governing body of the movement. We concluded that he would inform us when the council would meet. A few days later I received the following postcard from him in Polish: "My dear nephew! Aunt Council is interested in you, and wants you to come visit her at her place in two days time." I kept the post card, but it was lost in the concentration camp.

Relations Between Jews and Poles

It is to be understood that there were Poles who jumped into the homes left by Jews, but I don't recall too many instances of Poles informing on Jews, except one time when a Jewess wanted to sell her fur coat to a Polish woman, who was involved with a Polish Gendarme. It is difficult to say whether the woman actually informed or the gendarme obtained the information by chance. The Jewish woman was arrested and shot to death. (It was forbidden to keep fur coats). In spite of this, a Jewish woman, who had converted to Christianity before the war, continued to live among the Poles, did not come into the Ghetto, and no one informed on her!

Family Likverman

Camp Yedlana

On March 28, 1942, I was sent to Camp Yedlana. We were 30 young men from Kozienice who were there. It was not an enclosed camp. Altogether a few huts, unfenced. A German firm employed us. They were responsible for paving roads. First of all, we cleared roots that grew at the roadsides. The name of the firm was Paul Gatz. The food that we received was insufficient: about 350 grams of bread, margarine and a liter of soup, which one of us would cook. At the end of two weeks, when we saw that there was no freedom on the horizon, and there were no facilities at the place, such as: showers, and a change of clothing, I turned to the one in charge, and requested that he send us home for a day. "We'll both go", he said. "I'll bring food and clothing for all." (It was to be understood that he would get special pay for this.) The German agreed and even suggested that I conceal my yellow Star of David. We made the trip several times, about every two or three weeks. When I arrived home I would distribute letters that I had brought from the youngsters to their relatives, and at the end of a couple of hours, the relatives would bring packages of clothes and food. The packages were wrapped in two sacks, and each of us took a sack on his bicycle, and brought the packages to the camp.

[Page 507]

Once I was caught by the gendarmes at the exit of the Ghetto, but through the intervention of the German who was responsible for us, I was freed. I was in this camp for about two months. From there we were taken to a place further away, Krushina. There we worked for about eight months, until December of 1942. There were supply camps there of German firms who provided food for the German Army. The work was hard and the food insufficient, but we had the feeling that we were needed, and perhaps the war will come to an end?

The Expulsion from the Ghetto of Kozienice

Before Yom Kippur of 1942, rumors reached us that some thing was going to take place in the Ghetto. The number of shootings of Jews increased among those who had been going out to the villages to buy food. The number of those starving, and Typhus sickness increased, especially among the Jews who had been brought into the Ghetto from the surrounding towns and villages.

An organization called "A Drop of Milk" fed hungry Jewish children

I received permission from the German in charge of the work, to bring my parents and sisters to the camp. On the eve of Yom Kippur, I arrived with that German, on our bicycles, at our home, to bring back clothes food and letters, to my comrades. I tried to convince the parents to come to the camp, but they didn't want to. "What will happen to all Jews – will also be our fate!" The Jews of the city did not understand what fate awaited them. They thought that they would be exiled to distant places. There was no communication between the Ghetto and the outside world, and no news reached the Ghetto. I suggested to my parents that I remain with them, but they convinced me to return to the camp, where it would be best for me. Perhaps there the chances would be better. On this occasion, they told me that in case the Ghetto was eliminated, they will hide for me in the cellar, merchandise and a portion of the family jewels. On Succos, rumors reached us that the Ghetto had been eliminated. The mood in the camp was difficult. We were depressed!

I Traveled to Our City

A week later, I traveled with that German to our city to find out what had happened. Every trip of this nature was frought with danger. I didn't enter the Ghetto. Instead, I went to the dentist for whom I had worked before I had been sent away to the work in camp. When he saw me, accompanied by a stranger, he was frightened. He told me that the Jews had been sent out of the Ghetto by train, and he almost cried. I felt that something serious had occurred. He told me that 50 Jews had remained in the Ghetto, and that only Polish firemen were guarding Jewish property. It was forbidden to enter the Ghetto, but there was no permanent German garrison there.

I didn't hesitate for a moment, and "my" German and I went to the Ghetto. When I went through the gate, I saw a number of people on the street, but when they recognized me, they came towards me.

[Page 508]

They were surprised to see me since they thought that they were the only ones left alive. They didn't know to where the Jews had been sent, but the Germans had left them to gather up the possessions and straighten out the place. Most of them were skilled laborers, who had worked for the Germans, and some were the Jewish Police and their commander. The Germans had promised the police that they and their families would remain alive. But they too, were finally sent away with all Jews. The "Jewish Police" in that place, helped the Germans carry out the expulsion!

I went with the German to our house in the ghetto. Like all houses it was open and all possessions and furniture were in it. It had been searched and everything was disturbed and upset. At the moment that I came out of the cellar, a Jewish girl, Chaya Zucker, one of those who had remained in the Ghetto came running and urges us to flee immediately, because the Germans had been informed about us. We fled immediately, and as I found out later, a gendarme had actually come looking for me. At the exit of the Ghetto, a Polish fireman tried to stop us, but the German with me drew his gun and threatened.

I returned to the camp. There they were all waiting to hear from me. Later on, a young man who had been expelled from the Ghetto, returned and told how the people of the Ghetto had been sent to Treblinka, where they perished. He had escaped in a freight car loaded with clothing. The sorrow in camp was great. At that time the Germans who employed us, assured us that we were "necessary" and "useful", and therefore we were alive. In the meantime, there arrived in our camp, a group of girls from Radom. In all of the surrounding camps there were concentrated about 1000 Jews. At that time, we had already decided that if they should come to destroy us, we would resist forceably. But we had no arms!

The Elimination of the Camps

On December 18, 1942, the camps in Krushina and Bertudzia were eliminated. During work hours the gendarmes came and ordered us to put down our work tools, and return to camp. There we were told to sit on the ground with our arms folded. They led us, on foot to one of the camps in the area. We were strictly guarded. The supervisor of the action was an SS officer. The others were 3 or Gendarmes, Germans, Ukrainians, and Lithuanians. The supervisor chose about 30 to 40 strong young men. We were assembled in a large hut, while the 30 to 40 remained outside, under guard. The first 10 were ordered to proceed to a large pit at the edge of the city. Four Germans accompanied them. At the pit they were ordered to kneel! The young men felt it was the end and they attacked the Germans. The SS man and a young man fell into the pit. During the struggle the young men began to flee. Six of them were killed and four succeeded in fleeing to the forest. In that forest we were assembled by the Germans in a hut. All night we were crowded into it without food and water. The guards would not consent to bring us water.

[Page 509]

The next morning, everything was conducted with running, shouts, and beatings. Shots were also heard. Afterwards, it became clear to us what had occurred. The Germans took 10 men out of the hut to the trucks, and 10 others were run into the field where they were gunned down by machine guns as they were running. The wounded fell among the dead. I met some of the wounded a few days later. One of them told me: "The Germans screamed that we should run. We ran and we heard shots. I fell, and others fell on top of me. I lost consciousness. Only in the evening did I revive, and I saw the Poles pushing the bodies into pits." The Poles told me that Jews were still alive in Shidlovtza. Only after we saw a few of the wounded with bullet holes in their clothing did we believe their story.

Kozienicer Jews working under the supervision of Rembalski

Judenstadt Shidlovitz

Only after the action did the trucks with those who were saved, move. They were guarded by a few Ukrainians in each truck, who were armed with rifles. They began to threaten and demanded gold, jewels and watches. They removed our clothes and succeeded in robbing a great deal of loot. It was obvious that they had experience in this. In this way we arrived in Shidlovitz at the end of December, 1942. There had been a Ghetto there which had been evacuated. Now the Germans decided to set up a concentration camp for gathering the Jews who were still in the area. They called it "Judenstadt". We were about 500 Jews, the first in the place. There was no where to live. It was really a brick factory. Jews, whom we met, told us that everyone had to fend for himself. We received a daily ration of 100 grams of bread, 1 slice, and a liter of poor quality soup. Even this was hard to come by. Every day they brought in additional Jews. There were also Jews who had turned themselves in, because they were unable to continue hiding out. Others thought that they would be safer in "Judenstadt" than among the Poles. When I arrived there, I was broken and exhausted. Until then I thought that my labor was essential to the Germans, and that they would leave "productive" Jews alive. I was taken directly from my place of work, dressed in work clothes, and I had no other clothing to exchange for food. I was hungry and depressed.

My Girlfriend

While still in the previous camp, I had attached myself to a family that had a daughter my age. After losing my own family, I attached myself lovingly to that girl. We were saved in the same way – on the trucks and not in the field where Jews were shot. When we came to Shidlovitz, they sold some gold objects for food. The girl refused to eat unless they would feed me also, and in that way I became part of the family, even though it made it difficult for her. I didn't know how long we would live there, before I became aware of the fact that this was but a way station on the road to the death camp.

[Page 510]

I thought about what to do: To attach myself to those Jews who remained after the elimination of the Ghetto in the city of my birth? Or to go to the camp to remove the bottle with the jewels that I had buried in a secret place, and return to Shidlovitz in order to exchange them for food? Here we didn't work, and the days passed slowly, and the cold was unbearable. When I told my thoughts to my girlfriend, she didn't agree that I should go. She suggested that she go by train, since she didn't, look Jewish. She went in the morning, returned and brought half of the treasure that I had buried. On the way she also found out that her brother who had been among the first ten to rebel, and had fled from the pit, was still alive. This family had relatives in another camp. When they heard about the elimination of our camp and that we had been sent to Shidlovitz, they persuaded the Germans to send a truck, in order to bring additional Jews to their camp. When the truck appeared in Shidlovitz it was with difficulty, filled with Jews; among them, this family and myself. On the morrow another truck was sent to bring Jews from Shidlovitz, but it became obvious that the "Judenstadt" was surrounded by SS, and all of the Jews were sent to Treblinka. It turned out that ours was the last truck that left Shidlovitz for the camp. In this way I was saved, at the last minute. A few days later, I fell ill with Typhus, and was saved with difficulty.

Camp Pionki

On the 6th of January, 1943, we arrived at Pionki, at a gun–powder factory, that had existed there from the time of the Poles. They worked there in shifts. In the camp there were 4000 Jews. In addition to the Jews, 8000 Poles worked in the factory. The Poles were given the choice: To be sent for forced labor in Germany, or to remain there. The Poles went home every day, and received a small salary. We, the Jews, didn't receive any salary, only a bit of food. 250 grams of bread, 30 grams of jelly, and 2 liters of soup daily. The Germans, who supervised the work, were interested in having the work flow smoothly, and therefore it was comparatively quiet. The SS and Gestapo were hardly ever seen. As much as we were able to we slowed down production, we did (together with the Poles). But serious sabotage was not effected. It was clear to us that if the factory would be eliminated, so would we. In the camp, there were a Jewish doctor and nurse, a police official, and a few policemen. Afterwards there arrived the head of the community from my city, and he was appointed elder of the camp. (Obviously he had been recommended by the gendarmerie of Kozienice.) Because the production caused our clothing to wear out, due to the pollution, we received work clothes as we needed them.

The Attitude of the Poles

The attitude of the Poles towards the Jews, was, in general, good. We worked together and felt that we were in a similar situation with a common enemy.

[Page 511]

Besides which the Poles needed the Jewish skilled–workers, because after the elimination of the ghettos, there was a tremendous shortage of skilled–workers. The work in the factory lasted eight hours, and there was time for other work, which could be done for the Polish workers, who needed a coat or a pair of shoes. A Jewish skilled–worker would receive the work, and suggest that another Jew take his shift in his place for a fee. (The cost of a days work was 2 kilograms of bread.) Both would earn in this way and the Pole would get a coat or a new pair of shoes for money or food.

The supervisor of the factory, Captain Brandt, was quite liberal in his attitude towards Jews, and wasn't interested in oppressing them. At times, additional groups of Jews arrived at the camp. Once a group of girls from a bunker in the Warsaw Ghetto arrived. They told us about the revolt. But we did not believe them. How come the Germans let them live? Before we arrived at the camp, ten young men who had fallen ill with Typhus, were shot to death. When we, who were ill with Typhus (I among them) arrived at the camp, we didn't tell the Germans, otherwise they would have killed us also. After a week passed I had to be well in order to go to work. Understandably it was difficult for me to lift my legs. In order to produce gunpowder, we had to use spirits (alcohol). Because there was a lack of vodka, and the Poles couldn't live without it, there was a busy trade in alcohol. It was very dangerous. Anyone who was caught with alcohol in his possession, risked his life. The Germans were clever. From time to time they would poison the alcohol. The poison had no taste. Some of the group were seriously poisoned and lost their eyesight. After the Germans were informed they would take them out and shoot them, with everyone in camp looking on. Once two young men fled, and were caught by the Gestapo. They were brought back to the camp and hanged with everyone looking on. Once the camp guards caught me and 4 or 5 other men, and led us out to the forest. There they commanded us to dig a pit. I was witness to the shooting of 5 or 6 men who had attempted to flee the camp. I had difficulty controlling myself, and not to strike, with the shovel in my hand, one of the camp guards, named Hurkshutz, who was responsible for the killing. At age 21 it was difficult to exert self–control, and very often the action preceded the thought!

Partisans

Once partisans invaded the factory. Shots were exchanged between them and the Ukrainian police. It seems the action did not succeed and one of the partisans was killed. I noted that one of the Poles who worked with me, made contact with the partisans. Not once did a substitute come to replace him at work, and he was absent. I decided to negotiate with him about my participation, but the partisans weren't interested in Jews.

[Page 512]

In the summer of 1944, the partisans took a couple, doctors, out of our camp. Dr. Feldman was an M.D., and she a dentist. Today they live in Haifa. It seems that the partisans were interested in them.

Einsatz–Gruppen

Once a few Jews arrived to sleep over. They told that they are obliterating graves, together with Germans, who have maps, on which the locations are marked. They dig, remove the corpses, and burn them to remove all traces. I heard the words but didn't understand. With the approach of summer, 1944 there was felt depression among the Germans, combined with optimism among the Poles. About this period i wrote after the war. A copy is to be found in "Moreshet". Near the Pionki Camp there was a small separate camp, for a few families, shoemakers and tailors, who worked at their trades for the Germans, and had satisfactory conditions.

To Auschwitz

On the 9th of Av (Tisha B'Av), in 1944, we were sent to Auschwitz. In order to send the people, they dismantled a train of sugar. 30 men stayed behind to dismantle the factory and send the machines to Germany. For two days we traveled to Auschwitz. There they separated the men from the women. They led us to the washing facilities. Then they dressed us in prisoner uniforms. Two days later SS officers came and made a selection. Most of those from our camp were sent to camps in the area. About 200 men, and I, among them, were sent to a camp in Vienna.

At the Camp in Vienna

There were 12,000 people in this camp, from all of the conquered European countries, most of them Jews. All of them worked in the factory of I.G. Farben. Each morning we went out to work accompanied by an orchestra. At the gate of the camp we were counted by the "camp–elder" (a German prisoner, a sailor on a battleship, who had murdered his wife, and was sentenced to a labor–camp). Besides this head count, there was also a head count by the SS, who guarded the camp, that was surrounded by a double, electrified barbed–wire fence. In the camp were to be found Jews from different countries. Relations between Hungarian Jews and Polish Jews were bad. When the Hungarians came to Auschwitz, the Polish Jews were the Kapos, and they mistreated the Jews from Hungary. On the other hand, in the Vienna camp, the Kapos were mostly Hungarian Jews, who mistreated us, and so there was a vicious cycle of hatred.

An Escape

Escape from the camp was almost impossible, due to the electrified fence and the guard towers of the SS and watch dogs. In spite of this two non–Jews escaped to the outside from their work places.

[Page 513]

When we returned from work, and the head count indicated that 2 out of 200 were missing, the SS declared an alert. The two were found and hanged publicly. The "camp–elder" announced the short list of charges and verdict. After the hanging we all passed by the gallows. As I passed, I didn't think any enlightening thoughts, but only about when it would all finally end, and we would be allowed to go to our blockhouse to receive our soup ration. All thoughts and feelings were dulled by our experiences.

A Good Kapo

There was no lack of evil Kapos. In this camp the Gypsies distinguished themselves by their cruelty, even though their families were exterminated in Auschwitz; but they didn't know of this, or so it seems. When I arrived in the camp, I joined a work battalion. Then we no longer engaged in laying the cables, but in repairing them, after they were blown up in bombings. This was actually easier work. The battalion consisted of 300 workers, and in command of every 100 men – a Kapo. Our Kapo was called Kazik. A Greek said that he was an electrical engineer, a member of "Hashomer–Hatzair" from Poland. When I had the opportunity, I dared and asked him myself. He didn't answer me, but tried to help me at every opportunity. Everyone said about him, that he was a good Kapo. About the camp in Vienna, and the difficulties there, I wrote immediately after the war. I sent the manuscript to "Morasha".

The Hospital at the Camp in Vienna

After three months in the camp, my situation worsened. As opposed to the labor camps in Poland, where there was the possibility to be in contact with Poles, outside the camp, and to obtain additional food (either for doing work or out of pity). Here we had to live on the camp's "menu", and actually starved. I tried to steal potatoes from the kitchen, but I didn't succeed and my situation worsened. I was stricken with swelling of the feet, but I avoided going to the hospital, because I knew that once a week patients were chosen to be sent to the gas–chambers. Finally, there was no alternative. I wasn't able to go to work, and went to the hospital. The hospital consisted of a number of huts. The personnel consisted of prisoners; most of whom working there after their outside work, for an additional ration of food. Most of the nurses were doctors. The food there was somewhat better. For those who were not bedridden, there was the possibility to earn a bit more food for cleaning up the hut, or some other work. A tailor earned extra food for sewing up hats. A prisoner's cap with a hard lining served as the sign of a dandy.

A Meeting with a Member of the Underground

When I felt better, I volunteered to clean the hut, in order to obtain an additional portion of soup. Once I was sweeping and humming a Hebrew song, when one of the patients called me. I approached him, and immediately saw that he is one of the camp leaders for he had a kew tied to his hanky.

[Page 514]

In the camp everything personal was forbidden. Even a fork or a napkin. But in the framework of their duties or their position, some of the special prisoners had a key of a hut or of a cabinet, which they kept tied to their handkerchief. He asked me in German: "What song is that?" "A Hebrew song." "Where are you from?" "From Poland." He began to speak Polish. "Where did you learn the song?" "In the branch of the Zionist Organization." And then he asked me in Hebrew: "How are you getting along in the camp?" And then proclaimed that he was ready to help me. On the morrow he told me that there was mutual help here. A secret underground organization, whose aim it was to help with food, clothing, and work, for the young people, who hadn't yet lost their identity. The members of the underground consisted of youths from various youth organizations. He asked me if I know other youths from the movement. I knew only one, whom I had met, by accident, in the hut. He was a member of the movement from Yugoslavia. He asked me how I wanted him to help me: To change my block or my place of work? I told him that my major problem was that of alleviating my hunger, and maybe getting into a block without any problems, but at my place of work, I was prepared to remain.

He answered me: "First of all, remain for another week in the hospital, in order to gird your strength." It became clear to me that he wasn't at all ill. He had come here to rest up a bit, and to change his place of work (this was the only opportunity to switch from a worse work situation). The underground group obviously had someone on the inside who arranged work places. They actually let me remain in the hospital, and I received from him additional bread, and finally he told me that arrangements had been made to transfer me to a different block.

I'm Set Up In a Different Block

The block in which I had previously lived, was considered a bad one. The elder of the block, who also had the duty of distributing soup, would leave the thick soup at the bottom of the barrel, and sell it for cigarettes. As opposed to this, the block into which I was transferred, was supervised by an elderly Jew from Germany, a Communist. He didn't make any trouble, and the distribution of food by him, was fair. He would also receive from the kitchen more food and thicker soup. In other blocks the ladle would hold 3/4 of a liter, but his ladle held a full liter. Only someone who has been in a camp, can appreciate the significance of such a minor detail. The young man who helped me in the hospital (I don't know his name) instructed me to get in touch with a young man who worked in the clothes storeroom, and from him I would receive an additional portion of food. Several times I went after work to meet this young man, and he promised to arrange something. Once I came to him and he said to me: "Return to your block, and the elder of the block will call upon you to receive an additional portion of soup."

[Page 515]

And so it was! The elder called me, not by name, but by the number on my arm. He looked me over from head to toe, and said that I needed the additional portion. It was the custom in the block, that after the distribution of the food, about 20 of the young men would receive an additional 1/2 liter of soup. A while later the elder called me and proposed that I become the pot washer. This job enabled me to receive several liter of soup. When I got this job, I proposed that my Jugoslavian friend come to me every evening to receive a liter of soup. In that way I widened the circle of mutual help. By the way, to this day I've maintained mail correspondence with that friend. He's in Canada, and works as a Professor of Chemistry. He signs every letter with his name, and the number of his arm. As I continued to wander, I was able to meet him on several occasions, and more than once we helped each other out.

The Kept Boy

There were very few youths in the camp between the ages of 15–17. Mostly they were treated well by the Kapos. There were several Kapos who would keep one of the boys for his personal messenger and servant, in exchange for additional food, but occasionally this relationship had a criminally romantic character. It once happened that one of the 1200 prisoners was missing. They immediately stopped the work detail, to which the missing prisoner belonged, at the gate. It became clear that the missing one was the "Mkept boy" of this Kapo. No one knew to where he had disappeared. The SS went out with dogs to look for the "escapee". A few hours later they found him unconscious, crushed by stones. They brought him to the camp, and after reviving him, he told that the Kapo wanted to have sexual relations with him, and when he refused, the Kapo had stoned him. They arrested the Kapo, and he was beaten viciously. I don't know what finally happened to him. As the cold became more severe, there were cases of men electrocuting themselves on the electric fences, in order to put a final end to their suffering. More than once the SS fired upon them before he managed to commit suicide.

I Imagined the End

With the War Front approaching, the Germans decided to evacuate the camp, and on January 18, 1945, at dusk, we were ordered to assemble. The evacuation began. We left the camp, on foot, under the strict watchfulness of the SS. We were dressed in camp clothing and wooden shoes. 12,000 men, we marched, on foot, all night in the frost. As it got dark, people began to flee. We heard many shots. Shots from the front, shots fired at those fleeing, and also at those who lagged behind. I lagged behind, and two prisoners dragged me. I don't know who they were. I imagined the end. I was freezing from the frost. Colors jumped before my eyes. When we stopped, I fell asleep on the road.

[Page 516]

Towards morning, we came to a brick factory. Many feet were frozen, and dead were not lacking. All day we rested, and in the evening they again took us out on the road. Towards morning we reached Glayvitz. There were several camps there, and we were "encamped" in the camp of the prostitutes. (We knew this from the beautiful and colorful huts that they had.) I couldn't walk anymore, I found some grains of barley there, and sat myself in a corner, and ate them. I had no desire to continue on the road, but I was afraid to remain alone. When I heard that we were going to continue by train, and that we would be given half of a bread I got up. For two days we starved. We had just left the camp, and they immediately began to push us into the railroad cars. We were packed in without pity, about 120 men in every car.

We Traveled For Six Days

An endless journey began. We traveled for six days, by way of Sudetenland, to Buchenwald. They did indeed distribute soup, once a day, but it never reached us. We didn't have any food utensils, and only a few strong–armed men got it. We were thrown several loaves of bread, but even they were seized by the strong. Once the train stopped under a bridge in Czechoslovakia, where passing workers were going to a factory. The workers threw us their meals. There were those among them who threw us their meals, returned to the city to get more and then threw it to us again. The Germans shot at them, but they continued to throw us bread. Already the first night there were dead in the car. The "strong" ones piled three dead on top of each other, covered them with a blanket, and used them as a bench. There wasn't any Kapo in the car. The strong were always able to leave for themselves a "bench". They would also remove the clothing from the dead, and wear them so they would be warm. During these six days, no soup reached my mouth, and no water or bread. When I had entered the car, I had with me some grains of barley in my pocket, and in Czechoslovakia, I had caught a few pieces of bread, and I shared them with an old man who supported me in the car.

In Buchenwald We Were Disinfected

We arrived at Buchenwald. From the train station to the camp, approximately one kilometer, we were able to drag our feet only by supporting each other. 12,000 of us had left Vienna – and only 6,000 of us reached Buchenwald. In Buchenwald we were disinfected, and we received new identity numbers. (My number was 122,898.) These numbers we sewed onto our clothing (there had to be order in the camp).

[Page 517]

In Buchenwald we didn't work. Every day additional transports arrived, and the crowded conditions in the blocks increased. Several times we were inoculated against contagious diseases. Once they took us out to a quarry in the hills. It took a half–day walk to get there. Each one took a stone and we returned to the camp. It seems that on that day the Norwegians were freed from the camp, because the Red Cross was coming and the Germans did not want them to see the overcrowding in the blocks. When we returned we saw the empty blocks of the Norwegians. All of the time that I was in Buchenwald, I didn't shower (until the 5th of March), because the showers and the courtyards around the showers were filled with corpses, which they hadn't yet cremated. I succeeded in attaching myself to a group that went out to clear away the ruins in Weimar. I was happy because it made time pass quickly. Among the ruins I found a towel and pants, and also a bit of food. But it was finished quickly. The Goyim dogged the Jews and didn't permit us to go out to this work. My friend, the Jugoslavian, (who didn't resemble a Jew) continued to go out to this work, and used to bring me also a bit of food.

The Work Camp Bisingen

From time to time the Germans sought experts. Once my friend and I were registered as carpenters and on March 5, 1945, a few hundred prisoners were sent away from Buchenwald. We traveled. On the way we received 330 grams of bread, 50 grams of margarine, and 50 grams of sausage. Camp Bisingen was a small camp in a valley. All of the paths in the camp were raised about 1/2 a meter above ground, and were made of wood. It seems that in the winter there is no lack of mud here. There were few prisoners in the camp, but in the shower there was a pile of prisoners' clothing. What had happened to these prisoners? To where had they disappeared? We worked there at the production of oil and gasoline from bituminous coal. All together we were about 1000 men, Jews, Poles and Russians. On April 17, 1945, we were taken out of there.

In The Transports

We went out on foot. We wrapped our feet in rags. Our objective was: Dachau, but because of lack of space, we ended up in Allach. This was also a former camp. The food – the worse. We received 160 grams of bread a day. We didn't work and there was no routine there. There were a few incidents of cannibalism. The men were very hungry. In the camp there were a few cats and we set traps for them. The Germans found bodies with missing limbs. Then they set guards at the morgue. On April 24, 1945 they packed us into sealed cattle cars. We were in a hopeless state. Remnants of starved humans. In the cars we received 320 grams of bread and sausage. In every car there was an aged SS man. Since the train stopped at times in the fields, we descended to gather grass and eat it.

[Page 518]

American Tanks

We had no idea of what was going on in the world but we sensed that the end was near. On April 29, 1945 we received half of a package from the Red Cross. On the 30th we heard shots and the SS disappeared. We went out of the cars and there before our eyes: American tanks! Some of the prisoners seized Germans and beat them but the Americans prevented it. I'm incapable of describing the joy. Men went crazy. They searched for food. There was one car filled with food, and it was seized. My friends and I found cereal. The prisoners began to leave the train, and went off in the direction of the German village, Staltch. We came upon a coffee house, where the German proprietors fed the prisoners. We searched for a place to sleep. It wasn't easy since there were many freed prisoners like us, and the Germans had locked themselves in their homes. Finally we were successful. A door opened for us. A German doctor lived there. His entire family hid in the cellar, and we, the two of us took their bedroom. We couldn't sleep because of the excitement, or because of the soft mattresses – as compared to the floor of the cattle cars.

When I awoke, we washed and put on the German's clothes. We went out for a walk. The Americans had opened a kitchen and were distributing food. During the first days when we walked, we enjoyed the freedom. We passed through towns and villages. Once we arrived at a village and the German family invited us. We were told that they had also been refugees and their father was a Communist (who had been a prisoner in the camps). We decided to move in with them, in their attic. In the meantime it became known to us that in Feldafing the camp inmates are being gathered. We went there. Understandably, we wanted to make Aliyah to Palestine. Once we met a group of Jewish youth and thought about setting up an agricultural training camp. We went to Feldafing, registered and each of us received clothing and a place to live.

Feldafing

There had been at the place a resort for the "Hitler Youth", and now the Americans had converted it into a DP Camp. The commandant of the camp was an American major, a Jew. The food was sufficient but there was nothing to occupy people. My friend began to work for "UNRAA" because he was fluent in several languages, and I worked in a dental laboratory. We were there three months. Propagandists arrived at Feldafing at that time and I heard how one Russian explained the victory of Comrade Stalin over Hitler's army, and he convinced the man to return to his homeland.

How Is It Possible to Make Aliyah

One time soldiers of the Jewish Brigade appeared. This made a deep impression on us. A meeting was called and the Israeli soldier spoke Yiddish. He stood on the platform with his rifle in hand, and spoke with tears. He warned against traveling across the ocean and requested that we wait patiently for Aliyah.

[Page 519]

After the lecture, I approached him and I asked: "How is it possible to make Aliyah?" It became clear that it was impossible. It became known to us that in Italy there exists the possibility to make Aliyah, and so we decided to travel there at the earliest opportunity. My friend knew Italian. We went to a camp of Italians, who were returning to their homeland, and we joined them. We reached Italy; a village where my friend had been a prisoner before the Germans took him to Auschwitz. They welcomed him nicely, and even returned to him some of his personal belongings that had remained in the village. From there we traveled to Venice, because we had heard that soldiers of the Jewish Brigade were active there. When there was nothing moving in regards to Aliyah, my friend enrolled in the University. At the recommendation of Prof. Luzzato, they accepted him without any credentials, because he had none. I began to work for a dentist in Venice, and when we were informed about an agricultural training camp, I left for Milan, where I met, for the first time, the representative of the movement, Shlomo Vidoklah, who now lives in Kfar Masaryk. He suggested that I join the training camp in order to strengthen the group of Shomrim who were there. In June of 1946, I made aliyah to Palestine on the illegal boat "Vog'vod". We reached the nucleus at Gan Shmuel. during the time of the disturbances and the War of Independence, I served in an aid battalion in Gal–On, and when the war ended we completed Ein–Hamifratz.

The Rabbi, R'meir Zlotnick Was Murdered in Kozienice

by Avraham Caspi

To the Honorable Rabbi Judah Avidah,

I received your letter, and I am conveying to you what I know about the heroic death of your holy brother, Rabbi Meir Zlotnick of Glovatshov, may the Lord avenge his blood. Unfortunately, I am not gifted with literary ability, because I'm a farmer, and in general, I am not drawn to the pen, therefore I'll convey to you the details in simple, but tragic language.

And so, that bitter day, when our parents and relatives were taken to slaughter and strangulation in the gas–chambers, was during the intermediate days of the holiday of Succos. Unfortunately, I cannot recall the day exactly. I only remember that it was the eve of the last days of Succos, but if it was on Hoshanah–Rabbah or the day before, has escaped my memory. It seems to me that it was a Sunday. On that day we all stood together with all of the Jews of Kozienice, in the city square, in the midst of the Ghetto, where we had assembled at the order of the German murderers, and awaited our fate! Suddenly I heard the voice of the wife of our Rabbi, R' Meir Zlotnick addressing me: "Avremele, Avremele!" I turned my head to her and she told me that the Germans had killed the Rabbi, because he hadn't come out of his house on time!

After the Germans led all of the Jews to the death railroad cars – about 80 of us Jews remained in order to clear out the Ghetto, and bury the dead, who had been killed during the action. I avoided going to bury the dead, because I couldn't stand the sight of the atrocity, but the comrades, who participated in the burial of the martyrs, told me that the Rabbi had been buried in a common grave, together with all of th Jews (women, men and children), after the murderers did not permit his individual burial. I remembered the exact date, in spite of the fact that many misfortunes dogged me since then. To my great sorrow, I cannot convey to you additional details in regard to his life, because in the last few years before the war, I lived in Lodz, and only once a year did I visit my parents in Glovatchov. I want to point out that the Rabbi, Meir Zlotnick, was a dear Jew, a man of principle, and beloved by the entire congregation. I will point out, to his credit, that he was very close to the affairs of the Holy Land. He conducted in his home a Minyan (prayer quorum of 10 men) of "Lovers of Zion", who used to pray there on Sabbaths and Festivals, and they would pledge contributions to the Jewish National Fund and the Keren Hayesod. His room was also decorated with portraits of the leaders of the "Lovers of Zion", and maps and pictures from the Land of Israel. We must remember that at that period, the 30's, not all Rabbis agreed with him, and I mention this to his credit.

This is the story of the tragic death of one of the great Rabbis of Israel, our dear Rabbi, may the Lord avenge his death. May his soul be entwined with the souls of the living, and may he rest in peace on his resting place, Amen.

[Page 521]

As regards myself: I made Aliyah to Israel in 1948, after being imprisoned on Cyprus for about 20 months. I settled in the Moshav, Nordia, near Natanya. It is a cooperative Moshav, that is ideologically affiliated with the Herut Party. In 1951 I got married, and a daughter was born. I work in the orchards. Of all of my abundant family, only I and my two sisters remained alive. One went to the United States, and the other to Canada. My father, mother and two younger brothers, holy and pure, perished in the Holocaust. I was never privileged to know their final resting place and they weren't buried in a Jewish grave. Their bones are scattered with the bones of the hundreds of thousands of martyrs in the gigantic cemetery whose name is: The Diaspora!

Respectfully,
Your faithful servant,
Avraham Caspi,
Moshav Nordia, Natanya, Israel.

[Page 522]

This Is How the Jews of Kozienice Perished

by A. Rotkovsky

Already a very long time ago, Jews lived in Kozienice and enjoyed the right to sojourn there.

A Bit of Statistics

The first Polish document in which Jews are mentioned is an illustrated Protocol of the year 1611. It is indicated there that in Kozienice there are 2 houses owned by Jews and 2 rented ones. In them are to be found 5 proprietors, 10 rent collectors, 6 butchers and 6 distillers of whiskey. At the start of the 1700's the Jews of Kozienice were occupied with the slaughter of cattle, the selling of meat and also with distilling whiskey. In 1765 there were already 1365 Jews in Kozienice and the surrounding villages who paid the head tax. In 1856, there were 2885 inhabitants, of whom 1961 were Jews. In 1860 there were 1950 Jews out of a total population of 3000. According to the census of 1897 there were already 3700 Jews of a total population of 6882. Right before the outbreak of World War II there were about 5000 Jews, who were mainly handworkers. The majority of Jews made a living from the shoe industry, which sold it's products to the east.

Small business men and merchants were but a small percent of the Jewish population. They were also mostly connected to the shoe industry. Besides tjris there were in the city a brewery, a mill and 2 sawmills, whose proprietors were Jews. During the fighting in 1939, Kozienice was heavily bombed by the German Luftwaffe.

The railroad of Kozienice that took the Jews to the exterminating camp of Treblinka

Many Jewish Houses Were Destroyed

Better situated Jews left the city, and went to relatives in other cities. The census of Jews which was carried out at the orders of the Germans, by the local Judenraat in January, 1940, indicated that there were only 4,208 Jews living in the city. The material situation of the Jewish population, right from the beginning of the occupation, was very bad. They didn't have the means to live. Because of the shortage in raw material (leather), the shoemakers had to cease working, trade died out, and occupation forces requisitioned the larger Jewish enterprises. In addition the Hitlerites levied on the Jewish community a number of "contributions" (in money and goods). Until January, 1940, the Jews "contributed" 26,000 Zlotys of a total of 126,000 Zlotys. Besides this they had to provide, on a daily basis 300 unpaid workers to do forced labor.

[Page 523]

The Ghetto

The Ghetto was set up earlier than in other cities, in the winter of 1939–40. This was a so–called Mopen Ghetto". Because of the bombing and the shortage of apartments, the Nazis removed a few hundred Jewish families from the central streets and squeezed them into the already densely crowded Jewish quarters. In these unsanitary conditions (a few families to a room), there spread disease and epidemics. The greatest number of Jews died of hunger. Many would willingly go to the various German "points", because there they distributed a bit of hot soup and a piece of bread. During the heavy winter frosts, tattered, barefoot Jews, worked at various labor. Those who collapsed from frostbitten hands and feet were common.

The Camp in Yedlin

Besides this, the German authorities sent out of Kozienice about 150 young Jews to forced labor in Yedlin (about 20 kilometers from Kozienice). There they worked 12 hours a day building roads and railroad lines. From the work camp in Yedlin, two Jews once escaped at night. They came back to the Kozienice Ghetto and hid in one of the attics. At the orders of the Nazis, the Judenraat and the Jewish Police turned them over to the occupying forces. They were returned to Yedlin, and there in front of all, they were shot to death. They were buried in the field near Yedlin. This was to be a warning to the remaining Jews.

Twenty Jews Shot

One of the Jewish survivors of Kozienice, Yitzhak Eliyahu Pearlstein, recalls that on Yom Kippur, 1942, 20 religious Jews refused to go to work. The commandant of the camp brought the Gestapo from Kozienice and they shot the 20 contrary Jews.

13,000 Jews in the Ghetto of Kozienice

In the Kozienice Ghetto there lived about 4,000 Jews. A short while before the great deportation, they settled in the Ghetto a few thousand Jews from Magnushev, Glovatshev, Ritshival, Shetshechov, Volya Klashtorna and other communities. By August of 1942 there already lived in the Ghetto about 13,000 Jews. The Ghetto was hermetically sealed with barbed wire and guarded.

[Page 524]

The Selection

On the 27th of September, 1942 (it was Succos) all the Jews were driven out of their homes to an assembly point. A selection was made, and they were driven to the railroad cars which stood at the train station ramp. During the "action" the Nazis killed on the spot more than 100 Jews, in the hospital, in their homes or on the street. On that day two transports of Jews from Kozienice were carried off to the extermination camp at Treblinka (altogether about 12,000 people).

What Did The Clean–Up Commandos Tell?

The clean–up commando, which consisted of 70 young Jews, afterwards gathered the corpses from the streets and the hospital, loaded them on wagons and brought them to the Jewish cemetery, where they were buried in a common grave. For two weeks the commando gathered up and arranged the things in the abandoned Jewish homes. In one such home – Yitzhak Eliyahu Pearlstein tells – "we found a decomposing body of a woman. She was lying on a bed. She was probably shot by the Gestapo on Succos during the great selection."

Furniture, bedding, laundry, clothing, shoes and so forth were carried on trucks to a German warehouse on Koshtshelne and Radomer Streets. After checking, the better things were sent away, and the worse ones sold to the Folk–Germans and the populace of the surrounding villages. The Jews who were occupied with this work, were later sent to Dombruvke (5 kilometers from Kozienice), where they dug a canal. A short while later they were taken in a military vehicle to the camp "Hasag" in Skarzshisko.

Kozienice in Judenrein

The old Jewish city of Kozienice became Judenrein. The few still left alive, vegetated or died in the German labor–camps in Pionki, Blizshin, Starachovitz, Skarzshisko and Ostrovtze. A few of them went through the hell of Auschwitz and Buchenwald. Only a counted few lived to see liberation in 1945. All the remainder suffered a horrible death at the end of September, 1942 (Succos) in the gas chamber and crematoria of Treblinka!

[Page 525]

The Terrible Nightmare

by David Goldman, Brussels

Dedicated to my little sister, Rivkele, who was gassed at Treblinka at the age of 11).

Our community, which counted about 5000 souls, consisted mainly of poor laborers: shoemakers, tailors and shopkeepers. In general, our town was indistinguishable from the surrounding Jewish communities. Market day was every Thursday on Targova Street. The trading was lively. They would bargain over prices, and shake hands when they consummated a deal. All Jewish children learned in Heders and Talmud Torahs, and attended the Polish elementary school, where Polish and Jewish children learned together. A goodly percentage of Jewish children also attended the Middle–School. During my school years, I didn't encounter any discrimination on the part of Polish teachers. With a few anti–semitic exceptions, they were all tolerant. The Jewish students had their own religious teacher, Gendzel, a tall assimilated Jew, who was well educated. His wife taught religion to the Jewish girls. As a small boy, I was always impressed by the ceremony in school on the 3rd of May, in honor of the Polish Constitution. The Polish official and his assistants would come to the House of Study. The Rabbi, R' Ben–Zion, would recite a special blessing, and the Jewish musicians would play the Polish national anthem. The entire population, out of respect, would hold their breath.

Different Winds Began to Blow

Different winds began to blow, when the criminal, Hitler, came to power in Germany. The economic situation in Poland was never bright. Polish reactionaries were taken by Hitler's methods, and they began to boycott Jewish shopkeepers, picket Jewish establishments, and in general, persecute the Jewish populace economically and materially. At that time there grew in our town a wonderful group of young people. It is amazing that from the ranks of such a poor population, there could develop such an exceptional, lively and outstanding group of Jewish youth.

Political Parties

On our street there existed all of the Jewish Political Parties. Not one was lacking. Zionists from the extreme right and the extreme left and religious parties of all nuances. The "Bund" and it's youth organization "Tzukunft" and children's organization "Skif", with Yonah Weinberg at its head. Folkists of various types with Chaim Berman and Yisroei Shpiegel at the head. The illegal Communist Party with its large number of devoted and dedicated fighters, who suffered and rotted in prisons and in Kartuz–Bereze. A number of them had gone to Spain to fight against Franco's Facism, with a deep–rooted faith that they would bring redemption to mankind – they gave up their young bright lives. We even had an Independent Party with Pinchas Birnboim, the lame, at its head.

[Page 526]

Kozienice youth was ready to fight for its accomplishments, and not once did there break out fist fights between the parties. We had intellectuals, poets, writers, teachers, an intelligentsia and sports enthusiasts. There was even a group of pigeon catchers and other anti–social elements, who gave the town its color. I remember the natural beauty around the town. The romantic fields, woods and lakes. I don't believe that a sensitive person can forget the place, where he was born and raised, where he breathed the air of the pine forests, where we used to spend every Shabbat with father, mother, brother, sister and acquaintances.

The material and political situation caused many of my fellow townspeople to emigrate, and therefore we find Kozieniceites all over the world. I believe that in our special circumstances this is a positive development.

I Come Home

When the German bandits attacked Poland on the first of September, 1939, 1 worked in Warsaw. I immediately took the last bus to Kozienice, in order to be with my nearest and dearest during the tragedy, which was to be enacted. On the 7th and 8th of September Kozienice was bombed and 10 Jews were killed. On the 10th the Germans entered Kozienice. We could not imagine that this was the beginning of the greatest tragedy in our history. Within 3 to 4 days the Germans burned the Synagogue and the House of Study, desecrated the scrolls of the Torah, and began to seize Jews for the dirtiest and most difficult labors, while cutting Jewish beards mercilessly.

I Cannot Manage To Flee

A significant number of Kozieniceites (among them the writer of these lines) decided to take walking sticks in hand and go to Russia. A few, with luck, crossed the border. I didn't manage it. The Polish guide, who led me and 3 other Jews, among them the Veterinarian Doctor, Gonshor, were caught by a German patrol on the Pulaver Bridge. We decided to sleep overnight in Gnievashov at Leizer Vasserman and smuggle ourselves across the border on the morrow. When we arose the next morning, ready to go, the guide, with the money and the horse and wagon, disappeared. Dr. Gonshor, due to anxiety, committed suicide. It is characteristic that upper class Jews took the humiliations imposed by the Nazi beast very hard. I went back home. Together with my parents, brothers and sisters, I remained in Kozienice until the final "deportation" to Treblinka, on the 27th of September, 1942.

To our crowded Ghetto in Kozienice, there came 5000 more Jews from the surrounding area. It is difficult to describe the situation of this unfortunate mass of humanity. Other comrades will certainly write about Ghetto life and the dark epoch, and the fate of our 10,000 martyrs. On the 28th of September they were no longer alive.

[Page 527]

The son–in–law of the barber–surgeon, Bendler, was also in the transport with his wife and infant child. Two days later, with the aid of a miracle, he managed to flee to Vulka, where hundreds of Jewish workers remained as slaves of the Polish director, Gortshitzki. He told about how our flesh and blood perished. Kozienice townspeople, with pity and love, hold high for many generations, their shining memory!

Three Murders

Of all who died of the torture of hunger, typhus and shootings there is engraved on my memory three murders, which I will never forget. A small, 10 year old girl went out to take care of the needs of her family, by obtaining a few potatoes. The gendarme, Zomer, (an Austrian) hid himself in the grass, and when the child approached, with the sack on her skinny shoulders, the German "knight" of civilization sprang out of his hiding place, stopped the child and said to her: "Let go of your sack, and I'll help you carry it." When the child bent down, this depraved Nazi shot her in the head.

A Jewish tailor had finished up a suit for a Pole, who lived on the "sands". A Polish drunk saw this Jew outside of the Ghetto. He quickly ran to find an SS man, and asked him to give him the suit after he will shoot the tailor. The SS man, on his horse, chased the Jew and shot him. When the Pole asked for his reward, he received a kick in the rear and the German "bearer of culture" took the suit for himself.

One of the most horrendous murders, was the murder of four important Kozienice women, among them Mrs. Danziger, Mrs. Freilich and two others. At the homes of three of them the Germans found old, worthless fur coats. The fourth, a young, elegant woman, had crossed to the other side of the sidewalk, which was forbidden to Jews. For this the Germans dragged her screaming into the forest, raped and then murdered her.

I, personally, am very grateful to the dear friends: Abraham Tenenbaum, Moshe Rochman and Abraham Gutmacher for their noble initiative in seeking all the bodies of our tortured brothers, and bringing them to Jewish burial. They really deserve very high praise!

In Camp Vulka

As I indicated above, after the destruction of our city about 400 Jews remained alive in Camp Vulka. I was one of them. Since I was a tailor, I didn't go out to road work. I did tailoring for a peasant who was connected with the Polish administration of the camp. After three "Actions" no one remained in the camp. My group was sent to Volanov, another group to Pionki, in the munitions factory, and the last group suffered the fate of the city, and was sent in a transport to Treblinka.

[Page 528]

Through the window of my peasant's house, I saw the transport of the remaining comrades of Camp Vulka. My father–in–law's son attempted to flee. I saw how the German bandits pursued him and shot him in a neighboring courtyard. I won't tell of my personal situation from that moment, when I remained alone surrounded by a hostile environment: on one side – the Poles, and on the other – Germans.

With a few short strokes, I would like to relate several episodes from my life until that beautiful day, the 16th of January, 1945, when the Red Army liberated our town.

Thanks To Two Polish Peasants

On a night of October, 1942, I went to Camp Vulka. I remembered a righteous and sympathetic family of poor peasants, named Psherva, in the village of Loye, about 6 kilometers from Kozienice. I will never in my life forget the name. He, a poor carpenter, with a small parcel of land, had a wife, three daughters and an old mother. My surprise at the time, cannot be described. The family received me in a very friendly manner, considering that every Pole, who helped our unfortunate brothers, was murdered and had his possessions burned. This was a colossal gesture! In a second village, Kenfetshki, about 8 kilometers from Kozienice, I became acquainted with a peasant, Kraskevitsh. This peasant was even more poverty–stricken than the first. He had a wife and two children, and a bit of land. This "mentsh" had the soul of one of the "hidden 36" righteous men – thanks to whom the world continues to exist. (They are called "Lamed Vovniks – the two Hebrew letters, whose numerical value is 36). These two peasant families did everything which was possible and even impossible, for me, in order to help me. Many times they risked their lives for me.

There were dramatic moments, when I and my peasants were in great danger – sometimes during searches by the gendarmerie, and sometimes during visits from the Fascist, Polish A.K., but we were always lucky. I must mention the fact that not all of the Polish nation was poisoned with hatred towards us. Brotherly hands were extended to me during this terrifying epoch, and this was a positive sign that the world had not yet been so poisoned, as some elements would have us believe, and that there is still enough room for understanding among races and religions. I must also point out that I was poor, and couldn't repay my peasants for their gesture. After each danger, which we escaped, the old peasant woman went to church and beseeched God to spare my life. The most difficult time in my life was at the beginning of 1944, when the German beast under the assault of the Red Army, was forced to retreat. The general atmosphere became less strained. We began to feel the end of the enslavement.

[Page 529]

I Flee

On the 16 of June, 1944, the Soviets reached the other side of the Vistula River. It is difficult to describe my situation, when we already felt liberation and the defeat of our murderers. My peasant, krashkevitsh, lived on the left side of the Vistula. The Soviets reached the right side of the river. Many peasants crossed over in boats. My peasant dissuaded me from doing so, arguing that the Russians are coming anyway, in a day or two. Unfortunately, I listened to him, and the Russians didn't cross the Vistula. The Nazis, seeing that the Russians were remaining there, returned and occupied the entire area.

The situation became critical. The Germans dug in, and we remained actually right at the front. On a nice morning in July 1944, the military authorities ordered us to evacuate the area in 3 hours time. Anyone who remained would be shot. The confusion cannot be described. The peasants fled with their possessions.

As a Jew, it wasn't easy for me to leave my hiding place. Not all Poles were sympathetic to us. I leapt down from the barn and took my walking stick, together with an old peasant woman. To my great surprise, she recognized me immediately as a Jew, but she didn't react, and we went on together. We noticed that the young peasants are being checked. I cannot permit myself this luxury, so I, Bami of Keltz, Henyek from Lublin and Velvel of Bialobzsheg, run. The field–gendarme chased me. I run faster than he does. I threw everything away, in order to be able to run faster. He shoots at me, and I clamor up a thick branched tree. The German runs past, seizes a young Pole, and thinks that he had captured me. The Pole defends himself, and the Nazi drags him to the checkpoint. I remained on my tree till late at night. It rained and my despair is indescribable.

I descended from the tree. I decided to rest up in an abandoned ruin, and maybe I would find something to wear. The next evening, I was stopped by an armed Polish patrol of the folks–Army. And again luck! He takes me into a courtyard, where tens of Poles were gathered in a group. Among them, many were armed, and I got acquainted with them. They suggested that I go with them. They conveyed some good news to me – that I'm not the only Jew there. Yisroelke Burshtein and his sister are there. For me this was an exciting episode. For two years I hadn't seen a single Jew, and hadn't spoken a single Yiddish word. When we were finally able to break out of this terrible zone, I was together with the peasants for three or four days. One of my peasant acquaintances advised me to leave the group, because the commandant is cin anti–semite, I took his advice. Yisroelke Burshtein and Chavale also left the group later.

[Page 530]

A Sympathetic Meeting With the Russians

Wandering in the forest, I came upon a group of Russians, decent people who had escaped prison. We established friendly relations, and we lived together in bunkers, which they had prepared. The Russian soldiers treated me decently, and we lived together as a family. Once, one of them asked me, if I was curious to see Jews? The question seemed to me like asking someone hungry: "Would you like to eat something?"

We went together about three or four kilometers deeper into the forest. We came to a place, where among the trees there looked out frightened Jewish eyes. Among them was Godl Zaltzberg, the red haired. We kissed each other for joy. Godl was there with a few young men from Radom, who had fled from the Pionki Camp. My Russian looked upon this scene with sympathy and tears in his eyes. He agreed to take Godl along with us. We bade farewell to the Jews and went away to the Russians. During an "action" in the village of Augustove we met Yisroelke Burshtein and his sister and we brought them to our group. Yisroelke became sick. The Russians only wanted to deal with healthy ones, so they left us. In September of 1944 there came to our bunker a guest: one of my Russians with a 17 year old, unknown Jewish young man. His name was Velvl from Bialobzsheg. The Russian left the pleasant young man with us, and shaking my hand, he vanished forever. Velvl, a short young man, with clever Jewish eyes, was intelligent and dynamic. He wanted me to arrange a visit to his "palace", meaning his bunker. I went with him to Kotziolki, where he and three of his buddies had their "residence". It was a crowded grave, where a fifth person couldn't enter. We sealed a pact of friendship. My new friends wouldn't let me leave. We were four young men and one older man, about 50: Zshuk of Keltz; Henyek from Lublin Velvl from Bialobzsheg; Yitzhak from Shidlovtze and myself.

The Nightmare Comes To An End

We five experienced indescribable adventures during the autumn of 1944, until that wonderful day, the 16th of January, 1945, when the Russian Army entered our town of Kozienice. We were so deep in the forest and in the snows, that it was eight days later before we became aware of the fact that we were already free, drunk with joy, mixed with sadness, we went back to our town. The nightmare had come to an end. A Polish peasant took us, free of charge, from the forest to Kozienice.

[Page 531]

With the Soviet Commander

We decided to turn to the Russian military headquarters. The Soviet Army made a very strong impression upon us. I can still see the placards on the walls of my town with the familiar quote from Ilya Ehrenberg: "Death to the German Invaders!" We tread our first steps as free men. I trembled when I saw the place, where there had been such an intensive Jewish life. Now everything was destroyed, and leveled to the ground. I stood before my home and recited the Kaddish. The tall, young, Russian Commander, who received us, recognized us as bedraggled Jews, who couldn't speak Russian, and said to us in his language: "Wait, I'll put you in touch with the top Captain of the region". "Nu, I see that you don't know any Russian. You can speak mame–lashon (mother–tongue–Yiddish) to me. I'm a Jew, named Lerman, Captain Lerman!" Seeing before us a proud, fighting Jew, you can well imagine our feelings, after the hell which we had been through. We saw, that in spite of all tragedies – our Nation lives, and will live forever!

Let Us Eternalize

I want to memorialize for eternity in our Yizkor Book all of the Kozienice martyrs, who fell in the war against the bloody enemy. Our fellow townsmen participated in the uprising in the Warsaw Ghetto: The Shabasons and others. There were those who fought the enemy in the battalions of the red Army: Krishpel and others. There were those who were prepared to fight the enemy in the battalions of the Palestine Jewish Legion. Our fellow townsmen, doctors, offered their lives in Soviet hospitals, in order to save soldiers: Aaron Shpiegel and others. Our comrades carried out sabotage acts in the French Maquis, and under the most terrible of conditions in the death camps. My brother, Shmil–Leib, who was deported from Drancy to Auschwitz, was one of those who bombed the gas chambers in the extermination camp, and paid for it with his young life.

Armed with Jewish humanitarian traditions and strengthened with Jewish faith, surrounded by a populace, which for centuries had been raised on hate for our people, and without outside help, Kozienice Jews did everything (with small exceptions of those Judenraat members) to save the honor of our people. And if 90% of us were destroyed, the fault is that of a poisoned humanity, which fed with hate and enmity towards their neighbors. Among those most guilty were the German murderers and the deep superstition of the backward Polish population, who helped us so little. We, the Kozienice survivors, will learn a good lesson from the past. We are active and live all over the world. We have not perished. Our children will proudly carry our flag of Yiddishkeit and humanitarianism: forever and ever! I hope that in the Yizkor Book will be written the names of the martyrs, who perished and didn't leave a friend or a redeemer.

[Page 532]

Rachele Pesach's Twins

by Gershon Bornshtein, B'nai B'rak, Israel

The twin brothers Gershon and Abraham Borenstein

Who of our Kozieniceites did not know Rachele Pesach's Twins? When the dark, devilish war broke out, fate separated us. The heart of my Godly mother shrivelled and turned to stone, when she became aware of the fact that one son of the twins had been selected, and she didn't know wherejto. At that time over 60 Jews were shot in the Ghetto of Garbatke – a small town near Kozienice, where my wife came from– I will never forget that day. The SS gathered all of the men near Tartak, not far from the railroad station, and told them to lie down on the ground. They walked on our backs and we couldn't raise our heads. Finally they told us to stand up. With rope they tied our hands and ordered us to load ourselves into box cars headed for Auschwitz. Before we left Garbatke, they told the women to bring food for the men. Each woman brought the last piece of bread. The SS gathered the food in one place, poured benzine on it and burned it. We rode for a day and a night, without food or water. On the way the SS took aboard people who had been waiting. At the beginning no one knew where we were going. Only when the train stopped did we find out that we were in the great hell!

Life in Auschwitz is indescribable. I'll never forget the picture of children kissing the corpses of their shot parents, saturated with blood. A short while later the second of the twins was torn from my mother. From Radom he had been selected for a transport to Treblinka. My brother had tried while still on Dembliner Station to write a few words and requested that the Bornshtein family of Demblin receive it, since he is on his way to his death. He also requested that his brother, Abraham, tell about his fate to his parents, and his wife in Kozienice. When our devout, mother became aware of it, she collapsed, cried days and nights and shed streams full of tears. Together with all the others, our devout mother was tortured. Her hot tears dripped until her pained heart ceased to beat, and the tears ascended to heaven.

[Page 533]

We Will Never Forget It!

by Yerachmiel Perlstein, Melbourne

On the 2nd day of Succos, it will be 20 years since the Hitlerite murderers destroyed 5000 Jewish souls from our city of Kozienice. Our parents, brothers and sisters tragically perished from chlorine gas and lime, which the sadists released in the sealed boxcars. Right on the spot, small children and older people were asphyxiated. Whoever didn't perish in the boxcars, was gassed in the gas–chambers of Treblinka. On the second day of Succos, all of Jews of our city of Kozienice already knew that on the morrow their lives would end. Parents bade farewell to their children, and children parted from parents. Sisters and brothers shook hands, crying tragically: "Tomorrow, we go to our deaths!"

How frightening and tearful those tragic moments seemed to be. People tried to save their lives in Camp Vulka, in Pionki, in the munitions factory, but not everyone was successful in this. On the second day of Succos a battalion of Ukrainians, Polish Police, and SS surrounded the Ghetto and the City with machine guns. At 5:00 a.m. all of the sirens sounded. All of the Jews were assembled in the marketplace, at the intersection of Koscielna and Lublin Streets. The old and the sick, who were unable to walk, were immediately shot. Mrs. Kleinboim, who owned a manufacturing shop was immediately shot. Benjamin Frish, Moshe Feingold, Lazar Walberg and many others were shot in their homes by the mad, wild animals. How tragic was the procession to the train – on the 2nd day of Succos. All day, the Ukrainians and SS shot Jews. At the train station, they began throwing our brothers and sisters into the boxcars.

Doctor Arnold Abramowitz, beloved M.D. Of Kozienice. He and his wife committed suicide during the Nazi occupation

The well–known, Dr. Abramovitsh distributed tablets to his wife and two children and they all dropped dead – by suicide. Immediately the boxcars left for Treblinka. For tens of kilometers, the cries and screams of our tortured brothers could be heard! The memorial day of the 5000 Kozienice families, the tortured, gassed and cremated, should not be forgotten by Kozieniceites. Those who saved themselves from the death camps and prisons, and those, who saved their lives in the Soviet Union, need to remember what happened to our city of Kozienice. All Kozieniceites, all over the world, from France, the U.S.A., who organize memorial evenings – receive my hearty wishes and brotherly regards. Unfortunately, we in Australia, are so few that we can't even organize a society of townsmen and arrange a memorial evening, in order to eternalize the day of the 2nd of Succos – the memorial day of the Kozienice martyrs.

Dr. Neuman of Berlin – May He Be Remembered for Good!

The remnant of Kozienice Jews all over the world bow their heads and respectfully mention one of the righteous of the nations, Dr. Neuman of Berlin, commandant of the military hospital in Kozienice, who helped and cheered Jews in the blackest days of the Nazi occupation. We respect his memory!

[Page 534]

This Is How I Parted From Kozienice

by Abraham Goldfarb Recorded by Yehezkel Harpenes, Beer–Sheva, Israel

In Beer–Sheva, I'm the lone survivor of Kozienice. I was young, when those terrible days, the days of the Holocaust, destroyed the Jewish people.

Like a Leaf in the Depths of the Sea

I remained an orphan, alone and abandoned, like a leaf in the heart of seas. Suddenly I jumped from childhood to adolescence, without a transition period. I was robbed of the supervision of a father and the love of a mother. I had to stand on my own two feet, to protect myself from the wild beasts who stalked us. Against this trap, I fought in various ways, in order to obtain a piece of bread which my instinct for life demanded. Therefore, I don't remember the good days that had existed when I was pampered by my parents. The Holocaust erased from my heart the glorious days of my town, which I wanted to write about for future generations, in memory of the town of Kozienice.

Abishel – Where Are We Going?

Two Rabbis: R' Elimelech and R' Aaron, lived on Magitova Street, not far from the Maggid's House of Study, for whom the street was named. I remember, when my father, Moshe Goldfarb, of blessed memory, went to pray. He took me by the hand and the two of us turned to go to the House of Study of R' Elimelech, of blessed memory. "Abishel, where are we going, do you know?" "Yes, father, we are going to the Rebbe." "And what will you do there?" "Pray!" "Do you know how to pray?" "Yes!" – I answered definitely. "We'll hear!" "I thank you, O'Lord ..." "And that's all?" "No, I know more." "So let's hear!" "Sh'ma Yisroel ..." "Very nice! Listen, Abishel, after the prayers approach the Rebbe and kiss his hand and say Gut Shabbas!" "Good, father." "How will you say it" "Gut Shabaas." "Fine!"

I was Privileged to Receive a Pinch from the Rebbe

My father, of blessed memory, participated in the Rebbe's service. Only occasionally did he glance at me to see if I was standing at my place. Mostly, it wasn't necessary, since I didn't move from my spot, and my eyes did not leave the Rebbe. I watched his every movement. I saw him bow before his Maker, and I had no doubt that his voice was heard in Heaven, and his prayers accepted. After the service, among the congregation that went to greet the Rebbe, and receive his blessing, were I and my father. When we got near, my father pushed me closer, and I succeeded in approaching, and how fortunate I was, when I was privileged to receive from him a pinch on my cheek, and afterwards a gentle pat, as if it were a velvet glove, which electrified me.

[Page 535]

The visit to the Rebbe occurred mainly on Sabbaths and holidays, and not on weekdays. On weekdays, it was difficult to synchronize our hours with those of the Rebbe, since we couldn't prolong our prayers as he would, because we had to prepare our merchandise in the store early, especially on the market day and the day before. We had to open very early in order to catch the farmers with their produce that they brought for sale. In our store we sold kitchen utensils, stoneware and other things which farmers needed. You had to be equipped with speed, efficiency and sharp eyes, even in the back of your head. Therefore, on weekdays, father went to pray very early, in the large House of Study, so that he could be at market early. When I grew up, I realized that I had to help out in the store, because the net on market day provided a livelihood for all the days of the week.

The Conqueror Began to Tighten the Noose

The cruel Nazi conqueror captured our city in September, 1939, and immediately began to tighten the noose around our necks. My father, of blessed memory, was a Jew with earlocks, a long beard and a quiet character. He always prayed with the congregation, morning and evening, as I indicated above. In face of the persecution that came upon us, he was even more diligent about going to the House of Study, quoting the famous parable of Rabbi Akivah: "When we engage in the study of Torah – we are in great danger and afraid – how much more so, when we refrain from study!" This did not please the unclean minions of the Devil, and they seized my father and beat him mercilessly, in the German fashion. This repeated itself several times. My mother pleaded with him to cease going to the House of Study, and to pray at home, to avoid going out in the street where the Devil reigned. At first he refused to listen to her, but the beatings he received – convinced him. In the meantime the situation had worsened. The Germans began to visit Jewish homes, in order to seize Jews for forced labor, and they did not skip my father's house.

When he saw the situation worsening, he decided to disappear. He hid in the basement and the attic. But it was already too late! His strength weakened, and he suffered a heart attack, and didn't have the strength to withstand the torture and degradation. He was confined to bed and didn't leave it. He was privileged to die in his bed, and be buried in a Jewish grave, with the honors that were due him. This took place before that terrible day when we were all led like sheep to the slaughter. He died during Passover of the year 5702 (i.e. 1942), may the Lord avenge his blood!

What Was the Objective of the Transport

In the meantime, all of us were concentrated in the Ghetto. Approximately 5000 inhabitants of Kozienice and about 3000 Jews from the surrounding area. We lived under inhuman conditions. The noose tightened from day to day. A group of Jews were taken for forced labor in the village of Dombrovka, four kilometers from Kozienice.

[Page 536]

There we worked at digging a canal. Also my brothers: Chaim and Meir, worked there. During Succos of 5703 (i.e. 1942) the destroying squads entered the Ghetto. They were the Gestapo and their helpers – the Gendarmerie composed of the inhabitants of the city and the surrounding area, who had volunteered for this task to make sure that it was carried out properly. They surrounded the Ghetto from the outside, so that not a single Jew should escape. With threats and blows they fell upon all the inhabitants, with whips in their hands, and removed to the outside with hysterical cries saying: "All of you, out!" Also the Jewish Police, approximately 40 in number, had to orchestrate the evacuation, and stood us in rows, in order to organize the transport. What was the objective of the transport? About this there was disagreement. For many of us life had already become unbearable. The terror and degradation inflicted upon us by the cruel enemy and his helpers in the Ghetto had been too much. Slavery was the rule, and there was no release, therefore many preferred to go elsewhere and perhaps live better. Their final argument was that it couldn't possibly be worse. This was the opinion of many. Others argued that it was a pity to leave. Here they were born, here they had lived and here was the place to die. Therefore they must prevent leaving the place. Who knows where they want to take us? Without doubt, it'll be worse there! But no one was given a choice, although there was the possibility to flee for some. Some tried their luck at fleeing, and also succeeded!

Abishel Remain a Jew!

After the degrading work had been completed, and the transport stood ready to depart, the Nazis removed 60 young men, between the ages of 15 and 18, and I was also among them. I stood beside my mother and she held my hand, as if she were afraid that someone wants to steal me away from her. Suddenly I was plucked out of her hand by force. She screamed, and I, being carried far away, heard her call out: "Abishel, remain a Jew. For the sake of God, don't forget? A Jew! Don't forget to say Kaddish for your father." My older brothers were not on the transport. They were in Dombrovka. My unfortunate mother saw how I remained alone. I felt her sorrow and was also sorry for myself: How will I continue life on my own? But nothing helped us. We were separated. The Jews were marched to the railroad station. The Ghetto was emptied, and only about two hundred people remained; the sick and crippled, who weren't able to walk the kilometer and a half to the train were shot. At the train station they packed them into cars, like cattle, and took them to Treblinka. Sixty young men and forty policemen – we remained in the Ghetto for the meantime. Also in Dombrovka there remained a camp with several hundred inmates, who worked there at digging the canal, and among them my two brothers: Chaim and Meir. In the transport headed for Treblinka, were to be found my mother Chana, my sister, Pearl and her husband, Abraham Luxenbaum, their daughter, Leah, aged 4, and their 2 year old son, Shlomo, my sister, Tzipe, and her husband, Moshe. There they died with all the martyrs, may the Lord avenge!

[Page 537]

Our Neighbor, R' Moshe Leib

The same sentence was imposed also on our neighbor the dearest of men, R' Moshe Leib, who lived with us in the same house at 20 Lublin Street. He was modest, an exceptional man, fanatically religious a scholar diligent in his work and in giving charity. An easy-going man who was beloved by all. He was, in everyone's eyes – a symbol; clean-cut and generous. He managed a delicatessen, and made a fine living. He was knowledgeable about medicine, and many people believed in him more than they did in doctors, because of his righteousness, or perhaps they preferred him to a doctor, because he didn't charge a fee for his help. He would go to every sick person who called upon him, even to non-Jews, on the condition that he wasn't rewarded for coming. On the contrary, if the sick needed financial help, he would gladly contribute.

We were his neighbors, and saw and knew everything he did. There was no limit to our respect for him. He was childless, and he adopted an orphan brother and sister, and raised them. The adopted son, Yosef, was killed at home, and the sister remained living. Ihis man deserves to have an entire book written about him, but to my sorrow, I lack the talent to describe his outstanding character. He also died a martyr's death. May the Lord avenge his blood!

How I Was Saved

Those who remained in the Ghetto were destined to complete the "final solution" for the local Jews. As I had mentioned, about 200 of us unfortunates remained alive.

On the morrow, they took us to clean up the Ghetto. Our initial work was to take the dead and dying in wagons to the cemetery. Many of the dying were buried alive. On the cemetery we found a large pit, and there we buried the victims. Afterwards, began the cleaning up of the city, meaning, assembling the loot from our homes in a central spot, and classifying it. Even here we bore witness to the terrible Holocaust. With our own hands we emptied our homes, in order to make it easy for our despoilers to divide the loot which was the fruit of our parents' sweat. When I began writing, I apologized about the fact that I've forgotten many of the events, but one episode I cannot forget.

In the village of Vilke, near Kozienice, there were only folk Germans (Polish collaborators), may their names be blotted out, because they served as volunteer gendarmes. All were bloodthirsty, but more than the others, a young man named Zomer. He was a sadist, who lorded it over us with an iron fist. It was a pleasure for him to persecute someone. He killed, and there was no one to stop him. Once I was also caught in his trap, and I was but a footstep away from death. I'll tell about the event. Once I attempted to smuggle myself out of the Ghetto, not in order to flee, God forbid. Such a thought didn't even occur to me.

[Page 538]

To my misfortune, I fell into a trap and Zomer caught me. I knew that no one could save himself from him, and indeed, I didn't argue with him. When he took out his pistol to shoot me, who would say to him: "Don't do it!" But God's Providence accompanied me, and there appeared that faithful man, the man of influence and ability, Abraham Shabbazon (who now lives in Tel Aviv). He saw the tragedy that was about to be enacted, looked at the young man, whom he knew to be a dangerous killer, and ran to help me. He was quite a distance from us, and when he saw the murderer drawing his pistol and preparing to pull the trigger, he shouted at him: "Stop!" In this way I was saved by a savior angel. We give credit where credit is due!

My Last Station

When we finished our work in the Ghetto, we were sent to Dombrovka. There I met my two brothers Chaim and Meir. When the labor was completed in Dombrovka, my brother, Meir, and I, were sent to Skarzisko. In this incarnation we were parted from our brother, Chaim. There were approximately 5000 prisoners in this camp. We worked in munitions factory until the end of 1944 when our captors felt that the enemy was approaching, in order to "save" us from them, so they wouldn't, God forbid "harm" us, they transferred us to Tzenstochov. That was our last station as prisoners, and there we were liberated at the beginning of 1945. I don't want to expand on the troubles and suffering of that period, therefore I'll only tell of the destruction of my town of Kozienice.

I Return to Kozienice

Immediately after I was liberated, even as the danger of the war still hovered over us, I didn't hesitate at all, and set out for Kozienice. The family instinct didn't permit my not returning at once to "home", as if my mother were awaiting me impatiently to see me healthy and whole, and to embrace me and see if I had indeed remained a Jew as she had instructed me before we parted! I went on foot; who knows how many hundreds of kilometers. For three weeks I made a mighty effort to reach home quickly. On the way I met armies and caravans, and grabbed some food here and there.

I continued until I reached Kozienice, my destination, the city I longed for since the day I had left her. I imagined how I would enter my home and appear before my mother. My heart pounded as I reached Lublin Street, and how great was my disappointment, when I saw all of the houses before our house – destroyed. When I reached my family's dwelling, in place of meeting my mother, who would embrace me warmly, and press me to her heart, as I had imagined, I found an overturned ruin, dirty, cold and dark. A dark bitterness clamped at my heart, mourning and disappointment, so that I couldn't even cry. Only then did I feel like an abandoned plant in a desert, some kind of cast–off limb. The world darkened for me.

[Page 539]

I wandered among the ruins, visited the ruins of the large House of Study, and looked for the bench, upon which my father had sat, may his memory be blessed. I found everything broken. I went to the small House of Prayer (Shtibel). The same destruction! "Is it possible?" I asked myself. "Hadn't the Rabbis prayed with devotion, and their prayers had been accepted? Why then had this destruction come about?" I passed through a few more houses, in which I had played and spent time with my friends, who were my buddies, but I found no sign .of life. Only darkness and shadow, ruins as if goats had pranced there. I had the feeling that evil spirits were pursuing me. I didn't see or meet a Jew. I said to myself: "I'm alone in the world, woe unto me, the last Jew!"

On My Father's Grave

Afterwards I recalled, that I'm not completely alone. Isn't my father buried in the cemetery? I'll go to visit him! I went up, therefore, to the cemetery. After searching, I found his grave, and then my stone heart melted and the source of my tears in my eyes. At first I sat near the grave. Then I spread myself on top of it and burst into tears. My eyes poured out the tears. That was the first time that I had wet my father's grave with tears flowing for hours, until I had no strength to rise.

I remembered my mother's last words: "Remember, Avramele, remain a Jew! Don't forget to say the Kaddish for your father!" Indeed, if there is still a quorum (Minyan) of Jews, I thought, I'll manage some way to say the Kaddish for my father. But where are you, my mother? How can I recite the Kaddish for you? What have 1 here, and whom do I have in this cruel world? It is not worth living anymore. I decided to lie here, next to the grave, until death would come and take me to my father. But death did not come, and the instinct to live forced me to rise up and stand on my feet. I returned to the city. I saw that there was no point in wandering around aimlessly. I said: "Kozienice, the faithful city, has betrayed us, and expelled her Jews, who saturated her atmosphere with Torah, good works and charity. She has abandoned her holy inhabitants, under the treads of the feet of animals of prey! It is not worthwhile that a Jew should any longer tread upon this profane ground." "Pour out thy wrath upon the nations who have not known Thee, and upon the kingdoms who have not called upon Thy Name for they have devoured Jacob, and his glory they have laid waste!"

It is only a pity on the holy and pure souls, that have been buried and remain here!

I parted from them, therefore, with a broken and depressed heart, and I left Kozienice, with the intention of never, ever returning there again!

Our Fate Was Already Sealed

by Abraham Shabason

Hunger and sickness reign in the Ghetto. In order to alleviate the situation, we organize a food kitchen and a hospital. The kitchen distributes hot meals and bread, daily!

I take over the supervision of the kitchen. I organize the personnel, consisting of capable people. Oewish police take care of the order. The work of the hospital is carried on under the supervision of Dr. Abramovitsh, and the head nurse is Salke Bendler. The situation worsened. I, Hershel Popyelnick and Leibel Fleisher provide the needy with wood, in order to heat their freezing homes. The help is but a drop in the ocean of need, hunger and sickness. The end of 1941 and beginning of 1942 were the most difficult months. The epidemics spread. The hungry were swollen, and were to be found everywhere. Those better off tried with their failing strength, to improve things, but what could they do? In 1942 the Germans brought to Kozienice the Jews from Magnishev, Ritshivol, and other towns. For a few days they were kept in Kozienice and then sent away. I spoke to the head of the Magnishev community. He told me that they are being sent to forced labor, but he didn't know exactly where. We handsomely bribed a Pole to find out for us where they were being sent, but unfortunately he returned without any information. He told us that after a day of traveling on the train, they were taken to a forest, but what happened to them there, he didn't know. Obviously this was already the death–camp at Treblinka, which had been prepared. At the time, we didn't know about it yet. This was the eve of Rosh Hashanah, 1942. The Hitlerites had brought to Kozienice all of the Jews from the surrounding towns and villages. We could see that the end was approaching. "On Rosh Hashanah it is inscribed; and on Yom Kippur, it is sealed!" Our fate was already sealed. On the eve of Yom Kippur, we already knew, that at the railroad station in Kozienice, the boxcars stand ready. Fear is on every face. Wild running in the streets. We prayed the Kol Nidre prayer with broken hearts. "Why, O'Lord, has this come upon us? Why and for what?"

At the headquarters there is a final meeting. The murderers demand a huge sum of money, obviously fare for the boxcars, which are waiting for us. We decide to go from house to house to gather up the amount. We divide into groups. I'm in the group with Hershl Perl. On Yom Kippur at dusk, we brought the murderers the agreed upon sum of money. No one sleeps. All are awake. Each one is sitting on his pack, ready for the final journey. On the first of the intermediate days of Succos, the sirens sound, from the city towers. The Ghetto is already surrounded. At each end stand armed German killers. Polish hooligans help them. The murderers show up in the Ghetto. They run from house to house. Whoever had not left his house is shot. In a few short hours all of Kozienice is already loaded into the boxcars!

[Page 541]

It's Hell In Life

by Gershon Bornshtein, Bnai–Brak, Israel

Gershon Borenstein

In September, 1939, the sky of Polish Jewry became darkened with black clouds. Which one of our families did not suffer this dark Hell? Only a select few, by a miracle, survived. None of the survivors can believe it.

My Father and Mother Perished

My father perished in Skarzshisko, where they quarantined a select group of skilled workers from Kozienice, to serve the Germans. By trade, my father was a cap–maker. He was called Moshe–Yitzhak Bornshtein, the tailor, Pesach's, son–in–law. My mother and my two sisters – Sarahle and Feigele – were selected, together with all Kozieniceites on the first day of Succos in 1942. In sealed box–cars, on a floor, disinfected with lime, they were deported. During the action their shoes were taken from them. Their cries reached up to heaven, when they were taken to Treblinka. My twin–brother, Abraham, was killed by the Nazi murderers, shortly before the evacuation. Of seven men in the family, two survived: Shabtai Bornshtein and myself, the remaining twin.

Hell in Garbatke

I was married in Garbatke, 14 kilometers from my birthplace, Kozienice. With my wife, Rochtshe Weisbart, and our only child, Sarahle, we lived in Garbatke, outside the Ghetto. Our hearts cried bitterly, longing for our families. But there was the threat that anyone who tried to enter the Ghetto would be shot. With an acquaintance, a Christian, I let my twin brother know that I wanted to come to Kozienice, to see my parents and brothers and sisters, for whom my heart yearned. My brother, Abraham, managed to contact a policeman from Kozienice, and they concocted a plan whereby a fictitious document would state that Gershon Bornshtein is needed in connection with the solving of a police case in Kozienice. For a handsome reward the policeman came to Garbatke and received from the commandant a permit to take me into Kozienice for the investigation. I made an agreement with my friend Sumer Pearlshtein, who lived in Garbatke, and had family in Kozienice, that he would accompany me. He agreed to this happily, and shared the expense, which was involved in this undertaking. On a lovely morning the policeman appeared with the necessary formalities, shook hands with my friend and myself, and took us to Kozienice. Everything according to plan!

I Want To Save My Child

The joy of my parents cannot be described. With tears and joy we conversed. The main reason for my coming was to turn over my only child to Christians. No one, at the time under the difficult conditions could forsee that it would be possible to hide. Besides this, my brother made an arrangement with a Christian, Oleshkevitsh, the former chimney–sweeper, with whom we had gone to school.

[Page 542]

Who wasn't acquainted with the city's chimney–sweeper and I gave that Christian my furniture, two new machines, all of my wardrobe and a sum of money. In this way did my wife and I decide to give our innocent child into the strange, Goyish hands. Shedding many tears, I parted from my parents, sisters and brothers, and also from my grandfather, Pesach Mandl, who cried bitterly into his beard, which the Germans had sheared off together with a piece of skin from his jaw. This caused him much sorrow. I will never forget his words: "I have no longer anything to live for. I want to die, because my beard was my adornment!" He took it very much to heart, until his holy, pure soul left his body a short while later, at age 75. He died in his own bed and in his own home. This was a great privilege during the time of the German occupation.

We Hear Shooting

On the way back to Garbatke, after sunrise, we heard, in the distance footbeats. With trembling and beating hearts, we lay down on the ground, in the forest, and listened carefully. The policeman suddenly, as if in water, disappeared, saying: "Go slowly! It's already not far to Garbatke. I am following you." When we neared the town, we heard, from time to time, the echo of shooting. I and my friend Sumer Pearlshtein, had decided to enter Garbatke. We parted, and each of us went to his own home. The few hundred meters to our homes was not an easy task. When I entered my house, my wife and child burst out crying, and told me that they were expecting an "action." I managed to calm them. Unfortunately it was true. The shooting came closer. This was proof that we were lost. A few minutes later, I heard wild knocking on our neighbor's door. He was Shalom Hoffman, by trade a boot–maker. "Open up! That's an order!" When he opened the door, two German's ordered him to show them where Jews lived, according to various addresses. An hour later we learned that he was lying, shot, not far from his home. When his wife and children learned this, they pulled the hair from their heads, because they couldn't cry.

The Jewish police of the Ghetto took him away to the small woods. No one of his family took part in his burial. In the same woods there was already buried a Kozienicer teacher, black Hava's son–in–law. The Germans had found him outside of the Ghetto, near Garbatke, where he would come from time to time to ask for help. He was also found shot. On the new cemetery there was already buried a certain Simcha Flamenboim, who had been shot near his home, because the German thought that he was wandering about outside the Ghetto. In fact he was at the Ghetto boundary. After a great deal of effort and for a goodly sum, the local Christians permitted him to be buried on the spot since the cemetery was in Kozienice, and how was it at all possible at that time to carry a corpse!

[Page 543]

The Germans Shot 80 Jews

The same morning in July, 1942, there came an order for all Jews to gather in a specific place, and that all Jews found in hiding would be shot. When all already stood in one row, all males and females up to age 14 were stood aside in one place. All of the older men were taken to the sawmill near the train station. At the same time they searched every house and the surrounding fields. Over 80 Jews, elderly and young and also sick, were shot on that day by the Germans.

The Gestapo Stomped on Our Shoulders

It was bitter and difficult to part with our children and families. The murderers didn't permit us to say farewell. When the small children stole over, to kiss their fathers. The SS man would beat the child. Till we were transported, we were forced to lie in rows, with our faces to the ground, and the SS men and Gestapo stomped on our backs. With each passing minute, we awaited the sound of machine gun fire. When the Jewish Police intervened in order to obtain a bit of water and piece of bread for us, they received the reply: "Not necessary, and too bad!" But in spite of it we were able to obtain a bit of water and a small piece of bread. The murderers discovered it, poured benzine over it and burned it. We felt then that our end was near. Until the deportation we lived as if in a Hell! Daily we would be assembled near the Jewish headquarters, in order to be assigned to the labor of unloading coal wagons, straw, iron and logs, or for loading. The work wasn't easy. We would pave roads, cut trees and lie in the muddy swamps. Everything moved at a fast tempo under a hail of bullets. When we returned home we had no strength left. We would barely make it home. Aftr the deportation of all men, 15 and over, there remained a few men, the women and children.

The victims who were shot – over 80 Jews – were dragged by hand, by the women and children, into the woods, where they dug a large pit! It was dreadful! The scene cannot be described. Children kissed the bloody clothing of their parents. The cries during the covering up of the dead in the pit, cannot be described. Together with the men who were shot, there was buried in that pit women and a number of children. From that small cemetery in the woods, there grew a large cemetery.

After transporting the men to an unknown destination, they tied our hands with rope and loaded us into freight cars guarded by SS personnel. For the entire journey no one could open his mouth to ask anything. In every car there were at least 40 Jews on each side. In the other half there sat SS men who were armed. If someone wanted to stand, he was struck with a gun. Long hours passed before we, dirty and hungry, arrived in the death–camp of Auschwitz. Together with us there were also transports of Christians.

[Page 544]

In Auschwitz

At the entrance of the camp there hung a sign: "Labor Makes You Free!" Afterwards we added to that phrase the rhyme: "From the crematorium, one, two, three!" Our hands were untied and we entered a reception center of the camp. At that spot we met many people. It was difficult to recognize them. They were swollen, scratched, emaciated and naked as they waited for the gas–chambers. These were the ones who were incapable of labor. They were no longer given even a swallow of water. The only thing which awaited them was the Zyklon Gas. Each one of us had to be interviewed by the Political Department, and had to be photographed. Everyone had to turn everything in; clothing and anything of value, since an order had been given that anyone who hid anything would be hanged. We saw this when we reached the camp: Two men were hanging on a gallows for hiding valuables, or attempting to escape.

After the disinfection, where everyone had to soak himself in chlorinated water, they shaved our heads and each one got a pair of striped pants, a jacket and a cap. We also received a pair of wooden shoes, and a number was tatooed on the left hand. Unfortunately, of those who had gotten earlier numbers, in a short time only a few remained alive. During the day we received another bit of water. Only in the evening, after two days of tribulations, did we receive our first 200 grams of bread, a bit of butter, watery tea, and also a written number, with a Star of David, to sew on the left lapel of the jacket. The edge of the Star of David was red–yellow. In the middle there was a "P" which stood for our country of origin, Poland.

Kozieniceites in Auschwitz

In the attic, under the roof of Block 18, where I was assigned to my block elder, Bartkovyak, I met Tuviele Schneider's son, Velvel Shpigelman, who was brought together with Abraham Ring, Yankel Zaygermacher's son, my mother's sister's husband, who had lived until the outbreak of the war in Paris and sent off to Auschwitz. It was supposed to mean that they were being sent to labor camps. They were also told that each one was able to send for his family and bring them to him. Arriving at Auschwitz, each one was able to see that he had arrived at an extermination camp.

How One Brother Saved His Other Brother's Life Without Knowing It

by Gershon Bornshtein, Bnai–Brak, Israel

The fortunate incident happened in a camp in Poland, named Wolanow–a labor camp for Jews, but there were many incidents of grief that preceeded this event.

The Germans took the Jews out of our city of Kozienice on September 1942. They left a few in a place to drain swamps, but we didn't stay there very long. After two weeks, they took the rest of us to Wolanow.

The first thing we saw when we arrived were six long, mass graves filled with 1,000 Russian prisoners of war in each. The marker read: "Here lie 800–1000."

The barracks had been built for the Russian P.O.W.'s. We found pieces of their overcoats, some of which still contained red star buttons of the Soviet Army. The Jewish townspeople who worked cleaning the camp after the Russians were killed, told us that they even found hidden gold rubles in the ceiling of the barracks. The young people were kept in the camp. Their parents were taken to Treblinka to be gassed and burned.

The first day they took us to work with Polish overseers. These men were more brutal than anything I had ever seen. One overseer asked if any among us were a tailor. I said that I was, so he put me to work making a suit for him whenever we were not busy working outside the camp making an electrical transformer. We also built barracks for the German soldiers who were part of an anti–aircraft battery.

The civilian German contractors were cement firms, which supplied the cement for building the roads. The Jewish inmates worked for the civilians. The contractors used Polish overseers, who were anti–semitic and very cruel. My first day, I was assigned to carry cement bags on the run–two bags at a time weighing 50 kilos each. We were watched over by German and Polish overseers who beat us with sticks. The name of the firm was Vonderveter.

The next day, we met the Commandant of the camp, a German named Bachman, a civilian about "6' 3" tall, and cross–eyed. He couldn't get into the army because of his grotesque appearance, but this rejection made him determined enough that he became a good Nazi. After about five or six days, Bachman made a selection of those unfit to work and told them he would send them back to the ghetto in our city, Kozienice, but the ghetto had already been liquidated. A few hours later, a truckload of Ukrainians and Latvians, who served the German S.S., came with machine guns. The Lithuanians and Latvians killed all those who had been selected as unable to work, and we were forced to watch the killings. The Lithuanians and Ukrainians were volunteers for the Germans and they were the ones who committed the murders.

We worked there for a while and were given little or no food. We were constantly hungry–hungrier than I had ever been in my life.

The Polish overseer found a sewing machine and he put me in a farmhose near the building site, outside of the camp, so that I could make him a suit. It was illegal to do this, and I could have been killed by the Germans right on the spot if I had been caught. He was greedy, and used me to make money for himself. Many farmers were in need of clothing, and since there were no ready made clothes, he had the farmers bring their materials to me and I would make their suits. The Polish overseer was paid by the farmers, and I got food in exchange for my work.

I now go back to 1940 and my home town of Kozienice. The Germans ordered that all Jews aged 16–55 must go to forced labor camps. My brother was five years younger than I. He was sturdy and healthy, and he volunteered to work for me under my name so that I could stay at home and work on tailoring brought in by the farmers. I would make them suits in exchange for food. We had more food than many other ghetto inhabitants.

My brother first worked clearing the swamps. At that time, people began to starve and we saw many swollen from hunger, and many begging house to house, but no one had any spare food to give them. My brother kept working, and when he became 16, he worked building a railroad line with other youths from our city. In 1941, he was taken to Kruszyna to lay railroad tracks. My brother was abused and beaten, but no one in that group was killed.

In September 1942, except for those working in the swamps, all of the Jews were taken to Treblinka by cattle cars. We worked for a Polish firm named Gorczicki at Wulka.

I had three sisters. The oldest who was then married, was Ethel and her husband was David. The younger sister was Sarah, who is now living in Rochester, and Gitl the youngest is married and living in Harrisburg.

Rumors spread that Jews were going to be sent away in cattle cars. A truck came from Kruszyna where Max was working. Sara and Gitl begged the driver to take them to Max. Ethel stayed home with her husband David, who worked at a confiscated Jewish owned saw–mill being run by the Germans. The Germans said they would let him stay there. This turned out not to be true.

I returned home that night and my mother was home alone. My sisters had gone to be with Max in Kruszina. I was despondent, and cried, but couldn't do anything to help save my mother.

The next day was Saturday, and we were told to take our belongings with us to the Gorchicki firm at Wulka. Farmers in horse drawn wagons took us to Wulka. Before I left, I saw my mother near the gate of the ghetto. With tears in my eyes and a pain in my chest, I kissed her. This was the last time I saw my mother.

Ethel came to Wulka. Every man who worked there had the right to bring a wife or sister. After three days, the Germans came and made a selection because there were too many Jews there. They selected quite a few of them to send to Zwolen. My sister gave her wedding ring to the Polish overseer, and he let her stay there. If she would have gone on that trip, she would never have returned.

David, Ethel's husband was an excellent shoemaker. He made shoes for the German S.S. officers. They put all the Jews on one street and took 500 at a time to the railroad station. An S.S. man for whom David made shoes, saw David and pulled him and about 60 other Jews out, so that they would clean up the city. The Germans took the Jew's possessions, some of which had been accumulated through the centuries. Some they kept, and some they sold to the Poles.

In January of 1942, all the Jews of Poland were sentenced to death by Hitler at a conference in Wannese near Berlin. Of course the Jews had no way of knowing about it then. Jews were not allowed outside of the camps, and if found breaking this rule, a Pole had the right to kill him on sight or hand him over to the Germans for a kilo of sugar or a litre of vodka. There was no place for a Jew to hide in Poland.

In 1942, after plundering Kozienice, the Germans sent David and others to a factory that made gunpowder in Pionek. Gitl and Sarah were in Kruszyna with Max. They worked with Max in laying the railroad tracks, suffering unbearable beatings the entire time. By April 1943, this work was finished. The Germans knew that some Jews were hiding in the woods, so they proclaimed that they would make five ghettos where Jews could survive and not be molested anymore. This offer was a lie.

One day, a few trucks came to Kruszyna. The Germans ordered ten men to come out of the barracks. These ten men were put into one of the trucks. Ten more men were then commanded to come out of the barracks. These ten men were shot in front of everyone. This procedure of alternately loading the trucks with men, and then shooting other groups of men continued until the barracks were emptied. A German civilian overseer had some Jews working for him and didn't want these people killed. He gave them a signal when it was safe to go to the trucks. Max was watching, and figured out what was going on, and when this signal was given, he followed this group to the truck and got on too. My sisters didn't know if Max had survived. After the barracks had been emptied, my sisters yelled out his name, and he waived his cap from one of the trucks. They knew he had made it alive. All of the women were then put on the trucks, and none were shot.

The trucks took the Jews to a little ghetto called Szydlowiec. Max knew that the ghetto would be liquidated a few days later. Ethel was taken to a munitions factory in Skarzisko. A truck came from Skarzisko to get laborers, and Gitl and Sarah volunteered so they could join Ethel.

There was a Pole who would deliver letters from one camp to another for money. He risked his life doing this, and eventually was discovered and executed. He had delivered a letter from Max saying that he was in Szydlowiec. I wrote back that if he could get to Wolanow safely, he should come. The next day, he arrived with about ten friends. They came to my camp illegally, but staying in Szydlowiec offered a certain death. They stayed inside the camp even though the Jewish police and the registrar knew about it.

I was still working for a Polish overseer making suits at that time. Since Max was a tailor, I took Max to work with me and we worked together. We both slept on the same bunk inside the camp. This continued for about 7 or 8 months. He lived on my rations.

During this time, Max contracted typhoid fever and could not stay in the barracks. It would be a death sentence if he was discovered ill and unfit for work. A nearby farm girl, who lived on Christian papers, took him in and cared for him. She gave him food and medicine and let him sleep about the stove. If it were not for her, he wouldn't have survived. She may have been a Jewish girl from Warsaw, hiding from the Nazis.

The firm finished work on the transformer, so we were taken to work at other places. We went to work in a big city called Radom–about 15 kilometres away. We went by truck, and as we left the gate, the Jewish police counted how many went out. The German Commandant Bachman suspected that illegals were living in the camp, and the registrar had orders to look for illegals and to keep them in the barracks, and not let them go to work that day.

I had a suspicion, and told Max not to stay in the barracks, but to go to work with me. When we went out, the Jewish policeman counted us, but did not stop us. Coming back from Radom at the end of the day, we saw a truck of Ukrainians coming from the camp. They were drunk and singing. When we arrived at the camp, the illegals were all laying dead on the ground.

Max couldn't go back into the camp anymore after this happened, so he and the others stayed in the nearby woods. They bribed a Polish driver who was going to Radom, and they were dropped off near the ghetto wall. They climbed over the wall, and a Jewish policeman caught them and threatened to hand them over to the Germans to be killed. They were put into a Jewish jail in the ghetto.

A girl in Radom had been in the camp at Kruszyna and knew Max from there. She found out that Max was in jail and because she knew the jailor, she got Max out of the jail. He stayed in the Radom ghetto for a while and then went to a different camp at Pionki.

From Radom, I was taken to Auschwitz where Mengele made a selection and took out the sick. The rest went to a camp near Stuttgart and from there we went to Dachau. The Nazis took 10,000 to 12,000 Jews from Dachau to the Tyrolean mountains near Innsbruck. The Germans believed their own propoganda about the Jews, and thought the Allies would treat them better if they let these Jews live.

Two days later after I left Dachau, Max was brought to Dachau. He had dysentery on the road to Dachau and his clothes were soiled. He threw his clothes on the road, and later found a braziere by the road. He used this to hide scraps of food he found as he walked. He arrived in Dachau with only the braziere.

At the same time, my sisters were brought to a camp near Dachau called Allach. Just before they were liberated, Ethel got hit by a German shrapnel, and the Americans took her to a hospital in Munich. Sarah and Gitl went to Dachau to look for anyone who survived and found Max sick with dysentery. They didn't know about me. They found a non–Jewish man from Kozienice with whom I had talked before i went to Innsbruck. He told them they killed everyone in the transport and brought back the bodies, but he was mistaken because the bodies were from a different transport.

My sisters didn't want to believe that I was dead. A man from Radom came to Dachau and said he had been at the Austrian border. He told my sisters that he knew me and that I was alive. Sarah hitched rides with U.S. soldiers to Garmisch. I was summoned to the American commander of the displaced persons camp and was re–united with Sarah. We returned to Munich and my sister told me that all of us brothers and sisters had survived. After a while, my brother–in–law David found out that we were all alive and came to join his wife and us.

As far as we know, we are the only family with five children and a brother-in–law, all put in different camps, who all survived. Thank God and the U.S. Army for our liberation.

Surviving the War

by Zygmunt Berneman

I was seven years old when the war broke out. In my mind thoughts began drifting to my own childhood. How sorrowful. As a little boy, I remember living with my father, mother, Chaskel and Bacia, my older sister Tema, and my very young sister Mindale. Our apartment was a front store with a door and window facing the street. Near the window stood a sewing machine (my father was a tailor) and three beds. I could still see my father bent over the machine, he could not see well and could not afford glasses, yet he had to make a living for us. My mother helped him and at the same time cared for her children, cooking, and cleaning. In the same large store lived my grandmother with her son Tzalel and daughter Reisel. They hung curtain as a partition so the back of the store belonged to my grandmother. It was dark there. The cooking was done where my grandma lived. There was only one stove for the two families. As a seven year old boy, I did not know any better, many families in Kozienice lived this way. Our lives changed drastically when the war broke out. We feared the Germans' brutal actions. Jews were beaten up, taken to work, and some never returned. My father had very little work because peasants from the neighborhood villages were not allowed to do business with the Jews. We were poor and hungry, but we were still together. In 1942, all unemployed Jews had to be deported from Kozienice, that was an order from the Nazis. A Pole, engineer Gorczycki, employed people to dig canals for irrigation. He told the Nazis that the Jews could do that work as unpaid, slave labor. At this time I was nine years old, and not fit for that type of work. My uncle Tzalel bribed the engineer and he allowed us to take my sister and myself to work. We dug the canals in Wolka, a village. *The* rest of the Jews from Kozienice, including my family, were sent to Treblinka. Our work in Wolka did not last long, only one month. Then the Germans evacuated us to Skarzysko–Kamienna, an ammunition plant. Here, again, my uncle Tzalel managed to bribe the lager leader of the camp, and my sister Tema and I remained in Skarzysko, as fit to work. My uncle gave away a camera, a Leica, then the best on the market. Tema was working with my uncle in the same factory. I was to young so my work was cleaning the barracks, sweeping the grounds of the camp. I had to prove myself useful. In the same year typhoid broke out in camp Skarzysko. My sister Tema became ill– the Germans killed her. I was still with my uncle until 1944 when the Germans began to liquidate camp Skarzysko, the Hassack ammunition plant, and they sent us to Czestochowa, camp Pelcery. There I remained only a few days and was then shipped to Buchenwald. I now was alone. My uncle was sent somewhere else. After the selection in Buchenwald, where people were sent to crematoriums, I was picked to select clothing from the dead people. In Buchenwald, where people were sent to crematoriums, I was picked to select clothing from the dead people. In Buchenwald, were not only Jews but Russian POW's. They looked even worse than us Jews, human skeletons. I was lucky, the Gestapo gave me some domestic work and I had better food than the prisoners. When I came back from my work to the barracks to sleep, I brought some food for the inmates. In my barrack was a Soviet general. I used to give him food that I brought from the Gestapo.

In 1945, we were evacuated together, to Bergen–Alsterlager, aviation plant. I still did domestic work at the Sturmfeurers office and managed to get food for the Soviet general. We were together for five months, until the war ended. Why I was so lucky, I would not know? (Maybe, my parents watched over me.) The Russian general turned out to be a Jew, which I found out later. His name was Goldberg. After the war, as gratitude for what I did for him, we traveled together to Chechoslovakia – to Prague.

I was alone, not knowing where my uncle was. General Goldberg was a very high rank official in the N.K.V.D. We came back to Germany to a town Baucan, near Dresden. Here, General Goldberg became commander of the town. Not knowing where to go, and being completely alone, he took care of me. He was going back to Russia and took me with him. Still a minor, I was put in a foster home, where I received an education and learned to be an electrician. We lived in Ural and kept very close with my general – whom we called Dziadzia (uncle) with love. Time was passing pleasantly. I became an electrician and was employed in a theatre in Swierdlowsk. I met there my wife and together with her family we were planning to go back to Poland. I still wanted to find out where my uncle Tzalel was. With tears in our eyes, my general and I said goodbye to each other. I found out that my uncle was in the U.S.A. and then he brought me to the U.S.A. We had some very good years together, until he died. Blessed be his memory.

Testimony of Gittel Mantelmacher Weinstock, Etta Mantelmacher Gutman and Sara (Chaisurah) Mantelmacher Milstein

by Gittel Mantelmacher Weinstock

The Germans arrived in Kozienice in early September, 1939. They created a ghetto in which all the Jews were placed. The young people were put to work either building drainage ditches or other labor. There was no food in the ghetto and everyone was starving.

Later in September of 1942, we found out from some Poles who worked at the railroad station that the Germans were preparing railroad boxcars to take the Jews away. Our brother Moishe had been taken earlier to a work camp in Krushina. When a truck came from there, my sister Chaisurah and I begged the driver to take us back with him.

We worked in Krushina digging ditches. In December, the work camp was liquidated. Most of the men were killed and the rest of us were transported to the small town of Shildloftze. They put us in the old Jewish ghetto, from where the Jews before us had been taken to the Treblinka gas chambers. None of the buildings had windows or roofs. We met a lot of Jews who had worked on the drainage ditches with us in Kozienice. There were also Jews that had been hidden by the Poles that were brought here. In this way, the murderers fooled our brothers and sisters, saying that this is how we could stay alive.

When we came to the ghetto, we realized that we wouldn't be staying here very long. We found a Polish newspaper that said the Jews who would work in the ammunition factories would be the last to be sent on the cattle-car trains. My oldest sister Etta was already in Skarzhisko, where Jews had been taken to a factory to make bullets.

Two days after we arrived in the Shildloftze ghetto, the Germans came with a truck and rounded up the healthy young people for work. We went of our own free will to the Skarzhisko factory, because we knew that to go on the cattle cars meant certain death. We wanted to save ourselves in any way we could.

We came to the Skarzhisko camp at night. There we met others from our home town of Kozienice. They told us that in a few days the Jews in the Shildloftze ghetto would be liquidated. Sick people and pregnant women who couldn't work were sent back to Shildloftze for execution. Later we learned that the Germans killed a lot of the Jews in Shildloftze by machine guns. The rest were sent to Treblinka to be gassed.

Life in Skarzhisko

My job was to make bullets. We worked 12 hours a day, one week on day shift and the next on night shift. The work was rigorous and we were watched constantly. If any defects were found in our bullets, we were given 25 lashes with a whip. They took our clothes off for the beating. My sister Etta once received such a beating.

Once when I came in to work, I went to the bathroom. A young man was next to me. The commandant came in with his gun drawn, yelled something, and shot the young man. I couldn't look. When I opened my eyes, the boy lay dead at my side.

In 1943, typhoid fever swept through the camp. It was very contagious. Etta was the first in the family to catch it and was unable to work. Every week, the Germans wrote the names of the sick on a list. These people were taken out and killed. Even though she was delirious, when Etta saw the Germans' dogs enter the barracks, she knew that she had to hide. She bundled herself in a pile of featherbeds, next to other such bundles. When the Germans came in, they ran their bayonets through all the bundles. Etta was stabbed slightly, but she didn't make a sound, for fear of being discovered.

Later, Chaisurah caught the fever and was put on the list. I learned that the next day all of the sick people would be shot, so I took Chaisurah to work with me. In the meantime, the Germans were looking for her and could not find her. By some miracle, I never caught the dreaded typhus. Life in the camp took its toll on us. People starved daily. We were all emaciated, with sunken cheeks, glassy eyes, bloated stomachs, and stick-thin legs. It was truly a miracle that all the members of my family survived.

In the summer of 1944, as the Russians approached, we were moved closer to the German border. We were in a camp named Chansdeckau, where we did the same kind of work. When the Russians came even closer, in December 1944, we were transported into Germany, to Bergen-Belsen. Later, we were moved to Dachau, where we stayed in a connecting camp called Allach.

The American troops entered our camp on April 29, 1945 and liberated us.

[Page 545]

Memories of My Birthplace

by Gershon Bornshtein, Bnai–Brak, Israel

I was born in a hunch–backed house, on a crooked street in Kozienice.

My Teachers

I started my education with the teacher, Yisroel–Mendele. When my mother took me to the Rebbe for the first time, she distributed sweets and nuts to all the children. The Rebbe's (teacher) home consisted of one room. His wife was a sick Jewess, who was always in bed. He lived penuriously, was modest, quiet and with a constant smile on his face. After learning, in the evening, we used to help him drive his two hens into his one and only room. Afterwards the Rebbe would take all of us home. From the Heder I went to a second teacher, who was called "the Warsaw teacher". This one was an "intellectual". His beard was always trimmed. He and his wife were well–dressed. The room was a lot more airy and near a large courtyard, where we used to play a few hours each day. When I got older, I was transferred to the teacher, Shlomo Tabatshnick. Until my Bar Mitzvah, I studied with Rabbi Lozer. With him we boys already learned Torah and Mishnah. With him we studied until late at night, because the older boys studied every morning in the Polish school, and cdme to him afterwards. The Rabbi would take us to the synagogue for the afternoon and evening prayers.

When I completed my Heder years, I went to Betar (Zionist Revisionist School) where I studied Yiddish and Jewish history with the teacher, Yoel Weintroib, in the Yiddish Folkshule for the courses organized by the "Bund". The last time I met the teacher Weintroib was after the deportation. He perished in the Warsaw Ghetto during the final uprising. He had gone from Kozienice to Warsaw, thinking that there he would save himself. His wife, Gitl, of the Shabason family, perished together with all of the others.

Zelig Shabason

The Beginning of the End

On Thursday, the 1st of September, 1939, the day of the Polish mobilization, I found myself in Warsaw. The streets were crowded with heavy military traffic. I barely pushed through with my truck, of which I was the driver. The Jewish population was disturbed. I arrived at the highway to Kozienice and it was loaded with the military. As I drived through the darkened towns of Piasetshne, Ger, Vorke, and Glovatshov I saw the entire Jewish populace on the streets. No one was sleeping. In the large market-square of Vorke, Jews fell upon me and asked in a fright: "What's happening in Warsaw?" The large bridge over the Pilitza is guarded by the military. They checked my documents, and I drove on to Kozienice. When I parked on Koshtshelne Street, I was overwhelmed with questions, as had been the case in Vorke.

[Page 546]

In Starostvo and in the city–hall there was a commotion. They were saying that the bridge over the Pilitze has been bombed out by the Germans. Eight days after the mobilization, the bankruptcy of the Poles was complete. The military deserted, together with civilians in an endless stream to the east of the Vistula River. The Jews of Kozienice ran to hide in the forests, and the villages among Goyish acquaintances. On the 9 day after the mobilization, Friday in the morning, the enemy squadrons of bombers appeared in the skies, and chased after those who were fleeing. The planes dive and bomb the streets of Kozienice. After the explosions, I could'nt recognize the place, near my house on Koshtshelne Street.

From Abraham Moshe Aaron Litman's house, a big pile of rubble remained. From under the ruins, they dragged him and his youngest son, badly wounded. His wife and two daughters were dead. These were the first Kozienice victims of the murderous Nazi Army. At night, by the light of a small lantern, they buried the victims speedily on the cemetery.

Kozienicer Jewish young men digging a canal

The Initial Days of the New Regime

On the morrow, the first military patrols showed themselves, as they run through the city. The city was like dead. The populace was in hiding. The German military marched all day and night in the direction of the Vistula River. A day later, military personnel in black uniforms, with a large skull on their caps, and others in brown uniforms with swastikas on their left armbands, appeared. These were the Gestapo, the SS and the SD. At dusk, I went out of my hiding place, because I noticed a large group of Poles with sacks both full and empty. The barbaric Poles were accompanying the soldiers in black uniforms, showing them Jewish businesses, which were broken into and looted. Before I was able to orient myself as to what was going on here, I saw a group of Jews being escorted by the military, and the Poles chasing and screaming: "Jew! Jew!" They were helping to drag Jews out of their hiding places. And now they noticed me. Before I could escape, I heard a yell telling me to stand still. If not, he'll shoot. They took me together with the group of Jews. On the way the Germans continued to beat us with the stock of their rifles. I and two other Jews were taken to the train. There a motorized unit was stationed. They told us to tear off branches and cover their pantzer vehicles. When we finished this work they freed us.

The second group of Jews were taken by the Germans to the priest. They drove the priest out of his house, threw his things out and told the Jews to prepare his dwelling for them as quarters. In doing this they beat the Jews mercilessly. Leib Bayer's son, Yisroel Shlomo, they harnessed to a plowshare and told him to pull it. As he was doing this they beat him murderously. There were also a few elderly Jews with beards, which the Germans sheared off, and in doing this they cut up their faces till they bled.

[Page 547]

They Again Captured Me

They again captured me for forced labor. They took me to the SS. There I also met my friends, who were chopping wood and clearing the courtyard. They ordered me to wash automobiles. An officer asked my name. When I answered him, he told me that I'll be his chauffer, and that I should take care of all the automobiles, motorcycles and jeeps. He called me into his office, and told his adjutant to write a note indicating that no one was to bother me, and no one should take me for forced labor, and that I'm permitted to be out during curfew hours. He was chief of the gendarmes, an SS man. Going out, I saw that they were loading cans of gasoline on a small auto. SS men seated themselves in the auto, and drove out of the courtyard. Later, the SS man came out, and told me not to go home, but to wait for him. When it got dark, he asked me if I knew where the synagogue and House of Study were located. I told him that I knew, since I had no alternative. Approaching the synagogue, I saw that soldiers were busying themselves, going out of the synagogue and the House of Study with empty jerry–cans of gasoline. On the street it was deathly still. Suddenly flames burst out from all of the doors and windows of the House of Study and the synagogue. Both buildings were engulfed in flame. Houses in the vicinity caught fire from the flames. Jews ran to and from in great commotion. The enraged soldiers were beating everyone, who fell into their hands. They were shouting that since Jews have set fire to the synagogue they must extinguish it. They pushed the Jews to remove the burning holy books. I also noticed that the soldiers were pulling R' Yosef, the city Rabbi, together with R' Yankele. R' Yosef was carrying a Torah Scroll and was badly beaten.

The soldiers pushed R' Yosef deeper into the fire, and ordered him to dance. At this the soldiers sang their song: "When Jewish blood spurts from the knife ..." The soldiers then jumped into their vehicles and drove away. The Synagogue of the Maggid, of blessed memory, and his House of Study burned to the ground. R' Yosef fell in a dead faint, and later died as a result of the beating. A short while later the Rabbi, R' Yenkele also died. On that day the murderers also set fire to the Palace, as it was called. In this way they celebrated their victory over Kozienice!

Kozienicer ghetto fenced with barbed wire. Anyone found outside the fence was shot on the spot.

The Difficult Winter of 1940 Approaches

The Germans issued a decree, that all houses, in which Jews live, were to be designated with a red Star of David. Jewish houses were broken into and robbed. Pain and want ruled. Epidemics and sicknesses spread. I remember the first victims of hunger and sickness. Later an order was issued that all Jews, who lived among Christians, must leave their homes, and go over to the Jewish side. A workers brigade of all classes was organized. Life was regulated by the Jewish Council, at whose head stood the leading householders of the city. The section of the city where Jews lived, was encircled by barbed–wire, and a Ghetto was formed. Jews smuggled themselves out of the Ghetto, in order to obtain a bit of food, to sustain their souls. Later there came an order, that the Ghetto is sealed. Anyone who leaves will be shot.

[Page 548]

Once, at noon, there began a run. Jews were running to hide. I saw that the gendarmes were accompanying Abraham Litman and his son, Yechiel. They were going in the direction of Koshtshelne Street. They come to their house, which had been bombed. It didn't take very long before we heard several shots. First, the son, Yechiel, fell and shortly thereafter – Abraham Litman. From afar I saw my father and my younger brother. The murderers noticed them and gave them an order to bury the dead on the spot, where they were shot, near the mound of grass. My father brought several Jews with lanterns and they buried the two victims. Two days later, my father took several Jews, and late at night, with lantern light, they speedily exhumated the two martyrs, and reburied them on the cemetery.

The End of 1941 – The Beginning of 1942

Jews died of hunger and of Typhus. There was not a house without a victim. A hospital was established, with Dr. Arnold Abramovitsh at it's head. Brigades of nurses worked day and night, but there was a lack of medicines. Hungry and swollen Jews wandered through the streets, and others became beggars. A folk kitchen was set up, but where do you get produce? The communal leaders approached householders, to help with whatever they can. And they did help! I remember the long lines at the kitchen: half swollen, barefoot, in tattered clothing, bent over Jews, who had been merchants and prominent householders. My father would stand for long hours distributing the food and worried over the fact that people were being embarrassed and insulted. Once there was a commotion: The gendarmerie was holding a group of workers, who went from their work at the canal. They beat them mercilessly and then shot them.

At the beginning of the German occupation, Jews tried to organize to help the hungry and the sick. Magen-Dovid Adom in Kozienice to help the children in the Ghetto.

My father ran in that direction. Perhaps he could save someone? The Council used to bribe the murderers with money, or with very valuable merchandise, but this time, unfortunately, he was too late. Jews would trade their last possessions for a bit of corn in the nearby villages. These Jews were discovered with the bit of corn, and they were shot near the Dombrovker Bridge. At the time the following fell: Leibl Fishboim, Yosl Tentzer and the third victim – I don't remember. My father wanted to put them in a wagon and take them to the cemetery, but the murderers didn't allow it. They were buried not far from the bridge. Leibl Fishboim's wife, Feige, together with her three children, were sent to Treblinka.

The End of the Kozienice Community

The Jews of the surrounding towns, were driven into Kozienice. This was shortly before the Holidays. On the last Yom Kippur, services were held at the lame Berish's home. The Cantor for the last arrived to tell us that boxcars had arrived at the train station. According to what we heard from them, and what had happened in other cities, we understood tht the boxcars had been brought in order to remove us. The murderers also decreed that in 48 hours, we should deliver to them a sum of money, meaning that the Council should pay the travel expenses for everyone. My father, together with others, ran around to collect the money.

[Page 549]

On the second day of Succos, at night, the Ghetto was surrounded by Gestapo, Ukrainians and Polish fire–fighters. Large trucks came from the Pulver Factory in Pionki. They loaded on tens of workers and drove off to the camp, which was being established there. A Ukrainian soldier pushed me aboard one of the trucks going to Pionki. Early in the morning, the murderers drove all of the Jews from their homes and stood them in rows, on Koshtshelne Street. Whoever tried to get out of line, was shot. Afterwards they robbed the homes and searched for hidden Jews. In Kozienice they left behind a group of Jews, among them – my father, and my older sister, Feige. My younger sister, Esther, and my mother, Chaya–Neche, went with the transport. Feige had a nervous breakdown. A Polish fire–fighter informed on her and they removed her, so to speak, to the hospital. There they shot her, and Poles buried her there. On the morrow, my father and a few other Jews, went there, removed her, and buried her in the cemetery. That day they killed in Kozience more than 30 victims: the sick and old, who couldn't go off their beds. Among them was the Glovatshover student, Albert, who studied in the Kozienice Gymnasia. With this the evacuation ended. Being for a few days in the Pionki Camp, I came back to Kozienice, thinking that I would be able to remain there.

The End of 1942

A whole night I went through the forest, until I came to Kozienice. Patrols guarded the approaches. A few Jews helped smuggle me in. In the Ghetto, on the streets, could be found all sorts of valuables. The Germans were selling them for next to nothing, to the Poles. The Poles were standing around the Ghetto with sacks in their hands. My father took me to the Maggid's small synagogue. In a corner stood a stool and a high bed, where the Maggid used to sleep. My father carried out the stool, broke the bed and together with the scraps of the library and old holy books, he burned it all in the courtyard. My father found books written in the hand–writing of the Tzaddik. We took them with us, and quickly left the spot. We put the books and papers in a box and buried them in a nearby courtyard. A few days later, the Germans rounded up the remaining Jews and a division of the Polish police was supposed to accompany them to Radom. On the way, they shot Elimelech Orbach, when he tried to escape. He was buried near the railroad tracks, which lead from Kozienice to Radom.

Family Isochor Shabason

[Page 550]

1943– 1944

I ran away to Warsaw. A day later, my father also arrived. We met in a place where my younger brother had already been from before. We were hiding by a Christian girl, who had worked for my mother's brother as a saleslady. She had taken upon herself to save whomsoever she was able to. A few days later a few Jews from Kozienice came, whom she had brought out. The number of people, whom she saved: 3 children and 18 adults, for whom she had arranged several shelters. Polish hooligans betrayed us, but bribery money helped us get away after a good scare. All the time we would move to a new place. We experienced the uprising in the Warsaw Ghetto. We found ourselves near a fence of the burning Ghetto. We also awaited the Polish uprising in 1944–. The battle broke out and blood flowed; this time not Jewish blood. Jews came out of their hiding places. After 6 months of heavy fighting, the uprising was quelled. We hid ourselves again.

In January of 1945 We Were Liberated

In January of 1945, we were liberated by the Red Army. Warsaw was in ruins. We were completely exhausted, swollen, sick and ruined. Father said that we must return to Kozienice. We went on foot, because there was no other way of transportation. In the streets there were still battles. The Russians were chasing the Germans. We went along the highway that leads to Kozienice. We reached Ger. The city was empty. Once Ger was filled with Jews from all over the world. We met Jewish soldiers, who were marching with their units. In two more days we arrived in Kozienice. We did not see a living human being. We were the first Jews. The patrols told us that the Poles hid themselves during the battles. At the home of the family, Shitshek, only the old Christian woman remained in the house. We slept there overnight. On the morrow we became aware of the fact that the commandant of the city is a Russian Jew from Odessa. We went to him. He spoke Yiddish to us. We went with him out on the street. The entire Jewish neighborhood, from Koshtshelne Street to the train was destroyed, torn up by its roots. As the Poles related, the Germans, with the agreement of the City council, sold, or gave permission to dismantle the houses, so that there would be no memory of them. Besides us there came to Kozienice, my wife, Bayle–Gitl (maiden name, Kelmanovitsh) from Lentshno, my father, Abraham, my brother, Gad, his wife, Miriam and my father's sister's child – Yeshayahu Shuch. A few days later, there began to arrive individuals, who were saved from the camps.

[Page 551]

We Leave Forever The Cemetery

I went with my father to the cemetery. Not a single tombstone remained. They were used for paving sidewalks. The fence had been dismantled. The Poles took away the bricks. There was no sign of the Maggid's tomb. My father recited the "Lord full of mercy" prayer and we said the Kaddish. We left the cemetery forever. A few days passed and the old priest sent to call for my father. We both went. He took us into a cellar and said: "This is what I hid away!" There we found tens of Torah Scrolls, prayer books, and bibles. A cellar full. My father took a Torah Scroll, which was still in good condition, and arranged for a prayer quorem (minyan). I found my Tallis at the home of a Christian, where we had hidden our things. This is the only Tallis, which was left in Kozienice after the Holocaust. On the holiday of Pesach (Passover). Shiele Becker led the prayer service, wearing the Tallis on the first day of the holiday. A few days later we bade goodbye to our destroyed town of Kozienice, and set out on our way to the Land of Israel!

The Difficult Martyrdom of Kozienice Jews in the Camps

Kozienice Clews, who were not evacuated to Treblinka went through a difficult martyrdom in various camps in Poland. They crushed boulders in the stone quarry at Blizshin; they dried swamps at Gortshitzki on the Vulke River; they built barracks in Valanov; they worked in the munitions factory in Pionki; worked in the factories of heavy industry in Starachovitz, Shidlovietz, Skarzshiska and Pulavi. Blood and sweat accompanied them in their martyrdom!

[Page 552]

We Buried 34 Jews

by Yosef Chlivner, Paris

After the arrival of the Jews from the neighboring towns, they began to spread rumors in Kozienice, that they would send us for forced labor to the Russian areas, but we didn't know any details. All of the news came from the Judenraat. We would always see groups of Jews at the Judenraat, discussing it with each other, but no one actually knew anything. This was driving us crazy. We consoled each other, by saying that they couldn't possibly arrange it, and supervise us, such a large city full of people.

Regards from Radom

As we wandered around so absorbed, there came regards from Radom, saying that there, a portion of the Jews had already been removed from the Ghetto. They took them to the train, sealed them into boxcars, and transported them to an unknown destination. This struck us like a cold shower. Our Ghetto looked like a boiling cauldron. Jews ran around and don't know what was happening to them. I don't have the strength to write about the last two days in the Ghetto. My writing doesn't contain even half of what actually took place. You could see that the people were running around and didn't know what to do. A portion of the Jews wanted to be sent to forced labor, because maybe they would be more secure there. Others wanted to pay money, so that they would be allowed to work in the fields around Kozienice. But the supervisors of the work, the Poles, chose only younger people.

Whatever Will Be – Will Be

I, Yosl Chlivner, a son of Betzalel Chlivner, was chosen to cast my lot with all Jews. Whatever will happen to them will also happen to me. I couldn't leave my mother and an ill sister. My father died 8 days before the evacuation. He was the last Jew to be buried in the Kozienice Cemetery. I decided to remain with my family, and suffer the same fate as all other Jews. The last Shabbas, when I looked into the Judenraat, I could already see that everything was already emptied, and no one was there. The gendarmes had seized all documents and all the members of the Judenraat had been sent to forced labor in a Camp. Only then did I really understand that they would also send us away. I came home, but I didn't say anything. On the last Shabbas my brother, Simcha Chlivner, came home. He was drafted for labor. He said that he wants to go with us during the evacuation. Even then we didn't know that we were going to be sent to our deaths. We believed that we were going to be sent to forced labor. But, unfortunately, the opposite turned out to be the case.

[Page 553]

The Sirens Began to Sound

It was our last Shabbas, the 23 of September, 1942. I well remember our last hours in the Ghetto of Kozienice. That night we already didn't lie ourselves down to sleep. We waited to see what would be. Sitting like that, sunken in thought, we heard the sirens begin to wail. We took our shoulder knapsacks and prepared to embark. At the time our neighbor, Chaim Eisenmeser, came in with his wife, and.–a daughter–in–law with a small child. That scene I cannot forget, My mother went out, kissed the Mezuzah, and cried. Our neighbor, Chaim, said to my mother, that he hopes we will live to return. He finished his words in a sad demeanor. We went out on Magitova Street. I don't know where we had gotten the news, that when the sirens wailed, we must go outside, and not lock our doors. Everyone just seemed to know that it must be so. On Magitova Street we could already see Jews from all the streets with their packs on their backs, and their children on their arms.

We Were Far From Realization

How terribly sad it was for us then! We didn't realize ourselves of what kind of situation we were in. In this way we entered Targova Street.

Here, many people were gathered. We happened to stand near Pesach Mandel's door. We stood by fives. Our five consisted of myself, my mother and sister, my brother and Chaim Eizenmeser's daughter–in–law with a small child in her arms. On the other side of the street, Jews were also lined up the same way. The middle of the street was empty. In the empty space, the Jewish police and the gendarmes paraded.

Whoever Has 1000 Zlotys – Remains

We stood this way and waited. Dead silence! No one spoke. Afterwards the gate of the Ghetto opened. Then we heard an announcement: Whoever will pay 1000 Zlotys – will remain in Kozienice. I didn't even dream about it because I didn't have that amount. It wasn't a very large amount at the time, but I didn't have it. The gendarmes went to and from. When they came to us, stopped and ordered us to step out, because we were still young, and we will remain here. I told them that I don't have the 1000 Zlotys, but they didn't converse with us, but pulled us out of–line, so that we couldn't even bid farewell to our families. We stopped at the intersection of Lubliner and Targova Streets. We beheld a tragic spectacle. In groups of 600 the Jews went out of the Ghetto to the train. And so it was until the end. Who could imagine that Jews are being led to their deaths. If someone lost a pack, the gendarmes picked it up and returned it to him, so he could take it along, since he would need it.

[Page 554]

Back Into the Ghetto

I stood, looking, and didn't know myself, what is going on. In a short while the man in charge of the transport, came, opened the gate of the Ghetto and told us to enter. We sat down on the steps of acquaintances. Yisroel Yitzhak Frish's house. We didn't speak, because our hearts were heavy. The day was hot, and the sun burned. I stood up and looked around. I'm on Magitova Street. What a deathly silence; like on a cemetery. Here, not long before, it was bustling with Jews in every corner. Now I'm wandering alone on the street, and do not see any of my acquaintances. I couldn't remain there long, and they came into the Ghetto and counted us. It was correct; 60 men. Afterwards they wrote down our names. Yoel Weintroib was also with us. In the midst of their writing, we suddenly hear shots. We sensed that the shooting was not far from us. We became restless, because we didn't know what this meant. We thought that the shooting was on the street that we were on. The man in charge of the transport calmed us. In two weeks we'll also be taken to the same village, to our families. After writing our names, we were able to sit down. We were both hot and cold.

We Go To Dig A Pit

Sitting like this, a gendarme came along. He picked 15 men and ordered them to go to the Jewish cemetery, to dig a pit. I was among the 15, and commandant was Yisroel Tenenboim. We went to the cemetery and began to dig a pit, not knowing for whom or why. Soon we saw that from all sides wagons were approaching. We began to understand that corpses of dead Jews are being brought to us. And so it was, unfortunately. As the first wagon arrived, the peasant told us that all of the Jews who were in the Jewish hospital, had been shot. Now we knew what the shooting that we had heard, meant. Then there arrived more and more wagons filled with the shot victims. We removed the corpses and lay them on the ground. We had to bury women, together with men, because we had no alternative.

We already had about 20 corpses in the grave, and were ready to cover it, but a gendarme came along. He was the greatest hooligan in Kozienice. He told us that there were 34 corpses and the grave is too small. We had to remove the 20 corpses, and make the grave bigger. The victims had been so horribly shot that it was difficult to recognize anyone. One of them I did recognize. He was one of our 60 who had remained behind. He was from Glovatshov.

We Leave the Cemetery

On the morrow, in the morning, I saw notices on all of the doors, in Polish and German: Whoever Opens a Door Will Be Shot! Imagine my Kozienice, where I spent my best years. Kozienice, where I felt that everything was mine, all the fields and the woods, all the lakes and stones. But now, when I look around and see no one, I feel like a stranger in my birthplace – Kozienice. All doors are closed. Packages roll around on the streets. When I returned to Targova Street, I met the remaining people from our group sitting on Yitzhak Frish's stairs.

[Page 555]

Candles – Your Father Lights
by Gershon Bomshtein

It cries for you thy father His holy victim, who perished at the Nazi Holocaust.
Extinguished forever your bright eyes, where does one find your grave, to weep over you?
Gestapo, SS accompanied you to Treblinka, shrouds for you – no one sewed.
Your holy ashes wild winds scattered, among stones, thorns and wild grasses.
After you nothing remained of the torn clothes (at death) your holy soul should rest in Eden.
Shameful and terrible was your torture, no mother no father – heard your cry.
Father, mother, where have you disappeared? I, your child, seek you, and can't find you.
Tragic, for Auschwitz, was the road of your parents dark nights and tortured days.
The hands bound, tied with rope, looking from afar, to see your last glance.
Not skipping a day or a night, always dreaming of you, about you, my child, I thought.
The nights – in terrible dreams enwrapped. Your father's heart bleeds, from the eyes tears drop.
In the dream having seen your beautiful blue yes, how you, my dear one, sucked your mother's milk.
I wanted to caress you, pull you close to my heart, to still my hunger, thirst and pain.
Praying to God, for your holy soul, that the day should come to take revenge.
With memorial letters, printed on paper, is the only memorial – which has remained after you.
The memorial candle – your father lights, for you, my dear beloved, unforgettable child.
May it be glorified and sanctified your great name, wait, my child, for the world–to–come.
Forever, in my memory – you will be, my dearest child – Sarahle, the daughter of Rachel and Gershon.

[Page 556]

On the Occasion of the
22ⁿᵈ Memorial Anniversary of My Little Town
by Shmelke Shpigelman, Montreal

Shmelke Szpigelman

Kozienice was a small town like other small towns. But it was nicer and I loved it more, because it was my little town. On Magitova Street, the Street of the famous Kozienicer Maggid, our house stood and there I was born.

Everything On Our Street!

I loved the street. There stood the Synagogue and the House of Study, the Rabbi's house, the small House of Prayer (Shtibel) where Mishnayos was learned, also the Maggid's Shtibel, and the house where the famous Maggid used to live. To us on that street would come Jews from all the cities and towns. They would bring their slips of paper (kvitlech) with requests on them, to the well–known Kozienice Rabbis. They would also visit the Maggid's Shtibel, or look in through the window at the Maggid's high bed, where he used to sleep. On our street, Jews, who had come to visit parent's graves, or the graves of the righteous on the ancient cemetery, would stop off. They would place their "kvitlech" among the old moss–covered tombstones and request the righteous should pray to the Almighty on their behalf.

On our street brides would be led to the canopy. Musicians (Klezmer) would play and cause the town to rejoice. Funerals would also pass through our street. When we would hear the wailing from a distance, and the sing–song voice of the old beadle (Shamas), R'Mosheh: "Charity will save you from death!", my father would put aside his work, put on his kapota (long black coat) close his shutters, and accompany the funeral procession. When I was a small boy, I would stand by the window, and listen to the cries of the deceased's relatives. Sadness would overcome me as I would think that such a thing could some day happen to my own dear parents. I only prayed to God that he not let this happen, and that I should die in their stead.

Through our street, observant women, with heart–rending cries, would run to the House of Study, to the Holy Ark, to beseech on behalf of a seriously ill relative, who could no longer be helped by a human doctor. Everything on our street!

A New Generation

But our town did not consist only of Magitova Street. Into the lap of our town was born a new generation, a worldly one, that was in conflict with the old ways, which did not carry "kvitlech" to the graves of the righteous, which did not cry into the half sunken tombstones of the deceased Rabbis. This was a new generation, which broke loose from the cramped House of Study walls, and began the learning of worldly studies. It was a generation, which saw it's future in the struggle for progress. It established worldly schools, produced theatre plays, arranged readings, and occupied itself with physical culture.

[Page 557]

We had all of the political parties, which existed among Jews at that time. Our town had a small lake and a beautiful larger lake, where the young people would bathe and sun themselves on the shore. In the quiet Pine woods, with which our town was surrounded, our young people would spend their free time, enjoy the good fresh air, and dream their youthful dreams. On the north side of our town there was a courtyard with a park. From the courtyard there led a path which was called the "hinter courtyard". This was the "lover's lane" where lovers would walk by the light of the moon and bright stars. On the bridge over the stream they would swear eternal love. These were two worlds, which were often in conflict, but still united.

How natural it was, when our fathers were celebrating the 3rd Sabbath meal in the House of Study or the "Shtiblech", we would at the same time be promenading back and forth on Lubliner and Radomer Streets, conversing and flirting with our girlfriends. A Jewish town, a Jewish life, a Jewish Street, once – you were! Oh how close you are to me! You live in my heart, and in my heart you were not destroyed!

If He's a Jew – He is Abandoned!

The German hordes tore into our town on the 3rd day of the war and took the majority of the Jews into the garden surrounding the church. They sheared off the beards together with pieces of skin of our grandfathers and fathers. They forced us to do the most degrading and dirty work, in their effort to kill in the Jew – his humanity. The Fascist bandit did not distinguish between the observant and the free–thinkers. If he's a Jews – he's abandoned!

Later they made a Ghetto for all of the Jews, and surrounded it with barbed wire. Many died of hunger and epidemics. Jews were shot when they stuck their heads through the Ghetto barbed wire, in order to beg a piece of bread from the Christian passers–by, in order to still their hunger. The town was spread throughout with graves of Jews who had been shot, when hunger drove them outside of the Ghetto to gather a bit of food for their hungry and swollen children. They were sent to Auschwitz and other concentration camps, the most beautiful sons and daughters of the town. But all this did not satisfy the German beasts. In their plan to exterminate all Jews, the German murderers did not make an exception of the Maggid's town.

The Evacuation

On the 2nd day of Succos in 1942, early in the morning, all Jews were driven from their homes. The sick were shot in their beds. The murderers stood us in rows, and took us to the train. They were told that they were being sent to forced labor. The Jews were packed into boxcars, like herring in a barrel (many suffocated from the crowded conditions even before the train started to move). They were all taken to Treblinka and on the 2nd of the intermediate days of Succos were led into the "showers" (gas chambers).

[Page 558]

The German murderers fooled them even before their deaths. The gas chambers were set up like real showers. They were all gassed and then cremated in ovens. Only one managed to survive the Kozienice transport. This was Shimon Rozental, who was attached to the "infamous Sonder–Commando", and later during the uprising fled. He is now in Israel.

An organization called "A Drop of Milk" fed hungry Jewish children

The Jewish Nation – Lives

There are no graves for our martyrs. There are no tombstones for our nearest and dearest. There are no Jews and no Jewish life in our little town. There is no memory of a Jewish house. The Jewish streets were burned. Jews no longer pray in the Houses of Study and Shtiblech, because they no longer exist. Jews will no longer come to parents' graves and shed their tears on the moss covered tombstones of the righteous. The German bandits damaged and destroyed them, and burned the Jews together with their Rabbis. They will no longer learn in the Jewish schools; no longer will Jewish theatre play, because both the audience and artists perished. No longer will they converse and promenade on my town's streets. Dead – are the people! Dead – is my little town! But the Jewish nation is not dead. Hitler and his helpers did not accomplish their task. My little town, together with hundreds of other cities and towns are dead. Six million Jews perished, but the Jewish nation lives on! We, the survivors, will fight on with all democratic forces for a world without cruelty. We strive for a world, in which all nations will live at peace!

[Page 559]

An Unusual Lady

by Yechiel Shabason, Ramat–Hasharon, Israel

Miriam Shabason. A Polish girl who at the risk of her own life saved over 20 Jews. After the war, she married one of the survivors and made her home in Israel.

I'd like to present here an overview of the life of a young lady, who was torn away from us in the full bloom of her life, and who sacrificed herself for Jews during the time of the Hitler war. Few people helped save our sisters and brothers from extermination. This type of woman was found in Kozienice, an exception to millions of Poles. She put her life in danger, in order that more Jews could tear themselves out of the claws of the Hitlerite death machine. Not daunted by any difficulties, she began a rescue operation at the time we were incarcerated in the Ghetto, and surrounded by fences and barbed wire. When a stranger's foot could no longer tread in the Ghetto, she came from Warsaw, and waited for the moment to enter the sealed off Ghetto, to visit the Shabason family. This was the blond girl, Marisha, who was born in Warsaw to not wealthy, but respectable, Christian people.

There were four children in the family. Marisha was the youngest of three sisters and a brother. After graduating from elementary school, she began working for a member of the Shabason family, who before the war had a butter establishment. She came to work as a sales–helper. During the day she worked in the establishment, and in the evening she used to study in the business school. During the summer she would come for vacation to Kozienice. She would feel very much at home with the Shabason family.

Marisha Helps

The bloody war came. The murderers rob Jewish businesses, and drive the Jews from their homes. Marisha saw what was happening to the business and home of the Shabason family at number 7, Aleya–Yerozolimska. There was no lack of pogromists and hooligans, who waited for the opportunity to rob. With all of her womanly strength, she protects the business, arguing that everything belongs to her, and in this way saves the entire fortune. When the Jews are driven from their homes into the Ghetto, she also takes over the Shabason home. From time to time she runs down to Kozienice, to find out what is happening there, to the Shabason family. She would spend a few weeks in Kozienice, and then return to Warsaw. In Warsaw, she was acquainted with a Jewish tailor's family on Dzshelne Street. The tailor would sew cloaks for the business. She would, at great sacrifice, enter into the Warsaw Ghetto, in order to help sustain them, putting her own life in danger. And this tailor's family gave birth to a little girl. Now the question arises: What is to be done with the new–born babe? After smuggling herself out of the Ghetto, through cellars and underground passageways, she consults with her brother, Yozef, about rescuing the child. They decide to use the Transport facilities, which are removing Jewish possessions from Warsaw, and where her brother works.

[Page 560]

On a beautiful day, when a large wagon of the Gestapo drives into the Ghetto to bring out Jewish goods, Marisha already finds herself in the Ghetto, by the Jewish family. She brings the child wrapped in a sack. The parents stand in a corner, and gaze upon the tragedy. At that moment she hands the child over to her brother, and he hides it in the storehouse where the feed for the horses is kept. The large flat wagon moves from its spot. Marisha loses no time. By various ways she gets out. On the other side of the Ghetto, her brother waits on the flat wagon. She takes the child from him and takes it home with her. But in her home she cannot keep the child, for fear of her neighbors, who know that she isn't married. A few days later the child is moved to a safe place.

The Last Summer

This was the last summer for Kozienicer Jews. They already knew that their fate was sealed. Every one would ask himself the question about how he could possibly save himself, but no one could see a way out.

This was a few weeks before the liquidation of Kozienice. With self–sacrifice, she began to save whomever she could, and as speedily as possible, because time was short. She already knew what evacuation means, and to where the Jews would be taken. In Warsaw she had connections with the

Jewish Underground, which already knew of the Final Solution for Polish Jewry. She provided false documents for both women and men. In this way she would each time bring someone to Warsaw, where she had a place for them in her home. On dark nights she would skirt through field and forest, bringing a man, a woman or a child to the nearest train station. For 20 kilometers she would travel on foot, and from there she would go by train to Warsaw.

She would be afraid to take the train in Kozienice, and in order to avoid having people inform on her, she would go by foot to the nearest train station. Once when she was bringing a six year old boy who today lives in Israel, and already has his own children, she was nearly discovered at the train station in Demblin. Fortunately she was able to convince the gendarmes. The train arrived, and she was able to save herself from them. In this way, during several weeks, day and night, she was able, by not wasting a moment, to rescue from the murderous hands, tens of Jews and bring them to Warsaw.

What More Can Be Done?

But here the question arises: What more can be done? In 1942, the Germans had already looted all of Europe. Death hovers over Jews in every corner. The ghettoes are being emptied and liquidated. The uprising in the Warsaw Ghetto is suppressed with fire. And on top of it all, the Polish hooligans allied themselves with the German murderers, and helped them in their work. They go from house to house, not to mention streets, to search for hidden Jews. And here, she had assembled about 20 Jews, among them small children. How can they be saved? They are living human beings. You have to worry about feeding them. But it is obvious that her luck doesn't leave her. She manages.

[Page 561]

Four Groups

She consults with her brother, Yozef. The people are divided into four groups, in different places. One group, of eight people remains with her and her brother. The second – is taken out of Warsaw, to her cousin, where she makes room for them. The third group she takes to a suburb of Warsaw, and the fourth group, not far from her own house. If one group is caught, at least the others will be saved. One group was protected with a double wall, so that in case of knocking, they would have a place to hide. A second group dug for itself a cellar, so that if someone knocked at the door they would all go down into the basement. She maintained contact with all the groups, and used to come from time to time to see them, and find out if everything was all right. When she would visit the groups, she would disguise herself in various outfits, so that she wouldn't be discovered. But as was said, her luck held. Her father and mother used to visit us from time to time in the evening hours, so they wouldn't be noticed. Unfortunately, they couldn't help us with anything, except with a kind word, and with the devotion of their daughter and son. In this way we sat until 1944 when the Polish uprising broke out.

Where Do We Go?

Marisha lost contact with the remaining groups. Warsaw was heavily bombarded, and burned. The uprising was quelled, and the population is driven out of the city. Marisha decides not to part from her group. She could have left with the Polish populace, but she decides: "I'm remaining with you! Whatever will happen to you, will also happen to me! We've held on until now, let us hope that we'll live through it!" Yes, but where do we go? She doesn't meditate too long, and goes out among the burned houses. There she meets a Polish Colonel, Kovalski. He now lives in Israel. He is wandering around with several other Jews, whom he had saved. He is also seeking a way out!

They decided to seek out a cellar among the burned–out houses, and there to dig a bunker, in order to hide until the Liberation. But when will Liberation come? No one knows. And will we survive? Also no one knows this. But, as was said, there is no other way – time is short. We gather some food and containers of water. We go down into the cellars under terrible conditions, because among us there are several wounded. We live this way for more than six months in a dark bunker, until the 17th of January, 1945.

We Crawl Out Of The Bunker

After a short offensive of the Red Army, we crawled out of the bunker at 22 Shenna Street, broken and ill. We dragged ourselves behind the military that had liberated us. We lifted our eyes to heaven. Have our sufferings ended? We search for the first groups, but who knows if they're alive? After a few days we are made aware that the other groups live, and no one is missing. Marisha gathers together her survivors. She goes to Kozienice. Maybe she'll find someone alive? But unfortunately no one is alive!

[Page 562]

Miriam Daughter of Abraham and Sarah Our Matriarch

Marisha wants to leave this bloody soil. She no longer belongs to that nation, which helped exterminate so many millions of Jews. "Your people – is my people; your God – my God!" (from the Book of Ruth, in the Bible). After months of wandering with the remnant of the Jews, she arrives illegally at shores of Palestine in 1946. There she marries a Miriam Shabason, daughter of Abraham, our Patriarch and Sarah, our Matriarch, according to the laws of Moses and Israel. Her husband is one of the survivors. After a few years in Israel, she was invited by her family to come to Columbia, but she longed for Israel. In 1966 they decide to return to IsraeL They settled in and made a fine living, but unfortunately she was torn from us in the full bloom of her life. She died on May 22, 1966, and was buried on the cemetery in Holon, Israel. There stands on her grave a tombstone with her unforgettable name: Miriam. She was born for the Jewish People and was taken into the bosom of the Jewish People! WE HONOR HER MEMORY!

Drops of Humanity In a Sea of Cruelty

(Note from the editor of this translation: the page numbers shown in the following paragraphs relate page numbers for this translation.)

In the years 1939–45, so many had helped the Hitler gang torture and murder Jews. For many it was almost a national obligation: to get rid of the Jews. Let there, therefore, be recorded again and again the few exceptions among the righteous of the nations, who sacrificed themselves in order to save Jews. The unknown author of the Kozienice Holocaust book tells us on page 497 and following of this translation about the heartfelt attitude of Dr. Neuman, a German military doctor, towards the Jews of Kozienice. Our friend, Yechiel Shabason, tells us on pages 633 and following of this translation of a noble Polish woman, who later attached herself to the Jewish People, and helped, with so much self–sacrifice save Jews.

Our friend Leibele Fishtein tells on page 649 and following, of a humane act on the part of three Germans: Gustave Hartman and Milkah of Kassel and Heintz Baumbach of Dresden. Our friend Zelick Berman on page 532 and following of this translation, tells of a simple, Polish peasant, Sabat, who sacrificed himself for a friend in a time of trouble. Our friend Rivke Pearlstein on page 672 and following of this translation, tells of an unknown Polish peasant, who stretched out a helping hand to unknown women in time of stress. They and tens of others were but rare drops in a sea of cruelty!

[Page 563]

Kozienice on the Threshold of Destruction
by Leah Gelbard, Tel–Aviv

At the beginning of September, 1939 the Germans bombed our town. It was the first sign of what was to come. I don't think that our town was bombed because it was a strategic point. But I'm sure that we were bombed because we were a Jewish town. The Germans had another reason, and that was to convince the Poles and the antisemites, that their hearts' desire is drawing close, and the "Jewish Problem" was to be solved forever.

The Town Reacted With Fear

The bombings continued for several days. The first victims fell, and the town reacted with fear. The faith: that the Lord would help – seized many, and it became the support of the masses. The Jewish mind began to seek ways: From whence will our help come, and how to flee from the Holocaust? On the first night of the German conquest the sun sank amidst streaks of flame – a sign of what was to befall us. Night fell. Fear seized the House of Israel. The town sealed itself behind lock and bolt. But the piercing question: What to do? – did not give us any rest. How to save the soul from the approaching Holocaust? Shots pierced the air. The judgement has reached every Jewish home. Who was wounded by the bullets of the enemy? Who is next? Eyes do not close. The mind doesn't stop seeking a gate of hope, and so it was until the light of morning. After a few days had passed, the tanks and armored cars arrived. The tooting of the horns was like salt strewn on death dealing wounds. The murderers did not cease, and displayed their strong arm tactics. Every Jew who was caught in the street was seized. Among them also my father, R' Yaakov Sherman, of blessed memory. The prisoners were assembled by the murderers in the square of the Catholic Church, and there they were tortured for 6 days. My mother, Tsharna, of blessed memory, remained in the house with 6 small children, among them, myself, the oldest. Our mother bemoaned secretly, and was careful not to reveal to us her fears concerning father's well–being. During the imprisonment the murderers confiscated all of father's money, his jewelry, his watch, his ring, and in this way our source of livelihood was broken.

In the town the first "Action" began. Young men were recruited for forced labor in Radom. We had no doubt about what the work would be. Every one, who had the courage and opportunity to part from his family, tried to flee, and escape to the Russian Zone. But generally only a few succeeded, and the majority made peace with their fate, and waited for the bitter end. In the meantime father returned home exhausted, hungry and depressed. In his heart flickered a spark of hope. He hoped that for the meantime, perhaps he could help us. Our joy was great at his coming, but it didn't last long.

[Page 564]

Does Yaakov Szerman Live Here?

Ya'acov Szerman

On Shabbat eve, we sat around the table. Father recited the Kiddush, and each word that he pronounced pierced the hearts of the youngsters. We were seized with fear and also joy. Suddenly, heavy footsteps were heard. The door opened with a noisy bang. Seven policemen entered. At their question: "Does Yaakov Sherman live here?" we answered: "Yes!" The policemen ordered father to stand, turn his face to the wall, raise his hands, and if he disobeyed they would shoot. We stood like turned to stone, without uttering a word. The policemen began their search. They overturned the entire house. Everything that they found they confiscated. The leather skins, that father had kept as our security, the murderers loaded onto a wagon. After they emptied our house – they arrested father. From then on, we never again saw father. He was swallowed up in prison in Radom, in very difficult conditions, and if not for the bread which we smuggled to him, father and the other prisoners would have long before perished from starvation. The murderers put father on trial. It lasted for 6 months. He was convicted of concealing merchandise, and sentenced to 2–1/2 years imprisonment. From the time of his sentencing, all traces of my father were lost.

Famine Plagued the Ghetto

At the end of 1940 a Ghetto was set up in Kozienice which was fenced in by barbed wire. All of the Jewish inhabitants were concentrated by the murderers in the Ghetto. Famine plagued the Ghetto. Whoever tried to escape was shot. We felt that the noose was tightening around our necks. People became swollen with hunger, and died before their time. The anticipation of complete destruction seized all of us and wasn't long in coming. A few hours before the elimination of the Ghetto, the truck for those forced to work, arrived. Among them, also I was taken for labor. After traveling they brought us to Camp Pionki, to work in the munitions factory. We were divided into three shifts. Each one worked 8 hours. Our salary was a pittance: 200 grams of bread a day (2 slices) and watery soup. The management of the factory was cruel; beatings, hunger and torture were our lot. One day we were witness to a disturbing occurrence. We were gathered in the central field of the Camp, where the murderers, this time Ukrainians, had set up a gallow. Four Jews were hanged because they had hidden a small can of alcohol.

For hours the bodies swayed in the wind, that pushed them to and from, and we were forced to stand and watch this fearsome sight which we would never forget. We knew our days were counted. Daily we waited for the bitter end, and if it was slow in coming, we felt it would come and we wouldn't escape it. In the meantime the crematoria in Treblinka and Auschwitz worked full blast. The pressures on them prolonged our days. Each day a new atrocity was revealed to us. Whoever felt sick for a day or two was eliminated. They would find signs of Typhus, and ordered him taken to the hospital. On the way to the hospital, the sick were told to dig a grave, and were shot to death.

[Page 565]

These incidents occurred daily. I'll never forget that bitter and disturbing day, when a group of the SS chose 100 Jews, whose faces didn't please them – and they were shot to death nearby, before our eyes. One day at the order of the commandant we were assembled. He asked that any of us who wanted to return to the main camp, volunteer and raise his hand. Three times the commandant repeated the question. Each time I raised my hand, and in spite of it I wasn't chosen among the volunteers for that camp. BECAUSE FATE WANTED IT THAT WAY!

As time passed we learned that the volunteers for the main camp, disappeared, and no one knew where they met their death. So we continued to live in the Nazi Hell until June of 1944, with dangers stalking us daily. In this month the murderers transported the remnants to Auschwitz. The trip to Auschwitz lasted 2 days, in sealed boxcars, accompanied by SS, and we received no food.

Exhausted and broken we finally arrived at Auschwitz. After de–licing, and the gift of two hours, standing naked, without anything, we were given new clothes. When we were dressed, we couldn't recognize each other for our appearance had changed so much in but a few short hours. 100 women were gathered in each Block, and we were there for about 6 weeks. During this time we weren't forced to labor, but we were starved for bread. Every morning, between 3 and 4:00 a.m. we were lined up and counted, and it lasted until 8:00 a.m., until the SS man was sure that no one was missing. The columns of smoke rose into heaven from the chimneys before our eyes, 24 hours a day. Through the barbed wire fence, we were witness to the infamous selection process: Left, right. Our eyes beheld dreadful scenes of how children parted from their parents, husbands from their wives and wives from their husbands. From Auschwitz we were ordered to go to Bergen–Belsen. An invisible hand watched over me during that time at the gate of Hell. From Bergen–Belsen they took us to the munitions factory "El–Sting", near Leipzig. There we were tried and tested with hunger and back–breaking labor, until we were again transferred to the death–camp, Bergen–Belsen, where hunger and Typhus reigned.

We Were Like Dreamers

Sick with Typhus and unconscious, I lay, when the English burst into the death camp, in March, 1945. The joy of the Liberation cannot be expressed in words. We were like dreamers. Who was like unto us? Who could compare to us? Immediately after liberation, we found a bread storehouse. Our joy knew no bounds. Everyone grabbed bread according to his hunger, feeling that the days of hunger were at an end. But it immediately became clear to us that the murderers had deceived us. They had poisoned the bread. When we fed it to one of the camp dogs, he died. In this way, thanks to our caution – many were saved, and we prevented poisoning. Slowly I recovered, and my strength returned. Among the survivors I met my future husband, Shlomo Gelbard. His determination to leave the despoiled soil of Germany, and go up to the homeland, the Land of Israel, was strong. Here, in Israel, we built a house, and established a traditional family. Our children: Yaakov, Ephraim and Ruth, who were born to us in Israel, received a Jewish education, traditional, and the words of the Prophet were fulfilled in us: "And I brought you to the land of Israel, and I gave you the spirit – and you lived!"

The Szerman Family

[Page 566]

The Wind Rocked Them Like Hanging Laundry

by Leah Gelbard, Tel–Aviv

Leah Gelbard – Israel

First I want to introduce myself. I'm the daughter of Yenkl and Tsharne Sherman. I was born in Kozienice. We were 6 children: Moshe (the oldest), Leah, Devorah, Rivke Pinyek and Feigele – the youngest sister.

A Few Words About Kozienice

Kozienice was a prominent city. To us they would come from tens of surrounding towns and villages to take care of various affairs in the government headquarters. The population was about 8000. Like in all of the cities and towns in Poland, the populace was mixed – not all of one class. The most prominent positions were held by the small businessmen and merchants of all kinds, beginning with textiles, manufacture of shoes and food to the restaurants, bars and other establishments which suited the different classes.

All Worked Hard

Jews made their living, not only from the city's population, but also from the villagers, who used to bring life to the city during market days and fairs, when peasants would bring their produce: potatoes, eggs, apples, pears, milk–products (butter and cheese) and wagon loads of wood. After standing with their produce, for a few hours outside, and selling their products they would immediately enter the bars, in order to warm themselves with a shot of vodka, some good food, and then end up buying food products. Also the handworkers occupied a prominent place in the economic life of our city. Can you imagine a town of tailors, shoemakers, carpenters, tinsmiths or smithys? Although the handworkers worked from early morning to late at night, to support their families – there were no really wealthy in the city: Not among the merchants and certainly not among the handworkers. All worked hard in order to support their families. But in spite of the daily economic situation, our city possessed a beautiful, intelligent youth, which gave our city courage and honor.

Eliezer Wasserman   Tsherna Sherman

Parties and Schools

The varied economic activity also influenced the political and spiritual life. We had members and adherents of all of the political parties and youth organizations, beginning with Zionist youth, to which I belonged, to the Revisionist Party, and its Youth Org., Be tar, Hashomer Hatzair, Poale Zion, Freiheit, Scouts, Bund and Communists. The organizations had larger and smaller libraries in order to enrich the knowledge, the party activity, and affiliation and devotion of the members. Also as far as schools were concerned, we were not backward. Besides the two elementary schools, there was a business school and a Tarbut (Culture) school.

From the right: Neche Waserman and her daughter Khava Kohn

[Page 567]

Thanks to the Maggid of Kozienice

Our city also had a unique reputation in Poland and in the entire world thanks to the Maggid, whose name had become a legend. Still during my time there lived two Rabbis of Kozienice Maggids descent: R'Arele and R'Elimelechel. Hassidim from all the ends of Poland and also from overseas came to them. R' Elimelechel died 2 years before the war.

Shifcha and David Waserman

Kozienice Rebels Fell in Treblinka

In the heroic uprising of the Jews against their German hangmen and their Ukrainian bootlickers, which broke out on the 28th of July, 1943, in Treblinka, the following Kozienice Rebels died:

MOSHE SHERMAN
ALTER KOHN
ISSACHAR KOHN

WE HONOR THEIR MEMORY!

[Page 568]

This is the Way We Saved Ourselves
by Chaya–Rivka Shildkroit, Haifa

My maiden name was Chaya–Rivka Kestenberg. Now it's Shildkroit. I was born in 1904– in Kozienice, and got married in 1926 in Demblin, where I dwelled all the years, and lived nicely. My husband was shot by the murderers in Buchenwald. I, and my children remained alive in the Demblin Camp from which I, and my 3 daughters: Rachel, Andziya and Blume, were liberated. My son– was liberated from Buchenwald.

We Flee

When the war broke out, I and my family found ourselves in Demblin. The first bomb fell not far from us, on the airport. The bombing continued. All fled, to wherever they could. We ran to Riki. Also in Riki the bombing caught us. So we ran again from the city, under the mill, near a swamp. The planes swooped low and fired their guns at several hundred people, who were lying on the ground. Many perished. We had nowhere else to run – everything around was burning. By a miracle we got out of there, and ran in the direction of a village, about 12 kilometers away.

We Began To Be Miserable

After a few days had passed, we returned to Demblin. There, we already met the Germans. It is to be understood that we found empty homes and businesses. We began to be miserable. We were sealed into a Ghetto, and driven daily to forced labor. In this way we lived, suffering until the end of 1941. During the first selection, we were all forced into the market place. The Gendarmerie and the Judenraat picked out those capable to work. I sneaked in among them, and in that way, for the meanwhile, saved myself. A short while later, the 2nd selection took place. For money, I was able to get my husband and my son work at the railroad. I, and my two daughters, age 5 and

11, were sent out. We began our march from the market–place in the direction of the railroad. It is to be understood that we were surrounded by patrols, and marched in rows of four. I began to plan how to run away with the children. We couldn't run away all together. My older daughter didn't want to flee first. I arranged with her, that I would flee first with my little girl, and that she should follow. In this way, we managed to flee.

The opportunity came when a large number of Christians happened to be near our column. We took advantage of the opportunity and squirmed out of the line. We ran to a Christian acquaintance. After me ran a woman who was being chased. I thought that I was being chased, so I re–entered the line. I got close to my daughter and told her that she was to go first now, and that I and my young child would follow her. She obeyed me and ran from the column.

[Page 569]

We Hide in a Toilet Shack

By the side of the road there were Christian houses, but no one wanted to hide her. She went past the houses and hid herself in a pit in the field. Later I managed to flee with my small daughter, and again a woman ran after me. We also ran to the Christian homes. We asked a Christian to hide us for a payment. He was afraid. He told us to run deeper into the fields, where he showed us a toilet (shack), in which we could hide ourselves. We all went into it. Through the cracks, I noticed my older daughter looking for a place to hide. I began to call her, and she joined us in the shack. I arranged with the Christian, that when nightfall came, he should come for us and take us back into the city. All of this for a good price, of course. We had learned that the Germans had left 200 Jews in the city, who had ransomed themselves for a large sum of money.

A Christian Takes Us to the City

We impatiently awaited nightfall. The Christian came to us, when it was already quite dark. He proposed that he take us two at a time. I sent my older daughter and the woman as the first pair. He told me and my small child to lie in a furrow, where we covered ourselves with leaves, so that no one would notice us. We arranged for a signal, which he would give when he would return for us. He finally came to take me and my child, but he didn't know how much to ask for, so he requested that I give him my child's fur coat. He took us to the outskirts of the city and left us standing there. That's where the woman and my older child were supposed to be waiting for us. I got myself into a courtyard of a family, where I found the woman and my daughter.

In the Demblin Camp

This way I saved myself and my two youngest daughters. The oldest daughter, on the day of the selection, had been at her forced labor. She wanted to flee from the labor and come to the city, but the man in charge was one of my customers, and he wouldn't permit her to go out of the door. All night she tore the hair from her head. Before dawn he let her out, and this way I was reunited with my three daughters. My husband and son, Abraham, were detained during the railroad inspection. Afterwards, as soon as the train was emptied of Jews, I brought my husband and son back to the city. Before we went into the camp, we were all stuck in a cellar, at the home of the gardening supervisor; understandably, for a large sum, until we were registered for the labor camp legally, to join all of the other workers. I want to mention the searches in the Demblin Camp. If anyone was found with money or other valuables, he was shot and the body was left with a sign as a warning to others. At that time, I worked in a bunker with rotten potatoes. We left the bunker in rows of four. Standing in line, with my middle daughter, Chana, I took off my belt with the gold pieces, and buried it in the sand under our feet.

[Page 570]

When my oldest daughter, Rachel, who worked in the payroll office, went to the shack to dispose of the belt, an officer followed her. Two other officers were in the vicinity. She also had with her, a $20.00 American gold piece and 10 gold rubles. For a good bribe, the officers let her go. Between the boards of my bed, with the help of a knife I hid the gold pieces, in order not to have them with me. In this way we all saved ourselves. After two years, we were transferred from the Demblin Camp to Tshenstochov. I, and my three small children remained alive. One day before the liberation of Tshenstochov, the Germans sent my husband and my son to Buchenwald. There my son was liberated and my husband was killed.

My Family

I'm listing the names of my family members, who perished during WWII: My father died in 1942 in his own bed. In Kozienice, Yechiel Kestenberg was an upright man and a devoted friend of the Rebbe. I remember how he ran a decent Hassidic household. Our livelihood came from a food store and from dealing in grain. My brother, may he rest in peace, perished, together with his entire family. His name was Moshe–Yosef Kestenberg. His wife's name was Sarah; the oldest daughter, Rashke, and two sons: Yitzhak and Alter. My sister was married to Shmuel Epstein. They had a daughter, Rivkele and a son, Yehoshua. My aunt was named, Chaya. Her husband was Moshe Shapiro, their daughter, Yehudit, who had a husband and two children. My father's brother was named Chaim–David, and four children. One daughter was named Chaya–Devora Kestenberg, and the other Rachel. The two sons were named Shmuel and Yisroel.

Page 571]

A Humane Deed

by Leibele Fishtein, Ramat–Gan

Radom

On the 2nd day, after the arrival of the Germans in the city, a small Gentile boy pointed at me. He indicated that I was a Jew. The Germans immediately took me away to the post office, and there turned me over to the district "Fuehrer11". The "Fuehrer" wore a military uniform with four stars on each arm. He stretched out his arm in the "Heil Hitler" (may his name be blotted out) salute, and told the Germans to leave the room.

Good–Day, Little Jew

The "Fuehrer" approached me, extended his hand and said: "Good day, you little Jew." At that moment I was confused; should I shake his hand or not? Perhaps he'll hold my hand with one of his and with the other take out his revolver, which was in his leather holster. I extended my trembling hand to him. In either case he could do with me as he wished. "Don't tremble," he said to me. "Don't be afraid. I'm fond of Jews. My best friends were always Jews. Are you hungry?" He doesn't wait for my answer. He goes into the adjoining room and brings out 2 rolls, a chunk of salami, a pot of coffee, and puts them down near me, on the desk. I stand in the same position as before and think: Am I perhaps condemned to death? Before carrying out the sentence, the prisoner is well fed! He even put a pack of cigarettes into my pocket, without even asking if I smoked.

He went to the door, turned the key and locked it. Afterwards he lowered the black paper curtain on the window. "Sit, little one", he said to me – giving me a stool at the desk. "Drink your coffee, and take the salami. Have you got a wife, children? It'll be for them." I sit myself on the stool, but I don't touch the food. I think: Maybe it is my last meal? It is also possible that there is poison mixed into the coffee. "Why don't you eat?" "I don't have an appetite!" "Don't be afraid. I'm friendly to Jews." With those words I noticed the truly sympathetic expression on his face. The doorbell rang. Before he answered it, he said to me quietly: "There in the adjoining room, there are various things lying on the shelf. Put everything in order, similar things together." I went into the room, where there was a huge pile of military clothing. I put each one in a separate cubby. It didn't take long. The "Fuehrer" came in with another, also in military uniform, with 3 stars, about the same age, 52. He shook hands with me and says to me: "I'm named Milkah, I am also friendly to Jews, like my fellow townsman here, the "Fuehrer", Gustav Hartman. We're both from Kassel." He took out a pack of cigarettes, and gave it to me. They saw how nicely I had arranged everything in the cubbies, and they called out enthusiastically: "Wunderbar! Wunderbar how you've arranged it all. You will remain with us till the end of the war!"

[Page 572]

The Situation Got Worse

From day to day the situation of the Jews here in Radom got more difficult. It was impossible to get bread. The lines at the bakeries were very long. A Jew would stand in line, and the Goyim would point him out to the Germans, who would throw him out of the line and also hit him a few times. You couldn't appear on the streets. When the Goyim would point out a Jew, the Germans would take him for forced labor. Many would come home bloodied and even crippled. Many never saw their homes again. Either they were sent away, or they were beaten to death at their forced labor. I had a wife and f children. At my work, I had enough to eat, but to take something home to my wife and children was impossible. In my home they suffered from hunger. I decided to tell my chief that my wife and children are starving. As soon as he heard this, he said the following to me: "We will remain here longer tonight, until everyone leaves." When all had already left and the place was empty, he took me into the food storage, where they kept what parents and wives had sent to their soldier sons and husbands. He felt all of the packages, put one of them aside and said to me: "In this package there is a lot of food." He tore off the label with the address, opened the door of the burning, pot–bellied stove, and burned up the address label. On the morrow, in the morning, as soon as I arrived at work, he told me to take the package, and ordered the other German to take me home, and also to turn over the package to me at my home. In the sack we found: Salami, chocolate, coffee, sugar and preserves. The German, who had helped us unpack the package, said to us: "When you'll finish eating everything in this package, I'll bring you another package of food. The accursed SS dogs can eat dust." This same German took me home a number of times with packages of food like this. To his credit, it is worthwhile mentioning his name: Heintz Baumbach of Dresden.

How We Were Saved

At about the third selection which took place in the Radomer Ghetto, we knew nothing, but it seems that our Germans knew all about it, and exactly when it would take place. Our German called together all of the Jews, who worked at that post and said to them: "Today, all of the Jews will work the night shift. None of you is to return to the Ghetto." At that military post there worked more than 20 Jews: Shoemakers, tinsmiths, painters, cabinet makers, joiners, and decorators. In the Ghetto, we almost had no one left, because during the first and second selections, our wives and children had already been sent away to Treblinka. We would sleep at the homes of acquaintances, or with strange families.

The night shift had to work at #7 Kilinskego Street, but instead of working, Hartman told us to go to sleep, only that it should be quiet, so that no one would know that Jews are in hiding there.

[Page 573]

On the morrow, after the 3rd selection, Hartman told all the Jews to line up, and ordered that two of the Germans on the post take us to Shvarlikovska Street, to those who had been selected as "fit for labor!" Before we marched away, Hartman called the SS men, who stood guard at the gate of the camp, and said to them: I'm sending you a group of Jews. For a few nights they've been working the night shift. Let them into the camp, and let them come out every morning to come to me to work. "This is the District Fuehrer of the Defense Post, Hartman, speaking." In this way we were saved from being evacuated to Treblinka!

Two unknown Jewish orphans in ghetto of Kozienice

I Went to Kozienice

My wife and children went to Treblinka. The only ones left to me were: my mother, and 3 sisters in Kozienice. I developed a terrible urge to see them. But how do I get to Kozienice? (Kozienice had not yet been evacuated). I went to Hartman, and poured out my heart to him, and begged him to let me go to the Ghetto in Kozienice. He thought awhile, took paper and wrote out a "permit", indicating that I was traveling with military post letters to the post in Kozienice. He called in Heintz Baumbach, told him what we had been talking about and said to him: "Heintz, you are going with him to Kozienice. You are to take him to the Ghetto, and you go to the post. On your way back, go past the Ghetto, and bring him back with you." This was a risky business for both the German and myself, but we succeeded!

On the very same day I entered the Kozienice Ghetto. At the gate stood Abraham Shabason, and he let me in. After my first steps into the Ghetto – I became mixed up. I knew the Radomer Ghetto very well, but something like the Kozienice Ghetto, I had never seen. Skeletons were sitting by the gutters in torn clothing. They were picking up something from the ground and putting it into their mouths. Gloomy children with yellow faces lie on the bare ground, and search for something in the sky. I wondered to myself: Where has their childhood gone?

I see people, but recognize no one. And I had known them all so well, and now they're not the same. All so aged, dried up – living skeletons. They walked and did not look around. Their heads were bent. Even the houses, which were always so well kept, now look crooked and dirty. The once beautiful town, now looks like one big mess!

This is My Sister, Rachel–Leah

I came into the home of my oldest sister. One room. She's alone! All of the 18 people, who lived here were now at work. As soon as she saw me, she cried out: "Leibele!" We fall into each others arms, and cried spasmotically. When we recovered, she lifted her head. "My God! This is my 35 year old sister, Rachel–Leah?" She looks like an old woman, gray and yellow. Her flesh hangs, and her two cheeks sunken. "Where is your Sarahele and the children?" She didn't know, that it was already over a month, since they'd been swallowed up in Treblinka. But I didn't want to tell her this. They still didn't know that Jews were being taken away to be exterminated. So I told her, that they were at home, in Radom.

[Page 574]

My Mother's Last Tears

By my 2nd sister, who lived in a wooden chamber by the water "Flowing Plimpl" – I also didn't meet anyone. Only a bed stood there, in which my abandoned, beloved mother was laying. I bent over the bed and kissed her face. Feeling the kiss, her eyes opened, looked at me, and a few tears, like pearls, rolled down over her sunken cheeks. She couldn't speak a word. I again bent over her and kissed her tearing eyes. When I lifted my head, her eyes were already closed. I began to shout: "Mama, Mama!" But the eyes did not open, as if she had suddenly fallen asleep. I remained standing motionless, not knowing what to do. With my hand I touched my face. The wetness of her tears reached my lips. I felt the taste of my mother's last tears.

The door opened, and my two sisters came in. They fell upon my neck, and together we cried bitterly. One sister told me that the Germans had shot her husband for bringing home a piece of bread. The second, the youngest sister, told me that her husband had been sent away to Shitshki for forced labor, and that there he was shot on Yom Kippur, when the Germans caught him praying, wrapped in his Tallis (prayer shawl). In the midst of my "enjoying" my nearest and dearest, the door opened and a Jewish policeman came in and told me that a military vehicle was waiting for me at the gate. I went over to the bed and gave my mother a farewell kiss, which, it seems, she no longer felt. I bade farewell to my sisters and went out. At the gate, I turned and took a last look at my birthplace, Kozienice. Going back to Radom, there stood before my eyes: The Ghetto, my mother, my sisters, and my birthplace. Three weeks later there didn't even remain a trace of what I had seen. They were all taken to Treblinka.

MAY THEIR MEMORY BE SACRED!

[Page 575]

How I Saved Myself

by Sarah–Mindel Kestenberg, Haifa

I was born in my beloved city of Kozienice, which I will never – till the end of my life forget. In 1926, as a 16 year–old girl, I went to Warsaw, where I got married, and lived with my husband and 3 children.

On September 1, 1939, Hitler attacked Poland. Two days before this, on Friday, early in the morning, German planes flew over our heads – but no one imagined, that war would break out. Warsaw held out for a month, before succumbing to Hitler. There was nothing to eat, no water or electricity. I then lived in an apartment at 3 Tvarde Street. The bombing was terrible, and all of Warsaw was aflame. Ten minutes before my building was bombed, I decided to remove the panes from my windows so that in case of emergency, I would be able to save myself and my family by escaping through the window. After removing the panes, a bomb actually fell on the house in which we lived. Through the window, we crawled into the street, where many corpses were laying. We went to Panske Street, to the synagogue. My husband went to the Vistula River to bring some water. Together with my husband I went to find out who was still alive in the family. We searched for a corner for ourselves and the children. At my relatives, and at my husband's relatives it was crowded, and there was no room for us. I had nothing with what to feed the children, and no clothing to change them into, because everything had been burned in our apartment. In Warsaw there wasn't any bread. An aunt of mine took my oldest child, an 11 year–old boy. He sold cigarettes in the street, in order to earn enough to buy a piece of bread.

Hunger and Want

The hunger didn't lessen. For bread we stood in line day and night, and often didn't get any. There were occasions when I got up from my bed in the middle of the night, in order to get a piece of moldy bread for the children. When I would stand for many hours, and finally my turn would come, a Christian would recognize me as a Jewess, and the Nazi, who preserved order, threw me out of line. I remained without bread. We could go out on the street only until 7:00 p.m. For appearing on the street after that hour you received a bullet in the head. The last, remaining Jewish businesses were ransacked by the Germans and their contents removed on German trucks. I saw this with my own eyes on Genshe Street, where there were Jewish establishments of piece goods. The Germans also seized Jews for forced labor.

[Page 576]

An aunt of mine, who came from Kotzk, told us that it was better there than in Warsaw, and she took my two daughters, Tzipporahle and Chavale, to her. I escorted them part of the way, because Jews were no longer permitted to ride the trains. I never saw my little girls again. I didn't have the opportunity to visit them. We decided to go to the Russians, just like many of the Jews at the time were doing. We left our son with my aunt, and my husband and I went to Bialostok, where a brother of my mother lived. In Prage (a suburb of Warsaw), we managed to get ourselves on a train. We came to Radzin, where we had to change for a different train. There was a commotion. Jews were being seized for labor, and they were being beaten. Everyone ran to hide. We hid in an attic, belonging to Jews. We were there overnight. In the morning, we continued on foot to Bialostok. It was already bitter cold in November of 1939. We came to Malkin, and went to a Christian. This was the point at which we wanted to cross the border. Two SS came in and took my husband, and 3 other men. An hour later they came back. They told us that they had already dug the graves for themselves, when a young Christian called the SS men away, and in that way they escaped and prevented their deaths.

We Got Lost

We went back to Warsaw. It was night and cold. We were hungry, sleepy and tired. We came upon a peasant's dwelling. There we spend the night. At 4:00 in the morning, we had to leave the house, because the peasant was afraid that he and his family would be killed. We went a short way and we heard "Halt! Halt!" We began to run in the direction of the forest, in order to save ourselves. We wandered around and got lost. My husband returned to Warsaw, and I ended up in Bialostok.

I was without money. I went to my uncle. He allowed me to remain with him, but it was very crowded. There were many refugees. On the morrow my son came from Warsaw. A Christian had had pity on him, and helped him cross the border. For the two of us there was definitely no room at my uncle's. I found a place in a synagogue. The crowded conditions there were indescribable. We slept on hard benches. We had nothing with what to cover ourselves. From my husband I heard nothing!

We Go To Russia

People were registered for work in Russia. I also registered. This was in 1940. In a few days we were sent in cold cars on a two–week trip. We arrived at Tshelyabinsk in the Urals. I was assigned as a helper in construction work. I rolled wheelbarrels filled with sand and cement. Two women had to pull a wheelbarrel. Even for men this was difficult labor! How much more so for women! Not once did I fall down at work. The Russian women laughed at me, saying that the "Jewesses" can't and won't work. They have white hands, and want an easy life. My wages weren't enough to buy the 400 grams of bread that I was entitled to daily. For some frozen potatoes you would have to stand a whole night in line.

[Page 577]

During the war with Finland, the situation became worse and more difficult. We got no food. My buyer and supporter was my 12 year–old son. I saw that we would die from hunger there, but we were barefoot and naked, without any money for expenses. I had already sold the last coat that I had from Poland for 400 rubles. With a mighty effort I obtained two railroad tickets. But it was impossible to get to the station. We dressed ourselves like Tarters, with great difficulty and finally managed to get to the station. We arrived in Moscow and from there went to Kiev.

We Go Back

The streets of Kiev were filled with Polish Jews. After many protestations we were allowed to travel freely. I received a ticket to Kovel. We arrived in Kovel at 8:00 in the evening. I had no one there, not any relatives and not any acquaintances. Jews were returning from the House of Study. I went over to a Jew and told him about my situation. When I told him that my birthplace was Kozienice he took me to Yonah Roisman, who was a Mohel from Kozienice, and who was living in Kovel. He told me that also Yisroel–Itshe Briks was in Kovel. On the 2nd day I traveled to Bialostok, to my uncle, in the hope that I would hear something about my husband.

My uncle told me that on the day after I had left for Tshelabinsk, my husband had come to Bialostok. He went to the employment bureau and requested that he be sent to the same place that I had been sent to. So they sent him where they wanted to. I knew the place but to reach each other we were unable, because my husband had signed a contract for two years. I fled to Kovel. I didn't get any work. Like previously in Bialostok, also here in Kovel they were seizing the Polish refugees, and were sending them in closed coaches to Siberia for forced labor. People were concealing themselves, and also I was hidden in a cellar for two weeks. My 12 year–old son used to get from a baker, rolls and bagels and sell them in the market place. With what he earned we managed to live.

A month later I received a letter from my husband from Berditshev with a permit to come to him. We were together for a month, until the war broke out between Russia and Germany. We again began to wander, and in this way we came to Siberia. In 1946 we returned to Poland, where my husband died in 1955. I and the children, two sons, went to Israel in 1957. My oldest son was married, and the youngest one is in the Israeli Army.

[Page 578]

We Envy the Dead

by Reizel Greenberg (Ankerman), Netanya, Israel

My father, Getzl and my mother, Henye–Tzirl knew many of the Kozienice people who remained alive. We lived on Lubliner street, number 28, in the house of my grandmother, Tshame Devorah Mandel.

I Was an Embroiderer (Needle Worker)

I was one of the full–time needle workers, known not only in Kozienice, but also far from our town. The years of my working among the needle workers, were years of energetic life for hundreds of Kozienice young men and women. Our employers were Chaim "Samochod", his brother, Alter, and his sister, the "black", Ethel. A larger undertaking in the branch was for many years run by Miriam Feigenbaum and her two sisters, Altele and Sara–Reizel, the daughters of Mordecai Nuta, the Shochet. Besides these there were tens of enterprises, in which there were employed, at needle work, young girls. Our work, ignoring the fact that it was difficult and monotonous in unsanitary conditions, was accompanied by singing, as was the custom among young people.

In 1913, I was married and left Kozienice. I settled in Shetshechov, the birthplace of my husband Moshe Greenberg. After the outbreak of the War, I was forced to leave, and attempted to settle in Gniewaszow. I had to leave because of our Polish neighbors, who informed the Germans that we had a great deal of merchandise, and that we had given the Polish authorities money to prepare the war resistance.

Reizl and Moshe Greenberg

Back to Kozienice

Also in our new dwelling place, my husband, daughter and myself, were not able to remain for a long while, because the German murderers began to drive the Jews of the small towns into the bigger towns. On German orders, the Jews of Gnievashov had to move to Zvolin, but I was drawn back to my birthplace, where my parents and relatives lived. The Kozienice Jews were already enclosed in the Ghetto. This was at the end of 1941. The situation of the Jews was atrocious. This was the beginning, when the Germans had thrown the Jews of the surrounding towns into Kozienice, and from there, together with Kozienice Jews were transported to the death camp at Treblinka. The area of the Kozienice Ghetto was strictly limited. In every Jewish house there were added Jews from the surrounding towns. The Germans, together with the Judenraat and the Jewish police, jammed into each house so many people, that the crowded conditions were unbearable. Many had to sleep on the floors. Dirt and the crowded conditions caused many illnesses, which decimated the Jewish population.

The coming of the Jews terrified the Kozienice Jews. We weren't aware of the reason why Jews were driven out of the towns and villages, but the confusion, disorganization, and fear were great, because it was clear that no good could come of it.

[Page 579]

We Flee Kozienice

Due to those conditions, my husband and I decided to move to Brezshnitze. For the price of gifts and money, which we gave to Polish engineers, they took us for forced labor on the canals. At that work there were employed hundreds of Kozienice Jews. The work involved digging the canals with shovels. This was done to dam the water from the fields, and the earth that was dug up, was brought with wheelbarrels to the surrounding fields. With us we had our Sarah–Malkale, who was then 6 years old. Every time we knew that the Gestapo was coming, we would quickly turn our child over to the paid people of the village, who would hide the child in the surrounding woods. I emphasize that at the time there were no longer any Jews in my birthplace, Kozienice. Our situation at the time was difficult to describe. We knew what was awaiting us. And on top of it, the work conditions were inhuman. November, 1942. Cold, frequent rains and frost. We slept in the fields. We nourished ourselves on beets which we stole from the fields.

Bullets Showered Us

On the 11th of November, 1942, when we were at work, a hail of bullets showered us. We began to run, wherever our eyes carried us. We understood that this was our end. A few fell dead on the spot. Among those shot were: Yosele Beirechs, and Lipshe, the daughter of the woman who sold fish. I no longer remember the others who fell. All night we wandered in the surrounding woods, and were afraid to approach the place of our work. We were not sure of what to do. In the morning we decided to find out what had taken place in the camp. When I say "We", I mean: myself, my husband and our child. Carefully we approached the place, where we became aware of the fact that all of the Jews with whom we had worked, had, after the shooting, been taken away in Gestapo trucks. Mentally and physically broken, we stood by the pit, in which there lay 13 Jews from Shetshechov, who had been shot, and among them, my brother, Yitzhak, of blessed memory. Unable to see any other way out, we decided that we must save our only child. It was clear to us that we must turn the child over to Christians.

The children of Getzel Ankerman

We Hide Our Child

The earth under our feet burned. Each minute was too long. We decided to turn the child over to a Polish family, that didn't have any children of their own. Understandably, this also involved a payment. We understood that our fate was sealed. Maybe, by a miracle, the child will remain alive. We turned our child over, and I and my husband went away, wherever our eyes led us. We wandered for days and nights in woods and fields, avoiding people. From time to time, at night, we attempted to knock on the door of a peasant. Among others, we decided to go to a poor peasant in the village of Zdinkev, to the not far from Gnievashov, about whom we had heard that he was hiding Jews.

At hat time we still had some money with us. The peasant's name was Bochenek. He took us and told us to go into the grain silo. In the silo there were two bundles of straw. My husband and I were exhausted from many sleepless nights.

[Page 580]

Where Are the Jews?

In the silo there was a pit. We went down into the pit and covered ourselves with the two bundles of straw. We fell asleep. We were awakened by the barking of the village dogs. Afterwards, we heard a knocking on the peasant's door. The A.K. were demanding that the hidden Jews be turned over to them. The peasant denied that he had any hidden Jews there. We heard all of this with our own ears. The A.K. then took Bochenek out in the snow, and beat him with thick sticks, demanding that he bring out the Jews. Afterwards, when the bandits did not stop beating him, Bochenek said that the Jews had been there hut that they had already left. Then they asked: "Where have the Jews gone?" Bochenek answered: "Would a Jew say where he's going?" We heard these words, and to this day they ring in our ears. Before leaving, the A.K. came into the silo with a dog, and lit it up with a flashlight. Seeing the silo empty, they left.

In the morning, Bochenek told us that three days earlier, the bandits had taken three Jews from his house, and shot them on the spot. After that conversation, we left Bochenek's home. We came to a place about 20 kilometers from our previous place, and hid ourselves in an out–of–the–way hut, which belonged to a woman named Gavelek. We hid ourselves there, without her knowing it. By day we were in the hut, and at night my husband went to acquaintances and brought sufficient food. In this way we "lived" from the beginning of 1942 until the end of 1943, not only in that hut, but also in a few other places.

How Shime Zuckerman Perished

During the last days of the year, 1943, we experienced a frightening event. Not far from the hut, in which my husband and I found ourselves, in the same village of Opastvo, a neighbor of ours, Shime Zuckerman was hiding out with his bride, Chaya Levita. Once, Shime went in to his peasant, where he was hiding his precious possessions. The peasant, knowing exactly when Shime was supposed to come, informed the Gestapo in Kozienice. When Shime entered the house, there were already two Gestapo agents waiting for him. His bride, Chaya Levita, was waiting outside. Shime fought with the Gestapo agents. It seems that the Gestapo did not want to shoot him on the spot. They tied him with rope and took him away to Kozienice, where, after administering frightful torture on him, they shot him.

Chaya Was Already Dead

Chaya fled and hid herself in the surrounding fields and woods. The murderers knew that Shime had not been alone, so they spread the alarm to all the units of the firefighters in the nearby village. There began a wild chase after Chaya Levita. After two days of searching, one of the local inhabitants found Chaya in a potato pit. They informed the Gestapo in Kozienice, who came, threw Chaya into the trunk of their taxi, and took her away to Brezshnitze. When they opened the trunk, Chaya was already dead. Her grave is behind the cemetery, in the village of Slavikov. Learning about this incident our own uncertainty increased to its highest point. We were envious of those who could no longer feel any pain. I didn't want to fall into the hands of the murderers alive.

[Page 581]

I Wanted To Commit Suicide

Not far from our hiding place passed the train to Kozienice. I had decided to put an end to my life. I begged my husband and tried to convince him that we must end our suffering by committing suicide on the tracks of the train. But my husband informed me that he would fight for his life with his remaining strength. We lived frozen from the frost and snow. I became ill with a high temperature. My lips were burning.. I wanted a drop of water to wet my dry lips. At night my husband went out of the hut. He found a container and brought some water, but it quickly froze. In order to obtain a bit of water for drinking, I had to put the frozen container against my burning body. Under such conditions, my husband, Moshe Greenberg and I managed to survive the year, 1944. Many years, after being liberated from the German bandits, we found out that our child, Malkele, had been murdered by the Christian, where she had been in hiding!

[Page 582]

How I Was Saved During the Holocaust

by Aaron Kestenberg, Tel Aviv

Ahron Kestenberg – Israel

Before I describe how I was saved from the Nazis, and how I got to Israel, I want to point out that my parents, Moshe and Luba, of blessed memory, were Kozieniceites from many generations back. My father was a son of the prolific Kestenberg family and mother was a daughter of the Rechthand family. My mother's grandfather, R'Aaron, served as the Kozienice Rabbi for 40 years. He named himself Rechthand (Right Hand) because he had been the right hand (assistant) of the Maggid of Kozienice. My parents got to Warsaw a few years before WWII. With the outbreak of war, the family numbered five children, Fishel, Yaakov, Shlomo and 2 sisters, Rivka and Nechama. I and my brother Yerachmiel, were the lone survivors of the entire family.

I Remember Kozienice From My Childhood

Kozienice I remember from the days of my childhood. I was then 6 years old. It was one year after the Balfour Declaration on November 2, 1917. This created an impetus for Aliyah to Eretz Yisrael. I remember how all of the Jews of Kozienice accompanied Chaim Aaron to the railroad station with a band and with the blue–white flag. Chaim Aaron was among the first to make Aliyah to Eretz Yisrael. This event penetrated deeply into my memory. At age 18 I joined a Kibbutz near Warsaw. After a year, I left the Kibbutz, in the hope that I would at sometime get to Eretz Yisrael. This dream was realized only after I had been through the seven levels of Hell.

It began with the conquest of Warsaw by the Germans. After the heavy bombardment, that lasted for 4– weeks, and at the heels of the army, came the SS and the Gestapo, who began to seize Jews, to clean up the wreckage of Warsaw. A terrible period began, which never had its equal in all of Jewish History. Daily we were faced with the dilemma: What would the day bring? And what would the morrow bring? Decrees and death were our lot. Hunger ruled in every Jewish home. The Nazis would pick especially on those Jews who had been seized to repair the damage they had done to Warsaw. Once they seized my father, and when he returned at night, it was impossible to recognize him. His beard had been shorn, and he had been beaten and was wounded. I was seized many times for labor, until I decided that I would disappear at the first opportunity.

The Nazi Didn't Find Me

It happened on one black day. All days were then black. A group of 100 Jews accompanied by 2 Nazis passed in front of our store. One of the Nazis dragged me out of the store and ordered me to join the group. I joined. So many Jews and only 2 Nazis! I began to think about fleeing. I said to myself: "I'll leave the line, that was walking on the road, go up on the sidewalk, and get lost among the passersby." I went up on the sidewalk, and joined the passersby. I began to run. In the yard of the first house I found a hiding place – an open storage shack. I closed the door and in this way I was saved. From within, I heard the Nazi curse. When I exited, towards evening, my father told me how the Nazi, with his gun in his hand, had searched for me, but couldn't find me.

A. Kestenberg his mother and brother

[Page 583]

In the morning, early, I went to the train station of the line to Shedlitz, and from there I crossed the border. After many difficulties I got to Bialostok. I had the feeling that I had left Hell and entered Paradise. A few months later, my brother, Yerachmiel, arrived with tragic news from Warsaw. At the beginning of June, 1940, the situation changed, also in Bialostok. Jewish refugees were sent en masse to Siberia. As fate would have it, my brother and I were separated, and I didn't know where he was until I made Aliyah in 1942.

My brother made Aliyah to Israel in 1959. In 1943, the most terrible of all news reached me: About Treblinka, and Auschwitz, where my family perished. Up to the last moments of my life – I shall never forget!

> Where are they all, O Lord of the
> Universe?
> The dear parents, the sisters and the
> brothers The holy, and the pure one.
> The souls – where are they?
> Of the infants and the children,
> Of millions of Jews?
> Your mercy, where is it, O Lord of
> the Universe?
> It is written in your Torah: "Do not
> take the mother together with
> the children!" We shall therefore cry
> over the destruction The great,
> terrible and awesome one!

Pesye Had Regrets

Pesia Shereshenski – Israel

In the summer of 1939, Pesye Sherevsky–Yazin was a teacher and administrator of the "Beis–Yaakov School" in Brisk. After a semester of work in the field of education of Jewish girls, she went, during vacation, to her parents home in the Hassidic town of Kozienice. Her father was the Rabbi in the town of Ostrolenko, near Lodz. She had been born there. In 1939, her father and his family already lived in the city of the Kozienicer Maggid, where he was the head of the Yeshiva. And there is where Pesye went at the end of the term, for the High Holidays. It was here that she was caught by the war. Days flew by and the War of Amalek (a nickname for Nazi Germany) showed its Hellish face. Once Pesye went out of the house and she was seized for forced labor. She was dragged to the Nazi headquarters where she was set to work washing windows. They made her take off her blouse, dip it into the pail of water and with it, wash the windows.

[Page 585]

My Mother Was Named Rachel

She stood and washed. Suddenly she saw a strange sight: Dr. Yosef Gonshor is being brought in. Dr. Gonshor, a convert to Christianity, was the Vice–Mayor of Kozienice, and much beloved by the Poles. They didn't know that he was a convert and thought that he was a born Samorodner Pole. He was being brought in screaming, and being beaten. "Admit that you're a Jew!" the Germans shouted at him and beat him. His blood flowed, but he didn't utter a word. They brought out a Torah Scroll and ordered: "Stomp it with you feet!" But he didn't move, so they beat him again and again, but didn't get anywhere. Non– Jews gathered and began to argue: "What do you mean he's a

Jew? He is one of us!" But the Germans answered: "We know better." And they continued beating him, until he fell unconscious. Then they let him alone.

The non–Jews carried him away in their arms. Pesye helped them, supporting his head. Suddenly she hears him utter something. She bends her head down to him and he says to her, in Yiddish, groaning: "I also once learned. My mother was named Rachel. Now my mother will be pleased with me." Afterwards he died! Pesye thought to herself: "Go, try to evaluate a Jewish soul! Only the slightest trace of Jewishness could be found in him, asleep within him, almost extinguished, but when necessary, it martyred itself!"

R' Eli, the Hunchback

A while later Kozienice saw an entirely different kind of martyrdom. There was in Kozienice a Jew, R'Eli, the Hunchback, he was called. He was a very secretive person. No one knew where he came from and who he was. He was to be found in the city garbage dump, but only at night. By day he would be found on the cemetery. Entire days he would spend lying on the grave of the Holy Maggid. Besides this he was also seen at funerals. He would trail behind every funeral. This is the way R'Eli would conduct himself all the days of the year. It would be entirely different when R'Arele would come to the city. Then R'Eli would come alive. The Rebbe, R'Arele, would seat him next to him, and in general befriend him.

As is well known, the Rebbe, R' Arele, was a great musician, who played the fiddle. When he would come to Kozienice, his custom was, on Saturday nights, to go to the Holy Maggid's small House of Prayer, put on the Maggid's Kittel (white robe), take the fiddle and play. Even there he would seat the Hunchback, R'Eli near him. No one knew the secret and the reason for it. But supposedly that was the way it had to be. When the Hunchback sensed, no one knew how, that the Nazis were planning to harm the Maggid's Shul, he would beat them to it. On a dark night, he removed from there the Torah Scrolls but he was caught at it.

And this is the way the Germans punished him: In the Maggid's Shul, in front of the Holy Ark, they scattered and tore the Torah Scrolls, until there was a large pile. They then tied the Hunchback and lay him upon the large pile of parchment. With ridicule and laughter at his defect they did it. The Germans were especially cruel to those who were crippled. They were the first to be exterminated. Probably because the cripples served no practical purpose, and on top of it had to be fed. It is also likely that they hated the feelings which cripples aroused in others: pity, charity and kindness.

[Page 585]

The Germans had regressed to the ancient Greek barbarism whereby they would put to death a deformed child, for so–called aesthetic reasons, so that nothing deformed or ugly would exist in the world. With derision and sport they threw the Hunchback, R'Eli to and from, among the pieces of parchment, and with especial pleasure they would bang him on his hump.

Outside, all around, stood the entire city, Jews as well as Goyim, whom the Germans had assembled to see this wonder. Then they set fire to the parchment! Jews, outside, saw the smoke through the windows, and they understood, that it had begun, but not a voice was raised. The Hunchback did not groan or cry out. He accepted the torture with love, as if the body wasn't his. This is what people later told, who were actually inside. His – was only a soul – and the soul the Germans were unable to touch. His face was pale yellow, just like the parchment, and he himself looked exactly like a Torah Scroll. Parchment doesn't burn quickly, and death did not come to R' Eli quickly. It was a long dying! A long Martyrdom! The Holy Ark caught fire from the Torah Scrolls, and soon afterwards, the entire Maggid's Shul was in flames. It had even been held sacred by the Goyim. The street, on which it had stood, was called "Magitova". The walls had been inscribed with the writing of great people, who used to come to the Maggid. There was even an inscription in the handwriting of the Polish Nobleman, Poniatovski. He was much esteemed by the Poles. The entire city stood and cried over the burning Shul. But the tears that were shed couldn't quench the flames. Pesye also stood here. She cried and thought about Eli's martyrdom, and she regretted that she had once in her heart questioned whether or not it was a worthy generation!

(From the Jewish Daily Forward, 1949)

Hitlerite Barbarism!

On Simchas Torah in 1939 the Hitlerite barbarians forced Kozienice scholars, and prominent citizen to pour kerosene and burn Torah Scrolls, and Holy books of all kinds on the spot of the Maggid's Shul in Kozienice.

[Page 586]

The Germans Ordered Us to Dig a Pit

by Leibele Fishtein, Ramat–Gan

Chaim Zaltzberg, who today lives in Canada, tells of an atrocity, whereby and why the Hitlerites had shot to death a minyan of Jews. This occurred in 1942, in a work camp, in the village of Shitshki, near Radom. On Yom Kippur morning, a minyan of young people put on their prayer shawls, and conducted their services. They were so engrossed in their prayers that they forgot to appear for their "line up". When they reminded themselves, it was already too late. Everyone had already long before gone out to their labor. They remained this way in their bunker all day, and prayed. In the midst of "Neilah the closing service", the Gendarmerie came from Radom, and ordered that they all come out to the square, wearing their prayer shawls. A few minutes later, when we returned from work, we found nobody left in the barracks.

At that moment we heard shots. We asked each other: "Who knows, maybe they've shot them?" a few minutes later, there returned from the woods "our" Germans, together with the Gendarmerie, joyful, as if they had just then returned from a good meal. They ordered us to line up. One of the Germans removed several men from the line–up. I was among them. They ordered us to take shovels – and led us into the woods. The Germans commanded us to dig a pit. How long the digging took, I don't know! I only remember the shouting of the Germans: "Make the pit larger! Even larger! So that there will be enough room for all of you." The word "larger" threw us into a panic. Who knows? Maybe we are actually digging the pit for ourselves? In burying those that had been shot, I recognized four from Kozienice: Moshe Greenshpan, Moshe Greenberg, Moshe Feigenboim and Menashe, the son of Chaim Samochod.

[Page 587]

I Sit In the Forest, Lonesome, Alone

by Rivke Pearlstein

I sit in the forest, lonesome, alone,
In my heart suppress a quiet sobbing,
Without occupation and without a home,
My wandering has no destination.
Wrapped in terror and fear,
Long forgotten what it means: to be sated
On the way of wandering.
To myself I think and talk,
Darkness all around, cold and late,
The eyes crying, broken, tired,
I ask God to put an end to the war.
How to save oneself from Hitler's hands,
Not to be burned alive,
Give advice, somebody tell me,
From my eyes drip a prayer–tear.
My God, my God, I murmur quietly,
Merciful and pitiful God – with great
feeling,
Tired, exhausted I fall asleep,
But a few numbered minutes run by.
The entire forest and everything around
Was quiet and mute.
An echo is heard there …
I remember to this day every word.

Don't worry, my child, don't cry and
bemoan,
Your redemption will come, the bright
day.
The sun will rise for you,
And for all Jews who cry.

You will yet sing songs in your own land,
And dance the Hora, Hand in hand,
Joy seizes me intimately,
Because I have felt the Image of God.
The eyes shone, the face beamed,
From my sweet dream, my health revived,
Suddenly I heard strong thunder,
And my sweet dream was shattered.
I sit in the forest, lonesome, alone,
In my heart suppress a quiet sobbing.

[Page 588]

A Preordained Thing

by Mira Sobol, Melbourne, Australia

My name is Mira Sobol, born Lipman, from the small town of Kozienice. Before WWI the town was under Russian occupation. The Czar did nothing to lift the cultural or economic level of the population. Because of it the Jewish populace lived in poverty, and only a few achieved either high school or higher education. The predominate portion of the Kozienice population was engaged in shoe production. More than 50% produced, handled and sold shoes. We lived in very bad conditions. Very often, six and seven people to a room. Earnings were minimal. The vast majority worked and earned only a few months of the year, and in the remaining months, didn't have enough for daily expenses– With the impoverished masses, the Polish government conducted a constant struggle. On the one hand they would subsidize with significant amounts, and on the other hand they would propagandize, so that buyers would not come to Jewish enterprises. This was what the former Polish Minister of the Interior called: The Economic War Against the Jews." Besides which they engaged in physical warfare against the Jews with their fists. They would beat them on dark streets, tore at their beards, threw rocks, demolished Jewish homes, and even killed Jews. But all of this was Paradise compared to what happened when the Hitler hordes occupied Poland.

As long as it was possible, the Jews of Kozniece took care of poor, needy children and orphans.
Representatives of Tipat Khalav (Drop of Milk) are providing baths and haircuts to the children in the ghetto of Kozniece.

Beatings and Shootings

Immediately, in the first weeks of their coming, the Germans drove the Jews into the Ghetto. During this activity, they beat, shot and robbed Jews. The majority of the Jewish populace had to depend on support, and when the support wasn't enough to maintain life, people died of hunger. It was a daily occurrence, to see swollen, hungry children and adults, begging. Those, who were able to help these living dead, became fewer day by day. Finally the time came when the small number, who only had enough to eat, became deaf and dumb to the beggars.

My family did not suffer hunger during the German occupation. My father had, before the war a leather business, and there remained enough merchandise on what to live, and support his family. When the Germans took the Jews out of the town to Treblinka, my entire family saved itself from the transports, by volunteering for the labor camps. At the end of 1942, the Germans liquidated the labor–camp, and took the people into the concentration camps in Skarzshisko and Pionki. My father and mother, and also my first husband, tragically gave their young lives to the bullets of the German murderers. I succeeded in turning over my four–year old son to a Polish family. I and my younger sister were able, as Christians, to go to Germany, to work, and in this way, by a miracle we saved our selves from annihilation.

Today, when I think of it, how the weak, helpless women and small children were able to overcome the great cataclysm and escape alive from the murderous hands, I see in it a great miracle and pre–ordained thing. And in spite of the fact that I am not a strong believer, I do indeed believe that a supernatural hand supported us and led us out alive from the greatest danger, in which Jews had ever found themselves, in all the long period of their history.

[Page 589]

Blood Flowed

by Gershon Bornshtein, B'nai–B'rak, Israel

Our grandfather, Pesach Mandl, or Pesach Schneider, as he was called, was one of the oldest householders in Kozienice. He had been born in Kozienice, and there he raised five sons and five daughters, grandchildren and great–grandchildren.

My Grandfather

Pesach Mandel

I remember, when we the grandchildren, used to come to our grandfather, of blessed memory, our greatest joy was to pat his shining, silky, white beard. It was also a pleasure for him, and he was overjoyed by it. He would groom his beard as if it were a precious diamond. Before every joyous event, he would groom his beard with a fine comb.

I want to point out that Pesach Schneider was the only tailor in the Rabbi's courtyard. He worked and sewed by the light of kerosene lamps, until late at night, and still did not miss a single afternoon or evening prayer in the House of Study. All of his ten children he raised and married off through his hard work, and waited patiently for his heavenly reward in Paradise. Unfortunately, he waited until the German Hell arrived. Our grandfather's courage and joy lasted until the German murderers occupied our city, our dearly beloved city of Kozienice, which was famous throughout Poland for it's Hassidism and it's Maggid.

When the first motorized armored vehicles lined up on Koshtshelna and Targova Streets, my grandfather had the urge to see the Germans. When he came to Yisroel–Abraham Schneider on the corner of Targova and Lubliner Streets, an SS officer approached and began to tear my grandfather's gray beard. Then he knocked on the tailor's door to bring him a scissors. My grandfather stood with trembling hands and feet, like an imprisoned lamb, waiting for the end. With his dirty bloody hands the SS man cut off the left side of grandfather's beard and in doing so also tore out flesh from his face. Blood flowed on my grandfather's Kapote (long black coat) and the blood pounded in his heart, when the wild SS man lit a match and burned grandfather's cut beard. Covered with blood, my grandfather suffered from his damaged beard, and from the burning of the old Maggid's Shul and House of Study.

Every one of us remembers, when we small children used to go with father to pray in Shul and repeat word for word, the chanting of the Cantor. Our unforgettable mothers would give us food, wrapped in hankerchiefs, to take along, in order, from time to time, to satiate our hunger. When the food supply would run out, we would run outside of the Shul to play. To this day, there rings in my ears, the sweet, gentle voice of Aaron–Berish, who used to cover his face with his Tallis, holding his hand at his ear, so that his gentle voice would ring out more clearly. Or the praying of Melech Chaim Pinchasl. The blowing of the Shofar still echoes from the old Maggid's Shul, which the Germans, may their names be blotted out, had burned.

[Page 590]

During the early days of the occupation, on a Friday night, the Germans poured gasoline on the inside and outside walls and drove the Jews out of their homes onto Magitova Street. Accompanied by wild Gestapo shouting and beatings, the Jews had to dance around the burning fire, which was devouring the Shul and House of Study. Those two scenes, mentioned above, accompanied my grandfather wherever he went: 1) The burning of the Maggid's Shul and House of Study, where he would daily praise the beloved name of the Holy One, Blessed Be He, and 2) the great tragic aggravation of his shorn beard.

The two great desolations, which he experienced in his great old age, had a powerful negative influence on him. He would isolate himself as much as he could, in order not to have to look upon the Nazi murderers. His gentle, beautiful beard he tied with our grandmother's head kerchief, and shortly, after these tragic experiences, his gentle heart stopped beating, and his soul was martyred in the Ghetto. In his funeral not even a single child or grandchild was able to participate. Only a few Jews from the Burial Society and his brother's son, Ben–Zion Mandl, accompanied him to his eternal resting place.

[Page 591]

My Heart Dripped With Blood

by Rivke Pearlstein, Haifa, Israel

For many years, the Chmielnitzky family lived in Yedlnia. We had an haberdashery manufacturing plant there. We would buy in Radom and sell to the Christians of the town. We lived quite peaceably, and the Goyim trusted my father. Our family consisted of sisters, brothers, daughters–in–law, sons–in–law and grandchildren. Our home was open to the poor Jews, who used to pass through our town. We were always open–handed about helping those in need. This is how we lived until 1939.

Rivka Pearlstein – Israel

My father and my mother came from Kozienice. My father was the son of R' Avigdor Yosef Chmielnitzsky, a fine Jew and an upright person. My mother, Nechama Leah, was the daughter of R' Itshe Feigenboim.

We Move To Kozienice

At the beginning of 1939 we decided to move to Kozienice. We moved into the house of my uncle, Aaron Berish, on Lubliner Street. There we decided to open a yard goods business. We had barely opened the business, when the merchants began to complain that the situation is very difficult. It didn't take long and the War broke out. It ruined our fortune and our family.

We Flee and Return

Once, on a Friday, when we were preparing for the Sabbath, we suddenly heard the sound of bombing not far from us. But nobody could imagine that the murderers would soon arrive. The first bombs fell and everyone ran into his corner. The first bombs brought with them some victims, the Lippman family. I and my two sisters fled to the forest, where we suffered hunger. At 5:00 p.m. we returned home, where we found the entire family. On Shabbat, before dawn, Jews from Kozienice fled the city. Some fled to the villages, and others to the forest. Panic ensued. We survived that Shabbat in great fear.

On Monday, the German murderers entered Kozienice. Several Jews arrived with the news that the Germans are very polite, so we returned to the city, great destruction greeted us. All of the business establishments were damaged. All of the merchandise was scattered on the streets, and entire

Jewish properties destroyed. Since we had no alternative, we adapted ourselves to the fear and terror. Suddenly an order was issued: That all Jews must abandon Radomer and Varshaver Streets. We were shoved into the Ghetto. It became overcrowded, and the noise,– great. We also adapted to this, and we hoped that God will not abandon us; that better times are in the offing. In this way we lived until the tragic destruction of our large family.

[Page 592]

During the intermediate days of Succot, all of the Jews of Kozienice were sent out to Treblinka. Only a small number managed to save themselves. I was in Camp Vulka. This was a village not far from Kozienice. I was together with my husband, Yenkel Vildenberg, my sister, Tovah, my mother, Raizel Zucker, her son Leibl, and many other Kozienice Jews., We worked hard. This took a number of days. Later, all remaining Kozienice Jews were sent to Skarzshisko, but we worked at digging canals. Two days after we arrived, we were all called into the square where a "selection" took place. A number of women were chosen, among them my sister, Tovah. They were taken in wagons to Vohlin. Many Jews decided to flee. When the Germans saw that they didn't have enough Jews to send out – they arranged another "selection". 1 was chosen during the second "selection". On the way we suddenly understood that the Germans had deceived us: They weren't taking us to Vohlin for labor, but to Treblinka.

I Flee

I decided to flee. I sprang from the wagon. I saw a Christian walking with a Jewish girl. The Christian told her to go into the forest, and he promised her that he would help her. I approached the girl and asked her to take me with her into the forest. The Christian wouldn't hear of it. I begged and offered money, but he won't listen. I warned him that if he won't permit me to go with the girl – she won't go either. The Christian went away, and the two of us went into the forest. The girl told me that the Christian had promised her to come at night and take her to "Vulka", to the labor place, but he did not come.

We remained in the forest for three days and three nights. We huddled together against the cold and the hunger. We had no food. We were dressed for summer. We were envious of those who had traveled on. We couldn't remain in the forest, but we didn't know where to go. Each step we took was terrible for us. Finally we assembled enough courage to go further into the forest. In either case we had nothing to lose. In this way we traveled for an entire day. Finally we crawled into a small village. Where shall we turn to, first? We begged of God to lead us in the right direction, so we would encounter people who might help us. The first house was a mill. We decided to enter the mill. Suddenly it occurs to me the thought that in the mill we might find Folk-Germans. We continue on our way, until we came to a small house. We decided to enter.

[Page 593]

We Hide Out With Two Female Peasants

Kozienicer young men working under the supervision of Rembalski

In the house we encountered two female peasants: An older one and a younger one. They were eating breakfast. We introduced ourselves as Christians, but they recognized that we are Jewish women. They calm us, and bid us not to be afraid, since they know everything and they tell us that during the night they had four Jews with them. According to their description, these were Jews from Kozienice. We stayed with them. They were alone and had no one else. They were impoverished, but they shared their food with us. We were tired and hungry. We ate with a hearty appetite. The women went to the fields to work, left us alone in the house, and locked the door from the outside. They allowed us to sleep in their beds. For us this was the greatest fortune. When we awakened from our sleep, we began to think about what to do next. We couldn't remain there. All of our proposals seemed unrealistic. In the evening the two women returned. They fed us. We sat together and thought about our situation and the great danger to these two women. They promised us that they will take us to Vulka. Understandably, this was for us a stroke of luck. Unfortunately, our joy did not last long. The women had second thoughts. They figured out that they couldn't go with us to Vulka, but they will introduce us to a Christian acquaintance, an upright person, who knows the way. They'll ask him to take us to Vulka. We were naturally afraid to go with a strange Christian at night, but we had no choice, so we agreed to the proposal. They got in touch with him, and he came to us.

We saw that he was an elderly peasant from the same village. He made an excellent impression upon us. We told him what we wanted of him, and promised him 60 Zlotys, if he would get us safely to Vulka. The peasant calmly listened to us, and then told us that he had a better plan. Since he has a large farm with chickens and cows, and doesn't have a wife, he would be amenable to taking us in, and we would be responsible for running the enterprise. We would lack nothing.

He has a large house, and we have nothing to fear, since there are no Germans in the village. We were afraid to live with a Christian in the village, so we thanked him for his kindness, and told him that since our parents were in Vulka and must be worried about us, we request that he have pity on us and take us to Vulka. We will never forget his attitude towards us.

[Page 594]

Back To Vulka

All night we didn't sleep. We could barely wait for the fortunate moment. In actuality, at about 4:00 a.m. he knocked at the door. We were already waiting for him. We bade a fond farewell to our hostesses and repeatedly thanked them for their nice attitude towards us. Then we left. We went, in the dark night, with great fear and pounding hearts through fields and woods. Who knows where the Goy is taking us? But, thank God, we reached our goal. We parted from him fondly and he wished us well. He didn't want to take any money. We repeatedly thanked him, and from great joy, we burst out crying. He returned to his village. This was at 10:00 o'clock. All of the Jews were at their labor, so we went into Christians and waited until 12:00, when all returned for lunch. When they all came, and saw us, they fell upon us with questions. We told them about our adventures. We remained in Vulka and went to work together with all of the others, but our good fortune didn't last long.

In Skarzshisko

A week later Germans came with large trucks, upon which they loaded us like sheep. A few fled, and they were shot. They told us that they were taking us to Skarzshisko for labor. When we arrived there, they took us into a large barrack, which was called "Ogulnik". There we found many Jews from various cities. In the morning we were taken out for a lineup. Decrees were read to us. Whoever opposed them would be shot immediately. After the lineup we were assigned to different work places. The leading place of work was a munitions factory. I was assigned to a machine. The supervisor was a Polish Christian. I strained with all my might to please my master, in order to be able to remain at the work. In this way the days flew by as well as the weeks and months.

Each day brought with it new troubles. People arrived and people were taken away. They beat, they killed and they hanged. We went through a living Hell, but with hope that we will live to see better times.

Troubles

Besides the fact that my husband, Yaakov Vildenberg, of blessed memory, was also in Skarzshisko, we were only able to meet at the gate, where the shifts would change. We lived like that until a Typhus epidemic broke out. My husband became sick. There were no medications and everyone died. With this, my troubles did not come to an end. The Typhus spread, and I also became ill. I was taken to the hospital, where I lay with fever. We didn't receive any food, because our female supervisor, Lola, a Jewish woman, took all of the food for herself.

[Page 595]

Ignoring my illness, I wanted to get out of the hospital as soon as possible in order to return to my work. The longer one remained in the hospital, the less were his chances to remain alive. Each day selections were made and patients were sent to the gas chambers. One night I dreamed that my parents were warning me to get out of the hospital as quickly as possible. I got up in the morning. My head was swinging. My feet can't carry me, but in spite of this I request of the supervisor that she sign me out of the hospital, because I want to return to work. As luck would have it, I was rescued from certain death, because two days later a selection was made, and the majority of the patients who remained in the hospital were sent to the ovens. And so we remained, quite a few Kozeniceites, until 1944. In August of 1944 a number of workers from Skarzshiska were taken to Tshenstochov. Here everything began anew. They began to distribute the workers among various machines. I was assigned to difficult labor. My supervisor was a Jew from Kozienice, A. Viltshik.

Once, at night, the best workers were selected. Then it appeared that I was a saboteur who does not work well. They took me to the guardhouse, whipped me thirty times on my naked body. While this was taking place, the German threatened to shoot me. I begged and pleaded that I wasn't guilty of any thing. To this day I can't forget how lucky I was that I remained alive.

You Are Free!

The Liberation came unexpectedly on a bright winter day, in 1945. We didn't believe our eyes. All at once we see Russian soldiers. They are coming. "You are free!" We ran to the gate. We found it open. Each one shouts to the other: "We are free!" Then our real troubles began. We don't know where to go. We run to the city, to Tshenstochov. I am quite alone and abandoned. I don't have to whom to turn. I try to stay with my own sort of people, who are acquaintances from Kozienice and from the camp. They are Devora and Eliezer Weinberg, and Feige and Gitl Friedman. Together with them I went to Gnievashov, and from there, on foot, to Kozienice. A Christian showed us the way.

It's Thursday. In Kozienice the Fair is taking place. I look around and everything is empty. Where are all the stalls? Where are all the Jews, the merchants and dealers from Radomer Street? Of our family no one remained, I'm all alone! Fear envelops me. I don't know where to go. Everything looks like a cemetery to me. I wandered around like that for an hour, until I succeeded in finding Abraham Shabason. He told me that there are a few more Jews there, among them: Paula Luksenburg. He goes with me to Lubliner Street. We go to the house of my uncle, Aaron Berishes. With fear and a pounding heart, we went into our house. Overcome with emotion, I fainted. In the kitchen I found our closet. We found a Christian family in our house. I also found our possessions there. In the third room they had books. My heart dripped blood at the sight of what had been done to our home.

[Page 596]

I girded my strength, and strongly desired to take in everything – for all eternity. I went up to the attic, where we had hidden a scroll of the Torah. I believed, that maybe the unclean hands of the murderers hadn't damaged the holy books. All I found there were old, torn books, prayer books, high–holiday prayer books. I froze in my tracks and couldn't move. I cried bitterly over my family, that had so tragically been martyred for the sake of the Sanctification of the Name of God. I can no longer remain in this cemetery, so I traveled to Yedlnye, to my former home, where we had lived and enjoyed a nice life. There, I didn't meet anyone from my family. Four Jews had remained alive, who had lived together in the same house for twenty years. We were overjoyed to see them alive and we cried bitterly. I remained there for five days and then went on my way. I found no resting place. I seeked. Maybe I'll still find someone from my family.

Life Flows On

From there I traveled to Lodz. There I met with Yaakov Korman from Kozienice. Lodz is a very big city and there you can meet people. I had seen that life continues. A living human being must eat and clothe himself. Having no alternative, I took myself in my hands. I remained in Lodz for a longer time, until the time arrived for Jews to leave Poland. I arrived in Stuttgart. There I found many Jews from Kozienice and Radom, who were my acquaintances from before the war. There, in Stuttgart, I became acquainted with my husband, who also had come from Kozienice. We decided to get married and then we remained in Germany for four years. We had a manufacturing plant, and lived very well. Life flowed on!

I gave birth to a son. We were overjoyed, but our joy mingled with sadness. We were nostalgic for relatives and friends, especially when we were celebrating a joyous event. But we had no choice. Such was life, and it cannot be changed. In 1949, we left Germany, and the good life there, and we went with our beloved son, Moshe, to Israel. Today he is already a Sargeant in the Israel Defense Forces.

In Israel, we met my uncle, Elimelech, who had gone to Israel quite a few years ago. We lived with him for two years in Kiryat–Chaim (near Haifa), and then we moved to Haifa. I gave birth to another son, Nachum (consolation) I named him Nachum after my mother, whose name had been Nehama (consolation). With this I end my memories of our city of Kozienice, which, unfortunately, is now yuden zein.

[Page 597]

How Tzipporah Weisbord Saved Herself

by Abraham Tenenboim, Warsaw

From the letters of Yadviga Marks, whose name will be mentioned here frequently, we became aware that on a frosty, December night, in 1941, Haskell Weisbord sneaked out of the Kozienice Ghetto with his 11 month old daughter, Tzipporah. Afterwards, as he wandered all night through woods and fields, he came to Yadviga Marks in the resort town of Garbatke, some tens of kilometers from Kozienice. From the letters we find out that Tzipporah, who was later called by the name of Bozshenka, was badly frozen, and her body broke out in a rash. There were Jews in Kozienice, who knew that the woman, Marks, and her husband were prepared to accept payment, or for a promise of further reward, were ready to hide Jewish children. Haskell asked her to take his little daughter to his sister, Eva, who lived with his second sister, Miriam, in Warsaw. In this way, the little Tzipporah came to Warsaw at the end of December in 1941. The Warsaw Ghetto, in those days, was a Hell. Thousands of Jews were taken each day to the Umschlag–Platz (Selection Place), and from there to either Maidenek or Treblinka.

Eva Weisbord decided to use her Arian appearance, and with the help of the Marks woman, she obtained Arian papers, with which she planned to go to Germany to work. In order to carry out her plan, Eva went to Maria Lach, Mrs. Marks' sister, who lived on the banks of the Praga. Eva arranged with Mrs. Lach, that if somebody from the Weisbard family will, after the great world conflagration, remain alive, and little Tzipporah remain alive, they will not request that the child be returned to them. Eva asked the Lach woman to give the child to a childless family. It means that the husband of Mrs. Lach, a railroad man, found the child and brought her from the Province of Bialistok. Eva said that the childless family should be told that during the evacuation of Poles from the Bialistoker Region, the Germans had forbidden them from taking the child with them. Maria Lach liked this plan very much, and she went to the childless family, named Skovronski.

Tzipporah Becomes Bozshenka

The Skovronski family took the child. They had no illusions about the danger, which they faced in hiding out a strange child. But in spite of all, they decided to save the child. What they went through cannot be described. The most difficult task was registering the child in the birth registry. By a mighty effort they managed to register the child in a small village registry as Bozshenka Skovronska, who had been born on the 2 of February, 1942. It wasn't long before the Hitlerites took Mr. Skovronski away to a concentration camp. During the August Uprising, the apartment of the Skovronski family was ruined. Mrs. Skovronski was left without a provider, without an apartment and without a livelihood. On top of these troubles, Bozshenka became ill several times. Having no alternative, she kept the child in a cellar on the cold floor. Thanks to miracles, the little girl was saved.

[Page 598]

In this way the child grew up as Bozshenka Skovronska. At age 8, a neighbor whispered in her ear, that the Skovronskis were not her real parents. But the little Bozshenka understood that this secret was not to be discussed with her parents. She buried the secret deep within her small heart.

Bozshenka Is To Be Married

Years passed. Bozshenka grew up. Troubles and need had obviously not had any influence, because she was a beautiful and well endowed young lady. At 19, she became acquainted with Yanush Tzsharnetzki and they decided to marry. Before the wedding, Bozshenka told her mother the secret, which she had buried deep within her for years. With tears in her eyes she begged her mother to tell her the truth. Mrs. Skovronska told her about Maria Lach, and how she had supposedly come from the Province of Bialistok. Bozshenka contacted Mrs. Lach and tried to persuade her to tell from where she comes, and who had brought her to the Skovronskis. Maria Lach remained silent. She didn't want to tell her anything, but she sent her to her sister, Yadviga.

Yadviga Marks Remains Silent

Yadviga, who had displayed so much heartfelt concern for Jewish children, and saved so many of them, must have shed a tear over the tragic fate of Bozshenka, but she filled her mouth with water and remained silent. She doesn't want to tell the truth. Having no other alternative, Bozshenka turned to the "Red Cross". She told what she knew about herself from the Skovronskis and requested that the "Red Cross" demand that Yadviga Marks tell the truth. It was of no avail – Yadviga remained silent!

Eva Weisbord saved herself from the great world conflagration. After much wandering, she came to America. She got in touch with Yadviga Marks and asked her to help find the little Tzipporah. Eva knew that she had been saved, and she requested that Yadviga give her the address. Yadviga answered the letters, but she managed to avoid writing about Tzipporah, and finally she conveyed some false names of the missing Tzipporah. She refused to give even her sister's address.

Eva Requests That I Help

In the autumn of 1963 I got in touch with Eva Weisbord. She had, in her letters, written to me quite a bit about how she had, at the end of 1941, turned over the child to Maria Lach. She requested that I help her. I understood that the secret could be uncovered. I contacted the "Red Cross", acquaintances and good friends. Finally, when I already knew Tzipporah's address, the thought began to bother me: How was I going to tell Tzipporah-Bozshenka the truth? I was afraid, that if I tell her, that she is Jewish, there will begin for her a new tragedy. I didn't know in what kind of an atmosphere she had been brought up. But I did know that now she already had a husband and a child.

[Page 599]

I Told Bozshenka Her Secret

How does one begin to speak to her? I decided that during our first conversation I would tell her the truth. I telephoned her and invited her to come to me. I told her everything: About her background, about her childhood, about her parents who had perished, and finally – about Eva, who had been searching for her for many years. Yadviga Marks now knew that she couldn't keep the secret any longer. Seeing that she was being attacked from all sides, she finally sent Bozshenka's address to Eva Weisbord. When Eva received the address – she already had letters from Bozshenka on her table. I've here given but a few moments of the dramatic life of Bozshenka. fa order to tell all, I would have to write a book.

[Page 600]

My Tragic Experiences

by Rachel Dorfman–Kestenberg, Tel–Aviv

My family lived in Kozienice for many years. My grandparents also lived there. My father was Shmuel Kestenberg, a butcher. We lived on Pieratzki Street. When the War broke out, I was 15 years old. Before the evacuation to Treblinka, I and my sister, Tovah, went to the Christian, Gortshitzki, and remained there working.

In Skarzshisko

A short while later, my sister and I and other Kozienice Jews, were sent away to a labor camp in Skarzshisko. There we experienced hunger and cold, and had to work hard. The terrible conditions made both of us sick, but even sick, we had to perform our labor, because we were afraid that if we didn't, the Germans would shoot us. We would help each other so that the work was performed. But to my great sorrow, my sister was unable to carry on, and in 1943 she died. She was exactly 20 years old. Her death had a very bad affect on me. I broke down. Sick as we were, we were sent to Tshenstachov, to another labor camp, where we worked on ammunition.

Finally – Liberation

In this way we suffered until the end of 1944. In January, 1945, we were liberated by the Red Army. Understandably, we didn't loiow what to do or where to go. We three, Kozienice girls, I, Polia Shpigel, Leah Kohn, and her husband, Shalom Kohn, decided to go on foot to Kozienice, because there were no trains as yet, and we had no money. We didn't know to whom to turn for help. We were barefoot and half naked, but we didn't anticipate any difficulties. We wanted to get to Kozienice as quickly as possible, hoping that there we would find our families.

It Became Bitter and Dark For Us

For 10 days we walked on foot. We would pass through villages and beg the Goyim for food. There were Christians, who not only fed us, but also permitted us to sleep over. More than once we had to sleep out–of–doors, until God helped us and we finally arrived in Kozienice. It became bitter and dark for us, when we came into Kozienice and saw the destruction which the Germans had inflicted on our city. All of the Jews had been killed, the houses burned. We searched for Jews, but found no one. We saw that there was nothing for us to do in Kozienice, so we decided to travel to Lodz.

Kozienicer Jews drying swamps in Vulka – Kozienice

[Page 601]

From Lodz To Israel

In Lodz we met some Kozienice Jews, and they told us that all of Kozienice Jews had been cremated in Treblinka. Hearing this we completely broke down. But God was merciful to me, and I met my husband to be, Nasan Dorfsman, and we were fortunately married and decided not to remain in accursed Poland but to go to Israel, to our own homeland. Good friends advised us to travel to Germany, and from there to Israel. That was what we did. Today, thank God, we live in Tel–Aviv. My husband is a butcher. We have a son, Shmuel, who is an officer in the Army, and a daughter, Sarah, who is a high–school student.

[Page 602]

This Was the Way I Was Liberated

by Shalom Kohn, New York

In 1942, in my early youth, just as the Germans occupied our city of Kozienice, I was also drawn into the bloody struggle, because on my forehead I bore the mark of a Jew.

We Lived In Fear

The Nazis took me to a forced labor camp on the outskirts of Kozienice, a town call Vulka, together with 500 other youngsters. We remained there for a month. From that forced labor camp they took a large portion of the people to Volanov. There we labored under difficult conditions. For the least infringement, we were threatened with death. Each day I saw the deaths of innocent victims. We lived in fear. I longed for my former home, and family. I and a few friends decided to flee from the camp and return to Kozienice. My doubts and hesitation cannot be described. Finally we concluded that we must make the attempt, even though failure would mean certain death. We sneaked out of the camp, and like an arrow from a bow we were carried along by the impetus. Fate, however, had decreed otherwise. On the way we were stopped by an SS Patrol. We were put in their truck and taken into the forest. We felt that they were going to shoot us. But a miracle happened. The truck swerved off the road and got stuck. Then the SS men ordered us to go into the forest.

From the right: Neche Waserman and her daughter Khava Kohn

We Flee

We walked as if going to our deaths, but seeing that the SS men were preoccupied with fixing the truck, and were not following us too closely, we got further away from them and began to run quickly.

We heard them firing at us, but the trees protected us. We ran as if we were deer and not humans. After a great deal of wandering around, in great danger, we arrived back in Vulka. They began to interrogate us. Fortunately, we weren't held too long in that camp, and I was sent with a transport to Skarzshisko.

Without Pity

The way to the other camp was accompanied by terror: Bullets flew over our heads. The scene is still vivid today before my eyes: How Dinahle Rosen's husband was shot dead. Many other people, whose names I cannot recall, also fell victim. We were driven, like cattle, accompanied by beatings, without pity. In Skarzshisko our clothes were taken from us. We stood before a new commission. The investigation lasted a whole night. We washed at faucets, where there were lying corpses, and persons who had passed out. Finally we were assigned to coal mining, about 25 kilometers from the camp. Under heavy guard we were taken to work. At work we were terrorized. If someone got lazy or engrossed in thought – he was immediately shot, and as a result there were daily victims. When we would go to work no one could be sure that he would end the day.

Chava Kohn and her children. Only one boy survived. All others were exterminated in Treblinka

[Page 603]

From time to time, a truck would come to take people to their deaths. Among those shot in the camp, were: Shmelke Rozentzveig and Nuta Lipman. Motke Honigshtok was shot for no reason at all, when he went out of his barracks, because the murderer just wanted some target practice. In such circumstances, we lived and labored!

Finally Liberated

From Skarzshisko I was taken to Tshenstochov, where I remained until my liberation. This occurred on January 17, 1945. From this camp, the Nazis were taking people for extermination until the very last day. We were swollen from hunger. We felt that the bloody murderer, Hitler, was facing a bitter end. This gave us the hope and courage to endure, and to hold out in order to see peace restored to the world. Shortly before the liberation, we were taken to a new kind of labor. I already had no more strength to drag my swollen feet. A warm thanks to the camp's Jewish policeman, who, in Polish, would shout to get up and go out to work, and in Yiddish would whisper to us not to go but to lie where we were! I regret that I don't remember his name, because he actually saved tens of lives. The approaching sound of cannons was getting closer. This was the announcement that our liberation was at hand. The Russian military came closer with a heavy bombardment. The camp guards fled like scared rabbits. In this way we were liberated. There, in Tshenstochov, I met the Kozieniceite, Lola Meltzer. We decided to marry, begin a new life, and build a home and family!

[Page 604]

Comfort and Sadness

by Avigdor Zilberknopf

Finally the time has come,
To take us out of slavery,
A life full of joy Brings for us the new
age.

We greet nature
So helpful and fine,
Also the rays which can't be counted
Of the sunshine.

At night in the quiet,
We greet with feeling,
Also the bright moon.
What we think and dream,
All is declared to her.
Without the heavenly gift,
When the heart is filled with longing,
It pains, and lacks the friendship,
It reminds us of once upon a time,
How we lived satisfied,
Like everyone, also we Jews.
Today, much suffering, without
measure.
O', her comfort no longer helps,
She can no longer shine for us,
Because we are heavily ruined,
And have lost everything.
Today, only now are we born again,
To life we are further led,
There isn't much that has remained for
us,
But to reminisce, and be driven.
Like swimming away in the ocean,
Like shadows we crawl.,
But we question ourselves and we
seek: Maybe, maybe…We'll find.

[Page 605]

Ach, the Tragic Joy

by Leibele Fishtein, Ramat–Gan, Israel

The day of liberation in the German concentration camps, was the most joyous and tragic day of our lives. One who didn't experience it by himself cannot have any concept of the taste of joy mixed with sadness.

You Are Free!

"Out of the barracks! You are free! The Allied Armies are already here!" The healthy ones yell "Hoorah!" and run like wild animals. The sick crawl off their beds on all fours, stand, run and fall; fall and run. Some remain lying, and never rise again. They had survived only long enough to hear: "Hoorah we are free!" Some were lying crouched in their places and no longer understood the meaning of the word "Free". They were already battling the Angel of Death and no longer heard what was going on outside.

Arnold Vaksman, my neighbor from the Pritshe (boards that served as beds), a Doctor from Budapest, danced with a long loaf of bread, which he was holding on his shoulder, just like a soldier shouldering his rifle. He had seized the bread from a German storehouse, which was now abandoned, and he shouted wildly in a sing–song tone. His eyes were shut, and his head he shook wildly in all directions. By his dancing – he appears to be drunk. A few days later, I saw him running around, wrapped in a torn blanket, and his head tied around in rags. His eyes were downcast, as if he were seeking something on the ground. He sees no one. He doesn't speak, acting as if he were struck dumb. It seems that he's gone out of his mind. What kind of a day that was – I don't remember. Cold or warm, sunny or cloudy, a day, a day, which quickly passed.

Where Does One Go?

When it got dark, the question was: Where does one go? Again back to the same holes, on the same Pritshes (boards that served as beds)? Or to remain under the free sky until tomorrow morning, and breathe in the free air once and for all. And tomorrow? Some, as tired as they were, fell asleep out–of–doors. Some turned back to their Pritshes, burying their faces in their hands, and spasmotically crying aloud: "What do we do? Where do we go? Out to the wide world? Where is the world? Does it still exist? Oh, no!"

Could I possibly hope that someone of my nearest and dearest is still alive? Why did I live to experience such a tragic joy? A few days later the German restaurants were filled with Jews. They drink as much as they can. One stands on a bench and declaims in a sobbing tone: "Drink, brothers, drink! Get drunk and drown what's inside of you!" A second person delivers a speech about revenge, and a third figures out the names of his relatives (who perished) and chokes from his tears!

[Page 606]

A Few Years Passed

A few years went by. Again I married, and children were born. A new plague struck, which doesn't let up for a moment. Day and night, a psychological plague. Perhaps my husband is alive? Perhaps my wife? Maybe he'll come soon? With whom shall I remain? From whom shall I separate? In the street I encounter my wife – my husband. My heart pounds. The knees bend. The eyes swoom. So many years have passed. It is difficult to recognize; both have grown so old!

But maybe... We pass. We stop and look back for a long while. Why didn't I ask her name? I'm afraid a tragedy! Two wives! What will I do? Soon two opinions begin to clash within me: Did I do right or wrong? I didn't feel as if I were walking in the street, but that I sit before a screen and see my whole life pass before me.

Sarahle – I Impetuously Cry Out

The doorbell rings. I open the door and remain standing in a frozen position. Opposite me she stands immobile, with very tragic, expressionless eyes, that look me over. "Sarahle!" I impetuously cry out and spread my arms to embrace her and hold her tight, and ask: "Where have you been for so long? I've searched for you everywhere!" At that moment she drew back and my arms remained stretched out in the air. For a long while I stood like that, like a mummy, and didn't know what to do. I just looked at her with pleading eyes. I noticed, that suddenly there grew in her hands a 3 month old child, glued to her breast. Near her stands a 6 year old boy. And another one smaller, and yet another one even smaller. Three children in a row. They stood silently with uplifted eyes, looking at me, as if they don't know me.

I strained myself, and wanted to run to them. They all together at once withdrew from me, further and further. I begin to chase them and cry out: "Sarahle! Yitzhakl! Eliezerl! Itele! Goldele!" In the midst of this I feel that a hand is shaking me and awakens me from my sleep.

What Were You Shouting About?

"How come you were shouting like that?" "Nothing, I was having a dream!" "What sort of a dream was it that you were shouting like that; Sarahle? Tell me, I also want to know." Tell her that the same dream repeats itself to me very often, and that I'm a broken man for a long time afterwards. At home, I must play the role of a laughing clown. From the children, I must for the meanwhile, withhold a secret that I had already once before been the father of four children. They are still too young. It is still too early. Another secret, I must keep from my wife: The day of the deportation of my beloved first wife and children is for me, for the rest of my life, a fast day. My wife prepares for me to take to work, but I eat it only at night. All day my thoughts are busy with thousands of pictures of events that took place before our tragic parting forever. Tears roll onto my work table. My eyes are overflowing with wetness. When I return home from my work, my wife asks me: "What's wrong with your eyes? They're swollen." The opportunity has come. What shall I tell her? My eternal crying. An inner absess. That bothers me without a stop!

[Page 607]

Can Nature Tolerate Such a Thing?

by Avigdor Zilberknopf

The time has come, O, the time, the moment
With shining eyes, how crazy, how strange.
You're fortune so superfluous, so late, already
too old,
Remove your rays – they are already too cold.
Time, O, the time of loneliness and fear,
From suffering wounds – a feeling arose
From a dying elder, from the world resigned,
Far away from life, death already governs.
Time, O, the time of Terrifying storm,
Which destroyed everything, which scattered
everything,
Which put an end to everything, which will
no longer return,
A shiver seizes, and the limbs break.
Time, O, the time, when blood flowed,
Like an overflowing river – it poured.
Also the tears of children were of no avail,
Like lambs in the slaughter house, they were
slaughtered.
Time, O, time, which on the altar burned and
broiled, he, the murderer.
Like steers in a barn, they packed the victims,
Where is he, the helper, with his great pity?
Time, at that time, where were you?
God of vengeance – You saw everything.
Can such a thing happen in the world,
Can nature tolerate such a thing?

[Page 608]

What Fellow–Townsmen of Kozienice Tell

by Tzvi Madanes, Tel–Aviv

Shimon Rozental, the active participant in the uprising in Treblinka, tells of his experiences under the Nazis, until his liberation. At the end of 1942, all of the Kozienice population was taken to the train, guarded by SS murderers. By their brutal treatment, everyone understood what was awaiting them. Many Jews perished, even before they entered the boxcars, among them: Dr. Abramovitsh, his wife and children, who poisoned themselves before the Nazis had a chance to kill them. The train was filled. Like cattle, the Jews were taken to Treblinka, in sealed boxcars, without water or air we were pressed against each other.

We Were Taken to Wash Ourselves

Through the small window which was closed with bars, we could see the way to Treblinka. In this large Concentration Camp, we were "greeted" by SS murderers, dressed in white cloaks. They told us to quickly line up and remove our clothes, because we were soon to be given work clothes, in order to go to Bialistok or Volkovisk. A crisis ensued. In the center there grew a mountain of clothing, until we all stood naked. Immediately the womens' hair was cut off. The camp administration chose a few healthy Jews for various jobs in the camp, and the remaining mass of thousands of Jews, was taken to the gas–chambers. They were told that they were being taken to the showers to wash themselves. The naked people were chased along a path, which was surrounded on both sides by a thicket of trees, so that the remaining people in the camp couldn't see that this was the last road.

The unfortunate people were accompanied by an SS guard and specially trained dogs, who fell upon the people like angry wolves. With yummering cries of "Shema Yisroel" (Hear O' Israel), the victims went to the gas–chambers. Into the chambers they drove as many as they could, and when they were packed, the floor opened and the victims fell into the cellar, where they were gassed. This took no more then about 15 minutes. Then the door of the cellar opened, and the victims were carried out on stretchers, so that they could be burned in a large pit, which burned day and night. In this way thousands of Jews perished daily in a shameful and brutal way.

Kurt Frantz Seeks People For Labor

I, Shimon Rozental, am one of 50 people who were chosen for labor. Kurt Frantz, with two revolvers on his hips, goes among the people and looks over the naked bodies. With all of his strength he beat us, and whoever did not please him, he shot immediately. As my luck would have it, I was able to tolerate the beatings, and as a result I was chosen for labor. Our work consisted of sorting the clothes of he victims. I was engaged in this work for about 5 months. I would labor from before dawn until dark and every small infringement carried with it the threat of death. Since shooting was such a mild penalty, they used to hang people.

[Page 609]

Why I Was Beaten

Kurt Frantz would hang people by the feet, and in this way the victims would suffer for at least 12 hours. My comrade, who slept near me, a Jew from Demblin, a wild person, confessed to me that he was planning to escape. I helped him as much as I could. My friend left. What happened to him, I don't know. But, the next morning, at the lineup, it was revealed that there was someone missing, who had obviously fled. Since he slept next to me, I and two other Jews, were taken to Kurt Frantz, in order to punish us. He told us to get undressed and lie down on a bench. He had a long whip, with a metal tip. We were sentenced to 50 lashes. The sadist would beat us and we had to count. The first were unable to count to 50. He smashed their kidneys and they fell into a faint. The lashes that my comrades failed to get, I received. During the whipping, he yelled at me: "You accursed Jew, you haven't counted accurately." Having fainted away, I was carried to the barracks. Fortunately, there were two Jewish doctors in the barracks, and they managed to save me. Thanks to them, I survived. On the third day I was forced to go to work, even though I didn't feel as if any limb of mine was whole. To this very day, I have scars of those lashes on my body.

The Pit Which Burned Constantly

In our work camp, the camp supervisor was the Jew, Galesky, from Lodz. He was a lawyer. Another was a Dr. Oranzshitzky, an officer in the Polish Army. There was also a barracks' commandant, a Jew, fine and devoted, from Warsaw, and another person, by the name of Kurland. He was also a doctor. His office was 200 meters from the camp, near a large pit. When the transports arrived, the weak were taken to the doctor. The pit was surrounded by barbed wire, and camouflaged, so it couldn't be seen. This was where the Doctor was. When a person was brought to the doctor, and the doctor approached him, the adjutant, a Ukrainian, shot him with his revolver, which was equipped with a silencer. The victim fell into the pit, where there was a steady fire, which couldn't be seen.

There was also a German, Sepp. When children arrived, this Sepp took them to himself. In the dark pit, on the other side, he had a large boulder. He would grab each child by the legs and beat his head against the boulder, until he died. He then threw the dead children, like slaughtered chickens, into the pit, in the vicinity of the burning Hell. There was also a Jew from the city of Ochote. His job was to inform the German murderers about his fellow Jews. He would also listen to the complaints of the Jews. The Jews, who worked in the camp were divided into groups, each according to his profession. For example: shoemakers, locksmiths, cabinet makers, and so on.

[Page 610]

How Shlamek Perished

Among the shoemakers there was Shimon Rozental, who was in charge of the shoe department. The department was located in a large barrack, which contained a very large table, at which there worked about 25 Jews. In the same barracks there worked a Jew from Tshenstochov, Galster. His job was to make ammunition containers from the scraps. His eyes would spy out the people in the department, and when he observed something suspicious, he would immediately convey it to the camp commandant. The culprit would immediately be taken to another camp for extermination. In the same camp there also worked Gedalyahu, a neighbor's son. Shimon Rozental kept him close to him, by force. People worked there with their bit of remaining energy, because the 200 grams of bread (2 thin slices) were insufficient for survival.

Galster had a box of bread, which he kept tightly closed with a lock. Since we could smell the bread, our hunger would increase. My neighbor's grandson, Shlamek, went mad, used the moment when Galster wasn't around, and fell upon the box, and with his hands and teeth tore and bit at the lock, until he broke it. His eyes flashed fire, when he saw the bread. He took the bread and then closed the box. When Galster came in, he immediately noticed what had happened. He turned to Shimon Rozental and demanded that he tell him who was responsible. "If not", he said, "you and another ten will be exterminated! You don't realize who I am!" Shimon begged mercy from him, and promised him that they will provide 10 loaves of bread for the one that was taken, if he would only ignore what had taken place. Nothing helped! He stood someone up against the wall, and forced him to reveal who had taken the bread. On the morrow, at 8:00 a.m., at lineup, Shlamek was taken to a death–camp. There he perished!

Kozieniceites in Treblinka

Moshe Sherman, Alter Kohn and his son Issachar, worked at sorting things, until the uprising, which took place in the Camp. It is also worthwhile mentioning, that in that great Hell, where people died over a crust of bread, there was an SS man, who is worthwhile mentioning. He made himself invisible, when Jews were able in some way, to obtain a piece of bread. Thanks to him, many Jews were still able to carry on with their work. There was a group of Jews who were transported daily from the camp. The SS man, would accompany them as a guard. The work consisted of cutting young branches from trees, and making them into brooms for the Camp. Outside where they were, they were able to arrange for the purchase of food items. The SS man would act dumb and not notice what was going on. In fact, he himself would carry the sack of bread into the camp. He also knew that the money, with which the bread was bought, belonged to Shimon Rozental. Understandably, he was well rewarded for this, but he was worth it because, with his help he saved people from hunger.

[Page 611]

Shimon Rozental Saves Salke Bendler's Husband

Coming to Treblinka, Salke Bendler's husband met Shimon Rozental and poured out his heart to him. He begged to be saved, because, if not, he'll cut his wrists, in order to escape further troubles. Shimon contacted another person from Tshentochov, nicknamed "Shneltzug", and requested that he help smuggle Bendler out of the Camp. The other agreed and organized the escape. We loaded packs of work clothes for the camps, so we prepared a truck with a window, and hid Bendler under the packs. Shimon warned him: "Remember, when the train approaches the mountain, it slows down. There you will jump out. In your valise we put money, to help you save yourself. And when you arrive in Kozienice, tell them about the death–camp here in Treblinka."

From the right: Pola Eichenbaum, Salke Bendler and a friend in 1928

The train left, accompanied by our best wishes. Everything went as planned. Bendler leapt off, not far from the mountain, and he managed to return to Kozienice. He was able to convey the bitter regards from the huge death–camp, Treblinka. But nobody wanted to believe him. They all said that he must be crazy. But, unfortunately, everything that he told them, was the tragic truth. When the remaining Jews, who buried the dead, and cleaned the houses, came to Treblinka, they saw with their own eyes, that everything he had told them was the absolute truth.

The Uprising in Treblinka, July 28, 1943

Seeing that thousands of people were being burned daily, there occurred the thought to rise up in revolt and free ourselves, or at least, blow up the Camp. The group which organized the uprising in Treblinka, consisted of 12 people: Shimon Rozental, Dr. Choronzshitzky of Warsaw, Engineer Galevsky of Lodz, Kurland of Warsaw, Reizman of Vengrov (He survived and lives in Paris), Engineer Boimeister, and six others, whose names I cannot recall. This was the Central Committee of the Uprising. The uprising was announced and a date was set. But since Obersturmfuerher Kurt Frantz caught Dr. Choronzshitzky at some preparatory work, which could have been a disaster for many Jews, he jumped through a window and fled. Kurt Frantz's dogs chased him. When the Doctor saw that he was in danger of being caught he swallowed poison tablets. Kurt Frantz did everything to save him, and to obtain from him the secret information, but Dr. Choronzshitzky died a hero. Because of this, the Uprising was postponed until the 28th of July, 1943.

The "Court" Jews Prepare Arms

The preparation of arms and ammunition was given over to the "court-Jews", as they were called. Those, who worked in the camp as smiths, shoemakers, tailors, hatters, furriers and mechanics. These people knew all the secrets of the Camp, and especially where the ammunition was stored.

[Page 612]

Each was assigned a task, to which he was most suited. There was a tailor with two sons. One would clean the bath rooms of the camp commandant, and always had with him a broom. He obtained access to the stores of hand–grenades, made a duplicate key, and every chance he got, managed to remove a couple of hand–grenades, which he turned over to Shimon Rozental, who would bury them in the sand near his work place. In this way 83 hand–grenades were assembled. Another Jew managed machine guns from the huge munitions warehouse in the Treblinka Forest. This was a very complicated procedure, and with great devotion, over a period of time 45 machine–guns were removed. It was also decided, that the mechanics, who worked with tanks, should, before the uprising, sever the chains. Those, who worked at other technical work, were to sever the telephone lines. It was decided that the administrators of the Camp, should be killed, even before the uprising itself.

The Death Sentence In The Shoemakers Department

Straws were drawn to decide who was to carry out the death–sentence in the shoemaker's department. It was decided that when the camp commandant will come to the department, Shimon Rozental should measure him for a pair of boots, and that he should be finished off from behind. And so it actually happened. Mishe, with the crooked head went and invited the commandant to come and be measured for nice boots, and while this was taking place someone came up behind him and clubbed him to death. His body was wrapped in a sack, and hidden among the piles of leather. The same thing happened in all departments, on the eve of the uprising, in which about 1000 people took part. A day before the uprising the barracks were disinfected, but this time there was a much large percentage of benzine in it, so that it would burn better.

We also dealt with the problem of how to deal with the Ukrainians, who stood guard at the 12 towers which circled the Camp. We also appointed 25 commanders, among them our fellow townsman, Shimon Rozental. It was decided that when Kurland will come into the courtyard at 3:30, where all the Jews were working, and he lifts his shovel, it will be a sign that the uprising has begun!

Abraham Tenenbaum and Abraham Gutmacher near a stone in Treblinka

Kurland Lifts His Shovel

Kurland came into the courtyard at the designated time, and gave the signal. All of us, as if we were one man went out to do battle. Each one had his weapons ready and took up his position. At that moment, the SS man, Kive, appeared. He was the first victim. Everything went according to plan. All of the barracks started burning. Our fighters fell upon the Germans and the Ukrainians with their hand–grenades. Those who were responsible for the attack upon the watch–towers, managed to convince the Ukrainians to come down, and if not they were warned that they would be burned alive.

[Page 613

When one hesitated, his tower was set afire with the cry: "Revenge!", and the tower burned. We fought about 150 Ukrainians. Many of them fell and others fled. The Camp was burned. The communication lines were cut and our fighters reached the main gate of the Camp. Beside the weapons, which each fighter had with him, he also had a poison pill, so that he could kill himself if he saw he was in any danger of being taken alive by the Germans!

The Gate is Open!

The gate was broken open. Everyone was free to leave for any place he desired, in order to save himself. In this struggle many heroic fighters fell, among them our fellow townsmen: Moshe Sherman, Alter Kohn, his son Issacher, and quite a few other Kozieniceites.

And What Next?

When the camps were liberated by Russian and Allied military personnel, and the stream of luck, eased the deathly white pallor, of the emaciated faces, we began to hope that maybe someone had still survived. But now, instead, there came to light the great tragedy of the Jewish People. Jews, once again, took the wanderer's cane in their hands and set out into the wide, wide world. Our fellow townsman, Shimon Rozental decided to wander no longer. He set out for Israel, to the warm sun, which would heal his deep wounds. His pride is Israel, his Jewish home, his wife and children, who live in Israel, faithful to their Jewish tradition.

May these few words eternalize the slogan: "Remember what the Amalekites did to you!" They exterminated Six Million Jews!

The monument in memory of the Polish Jewry in Treblinka

[Page 614]

For The Merit of My Father,
May God Avenge His Blood

Yerachmiel Fleisher, as a child, together with all Kozienice Jews, lived through the bloody threat of extinction. The Germans undressed him completely and made sport with him. They ordered him to run around the church garden, among the rows of soldiers, and every soldier beat him a few times. Why? How come? For four days the young Yerachmiel was tortured in this way. When the order came to free the Jews up to age 16, from the church garden, there was among them the bloody youth, Yerachmiel, who had many wounds on his body.

We Go Home

Where does a Jew have a home? Our city was a ruin. The Jews who had been held in the church, were freed, after six days of torture. The Judenraat sent Jews to forced labor in Yelna–Koshtshelna, at the railroad. This, of course, was forced labor, without pay, but with beatings. Before the transportation to Treblinka, Yerachmiel Fleisher came home to his family. At home there was destruction and wailing! Everyone feels that death is approaching. With bitter tears, the Jewish mother bewails the tragic fate of her offspring.

The Ghetto is guarded. It is impossible to save oneself. My father, of blessed memory, takes me by my hand and gives me to understand, that it is not a good idea for us to remain together. Every one must go in a different direction, perhaps in this way some will survive. My father tells me that when Jacob (in the Bible) went forth to meet his brother, Esau, he divided his family into three camps, and that we must do the same. My father holds my hand tightly, and we walk in the Kozienice Ghetto. It is dark in the street and also in our hearts. We were not far from the barbed wire, so they opened fire on us. My father commanded me: "Run Yerachmiel!": I no longer saw my father. I climbed over the wire, and ran, wherever my eyes led me.

I Came to Dombrove

There was a Labor Camp there, which contained many Kozienice Jews. I wasn't able to stay there too long, because I wasn't registered in that Camp. But I decided to stay and see what fate would bring. A day after the transportation of Kozienice, the SS came to choose fresh victims, who supposedly were to be taken to Shidlovtze. A day later, we already knew, that all of them had been shot. Among them, Motl Tzeitfinger and his wife. On a particular day 100 people were chosen to go to Volanov. Shmerl Soffer's son attempted to flee, and was immediately shot. From Volanov, we were sent to various labor camps. Daily people fell at their work. Every month there was a selection, for a grave that had been dug, right on the spot!

[Page 615]

I Was Covered With Warm Blood

There was a new selection of 120 people, among them Abraham Sapirstein and many other Kozieniceites. We were supposedly being sent to new labor. Meanwhile we were being driven to the fences. We already felt that we were being led to our deaths. At that moment there arrived a group of Ukrainians and SS with machine–guns. They opened fire on us. At the sound of the first shot, I instinctively threw myself to the ground. I became covered with fallen victims and warm blood. The Ukrainian and SS murderers did their bit of work. All of the 120 were lying like slaughtered hens, and they, the murderers, went off, on their way.

Night fell. A group of Jews came to bury the corpses. I felt them inspecting my clothes. They realized that I was alive, so they ordered me to flee immediately! I hid myself under a barrack. There I lay for three days and listened carefully to what was taking place. Together with me there were in hiding the two children of Yosef Lichtenstein. When things calmed down a bit, I went to Radom, to a new work place. There the terror was exactly the same there as it had been in Volanov!

The Days Drag Along Slowly

Jews wanted to save themselves. They planned to flee, but it ended up with new victims. The remaining Jews were taken to another place. They sent us to Tomashov. The Camp commandant assured us that here, in this place, nothing will happen to us. From here we will go to Auschwitz. The days dragged endlessly, each one like a year. Our strength faded. We wanted to hold out and get stronger in order to survive until the day of liberation. They took us to Auschwitz. In Auschwitz a selection was made immediately. The women and older people were taken to the gas–chambers.

They sent me to Stuttgart. I saw that the gates of Hell were being closed to me. This gave me the strength to continue on my way to other German labor camps, until I was liberated and born anew. In the decisive moments of life or death, right or left, Yerachmiel Fleisher saw his father and felt as if he were still holding him by the hand, and leading him onward towards life!

[Page 616]

Yehudah Hoffman Survived the Camp

This was an autumn eve. I and a few other Kozienice families were invited to the family of Chayele and Yaakov Adler. Among the guests there was also Yehudah Hoffman, of blessed memory. Our conversation revolved around our city of Kozienice, and our former lives there, before the Great War.

Mordkhai Borenstein – Israel

Are You the Brickmaker, Rozenboim?

This was the word that Yehudah Hoffman received and he told: In Auschwitz he saved from death our fellow townsman, Rosenboim, who had a brick factory in Kozienice. His story made an impression on all who were present. It became quiet. "I had met Rozenboim in Auschwitz, where he and another were dragging a large pot of soup. His hat was falling over his eyes. I had the impression that the pot of soup was dragging him, and I asked him: 'Aren't you the brickmaker, Rozenboim?' 'Yes, that's me.' 'Perhaps you can give me a note to the cook to provide me with an extra portion of soup, because I no longer have the strength to drag my feet?' I was also concerned about someone noticing him giving the note to the cook." "I," Yehudah Hoffman told, "was a carpenter in the camp." Being curious about whether my note had gotten to the right address, approached the window of the barracks in which he slept. 'Yehudah! You have been sent to me like an angel from heaven. They've stolen my number with my pyjama, and if I don't have it by morning, I'll be shot. Yehudah recorded the number and went to enlist aid for Rozenboim. When the exhausted bodies were lying in their cots, Yehudah approached the window and gave Rozenboim the pyjama with the correct number. This way Rozenboim was saved from a certain death.

Yehudah Survived the Camp

Yehudah survived the camp thanks to his capable hands. When the war ended and the gates of the camp were opened for the tortured, there appeared new roads to the great world. Yehudah Hoffman, of blessed memory was always a member of a Socialist organization. But after the war, he made an evaluation of all the Jewish workers' parties and their platforms, and decided that a Jew can be free only in Israel. Coming to Israel, he accepted everything with love and satisfaction. Only one thing bothered him: His children, who were still alive and were not with him. He did everything like a dear, devoted father, and lived to see his children, and had joy and satisfaction from them. But, unfortunately, dark fate decided otherwise. On an early morning, when Yehudah, of blessed memory, was going to work, he was killed by a devilish automobile, and his life and joy were snuffed out. May His Memory Be Blessed!

[Page 617]

God, Is Your Judgement Just?

by Mordecai Donershtein, Ramat–Gan

Yehuda Hoffman – Israel

When I remind myself of you Kozienice,
In which everything was contained,
Then my eyes are filled with tears
And my heart dies within me.
You contained in yourself,
Religious Jews and Rabbis,
Proletarians and Chalutzim (Pioneers),
And just plain folk.
Libraries and Yeshivas,
Many Hebrew Schools, and also a Talmud
Torah,
There flourished a Jewish life,
Without fear and dread
And they worked there
With vigor and bitterness and labored:
As cutters and sewers,
Of shoes, day and night.
One would sell the boards,
Another thread and leather.
With shoes were occupied:
The Rabbi, the judge, and others.

When Friday came,
And the Sabbath candles lit,
The town enwrapped in Holiness,
And the people in enthusiasm
As soon as the Sabbath came,
The troubles and cares left.
Each one hoped
With faith in a better tomorrow.
Some to the Rebbe's table, for the leavings
With enthusiasm ran,
And some to the forest and the field
Where they wanted to meet their joy.
Also in all of the institutions,
Among the different parties,
The debates were heated,
And even louder the arguments.
In this way they lived there,
Days, nights and months,
Everyone believed in something:
Some in the Messiah, in Revolution, or in
certificates.

[Page 618]

Until on an early morning,
Hitler declared war on us,
Robbed, killed and burned,
And spoiled the entire dream.
Separated children from their mothers,
The old and the sick from their beds,
Only fear and hunger reigned,
At the command of the Hitler Satan.
And everyone was taken,
By force and bloody beatings,
Loaded up and set to Treblinka,
And the city left smoldering.
So I live – in our own land,
And I ask myself: "Did it all happen there"
"and how were you dear God,
Able to observe it all?"
My heart cries without tears,
The eyes becloud, and the head breaks.
I ask you, My God,
Is Your judgement just?

[Page 619]

In 1939 I Separated From My Family

by Tzila Kirshenblatt

I, the daughter of Yitzhak and Leah Kirshenblatt, was born in 1925, in the city of Kozienice on Targova Street. My father was a hat maker, and my mother a housewife. We were eight brothers and sisters. My sister, Devorah, was married in Warsaw. My sister, Ita, married in Kozienice, and then moved to Warsaw. I was the youngest of the sisters. I also had 5 brothers: Fabi, the oldest, was married in Kozienice, moved to Pionek and raised 5 children. Mendl married in Kozienice and raised 3 children. Shammai married in Kozienice. Shlomo married in Kozienice and moved to Pionek where he raised 2 children. Siyuma went in 1939 to Russia. There he married and returned to Poland in 1940. We lived in peace and tranquility until 1939.

After the German conquest, I separated from my family. In 1940 the Germans took me to a labor–camp. From then on, I no longer saw my family, and remained alone to this very day. In the camp we dug water tunnels. The sanitary conditions were miserable and the food terrible. Afterwards they took me to Skarzisko. There I worked at the production of rifle ammunition. Conditions were very difficult and I got almost nothing to eat. At that time I became ill, and lay in bed, but the Germans forced me to continue working 12 hours a day. Afterwards it became clear that, I was ill with Typhus. For several days I lay with a high fever. Since I had no choice, I was forced to continue working, because if someone was out ill, for three days, the Germans would kill them.

At the time I had but one change of clothing. In the courtyard, near my workplace, water flowed, and there I found soap. One day I went out to wash my blouse, and was caught by my labor supervisor, who whipped me 25 times. I was forced to count the whipping, for as long as I was being whipped. When he finished his "work", I was unconscious. On the morrow, the Germans forced me to complete my quota.

In 1944 I was transferred to Tzenstochov, and also there I worked at backbreaking labor. The Red Army liberated me. I traveled back to my home in Kozienice, in order to see what fate had befallen my family and relatives. To my astonishment, I didn't find even one of them. I returned to Tzenstochov, after I had despaired of finding my parents. There I found work and supported myself until I met my present husband. Together we traveled to Germany. In Germany we were married in 1945, and made Aliyah to Israel on the ship, "Yagur", which was an illegal one. The British caught us, and after a short battle, they overcame us, and dragged us to a detention camp on the island of Cyprus, where we remained for close to half a year. After we received an Aliyah permit, we came to Israel. We settled in Israel, and established ourselves. In time, two children were born to us, and we established a new generation in Israel.

[Page 620]

Know, What Amalek (Germany) Did To You!

by Sarah Madanes, Tel Aviv

Where are all of the members of my family? Where? Why did they fall victim? Victims of the German nation, and all of it why? O' why? Because They were Jews!

Sara Madanes – Israel

It may be that my narrative will be different. I will not be able to tell about the city of Kozienice because I was born in Eretz Yisrael. But I also have something to say, perhaps not about the city, but about the terrible tragedy that befell my people. Often, in our home the topic of the Holocaust and the courageous spirit comes up in our home. Who can forget the slaughter? To this day we can't make peace with the facts: 6 million Jews were wiped out, only because they were Jews. Except for a few monuments, what memorializes their memory? The Memorial Book of the Martyrs of Kozienice, the birthplace of my father, and the Memorial Book of the martyrs of Harovishov, the birthplace of my mother, will memorialize my family, which to my great sorrow, are known to me only through the books. By way of deception that they were taking them to labor camps, the Nazis took their victims to extermination camps. It is difficult to describe how they felt in the sealed boxcars, standing pressed together, without food or water, and on top of it they knew that from the place to which they were being taken they would never return. The Jews knew what was in store for the elderly and their parents. More than once children risked their lives to save parents. My family can serve as an example. The two sisters, Franka and Sarah Braunstein hid their mother. Everywhere they went they took their mother, in secret. They stole food for her, and thanks to them, my aunt Tzipporah (their mother) is here, may she live to 120. There were more than a few such examples in this war of extermination, but in this Holocaust, Hitler did exterminate men, women, the elderly, infants and children in camps encircled by electrified barbed wire, until he put an end to them.

[Page 621]

There Was Once a Town, Garbatke

by Gershon Bornshtein, B'nai–B'rak, Israel

Until the outbreak of WWII, there lived in Garbatke close to 100 Jewish families. The town was famous for clear forest air and comfortable mansions (Hotels) to accommodate guests in the summer season. Guests would come with their wives and children from Radom, Keltz and the surrounding areas. At Passover time merchants would come and also manufacturers and hand-workers, to reserve their hotels or cottages. Realtors were engaged in this and this was one of the Jewish livelihoods. On the train stations there would await the guest drivers with horses and wagons, lined with straw, and covered with blankets. No other form of communication existed. This seasonal occupation was conducted by the inhabitants of Garbatke, and from it they would survive the winter months.

Garbatke Was Tied to Kozienice

Administratively, Garbatke was tied to Kozienice, where they would pay taxes, and use the courts. Garbatke did not have it's own Rabbi. It was tied to the Jewish community of Gnievashov, and from there they would get their birth documents. Their dead were buried in Kozienice or Gnievashov. This was also true of the bath–house and Ritual Bath. Garbatke needed a Ritual Slaughterer, so they advertised that whoever would build a Ritual Bath at his own expense, would be appointed Ritual Slaughter. He was also engaged in teaching Torah and commentaries to the boys up to Bar Mitzvah age, and had to officiate as Cantor and Mohel. When they appointed the Ritual Slaughterer they finally got their own Ritual Bath. This way they solved one of their major Jewish problems.

Small business men of all kinds lived in Garbatke: notions, housewares, food/piece goods and even nails were sold there, at times under one roof. It wasn't easy to raise children there, and set them up, but in spite of it they lived satisfied. Once a week there was a fair in town. On that day, tailors, hat makers and other merchants would come from Kozienice. The village peasants would bring cheese, eggs, hens and fruit. This way Garbatke was provided with everything. On Thursdays the housewives prepared for the Sabbath. Mothers would bake Matzoh farfel, egg cakes, rolls and twisted Challos. After changing the children into their Sabbath finery, the father would go with them to pray in the House of Study. Mother would already have lit and blessed the Sabbath candles. The Holy Sabbath had begun.

Garbatke youth was satisfied, when young guests came to flirt with them. During the long winter evenings the maidens would knit, and read books. The young men would play at dominoes or chess. There was no cinema in Garbatke. From time to time an amateur theatrical group would come from Kozienice, or they would travel to the cinema in Kozienice. It was nice and they were fortunate. For some easier and for others more difficult, but all were satisfied. They would also solicit for the Jewish National Fund from the summer guests; and also for other causes.

[Page 622]

During the summer Garbatke came alive, in spite of the heavy work. After the guests left, a stillness descended on the town. In this way Jewish life continued until 1939. And from 1941 on, Garbatke Jews lived in a Ghetto.

The 12th of June, 1942

On a lovely morning on the 12th of June, 1942, the SS surrounded the Ghetto and shots were heard. Everyone understood that the evacuation is approaching. Tens of Jews had already been shot. Men, 16 years old and older, were gathered together in one place, and taken to the Tartak (saw mill), where the boxcars were waiting. The Hitlerites loaded on over 100 men, with their hands tied and took them to an unknown destination. Only when we were unloaded from the boxcars, did we realize that we were in an extermination camp, Auschwitz. A while later the Hitlerites eliminated the labor–camp at Pionki, where for the slightest transgression you could be hanged or shot. The labor–camp was guarded by Ukrainian robbers and SS.

From the few Garbatke Jews we found out about the dark fate of those who had remained in Garbatke, where the majority had been shot. Some of the women and children were evacuated to Zvolin and from there back to Garbatke. In boxcars, they were later taken to Treblinka, the extermination camp. The Garbatke woods remained uninhabited, without Jews. The Goyim stole the bit of goods that Jews had stored there. In a forsaken corner overgrown with pines, in the small woods, were buried all together, women, men and children. During big storms and rains, the trees rustle, as if they were humans crying over their dark fate. It is worthwhile mentioning, that around Kozienice there were other small towns with Jewish populations. All were destroyed. In Glovatshov there were 25 families, in Shetshechov, 120 families, in Yedlnie, 15 families, in Ritshevol, 60 families, in Magnushev 80 families, in Mishev, 25 families, in Yablone, 13 families, and in Pionki more than 30 families.

[Page 623]

A Small Number of Garbatkeites Remained Alive

by Yitzhak Tzimerman, Jerusalem

12 kilometers from Kozienice, surrounded by a forest, was to be found Garbatke. The inhabitants occupied themselves with real estate and fabricating. Garbatke was also known as a resort. About 70 Jewish families lived there, most of them handworkers and small merchants. When the Hitlerites marched in 1939, they levied a heavy fine against the Jews. Jews were driven to heavy labor, and were beaten till the blood ran. The Hitlerites searched for arms, and at every opportunity stole whatever they could find. Later they sent us out for labor in the woods. In 1941 they forced the Jews into a Ghetto, where they also brought the Jews from Yablonov (25 families). In the Ghetto it became crowded. People went hungry and died from Typhus. On the 12th of July, 1942 (12th of Tammuz) during the early morning hours, the Ghetto was surrounded. Close to 100 Jews fell victim to shooting. They were buried in the Ghetto. The remaining men were sent to Auschwitz. The women and children were sent to the Pionki Ghetto.

Those capable of labor were put up in the Pulaver Factory, and the remaining Jews were taken to the Zvolin Ghetto; from there back to Garbatke; and from there packed into boxcars and sent to their deaths. The Jews from Garbatke, Pionki, Zvolin, Kozienice, Keltz and Radom worked in the Pulaver Factory. The factory was encircled by barbed–wire, and guarded by Ukrainians. Jews were working under miserable conditions, and on top of it they were beaten and even killed. In 1944, with the start of the Russian offensive, the Hitlerites packed the few Jews into boxcars and took them to Auschwitz, and from there to various work–camps. In 1945 there remained only a handful of Garbatke Jews. They immediately departed, seeing that it was impossible to build a new life on the soil which was drenched with blood and death. The majority of those who remained alive settled in Israel, where they had the opportunity, in 1948, to fight for the liberation of Jerusalem. Others once again sought their good fortune in other lands of exile.

ON JULY 21, 1942, 100 JEWS WERE SHOT IN GARBATKE.

WE HONOR THEIR MEMORY!

SECTION 7 - NECROLOGY

God

Full of mercy, who dwells on high,
Grant rest beneath the shelter of your Presence.
And in the exalted ranks of the holy and pure
Who shine as the brightness of the firmament,
To the souls of
The six thousand members of the holy congregation of

Kozhenitz

Men, women and children
Who were killed, slaughtered, burned, strangled
And buried alive by Hitler's executioners
And their evil servants, (May their names be blotted out),
In the years 1939 –45.

May their resting place be in the garden of Eden!
And so, may the Lord of mercy bind their souls in the Bond of life.
The Lord is their inheritance,
And may they rest upon their couches in peace,
And let us say, Amen!

[Page 624]

Martyrs of Garbatke
**Who were shot, gassed and tortured by Hitler's executioners
and their henchmen in Garbatke and the death camps in the years 1939-45.***

- A/B/F -

Aidelman Mayer, wife, daughter and son
Aidelman Shlomo, Natan, Chana and 3 children
Ainshindler Khaim, wife Khana and 3 children

Baginski Mayer, wife and 4 children
Bornstein Rachel, & Sara Feiga
Breitman Debora, Menashe and Tzirla
Breitstein Yankel, Reizel, Joseph, Pesie and Rebeka

Flamenbaum Ester
Flamenbaum Hershl and Sala
Flamenbaum Israel, Khana, Moshe and Shmelke
Flamenbaum Izik, Khaia and 2 children
Flamenbaum Khaim, Bela and 2 children
Flamenbaum Leibl, Khava, Ester, Zvi, and Hene
Flamenbaum Mala and Ester
Flamenbaum Menashe, Rachel and Ester
Flamenbaum Mendel, wife and 3 children
Flamenbaum Moshe, Bela, Motl, Sheva and Bluma
Flamenbaum Pinchas, wife and 2 children
Flamenbaum Shmiel-Zvi, Khama, Abraham
Flamenbaum Simcha, Toba and Joseph
Futerman Gela, Menashe and Sara

- G/H/J/K/M/P/S -

Green Rebeka
Gruberg Khaim and wife

Hitlsman Sara, husband, Bracha, Itka, Gershon and Moshe
Hofman Shalom, Salka, a son and 2 daughters

Jacobson Jacob, wife and 4 children
Jacobson Moshe, wife and 2 children
Jacobson Shlomo, wife and 2 children

Jacubson Hersh-ldl, wife Mordekhai, Khava and Shlomo

Kizshberg Ickhok, Adka and daughter
Kirshberg Shmelke and Ratze Kornblum Leah
Kun Aron, Toba and Ickhok

Lederman Benjamin, wife and 2 children

Mendleman Nehemia, Khane and Rivka
Milberg Zelig, Malke and Hershel

Perelstein Abish, Sarah, Noah, Pinchas and daughter
Perelstein Sheva, son and 2 daughters
Pruchnicki Eliezer

Sukno Aron, Pearl, Hersh and Israel

- T/W/Z -

Tirangel Joseph Khaim
Tirangel Shlomo, wife, 2 sons and 2 daughters

Waksman Eli, Khava and five children and grandchildren
Waksman Israel and Mother
Waksman Shlomo and wife
Waksman Shmuel and Pola
Weingarten Motl, wife and 2 children
Weingarten Zonde and 3 children
Weisbard Jacob, wife Khaia and 2 small daughters
Weisbard Sender, Bracha, Itke, Gershon and Moshe
Weisman Shalom, wife, Jacob, Rebeka Chaia and Yechezkel
Weitzman Moshe wife and 3 children
Weltman Ester and Mendl
Wertman Moshe, Sheindl, Uri, Reizel and Zindl
Winograd Eli, Khana and 2 children
Winograd Kalman, wife, Hershel and 2 children
Winograd Matis, Sheva, Mindl, Motl, Gedalia, Moshe and Sara
Wolman Kalmen, Debora, Yechiel-Sumer, Alter, Joseph, Eliezer, Ita and
Tzipora

Zalzman Abraham and Toba
Zalzman Joseph, Frimet and Dunia
Ziman Szmuel-David, wife and 2 daughters, 2 son-in-laws and
grandchildren

Zimerman Manes

* Residents of Garbatke killed in Garbatke itself, as well as those deported to the death camps where they were murdered.

[Page 626]

A Tear on Your Grave

by Betzalel Madanes, of Blessed Memory

Translated from Hebrew

There, to the green, grassy grave
dews come from all ends
Birds fly from great distances,
To say the Kaddish over your grave.

Stalks of corn rustle in the fields,
Birds sing in the forest,
Heavenly quiet, sad songs
From the depths of their hearts, about their homeland.

The light of mourning burns, it burns,
For you, the one and only of the nation;
Dark, black, flaming shadows
Show the way to the grave there.

The light is not extinguished
They light the shadows of your resting place,
when at night there is heard sometimes
A cry, a plea, for a word from you.

Yummering, crying in the depth of night,
They drank your blood with mockery,
A Jew has just fallen, a Hero,
With the words: God is One!

Tired, broken from the torture,
You went out there to do battle,
Mourned your brothers who fell,
Mourned the night of exile.

Only late at night, like a cry
The silence passed,
Lonely, all alone,
You reminded yourself of the great destruction.

He sits alone, like a stone,
The eyes pour out a lake of tears,
No one feels his torture,

Only a voice from afar let's itself be heard.

Now, brothers arm themselves; there the battles
In the cellars by the murderers there,
Tied in chains, we give our souls,
"Hear O' Israel" – their last word.

Soon the last word disappears,
There already lie new victims, a number.
There grow already new, fresh graves,
Like mountains in the midst of a valley.

Resounding, storms, rustle the winds,
The moon ceased to shine
There under the black clouds,
The fallen heroes – they will be bewailed.

The stars do not cast light,
Everything is enwrapped in sadness,
Nightingales have ceased their singing,
It darkens more and more.

The voice calls further,
From deepest pain and heartfeltness,
The voice gets louder, louder
to the throne of glory, to the Holy Bench.

Tear the chains of your children
Who are tied to the Diaspora,
Let the sun shine in the east already,
To heal their wounds.

–Light the day became,
The sun already rises in the east,
The black cloud has disappeared,
The Jewish Nation – Arises!

Tzalke Mandanes was born in 1909. Already in the Heder, he had distinguished himself with his extremely sharp mind. As a youngster he joined the Zionist Organization, and instantly became beloved, thanks to his good sense, and his literary and dramatic abilities. His closest friend was Naftali Mandel of blessed memory. They were inseparable, and suffered the same tragic fate at the hands of the Nazi murderers.

WE HONOR THEIR MEMORY!

[Page 628]

The Last Time in Kozienice

by Moshe Ruchman, Pardes–Hannah, Israel

Mosze Rochman

After a mighty effort, the Polish Government was successful in obtaining the release of her citizens from Russian prisons. Their only crime had been that they were Polish citizens. For this crime I was sentenced, under the famous Article 58, to 10 years imprisonment. In November, 1948 I returned to Poland.

The Same Wagon and the Same Horse

At 11:00 p.m., I arrived at the city of my forbearers, Kozienice. At the railroad station, I encountered the same wagon and the same mail horse, and the two old–time workers, who knew me. They were happy to see me and asked about my experiences. Since not even a single Jew now lived in Kozienice, they advised me to go and sleep in the Leshish Hotel. There everyone knew me, and after questions from me and from them, I went up to my room, to spend my first night in Kozienice, since 1939. On the morrow, I borrowed from my friend, the Pharmacist, Yanechek, 4000 Gulden, since I didn't have a cent in my pocket. I visited a number of government offices. I spoke with inhabitants, and heard a great deal about the War, the Ghetto that had been eliminated, the sufferings of the Jews, and the details about my family, until their extermination in Treblinka. I saw and visited the entire length and breadth of the city. The entire Jewish quarter, from Targova Street, along Lubelska and Bzhuska Streets – there wasn't a sign of a Jewish house. Of all the Holy and Historical edifices, like the home of the Maggid, of blessed memory, the House of Study, the Great Synagogue, there was no sign of Jewish life.

I Searched for the Remnants of Kozienice

On that same day I left Kozienice, on the way to Lodz. After I obtained the address of Dorfman, the husband of Malkale Mandel, I found in Lodz some Kozienice families. From there I traveled to Vorotzlav, to my cousin, Abraham Gutmacher, who had married Shevale Burshtein, the sister of my friend, Yisroel Burshtein, who died, after torture, in a Nazi camp.

I also visited Valdbzheg and towns in the vicinity, since in western Poland there had been heavy concentrations of Jews, who had returned after the War. Among them I found Jews from Kozienice, who were survivors. They all recognized me, and greeted me nicely. I also visited Yerachmiel and Rachel Pearlstein, and established a warm relationship with them. After a few months had passed, in March, 1949, I returned to Kozienice as the representative of the city's Jewish committee, at whose head stood Abraham Tennenbaum, in order to prepare for the exhumation of the martyrs who had been slain by the Nazis in the Kozienice area.

A memorial evening after the Kozienicer martyrs in Waldbzheg. Year 1948.

[Page 629]

This required a great deal of courage on my part. Not only because of the difficult work, but also because of the danger, since not a single Jew had remained living there. I rented a room in the village of Budi, near the city, from the peasant Voitchik. First of all, I had to locate each grave. After questions and explanations from local people and all sorts of officials, we located the graves that were at least partly within the city boundary, and partly within the boundary of surrounding villages. Only after I had a list of all the graves, was I able to tackle the technical arrangements connected with exhumation. After meetings and discussions with all sorts of authorities, we set the exhumation for April 25, 1949. I hired workers, I opened graves, I prepared coffins and shrouds, in order to gather the martyred bones, and remove them to an assembly point, from where the funeral would be conducted. The coffins and shrouds for each martyr were ordered and prepared by my friend, David Golomb, who represented the Jewish Community of Poland. He was active in this till the end of the exhumation, and deserves praise for it.

April 25, 1949 – The Day of the Exhumation

Almost all of the Kozienice Jews, who were in Poland, about 15 men and women stood from the early hours of that day, on their feet, in the Leshish Hotel. From Lodz, there came: Moshe Dorfman, Ben–Zion Mandel, Nissan Greenspan. From Vorotzlav: Avrahamele Gutmacher; from Valdbzheg and the surrounding area: Abraham Tennenbaum, Rachel Pearlstein, Ratza Vasserman, Chaiml Zaltzberg, Feivel Reisman, Yisroel Sherman; and from Lignitz: Yitzhak Hoffman. The committee of Kozienice Jews worked hard. Each one obtained workers, transport, coffins, shrouds and went according to instructions to open a grave. They assembled the bones in the coffins, and brought them to the assembly place, which was the hall of the fire department, on Lubelska Street, opposite the flour mill of Pinchas Freilich. A number of graves were opened right on Hamarnitzka Street – in the center of the city. Abraham Tennenbaum opened the grave of the wife of Arthur Bornshtein and her children. According to the stories on the street, they were taken to be shot when the woman who hid them informed on them, because she wanted their possessions. .

On the same street, closer to the cemetery, in the courtyard of Yoshkowitz, they opened the grave of Yosef Shvartzberg, son of Shmerl. The Nazis had found him in the storehouse, when he was making soap.

In the village of Budi, I opened the grave of Yehezkel Weisbord, his brother-in–law, and the brothers Feigenbaum from Glovatz'ov. They had been taken there to be killed, after they weren't successful in their attempt to flee the Ghetto, after they had learned that on the morrow the evacuation to Treblinka was to take place. Their hiding place became known to a Jewish informer, Abraham Kreitzberg, who brought the Gestapo, which took the martyrs away and shot them close by. After this, I opened the grave in Stzhelnica. Here there were buried the martyrs, Chayale Freilich and the wagoner of the Tzemach family. I was also present at the opening of the grave on the way to the Vistula River.

[Page 630]

I was invited there specially, since we couldn't find the place. Finally we found the grave on the left side of the road. We also opened the graves on the road to the village of Volka. There the martyrs were slain by the Nazis, because they had gone to buy food. After we brought the coffins with the martyrs to the assembly point, we set the funeral for 4 o'clock in the afternoon.

The Funeral Procession

At exactly 4:00, we put the coffins in a truck and a wagon, in order to bring the martyrs to a Jewish grave and eternal rest in the Jewish cemetery. The funeral procession began to move from the assembly point. At its head there marched Abraham Gutmacher with a large floral bouquet. At his side were Rachel Pearlstein and Ratza Wasserrnan. After them there marched the band of the fire department. Afterwards marched the government representatives: The governor of the province (Starosta) and all of the senior officials; the leaders of the political party; the members of the city council and its chairman; the representatives of the official agencies, and the citizens. After them came the coffins of the martyrs which were escorted by all of the Jews of Kozienice who had come to the funeral. To the rear marched many Poles. It seemed to me that all of the inhabitants of Kozienice had turned out to pay final tribute to the martyrs of the city. The funeral procession went through Lubelska Street, turned into the 11th of November Street and continued towards the Jewish cemetery. On the cemetery there was already a large communal grave prepared, about 20 meters from the entrance. After we unloaded the coffins, I gave a eulogy in the Polish language. After me, the head of the city council, the secretary of the Communist Party, Abraham Tennenboim, and my friend, David Golomb, eulogized the dead. We closed up the grave, recited the Kaddish, and dispersed. We, the remnant of the Jews of Kozienice, were photographed for the last time at the fresh grave. We felt that the rich past of the Jews of Kozienice, that had begun hundreds of years ago – was eliminated by the Nazis, during WWII, and came to its end with this final photograph. This past we were able to memorialize with two memorials. One was a large tombstone on the fresh grave, and the second memorial we were able to set up with the help of my friend, Yoel Litman. It was a marble plaque on the wall of the Holocaust crypt on Mount Zion in Jerusalem.

[Page 631]

The Exhumation of Kozienice Martyrs

by Ratze Vasserman, Holon, Israel

Ratza Waserman

I feel a shiver when I remind myself of what the German vandals did to our magnificent city and her thousands of Jewish inhabitants. I tremble at the memory, that in the town where I was born and raised, there, in that town, where I spend my childhood, there where my fondest hopes, and childhood fantasies were woven, that there, a terrible destruction overcame our nearest and dearest, and put an end to the magnificent Jewish community – made it a heap of destruction!

The Heart is Tense

The heart is tense at the thought that we are a remnant that has remained after the destruction of our town, and that we are the "Last of the Mohicans" of our magnificent Jewish community, which had with its rays of light and learning, enlightened Polish Jewry. Who could have imagined that a small group of Kozienice Jews would have to mourn our community, in which there lived and taught one of the founders of Polish Hassidism, the world renowned scholar, the Maggid of Kozienice, of blessed memory. No! Nobody would have imagined it, that the Hitler murderers would destroy the city, which had a history of hundreds of years of Jewish life and achievement. Unfortunately, it is sadly a tragic truth that the Hitler murderers and their cohorts were successful in erasing our city, and we don't even know where the final resting place of our families is!

With Tears I Write These Lines

I remind myself of the beautiful youth that existed in Kozienice. The youth was thirsty for knowledge. All of the organizations were filled with young people. The libraries were always filled with readers. From Warsaw there came speakers who lectured on literary and political topics. The youth attended and listened and then discussed all of the topics. The Kozienice youth brought light and knowledge to the town, and Kozienice was proud of its youth. Kozienice also had a large number of labor and professional associations. Almost all of the workers belonged to associations, which were well organized and informed. Until a sharp knife fell and cut off this dear, beautiful youth.

The survivors of Kozniece accompanying the exhumed remains of holy victims on their last route on April 17, 1949

No One Will Ever Forget This!

And how can we forget this enlightened city, in which I was raised as a free soul? With respect we'll mention the heroic struggle which our parents, sisters and brothers carried on against their oppressors, until the last day of their lives. We will set up a living monument to our tortured community.

[Page 632]

This will be – a Yizkor (Memorial) book. When we will open our book, there will be spread out before us your torture and difficult life which you experienced. Your lives will serve as an example for all of our future generations. You will constantly be our inheritance and support! Your last words will be for us a holy will and testament, so that we may never forget the fearful crime which the Nazi murderers carried out on our nearest and dearest. **WE WILL NEVER FORGET IT!**

It Was Right After the Great Destruction

Our town was destroyed and laid to waste. The Jewish quarter had been entirely erased, and to return to Kozienice could not even be considered. We, the small group of survivors, Kozienice Jews, either from the Soviet Union, or from the camps, came together in 1948 in Lower Silesia, by our friend, Abraham Tennenboim. The major topic at our first get–together was: the exhumation of our murdered Kozienice Jews. We turned to our fellow townsmen in Brazil, for the financial support necessary to carry out the exhumation. Our fellow townsmen, in Brazil, responded positively and immediately provided the material help that was needed. We immediately delegated Tennenboim to go to Kozienice, to take care of the formalities necessary for the exhumation. In April, 1949, we a group of 18, consisting of: Benzion Mandel, Chaim–Itshe Provizor, Moshele Rochman, Abraham Gutmacher, Shmuel Sherman, of blessed memory, Chaim Zaltzberg, Chemya Reizman, Rachel Pearlstein, Yitzhak Kleinman, Mindi Bieganyetz, Moshele Dorfsman, Nissan Greenspan, Abraham Tennenboim, the writer of these lines, and two other Jews, whose names I do not remember, and the representative of the Central Jewish Committee in Poland, Chaver Golomb. Terror seized us when we tread on the earth of our home–town. The Ghetto was destroyed, only grass. It couldn't be recognized that here there once lived a flourishing Jewish community.

It took 4 days for us to gather the bones of the murdered and shot Jews. On all the roads around Kozienice and also in the city there lay the remains of men, women and children, who had been shot. For example, near the lake, not far from the hospital, were dug up the remains of Alter Bornstein's wife and two children. By the Shtshelnitze, we dug up Chantshe Dantziger, Chayale Freilich and the Jew, whom the Germans had forced to dig their grave. This was the Jew, who used to distribute beer from Yonah Tzemach's brewery. He had been thrown live into the grave and then covered up. Shmuel–Abraham Tzeitfinger's bones were dug up not far from R' Yenkele's home. There they also dug up the bones of Yankl Shmeiser. Near the barges there were dug up the corpses of the Kutsher brothers from Glovotshev, Yehezkel Veisbord, his wife's sister, Sarale Mekler, and also Tzalke Kreitzberg. On the way to the village of Dombruvke, there were dug up the corpses of five Jews. Among them was Moshe Kestenberg's wife, Rivke. The names of the other four, we weren't able to establish with certainty.

Ratze Waserman, Abraham Gutmacher and Roche Perlstein in front of the funeral procession.

[Page 633]

Behind the courtyard, on the Vitestve, they dug up the corpse of a 17 year old girl, who, according to the information provided by the Polish inhabitants, was shot by German gendarmes. In the village of Dudof, on the field, near a small lake, they dug up the corpses of four Jews, whose names, unfortunately, were not identified. In a portion of the not yet rotted clothing, we found a gold engagement ring, a pocket mirror, and a portion of a document with the name Grinshpan, which had been issued in 1942 in Radom. On the "sands" was found the corpse of Moshe Fine's wife, Brandl. She went outside of the Ghetto in order to search for food for her children. Coming back she encountered a gendarme, who knocked her down, and choked her to death with his boot. Near the stream, not far from the bridge, we dug up three Jews, whose names we couldn't establish. Not far from that spot where the Zamoisky family lived behind the hill, we dug up three Jews. Not far from the village of Vilke we found the bones of Tsharne Shermeister. A bit further away from the railroad station there were found the corpses of two Jews, but unfortunately we were unable to identify them.

Altogether, 32 Jews were exhumed. During the exhumations a Polish government doctor was present. The bones of those who had been shot and murdered, we wrapped in white linen, and placed in a coffin. Afterwards we arranged a funeral procession, accompanied by an orchestra, with the participation of Polish officials. The funeral procession proceeded through the area that had formerly been the Jewish Ghetto, through Radomer Street up to the cemetery. There they had prepared a communal grave. The coffins with the martyrs were lowered into the grave. Eulogies were said by Abraham Tennenboim, Moshele Rochman, the representatives of the Jewish Committee and a representative of the Polish government. The entire crowd recited the Kaddish, and in a sad mood, with broken hearts, we parted from our martyrs, who had been murdered, only because they were Jews. WE HONOR THEIR MEMORY!

A funeral of 34 Jewish bodies dug out at the end of the war in Kozienice. A Polish music band follows the caskets.

[Page 634]

The Exhumation in Kozienice Martyrs

by David Golomb, Holon, Israel

When I, the authorized representative of the Central–Committee of the Jews in Poland, David Golomb of Lovitsh, sat after the War with Moshe Rochman of Kozienice in the Lodz Kibbutz, he requested that I carry out the exhumation in his home city. I honored his request and set to work. In Kozienice, I didn't find a single Jew. This pained me greatly, because as I well knew, Kozienice was, before the War, one of the nicest Jewish cities, which was renowned throughout the world.

Abraham Tenenbarum digging out the remains of the family Borenstein.

And You Shall Bring Up My Bones

I set about doing the exhumation and carried out the words of the biblical verse: "And you shall bring up my bones!" I immediately posted placards signed by the mayor, that in the hotel in Room 10, the representative of the Central–Committee is to be found and anyone who had information concerning Jews, who were murdered by the German bandits and their cohorts, can and must give this information in Room 10. Already on the 2nd day, people came to me and told me about various incidents. I immediately ordered coffins, according to the instructions of the health department. I bought linen and hired 4 people, who would help me dig up the corpses, and bring them to a Jewish grave.

I remember that the carpenter, who made the coffins, told me a secret: that a Christian, who had taken away from a woman with two sons, her jewelery and money, had in an unashamed manner turned them over to the SS men. The unfortunates were shot near the home of this Christian and there they were buried. We did, indeed, find them there. I remind myself of another incident. We stood near a grave more than 4 hours, till we were able to remove all of the bones. At another grave we found an identity card and an engagement ring. I gave it all to Abraham Tennenboim for the Historical Institute. In another grave we found a pearl, a bottle and a small box. A saying states that "shrouds do not have any pockets", but even so we found things among the victims.

A Miracle Occurred

When I returned to my hotel, there came to my room a Christian, who told me that not far away, there lives someone who knows where a Jew, who was shot, lies buried. I immediately went to that address. A little girl told me that her father wasn't at home. Later it turned out that her father had killed a Jewish passer–by, the day before. A miracle!

It wasn't easy to carry out the exhumation. We set the funeral. A few days before the exhumation the remnant of Jews from Kozienice had begun to gather. It was already dark. All of us and the department of health workers, who accompanied me all day, went out of the hotel. We were approached by a young Goy, who drew a revolver and ordered us to "Halt!" You can well imagine that we were frightened.

[Page 635]

I thought to myself: "Saved from the War, and now to find my death in Kozienice!" He led us a long way. Suddenly we were approached by Avramele, Moshe Rochman's cousin, with the militiaman, who had accompanied me during the entire day of the exhumation. I asked the militiaman to take us to the O.B. As it turned out later, nothing would have happened to the drunk if he had shot us, because the very next morning, early, he was marching through the streets, free as a bird.

They Honor the Jews

When I met with the representatives of the O.B. in the county building, they proposed that the funeral be accompanied by music. I told them that for Jews it is forbidden. They made this a condition for the funeral to take place. You can therefore actually see in the pictures that leading the funeral procession is the State Orchestra, and following the orchestra are the surviving remnant of Jews. The intent of the Polish officials was to display before the Polish populace, the fact that Jews are being honored. I would have appreciated their not honoring us so! When the procession went through Kozienice streets, all businesses were closed. Through the entire route the orchestra played the funeral march of Chopin. Many Christians came to accompany the funeral. While they were preparing the large communal grave for the 32 martyrs, the remnant of Jews surrounded and sealed off the tomb of the Maggid, of blessed memory. After lowering the 17 coffins into the grave, the survivors recited the Kaddish and "Lord full of mercy...." in unison.

My Eulogy

I eulogized the newly interred in a Jewish grave, with the following words: "Fathers and mothers, brothers and sisters, children and parents, Tzaddikim and Hassidim, tailors and shoemakers, porters and wagoners, intelligentsia, youth, and doers of every sort, you who were so cruelly deceived in your hopes; workers who hustled all week, in order to prepare bread and herring for the Sabbath; all of you, who all of your lives awaited the Messiah, and in the end were in a murderous fashion tortured and shot. For you I will, today, here, in the name of all of the Jews of the entire world, we express our protest, and tell the world, who saw all this take place and remained silent! NEVER AGAIN! We cannot forget so many tears for the innocent blood, which you, dear souls, shed. We can still hear the screams of the children, who were torn away from their mothers, who did not have the privilege of being able to bear and give birth to their own children.

We Demand Revenge!

[Page 636]

If someone should remain alive from those who survived the Hell, take revenge for our innocent blood! We, those who've remained alive, and had the privilege to gather up from the woods and fields the remains and bring them to a Jewish grave in your home city, swear, over this fresh grave, that we will not rest, until the murderers and their cohorts are punished. May my words serve as a Kaddish, and Eternal Light for those, who we weren't able to bring to a Jewish grave. There is no consolation, which could possibly console your premature and murderous deaths. May their souls be linked into the chain of life!

Abraham Tenenbaum and Ickhok Kleiman lowering the casket into the mass grave.

[Page 637]

Kozienice, 26 April 1949 - Permit and Exhumation Protocol

by David Golomb, Holon, Israel

(Translation of Polish Document)

**KOZIENICE, 26 APRIL, 1949 COUNTY–CITY HALL OF KOZIENICE
COUNTY DOCTOR HEALTH CERTIFICATE: 13 SEPTEMBER, 1949**

PERMIT

Based on the Statute of 17 March, 1932, about the burial of the deceased and establishing the cause of death (no. 35, section 359) and Disposition from Ministry of Welfare from 30 November 1933, about the above matter (no. 13, section 103), I permit the Representative elected by the Central–Committee of Jews in Poland, Mr. David Golomb, to execute the exhumation of the bodies of Jews murdered by the Germans, during the period of the occupation, in the area of the County of Kozienice (town Kozienice, County Brzeznica and County Kozienice) and transfer of the above mentioned bodies, to the Jewish Cemetery in Kozienice.

The permit is issued under the following conditions: 1) The bodies can be exhumed and transferred to the Cemetery in the presence of the County Sanitation Department. 2) The bodies have to be stored in sealed wooden crates. 3) The exhumation is to be carried out only during evening hours. 4) The burial of the Jewish bodies is to take place on the 27 April, 1949 on the Jewish Cemetery in Kozienice.

The responsibility for the execution of the above conditions is delegated to Mr. David Golomb.

Exhumation Protocol

On the 26 April, 1949, there took place the exhumation of the Jewish population, murdered by the Nazis in 1942 in the region of Kozienice and surrounding villages, carried out by the Jewish Committee: Head, Abraham Tennenboim; members: Moshe Rochman and David Golomb, in cooperation with the representatives of the local Mayor's Office, Mr. Marian Woinovski and County Office, Mr. Juseph Domanski.

The burial grounds of the murdered were in the following places: Town of Kozienice – 15 victims; area of County Kozienice – 14 victims; and County of Brzeznica – 3 victims.

At the time of the exhumation, the document of Abraham Grynsztajn (food card); two pocket mirrors; wooden cigarette box and a gold wedding ring were found.

[Page 638]

All bodies in a state of decomposition were deposited in 17 wooden crates (coffins) and buried on the 27 April, 1949 on the Jewish Cemetery in Kozienice, on Radomska Street, in a common grave. Items found by the bodies, were removed by the head of the Committee so that they could be presented to the Historical Society of the Jewish Committee in Poland. The Jewish inhabitants of Kozienice, representatives of the City Mayor's Office, Communist Party and Public Security took part in the burial ceremony. The burial ceremony ended on 27 April, 1949 at 8:00 p.m. This Protocol was finished and signed in six exact copies.

Head of County Office Representative of Police Head of Exhumation Committee Members of Exhumation Committee

Kozienice, 28 April, 1949

[Page 639]

Kozienice – Judenrein

by Levi Reznik, Bogata

The mind cannot accept that Kozienice, which was renowned and world-famous, is today – Judenrein. Kozienice, where Goyim, when they would pass the holy Maggid's shack, would bend their heads out of respect, and mumble a prayer with their lips, that the Maggid should help them – is today Judenrein. Kozienice, which on the 12th day of Elul (August) became one great boarding house, when from all over Poland, Jews and dewesses would come to the Maggid's tomb; old men and women, children and entire families, in order to request a good year that was to begin the next month, for all of Israel – that Kozienice is today dudenrein. Kozienice! You, my town. There where the cribs of my nearest and dearest stood, you are today, O'voe dudenrein!

How Could It Have Happened?

How could it have happened? And why did you, democratic world, stand by and look on while people born in the image of God, be led like dumb lambs to the slaughter? Why were you quiet, O' world?! A curse on you, world, for our fearful tragedy. You, the Germany, of Heine and Goethe, of Wagner and Strauss, cursed forever. A world of curses on your dirty, cannibalistic body. Oâ€™ God of Revenge do not rest, but bring plague after plague, for our brothers and sisters, for our fathers and mothers, for our children and for the infants in the schools. Our days were beclouded. Our laughter became wailing. Our food was salted with tears, and our drinks were mixed with blood. Lord, full of mercy!

Can you ever console your orphaned people?! Gravediggers did not dig graves, Mourners didn't sit the 7 days of mourning; no Kaddish was recited and no tombstones were set up. An orphaned nation doesn't know when to light the annual memorial candles. It only knows the names of Treblinka, Auschwitz, Maidenek, Chelmno, and Bergen–Belsen – all of Poland one mass grave. Death by choking, death by burning. Six million Jews, mine, yours and ours, gave up their souls in the death factories. May the Nazi–German name be erased forever!

Blood Drips From Every Letter

Our history is pitch black. Blood drips from every written letter. Death cries out to us from every corner. The hands of 6 million Jews hide the sun in the heaven, begging revenge for burned–out lives, for the scattered ashes on Poland's bloody fields. You were small in area, my town of Kozienice. Your population wasn't large. You were poor all week. Your shoemakers, needle workers, tailors, smiths, carpenters, and others worked late into the evenings in order to support wives and children. But you were festive in your ways, and Sabbath–like in your talk. Joy and laughter echoed from your humble homes. Mystical, Hassidic melodies, and work songs were mixed together in one great symphony.

[Page 640]

Kozienice feet danced Hassidic and modern dances. From your poverty stricken streets, my Kozienice, your libraries shone like streaks of light. Also your institutes and associations. And all around this like a wreath of flowers you were encircled by the Hassidic legend of the Holy Maggid. Today you lie, holy princess, Kozienice, in ruin. Your streets and homes stand wrecked by the murderous German bombs. Your Jewish streets, your Jewish houses are abandoned, and there is no memory of the Maggid1 s shack, of the cemetery, where your former Kozienice inhabitants had found their eternal rest.

Kozienice, you've become Judenrein. All is destroyed, that was Jewish in you. An eternal curse should hang over Kozienice skies, for those who destroyed you, and on those who stood by and watched your destruction.

Be Consoled, Surviving–Remnant

Israel is not a widower. The Jewish nation has not been wiped out. The prediction of the greatest monster and his Nazis has not been fulfilled: That the Jewish people and Jewish nation will be exterminated!" The Jewish nation lives, and will live. The 2,000 year–old dream of a reborn Jewish State in Israel has been fulfilled, so we are once again a nation among nations. From the ruins of the Warsaw Ghetto, and from the destroyed ghettoes in all of Poland, they, the surviving ghetto–fighters, escaped through filthy tunnels, and across thorny roads, carried on leaky ships over stormy seas, until they were united with the heroic Israeli youth, and established a Jewish state, renewing and revitalizing the Heroic Names of the Ancient Maccabees.

Nazis having a good time cutting off the sidelocks of a religious Jew in Kozienice.

Editor's Note: Another source claims: "Photograph taken in the Bergen-Belsen concentration camp shows Adolf Eichmann (2nd R) smiling while German officers cut a Jewish prisoner's hair."

A memorial evening in Stutgart, Germany in 1946.

On the fourth anniversary of the evacuation of Kozienicer Jewry to
Treblinka. Survivors gather in Stutgart, Germany for a memorial.

[Page 641]

Kozienice In 1966

by Abraham Tennenboim, Warsaw

Kozienice without Jews. These words before 1939 ago would have rung in my ears as an unbelievable nightmare. Today it is an actuality. The ruin of Kozienice can be seen, as soon as you cross over the bridge, where Lubliner Street begins. On this Street there once lived thousands of Jews. From all of the houses, which belonged to Jews, there have remained only those which were considered the biggest and nicest houses in the city: Leizer–Itshe's house, Pinchas Freilich's mill and two small houses. They are on one side of the street. On the other side of the street there stand only two houses: Aaron–Berish Feigenboim's and Moshe Medalyon's. All along Lubliner Street, from the bridge to Leshitze's house there is no sign of the former active Jewish life. Waste! Only the waterfall from "Plimpl" still flows, as formerly, during the good Jewish times.

The Brovarne Street – That There Was Once

There is no sign remaining of all the surrounding big or small streets, where Jewish poverty had existed. The Brovarne Street, that had once existed here! Here there lived: water–carriers, washer–women, Laufers (who went to the villages), smiths, and just general impoverished people, who would go from house to house, begging. Here we would see the rope–maker, in front of his home, braiding the strands of rope. Here was the messy place where the unfortunate poor would sleep. The steam bathhouse and Ritual Bath were also located here. The Brovarne Street was located near the bank of the river, and therefore it was often, in springtime, flooded, when the river overflowed its banks. Also the big house of Ite Leibish disappeared. On the site, apple trees are now growing.

For all eternity the neighborhood has disappeared where religious life had been concentrated. On the street of the Central Synagogue, House of Study, the Rabbi's house, and the Maggid's prayer house there are now built up large apartment houses. From Magitova and Targova Streets all Jewish homes have disappeared. Like one in a daze, I step on the ground of the former hundreds of years old Jewish life, and I just don't know where I am!

Here I Was Born!

Here at number 29 Lubliner Street, I was born. Hundreds of thousands of Jews now stand before my eyes. My feet lose their steadiness. My memory tortures me, that the objective to erase every sign of Jewish life was accomplished. Now as I walk on this earth, I remind myself, that when we carried out the exhumation of the Kozienice martyrs, we found everywhere where we dug, the graves of murdered Jews. It simply means that the soil of Kozienice is drenched with Jewish blood. The picture of destruction ends on Radomer Street.

[Page 641]

This was the boundary of the Ghetto. The right side of the street is unharmed. And that half of the city is just as it was one hundred years ago. The substantial house of Mintzberg, the brewery and big house of Yonah Tzemach, the house of Yankl Birnboim and some other Jewish houses have not been changed. But Yiddishkeit (Jewishness) – has disappeared. In place of the Friday night Sabbath candles, which used to sparkle in the windows – there hangs a cross.

Who Vandalized the Tombstones?

The ruin of Kozienice can also be seen when you come from Radom. In the Radomer Woods stood the cemetery, which was completely destroyed. To this very day, I haven't been able to establish with certainty who was responsible for vandalizing the thousands of tombstones and where the bricks of the fence had disappeared to. Here and there stand some broken tombstones. Only four complete tombstones are to be found in the graveyard, lying turned over with the lettering facing the ground. The mass grave of the 32 exhumed martyrs, with the memorial stand as if orphaned. When we mention the mass grave, we must indicate that the condition of the monument and its foundation require a fundamental renovation and reconstruction. The grave is the only sign of Jewish life in Kozienice.

[Page 643]

Kozienice, the First Saturday in May, 1926

by Mosze Rochman

At three thirty A.M., I heard a light knock in the window of my room. I grabbed my jacket and in a few seconds I knocked in the window of Shmuel Kohn. He walked out on his toes. From a side street of the Rabbi came out Shlomo Bukhner and Lutshi, after them ran Moshe Shwartzberg. We started to walk towards the Radomer Street. On the way we met already Moshe Kestenberg, Hillel Waserman, Israel Burstin, Aron Tabatshnik, Isokhor Frish, Levi Shabason, Jankel Zilberberg and Velvel Korman. It started to dawn. The air smelled with the smell of Acacia, it was so quiet around. It made the impression that because of the Sabbat, God spread out his wings over the roofs of Kozienice, not to disturb the sweet Sabbat rest of His Kozienicer Jews. From the Radomer Street we walked through the forest to the village of Budy. Before the village we sat down to rest on the grass. Shlomo Bukhner collected 20 cents (Groshi) from everyone. This money everyone saved up for this morning hike.

A few minutes later we were all sitting around a wooden table in the back yard of Mrs. Voitshikova. On the table we were served: butter, cream, hard boiled eggs and two homemade large pumpernickle breads. We ate with such an appetite, like we wouldn't eat for months, and we had the impression that such a breakfast we couldn't get anywhere except at Mrs. Voitshikova. At the end we drank fresh warm milk just taken from the cow.

Mr. Bukhner paid for the breakfast and the woman invited us to come the next weekend again.

We went back to the forest and everyone felt now rested and refreshed. After a while we parted into two groups and started to play handball. The game became interesting and we became so involved, that we did not notice how fast time was running and if not the fact that we noticed an older group going home, God knows how long we would still be playing. The older group was Melekh Waserman, Shlomo Kestenberg, Eli Huberman with Sara Kohn, Hershel Rokhman with Brandl Olshina, and Ber Zilberberg with Khaia Flamenbaum.

For the remaining money we bought a bucket of Acacia for everyone and we were on our way home. Coming back to the city we found only two stores open on the Radomer Street. The streets were already full with people strolling in their Sabbat clothing. We realized that we missed already the evening prayers. Who knows what a spanking we would get from our parents if not for the big bucket of Acacia that everyone brought home.

The Village Budy, April 1949

On the field across the little house of Mrs. Voitshikova were assembled around a wooden casket, covered with white linen: Nissen Greenspan, Moshe Rokhman, Khaim Zaltzberg, Ratze Tokhterman, Moshe Dorfman, Ben–Tzion Mandei and Favel Reisman. Inside the casket were the bones and pieces of the bodies of Khaskel Weisbord and his sister–in–law and the brothers Feigenbaum from Glovatshov. They were just dug out from the grave full of water.

Mrs. Votshikova just told me this story:

Because of the rumors that the following morning the Jews of Kozienice will be deported to Treblinki, the four youngsters sneaked out at night from the ghetto, and were hiding in the silo of Mrs. Voitshikova in the village of Budy. They may have survived if not for the traitor Avrom Kreitzberg may his name be blotted out. He brought the Gestapo over and showed them the place where the four victims were hiding. They were forced out into the field and were shot while

this dog Kreitzberg was watching on. One of the brothers Feigenbaum tried to escape but was hit by a bullet from the Nazi. To hide the murderous act they forced Mrs. Votshikovas husband to dig a grave and bury the four Jewish victims. Now we took out the remains of the four murdered victims, brought them to the Jewish cemetery and laid them to rest in one mass grave together with other martyrs dug out in different places around Kozienice. This dirty informer Kreitsberg died later. Like all other Jews the Germans used him as long as they needed him and then he was to them a Jew like all other Jews.

Israel 1953–54

From here, from Israel I am sending this message to all survivors of Kozienice. The voice of our martyrs raped and slaughtered in Treblinki, in the village of Budy, in the village of Vulka. On the hills and roads in the vicinity of Kozienice calls you not to build another Kozienice among other nations. Enough slaughters, pogroms and executions. Build a Kozienice in your own land, where you can meet your enemies on the battlefield like all other nations of the world. Make an end to the Jewish diaspora, make an end to the unpunished slaughter of Jews. Come together with your children to live in our own land of Israel.

(Left) This is the way the Kozienicer Cemetery looked after the war. A complete ruin.
(Right) On the Kozienicer Cemetery remained only one tombstone turned over.

(Left) Hard to recognize the market after the Shoah.
Right) This house once belonged to a Jewish owner Idl Zilberberg. Now this is City Hall.

(Left) The Kozienicer Railroad Station. From here Jews were sent on their last way to the extermination camp in Treblinka.
(Right) On the Targova Street there were many jewish small houses. A big apartment house was built.

Berl Rochman and his family in 1942.

(Left) Leah Rosen and Tisl Braun (Right) Isral Sheva and Khaim Rochman

(Left) Mayer Sirota and his wife (Right) Eliezer Grudniak and Ester Apelbaum

Kozienice in the World

Shalom Melzer, President of the Kozienicer Society in Paris.

Rabbi Funk and Isoskhor Lederman unveiling a monument of
Kozienicer Martyrs in Rio de Janeiro, Brazil.

[Page 647]

Members of Avodat –Yisrael Go On Aliyah

by Chava Shapiro, Kfar –Hassidim

It was a special night of "watching", the night before the first chalutzim of Avodat –Yisrael went up to occupy their own land at Charbaj, which is close to the Kishon River (today Kfar –Hassidim). The houses of the Rebbe on Magitove Street were lit up with kerosene lamps and silver candelabra. At the set tables there sat: The President of Avodat –Yisrael, the Rebbe, R'Yisroel Elazar, a righteous man, of blessed memory, next to him, may they be distinguished for life, to his right, Rabbi Shalom Shapiro, the Secretary, R' A. A. Zuckerman, and all of the members and Hassidim – around the tables. The rooms were filled to capacity, and many gathered outside due to lack of space. The balcony at the entrance was decorated, and on a gigantic white banner there were embroidered in blue "Book and Scythe", and "Torah and Avodah (Labor)". It was magnificent embroidery which I had done. The banner waved proudly above our home, and had the privilege of going on Aliyah with us, and to wave over the territory of Kfar –Hassidim. To my sorrow, cruel hands removed it from the flagstaff, tore it and threw it into the Kishon River. To this day I'm grieved over it. In my soul I embroidered it. Too bad for the symbol that was lost.

On That Night No One Shut An Eye

Even an infant in its crib could feel the rising excitement. The entire gathering was moved and excited at the thought of escorting the first Chalutzim to Ertz –Yisrael. The Hassid, R' Yechiel Elazar and his son, may God avenge their blood, stood on guard and preserved order. From time to time, shouts of joy were heard: "Come and Let Us Go Up" from the mouths of: Abraham Yakl Freilich, R'Yaakov Eliazor – a merchant in skins, may the Lord avenge his blood; R'Elimelechl – the bookbinder; R'Aaron Berish; the dedicated Zionist: R' Motl Potshnik, R' Shlomo Zalman, R' Shmuel Motl Alters, Pinchas Freilich, R' Aaron Gutman, our devoted Bible teacher, and his son, Kaddish, the silversmith, R' Michael, the watchmaker, R' Shlomo who was the teacher of the Rebbe's children, and the Hassid, R' Moshe Yakl. All of us, as one, felt that we were participants in the celebration. Sparks of hope were kindled in the hearts of all, and the desire to go on Aliyah beat in the hearts of those who had never even thought about leaving the diaspora.

The Heart of the Rebbetzin, Bruchale, Was Frightened

In the adjoining room sat my sainted mother, the knowledgeable, and wise Rebbetzin, Brachale, of blessed memory, and observed the goings –on with joy mixed with fear. She believed that her sons are sacrificing their souls for the good of Eretz –Yisrael, but in her deep understanding she could foresee the heavy responsibility, that her sons are taking upon their shoulders. Therefore her heart feared.

[Page 648]

The hands of my sister, Chana Golda, who was well educated in Torah and science, were heavily occupied in anticipation of the journey. My dear sister, who devoted her soul to the Holiness of Eretz –Yisrael, used to, in the first years of settlement, in Kfar –Hassidim, go from hut to hut, and attend to everyone who was sick. She made a trip back to Poland and was stuck there, without a chance to return. She perished there in the Holocaust, may God avenge her blood.

Until the wee, wee hours we sat and discussed details. The President spoke and explained the heavy responsibility that each member had taken upon himself. Spontaneously, we answered that we would do and accomplish all!! With a prayer that God shine his countenance on them and make them successful – they dispersed.

R'Tzuddok Didn't Let Go of the Torah Scroll in His Hands

On the morrow, in the morning after morning prayers, once again multitudes gathered at our house. The house hummed like a rushing stream. The President took out the Torah Scroll that was to go on Aliyah with us, and gave it to R' Tzuddok Simonhoz, of blessed memory, one of the first chalutzim. R' Tzuddok didn't let go of the Torah until he went up on the boat. AT 10:00 a.m., the procession went to the railroad station in Kozienice. At its head marched Râ€™ Levi Godel with the banner. In reverence he pressed against his heart. He would sit and learn from a volume of the Talmud in his store, and between customers would engage in learning. He had closed his store to carry out this holy function. During the procession, under a canopy, we danced and embraced the Torah, with our souls uplifted with song and melodies, accompanied by the City Orchestra. At the end of two hours we got to the station. As the chalutzim went up into the cars, the crowd burst out in song that penetrated the seven heavens: "Our Hope has not abandoned us!M This song was sung with the reverence of the final prayer of the Yom Kippur Day (Neilah), in the hope that it would open the gates of Heaven. From the eyes of all, tears flowed, and in everyone's heart there beat Hope!

When he became the Rebbe of Kozienice, R'Yerachmiel Moshe instituted the custom that each Hassid, upon coming to him with a request, would have to give a contribution for the resettlement of Eretz Yisrael. A special plate for this stood on his table. If a Hassid did not put his own money into the plate – the Rebbe himself would put his own money into the plate!

From the book: Beit Kozienice by Rabbi A. I. Bromberg

[Page 649]

The First Steps of Kfar Hassidim

by Malka Shapiro, Jerusalem

As the Moshav, Kfar –Hassidim completes 20 years, there arise in our memory the birth pains of the Moshav and they reflect all of our strivings.

The Great Awakening

I remember the great awakening that occurred in the city of Kozienice at the time when the members of "Avodat –Yisrael" prepared to leave Poland. A large crowd from nearby cities and villages came and wanted to go on a pilgrimage to Eretz Yisrael. Since Rabbi Yisroel Elazar Hopstein, a descendant of the Holy "Maggid", son of the Tzaddik of the generation, Rebbe Yerachmiel Moshe, of blessed memory who is President of the organization, is going on Aliyah – certainly the day of redemption is certainly approaching. A great procession, accompanied by song and music, went to the station, and over it fluttered the blue and white banner, that the sister of the President, Chava, had embroidered on it in letters of gold HAvodat –Yisrael Org.", and the entire city rejoiced and made merry.

Emotion of a Different Sort

I remember also emotion of a different sort on the part of the people of the city, when the members returned from Eretz Yisrael, and told of the great hardships, and even though they praised the President, who was ready to give his life for his fellow members, and he led them through every danger, there were complaints that exceeded all bounds, and even reached the ears of my mother, the sainted Rebbetzin, Bracha, Tzipporah, Gitl of the house of Tzernobol, of blessed memory, who suffered because of the hardships imposed by her son on Jews. In spite of this, she accepted it because of her love of the Holy Land, and she didn't prevent her other children from going.

We Left Grodzshisk

A short while after these days, we left Poland, and went out from the house of Grodzshisk. My father –in –law, the righteous Rabbi, and my mother –in – law, the Rebbetzin, parted from us in tears, but didn't prevent us from making the trip to the Holy Land. They and all of the family and the entire congregation of Hassidim accompanied us to the train, and the Hassidim parted from us with traditional songs, which we did not forget all of the days that we suffered in the Land. The first hardships of Eretz –Yisrael we experienced in Haifa. After trying all sorts of factory work, and after quite a bit of suffering, my husband, the Rabbi of Grodzshisk, Abraham Elimelech, went up to Jerusalem. Since he was an expert in engineering and electricity, he began to rebuild his life anew in those fields.

[Page 650]

We Turned Towards Kfar Hassidim

I, in the meantime, took my daughters, and turned towards the Moshav "Avodat –Yisrael" which had been founded by my brother, Rabbi Hopshtein, and the members of my family, and had developed after members of "Nachalat –Yaakov" and "Hapoel Hamizrachi" had joined, into Kfar –Hassidim. We hoped that the parents, the brothers, the sisters and the families, would soon come up to us. They also hoped for this, but neither I nor they were to be privileged to experience this.

We Reached the Fields Covered With Thorns

It was summer. The wagon pulled by mules moved heavily on the rutted roads. We passed over the Kishon River. The members of Avodat –Yisrael had immediately set a bridge over it, when they had settled the land. But the bridge would be wrecked from time to time by the Bedouins, who were camped in the area, and in the rainy season when the Kishon overflowed, it was swamped and had to be repaired, but we crossed over it safely. The sun disappeared in the west, past Mt. Carmel, and to the east and south the hills darkened, those which surrounded the Zevulun Valley. We came across fields, sown with thorns, which covered us, the wagon, and the mules. The sad wail of jackals filled the air, and it seemed to me that this wailing had not ceased here since the Temple had been destroyed and since Rabbi Akiva had seen jackals on the Temple Mount and rejoiced saying: "Since the evil prophecy has been fulfilled, also the prophecy of consolation will be fulfilled (that the land would be rebuilt)". We who had come to rebuild it certainly felt this seeing the progress that had been made.

We Reached A Hill Covered With Thorn Trees

We reached a modest hill covered with thorn trees (now "Kfar Hanoar Hadati"), huts of wood scattered among the bushes, and wild –life appearing before our eyes. Here a cow grazing near the hut, there a tethered calf. People bent over their work, uprooting weeds, digging in the soil, fixing stoves for cooking among the rocks, digging a well in the depression. Joy fell upon us. Through the silence of dusk the sound of tools was replaced by the murmur of prayer from the hut of the synagogue. Immediately members and my family came to greet us. Their faces were tanned and like ancient water gourds. My brother, President of "Avodat –Yisrael" was somewhat changed. His pleasant expression remained only in his blue eyes. I asked how he was, and he answered: "My life is entwined with the lives of tens of families in Israel, with their troubles – I suffer, and when they are at peace – I am at peace. Would the Glory of God shine on the works of our hands!"

We came to the wooden hut with its cracks. Openings covered with nets served as windows. The walls which were somewhat decorated with needlework, which my sister, Chana, of blessed memory, had brought with her from Poland. A number of years previously she had gone on Aliyah, and now she had come here from Jerusalem, in order to aid in the building of the Moshav. Her sense of the beautiful had not left her, and it found its realization on the bare, ugly boards of the hut.

[Page 651]

We Came Upon Hard Times

Night darkened and the members of the Moshav came to greet the President upon his receiving us as guests. The elders among them said that it was a privilege for them, that a reed in the ocean of waste, had given them the opportunity to build the Moshav in the name of the Holy Maggid of Kozienice whose grandson is now their leader. There began mixed religious and secular discussions. Finally the practical secular items came to the fore, and the Moshav matters were discussed. When I saw the sparks of joy on their poor faces I said: "Certainly, the good that is hidden from the eye, is hidden in their suffering. And then there was revealed to me the incidents of their suffering: Attacks by their Arab neighbors when they drew water from the Kishon, and when they plowed their bare fields. One hand holding a gun and the other a scythe. The draining of the swamps, which endangered the health of the members, and still the malaria mosquito reigning over all. The kerosene dripped out of the small kerosene lamp and the long shadows danced on the walls. Silently decisions were adopted for work arrangements and the schedule for Torah learning. They also decided to augment guard duty at night so that it would include three, in order to make it easier on the President, who doesn't sleep, and is ready nightly to mount his horse, in order to frustrate attacks. The members left the room with words of encouragement, and disappeared into the darkness of the night, which swallowed the hill, its trees and huts, and the mountains and valleys all around. An enthusiastic evening prayer broke out from the synagogue hut, and it seemed as if the stars at the dark blue peak of the heaven whispered to us about a future of good fortune and peace.

We Came Down From the Hill

The national organizations, the Jewish National Fund and the Keren Hayesod, planned the layout of the Moshav, in the valley at the foot of the mountains of Zevulun. We were happy to descend from the hill, where we were isolated, and the Bedouin would ambush us from the mountains. We moved the huts from the hill to the wide valley. Also the members of "Nachalat Yaakov", which had been founded by Yablona Hassidim, came down with us from their hill to the valley. Also the members of "Hapoel Hamizra chiH joined us, and the Moshav grew.

Kfar Hassidim Became a Swamp

The rainy season approached, and the winds blew from all four directions, and a number of huts were blown away. The rains poured down heavily and the swamp grew. Our entire valley, which was called by its new and common name: "Kfar –Hassidim", became a sea of swamp, and the members suffered the worse. Disease increased and it was impossible to get to an infirmary, which had been set up by the Kupat Holim on the central hill. The stone stoves, which had been built outside were being demolished, and the iron stoves, which had been provided by the Keren Hayesod, couldn't be used, because there was no wood with what to kindle them (the road to the mountain on which the thorn trees would be cut, was closed).

[Page 652]

No Water in the Moshav

In the work of drilling the well, which was at the foot of the hill it was impossible to continue at this time, and the well above, where the water was pure, the Arabs had contaminated by throwing the corpse of a cow into it, so that using the water was dangerous. And since there was no water in the Moshav, and the way to the Kishon strewn with wagons, which couldn't be pulled out of the way. Even the mules were stuck up to their bellies in the mud. It seemed as if the world had become .a wilderness. Even inside of the hut we suffered from the blessed rain, because we hadn't rainproofed the hut sufficiently. The huts of the other members had been built before ours had been.

Once again, I stood before a situation I hadn't anticipated. My brother, the President of "Avodat –Yisraer aged twenty and some years, who at home hadn't moved on his own or left the Torah desk, he, who was a gentle soul, rose up first and went out to inspect the swamp; The desolate land requires its builders to be devoted. We must provide support and medicine for the members from whatever source even by way of miracles!" And the members of the Moshav, when they saw their President, Rebbe Yisroel Eliezer of Kozienice, and his brother –in –law, Rebbe Shalom, in the wagon being pulled with difficulty, immediately harnessed their own wagons and went out to the swamp, on the way to the hill. And also this brother –in –law, is a descendant of holy forefathers from ancient times, and is already engaged in the labor of the Holy Land with all of his heart and soul, ignoring reality. His wife, Chava, the sister of the President, who had embroidered, at home, the blue –white banner with the gold letters, did not fear either illness or pain, nor difficult labor, and with devotion she serves besides him.

Kozienicer contributing a Torah scroll to a synagogue in Kfar Khasidim, Israel.

Finally The Rains Ceased

Finally the rains ceased and the thunder and lightning quieted down. The swamp dried up a bit, and the sky wore its blue "tallit" once again. The members went out to plough the fields. They prayed. The Holy One, Blessed Be He, blessed at this time the works of the hands of those who went out to work the Holy Land which had been promised to the descendants of Israel. And I, when I went down with the cow to the valley, where the shepherd gathered the herds. The birds began to nest in the trees, with the settlement of the Hassidim. The red anemone flowers which had blossomed on the hill and in the valley smile at the wagons which are being pulled amidst song and melody. Then I felt in my heart: Perhaps the melodies of the Baal Shem Tov (founder of Hassidism) and his holy convocations are hidden among the thorn trees there in the niches of the mountains, at the point where the sky and earth kiss, and that is what gives spirit to those who go to to the desolate field through intimate contact. And perhaps the spark of the Ari (Râ€™ Isaac Luria, of mystic fame, who lived in Safed) and his devotion and attachment to the Holy Land took hold of them in order to actualize part of the vision that always enwrapped itself around the house of our forefathers, of blessed memory, in the Diaspora.

[Page 653]

Blessed be the Moshav Kfar –Hassidim, that was privileged to become an example to the God –fearing who plough at ploughing time and sow at planting time, and harvest at harvest time, who engage in charitable and righteous deeds, and set aside time for the study of Torah. May it be Thy will that they be sated from the best of the land below, and from the produce of the heavens above until the coming of the Redeemer!

[Page 654]

Avodat –Yisrael on The Banks of the Kishon

by Sh. Shalom

Several weeks after the settlement of these Hassidim on the land of "Nachalat –Yaakov", other Hassidim came up with their young Rebbe, of the descendants of the Maggid of Kozienice, on different land closer to Haifa, and they also established a new village, that was called " Avodat –Yisrael", the name of the Maggidâ€™s book. Also the founders of this village passed through by the house of grandfather, of blessed memory, and also to them there attached themselves one of my family as a teacher and leader. He was my younger brother, Yitzhak. My brother and I used to visit each other at night, mounted upon horses, and in this way I observed the birth –pangs of this settlement point. The young Rebbe, who was called "The President" by his people, and also his brother –in –law, who had made Aliyah with him, the son of the Rebbe of Grodzisk, were related to us, one on my father's side and one on my mother's side. The wife of this brother –in –law, the sister of "The President" was "renowned" for her beauty. Quickly she also became famous for her expertise in milking cows, for the speed with which she could harness a pair of mules, in order to bring barrels of water from the Kishon, and her wisdom in construction which she displayed.

Healthy Jews, good –hearted and of righteous spirit, broad –shouldered and strong –armed, men of the soil, smiths, carpenters and laborers from the country towns, and from the Hassidim of Kozienice, who were outstanding in their height, who while still in the Diaspora would bend iron bars at weddings in their Rebbe's home, would display some of the approaching Messianic era, when the Eretz –Yisrael mules would submit immediately to them and they would go out each morning to their labor as the Jewish "cantor" would chant his merry melodies to the words: "On the Sabbath Day an offering of two impeccable yearlings."

(From the book: "The Aliyah of the Hassidim")

And from here would travel and reach the territory of another forefather, the Maggid of Kozienice of blessed memory, whose home and courtyard stand complete "to this day" like a precious corner in the town of Kozienice. Someone who had visited in his youth, on a Sabbath, that house, and parted with the words: "A peaceful Sabbath" from the empty room, as he was retreating backwards with his back to the door, and his face to the inside of the room, can now relive that experience, which the simple and sparkling words of his mother aroused.

The small room of the holy Maggid, which breeds antiquity, and every piece of furniture on a child scale, the small bed, the small chair, the child's high – chair, where the Maggid would sit all day, wrapped in his Tallit and engaged in the study of Torah. The open book, resting on the shelf attached to the chair front, his holy book: "Avodat –Yisrael" – she would finish her story in a tone of wonderment – that this is the foundation and the bridge to the labor that our chalutzim are today performing in Eretz –Yisrael. And that its signs were visible there on the Sabbath at dusk, when the souls return to their resting place in Paradise.

(From "The Candle Is Not Extinguished")

A group of Kozienicer in the foerst of the martyrs in Israel.

[Page 655]

Our Landsmanschaft in Israel

by Tzvi Madanes, Tel–Aviv

The Kozienice Landsmanschaft in Israel is younger than those in Paris, Brazil and America. They already have served their internship of tens of years of work in helping out fellow townsmen, who are new. This problem did not exist in Israel, by us. Each immigrant established his nook, according to his abilities and possibilities. Our landsmanschaft was founded right after WWII. When our refugees brought with them the great tragedy of our city and her destruction, we took it as our holy duty not to forget our martyrs, and not to stifle their last outcry. The committee in Israel took upon itself the responsibility to carry out our holy duty towards our martyrs and put out the Memorial Book of our city, in order that the blood and tears not be obliterated. Our first work was to set up a memorial, in memory of the Kozienicer Martyrs, on ML Zion, in the Holocaust Cellar, among all of the obliterated Jewish communities.

The executive committee of the Kozienicer Society in Tel-Aviv, Israel.

One Thousand Trees In The Forest Of The Martyrs

Our second objective was to plant in the Forest of the Martyrs on the road to Jerusalem – 1000 trees. Among the trees we set up a memorial. To this ceremony there came members of the committee and tens of fellow townsmen. Rabbi Nurok's words moved boulders. The trees, as if in mourning, bent their heads, and we felt that we are fulfilling the last will and testament of our martyrs: NEVER TO FORGET! Our third step was to publish this Memorial Book, together with all of our fellow townsmen all over the world.

At first we were pessimistic: When will we be able to realize such a great undertaking with so many aspects. But already at the first meeting of the committee all of the members pledged large amounts, which greatly encouraged each one of us. As Chairman of our Landsmanschaft in Israel, I took it upon myself to greet all of the male and female members of the committee and of the editorial committee. Thanks to their active work, the book was published. I also want to greet the fellow townsmen who encouraged us with greater sums of money for the Yizkor Book. These are the families: Tova and Levi Mandel, Mordecai Donnershtein, Leah and Shlomo Gelbard and Yedidya Berneman (Belgium). I want to greet our townsmen in Israel for their participation in writing and funding. We are also closely bound with all of our

Landsmanschaften in the whole world, and we hope to carry out our task with honor. It is also worthwhile mentioning, that during the time there turned to us members who wanted loans. We had no special funds for this purpose, because everything had been set aside for the Yizkor Book. But every member, who turned to the committee, had his request acknowledged. Our committee consisted of the following: Chairman and Secretary – Tzvi Madanes

Correspondence – Leah Gelbard

In the executive committee the following members took part: Tova Mandel, Elimelech Feigenboim, Levi Mandel, Zelik Berman, Mordecai Donnershtein and Chaya Adler.

The Editorial committee consisted of the following members: Tzvi Madanes, Levi Mandel, Mordecai Donnershtein, Ratze Vasserman, Zelik Berman, Elimelech Feigenboim, Yerachmiel Kestenberg and Leibl Fishtein.

[Page 656]

The Kozienice Landsmanschaft in Paris

by Yitzhak Shamis, Paris

In 1933, some Kozienice townsmen came up with the idea to found a
Kozienice Landsmanschaft in Paris. At the time it was a necessity, because
there had been an immigration of many townsmen from our town of Kozienice.
A portion of our townsmen had come without any means and they needed
help.

The Founding –Meeting

The first founding –meeting took place in the Jewish Quarter, Belleville, in
a Jewish restaurant and a large number of Kozieniceites participated. The
gathering elected a committee of the following members: Chairman – David
Eisenboim, Secretary – Yosl Eisenboim, Correspondent – Volf Reishappel, and
a few other people. There were immediately set up a fund and a sanitary
committee, whose job was to see to it that material and also medical help be
provided for all in need. We immediately joined up with the Central Federation
of Jewish Organizations in Paris, whose obligation was to conduct cultural,
material and also social welfare and fight anti –semitism and for equal rights
for the Jewish immigrant masses. We had to legalize the illegal Jewish
immigrants, which at that time couldn't find employment and did not receive
resident permits. The Federation had contacts with the administration. In
many cases she enabled workers and handworkers to establish themselves in
France.

We Worry About A Cemetery

When we were legalized, there arose for us the problem of providing for
ourselves our own cemetery. This was the basis for our Landsmanschaft in
Paris. We set up a general monument with each city inscribed on it, and we

eternalized the names and photographs of those who perished. This created, to a certain degree, a tie between the townsmen and the societies. Every eve of Yom Kippur, all of the societies came to the cemetery, and prayers were conducted and we honored the memory of our nearest. This involved a large expense, and then there was support from all of the societies to cover expenses. This way we conducted our community affairs and our society grew. A large number of townsmen became members, and it beared the character of a large family. The frequent meetings and social activities, which we arranged were very successful. We would discuss various current problems and we would share memories about our town of Kozienice. Afterwards we drew into our organization the leftist element which consisted of the syndicalist workers, such as Yechiel Zucker – a very capable community worker, Yerachmiel Serota, who was experienced in communal work, Shmuel Goldman, David Weitzman and many others. Together with them we organized the first welfare action for our needy families in Kozienice, which yielded very good results, because quite a few families in Kozienice benefited from our help.

[Page 657]

Persecution of Jews

When the Hitlerites occupied France, they immediately began to persecute Jews. Everyone tried to find a way to save themself. Many Jews went to sparsely inhabited places, where Jews were able to hide out. But it didn't take long and the Nazis and their helpers among the French collaborators caught Jews and deported them, not sparing children, the old and the sick. Each day they sent away, to the infamous concentration camp, Drancy, large masses of Jews, and from there they were deported to the Hitler Death Camps, where they perished. Many had perished in the French Resistance.

We Renew Our Activity

After long years of troubles and torture, when the Nazi Army was smashed by the Allied Armies, in France and we were liberated, we saw the terrible destruction which had come upon European Jewry, and among them – our town of Kozienice. Then we faced the difficult problem: How to renew our activity, in order to give help to our fellow townsmen, who had the good fortune to survive, but without the means to carry on their lives. There came men without wives, women without husbands, children without parents, the sick and the broken. This way we started our first rescue operation, which was successful.

The first meeting took place at the home of our long –time President, Shalom Meltzer. The following took part: Shalom Meltzer, Yitzhak Shamis, Yechiel Shamis, Gutman Meltzer, Morris Meltzer, Yerachmiel Serota, Shabbtai Kamer, Abraham Shamis, Shalom Chlivner, David Radovitsh, Nagel and his wife, Teme Potashnik. We immediately got financial support from all present, and distributed the proceeds and began a steady activity.

We Worry About the Sick

We set up a Health Committee, whose job was to care for the sick children without parents, and to visit sick townsmen in the hospitals and distribute help to them. At the head of the Committee, stood Mrs. Potashnik, thanks to whom, many fellow townsmen were helped. We also took part in community activities, which took place in the Jewish community. We contributed annually to the old –age homes, to the appeal for the children's colony, which sent children to Israel for summer vacation. We also supported the memorial to the unknown Jewish Martyr, which the great personality, Shneerson, headed. The House of Documentation reflects the great tragedy which befell European Jewry. We arranged an annual memorial evening for our town, in which many townsmen participated. Our fellow townsman, the well –known cantor, Fleisher, chanted the prayers and a general Kaddish was recited.

[Page 658]

We are in contact with our Israel fellow townsmen, about various problems which concern our town. We took an active part in putting out this Yizkor Book, which eternalizes our families who perished. We organized a committee, which consisted of: Serota, Elani, Mrs. Potashnik, and the Dimant brothers. They carried on the work, which yielded good results. We occupy a respected place in the Jewish community of Paris.

In Memory of Our Fellow Townsman, Peretz Gelberg, of Blessed Memory

Peretz Gelberg was born in 1906 in Kozienice. His first activity was in the "Bund" Party, but in 1933 he turned to the Zionist Organization. He joined "Hechalutz" and prepared to go on Aliyah to Eretz –Yisrael. In that year he also married Rivke Herbst, and in 1934 went to Palestine. He crossed the Mandate boundary by way of Egypt. As soon as he arrived he joined the forces of construction laborers. In 1937 he went to Kfar Yonah and was accepted into MIrgun BorochovH, which prepared its members for settlement on the land. A few months before the outbreak of the War, his wife also came to Palestine, and they began to build a family. In 1940 and 1945 they gave birth to two sons, who were raised in the love of the land. Peretz was a member of the

"Hagana", and in spite of his advanced age, stood guard duty during the riots and the War for Independence. All of his life in the land was dedicated to fruitful labor and the rebuilding of the land. At age 63, on April 22, 1969 he passed away. May his memory be blessed!

[Page 659]

Our Kozieniceites in Paris

by Yerachmiel Serota, Paris

The Kozienice Society in Paris was founded in 1933 by: Shalom Meltzer, Shabbtai Kamer, Gutman Meltzer, Avrahamtshe Shamis, Zelik Eidenboim, David Eidenboim, Yankl Birnboim, the three Reichappel brothers and others. At the beginning the Society concerned itself with a cemetery and with mutual welfare. Actually there already existed in Paris several Societies, which had been founded by Jewish immigrants from Poland, in order to help Political Prisoners in Poland and support a Progressive Jewish newspaper, a Library and Theatre.

The executive committee of the Kozienicer Society in Paris.

We Found a Patronat

A limited activity was conducted by the Culture Council. Already in 1927 – 1928 we founded a Patronat, which was conducted by Radomer, Kozienice and other surrounding fellow townsmen. The first meeting took place at the home of our member and friend, Shmuel Leib Goldman. In his home was laid the foundation stone of an organization called the Patronat. A committee was chosen to work in the Patronat, which consisted of progressive elements, who had come from Poland with the baggage of communal activity experience.

From time to time the Patronat organized readings, outings, visits to museums. It was, so to speak, our second home. We conducted ourselves brotherly and friendly. The immigrant, who came at that time to Paris, did not feel lost; quite the contrary; he immediately found a comradely atmosphere. Many came illegally. The Patronat concerned itself with obtaining employment, even illegally, for each one of the newcomers. Every one in the Patronat had his acquaintance, his friend his comrade. The approach to work in Paris, was not like in Poland. Here, each one had to go to a small trade school, to learn the local methods of work. We saw to it that one of ours was not exploited by strange elements. We exerted ourselves to see to it that the newcomer should do his learning among familiar comrades and become fit for work. It was also a necessity because of the language. It is very bitter for an immigrant when he has no one with whom to exchange a word in his mother tongue. He feels like one who is dumb. And another factor, not unimportant. The immigrant who has no friend or family, begins to search for a fellow townsman or a friend.

The first immigrants, after 1905, were, mostly, political refugees from Russian Czarism. They went through quite a hard time, until they were settled. Many had to leave France and Oee further.

[Page 660]

In 1926, There Was Already Jewish Life in Paris

After WWI, when Poland became independent, the immigration of Polish Jews to France expanded because of economic and political reasons. In 1920 an economic crisis broke out in France. Many immigrants couldn't find employment, and had to return. At that time, Jewish communal life was less developed, and this made the life of new immigrants even more difficult. In 1926 and 1927 there was already a Jewish life in Paris. You already didn't have to look for acquaintances in the coffee –houses. Many of our Kozieniceites already had their own homes, and we had where to spend an evening and discuss the old and new home. We had a place to set up a rendezvous with a fellow townsman and an acquaintance. Once at Meichael Nagel's, at Savell Friedman's and at others.

I want to mention that Savell Friedman and his wife, Ida, and their sons, Paul and Marcelle, were shot by the Hitler bandits a few days before liberation in Perigo – a provincial town in France.

Our second home was there, by them, Kozieniceites were, in general, employed. The main problem was the problem of proper papers. At the moment this problem was solved, the immigrant could breathe free. I remember, that not long after my coming to Paris, many of my friends and acquaintances came to me. In a short while we became a large group of Kozieniceites. We had a good word to say about everyone, to encourage them, to help them look for a hotel, and whoever didn't have papers, we would provide him with a place to sleep. The Patronats at the time concerned themselves with all of the on –going problems and needs of the immigrants.

We Join A Society

A few years later the Patronats joined the Societies which had been organized in Paris. Until then the Societies had only been concerned with burial ground. At the moment that we joined them, they began entirely different activities. First of all, we had a definite communal experience and a different approach. We blew new life and soul into the Kozienice Society. We decided to hold new elections. A few of our group were elected to the committee: Shmuel Leib Goldman, Zucker, Savel Friedman, and myself. We arranged help for the needy and also concerned ourselves with communal activities. We arranged an annual Ball, where all Kozieniceites and friends from surrounding outskirts came together to enjoy a happy and homey atmosphere. There was always friendship in our Society. The majority of Kozieniceites in Paris were members. Every activity which we organized was always successful. Our Society, like all of the others, consisted of people of all classes, even though we were all united. We straightened out every misunderstanding, and always handled with tact, so that our community did not suffer.

[Page 661]

200 Kozieniceites Perished

So our work progressed until 1940, when the Hitler murderers occupied France and began their criminal activities. Some of us immediately mobilized ourselves into the ranks of the Resistance, together with the French, who did not want to bow their heads to the murderers. Many Kozieniceites hid themselves in towns and villages. Almost 200 fellow townsmen perished in the concentration –camps, crematoria and gas –chambers. After this terrible Holocaust we were once again obligated to organize immediate relief for all of the needy. We immediately renewed our activities. All, who crawled out of the nightmare, and from their hiding places, where they had spent more than four years, needed help. Our Kozieniceites who had the good fortune and remained alive, were like all others, ruined and broken morally and physically. Many families did not return. There were those who had lost a husband, a wife or children. All needed our help.

We Help – Israel

Many Kozieniceites, who had saved themselves from Hitler's Hell, went to seek their relatives over seas. We went towards them and helped them as much as we were able to. The committee at the time, which we had organized, is still engaged in that work today. As for example: President Shalom Meltzer, has had that position for 25 years. I, Avish Blatman, Yitzhak Shamit, Chili Gutman, Meltzer, Meir Nagel, and others, who joined later, such as Yankl Haberman, Chil Mandel, Abraham and Chaim Diament, Yitzhak Elani, Shmuel Kestenberg, our beloved Teme Potashnik (maiden . name: Krishpel) and many others. Besides the difficult problems that we had to solve, we didn't forget Eretz –Yisrael, who was carrying on her struggle for independence. Every activity on behalf of Israel was widely supported. To this very day we are in contact with all of Parisian Jewish community life. We do everything, to support every organization which has a humanitarian character, and supports friendship among the nations and peace.

[Page 662]

I Feel a Longing

by Leibele Fishtein

Why do I feel such a specific closeness when I meet a townsman? Only because of the Yizkor Book? Yes! This is a holy obligation. A steady Kaddish for generations to come, for our dearest who perished. The question arises: When the Book will already have been published, or a while after its publication, will this closeness disappear? It seems, that not! When you see a townsman, at that moment there appears before the eyes an unwinding tape of pictures of the childhood –years and of later youth: the celebrating in the lovely nature preserves, summer, the forest, the lake and the city, the lake by the "Hamer", the Yezshore, the walking around the church garden and the outing to the "Babyagura".

Winter: A pleasure, snow and ice. And most important, the way home to the high stove, where every night, it drew like a magnet, to a meeting, to a lecture, a reading, a debate, evening courses, and some with books under their arms to the Library. We are already established citizens of Israel, which we learned about in Heder, that .it is our land "flowing with milk and honey". The childhood dream was realized. Still there is a longing for what was once: the school and House of Study; to the former festive life, which ruled every Jewish person. Even those former week –days are glorified. Today as we meet someone from the family, we feel a strange nearness. The more we look at each other, the more we remind ourselves of the past, where we used to meet, also with those who are no longer with us. Cruel hands pitilessly cut them off. May their memory be Holy!

[Page 663]

Kozienice Landsmanschaft in Paris

by Shalom Meltzer, Paris

In 1937 I decided to found a committee of all Kozieniceites in Paris. I immediately set about realizing my dream. It was necessary because there had arrived at the time Jews from Kozienice, who had .to settle in Paris. For various reasons – they couldn't remain any longer in Poland. Many of the immigrants needed help. To whom could they have turned if not to Kozieniceites? In order to help them materially and to settle themselves, I called together all of those from Kozienice, who lived in Paris and founded a Kozienice Landsmanschaft. At that meeting I was chosen as President of the Committee. When the War broke out, I had to destroy all documents dealing , with the : Landsmanschaft, for security sake and unfortunately, today, I don't remember all that I had recorded up to the outbreak of War. At the gathering in 1945, which I had called, it was noticeable that many had perished. Before the War we had been 120, now only 68. This was with a post –war supplement of members. After the War there began to appear Kozienicer survivors, who needed support. We did everything to aid these fellow, townsmen. We also did much for those who went on Aliyah to Israel, and passed through Paris on their way. They also needed support and help. At the end I want to mention those Kozieniceites from Paris who so tragically perished at the hand of the Hitler bandits, and honor them. We honor their memory!

Shalom Melzer, President of the Kozienicer Society in Paris.

In Memory of Yoel –Aaron Birnboim, Of Blessed Memory

Yoel –Aaron Birnboim was born in Germany in 1947 to his father, Yitzhak, and his mother, Tzivia, of Kozienice. When he was still an infant he went on Aliyah. A short while afterwards, he and his brother Chaim, were orphaned of their mother. His early years of education were obtained at the Dogma School in Tel –Aviv. In 1956 he joined Kvutzat Yekinton in Manara. After he finished elementary school, he continued his studies at the regional school in Dafna. He distinguished himself in his grasp and ability to express himself, was well – liked as social director and at his work. His musical and dramatic talent were well known. Thanks to them he was the lively spirit at parties and social gatherings. He passed the required Air Force tests, and indicated that he wanted to be drafted into the Air Force, but the Kvutza objected and he was drafted into Nachal. (Working and Serving Pioneer Youth). During his military service, he fell in action on March 1, 1967, at age 20. May his memory be blessed!

[Page 664]

Our Participation in the Resistance

by Yerachmiel Serota, Paris

Our town of Kozienice has a rich past of struggle. Soon after WWI we fought, together with all Progressive elements of the Polish Nation against Polish reaction. I consider it my moral obligation to write in our Yizkor Book the part played by Kozieniceites in the Resistance, together with the French Nation, soon after the German Army marched into Paris. The soul of each one of us froze, when this happened. A black cloud hid the sun, as soon as we saw the SS bandits on Paris Streets. At first it was quiet. Jews could still go to work, but those who had the least bit of political sense, could foresee that they would do the same in France as they had done in the other lands they had conquered.

The Hitlerites Poison the Atmosphere

First of all, the Nazis psychologically prepared the French and poisoned the atmosphere against Jews and Communists. The two were always equated. All of the Fascist groups and periodicals were mobilized. All streets were posted with anti ¬Jewish posters and caricatures. The radio blared away all day, until late at night, that Jews are this and that. In one word: the entire Goebbels – Torah came out of the mouth of the French Goebbels, Phillippe Henri and his helpers. In the meantime the Vichy regime ordered that all Jews must register in their own areas. Even converted Jews who had been Christians for generations had to line up to register. The lists later made it easy to deport Jews to the gas –ovens. Later it was forbidden. for Jews, under threat of death, to possess a radio. Every few days, new decrees: Jews cannot travel in the coaches with Frenchmen; Jews may only buy food at certain hours of the day.

Frenchmen Help Us

Later there was issued a decree, that Jews must liquidate their businesses. A commissioner was appointed to oversee every Jewish business. In this way the Jew no longer had the possibility to earn his livelihood. The majority of the French population displayed the greatest sympathy towards their Jewish neighbors, and helped them in every way possible. Many Frenchmen hid Jewish fortunes. Those who had the good fortune to survive, got everything back from their friends and neighbors. There were many cases of French householders who didn't want to rent the businesses which had been confiscated from Jews, except when forced to do so. There were also Frenchmen who fictitiously bought Jewish businesses, moved into Jewish homes, and right after the liberation returned everything to their Jewish owners. Besides solidarity with Jews, the French by their acts carried out patriotic acts against Hitlerism. This way Jews lived in a steady nightmare, with the constant ' fear of new decrees and persecutions.

[Page 665]

A New Misfortune

It didn't take long and a new misfortune overtook all foreign Jews, who had lived for many years in Paris and her suburbs. Jews received a notice on May I", 1941, that they were to gather at specific points with a blanket, a cup, a spoon and shaving equipment. In one day 5,000 Jews were assembled, only men. They were tossed into wooden barracks, encircled with tall barbed wire fences in Pitivie, Bon –Loroland, about 50 kilometers from Paris. This was the first, great tragedy of the Parisian Jewry. The decree severed thousands of Jewish families, and caused tragedy to mothers, wives and children. Later it was permitted to bring to those arrested, a package of food by way of the gendarmerie, who guarded them day and night, as if they were criminals.

Some women managed to see their men through the wire. But the French gendarmes continuously drove the poor women away, and at the same time also threatened those arrested, and their wives and children, who had come to see their fathers through the barbed wire. The threat was that if they would carry on like this, they would turn over the guard duty to the German soldiers. In the meantime it was the French Police who were doing this dirty work. It went on like this for months. Many families remained without any income to live. We felt that further evil was awaiting us.

We Help Poor Families

At that time the Resistance began to grow stronger, and the solidarity activities in Jewish circles to help poor families. A number of the interned men managed to escape. For us, who had escaped, it was extremely satisfying. The Germans, meanwhile carried on with their dirty work. They sealed off the streets where Jews lived, and arrested all Jewish passers –by. At that time they no longer differentiated between foreign and French Jews. They sent us all to Drancy, about 10 kilometers from Paris. From that day on all Jews lived in constant terror. No one was any longer secure in his fate, and trembled, that he shouldn't be cast into Drancy or Compien, 50 kilometers from Paris. Ignoring the terror, the resistance developed from day to day. Illegal newspapers appeared. Ignoring the danger, which faced old and young alike, more and more took part in the struggle. Jewish, young communists, who distributed flyers on the wide boulevards of Paris, paid with their lives: Among them the sons of our comrades and friends: Tishelman and Bekerman.

When the communists decided to use arms in the struggle, the first attack was carried out against an SS officer in the Metro "Barbes", by a French Communist, Fabian (He later received the Grand Colonel). After the attack, the

Germans shot 100 men: half of them Jews and half – Frenchmen. Ignoring the terror which the Germans unleashed against Jews and non –Jews, there was an immediate upsurge in the Resistance in the Free Zone, where the Vichy Regime ruled, and in the Zone occupied by the Germans. There was also a third zone in the Alps, occupied by the Italians. In the Italian Zone, Jews were not under any pressure, until the Germans occupied all of France, after the capitulation of the Italian King.

[Page 666]

We Flee to the Free Zone

In the Free Zone there was organized the Central Resistance for all of France. We, a group of Kozienicer, Radomer, and Zvoliner Jews decided to pass over to the Free Zone. Three of us were naturalized Frenchmen: Myself, Greenberg and Yosef Bleecher of Radom. We decided to cross together. But it didn't occur that way due to various reasons. In October, 1941, I was one of the first in Limoges. From there I went to Lyon. In Lyon, our townsman, Itshe Elani, and his brother Abish were already to be found. Later there came: Greenberg, Bleecher, Issacher Funk and others. We were constantly in contact. Each one of us was looking for employment. Since we were Frenchmen, we didn't have any difficulty finding work. A while later we were able to bring our wives to Lyon. I had luck: I found a bit of a dwelling. For the while we were already a Resistance group.The one in charge of my group was a man from Lyon, an acquaintance, a comrade, and longtime activist, David Keniger, a very fine person. Later friends and comrades came from Paris. They had my address, so they sent the neediest to me. Every week I received valises filled with things, and this helped them a great deal, because to take things along with them was impossible. At the time it was frightful in Paris: Seizures and arrests. In 1942 they began the mass –deportation of Jews. No one knew, where they were being taken. They were packed into cattle cars, without food and drink. Many died on the way. But the greatest tragedy of Parisian Jewry occurred on the 16th of July, 1942.

July 16, 1942

Gestapo agents and French Militia, with bestiality, rounded up 32,000 Jews in one day: men, women, children and the elderly. It is impossible to write about the sufferings of our parents, sisters and brothers. The point to which they were dragged was the Veledrome d'Hiver (a sport's palace). Later they were all taken to concentration camps around Paris, and from there they were all deported. After these tragic events, there was a mass emigration. Jews ran. They looked for a hole, where to hide. Man hid in the towns and villages. Frenchmen of all classes, displayed great sympathy and made the effort to help us in this difficult moment, even though they were threatened with the same fate as the Jews. Many Jews fled to the Free Zone. But the border was closely guarded, by German field Gendarmes and also by Vichy Gendarmes, who weren't any less cruel. Non –naturalized Jews had to report every few days to the Police, and they couldn't move about without an official permit. Many Jews were sent to the Spanish border, where they were placed in wooden barracks, without sanitary facilities. French gendarmes and criminals guarded them. Many Jews, unfortunately, couldn't cross the border into the Free Zone. They fell into German paws and were deported. A lot of familiar friends arrived in Lyon, and many of my comrades stayed with me, until they found a place, where to lay their heads. The solidarity was great. We did everything in our power to help the newcomers.

[Page 667]

New Decrees

Right after the disaster of July 16th, Jews received a new gift: The Yellow Patch. At the same time it became forbidden to Jews to go to the theatre, the movies, and parks. It was difficult for Jewish children to understand that they could no longer play in the sand with other children.

Frenchmen proposed to their Jewish neighbors to take the Jewish children along with them, in order that they might continue to play in the parks. The same was also true of the Yellow Patch. Jews felt, that the "patch" would automatically separate them from the French populace. Fortunately the opposite occurred: The majority of Frenchmen greeted Jews in a friendly manner. There were cases where Frenchmen, in order to display patriotism and friendship to Jews, put on the Yellow Patch. At the same time there were checks in the streets. Many Frenchmen were dragged to the Police stations, and they were warned that if they would again be caught with the Yellow Patch, they would be deported together with the Jews. The French populace helped us a great deal in those tragic moments. This gave us encouragement. After the mass –deportations, the Germans began to steal Jewish possessions. All of Jewish property was transported to Germany.They broke walls and floors, and looked for gold and diamonds, but at the same time our morale grew.

The Resistance in France, and also the other occupied countries grew from day to day. With satisfaction we could demonstrate, that in the struggle all classes and parties participated: from the extreme right to the extreme left. The struggle against Hitler and his cohorts was carried with devotion and self –sacrifice. In the cities and in the provinces there was a commissar who commanded the Resistance. There were fighting units, sabotage units, who were concerned with arms, disseminating literature, and newsletters.

The Resistance Aids Jewish Children

We, Jews, had a special task: Together with the general Resistance, to hide Jewish children with French families. For that we needed a great deal of money. A cousin of mine, Madame Galtshtein, who arrived after the 16 of July, stayed with us. She had placed her two children with a French family, on the German side. Once we received a letter from the family, saying that an agent had come to them and asked if the two children, one aged six and the other seven and a half, whether they were Jewish. So she told them: No!

Afterwards the agent asked the teacher in school, and he also said: "No!" I and my cousin, who had joined a group in Lyon, conveyed this information to the women responsible, in the Resistance and she undertook a special investigation of the matter. Within three days time the two little girls already found themselves with us in Lyon. Afterwards we provided the girls with a safe place. With such dynamism did the group carry out the task of saving Jewish children.

[Page 668]

Right before the Liberation, something happened to a very good friend of mine, Meir Shalom Goldstein. He was an escaped German war –prisoner. He lived and worked far from Lyon at cutting lumber. His wife later came to him with two small children. When the Germans occupied all of France they began making changes in the cities and in the towns, and I received from him a very unpleasant letter. He writes that his wife and two children are about to be arrested. Twenty –four hours later I, with the help of the woman responsible, took care of the two children in Lyon. Soon afterwards, the parents also came, and this way, we were able to avert a tragedy.

Terrible Years

The years, 1943 –1944, were terrible. The revisions (searches) were a daily occurrence. Many Jews lived in hotels, which were especially terrible. As soon as we received information, that a search was to take place, there already were with me many of my friends, and we averted trouble. Ignoring my wife's serious illness, I did not neglect my work for one moment. At that time there were in Lyon, the son and the daughter of our not forgotten friend, Shmuel – Leib Goldman. They had left the provincial city of Vienne. The son, Marcelle, occupied himself by providing false papers for the Resistance. Looking for a birth certificate in the Municipality, he was arrested by the French Milita. The Resistance approached the Prosecutor of the Republic, and managed to free him. It is important to note, that also the Prosecutor was a member of the Resistance.

The daughter of Comrade Goldman, Dora, 15 years old, well developed, was occupied bringing arms for the Maquis and also served as the Courier to the high command of the Maquis. It is worthwhile mentioning joyfully that, the young Dora, who had been with me for a few months, was, after the Liberation, decorated by the French Government with the Croix de Guerre (War Cross). My cousin, Mrs. Galtshtein, (her husband was deported) also did tremendous work. Twice or three times a week, packages, flyers and newsletters were prepared in her home. And she, together with another comrade, distributed them disguised as food, in a food basket, to all sectors of the city. This was how it went on until the Liberation.

We Are Free!

The 6th of June, 1944, was for us Jews in France and for all French patriots, the most beautiful day of our lives. On this day the Allied Armies landed on French territory. In that year the Hitlerites suffered defeat after defeat. An anger seized their ranks. They felt their end approaching. The Partisans and Resistance became very active. Acts of sabotage became a daily thing. The most outstanding in the struggle were the French Railroad Workers. At the risk of their lives, they sabotaged German transports. As revenge the German murderers shot hundreds of fighters daily in the cellars of the Gestapo on Bertelo Avenue in Lyon. Also, we Kozieniceites, suffered victims. David Zucker, the Secretary of our Society, and Yitzhak Potashnik, were deported, and perished. Serge, the 19 year old son of Moshe and Shifra Wolberg, was shot by the French Militia in a small town, Maniek –Lavalle and drove into mourning his unfortunate parents.

[Page 669]

It was enough to go down to the Jewish cemetery in Lyon, and see the long rows of graves of the heroic, Jewish fighters, many of whom we had worked with. On the day of the Liberation, when the Jewish population of Lyon and representatives of the Resistance came to honor the fallen heroes in the struggle against the bloody murderers, we said to them: "Your struggle was not in vain. On this soil, which is soaked with tears and blood, we will build a world of brotherhood and love between nations."

WE HONOR THEIR MEMORY!

[Page 670]

Kozieniceites in New York

by Shmuel Reizman, New York

During the years, 1949 –50, when the American government eased the Immigration Law, and allowed almost 100,000 refugees into the United States, there gathered in New York and the surrounding area, some forty odd Kozieniceites, who had come from the camps of Germany and Austria. Most of them were young people, who had married and had children after the War. There were also among them a few families who had married before the War, and had the good fortune to survive the terrible War and reunite.

We Arrived Without Means

The majority had arrived without means, without money and without the possibility to resettle themselves. Almost no one had any family or friends, and those who met some distant relatives, found them cold towards the newcomers. They could not expect any help of any sort, or aid in settling in. The few tailors among them immediately found employment. A few of the shoemakers among them got some employment with the help of Motl Goldstein, may he rest in peace. Pinchas Shmelke's son was then an official in a professional association of Leather Workers. The vast majority of Kozieniceites found themselves in great difficulty. They simply didn't know where to turn. The so –called Kozienice Society, which had by then already existed for 40 years in New York, had quite a large membership and much money in the bank, did not show any interest in the newcomers. The reason? Those of the Kozieniceites, who had many years previously founded the organization, almost no one remained. Those, who headed the organization, were American born, and really had no attachment to Kozienice. This unsympathetic attitude towards the newcomers, they would display on every occasion, and they would tell about the experience that they had had with the Kozienice Rabbi, R' Yisroel Eliezer Hopstein, of blessed memory. When he came to America in 1942, they, under the urging of Kozieniceites then still living, had helped him. At every opportunity they emphasized what they had done for him. But the Rabbi would have nothing to do with them, since it wasn't befitting to the honor of the Kozienice Rabbi to take a part in their activities, and this pained them greatly. Later they would mention this at every opportunity. This was why the newcomers weren't accepted into the so –called "Kozienice Society."

The executive committee of the Kozienicer Society in New York. (in back, third from left, Victor Silver, then Mr. Reisman, then Sam Goldstein)

A House In Which to Warm Oneself

In those difficult times, when everyone was seeking a place to live, and warm oneself, and hear a good word from an acquaintance – the home of Moshe Kohn (Shlomo Berl's, who had come to America in 1937) was the gathering place for our fellow townsmen. Every Sunday a group of us would gather there to enjoy, receive regards and become aware of who of our acquaintances had arrived in the country, and where they were living and working.

[Page 671]

The fact that, at the time, Moshe Kohn was sick, and there wasn't much of a livelihood at home, did not prevent us from spending our Sundays there. The relation among the newly arrived Kozieniceites were warm and friendly. We would help each other in time of trouble, and enjoy ourselves very much, when a fellow townsman celebrated some joyous occasion. And so life moved on. Bit by bit all of the newcomers got settled with housing, employment, or were able to open some small business. The children grew up, and were sent to school and then to university. The contact among the townsmen did not weaken.

We Try Our Luck

Later we decided once again to try our luck with the existing "Kozienice Society". Perhaps we would be able, from the inside to interest them in our undertakings.

Ignoring the difficulties that they had caused us when we attempted to enter the Society, the hefty dues, which they had requested from a few of the older members, such as: Yitzhak Mandelboim and Matis Fishboim, of blessed memory, and Max Tennenboim, for long life, a large group of us became members of the Society. It quickly became clear that all of our efforts had been in vain. When the question of help for this Yizkor Book came up, or help for a fellow townsman overseas, setting up a memorial event for Kozienice martyrs – they didn't want to know of or participate in such things. All of these things we had to do on our own. When we turned to them about setting up a monument for the Kozienice victims on the cemetery, which they had, they stalled us with all sorts of excuses for two years. It turned out that they wouldn't support us, nor give us a proper place for the monument.

We Quit the Society

After deliberations of the temporary committee, which had already existed for a long time, we decided, that we "had to set up on our own", and that in order to carry out our undertakings, we would have to create an organization of newly –arrived Kozieniceites. We went to work, raised money and bought land for a cemetery. We carried out various undertakings, meet on various occasions and remain in touch with our members. Unfortunately, to our great sorrow, the new Kozienice Cemetery in New York was started with the grave of the 18 year old daughter of Chava Weisbard –Berger, who died in June, 1967. All of the townsmen express their deepest, heartfelt sympathy to the Berger family on their great loss.

[Page 672]

The Kozienice Landsmanschaft in Brazil

by Issachar Lederman, Rio de Janeiro

At the start of my report on the activities of our Landsmanschaft, I consider it my duty to greet all of the Kozienice Landsmanschaft in France for the idea to publish a Yizkor Book in memory of the destruction of Kozienice. You should be blessed for this holy idea. This will lead to a closeness of all Kozienice townsmen in all countries. Now a few words about our own Landsmanschaft. At the end of WWII, after the first tragic reports from across the sea, about the great Holocaust which overcame 6 million of our brothers and sisters in the old home, the Landsmanschaft movement in Brazil became strengthened. Daily new ones were formed. The object of their existence was a holy one – to bring help to the surviving Hitler victims. The help was great!

Rabbi Funk and Isoskhor Lederman unveiling a monument of Kozienicer Martyrs in Rio de Janeiro, Brazil.

We Found the Landsmanschaft

We Kozieniceites also understood that our obligation was to found one in Brazil. Essentially it was the two large cities: Rio and Sao Paulo, where there are to be found almost all Kozieniceites, in order to help our surviving townsmen in Poland and other countries of Europe. Although our total was small in the two cities: 32 families (mostly in Rio), we managed to raise a large sum of money. We immediately sent, by way of the "Joint", packages of clothing and shoes to Poland. We also helped the survivors, who came through Brazil, with everything they needed. We contacted the Kozieniceites in Poland, France, Israel and America and also with the Kozienice Rabbi, R' Yisroel Eliezer Hopshtein, who is in America. We also sent $200 to the Kozieniceites in Poland, for the reburial of the martyrs in a mass Jewish grave in the Kozienice Cemetery. They carried out this holy task with the greatest dignity. We also set up a monument in the Martyr's Tomb in the Rio Cemetery, in the name of our Kozienice Martyrs, as an eternal memorial. This was how we were united in a Landsmanschaft, in joy and in sorrow.

During Succos We Gather for a Memorial Evening

Each year, on Succos, we meet and make a memorial for our martyrs. We are sending you a number of notices about the memorial evenings so that they may be eternalized in our Yizkor Book.

[Page 673]

Kozienice Landsmanschaft Rio De Janeiro

We invite our townsmen and all of the Jews of Rio and the surrounding area to the unveiling of a Memorial Plaque

MEMORIAL PLAQUE

In the Tomb of the Martyrs on the Cemetery of Villa Rosalie
In Memory of our Martyrs on:

Sunday, September 19th (21st of Elul at 9:00 a.m.)
The assembly point will be at the Burial Society, 225 San tana Street
at 7:30 a.m., where buses will be waiting for all.

COME AND HONOR THE MARTYRS

The Directorate

Since we are a small group, its natural that our activity on the culture front is very limited. But still, we participate with other Polish Landsmanschaften in the Jewish life, and annually we participate in the observance of the 19th of April, which is celebrated by the Organization of Polish Jews together with the entire Jewish community. In conclusion, we will mention with honor our late townsman Yaakov Rechthand, of blessed memory, who devoted a great deal of time and energy to our Landsmanschaft. We hereby list the Kozieniceites who came to Brazil after the Holocaust: Moshe –Yaakov Eisenmeser, Tova Berman and her husband, Zelik Berman and his wife, Hese Honigshtok, Chaim –Yakl Hershenhorn, Mendel Vasserman, Tsharne Lederman, Chaim –Yakl Shvartzberg, Berish Shabason, Hershel Weinberg and his wife, Yechiel Shabason and his wife, Rachele Weinberg, son and daughter, Ephraim Kreitzberg.

To our Kozienice friends in Brazil!

Confirmation (Receipt)

Dear friends!

With this we confirm that we received a letter from our friend Potazshnik, that your aid – the $200 has already been received. This means that in fact the money is already in our hands.

At the same time we want to inform you that soon, in the next few days, we will approach our task. About the progress of our work, we will keep you informed. Last week we wrote you a detailed letter. In the name of our difficult and holy work, we express to you our heartfelt thanks for your initial and earnest help.

Fond regards from all Kozieniceites.
The Committee:
Chairman Tennenboim Secretary Tochterman Cashier Peredstein
Waldbzheg, February 12, 1949

[Page 674]

We also consider it our obligation to eternalize in our Yizkor Book, all of the Kozieniceites who lived with us in Rio, and death tore them away from us: Yaakov Birnboim, Shifra Birnboim, Tove Berman, Chome Berman, Shimon Berman, Berish Diament (Ritual Slaughterer), Hese Honigshtok, Daniel Weinberg, Rivke Lederman, Yakl Krishpel and Yaakov Rechthand. We Honor Their Memory!

With this I conclude the report about our Kozienice Landsmanschaft in Brazil. The Directorate of our Landsmanschaft:

Chairman: Issachar Lederman.

Vice–chairman: Berish Shabason.

Secretary: Benjamin Krishpel.

Treasurer: Ephraim Horvitz.

Members: Yisroel Bakman, Me lech Birnboim.

[Page 675]

Kozienites in Belgium

by Yedidya Berneman, Antwerp

Among the first Kozieniceites, who came to Belgium in 1906, was Eliezer Shipper, of blessed memory the eldest son of Yakl Shipper, of blessed memory. At the same time there also came Aaron Usher Eisentzveig, who was actually a Kozienicer son –in –law. He had married the sister of Chaim Chmielnitzky. After WWI there began a large Jewish immigration into Belgium. In 1923, Mordecai Shipper came to Belgium (today in Mexico City) to his brother Eliezer, of blessed memory, who by that time already occupied a prominent position among the large diamond –merchants in Antwerp, and in all the diamond –markets of the world. Later Mordecai's friends began to come: Moishele Berneman, of blessed memory, Liuba Potashnik, of.blessed memory, Ida Shipper and Yosef Kuropatva. In 1929 there came Yosef Lichtenstein, of blessed memory, his wife Dobra Potashnik and Bracha Weintroib (Shipper). During 1929 –30 there broke out the serious crisis in the diamond industry. Because of it, Yosef Lichtenstein, his wife, Dobra, and child, went back to Kozienice and perished during the deportation to Treblinka. Their son, Gedalyahu, remained alive. He was in Eretz –Yisrael, participated in the War for Independence, and returned to Belgium. In 1932 there came to Belgium: Moshe Ber Birnboim and his wife, Batshe Leah, Moshe Pearlstein and Israel Goldman.

In 1934, the crisis in the diamond industry was over, and the immigration from Kozienice was renewed. Then there came: Shlomo Kuropatva, Moshe Kuropatva, Gedalyu Potashnik, Ite Birenman, Zelik Kuropatva, Chaya Weintroib, Mordecai Donnerstein and Velvel Patashnik. Thanks to the humanitarian attitude of the Belgian population during WWII, Kozieniceites were able to save themselves, with the exception of the families, who were deported and did not return. Among those who didn't return were: Aaron Asher Eisentzveig and his wife, of blessed memory, Moshe Ber Birnboim and his wife Batshe Leah, of blessed memory, Chaya Weintroib and her husband Birnboim, of blessed memory.

After the liberation there came to Belgium: Dovrele Zaltzberg, of blessed memory, the daughter of Leib Ber Zaltzberg, who after terrible suffering, died, and found his eternal rest on the cemetery in Pite (Holland), Hershl Potashnik, Velvel Zaltzberg, Pinye Kirshenboim, Kalman Berneman, his wife, Chana Flam, Gedalyahu Lichtenstein, and Moshe Patashnik, who came from Israel, after he had participated in the War of Independence, and was among the liberators of Eilat. In general we want to emphasize that Kozieniceites in Belgium are well off. They cooperate generously when it's necessary to help fellow townsmen. We want to emphasize, that the immigration from Kozienice to Belgium was based upon the families: Shipper, Kuropatva,

Benenman and Potashnik

Pictures Tell the Story

5000 Jews lived in Kozienice before it was destroyed

We honor the memory of a few of them in these pictures

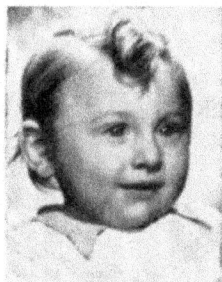

Top Row Left to Right: Yankl Shpigel, at 13 he works drying swamps in Vulka-Kozienice, Charl Bernat-Grandson of Sholim Meltzer - Perished during the German occupation of Paris, Motek Kalb

Middle Row Left to Right: Chaia Kreitzberg, Ickhok Berneman, Betzalol Karpik.
Bottom Row Left to Right: David Shames, Yekhiel Zaterman, Sheva Rochman

Page 500

משה און שיינדל צוקער.

בעריש און הדס־גיטל מינץ, געשטאָרבן אין יאָר 1938.

לייזער רודאָוויטש און זיין פרוי.

ס׳ש ט יי ע ן: מנשה און יששכר פלאַמענבוים. ס׳ז י צ ן: אליעזר און חנה פלאמענבוים מיט זייער שנור און צוויי קינדער.

page 500

Top Right: Moshe and Shaindl Tsuker

Top Left: Berish and Hadas-Gitel MIntz who died in 1938

Middle: Leyzer Radovitch and his wife

Bottom:

Standing: Menashe and Issachar Flamenboim

Seated: Eliezer and Hannah Flamenboim with their daughter-in-law and two children

Page 501

לייבל זיפערמאַן און וועלוול שפינגעלמאַן.

פון רעכטס, ס'שטייען: יעקב־צבי און רבקה טענענבוים, שרה־
נעכע און יעקב־משה באַנדמאַן, מרים לערנער, ... ס'זיצן:
יששכר, דינה, יונה טענענבוים, אסתר מידן־טענענבוים, און מאיר־
זאב באַנדמאַן.

ישראל וואָלבערג און זיין פרוי —
אומגעקומען אין וואַרשעווער געטאָ.

משפחה יואב. זיצן פון רעכטס: ישראל־בער יואב, יוכבד פאַטאַזשניק, עליזה יואב, רחל, שבע און יהודית.

Page 501

Top Right:

From right to left: Standing: Yaakov-Zvi and Rivka Tenenboim, Sarah-Nekha and Yaakov-Moshe Vandman, Miriam Lerner...

Seated: Issachar, Dina, Yonah Tenenboim, Esther Miden-Tenenboim and Meir Zeev Vandman

Top Left:
Leibel Ziperman and Velvel Shpigelman

MIDDLE
Israel Walberg and his wife arriving in Warsaw Ghetto

BOTTOM
The Yoav family: Seated from right to left: Israel-Ber Yoav, Yocheved Potashnik, Aliza Yoav, Rachel, Sheva and Yehudit.

Page 502

פערל-גאלדע ראטאפיא, געבוירן וואלבערג, איר מאן מאקס —
אומגעקומען אין וואַרשעווער געטאָ.

חיים-אהרון וואַלבערג און זיין פֿאַטער.

אברהם וואַסערמאַן און זיין פֿרוי, אומגעקומען אין לאַגער.

גרשון, צפורה און משה זאַלצבערג — אומגעקומען אין
טרעבלינקי, 1942.

Page 502

TOP
Right: Haim-Aaron Walberg and his father

Left: Pearl-Goldie Ratafie (nee Walberg) and her husband Max who were killed in
Warsaw Ghetto

BOTTOM
RIGHT: Gershon, Ziporah and Moshe Salzberg who were killed in Treblinka in 1942.
Left: Avraham Wasserman and his wife who were killed in a concentration camp

Page 503

חוה דאנערשטיין   משה דאנערשטיין

Page 503

TOP

RIGHT: Shmuel Leib Goldman, his wife Mali and his two children who were deported from Paris and were killed in Auschwitz

LEFT: Hava Birenboim and her two children who were killed in Warsaw

BOTTOM

RIGHT to left: Moshe Donershtein   Hava Donershtein
Below is Miriam Donershtein

LEFT: The Gelberg family: Raphael, Ezra, Zvi, Sima-Rachel, Israel-Menahem, Hannah, Moshe and Yehoshua

Page 504

Page 504

TOP:

Frisch family
Standing (Right to left) are: Issachar, Monik and Etta Baila. Seated are: Melech,
Golda, Mendel, Raizel Leah, Israel-Yitzhak, and Liova. The small child is Hanalleh

BOTTOM:

RIGHT: Issachar Shtatiner and his wife
Left: Leibl and Haya Salzberg who were killed in Treblinka in 1942

Page 505

Page 505

TOP:

Efraim Tishman, his wife, children and his mother Tema

BOTTOM

RIGHT: Moshe Lederhandler and his wife Gitel who were killed in Treblinka
LEFT: Golda Frieda and Meir Milgrom

Page 506

Page 506

TOP

Right: Bina and Golda-Leah Horovitz

LEFT: Friedman family
Standing: Baila Friedman, Haim Rakhman, Tova Friedman
Seated: Eliezer Friedman, his wife and grandchild

BOTTOM

RIGHT: Yosef and Malka Flamenboim
LEFT: Rela and Aaron Shtrypman, a brother-in-law to Yerakhmiel Sirota.

Page 507

Page 507

TOP

RIGHT: The family of Israel Spiegel. The only survivor was Paula. Standing: Aaron Spiegel

LEFT: Tsuker family. Seated are Avraham, Leibl and Raizel Tsuker. Standing: Shmuel, Haya-Rivka and Haim-Mordehai Tsuker.

BOTTOM:

RIGHT: Avraham and Hava Steinbach with their children

LEFT: Yaakov Rakhman and his wife

Page 508

Page 508

TOP

RIGHT: Betzalel and Sarah-Henya Madanet

LEFT: Betzalel Madanet and Naphtali Mandel

BOTTOM:

RIGHT TO LEFT

Yitzhak-Meir Madanet, Yaakov Madanet, Israel-Yosef – son of Betzalel Madanet

Page 509

Page 509

TOP

RIGHT: Moshe-Aaron, Haim-Meir and Yerakhmiel Rekhthand

LEFT: The children of Zippa and Yitzhak Khanft, Aaron Berish Fainboim's grandchildren

BOTTOM LEFT: The children of Elimelekh Walberg

MIDDLE RIGHT TO LEFT: The children of Yaakov Zilberman; The children of Tova

BOTTOM RIGHT TO LEFT: Lola Gutmakher;
Israel-Yitzhak Steinbach

Page 510

יצחק כץ   יוסף זאַלצבערג   ישראל קאַהן   ישראל זאַלצבערג   יחיאל זאַלצבערג

אלימלך פרידמאַן   עובדיה ראַזנפעלד   שמערל שװארצבערג   אליעזר שיראַטאַ

יעקב װילדנבערג   מרדכי וואַסערמאַן   ישראל וואלבערג   שמואל גאַלדמאַן   מרדכי גרינשטיין

משה מעלצער   שבתאי מאַנדל   יענקל מעלצער   ירחמיאל טעננבוים   יעקב רעכטהאַנט

Page 510

Top to bottom right to left

Row 1
Yehiel Salzberg, Israel Salzberg, Israel Kahn, Yosef Salzberg, Yitzhak Katz

Row 2
Eliezer Sirota, Shmerl Schwartzberg, Obadiah Rozenfeld, Elimelekh Friedman

Row 3
Mordehai Grinstein, Shmuel Goldman, Israel Volberg, Mordehai Vasserman, Yaakov
Veildenberg

Row 4
Yaakov Rekhthand, Yerakhmiel Tenenboim, Yankel Meltzer, Shabtai Mandel, Moshe Meltzer

Page 511

שלמה שטערנשטיין   משה צימערמאַן   מאיר־שלום אַבראַמאַוויטש ברוך־משה גרינשפאַן יחיאל־הערש האַנינשטאַק   אשר ווילדנבערג

חיה זלאַטע ווילדמאַן   הערש ריכטמאַן   ישראל־יצחק דימענשטיין נפתלי־הערש גרינבערג גדליה ברעכמאַן

שמואל בלאַטמאַן   מאיר־שלום אונגער יענקל מענדל גראָדניאַק ישראל גרינהויז   רעכטמאַן

הדס קאָרפמאַן   רוחמה צוקער   רייצע וויינבערג שרה אַלטע פּאַסטערנאַק מלכה יענטע דאָמב

Page 511

Top to bottom right to left

R. to l.

Row 1
Shlomo Shternshtein, Moshe Tsimerman, Meir-Shalom Abramovitch, Baruch-Moshe Grinshpan, Yehiel-Hersh Honigshtok, Asher Veildenberg

Row 2
Hersh Rikhtman, Israel-Yitzhak Dimenshtein, Naphtali-Hersh Grinberg, Gedalya Brekhman, Haya-Zlateh Weidman

Row 3
Rekhtman, Meir-Shalom Unger, Yankel Mendel Grodniak, Israel Grinhoiz, Shmuel Vlatman

Row 4
Malka Yenta Domb, Sara Alte Pasternak, Reitze Vineberg, Rukhama Tsuker, Hadas Carpman

Page 512

נעכע כ″ץ—צוקער   חיה צפורה מעלצער   מלכה כענטשינסקי   עטל זילבערצווייג   איטל בירנבוים

ראזא בערנאט   הינדע ראזנבערג   שרה הינדע ראזין   דינה רעכטהאנט   חנה רעכטהאנט

יורע גרינשפאן   ביילע רבקה גאלדבערג   גיטל בארנשטיין   פייגל זאלצמאן   פאלעט ראדאוויטש

שרה טעפער   חוה ראזין   רבקה שפינעל   עטע נאגעל

Page 512

Top to bottom right to left

Row 1
Itel Birenboim, Etel Zilbertzveig, Malka Khentichinsky, Haya Ziporah Meltzer, Nekha Katz-Tsuker

Row 2
Hannah Rekhthand, Dina Rekhthand, Sara Hinda Rozin, Hinda Rosenberg, Rosa Bernat

Row 3
Paulette Radovitch, Feigel Saltzman, Gitel Bornstein, Beile Rivka Goldberg, Yura Grinshpan

Row 4
Ete Nagel, Rivka Shpigel, Hava Rozin, Sara Takher?

Page 513

פייוול גרינבערג	משה וויינבערג	מאיר נוסבאָם	העגאך פראָמאַן

חנה שפירשטיין	שרה רבקה צימערמאַן	פערל פיעקאָלעק	שיינע געלבערג

לייב גרינשפאַן	יצחק משה באָנטמאַן אברהם יצחק פראָמאַן אהרון יצחק מעלצער

לייזער גראָדניאָק	שמואל שמיס	חיים דוד פראָמאַן	אברהם-לייב אווענשטערן

Page 513

Top to bottom right to left

Row 1
Feivel Grinberg, Moshe Vineberg, Meir Nussbaum, Heinich Froman

Row 2
Hanna Saperstein, Sara Rivka Tsimerman, Perl Piekalek, Sheyna Goldberg

Row 3
Leib Grinshpan, Yitzhak Moshe Vantman, Avraham Yitzhak Froman, Aaron Yitzhak Meltzer

Row 4
Leyzer Grodniak. Shmuel Shmis, Haim David Froman, Avraham-Leib Overshtern

Page 514

יחיאל צוקער   פרץ ראזין   לייבל שיפערמאַן   יחיאל שיפערמאַן   יצחק פּאָטאָשניק

מאָריס ראָדאָוויטש   רוזשע קעַטשינסקי   שרה כמיעלניצקי   יוכבד כמיעלניצקי

לייב אליעזר מאַנדל   צירל מאַנדל   יעקב מאַנדל

אברהם און דבורה כהן   יחיאל כץ, זיין פרוי און טאָכטער חנה.

Page 514

Top to bottom right to left

Row 1
Yitzhak Potashnik, Yehiel Shiperman, Leibl Shiperman, Peretz Rozin, Yehiel Tsuker

Row 2
Yocheved Khmelnitsky, Sara Khmelnitsky, Rozshe Khentshinsky, Morris Radovitch

Row 3
Yaakov Mandel, Tzirel Mandel, Leib Alexander Mandel

Row 4
Yehiel Katz, his wife and daughter Hannah; Avraham and Devorah Cohen

Page 515

Page 515

Right top
Rachel Overshtern and her children, Ita Leah (shot by the Germans),
Shloimele – killed in Treblinka

Middle right
Son of Shmuel and Hannah Overshtern

Top left: Charna Goldshvartz-Volberg with her two children. They died in
Warsaw ghetto.

Middle left
Feiga-Leah Bornstein and Feiga-Leah Arbeitman- died in Treblinka.

Two bottom pictures do not have captions

[Page 676]

The Book of Kozienice Finished and Completed

by Baruch Kaplinsky, Tel–Aviv

There lies before us The Book of Kozienice. It is not just any book. It is a monument on the grave of the 5,000 member, Holy Jewish Community of Kozienice, which had lived and struggled and so tragically perished. It is proof of a sum –total of 350 years of Jewish life in a Jewish, Hassidic Shtetl in the center of Poland. This sum –total did not come easily to us. Maybe there are in Poland many sources for the history of the Jews of Kozienice, but here, in Israel, in France, in the United States, in Brazil, the sources are few. A notice here, a few lines there, a hint in an encyclopedia, an item in a newspaper, and that's it. From these poor sources, we couldn't build a rich history of the Jews of Kozienice.

Memoirs

Therefore we made intensive use of memoirs. The Kozienice survivors wrote. I would even say that they wrote a great deal, and naturally, that which they remembered. Foremost the memoir concentrates on the tragic consequences of the Holocaust. On the other hand, communal institutions, the traditional ones as well as modern schools, political parties and the life – style were privileged with only a few meager lines. Too bad!

A Collective Creation

This book is a collective undertaking and creation of a hundred authors, who did not mutually discuss the contents of their work. Therefore our book is not free of contradictions, and duplications, in spite of the hand that erased, but with Jewish mercy. We wanted all Kozieniceites should have the opportunity to tell about themselves, about their relatives, about Kozienice and her history in their own words, in their own style and according to the way they remembered. As a result of this, the Book is not free of a nice amount of contradictions in dates and events, but not one of us wanted to be final arbiter and judge who remembered best. Maybe it would have been more logical if the Book had been composed entirely in Hebrew, the Language of Israel, the language of our children, the Sabras. Maybe it would have been more natural, if the Book followed the tradition of Kozienice Record Books, which were always kept in the Holy Tongue (Hebrew), but never reached us. Maybe it would have been more realistic if we had written the Book for future generations and not for ourselves. But, in spite of all, after long deliberation we decided: Let each one tell his story in the language that he finds easiest to use.

Thanks

At the end may we express our thanks to the initiators, gatherers of materials, memoir writers, and fund–raisers for the Kozienice Book. Congratulations to the tens of anonymous friends from Israel.

INDEX

Kirshenboim, 814
Kitzes, 79
Kizshberg, 750
Klainboim, 569
Kleiman, 767
Klein, 338, 339
Kleinbaum, 23
Kleinboim, 526, 633
Kleinman, 23, 761
Kleinnan, 23
Klezmer, 128, 354, 408, 491, 670
Kliger, 547
Klimatchuk, 316
Kloinsky, 23
Koffler, 23
Koffman, 23
Kohn, 13, 23, 215, 292, 320, 349, 397, 399, 453,
    684, 685, 721, 722, 723, 724, 732, 736, 775, 808
Kokhniks, 299
Kokos, 338, 409
Koplewitz, 37
Korman, 23, 219, 260, 262, 264, 268, 279, 286,
    306, 307, 386, 392, 399, 525, 547, 588, 717, 775
Korngold, 263
Kornwasser, 23
Koshkis', 418
Kotter, 478
Kovall, 478
Kovals, 220
Kovalsky, 471, 473
Kozienicer, 48, 49, 50, 51, 58, 70, 76, 84, 85, 110,
    115, 122, 134, 137, 138, 139, 140, 141, 142,
    144, 145, 146, 147, 149, 151, 158, 159, 162,
    163, 164, 168, 170, 172, 173, 174, 176, 180,
    182, 183, 184, 185, 186, 187, 188, 189, 190,
    198, 200, 215, 216, 217, 218, 219, 220, 238,
    250, 251, 256, 257, 261, 262, 271, 280, 281,
    294, 301, 305, 308, 337, 356, 357, 358, 369,
    382, 389, 392, 408, 413, 420, 450, 451, 452,
    459, 462, 463, 469, 472, 474, 475, 476, 487,
    493, 498, 499, 514, 535, 536, 539, 559, 561,
    608, 644, 657, 659, 669, 674, 703, 714, 722,
    756, 772, 775, 777, 779, 786, 789, 790, 795,
    799, 800, 803, 807, 810, 814
Kozlow, 282
Kramarski, 23, 465
Kraskevitsh, 628
Kreitzberg, 405, 571, 757, 761, 776, 812, 817
Kreizberg, 23, 229, 231, 307
Kreizenberg, 4
Krishpel, 23, 171, 259, 267, 285, 299, 300, 302,
    322, 323, 386, 408, 410, 496, 497, 498, 541,
    563, 631, 798, 813
Krishpels, 401
Kronengoid, 23
Kronengold, 23, 303, 419
Krongold, 569

Kruck, 387
Krueger, 528
Kruk, 269
Kubitchek, 405
Kugel, 158, 448
Kun, 750
Kupler, 23
Kurland, 731, 734, 735, 736
Kuropatva, 814
Kuropatve, 23, 496
Kuropatwa, 302
Kutscher, 23
Kutsher, 569, 761
Kuzmirer, 289

L

Lach, 718, 719, 720
Lahat, 227, 231, 599
Lampa, 291
Lampe, 478
Larski, 57, 303, 377, 542
Lederhandler, 829
Lederhendler, 25
Lederman, 25, 37, 69, 162, 167, 252, 267, 268,
    279, 280, 286, 292, 299, 301, 302, 304, 306,
    312, 314, 321, 376, 382, 385, 386, 392, 400,
    402, 403, 406, 420, 436, 438, 488, 497, 584,
    585, 592, 750, 779, 809, 810, 812, 813
Leibishes, 263, 327
Lenga, 25, 263, 595
Lerman, 25, 631
Lerner, 25, 442, 443, 467, 821
Leshtshinsky, 57
Levi, 25, 26, 81, 84, 86, 87, 88, 89, 91, 92, 111, 118,
    126, 137, 144, 145, 150, 151, 152, 167, 180,
    252, 322, 323, 327, 331, 356, 387, 448, 486,
    769, 775, 781, 790, 791
Levin, 329
Levine, 25, 63, 393
Levinson, 393
Levita, 699
Lichtenstein, 25, 225, 293, 302, 315, 389, 393,
    509, 546, 738, 814
Lieberman, 25, 331
Lifschitz, 151
Likerman, 599
Likorman, 599
Likverman, 25, 231, 498, 603
Limon, 393
Lipman, 513, 514, 708, 725
Lipmann, 302, 464
Lippman, 25, 712
Lippmann, 25, 37
Lipschitz, 152
Lisband, 25
Litman, 7, 467, 656, 659, 758

Nashelsky, 27
Neudorf, 27, 59
Neuman, 535, 536, 537, 538, 539, 634, 677
Neunold, 27
Neustein, 27
Nikolayevitsh, 476
Nisker, 402
Nissenbaum, 143
Nodelman, 408
Nomberg, 386, 389
Noodleman, 27
Noreck, 461
Noshelski, 428
Notis, 382
Notte, 16, 23, 25, 37, 132, 202, 220, 246, 302, 322, 323
Notteles, 220
Nussbaum, 27, 845
Nuta, 423, 695, 725
Nutes, 459

O

Oboge, 231
Oger, 411, 412, 451, 453, 454, 494
Okon, 27
Oleshkevitsh, 643
Olshina, 27, 775
Onipoler, 151
Oranzshitzky, 731
Orbach, 27, 322, 570, 571, 662
Orentstern, 285
Orgelbrand, 41
Ortshtein, 443
Oszerower, 151
Ovenstern, 220
Overshtern, 289, 290, 845, 849

P

Papieroshnik, 302
Parashinski, 571
Pasternak, 27, 841
Pat, 292, 293, 349
Patashnik, 814
Pearl, 15, 16, 18, 20, 22, 23, 25, 26, 27, 28, 29, 33, 38, 48, 51, 78, 285, 361, 365, 638, 750, 823
Pearlshtein, 643, 644
Pearlstein, 27, 37, 623, 624, 677, 707, 711, 712, 756, 757, 758, 761, 814
Peredstein, 813
Perelstein, 750
Perl, 544, 552, 642, 845
Perlov, 126, 363, 364, 525
Perlstein, 633, 762
Peter, 27
Piekolek, 27

Pikolek, 261
Piltz, 393
Pinczover, 261
Pinkhas, 335
Pinkhases, 220, 221
Pintschever, 27
Pitkkowitz, 551
Pittkowitz, 27
Pockshevinski, 436
Pokashinski, 316
Pokzshevinski, 459, 579
Polav, 537
Polkovnik, 412, 461
Poniatowski, 42, 43, 51, 92, 93, 94, 95, 103, 142, 149, 169
Pontsch, 27
Popelnik, 232, 448
Popielnik, 27, 263, 547
Popilnik, 332
Popyelnick, 641
Popyelnik, 544
Postasznik, 267
Potachnik, 392
Potashnik, 467, 496, 497, 498, 794, 798, 806, 814, 821, 847
Potasznik, 27, 37, 285, 302
Potshnik, 780
Prager, 152, 536
Prelutzki, 387, 388
Prilucki, 268
Prilutzki, 349, 353, 389
Prilutzky, 389, 392, 394
Proveizer, 289
Provizor, 761
Pruchnicki, 750
Psherva, 628
Purisever, 27

Q

Qger, 351, 411
Qventshtern, 563

R

Raban, 387
Rabi, 438
Rabin, 37
Rabinowitz, 28, 90, 119, 137, 143, 153, 203
Radovitch, 819, 843, 847
Radovitsh, 793
Radowitz, 28, 37
Rakhman, 289, 305, 466, 831, 833
Raphnowitz, 37
Rappaport, 28, 548, 588, 593
Ratafie, 823
Ravitch, 349

Shildkroit, 685
Shiperman, 847
Shipper, 6, 7, 293, 408, 411, 453, 814
Shitkovski, 316
Shitshek, 663
Shmeiser, 761
Shmeisser, 315
Shmelke, 16, 28, 49, 51, 83, 84, 93, 94, 95, 105,
    144, 145, 151, 166, 167, 171, 220, 295, 302,
    401, 506, 557, 562, 591, 669, 725, 750, 807
Shmis, 845
Shmueles, 220
Shneerson, 794
Shoikhets, 220
Shoykhet, 353
Shpiegel, 399, 452, 625, 631
Shpigel, 581, 591, 721, 817, 843
Shpigelman, 465, 506, 556, 562, 565, 646, 669,
    821
Shpigler, 309
Shtatiner, 827
Shternshtein, 841
Shtrypman, 831
Shvartzberg, 418, 488, 489, 590, 594, 757, 812
Shvartzboim, 443
Shwartzberg, 775
Sigelman, 547
Silberberg, 6, 307, 319, 320
Silberstein, 467
Silver, 807
Silverberg, 29, 37, 268, 285
Silverknopf, 29
Silverman, 29
Silverstein, 29, 302, 317, 318, 319, 322
Simenhaus, 29
Simonhoz, 781
Sirota, 29, 270, 279, 283, 285, 291, 312, 460, 465,
    478, 778, 831, 839
Skovronska, 719
Skovronski, 719
Skowronski, 96
Slonimsky, 401
Smyser, 29, 37
Sobol, 29, 37, 708
Sochachevsky, 29
Sofer, 491
Soffer, 738
Sokolow, 292, 293, 400, 401
Soloveitchick, 331
Soyfers, 314
Spector, 425
Spiegel, 29, 307, 350, 833
Spiegelman, 29, 37, 220, 295
Starkman, 37
Starovshtshik, 594
Statiner, 29
Statwohner, 37

Stavsky, 415
Stecker, 29
Steinbach, 833, 837
Steinbaum, 29
Steinberg, 214
Steinbock, 29
Stern, 117, 152
Sternbaum, 29
Sternstein, 29
Stinitzer, 118
Stockfish, 37
Streiman, 29
Stupnicki, 293
Stupnitsky, 386
Sukno, 750
Szabason, 241, 552
Szerman, 679, 681

T

Tabachnik, 32, 256, 300, 315
Tabatchnik, 426, 483
Tabatshnik, 775
Takher, 843
Teitelbaum, 32, 152, 234, 540
Tenenbaum, 5, 627, 735, 767
Tenenboim, 450, 453, 512, 589, 667, 718, 821, 839
Tennenbaum, 32, 38, 65, 279, 282, 283, 285, 291,
    756, 757
Tennenboim, 441, 758, 761, 763, 765, 768, 773,
    808, 813
Tennenholtz, 32
Tentzer, 661
Tepper, 32, 386, 561, 590
Tepperman, 32
Tirangel, 751
Tishman, 32, 829
Tochterman, 32, 813
Toibes, 390
Tokasz, 350
Tokhterman, 776
Tomashevski, 372, 594
Trag, 543
Treger, 216, 461
Tsholok, 413
Tshwok, 322
Tsimerman, 841, 845
Tsuker, 819, 833, 841, 843, 847
Tuchman, 32
Tuter, 385
Twersky, 472, 475
Tzaitvingel, 449
Tzeitfinger, 738, 761
Tzemach, 379, 442, 443, 450, 472, 477, 487, 757,
    761, 774
Tzemakh, 464
Tzernobol, 782

www.ingramcontent.com/pod-product-compliance
Lightning Source LLC
Chambersburg PA
CBHW062021090426

42811CB00005B/919

9 781939 561428